Introduction to Victimology

Contemporary Theory, Research, and Practice

Bonnie S. Fisher
UNIVERSITY OF CINCINNATI

Bradford W. Reyns
WEBER STATE UNIVERSITY

John J. Sloan III
UNIVERSITY OF ALABAMA AT BIRMINGHAM

NEW YORK OXFORD
OXFORD UNIVERSITY PRESS

Oxford University Press is a department of the University of Oxford.
It furthers the University's objective of excellence in research,
scholarship, and education by publishing worldwide.

Auckland Cape Town Dar es Salaam Hong Kong Karachi
Kuala Lumpur Madrid Melbourne Mexico City Nairobi
New Delhi Shanghai Taipei Toronto

With offices in
Argentina Austria Brazil Chile Czech Republic France Greece
Guatemala Hungary Italy Japan Poland Portugal Singapore
South Korea Switzerland Thailand Turkey Ukraine Vietnam

For titles covered by Section 112 of the US Higher Education
Opportunity Act, please visit www.oup.com/us/he for the
latest information about pricing and alternate formats.

Published by Oxford University Press
198 Madison Avenue, New York, New York 10016
http://www.oup.com

Library of Congress Cataloging-in-Publication Data
Fisher, Bonnie, 1959-
Introduction to victimology : contemporary theory, research,
and practice / Bonnie S. Fisher, Bradford W. Reyns, John J. Sloan III.
pages cm
Includes bibliographical references and index.
ISBN 978-0-19-932249-7
1. Victims of crimes. 2. Criminology. I. Reyns, Bradford W., 1979-
II. Sloan, John J. III. Title.
HV6250.25.F57 2016
362.88--dc23

2015011389

Printing number: 9 8 7 6 5 4 3 2 1

Printed in the United States of America
on acid-free paper

DEDICATION

Dedicated to the memory of the victims of the Sandy Hook Elementary School shooting, Newtown, Connecticut, December 14, 2012:

Charlotte Bacon, 6
Daniel Barden, 7
Rachel D'Avino, 29
Olivia Engel, 6
Josephine Gay, 7
Dylan Hockley, 6
Dawn Lafferty Hochsprung, 47
Madeline Hsu, 6
Catherine Hubbard, 6
Jesse Lewis, 6
Ana Marquez-Greene, 6
Chase Kowalski, 7
Grace McDonnell, 7
Anne Marie Murphy, 52
James Mattioli, 6
Emilie Parker, 6
Jack Pinto, 6
Noah Pozner, 6
Caroline Previdi, 6
Jessica Rekos, 6
Avielle Richman, 6
Lauren Rousseau, 30
Mary Sherlach, 56
Victoria Soto, 27
Benjamin Wheeler, 6
Allison Wyatt, 6

BRIEF CONTENTS

CONTENTS

ACKNOWLEDGMENTS

Each of us thanks the entire team at Oxford University Press (OUP) for their support, guidance, and attention to detail through the organizing and writing of this textbook. Sarah Calabi, who is no longer with OUP, was instrumental in our initial decision to partner with OUP and was enthusiastic and supportive of our early ideas for a victimology textbook with a solid theoretical foundation. Steve Helba, our current editor, and Olivia Caroline Geraci, our editorial assistant, have provided helpful feedback on reviewers' comments to chapters. We very much appreciated their willingness to discuss our responses, and support our decisions on how to proceed.

We also want to thank colleagues at our respective universities and elsewhere who were kind enough to take the time to provide valuable feedback during the conceptualization and writing stages. We thank the reviewers listed below who read chapters and provided critical reflective comments that inspired our thinking. Each of us read all of your comments, with colored highlighters in hand, and discussed each comment at length during several e-mail and telephone communications. We very much appreciate you sharing your time and expertise with us.

- Dick T. Andzenge, St. Cloud State University
- Kevin M. Beaver, Florida State University
- Karin Brown, Hardin-Simmons University
- Carrie L. Cook, Georgia College & State University
- Sarah E. Daly, Rutgers University
- Wendelin Hume, University of North Dakota
- Susan L. Miller, University of Delaware
- Jamie Price, Florida Atlantic University
- Elizabeth Quinn, Fayetteville State University
- Shannon Santana, University of North Carolina—Wilmington
- Debra L. Stanley, University of Baltimore
- Kathleen Fox Talbot, Arizona State University

- Rae Taylor, Loyola University—New Orleans
- Shaun A. Thomas, University of Arkansas at Little Rock
- Janet K. Wilson, University of Central Arkansas

We could not have written this textbook if we had not had opportunities to share our knowledge of and passion about victimology with our numerous students over the years. Our students, both undergraduate and graduate, provided each of us with valuable insights and perspectives that differ from our own and raised questions and answers that we had not considered but gave us pause for reflection. We thank our students for educating us and giving us the opportunity to educate them to critically think about and integrate victimological theory, research, and practice.

Individually, Bonnie expresses her heartfelt appreciation to her husband, Nick, and their daughters, Olivia and Camille, for their support and for stimulating her thinking through their questions and insights about victimization—its correlates and impacts, especially on females. Brad would like to thank his family, especially his wife Cassie and his daughters, Abby and Reese, for giving him a reason to work hard, and understanding what a huge undertaking this would be. Thanks also to Rocky, who is a dachshund, for being a great writing companion. John thanks his wife, Tavis, for her understanding and support during another major writing project and the Gulf of Mexico for providing him a wonderful respite when things got a little too tense!

PREFACE

Although criminal victimization is a reality that people experience every day, for most individuals it is a relatively rare event. That said, all of the authors have been victims of crime at some point in their lives, with each of them having experienced recurring victimization. Bonnie had two old cars stolen while she was in graduate school at Northwestern University during the 1980s; she reported both incidents to the police for both peace of mind and insurance money on the first stolen car that was never recovered. The second stolen car, however, was actually towed from a snow emergency route in Evanston, Illinois, in December during a lake-effect snow storm. When Bonnie told the police officer who had called (which at first she assumed was a prank her friends were playing on her) to tell her that her car was towed, she told the officer that her car had been stolen (and reported to the Evanston police) in September. He then politely asked Bonnie if she was sure her car had been stolen—to which she again answered yes—and then he replied that he had to double-check their records. Needless to say, she still had to pay quite a large sum of money to get her car out of the pound. More recently she had her GPS taken from her unlocked minivan, which was parked in her driveway, in the wee hours of the morning in July 2011. Fortunately, a police officer biking in her neighborhood saw a young man with a large backpack walking up and down driveways in her neighborhood. When the officer stopped the young man to question what was in his pack, the young man explained that he was looking for his friend who had asked him to hold the GPSs. A police officer arrived at Bonnie's front door with her GPS in hand before she even knew it had been stolen.

Brad has twice experienced credit card fraud victimization. Once, while still in graduate school at the University of Cincinnati, he accessed his credit card account online only to find a charge for around $5,000 had been made without his knowledge or permission. Interestingly, the perpetrator used the credit card information to pay the Internal Revenue Service for taxes owed. Although the credit card company quickly reimbursed the account and canceled the card, it was shocking to find such a large charge on the account, and further disconcerting was the fact Brad still had the actual card in his possession. Brad's second experience with credit card fraud victimization occurred during the 2013 holiday season, in which a different credit card company contacted Brad to alert him of changes to his account—specifically a change in the e-mail address associated with it. Upon checking his account he found that his contact information with the credit card company had been changed, presumably to the offender's, and a charge was pending with a skin-care company in New York City. Neither incident was reported to the police.

Unlike Bonnie's and Brad's property victimization experiences, John experienced a violent victimization while in high school. In September 1972, in a quiet residential neighborhood in Northwest Detroit, John was walking home from high school one day when he was confronted by an older man who walked him into a nearby alley and attempted to rob him at gunpoint. Luckily for John, a passing motorist saw what was occurring and intervened by driving his car into the alley, revving his engine and honking the horn. The gunman was scared off; the motorist took John to the local police station. There, John was questioned about what had happened, including being asked for a description of the gunman. John recalls not being able to provide much detail about the man because all he could remember was how BIG the gun seemed as it was pointed at his face (it was a .38-caliber revolver). The police promised to do what they could to "find the guy" and "bring him to justice." John never heard from the police again. After the victimization and fearful of another robbery, John rode the bus both to school and back rather than walking. For months afterward, John had recurring nightmares of the event, tried to never walk around the neighborhood alone, and even had his appetite affected. In short, John suffered trauma from the event.

Obviously, people who experience a criminal victimization suffer—some a great deal, others not so much—but *all* of them suffer negative consequences *in some way*. Whether having to deal with insurance companies to have stolen items replaced as the result of an automobile theft or burglary, communicating with credit card companies to deal with replacing credit cards, negotiating with their employers because they have to take time off from work to meet with police or prosecutors or go to court, or comforting a spouse or partner (or themselves) who is grief-stricken over what happened, criminal victimization *affects* people regardless of age, race, sex, social status, or educational attainment. Once one has been victimized, a chain of events is set into motion: Do I report this incident to the police? If I do, will they be able to do anything? What will happen if the perpetrator finds out I reported him or her to the police—especially if I know the perpetrator? Assuming the perpetrator is apprehended and prosecuted, what will the process be like? Is there someone I can speak with about the after-effects of the event? For some victims, these questions will never be answered.

Approach of the Book

This book examines the entire landscape of criminal victimization by presenting readers with an overview of the discipline known as *victimology*—the scientific study of victims, their relationships with offenders, the forces that caused the victimization, and the interactions victims have with the criminal justice system. Readers will notice that throughout the book, not only do we present information about what is known about various aspects of the study of crime victims, but we do so within a framework that is guided by *theory*. Because victimology is an example of a social science discipline—just like sociology, criminology, psychology, or political science—it relies upon theory as the basis for its investigations of the causes, consequences, and prevention of criminal victimization. In each of the chapters, we provide at least some discussion of the theoretical roots that have guided investigations into how and why criminal victimization occurs and its effects. Simultaneously, victimology is also very much an applied discipline. What that means is that victimologists seek to develop practical solutions to the problems posed by criminal victimization. Whether the solution is creating a rape crisis center to help victims with the horrific emotional impact such a violent victimization can have on victims and their families, or designing buildings and places to discourage opportunities for victimization to occur, victimologists have helped create and evaluate solutions to the problems faced by victims.

As you undertake the journey into the world of victimology, you also will find that victimologists have engaged in a large body of research, and this too will be highlighted throughout each of the chapters that make up this textbook. Some of this research has been groundbreaking and made a major contribution to what is understood about crime victims and criminal victimization. The point in sharing research findings is to show that theory, research, and prevention policy should be *interconnected* (although, as we will sometimes point out, that is not always the case). In science, a problem generates a theory, which in turn generates hypotheses that are then rigorously tested and retested. When enough of the hypotheses have been supported, we say the theory is confirmed. If the hypotheses are rejected, then the theory is not confirmed, and scientists can modify the theory or develop and test new theories. When a theory is confirmed, solutions that are theory-based or evidence-informed can be developed and tested in different settings, with different samples of people, and across time.

One theory repeatedly discussed in this textbook, *routine activity theory*, posits that criminal victimizations involve the coming together in time and space of three components: a *target* (whether a person, a business, or some larger institution); a *motivated offender*; and an absence of people—called *guardians*—who could stop the event from occurring. The core contribution of routine activity theory to both victimology and criminology is the notion of *opportunity*—that criminal victimization occurs when certain *opportunities* are presented. Also important is the fact that routine activity theory paved the way for practical solutions for reducing the risk of victimization. By disrupting the coming together in time and space of attractive targets, motivated offenders, and lack of guardians, *victimizations can be prevented*. Those disruptions may occur by changing people's routines, by reducing exposure to motivated offenders, or by increasing the presence of guardians. Thus, routine activity theory provides a solid foundation on which can be developed effective solutions to help prevent criminal victimization.

As readers move across the chapters, they will also find "spotlighted" specific theories, research studies, and policies. These "Spotlight" boxes are intended to provide readers with greater detail about a particular theory, set of research endeavors, or policies relevant to the substantive topic(s) covered in a chapter. For example, in the chapter that deals with the victimization of children, a "Spotlight on Policy" examines the ongoing scandal in the Catholic Church over priests sexually assaulting children, boys and girls, and the ramifications of that scandal.

Structure of the Book

We have divided the book into four separate parts. Each part begins with an introduction and provides a case study designed to illustrate the theme that guides the chapters making up a specific part of the book. Part I of the book, for example, consists of three chapters that present the origins of victimology and the major theories that have developed since the beginning. Taking an evolutionary perspective on the development of the discipline, Part I provides an overview of four different generations of researchers and theorists, with spotlights provided to illustrate what we believe are particularly interesting examples across the generations.

Part II of the book, consisting of six chapters, examines sources, trends, and types of victimization. Across these chapters, readers are presented with the basics of victimization: what happens, to whom, and how patterns may change based on various contextual matters (e.g., personal characteristics, time of day, location). Here, we also discuss sources of data on victimization ranging from data compiled annually by the FBI to national-level surveys administered to thousands of people to learn about their victimization experiences.

Part III of the book examines responses to, and the consequences of, criminal victimization. These chapters mark a transition to a different set of research questions than those that guided Parts I and II as we move into answering the question of what happens after victimization. The four chapters that make up Part III cover the topics of victim decision making, the consequences of crime for victims (e.g., physical, social, behavioral), responses to victimization, and the fear that victimization can generate not only among those who have actually experienced a crime, but for others as well.

Part IV of the book is, in our opinion, unique to victimology textbooks in that it is devoted entirely to efforts aimed at *preventing* criminal victimization using theories and research grounded in what is known as *environmental criminology*. Environmental criminology's focus is with the contextual factors—space, time, geography, and the natural or built environment—that influence opportunities for and victimization. Consisting of a single chapter, Part IV of the book reviews the theoretical foundations that underlie the prevention of victimization, with particular attention paid to opportunity theories, which are the keystone of most theories relating to preventing victimization. Several theories from environmental criminology, including defensible space, crime prevention through environmental design, and situational crime prevention, provide the rationale not only for *why* opportunity is crucial for preventing future victimizations, but also for identifying the mechanisms that can be manipulated to prevent victimization in the first place. The chapter also concentrates on *applying* the theories when developing efforts to prevent victimization. Here, we stress the fact that researchers and practitioners alike have tested the effectiveness of theoretically informed victimization prevention strategies that focus on reducing opportunities for crime, and discuss those efforts. We conclude the chapter by exploring the *collateral consequences* of preventing victimization, which involve what are known as displacement, diffusion of benefits, and anticipatory benefits.

In writing the book, we have endeavored to keep the student audience in mind, and so in each chapter we provide a set of key terms, discussion questions, and references that students can use to help them learn substantive content. We also provide many tables, figures, charts, and other graphical representations, again to help students visually grasp the substantive material. Finally, we have tried to adopt a writing style that is a bit less formal than one might expect in a textbook, one that is more conversational in tone and less "ivory towerish." While the three of us have been engaged in teaching and research in victimology a bit longer than most of our readers, we certainly do not have all of the answers, nor do we expect our students to have them. Rather, what we hope to encourage students who read this text to do is to ask questions, explore the patterns, and discover some possible answers to the problems faced by crime victims. Should we achieve those goals, we will take comfort in the hope that we may have inspired at least some of our readers to continue exploring victimology. With these introductory words in mind, let us begin the journey . . .

PART I

Origins and Theories in Victimology

Victimology is an integrated field of study that focuses specifically on victims of crime and their experiences. Because individuals with diverse academic backgrounds study victimology, it is somewhat difficult to synthesize the immense body of research concerning the plight of crime victims and tell a "single story." For example, a criminal justice scholar may view criminal victimization from a different perspective than a psychologist, a sociologist, or a nurse. Speaking to this diversity within the field of victimology, the authors of this textbook have backgrounds in political science, criminology, and sociology, respectively. Yet, despite the differences in our academic training, we have endeavored to represent the diversity of perspectives not only in our areas of expertise, but in the larger body of research that represents contemporary victimology.

In writing this textbook, our primary goal has been to use victimological theories to illuminate the circumstances surrounding criminal victimization—that is, to explain how and why victimization occurs. However, at the forefront we also offer a word of caution in interpreting these theories and the empirical evidence identifying the risk factors for victimization that are presented throughout the text. There is a somewhat fragile balance between identifying factors or characteristics that are related to increased risks for victimization and blaming victims for what has befallen them. In all cases, our intention is to reinforce the former—namely, that victims bear no fault or blame for their victimization. Rather, it is the offender's behavior and his or her actions that are responsible for the criminal event. This discussion is more fully articulated in Chapter 1 of the textbook but is important to keep in mind before reading further.

In reviewing the vast body of research examining criminal victimization, we have divided the textbook into four separate, yet interrelated, parts. Part I, which you are about to read, lays the theoretical foundation for the rest of the book. It is divided into three chapters; each examines the theoretical development and evolution of victimology theory from a generational perspective. In Chapter 1, the origins of the field of victimology are reviewed, including the academic origins of the study of victims and the first generation of victimology theories. This chapter also discusses the grassroots and political origins of the field, recognizing that many important milestones in the history of victimology occurred outside of academic settings.

Chapter 2 is one of the keystone chapters of the text. The chapter acts as a bridge between the origins of the study of crime victims and contemporary theoretical approaches to explaining victimization. Here, the pioneering second-generation work into lifestyle-exposure theory and routine activity theory is introduced. Theoretical explanations of victimization from this generation center on the importance of opportunity in facilitating criminal incidents, and the influence that victims might have upon the creation of such opportunities. These are recurring themes in both victimology research and the textbook. Part I of the textbook culminates in Chapter 3 with a discussion of contemporary theories in victimology. Many of the theories presented in this chapter are refinements of, or extensions to, the earlier opportunity perspective on victimization, with the inclusion of several notable theories from criminology that provide insights into explaining victimization.

The overarching purpose of Part I is to provide readers with a theoretical basis for understanding how and why criminal victimization occurs. Against this backdrop, patterns in victimization discussed in subsequent chapters are viewed not merely as descriptors of victimization, but as correlates (at a minimum) and possibly as determinants that can potentially be changed to reduce victimization risk. Part II reviews the sources, trends, and types of victimization. Part III examines responses to, and consequences of, victimization, along with highlights of the most up-to-date research on these topics, while Part IV discusses strategies for preventing victimization.

CASE STUDY #1

Project Payback—A Juvenile Restitution Program

In this first part of the textbook, we review the origins of victimology and provide an overview of the major theories that have defined the field and guided victimological research and helped influence policies and programs aimed at victims. In this case study, we present an example of a program that illustrates some of the key ideas presented in the first set of chapters:

- Seeking justice for victims is one of the core functions of victimology, and that quest is illustrated by a variety of programs and policies operating at the federal, state, and local levels of government;
- Criminal victimization does not exist in a vacuum, but rather occurs in a context that includes not only people, but people and places interacting with one another;

- The most successful programs and policies aimed at assisting victims are carefully crafted and take a holistic approach that considers victim, offender, and context.

Project Payback

Project Payback (Howard, 2011, pp. 97–106) is a juvenile restitution program that has been operating in the Eighth Judicial Circuit of north central Florida since 1999. Restitution programs involve offenders providing monetary payback—directly or indirectly—to victims for property loss or personal injury suffered. Howard (2011, p. 99) argues that the benefits of restitution to victims are clear: Offenders are held accountable—they see the direct consequences of their actions—and victims receive economic compensation for their losses and experience a criminal justice system that is responsive to their needs. Howard (2011, p. 102) argues that effective restitution programs are those that hold offenders and the criminal justice system strictly accountable—offenders for compliance, and the system for efficient collection of funds from offenders and maintaining enforcement mechanisms to ensure offenders' compliance. Project Payback uses an *offender accountability approach* in which juvenile offenders are held directly accountable to victims and the system is held accountable for ensuring that restitution is collected and enforcement mechanisms are in place for dealing with offenders who fail to comply.

Program purposes. According to Howard (2011), Payback's purposes include providing job skills training for juveniles to facilitate employment and payment of restitution; requiring juveniles ages 16 and older to be either employed or actively seeking employment, with those unable to find employment earning restitution through community service hours paid at the minimum wage; monitoring monthly compliance of juveniles ordered into the program; reporting on offenders' restitution compliance status with the court; initiating enforcement actions for noncompliance; making victims aware of when a case has been set for a noncompliance hearing; and informing victims about the status of the case.

Program specifics. Juvenile offenders who owe restitution are court-ordered to complete Project Payback as a condition of their probation. Payback accomplishes its mission by offering individualized job skills and life skills training and providing youth unable to become employed the option of completing "community restitution service" hours with monetary credit at minimum wage paid to victims. At the initial or intake appointment, a project staff member meets with the offender and his or her parent(s) or guardian(s) and reviews a restitution contract, which includes the offender paying a minimum amount of restitution of $100 per month. The offender and his or her parent(s) or guardian(s) then sign the contract. Staff also schedule up to two two-hour job employability assessments and training sessions for the offenders.

Job skills/life skills training. Training sessions are four to six hours in length and experiential in orientation, and they include both job training and life skills training via Morita Therapy (Morita, 1998) and Naikan principles (Kretch, 2001). Morita Therapy, a form of cognitive-behavioral therapy (Rothbaum, Meadows, Resick, & Foy, 2000), provides experiences that educate clients about nature and their lives, behaviors, emotions, and mental attitudes. Naikan therapy encourages youth to reflect on their relationships with others, including what they have received from and given to others, and the problems and difficulties they have caused others. A list of entry-level jobs and relevant information (e.g., business name, location, and minimum age or skill requirements) is updated annually and provided to Project Payback participants. A list of community restitution sites—by location, minimum age requirements, and type of work—is updated twice annually and distributed to youth who are not aware of community restitution sites within the community. Participants then contact the employer or community restitution site.

Program impact. Prior to Project Payback's implementation, an average of $166 per month in restitution was paid to victims in the county; in 2011, the average was over $3,500 per month. Since its inception, over 1,300 youth have been referred to the program and more than $545,000 in restitution has been paid to victims. In 2004, approximately 16% of juveniles enrolled in the program were terminated; in 2010, that figure dropped to approximately 15%. The program was expanded in 2000 to include all the rural counties of Florida's Eighth Judicial Circuit: Alachua, Baker, Bradford, Gilchrist, Levy, and Union—all of which have relatively small populations and few employment opportunities.

References

Howard, S. (2011). Project Payback: A juvenile restitution program. In S. Howley (Ed.), *Making restitution real: Five case studies on improving restitution collection* (pp. 97–106). Washington, DC: National Center for Victims of Crime.

Kretch, G. (2001). *Naikan: Gratitude, grace, and the Japanese art of self-reflection*. Berkeley, CA: Stone Bridge Press.

Morita, M. (1998). *Morita therapy and the true nature of anxiety-based disorders*. Albany, NY: SUNY Press.

Rothbaum, B. O., Meadows, E. A., Resick, P., & Foy, D. W. (2000). Cognitive-behavioral therapy. In E. Foa, T. Keane, & M. Friedman (Eds.), *Effective treatments for PTSD: Practice guidelines from the International Society for Traumatic Stress Studies* (pp. 320–325). New York: Guilford Press.

CHAPTER 1

Origins of Victimology

CHAPTER OUTLINE

Introduction
Studying Criminal Victimization: Theory and Research
Academic Origins of Victimology

- Hans von Hentig
- Beniamin Mendelsohn
- Stephen Schafer
- Marvin E. Wolfgang
- Menachem Amir

Grassroots Origins of Victimology

- The Civil Rights Movement
- The Women's Movement
- The Children's Movement

Political Origins of Victimology

- The "Law and Order" Movement
- The President's Commission on Law Enforcement and the Law Enforcement Assistance Administration
- Federal Legislation in the United States

Summary
Keywords
Discussion Questions
References

LEARNING OBJECTIVES

- Describe the purposes and scope of the field of victimology.
- Explain the functions served by research and theory in victimology.
- Summarize the contributions of the first generation of victimology theories and theorists.
- Explain the concept of victim precipitation and its importance in the academic origins of victimology.
- Describe the typologies developed by early victimologists and how they were used to explain the victim's role in the criminal event.
- Identify similarities and differences among the first-generation typologies.
- Analyze the grassroots origins of victimology.
- Explain how grassroots groups influenced the political origins of victimology and vice versa.
- Identify the outcomes of the political origins of victimology.

> *Often victims seem to be born. Often they are society-made. Sometimes the most valuable qualities render us easy victims. As always, mere chance, blind and senseless, is liable for what befalls us.*
>
> **von Hentig, 1948, p. 385**

Introduction

Every crime has at least one victim. According to the National Crime Victimization Survey (NCVS), which is administered by the Bureau of Justice Statistics, there were an estimated 6,842,593 violent victimizations and 19,622,977 household victimizations experienced in 2012 (NCVS Victimization Analysis Tool, 2014). And, while the NCVS estimates do not provide a perfectly clear picture of all victimization in the United States, the statistics do highlight the enormity of the issue of criminal victimization. The term ***victimization*** refers to events that harm individuals, households, businesses, communities, or institutions, and in cases of criminal victimization, this harm is suffered as a result of a violation of the law.

The concept of victimization is not new. Indeed, the notion of "victimization" dates back to ancient cultures and civilizations, and historically the concept was associated with taking the life of a person or animal to satisfy a deity. Over the centuries, the notion of "victim" has changed greatly. Today, the term ***victim*** is used in many contexts, is broadly interpreted, and is used to describe a range of human experiences. For instance, in the health care domain, the term is often applied to those who have cancer ("cancer victims"); when a natural disaster strikes, the label is applied to survivors ("hurricane victims"). This text focuses exclusively on a different type of victim: crime victims. ***Crime victims*** are those persons, households, businesses, communities, or institutions that are harmed physically, financially, or emotionally as the result of criminal acts.

It was not until relatively recently that scholars directed their research to studying crime victims and the circumstances surrounding their victimization. This is among the purposes of the field of ***victimology***. Another primary purpose of victimology is to ensure that victims are provided with the services they need and advocates on their behalf. Victimologists have diverse backgrounds, ranging from social work and sociology to economics, public health, psychology, political science, nursing, criminology, law, and medicine, and for this reason victimology is considered an interdisciplinary field. This diversity among academics, practitioners, and advocates working in the field of victimology is reflected in the wide range of issues studied by victimologists.

Victimologists conduct research into issues such as estimating the extent of different types of criminal victimization; explaining why victimization occurs, to whom it occurs, and where it occurs; what the consequences of that experience are for crime victims; victims' rights and remedies to their victimization; and the role that victims play in the criminal justice system. Overall, the study of victimology is concerned with the many *dimensions* of victimization. Throughout this book, these dimensions will be explored, with each chapter presenting a different dimension of the larger topic of victimization. Particular emphasis will be placed on research and theory, past and present, which has contributed to and continues to influence the field of victimology.

This chapter reviews two important areas within victimology: its origins as a field of study and the importance of research and theory to understanding the nature and extent of criminal victimization. We begin the chapter by examining the role of research and theory in victimology, including the role of hypotheses and their testing, data collection and analysis, and how the conclusions reached based on scientific study have influenced what is known about crime victims. Following this discussion, we examine the origins of victimology, including its academic, grassroots, and political beginnings.

Studying Criminal Victimization: Theory and Research

Victimology is a social *scientific* discipline. As is the case in any science, researchers in victimology use scientific research methods to develop theories, formulate hypotheses, gather information to test those hypotheses, and either support or reject them based on data collected. This research process allows researchers to develop theories that describe or explain the causes of victimization, advance knowledge in the field of victimology, and suggest possible policy or program responses to prevent victimization.

During the research process, researchers collect observable (empirical) data about crime incidents and victims and investigate relationships between or among variables. For example, a consistent research finding relates to the relationship between the variables *gender* and *victimization*, where males generally have higher overall victimization rates than females, but that pattern does not hold true for all forms of crime, such as sexual violence. To study this issue, a *victimologist* might collect information from crime victims (this information represents something observable or empirical) and discern if there are important differences between males and females that might explain the disparity in rates of victimization. In this way, victimology is similar to another field of study, criminology, a subject with which many readers also may be familiar.

Victimology and criminology are complementary areas of study. For instance, criminologists might read the latest crime statistics and consider why and how offenders broke the law. Victimology is the other "side of the coin." Instead of focusing on the offender, his or her motivations, and how the criminal justice system can best respond to illegal behaviors, victimologists consider crime from the victim's perspective. In doing so, victimologists study why, for example, certain persons, households, or businesses are targeted by offenders, and what puts these targets at risk for criminal victimization. In the study of crime, both of these perspectives are valuable and necessary. In other words, to understand the nature of crime and how and why criminal events transpire, it is also necessary to understand the nature of victimization. Whether victimology is a subfield in criminology, a separate field in its own right, or a distinct field with overlapping focus with criminology is an open question that will not soon be settled (e.g., Mendelsohn, 1974; Nagel, 1974). Figure 1-1 illustrates the possible relationships that the field of victimology has with the field of criminology.

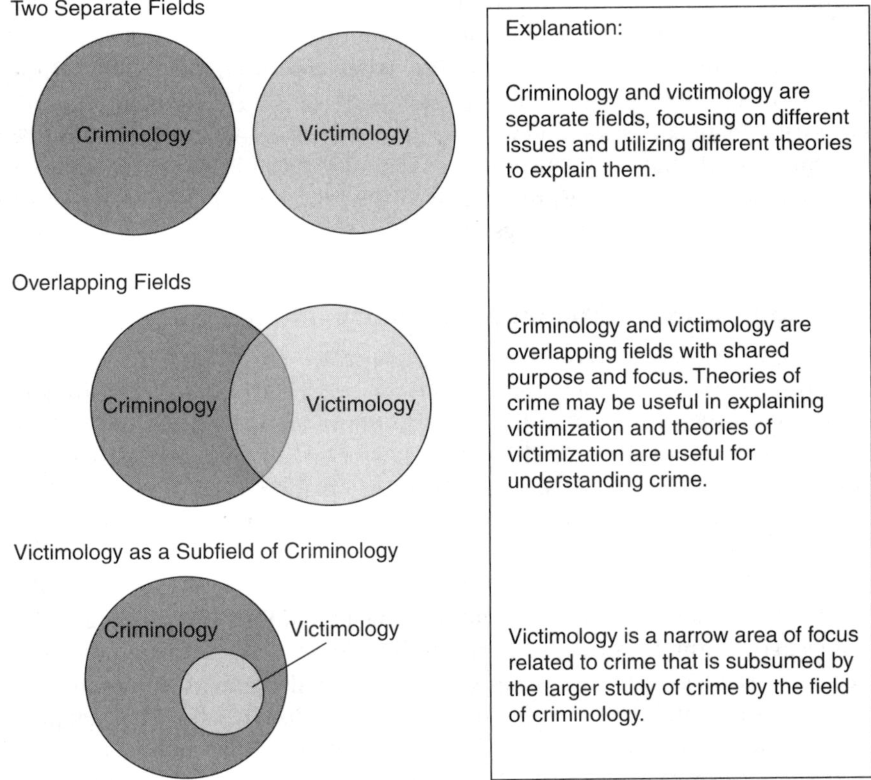

Figure 1-1 Victimology vs. Criminology

Victimology and criminology both use scientific theories that make statements about presumed relationships between or among observable variables. In other words, victimology research is guided by theory, whose statements are widely varied because there are many research questions related to criminal victimization that need answering. The previous example involving victimization rates between males and females could yield several interesting research questions. For instance, are victimization rates the same for males and females? If they are different, how are they different? What can explain this difference? Does this pattern hold for all types of victimization, or only some? Although there are many questions victimologists try to answer, a primary focus of contemporary victimologists is to identify what are called "risk factors" for criminal victimization.

The term ***risk factor*** comes from the field of epidemiology, the study of the patterns and causes of diseases. In epidemiology, risk factors are those variables that are associated with increased risks of disease or infection. For example, according to the Centers for Disease Control and Prevention (CDC) (2014), cigarette smoking is the number-one risk factor for lung cancer. This does not mean that every individual who smokes will get lung cancer, but smokers are at an increased likelihood of acquiring lung cancer compared to those who do not smoke. As previously noted, victimologists also try to identify risk factors for victimization. In victimology, then, risk factors are the variables, such as gender or race, that are associated with increased risks for criminal victimization. For example, living in a city and being outside late several nights every week increases the risk for robbery victimization compared to those who live outside a city or who live in a city but are not outside late at night multiple times a week. Again, this does not necessarily mean that every individual who stays out late will be robbed, but it does mean that he or she may be at an elevated risk of experiencing a robbery compared to others. Further, just as the medical field works toward disease prevention, victimologists work toward preventing victimization by educating people about their risks and providing them with concrete tactics they can use to reduce their risk.

Victimization research and theory have developed and changed over time. While many contemporary victimologists focus on victimization prevention and the identification and reduction of risk factors for victimization, early victimologists were interested in different issues. The various approaches taken by scholars studying criminal victimization through research and theory have evolved over four generations, each contributing to the development and advancement of the field of victimology. Theories of victimization from these four generations are reviewed throughout Chapters 1 through 3, with the *first generation* representing the academic origins of the field of victimology. The first generation is discussed in this chapter; Chapter 2 reviews the second and third generations of theories and theorists; Chapter 3 includes the fourth generation. Table 1-1 summarizes each generation's primary approaches to studying victimization.

Academic Origins of Victimology

Early victimologists viewed crime as an *interactive event* to which both the offender and the victim participated and contributed. Offenders clearly play a major role in

Table 1-1: Generations of Victimology Theories and Theorists

Generation	Primary Approach to Studying Victimization	Scholars Most Associated with the Generation
First Generation	• Focus on victim precipitation in the criminal event • Victim typologies created to categorize victims according to their contribution to their victimization • Earliest empirical research conducted to examine victim precipitation	Von Hentig (1940) Wolfgang (1957) Amir (1971) Mendelsohn (1974) Schafer (1977)
Second Generation	• Victim precipitation approach abandoned in favor of a focus on victimization opportunities • Major theories include lifestyle-exposure theory and routine activity theory	Hindelang, Gottfredson, and Garofalo (1978) Cohen and Felson (1979)
Third Generation	• Continued development and examination of opportunity as the cause of victimization • Refinements to lifestyle-routine activities perspective, including structural-choice theory and multilevel opportunity theory	Miethe and Meier (1994) Fisher, Sloan, Cullen, and Lu (1998) Wilcox, Land, and Hunt (2003)
Fourth Generation	• Further expansion and refinement of the lifestyle-routine activities perspective (e.g., gendered routine activities theory, feminist routine activities theory) and the application of criminological theories (e.g., a general theory of crime) to explain criminal victimization	Schwartz and Pitts (1995) Schreck (1999) Schreck and Fisher (2004) Wilcox, Tillyer, and Fisher (2009) Henson, Wilcox, Reyns, and Cullen (2010)

the commission of crime, for it is their behavior that ultimately is a violation of the law. However, the responsibility that the victim bears for the criminal event is less straightforward. According to Hans von Hentig (1948, p. 384), one of the earliest victimologists, "In a sense the victim shapes and moulds the criminal." In other words, von Hentig was arguing that victim characteristics and behaviors often influence criminal decision making. Explaining victimization as a "collaboration" between offender and victim, with each assuming some responsibility for the crime, is known as victim precipitation and was the hallmark of the first generation of victimologists and victimology theories.

There is no universal definition of victim precipitation or the various forms it takes. Nonetheless, ***victim precipitation*** implies that victims contribute to the criminal event that harms them. Victim precipitation essentially takes one of two forms: victim facilitation and victim provocation. In instances of ***victim facilitation***, victims, often unintentionally, make it easier for offenders to target them or set in motion the events that result in their own victimization. For example, returning to our robbery example, the person who is out late at night several nights a week and cuts through poorly lighted alleys to save time may facilitate his or her own victimization by presenting himself or herself as a relatively easy target to motivated offenders. Chapter 2 highlights the importance of opportunities in causing crime, and the hypothesis that victims may facilitate their victimization by enhancing these opportunities. ***Victim provocation*** suggests that victims overtly act in ways that result in their victimization. For instance, an individual who provokes another into a fight, and loses, is legally speaking a victim of assault, but is not without blame. It was he or she, after all, who provoked the assault. The contributions of the first generation of victimologists who conducted research into victim precipitation, including Hans von Hentig, Beniamin Mendelsohn, Stephen Schafer, Marvin Wolfgang, Menachem Amir, and others, are discussed below.

Hans von Hentig

For much of its history, criminology focused on the causes and consequences of crime in society, in particular why people engaged in criminal actions. Beginning in the middle of the 20th century, this began to change. In 1948, German criminologist Hans von Hentig (1887–1974) published his book *The Criminal and His Victim*, which presented the novel idea that victims—their characteristics, behaviors, and vulnerabilities—are important considerations in understanding why crime occurs. One of the primary ways in which von Hentig explained victimization was by creating a typology or classification scheme of victims. A ***typology*** is a research tool used to systematically classify or "type" characteristics or common traits.

In von Hentig's typology, he classified victims according to two dimensions: (1) *general classes of victims* and (2) *psychological types of victims*. Box 1-1 presents von Hentig's typology of victims based on their biological, sociological, and psychological characteristics. It is important to point out that von Hentig's research was undertaken many decades ago, and, as you will see, some of the terminology and assumptions he makes are extremely dated. However, his work is still considered influential because it introduced the notion that victims, in varying degrees, contribute to their own victimization, and his ideas spurred research by scholars in the first generation premised on this idea. Other early victimologists, notably Beniamin Mendelsohn, Stephen Schafer, and Ezzat Abdel Fattah, also categorized victims according to these characteristics.

As Box 1-1 shows, victim types included in von Hentig's general classes of victims are (1) young people, (2) females, (3) the elderly, (4) those with developmental disabilities or illnesses, and (5) a category including immigrants, minorities, and what he called "dull normals." In considering why certain individuals are targeted by offenders for victimization, von Hentig argued that individuals with these "attributes" carried an increased victimization risk due to their personal characteristics, which attracted offenders to them.

Box 1-1: Von Hentig's Typology of Victims

General Classes of Victims

1. The Young
2. The Female
3. The Old
4. The Mentally Defective and Other Mentally Deranged
5. Immigrants, Minorities, and Dull Normals

Psychological Types of Victims

6. The Depressed
7. The Acquisitive
8. The Wanton
9. The Lonesome and the Heartbroken
10. Blocked, Exempted, and Fighting Victims
11. The Tormentor

Source: Von Hentig (1948).

For the most part, von Hentig viewed the characteristics of the general classes of victims as bringing with them vulnerability, weakness, or a lesser ability to react and recover if criminally victimized. For example, young people, according to von Hentig, are especially vulnerable to victimization. He made the following analogy between young victims in society and the natural order in the animal kingdom: "Youth is the most dangerous period of life. Young creatures under natural conditions are the ideal prey, weak and easy to catch and savory" (von Hentig, 1948, p. 404). Overall, he saw youth as a risk factor for victimization because of the attractiveness of young people as targets and the added vulnerability that youth brings, such as physical weakness and susceptibility to the suggestions of others.

Von Hentig also identified females and the elderly in his typology as possessing risk factors for victimization, using arguments similar to those used to explain victimization of the young. Von Hentig's contention was that female, as a characteristic, was a form of weakness in human beings, particularly physical weakness, that resulted in the commission of crimes against females. Similarly, the elderly often lack physical strength, possess physical or mental impairments that make them "easy" targets, and have accumulated wealth, which is desirable to motivated offenders.

Box 1-1 shows that von Hentig's fourth category includes a group he termed "the mentally defective and other mentally deranged." He categorized "the feeble-minded, the insane, the drug addict, and the alcoholic" as falling into this class of victims (von Hentig, 1948, p. 411). While these personal characteristics seemingly have little in common, von Hentig saw each of these groups (e.g., the insane, drug addicts) as being less able or even incapable of responding to threats arising from their environment. Therefore, his argument was that persons with these characteristics make especially good prey for offenders. For example, of alcoholics he remarked: "The number of larcenies, robberies, rapes, and even murders committed on intoxicated people exceeds all expectation" (von Hentig, 1948, p. 412).

The final type of victims in von Hentig's *general classes* category includes immigrants, minorities, and dull normals. Once again, at first glance these descriptions seem to have little in common, and the meaning of "dull normals" is not immediately clear. Von Hentig used this term to describe those who are gullible or of lower intelligence—those who can be easily "suckered" or taken advantage of by criminals. From this perspective, von Hentig believed that these individuals, along with immigrants and minorities, all shared the common risk factor of being not only less capable of protecting themselves, but also less able to respond to the crime if they are victimized.

Von Hentig's *psychological types of victims* include those who are depressed, acquisitive (greedy), wanton (sexually unrestrained), and lonesome and/or heartbroken, and those he described as "blocked, exempted, and fighting." He argued that each of these psychological states is associated with an attitude (e.g., apathetic, submitting, cooperative, provocative) that makes the victim a more attractive target for offenders. For example, individuals who are depressed can be more easily exploited because they are often apathetic and not alert. In the same way, individuals who are acquisitive or greedy can also be easily exploited because their excessive desire for wealth overwhelms their better judgment. For example, someone who is acquisitive can be easily fooled by a con artist offering a quick return on an initial investment, as is the case in Ponzi schemes. A detailed example of the acquisitive victim can be found in Box 1-2.

Those who are wanton, sensual, or sexually unrestrained may be provocative to offenders, take risks, and/or find themselves in situations that are favorable to crime. The rationale for having a category for the "lonesome" or "heartbroken" is similar to von Hentig's arguments surrounding depressed and acquisitive victims. The idea is that people who are lonesome or heartbroken are easier for perpetrators to target and take advantage of because they are often alone and therefore less protected, and perhaps even more trusting of people they do not know. Blocked, exempted, and fighting victims are those who have "a self-imposed helplessness" that is attractive for criminals (von Hentig, 1948, p. 433). These are individuals who have gotten themselves into bad situations and cannot call the police for help. For example, robbing a drug dealer is at once a dangerous and safe offense. It is dangerous because the victim may have protection and retaliate, but it is safe because he is unlikely to

Box 1-2: The Acquisitive Victim

"In 1917 an illicit sugar trader, X, was found murdered in a deserted wood near the city of Dresden. At this time sugar was strictly rationed in Germany, but there were some possibilities to obtain sugar at an exorbitant price from illegal traders.

X had received a letter, telling him that he could have a vast amount of smuggled sugar, if he would meet the owners in a lonely wood at night where the sugar was supposed to be hidden. They were ready to strike the bargain if he could pay in cash.

In the hope of a substantial and easy gain X went alone to the place with several thousand marks in his pocket. There he was slain and robbed by three youngsters."

Source: von Hentig (1940, p. 304).

call the police. In this scenario, the drug dealer is the "blocked" victim. Victims of blackmail also can be considered blocked victims.

The final psychological type is called "the tormentor," which describes victims who are victimized over time and eventually turn on their offender, becoming perpetrators themselves. For example, a victim of intimate partner abuse for many years is finally provoked to the point of killing the offender. In considering von Hentig's typology and arguments, it is important to keep in mind the overall premise of his work—namely that criminal events are the result of an interaction of victims and offenders. From this perspective, not only do offenders affect victims, but victims influence offenders as well. This principle suggests that in many ways victims precipitate or contribute to their own victimization, an idea underlying both the first generation of victimology and the work of Mendelsohn.

Beniamin Mendelsohn

Beniamin Mendelsohn (1900–1998) was an Israeli defense attorney turned victimologist who became interested in the role of the victim in criminal acts as he prepared cases for trial. As a contemporary of von Hentig, Mendelsohn focused on the victim's contribution to the criminal event. In studying victim-precipitated crime he interviewed his clients prior to trial, asking them to answer as many as 300 questions, and concluded that most victims participated in their victimization to some degree (Mendelsohn, 1974). In 1947, Mendelsohn presented a paper in Bucharest, Romania, in which he coined the term *victimology* and advocated that the study of victims be a new and separate field from that of criminology (Mendelsohn, 1974). For this reason, Mendelsohn is often referred to as the "father of victimology."

Although Mendelsohn's work eventually widened in scope to encompass general victimology, which is concerned with all types of victims, his first-generation work in victimology focused on crime victims. Like von Hentig, Mendelsohn devised a typology of victims to better understand how victims ultimately contribute to their victimization, but his typology categorized victims according to their degree of responsibility for the crime. From this point of view, it is not only offenders who are accountable for crime, but also victims. Further, the responsibility assigned to either the offender or victim varies with circumstances, is not always clear, and is shared more often than not (Mannheim, 1965). Mendelsohn's typology comprises six categories and appears in Box 1-3.

Box 1-3: Mendelsohn's Typology of Victims

1. The Completely Innocent Victim
2. The Victim with Minor Guilt (also known as victims due to ignorance)
3. The Victim who is as Guilty as the Offender (also known as voluntary victims)
4. The Victim who is More Guilty than the Offender
5. The Most Guilty Victim (also known as victims who are guilty alone)
6. The Imaginary Victim (also known as simulating victims)

Mendelsohn's first type of victim, *the completely innocent victim*, bears no responsibility for his or her criminal victimization. Children, for example, who are targeted simply because they are children, are completely innocent. Mendelsohn also indicated that those who are unconscious are completely innocent victims. His second type, *the victim with minor guilt*, includes victims partially responsible for their criminal victimization, although their actions may be accidental or inadvertent. Those who inadvertently place themselves in harm's way would assume minor guilt for their victimization, because such danger could have been expected or avoided through awareness or planning. For example, someone who walks home alone at night from a bar and is attacked may have minor responsibility for his or her victimization. Mendelsohn's third type of victim is *as guilty as the offender*. He explained that these victims shoulder responsibility equal to that of the offender for their victimization. They engage in risky, deviant, delinquent, or criminal behaviors and in doing so accept the victimization risks. For instance, an individual who is insulted and challenged to a fist fight accepts the challenge knowing the opponent is going to try to hurt him or her. This individual voluntarily participates.

Mendelsohn's fourth type of victim is *the victim who is more guilty than the offender*. Mendelsohn considered these victims to be slightly guiltier than their offenders. They may provoke or induce offenders into action. For example, von Hentig's tormentor type described victims who eventually retaliate against their perpetrators, such as victims of child abuse or intimate partner violence. In this scenario, the perpetrator who is attacked (i.e., the abuser) has more guilt than does the offender (i.e., the victim of child abuse).

The fifth category of victim, according to Mendelsohn, is *the most guilty victim*. These victims are most guilty because they are responsible for initiating the actions that eventually lead to their subsequent harm. For instance, a robber targets a victim who fights back and kills him in self-defense. In this example, the robber accepts guilt because there would have been no injury if not for his behavior. Mendelsohn referred to his final type of victim as *the imaginary victim* to describe those who have not suffered a criminal victimization but may accuse another of offending against them, such as "paranoids, hysterical persons, senile persons, and children" (Schafer, 1977, p. 36).

Mendelsohn's typology contrasts with von Hentig's in interesting ways. Perhaps because of his legal expertise, he classified victims according to their level of guilt or culpability rather than based on their personal characteristics, attitude, or psychological state. For example, while von Hentig identified youth as a risk factor for victimization, Mendelsohn suggested that children were completely innocent, having no responsibility for their victimization. Further, most of the types of victims from von Hentig's general classes of victims would probably be classified by Mendelsohn as having either no guilt or minor guilt. This is a difference in approach between von Hentig, who focused on victimization risk, and Mendelsohn, who actually assigned varying degrees of culpability or blame to victims. The two typologies also overlap. For instance, von Hentig's tormentor type is an example of a victim who is "more guilty" than the offender.

These typologies and others like them (e.g., Fattah, 1967; Sellin & Wolfgang, 1964) were useful tools for victimologists to consider how victims factor into criminal events.

One such typology, developed by Stephen Schafer, bridged the gap between von Hentig's and Mendelsohn's typologies by considering victim characteristics as well as the victim's degree of responsibility.

Stephen Schafer

Stephen Schafer (1911–1976) was a native of Hungary and a criminologist at Northeastern University. He criticized existing victim typologies as incomplete and argued that typologies of victims should be derived from theory and guided by empirical observations about victim–offender relationships. It was Schafer's contention that much victimization is the culmination of a back-and-forth between the victim and the offender that varies according to the victim–offender relationship. Thus, for Schafer, the victim is an integral player in the criminal event.

Similar to von Hentig and Mendelsohn, Schafer proposed his own seven-category typology of victims in his book *Victimology: The Victim and his Criminal*. Schafer's typology was based on his concept of ***functional responsibility***, which means that victims (or potential victims) are responsible for not provoking offenders into action, while at the same time actively preventing their possible victimization. In other words, victims should have the smallest possible role in the criminal event by not enticing, provoking, or otherwise precipitating their victimization in any way. Schafer's typology is in Box 1-4.

Schafer's first type of victim is referred to as *unrelated victims*. These victims have no relationship with their offender, besides being his or her crime victim, and in this way all members of society are potential victims. For these types of victims, Schafer argued that the offender was totally responsible for the crime because the initiation of the crime was solely the decision of the offender. Schafer explained that, for example, victims of bank robbery, burglary, and other crimes who are selected only on the basis of situational characteristics or at random would be considered unrelated victims. *Provocative victims* are victims who initiate the chain of events that result in their victimization by "harming" the offender in some way. For this reason they share responsibility for the crime with the offender. Provocative victims might incite an offender into action in any number of ways. For example, an insult, an abrasive remark, a broken promise, or any other overt action that elicits a criminal response would be considered a provocation.

Box 1-4: Schafer's Typology of Victims

1. Unrelated Victims
2. Provocative Victims
3. Precipitative Victims
4. Biologically Weak Victims
5. Socially Weak Victims
6. Self-Victimizing Victims
7. Political Victims

As Box 1-4 indicates, Schafer's third victim type is what he described as *precipitative victims*. Schafer explained that these victims are similar to provocative victims in that precipitative victims initiate the criminal event. However, their behavior is not harmful to the offender; it is merely encouraging, enticing, or alluring. For example, careless behaviors such as failing to lock doors or leaving valuables unprotected might tempt those who otherwise have no criminal motivation. Schafer explained that these victims are not entirely blameless and therefore share some responsibility for their victimization with the offender.

Schafer labeled his next victim type as *biologically weak victims*. These are victims who are targeted *because* of their biological (physical) or mental characteristics and who have no responsibility for their victimization. Children, the elderly, and those with physical or developmental disabilities are all examples of "biologically weak victims." Although Schafer argued that, technically, these individuals do precipitate their victimization, they have no choice in the matter.

The fifth type of victim in Schafer's typology is what he called *socially weak victims*. Like biologically weak victims, socially weak victims are not responsible for their victimization. Schafer explained that these individuals are not regarded as full-fledged members of society, which makes them vulnerable to victimization. Accordingly, Schafer argued that blame for their victimization was shared between the offender and society. Immigrants, minorities, and members of certain religions who are victimized may be considered socially weak victims.

Next, *self-victimizing victims* are individuals who, according to Schafer, victimize themselves and include such individuals as gamblers, alcoholics, and drug addicts. They are, in effect, their own criminals. As such, self-victimizing victims are wholly responsible for their victimization.

Schafer's final type of victim is labeled the *political victims*. These are victim who are targeted by political opponents. Those who are unjustly slandered, maligned, or made out to be criminals by their competitors are considered political victims for Schafer. For example, Martin Luther King, Jr. was labeled as a "communist" by his political enemies. Likewise, the 1950s witnessed Republican Senator Joseph McCarthy's practice of accusing his political rivals of being "disloyal and treasonous communists."

Through their typologies, von Hentig, Mendelsohn, and Schafer categorized victims either according to their risk factors for victimization (von Hentig) or their (lack of) responsibility for the crime (Mendelsohn and Schafer). These early efforts to understand victims and the reasons for their victimization are representative of the first generation of victimologists. Other notable contributions were made by Fattah (1967) and Thorsten Sellin and Marvin Wolfgang (1964), who developed their own typologies of victim responsibility (Table 1-2).

Overall, each of the previously discussed scholars contributed to the academic origins of the field of victimology through their typologies. However, typologies are limited and were not the only method used by the first generation of victimologists to study crime victims and their responsibility for crime. In fact, Schafer (1977, p. 44) argued that "Certainly no victim typology can be perfect, and in our present state of knowledge even the best would be easily vulnerable for a critique." Advancing the study of victimology required moving beyond theoretical typologies to analyzing empirical victimization data. Several early victimologists contributed to this effort

Table 1-2: Spotlight on Theory: Other Typologies—Fattah and Sellin and Wolfgang

Fattah (1967)	Sellin and Wolfgang (1964)
1. *Nonparticipating Victims:* do not contribute to their victimization	1. *Primary Victimization:* individuals who are personally victimized by offenders
2. *Latent or Predisposed Victims:* are more likely because of their character to experience certain types of crimes	2. *Secondary Victimization:* impersonal victimization targets (e.g., retail stores, churches)
3. *Provocative Victims:* play a part in the crime by passively or actively encouraging the offender	3. *Tertiary Victimization:* the public or society at large is victimized
4. *Participating Victims:* make their own victimization possible or easier	4. *Mutual Victimization:* victims consent to their victimization and are also offenders (e.g., assisted suicide)
5. *False Victims:* are not true victims or have victimized themselves	5. *No Victimization:* there is no victim or the offense is minor and unrecognizable

Sources: Fattah (1967); Sellin and Wolfgang (1964).

(e.g., Fattah, 1971; Pittman & Handy, 1964), investigating variables such as victims' race or age, the presence of alcohol during a crime, and the relationship between the victim and the offender, but Marvin Wolfgang (1957) was the first to investigate the issue of victim precipitation by collecting and analyzing victimization data.

Marvin E. Wolfgang

Marvin Wolfgang (1924–1998) was a professor of criminology, legal studies, and law at the University of Pennsylvania for nearly 50 years. During that time he made innumerable contributions to the field of criminology, and in 1994 the *British Journal of Criminology* recognized Wolfgang as "the most influential criminologist in the English-speaking world." Although Wolfgang was a criminologist, one of his most significant contributions was research into the occurrence of victim-precipitated homicide, which was published in his 1957 book *Patterns in Criminal Homicide.* He defined homicides as victim-precipitated if "the victim is a direct, positive precipitator of the crime" and "the first to commence the interplay or resort to physical violence" (Wolfgang, 1957, p. 2). For example, if the homicide victim was the first one to threaten, show, or use a deadly weapon or initiate a physical altercation, Wolfgang considered the resulting homicide to be victim-precipitated.

To study victim-precipitated homicide, Wolfgang collected official victimization data from the Homicide Squad of the Philadelphia Police Department on homicides committed between 1948 and 1952. These data yielded a total of 588 homicide victims, 26% of whom Wolfgang (1957, 1958) determined had precipitated their own victimizations. Examples provided by Wolfgang of typical victim-precipitated homicides are provided in Box 1-5.

In addition to calculating the percentage of victimizations that were precipitated by victims, Wolfgang (1957) also identified the following factors common to victim-precipitated homicides: (1) the victim and offender had some kind of *prior relationship*;

Box 1-5: Examples of Victim-Precipitated Homicide from Wolfgang's Study

"A husband accused his wife of giving money to another man, and while she was making breakfast, he attacked her with a bottle, then a brick, and finally a piece of concrete block. Having had a butcher knife in hand, she stabbed him during the fight."

"During a lover's quarrel, the male (victim) hit his mistress and threw a can of kerosene at her. She retaliated by throwing the liquid on him, and then tossed a lighted match in his direction. He died from the burns."

"A drunken victim with knife in hand approached his slayer during a quarrel. The slayer showed a gun, and the victim dared him to shoot. He did."

"The victim was the aggressor in a fight, having struck his enemy several times. Friend tried to interfere, but the victim persisted. Finally, the offender retaliated with blows, causing the victim to fall and hit his head on the sidewalk, as a result of which he died."

Source: Wolfgang (1957, p. 3).

(2) there was a series of *escalating disagreements* between the victim and the offender; (3) the victim often had a *prior criminal record*; and (4) the *presence of alcohol* during the situation. To this last point, Wolfgang (1957) noted that in 74% of victim-precipitated homicides alcohol was present, compared to 60% of homicides that were not victim-precipitated.

Wolfgang's work provided empirical evidence that under certain circumstances victims are accountable for their victimization, at least as far as the concept of victim culpability, responsibility, or precipitation is defined. It also inspired the work of another first-generation victimologist, Menachem Amir.

Menachem Amir

Menachem Amir (b. 1930), a former graduate student of Wolfgang's, conducted empirical research focused on the topic of victim-precipitated rape. While Wolfgang used homicide data from Philadelphia to reveal that under certain circumstances homicides may be victim-precipitated, Wolfgang's conceptualization of victim precipitation had a legal basis. In other words, his examples from Box 1-3 demonstrate that in many cases homicide victims are killed in self-defense by those they themselves were attacking. However, there is no self-defense or comparable argument for rape victimization. Still, Amir (1971, p. 230) asserted that

> like the offender who creates situations in which he is apprehended, and thus becomes the victim of his own doings, the victim of sex crimes, by her relationship to the offender and by her behavior, which is often unconscious, creates the situation of her victimization.

Wolfgang's scholarly influence on Amir's research is apparent. Like Wolfgang, Amir collected data from police files. Even the title of his book, *Patterns in Forcible*

Rape, is similar to the title of Wolfgang's book. Further following Wolfgang's lead, Amir defined victim-precipitated rapes as those in which the victim actually or was perceived by the offender to agree to sex, but changed her mind beforehand or did not respond forcefully enough when the offender suggested sex (Amir, 1967). In other words, according to Amir, a victim is responsible for her rape if she changes her mind about sex, does not reject the offender vigorously enough, or somehow incorrectly sends the wrong signal that she wants to have sexual relations.

Amir collected rape victimization data from the Philadelphia Police Department for the years 1958 and 1960, which netted him 646 rapes. Primary among his findings was his conclusion that 122 (19%) of these victims had precipitated their own victimization. Amir also reported a significantly higher presence of certain characteristics among victim-precipitated rapes compared to others. For example, Amir claimed his analysis revealed the following characteristics as associated with victim-precipitated rapes: (1) victims were primarily between the age of 15 and 19; (2) alcohol use (by either the victim or both the victim and the offender); (3) victims and offenders knew each other; and (4) victims were more likely to have a "bad" reputation.

Using these findings Amir devised his own typology of rape victimization based on the victim's behavior, which appears in Figure 1-2. He conceived of rape as occurring within a continuum of victim responsibility, with some victims having no responsibility for their victimization and others being active participants in their own rape. According to Amir, the victim's behavior prior to the rape determines where along the continuum of victim precipitation she should be placed. For example, a *precipitative victim* may place herself in a risky situation that results in her rape, a decision for which Amir says she should take some responsibility for her victimization. Similarly, victims who behave *seductively*, by their language, their dress, or their manner, are either conscious or unconscious participants in their victimization and should bear some responsibility for their rape victimization.

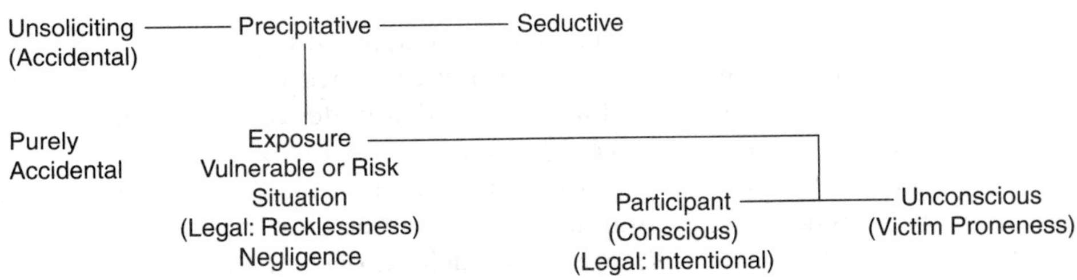

Figure 1-2 Amir's Typology of Victim Behavior
Source: Amir (1971).

Amir's research was met with heavy criticism on several fronts. His critics took particular issue with the implication that some rape victims have a psychological, if unconscious, desire to be raped (Doerner, 2010). Further, Amir's conceptualization of a rape as victim-precipitated was based in part on the rapist's *perception* of the victim's behavior, not necessarily her *actual* behavior—something over which victims have no control. Amir further suggested that victim behaviors may be contrary to how offenders believe women should behave, which allows them to rationalize victimizing women. For example, if a woman uses risqué language, dresses seductively, or has a "bad reputation," the offender may rationalize his criminal behavior by believing that she "deserved" her victimization or "had it coming to her" (Amir, 1971).

In light of his study's results, Amir (1971, p. 275) concluded that "These results point to the fact that the offender should not be viewed as the sole 'cause' and reason for the offense, and that the 'virtuous' victim is not always the innocent and passive party." This assertion not only led to a rejection of Amir's work but effectively halted the progression of victim precipitation as an explanation for victimization among academics in the field of victimology. One criticism of this line of research was that to assign victims responsibility—by arguing victim precipitation, facilitation, or provocation—was to blame victims for their own victimization (Fattah, 2000). ***Victim blaming*** was not only a critique of the first generation of victimology, but also a criticism of society's reaction to crime victims. Partially in response to victim blaming, grassroots advocacy groups, including the victims' rights movement, the women's movement, and the children's movement, also played influential roles in the development of modern-day victimology.

Grassroots Origins of Victimology

While the academic roots of victimology were growing, social forces throughout American society also were driving the development of the field of victimology. The civil rights movement, the women's movement, and the children's movement were each separately working toward the shared goal of highlighting the plight of crime victims and advocating for cultural, social, and political changes with respect to society's and the criminal justice system's treatment of them.

The Civil Rights Movement

The civil rights movement in the United States during the 1950s and 1960s concentrated on ending segregation of African Americans from many areas of social life, such as education, housing, and employment, and an end to other forms of discrimination, including discrimination in the criminal justice system. The movement furthered the causes of crime victims by highlighting the discrimination and unequal treatment suffered by both African American crime victims and African American offenders. For example, during this time relations between law enforcement and the African American community were very tense, with police, who were almost exclusively white and male, often viewed as little more than an invading army. As a result, black crime victims would often not report their experience to the police and therefore did not receive help in recovering from their victimization, nor receive justice for the harm done to them. Many African Americans who did contact the authorities felt that the police did not respond to their victimization in the same way as they would for white victims. Further, African Americans accused of crimes were also treated differently than were whites once they entered the criminal justice system. Police brutality, unequal treatment in the courts, and disparate sentences were all issues the civil rights movement sought to address. Highlighting these social injustices also underscored the need to help individuals who had been victims of crime.

The Women's Movement

During the 1960s and 1970s, as victimology was still developing, advocates for women, including the ***feminist movement***, championed women's rights issues related to criminal victimization. Although concerned with the treatment of women by social institutions such as schools, the workforce, and the family more generally, the women's movement was especially influential in two areas of criminal justice. First, the movement focused attention on the sexual victimization of women and the criminal justice system's response to crimes such as rape and sexual assault. For example, feminists in the 1960s were successful in getting states to repeal what were known as *marital exemption laws* (found largely in the South) that made it legally impossible for a wife to pursue rape charges against her husband for having sexual relations with her without her consent for as long as they were legally married. Today, marital rape is criminalized in all 50 states.

The second area in which the women's movement directed its efforts was spousal abuse—that is, physical assault perpetrated by a husband against his wife or a wife against her husband. Feminists argued that spousal abuse and the ways in which the criminal justice system responded to it were further evidence that society was dominated by men. For example, feminists claimed many police officers were reluctant to intervene in situations occurring behind closed doors within the context of a marriage. As a result, a cycle of physical violence was often repeated among the spouses. According to Lenore Walker's (1980, 2009) ***cycle theory of violence***, spousal assault often involves a tension-building phase, an acute battering phase, and a contrite loving phase. The cycle of violence is discussed in depth in Chapter 6 and illustrates that episodes of spousal abuse are often cyclical or repeated, which is why intervention by the system and services for victims who feel trapped and powerless are so important.

Feminists argued that victim blaming was a significant problem in instances of spousal sexual and physical victimization, and the poor treatment of these victims by the criminal justice system further demonstrated that women occupied a subservient place in society. Many victims of these crimes felt that the criminal justice system victimized them further by not believing them or taking them seriously, failing to punish offenders appropriately, or scrutinizing the victim's behavior rather than the offender's. The women's movement worked toward remedying these problems through providing victim services, shelters, and legal actions.

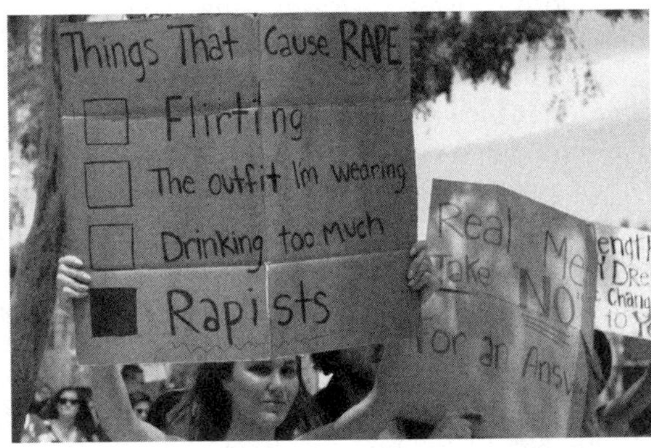

Protestors Responding to Victim-Blaming.

The Children's Movement

Like the women's movement, the children's movement advocated for better treatment of an underserved group of crime victims: children. Crimes against children, such as abuse and neglect, have occurred throughout history, as illustrated in the case of Mary Ellen Wilson in Box 1-6. However, recognizing children as a group of crime victims with special needs did not occur in earnest in the United States until the early 1960s.

Box 1-6: Mary Ellen Wilson

Mary Ellen Wilson before and after her ordeal. Photo credit: The George Sim Johnston Archives of The New York Society for the Prevention of Cruelty to Children

Mary Ellen Wilson is sometimes described as America's first victim of child abuse (Shelman & Lazoritz, 2005). While child abuse has existed throughout recorded history, it was Mary Ellen's experiences in the slums of New York City in 1874 that generated national attention and debate on the issue of child abuse. Nine-year-old Mary Ellen was confined to her tenement apartment by her guardians, who treated her cruelly and beat her frequently, until a humanitarian named Etta Angell Wheeler learned of Mary Ellen's plight and intervened. Since no laws existed to protect children from abuse or cruelty by parents or guardians, Wheeler appealed to the American Society for the Prevention of Cruelty to Animals (ASPCA). Henry Bergh, the president and founder of the ASPCA, and his attorney, Elbridge T. Gerry, were able to convince Judge Abraham Lawrence to take the case. Within 48 hours of learning of Mary Ellen's plight from Bergh, Mary Ellen had been rescued forever from her situation. Her story generated national interest in the issue of child abuse and led to the creation of the New York Society for the Prevention of Cruelty to Children. Mary Ellen described her lifetime of victimization to Judge Lawrence as follows:

> "My name is Mary Ellen McCormack. I don't know how old I am. My mother and father are both dead; I have no recollection of a time when I did not live with the Connollys; I call Mrs. Connolly mama; I have never had but one pair of shoes, but can't recollect when that was. I have had no shoes or stockings on this winter; I have never been allowed to go out of the rooms where the Connollys live except in the nighttime, and then only in the yard; I have never had on a particle of flannel. My bed at night is only a piece of carpet, stretched on the floor underneath a window, and I sleep in my little undergarment, with a quilt over me. I am never allowed to play with any children or have any company whatever. Mama has been in the habit of whipping and beating me almost every day. She used to whip me with a twisted whip, a raw hide.

(Continued)

Box 1-6: Mary Ellen Wilson (*continued*)

The whip always left black and blue marks on my body. I have now on my head two black and blue marks which were made by mama with the whip, and a cut on the left side of my forehead which was made by a pair of scissors in mama's hand. She struck me with the scissors and cut me. I have no recollection of having ever been kissed by mama. I have never been taken on my mama's lap, or caressed or petted. I never dared to speak to anybody, because if I did I would get whipped; I never had, to my recollection, any more clothing than I have on at present, a calico dress and skirt; I have seen stockings and other clothes in our room, but I am not allowed to put them on; whenever mama went out I was locked up in the bedroom; the scissors with which mama struck me are those now shown by Mr. Evans; I don't know for what I was whipped; mama never said anything to me when she whipped me; I do not want to go back to live with mama, because she beats me so; I have no recollection of ever being in the street in my life."

Source: Shelman and Lazoritz (2005, p. 7).

In 1962 Dr. C. Henry Kempe exposed the medical community to the pervasive issue of child abuse through a paper published in the *Journal of the American Medical Association* titled "The Battered-Child Syndrome." According to Kempe and his colleagues (Kempe, Silverman, Steele, Droegemueller, & Silver, 1962), ***battered-child syndrome*** occurs when a young child suffers repeated serious physical abuse by parents or other caregivers. This article raised awareness in the medical community and among the general public about the existence of child abuse. Also reported in this article were the results of a nationwide survey of hospitals on the incidence of battered-child syndrome. From their national sample of 71 hospitals, the researchers identified 302 cases, in which 33 of the children died and 85 suffered permanent brain damage (Kempe et al., 1962). Kempe and his coauthors (1962, p. 24) also called on the medical community to report suspected cases of battered-child syndrome to the authorities, remarking

> Physicians, because of their own feelings and their difficulty in playing a role that they find hard to assume, may have great reluctance in believing that parents were guilty of abuse. They may also find it difficult to initiate proper investigation so as to assure adequate management of the case. Above all the physician's duty and responsibility to the child requires a full evaluation of the problem and a guarantee that the expected repetition of trauma will not be permitted to occur.

Kempe's work provided advocates with evidence needed to argue for expanded rights and services for child crime victims, which were a reality soon after. Considered collectively, the civil rights movement, the women's movement, and the children's movement had a significant influence on the overall victims' rights movement, and eventually these efforts culminated to improve the lives of marginalized groups, including the lives of crime victims. Also central to the development and proliferation of victims' rights were the political origins of victimology, including the law and order movement, the work of the Law Enforcement Assistance Administration (LEAA), and key federal legislation.

Political Origins of Victimology

Over time, the previously discussed social justice movements, along with the growing academic interest in the emerging study of crime victims, coalesced, and politically the United States began to address the plight of victims of crime through federal victims' rights legislation. In part, this change was also driven by the conservatism of the law and order movement, the report on the state of crime in the United States by the President's Commission on Law Enforcement, and the work of the LEAA.

The "Law and Order" Movement

In some ways, the so-called "law and order" movement can be seen as a countermovement to the civil rights and women's rights movements. Increasing crime rates during the 1960s, along with unrest on college campuses, antiwar protests, rioting, and expanded civil rights, helped move a significant portion of the American public to the political right, fostering a new conservatism and a renewed focus on law and order. "Law and order" is a phrase that has been used in many contexts by presidents and other politicians from Thomas Jefferson to Richard Nixon to Bill Clinton (Oliver, 2003) with varying intent. In the 1960s and 1970s, as the ***law and order movement*** was developing and growing, the phrase was based on a particular philosophy of ***crime control***.

As a philosophy, crime control endorses swift justice, harsh punishments, and efficiency in the criminal justice process. Proponents argued that too many criminals escape the criminal justice system though "legal loopholes" (e.g., procedural law) that only protect criminals from arrest, prosecution, and punishment, while those who are victimized are left to fend for themselves. Combined with public fear of crime and media frenzy about rapidly increasing crime rates, politicians were able to argue for greater crime control and "get tough" approaches to the crime problem. Although the law and order movement was certainly not a victims' rights movement, its emphasis on punishment eventually led to an acknowledgment that victims had been ignored in the administration of criminal justice. This generated support for victims' rights and remedying the hardships suffered by victims of crime, such as victim restitution as a form of punishment. These shifts in attitude and the recognition that victims should be part of the criminal justice process were contributing factors in the expansion of victims' rights that was to come in the 1980s and 1990s.

The President's Commission on Law Enforcement and the Law Enforcement Assistance Administration

During the 1960s the issue of crime became part of the national dialogue as crime rates increased dramatically, race relations were strained, and prominent leaders were assassinated, including President John F. Kennedy, his brother Robert Kennedy, and Dr. Martin Luther King, Jr. The federal government's response was to create the ***President's Commission on Law Enforcement and the Administration of Justice***, enact the *1965 Law Enforcement Assistance Act*, and establish the Office of Law Enforcement Assistance. The President's Commission released a famous report in 1967 titled *The Challenge of Crime in a Free Society* that surveyed the entire criminal justice process as well as specific forms of crime and delinquency (e.g., drug abuse, organized crime) and made recommendations for improving the nation's response to crime.

The report made several recommendations for addressing the crime problem, such as improving education and training of police officers throughout the United States. This report also is important to the political origins of victimology because it suggested that efforts should be made to compensate victims of crime who suffer financial hardships—a significant step toward victims' rights. In fact, the Commission (1967, p. 38) suggested that the consequences victims suffer as a result of crime need more attention, concluding that: "One of the most neglected subjects in the study of crime is its victims." The Commission also undertook the first ever national victimization survey, which was the forerunner to the National Crime Victimization Survey (discussed in Chapter 4). Further, based on the recommendations of the President's Commission, Congress created the ***Law Enforcement Assistance Administration*** (LEAA) with passage of the *Omnibus Crime Control and Safe Streets Act of 1968*. The LEAA replaced and absorbed all of the functions of these previous entities.

As a unit within the larger U.S. Department of Justice, the purpose of the LEAA was essentially to improve the criminal justice system in the United States by administering federal grants to state and local agencies geared toward reducing crime. Specifically, the mission of the LEAA was fourfold: (1) to encourage states to develop plans to combat crime and delinquency; (2) to make grants available to states to implement these plans; (3) to help governments and agencies improve the criminal justice system by providing guidance and leadership; and (4) to conduct criminal justice research. The LEAA was abolished in 1982, but during its tenure it funded programs that trained and educated thousands of criminal justice professionals (Barker, 2010).

The federal *Omnibus Crime Control and Safe Streets Act of 1968* also established the National Institute of Law Enforcement and Criminal Justice as the research wing of the LEAA. The Institute was primarily concerned with researching the crime problem and the national response to it, which included funding research through grants to private organizations, colleges and universities, and public agencies (Varon, 1975). The LEAA is included as an early political force in the development of the field of victimology because the federal funding allocated by the LEAA was used to create some of the early victim service programs, such as victim-witness assistance programs (Dussich, 1986).

Federal Legislation in the United States

The law and order movement, the work of the President's Commission, and the LEAA provided the backdrop for a wave of state and federal victims' rights legislation that was to come in the 1980s and 1990s. As Box 1-7 illustrates, in recent decades

Box 1-7: Key Federal Victims' Rights Legislation

Year	Legislation	Year	Legislation
1974	Child Abuse Prevention and Treatment Act	1996	Community Notification Act ("Megan's Law")
1980	Parental Kidnapping Prevention Act	1996	Antiterrorism and Effective Death Penalty Act
1982	Victim and Witness Protection Act	1996	Mandatory Victims' Restitution Act
1982	Missing Children's Act	1997	Victims' Rights Clarification Act
1984	Victims of Crime Act	1998	Crime Victims with Disabilities Awareness Act
1984	Missing Children's Assistance Act	1998	Identity Theft and Deterrence Act
1984	Family Violence Prevention and Services Act	2000	Trafficking Victims Protection Act
1985	Children's Justice Act	2001	Air Transportation Safety and System Stabilization Act
1988	Drunk Driving Prevention Act	2003	PROTECT Act ("Amber Alert" law)
1990	Hate Crimes Statistics Act	2003	Prison Rape Elimination Act
1990	Student Right-To-Know and Campus Security Act	2003	Fair and Accurate Credit Transaction Act
1990	Victims of Child Abuse Act	2004	Justice for All Act
1990	Victims' Rights and Restitution Act	2006	Adam Walsh Child Protection and Safety Act
1990	National Child Search Assistance Act	2010	Tribal Law and Order Act
1992	Battered Women's Testimony Act	2011	Ike Skelton National Defense Authorization Act
1993	Child Sexual Abuse Registry Act	2013	Kilah Davenport Child Protection Act
1994	Violent Crime Control and Law Enforcement Act	2014	Sean and David Goldman International Child Abduction Prevention and Return Act
1994	Violence Against Women Act		

Source: Office for Victims of Crime (2014).

Congress has passed many federal laws focused on expanding services for crime victims and providing victims' rights, starting in 1974 with the *Child Abuse Prevention and Treatment Act of 1974*. In part, this legislation was fueled by the 68 recommendations made by the President's Task Force on Victims of Crime, which was created by President Reagan in 1981 to find ways to improve the lives of crime victims. While it is beyond the scope of this chapter to review every federal victims' rights law, a few examples are discussed in detail.

The ***Child Abuse Prevention and Treatment Act*** of 1974 has been amended several times over the years, but its original purpose was to provide financial assistance to the states and their communities for identifying, preventing, and treating child abuse and neglect in the United States. The act also established the National Center on Child Abuse and Neglect, which acts as a clearinghouse for information, technical assistance, and model programs related to addressing child abuse and neglect. In 2010, the Act was amended and reauthorized.

The ***Victims of Crime Act of 1984*** established the Crime Victims Fund, which allocates money to state victim compensation and local-level victim assistance programs. These funds are generated from federal bond and asset forfeitures, and fines and penalties paid by federal offenders. Subsequent revisions to the Act also established the Office for Victims of Crime, which administers the Crime Victims Fund. These funds support victims across the United States in their recovery efforts following a crime through victim assistance and compensation, training and technical assistance for victim service providers, and more.

The ***Student Right-To-Know and Campus Security Act of 1990*** (later renamed the *Jeanne Clery Disclosure of Campus Security Policy and Campus Crime Statistics Act* after Jeanne Clery, who was raped and murdered in 1986 in her dorm room at Lehigh University) originally was designed to mandate colleges and universities participating in federal financial aid programs to publicly report their annual crime statistics and engage in various crime-prevention activities. Like the previously discussed legislation, the *Clery Act* has been reauthorized and amended over time. The Act also requires these institutions to keep a publicly available crime log and provide timely warnings of crimes that may be a threat to students and employees.

The ***Violence Against Women Act of 1994*** was drafted by then-Senator Joseph Biden and signed into law by President Bill Clinton as part of the *Violent Crime Control and Law Enforcement Act of 1994*. It provided funding in excess of $1 billion to address violence against women by enhancing enforcement, increasing prosecutions, expanding services, and providing protections for victims of such crimes as domestic violence, sexual violence, dating violence, and stalking. The act was reauthorized and expanded in 2000, 2006, and 2013.

These federal laws and those listed in Box 1-7 represent successful efforts on the part of victimologists and advocates to address perceived issues relating to victims' rights and suffering. The policies and practices that exist as a result of these laws define how crime victims recover from their victimization and are an important element in the functioning of the criminal justice system. The victim's role in the criminal justice process, victim services, and victim assistance are discussed in Chapter 12, but these remedies exist in part because of the political origins of victimology highlighted here.

Summary

This chapter introduced victimology as a social science and focused on the three origins of contemporary victimology: its academic, grassroots, and political roots. While the concepts of *victimization* and *victim* are not unique to these origins, they did take on special meanings across these contexts. First, the first-generation academic origins of victimology focused on assessing the degree to which victims contribute to criminal events through precipitation, facilitation, and provocation. As such, researchers developed typologies that could be used to understand different types of victims and their responsibility for criminal victimization. At the same time, early empirical research in victimology was undertaken and the first studies of victim-precipitated crime were conducted. Second, the grassroots origins of victimology began as separate social justice movements aimed at improving the lives of marginalized groups but culminated in a realization that society was not taking care of its crime victims. The civil rights movement, the women's movement, and the children's movement drew attention to the needs of racial minorities, women, and children as victims of crime. Third, the political origins of victimology are illustrated in the conservative approach to crime characterizing the law and order movement, and the policy and law that was inspired by the President's Commission and the LEAA during the 1960s. One of the many policy descendants of these early political efforts is the *Clery Act*, which is highlighted in the "Spotlight on Policy: The *Clery Act*" box. Together, these three pillars of the origins of victimology overlapped in many ways, climaxing in the complex and multidimensional field that represents modern-day victimology research and services.

Spotlight on Policy: The *Clery Act*

In 1990, Congress passed and President George H.W. Bush signed into law the *Student Right-To-Know and Campus Security Act*. A primary focus of this new legislation was to require all postsecondary institutions that are eligible for federal financial aid programs to make publicly available their annual crime statistics. Specifically, institutions are required to report the crimes that were reported on campus as well as their security policies.

Beginning in 1991 and ever since, universities throughout the United States publish counts for on-campus murders, sexual offenses (forcible and non-forcible), robberies, aggravated assaults, burglaries, motor vehicle thefts, manslaughter, and arson. Related to their security policies and practices, institutions also include in the annual report the number of on-campus arrests related to alcohol, drugs, and weapons.

The *Student Right-To-Know and Campus Security Act* has been amended several times since its passage in 1990. These amendments occurred in 1992 and 1998. The 1992 amendment included, among other stipulations, the *Campus Sexual Assault Victims' Bill of Rights*, which affords certain basic rights to victims of on-campus sexual assaults. In 1998, the act was renamed the *Jeanne Clery Disclosure of Campus Security Policy and Campus Crimes Statistics Act of 1998*. These expansions of the act stipulated that institutions disclose the location on campus that crimes occurred, and that daily crime logs be available upon request. Subsequent amendments in 2000 and 2008 to the *Clery Act* focused on sex offender notification and require institutions to release information about the number of sex offenders on campus. In response to the mass shooting at Virginia Tech in 2007, Congress also amended the Act to address campus policy related to emergency response. As part of their emergency preparedness, schools must have mass notification systems and conduct yearly emergency drills.

Universities failing to comply with the provisions of the *Clery Act* could face civil fines imposed by the U.S. Department of Justice and the loss of eligibility as a recipient of federal financial aid (for more information about the *Clery Act*, see Sloan and Fisher, 2011).

KEYWORDS

Victimization	Victim	Crime victims
Victimology	Risk factor	Victim precipitation
Victim facilitation	Victim provocation	Typology
Functional responsibility	Victim blaming	Feminist movement
Cycle theory of violence	Battered-child syndrome	Law and order movement
Crime control	President's Commission on Law Enforcement and the Administration of Justice	Law Enforcement Assistance Administration
Child Abuse Prevention and Treatment Act of 1974	Victims of Crime Act of 1984	Student Right-to-Know and Campus Security Act of 1990 (Jeanne Clery Disclosure of Campus Security Policy and Campus Crime Statistics Act)
Violence Against Women Act of 1994		

DISCUSSION QUESTIONS

1. What is the relationship between criminology and victimology?
2. Do crime victims contribute to their victimization through victim precipitation? Why or why not? Explain your answer.
3. Are typologies helpful in understanding why and how individuals are victimized? Why or why not? Explain your answer.
4. Compare and contrast von Hentig's, Mendelsohn's, and Schafer's typologies. In what ways are they similar and/or different?
5. Do the empirical studies by Wolfgang and Amir show that in some cases victims are responsible for their own victimization? Explain your answer.
6. Can you think of some possible negative consequences of victim blaming? Explain.
7. In what ways did grassroots efforts to improve the circumstances of crime victims eventually succeed?
8. Explain how political efforts shaped the development of victims' rights.
9. Search your college or university's website for the annual crime statistics they provide as required by the *Clery Act*. Does your campus have a crime problem?

REFERENCES

Amir, M. (1967). Victim precipitated forcible rape. *Journal of Criminal Law, Criminology & Police Science, 58,* 493–502.

Amir, M. (1971). *Patterns in forcible rape.* Chicago: University of Chicago Press.

Barker, T. (2010). Law Enforcement Assistance Administration (LEAA). In B. S. Fisher & S. P. Lab (Eds.), *Encyclopedia of victimology and crime prevention* (pp. 525–526). Thousand Oaks, CA: Sage Publications, Inc.

Centers for Disease Control and Prevention. (2014). *Lung cancer: What are the risk factors?* Retrieved July 1, 2014, from http://www.cdc.gov/cancer/lung/basic_info/risk_factors.htm

Cohen, L. E., & Felson, M. (1979). Social change and crime rate trends: A routine activity approach. *American Sociological Review, 44,* 588–608.

Doerner, W. G. (2010). Victimology. In B. S. Fisher & S. P. Lab (Eds.), *Encyclopedia of victimology and crime prevention* (pp. 996–1003). Thousand Oaks, CA: Sage Publications, Inc.

Dussich, J. P. J. (1986). The victim assistance centre: Its history and typology. In K. Miyazawa & M. Ohya (Eds.), *Victimology in comparative perspective* (pp. 337–348). Tokyo: Seibundo Publishing Co. Ltd.

Fattah, E. A. (1967). Towards a criminological classification of victims. *International Criminal Police Review, 209,* 162–169.

Fattah, E. A. (1971). *La Victime est-elle coupable?* Montréal: Presses de l'Université de Montréal.

Fattah, E. A. (2000). Victimology: Past, present and future. *Criminologie, 33,* 17–46.

Fisher, B. S., Sloan, J. J., Cullen, F. T., & Lu, C. (1998). Crime in the ivory tower: The level and sources of student victimization. *Criminology, 36,* 671–710.

Henson, B., Wilcox, P., Reyns, B. W., & Cullen, F. T. (2010). Gender, adolescent lifestyles, and violent victimization: Implications for routine activities theory. *Victims & Offenders, 5,* 303–328.

Hindelang, M. J., Gottfredson, M. R., & Garofalo, J. (1978). *Victims of personal crime: An empirical foundation for a theory of personal victimization.* Cambridge, MA: Ballinger Publishing Company.

Kempe, C. H., Silverman, F. N., Steele, B. F., Droegemueller, W., & Silver, H. K. (1962). The battered-child syndrome. *Journal of the American Medical Association, 181,* 17–24.

Mannheim, H. (1965). *Comparative criminology.* Boston: Houghton Mifflin Company.

Mendelsohn, B. (1974). The origin of the doctrine of victimology. In I. Drapkin & E. Viano (Eds.), *Victimology* (pp. 3–11). Lexington, MA: D.C. Heath and Company.

Miethe, T. D., & Meier, R. F. (1994). *Crime and its social context: Toward an integrated theory of offenders, victims, and situations.* Albany, NY: SUNY Press.

Nagel, W. H. (1974). The notion of victimology in criminology. In I. Drapkin & E. Viano (Eds.), *Victimology* (pp. 13–16). Lexington, MA: D.C. Heath and Company.

NCVS Victimization Analysis Tool. (2014). Retrieved July 1, 2014, from http://www.bjs.gov/index.cfm?ty=nvat

Office for Victims of Crime. (2014). *Landmarks in Victims' Rights and Services.* Retrieved July 1, 2014, from https://www.ncjrs.gov/ovc_archives/ncvrw/2009/pdf/LandmarksinVictimsRights.pdf

Oliver, W. M. (2003). *The law & order presidency.* Upper Saddle River, NJ: Prentice Hall.

Pittman, D. J., & Handy, W. (1964). Patterns in criminal aggravated assault. *Journal of Criminal Law, Criminology and Police Science, 55,* 462–469.

President's Commission on Law Enforcement and Administration of Justice. (1967). *The challenge of crime in a free society.* Washington, DC: U.S. Government Printing Office.

Schafer, S. (1977). *Victimology: The victim and his criminal.* Reston, VA: Reston Publishing Company, Inc.

Schreck, C. J. (1999). Criminal victimization and low self-control: An extension and test of a general theory of crime. *Justice Quarterly, 16,* 633–654.

Schreck, C. J., & Fisher, B. S. (2004). Specifying the influence of family and peers on violent victimization. *Journal of Interpersonal Violence, 19,* 1021–1041.

Schwartz, M. D., & Pitts, V. L. (1995). Exploring a feminist routine activities approach to explaining sexual assault. *Justice Quarterly, 12,* 9–31.

Sellin, T., & Wolfgang, M. E. (1964). *The measurement of delinquency.* New York: John Wiley & Sons.

Shelman, E. A., & Lazoritz, S. (2005). *The Mary Ellen Wilson child abuse case and the beginning of children's rights in 19th-century America.* Jefferson, NC: McFarland & Company, Inc., Publishers.

Sloan, J. J., & Fisher, B. S. (2011). *The dark side of the ivory tower: Campus crime as a social problem.* New York: Cambridge University Press.

Varon, J. N. (1975). A reexamination of the Law Enforcement Assistance Administration. *Stanford Law Review, 27,* 1303–1324.

Von Hentig, H. (1940). Remarks on the interaction of perpetrator and victim. *Journal of Criminal Law and Criminology, 31,* 303–309.

Von Hentig, H. (1948). *The criminal and his victim: Studies in the sociobiology of crime.* New York: Schocken Books.

Walker, L. E. (1980). *The Battered Woman.* New York: Harper & Row.

Walker, L. E. (2009). *The battered woman syndrome* (3rd Ed.). New York: Springer Publishing Company, LLC.

Wilcox, P., Land, K. C., & Hunt, S. A. (2003). *Criminal circumstance: A dynamic multicontextual criminal opportunity theory.* New York: Aldine de Gruyter.

Wilcox, P., Tillyer, M. S., & Fisher, B. S. (2009). Gendered opportunity? School-based adolescent victimization. *Journal of Research in Crime and Delinquency, 46,* 245–269.

Wolfgang, M. E. (1957). Victim-precipitated criminal homicide. *Journal of Criminal Law, Criminology, and Police Science, 48,* 1–11.

Wolfgang, M. E. (1958). *Patterns in criminal homicide.* New York: John Wiley & Sons, Inc.

CHAPTER 2

Opportunity Theories of Victimization

CHAPTER OUTLINE

LEARNING OBJECTIVES

- Describe how the opportunity perspective is used to explain criminal victimization.
- Assess the merits of the opportunity perspective in explaining victimization.
- Identify and understand the four opportunity theories presented in this chapter.
- Compare and contrast the four opportunity theories presented in this chapter.
- Describe the measurement issues involved with testing opportunity theories of victimization.

Routine activity patterns and lifestyles in contemporary society create a criminal opportunity structure by enhancing the contact between potential offenders and victims.

Miethe and Meier, 1990, p. 245

Introduction

Why do some individuals, property, businesses, or organizations become crime victims while others do not? This is the question that the second and third generations of victimologists and victimology theories have sought to answer. The second generation transitioned victimology away from such notions as typologies of victims, victim precipitation, and victim blaming. These theorists instead focused on explaining how various kinds of opportunities were related to criminal victimization. In investigating the above question, the ***opportunity perspective*** posits that the root cause of victimization is the favorable combination of circumstances, time, place, and people, and that without such favorable combinations the chances of a victimization occurring are substantially reduced. The opportunity perspective, best illustrated by lifestyle-exposure theory and routine activity theory, focuses on identifying the circumstances that increase the risk for a victimization to occur. Research testing these theories has examined how the lifestyles and daily routines of people facilitate opportunities for victimization by exposing potential victims to, or bringing them into proximity with, others who are likely to take advantage of these criminogenic circumstances.

The third generation of victimologists and their theories better developed and refined lifestyle-exposure theory and routine activity theory. They discovered that the circumstances creating opportunities for victimization are more complex than the first and second generation of victimologists proposed. In particular, the third generation of theorists identified specific behaviors that increase victimization risk and developed innovative means to test theoretical concepts central to opportunity theories. Further, this generation extended the breadth of the opportunity theories by considering not only how certain victim behaviors create an opportunity for enhancing the risk of criminal victimization, but also how the characteristics of places contribute to the likelihood of victimization. Taking into account both individual-level and place-level characteristics, this multilevel view of opportunity was a major step that moved the field toward a fuller understanding of the correlates of victimization. This chapter presents the major contributions of the second and third generations of victimology theorists, including the development of victimization theories, their concepts, and hypothesized relationships for explaining why and under what circumstances victimization occurs.

The Opportunity Perspective: The Second Generation of Victimization Theories

People often take for granted the role of opportunity in their lives. For example, whether you have a date for Saturday night might depend on whom you sat by in class today, which provided you an opportunity to ask the person seated next to you to go to a party or see a movie. In general, opportunities are circumstances that are favorable to some outcome. Sometimes, this is a matter of being in the right place at the right time, or when it comes to criminal victimization being in the *wrong* place at the *wrong* time. The opportunity perspective of victimization focuses on the circumstances that make a situation more favorable to having a victimization occur. For example, an unguarded backpack or laptop sitting on a table in an isolated section of the university library provides an opportunity for theft. Overall, the opportunity perspective provides a broad framework for thinking about how circumstances favorable for a victimization to occur are created. Within this larger framework, there are two primary theories that explain victimization—lifestyle-exposure theory and routine activity theory. Over time, research into these theories and the broader opportunity perspective has resulted in core principles that explain and predict victimization.

In 1998, Marcus Felson and Ronald Clarke, two prominent scholars in the fields of crime prevention and victimology, published a research report with the United Kingdom's Home Office entitled *Opportunity Makes the Thief.* Their report summarized much of the research into criminal opportunities and listed and described "ten principles of opportunity theory." The 10 principles are listed in Box 2-1 as an introduction to the opportunity perspective.

Box 2-1: Felson and Clarke's 10 Principles of Opportunity Theory

1. *Opportunities cause crime.* There is no type of crime or victimization in which opportunity does not play a role; opportunity is a "root cause" of crime.
2. *Crime opportunities are highly specific.* Opportunities for victimization depend on the type of victimization and specific circumstances generating opportunities. For example, opportunities that result in sexual victimization are different from those for theft.
3. *Crime opportunities are concentrated in time and space.* Crime and victimization do not occur randomly—they are patterned according to where and when opportunities arise. Therefore, the places or times that have the most opportunities will be the places and times where victimization most often occurs. For example, most *residential* burglaries occur during the day (while most people are away at work) but most *commercial* burglaries occur at night (when no employees or customers are present).

(Continued)

Box 2-1: Felson and Clarke's 10 Principles of Opportunity Theory (*continued*)

4. *Crime opportunities depend on everyday activity.* Routine, daily activities facilitate opportunities for victimization. They bring together would-be offenders with potential targets. For example, the morning commute to work or school on a subway or bus may provide an offender with an opportunity to steal someone's wallet or purse.
5. *One crime produces opportunities for another.* Criminal opportunities are dynamic and change according to the situation. Case in point: What starts out as a convenience store robbery may escalate into an assault on the clerk, or worse, depending on how the situation unfolds.
6. *Focused opportunity reduction can produce wider declines in crime.* In contrast to displacement effects, it is possible that prevention efforts can be diffused. For instance, efforts to prevent victimization on one street may also help to prevent victimization on neighboring streets.
7. *Some property offers more tempting crime opportunities.* In considering crimes such as shoplifting, there are some products that provide easier opportunities or appear to be more attractive targets for victimization than others.
8. *Social and technological changes produce new crime opportunities.* Just as daily routines determine the distribution of opportunities, so too do social and technological changes in society. For instance, the life cycle of products (e.g., smartphones, iPads) establishes a demand for them and their desirability as a target for a thief. Online social networking (e.g., Facebook) is a relatively recent innovation that can be considered both a social and technological change that has produced new crime opportunities, such as identity theft or cyberstalking.
9. *Crime can be prevented by reducing opportunities.* Focused opportunity reductions can result in declines in crime and victimization rates. This strategy is a focus of situational crime prevention, which is discussed in Chapter 14.
10. *Reducing opportunities does not usually move crime to nearby places.* Critics of the opportunity perspective have argued that reducing opportunities for victimization of specific targets or in certain places merely moves the crime ("displaces" it) to other targets or places. Research reveals that displacement is neither a certainty, nor is it likely to be 100%.

Source: Felson and Clarke (1998)

If victimization can be explained as a function of opportunity, then the task left to victimologists is to identify which factors, circumstances, and features of each unique type of victimization create opportunities that are favorable for a crime to occur. This has been the primary focus of the two key theories in the opportunity perspective—lifestyle-exposure theory and routine activity theory.

Lifestyle-Exposure Theory

In 1973, the first National Crime Survey (NCS), later redesigned and renamed the National Crime Victimization Survey in 1992, was administered in the United States. The purpose of the NCS was to complement the Uniform Crime Reports (UCR) and provide a measure of criminal victimization that was not influenced by whether crimes were reported to the police. (These two sources of national crime estimates are discussed in detail in Chapter 4.) One important finding to come out of the NCS was the discovery that victimization had specific patterns. For example, males were found to have substantially higher rates of personal victimization than females. Those who were either never married or were separated or divorced had personal victimization rates that were double those of married or widowed individuals. Similar patterns of victimization were uncovered for other demographic characteristics as well, including age, family income, and race. These patterns suggested that victimization was not a random occurrence, and it disproportionately affected certain groups of people. The challenge became explaining these findings, especially since no theory existed to account for victimization patterns.

In 1978, Michael Hindelang, Michael Gottfredson, and James Garofalo published their book, *Victims of Personal Crime: An Empirical Foundation for a Theory of Personal Victimization*. They not only summarized the findings from the NCS but also presented a theory to explain patterns of personal victimization. In ***lifestyle-exposure theory***, they argued that different lifestyles expose people to varying levels of risk for personal victimization. These lifestyles, in turn, could be traced back to the personal demographic characteristics (e.g., age, education, occupation) of individuals. For example, since young people tend to spend more time out with friends (a lifestyle characteristic) than older people, they are more likely to be targets for victimization.

According to Hindelang and colleagues (1978, p. 241), lifestyles are "routine daily activities, both vocational activities (work, school, keeping house, etc.) and leisure activities." In other words, a person's lifestyle is his or her way of life. But lifestyle alone is not a sufficient cause of victimization: It is the nature of the lifestyle and the associated activities that either increase or decrease the likelihood of becoming a victim of crime. Unfortunately, the NCS did not collect information from respondents about their lifestyles or routine daily activities. However, Hindelang and colleagues detailed the precursors to lifestyle (i.e., age, sex, race, income, marital status, education, occupation) as well as the links between lifestyles and personal victimization.

The lifestyle-exposure theoretical model of personal victimization is presented in Figure 2-1. This model describes the causal chain in which personal demographic characteristics such as age, sex, and race can ultimately be used to explain why victimization occurs. The solid arrows forming the various linkages in the model

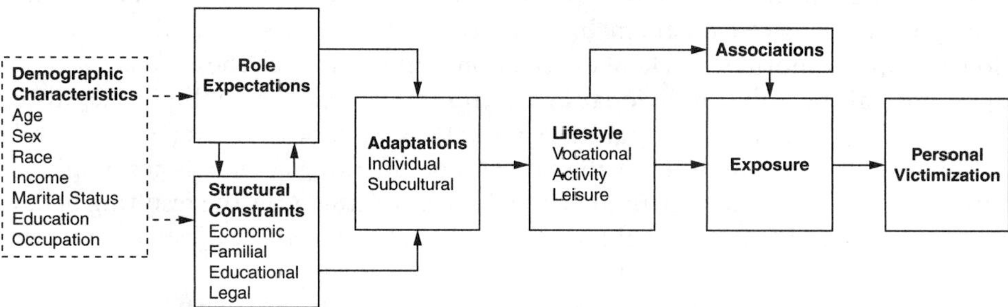

Figure 2-1 The Lifestyle-Exposure Theoretical Model of Personal Victimization
Source: Hindelang, Gottfredson and Garofalo (1978).

indicate causal relationships between theoretical concepts. The dashed lines around the demographics box in the model signify that demographic characteristics are not meant to cause role expectations or structural constraints. Rather, depending on individuals' demographic characteristics, they will have certain role expectations and structural constraints imposed on them.

The lifestyle-exposure theoretical model suggests that two important features of larger society influence the types of lifestyles people adopt—***role expectations*** and ***structural constraints***. Note, too, that the influence of these factors varies according to a person's constellation of personal characteristics such as race, age, and gender. Role expectations refer to "cultural norms that are associated with achieved and ascribed statuses of individuals and that define preferred and anticipated behaviors" (Hindelang et al., 1978, p. 242). Put differently, people expect others to behave in certain ways depending on their personal characteristics, and these expectations are imposed on us by the culture in which we live. For example, young people are generally expected to attend school, usually while living at home with their parents, graduate from high school, and either further their education or enter the workforce.

The other social factor that acts on us based on our personal characteristics is structural constraints. According to Hindelang and colleagues (1978, p. 242), structural constraints are "limitations on behavioral options that result from particular arrangements existing within various institutional orders, such as the economic, familial, educational, and legal orders." This means that individuals are limited in their choices because of the way society functions. In continuing with our example regarding young people, those under 16 are not allowed to legally drive, those under 18 are not legally permitted to purchase or smoke tobacco (although in a few states such as Alaska and Utah the smoking age is 19), and those under 21 cannot legally purchase, possess, or consume alcohol. Further, as noted previously, young people are legally required to attend school until a certain age (usually 15 or 16), but again this varies from state to state. These are all examples of constraints that are imposed on young people, ultimately limiting their behaviors. Similar arguments can be made for each of the demographic characteristics contained in the lifestyle-exposure theoretical model of personal victimization presented in Figure 2-1.

Of course, not everyone with given characteristics has the same lifestyle. Not all married people, or white people, or elderly people, for example, have the same daily routines. Taking this variation into account, Hindelang and his associates argued that individuals learn how to adapt, behave, and maintain their individuality within the constraints placed on them by role expectations and structural constraints. Some people conform to societal expectations; others do not. These behavioral adaptations can be either individual or subcultural. In some neighborhoods in big cities, for example, gangs use graffiti to mark the boundaries of their territory, while in some affluent neighborhoods the same border-marking activity is accomplished by enclosing a subdivision behind decorative gates. Either way, the resulting behavioral routines, or ***lifestyles***, should remain fairly stable. It is these lifestyles that then ultimately determine one's level of risk for personal victimization.

Hindelang and colleagues explained that variations in lifestyles determine whether individuals are exposed to times, places, and people that are conducive to criminal activity, thereby increasing individuals' personal victimization risk. People can also be exposed to high-risk situations through the personal relationships or associations they maintain. Generally, individuals spend much of their time around others who have similar lifestyles and personal characteristics. This is known as the ***principle of homogamy***—people tend to choose mates and friends from others like themselves. One example of the principle of homogamy is a gang member who spends his time participating in drug deals, arguing over territory, and engaging in other illegal activities with other gang members. Another example could be a college student who lives on campus, attends classes, and belongs to a sorority. Although these two people lead very different lifestyles, they both spend the majority of their time around people with similar lifestyles. When sharing lifestyles with those who are more likely to commit crimes, these associations can enhance the risk of personal victimization.

Finally, the last concept depicted in the theoretical model is personal victimization. Hindelang and colleagues' theory explains that there are differences in the likelihood of personal victimization among individuals because of differences in their lifestyles that either expose them to high-risk situations or protect them from these risks. Hindelang and colleagues also offered a set of eight propositions that are helpful in explaining personal victimization based on their lifestyle-exposure theory. These eight propositions are listed in Box 2-2, along with an example of a college student's lifestyle for each proposition. Our hypothetical college student, Sarah, is a 19-year-old freshman who lives on campus, frequents clubs and parties, and dates fellow students several nights a week.

Box 2-2: Propositions and Illustrations of Lifestyle-Exposure Theory

Proposition	Illustration
1. *The likelihood of experiencing personal victimization is directly related to the amount of time that a person spends in public places (e.g., on the street, in parks, etc.), especially at night.*	Sarah is theoretically at a higher risk for personal victimization because she spends many nights a week in public venues.
2. *The likelihood of being in public places, especially at night, varies as a function of lifestyle.*	Sarah has a lifestyle that frequently places her in public locations at night.
3. *Social interactions mostly occur between individuals who have similar lifestyles.*	Sarah associates primarily with other people her age, who are also attending college and spending their free time going to parties and dating.
4. *An individual's likelihood of personal victimization depends on the extent the individual shares demographic characteristics with offenders.*	The people with whom Sarah spends most of her time are demographically similar to her. They are likely the same age (18-24), come from the same socioeconomic background, are single, and so on.
5. *The amount of time an individual spends among nonfamily members varies as a function of the lifestyle.*	Sarah's college-oriented lifestyle does not leave much time for her to spend with herfamily, even if they live nearby.

(*Continued*)

Box 2-2: Propositions and Illustrations of Lifestyle-Exposure Theory (*continued*)

6. *The probability of personal victimization, especially personal theft, increases as the amount of time spent among nonfamily members increases.*	Sarah is more likely to experience personal victimization because she does not spend very much time with her family.
7. *Lifestyle differences influence the ability of individuals to separate themselves from persons with offender characteristics.*	Sarah's lifestyle does not allow her to have complete control over the people with whom she comes into contact, such as other students in her classes or party guests. Since property crimes and sexual crimes are common among students, Sarah may be at a higher risk for these types of victimization.
8. *Lifestyle differences are related to the attractiveness of the person as a target for personal victimizations.*	Whether Sarah ultimately becomes a victim depends on whether her lifestyle makes her or her property an attractive target for victimization to a would-be offender.

Source: Adapted from Hindelang, Gottfredson, and Garofalo (1978).

The eight propositions of lifestyle-exposure theory are similar to the theoretical concepts presented below in routine activity theory. Lifestyle-exposure theory explains that opportunities for victimization are generated through lifestyles that expose individuals to differing levels of risk. Routine activity theory explores this idea in more depth, explaining that exposure is just one important ingredient required to create an opportunity for victimization.

Routine Activity Theory

Following World War II, crime rates in the United States began to increase dramatically. Lawrence Cohen and Marcus Felson (1979) hypothesized the increases in crime rates were the result of changes in the daily ***routine activities*** of the U.S. population. In other words, people across the nation were changing the ways in which they lived their daily lives. Cohen and Felson (1979, p. 593) defined routine activities as

> any recurrent and prevalent activities which provide for basic population and individual needs, whatever their biological or cultural origins. Thus routine activities would include formalized work, as well as the provision of standard food, shelter, sexual outlet, leisure, social interaction, learning and childrearing.

They hypothesized that over time, the U.S. population began spending increasingly greater amounts of time away from home, thereby creating opportunities for more individuals to be victimized. Cohen and Felson assumed that the home was among the safest environments in terms of protection against victimization risk. At the same time, with a larger segment of the population now spending time outside the home, particularly as more women joined the workforce, residential property was being left unguarded and thus became a potential crime target. In either case, Cohen and Felson's argument was that large-scale changes in the American population's daily routines were creating ever-greater opportunities for victimization.

To examine the effect that changes in individuals' routine activities had on crime rates, Cohen and Felson constructed what they called the ***household activity ratio***, which took into account the number of married, female labor force participants and the number of single-headed households as a proportion of the total number of households in the United States. They argued that this variable represented the proportion of U.S. households at the highest risk for victimization, given the greater participation in activities away from the home. Cohen and Felson's initial research revealed that the household activity ratio was significantly related to each type of crime rate they examined (i.e., non-negligent homicide, forcible rape, aggravated assault, robbery, and burglary). However, merely being away from home does not by itself necessarily create more opportunities for victimization.

According to ***routine activity theory***, opportunities for victimization occur when suitable or attractive targets intersect with motivated offenders at the same time in environments with ineffective or no protection against victimization. Figure 2-2 depicts the three main concepts in the theory as a ***crime triangle*** (Clarke & Eck, 2005). Each of these concepts—motivated offenders, suitable targets, and guardianship—is discussed below.

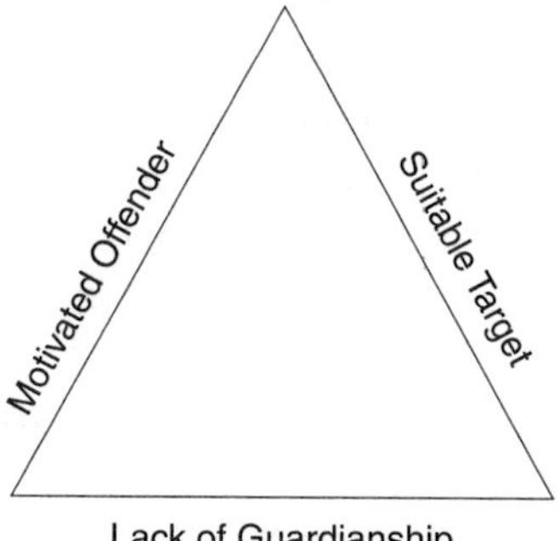

Figure 2-2 The Crime Triangle
Source: Clarke & Eck (2005)

Motivated Offenders

Routine activities research has generally conceptualized this component of the theory in two ways: (1) exposure to risk and (2) proximity to motivated offenders. ***Exposure*** refers to the accessibility or visibility of potential targets to potential offenders (Cohen, Kluegel, & Land, 1981). This concept is comparable to the idea of exposure discussed earlier by Hindelang and colleagues. For example, certain products in a retail store may be more exposed or accessible to shoplifters than others. Batteries, over-the-counter medicines, and snacks are easily accessible to shoppers and shoplifters alike, while other products such as prescription medicines, electronics, and tobacco are kept behind service counters (and sometimes locked up) and are therefore less exposed to risk. All else being equal, greater exposure to motivated offenders is hypothesized to increase the odds of victimization. ***Proximity*** to motivated offenders refers to the physical closeness of potential targets and potential offenders. For example, retail stores or gas stations located in neighborhoods with high crime rates may be more likely targets for robberies. This assumes that neighborhoods with high crime rates contain a higher-than-average proportion of motivated offenders.

Suitable Targets

Whether or not a target, be it a person, object, or place, is seen as suitable or attractive for offenders depends on the type of victimization that the would-be offender wants to commit. Cohen and Felson (1979, p. 591) described items attractive to thieves as possessing ***VIVA***: *value*, *inertia*, *visibility*, and *access*:

- **Value**. Value has two dimensions when considering target attractiveness. First, the item may have *monetary value*, in which case the thief will be able to fence the stolen item for a higher amount and make the crime worth his while. Second, the target may have *personal value* to the offender. For instance, perhaps to an offender with no means of transportation, an unguarded bicycle will be an attractive target because it can be used in the future.
- **Inertia**. Inertia refers to the weight or movability of items. Various household or personal goods are theoretically more suitable as targets if they are easy to move or conceal. For example, Blu-ray discs, DVDs, CDs, or video games are both lightweight and easy to conceal, whereas large flat-screen TVs are more valuable but more difficult to conceal and hence successfully steal.
- **Visibility**. Visibility is an aspect of exposure to motivated offenders. It is not likely that an offender will target an item if he or she does not know about its presence or specific location. For instance, perhaps during the holiday season, a retail store will keep the most sought-after toy in a locked showcase and require customers to make their purchase before transferring ownership.
- **Access.** Access or accessibility refers to the ability to approach or make use of the targeted item. For instance, a Las Vegas casino may appear to be an attractive target for robbery given the vast amounts of cash on hand. Yet, would-be robbers would have no access to the vault and, indeed, most likely no information about where the vault is located.

VIVA does not adequately describe why all targets are chosen, but it does offer some insights into target suitability with respect to property victimization, especially for crimes such as burglary and larceny. Further, the concepts of value, visibility, and access can be applied to essentially any type of target, including individuals. For example, for some offenders, harassing and threatening a coworker may be of some value, such as getting revenge, but an ability to do so may depend on visibility and access to the victim.

Table 2-1: The Elements of CRAVED

Element	Definition
Concealable	Items that thieves can conceal, either when carrying out the criminal act or afterward, make more attractive targets because they are easier to remove or they are more difficult to identify as stolen.
Removable	Comparable to the VIVA concept of *inertia*, removable items are easier to move, and therefore more likely to be targets for thieves.
Available	Similar to the VIVA concepts of *visibility* and *access*, items must be available in order for offenders to target them.
Valuable	Analogous to the VIVA concept, valuable items will generally be targeted because they can be sold by the offender for more money, or because the offender values and can enjoy them.
Enjoyable	Given the choice between items of comparable value, offenders usually target those that are more enjoyable to own or possess.
Disposable	Items that are easier or more likely to quickly be sold to others are more frequent targets of offenders.

Ronald Clarke expanded the VIVA concept of target suitability with his own notion of ***CRAVED***. According to Clarke (1999), attractive targets for property offenses such as theft, are Concealable, Removable, Available, Valuable, Enjoyable, and Disposable (Table 2-1). CRAVED items are also likely to become ***hot products***—items that thieves are more likely to target. Pires and Clarke (2011) have applied the CRAVED model to the poaching of 22 different and protected species of parrots in Mexico. They identified those species that are widely available and whose chicks are easily removed from the nest as the species most targeted by poachers. Interestingly, more valuable, disposable, and enjoyable species were not frequent targets because poaching that occurred in the 1980s reduced their availability.

Guardianship

Guardianship represents a protection against victimization, regardless of the mechanism used (e.g., security guards, alarm systems, and surveillance). As the number and/or the quality of guardians is reduced, the likelihood of victimization is increased. Routine activities research has considered two dimensions of guardianship: physical and social. ***Physical guardianship*** involves measures taken to make a potential target more difficult to victimize. For example, a homeowner may install extra locks on doors, purchase a security alarm or additional exterior lighting, bar the windows, or buy a dog. Each of these measures is a form of target hardening that makes the residence more resistant to crime. Recently, however, Meghan Hollis, Marcus Felson, and Brandon Welsh (2013) have clarified this component of the theory and explained that all guardianship is social, and that these target-hardening measures may be better thought of as dimensions of target suitability.

Spotlight on Theory: Social Guardianship

Personal responsibility: Those who have a special responsibility to act as guardians over potential targets. For instance, parents are responsible for keeping their children safe, and business owners are responsible for protecting their businesses.

Assigned responsibility: For some, protecting targets may be a part of their job description. For example, doormen make themselves visible in front of apartment buildings, and retail stores often hire loss prevention personnel to discourage and respond to shoplifting.

Diffuse responsibility: For others, protecting targets may be secondary to their primary function on the job. A housekeeper's presence may discourage trespassers, yet his or her primary duty is to clean and maintain hotel guests' rooms.

General responsibility: Some may discourage crime and victimization whether they intend to or not. For instance, bystanders, strangers, and passersby might act as social guardians and prevent crimes by their mere presence. Most offenders do not like the idea of committing a crime while there is someone around to see them.

Source: Felson (1995).

Social guardianship discourages crime through the presence of individuals who could potentially intervene if an offender decided to act. However, social guardians have differing levels of responsibility for discouraging or responding to crime: personal, assigned, diffuse, or general. The degree of the response by the guardian and the importance placed on it to thwart victimization is strongest at the personal level and weakest at the general level. The four degrees of responsibility related to social guardianship are illustrated in the "Spotlight on Theory: Social Guardianship" box.

Overall, the concept of guardianship is not unique to routine activity theory, but it is an important component in the dynamics of victimization (Felson & Boba, 2010). After all, if guardianship were not effective at preventing victimization, why would individuals lock their car doors, homes, and garages or take other routine measures to protect themselves and their property?

Refinements to Opportunity Theories

The third generation of victimization theories expanded on key concepts found in lifestyle-exposure theory and routine activity theory. The concepts were eventually combined into a single perspective because of their shared emphasis on the role of opportunities in explaining victimization and similar theoretical assumptions (Garofalo, 1987). This combined perspective—***lifestyle–routine activities theory***—explains that victimization is a function of four important concepts: exposure to risk, proximity to motivated offenders, target attractiveness, and a lack of capable guardianship. All else being equal, these aspects of opportunity are hypothesized to operate in the following manner:

- Exposure to risk increases likelihood of victimization.
- Proximity to motivated offenders increases likelihood of victimization.

- Target attractiveness increases likelihood of victimization.
- Guardianship decreases likelihood of victimization.

Important developments in lifestyle-routine activities theory were accomplished by the third generation of victimology theorists. These developments include the following: (1) the finding that opportunities for victimization occur at multiple levels of analysis, and the subsequent development of multilevel opportunity theory; (2) the introduction of structural choice theory, which focuses on opportunity as one element of the criminal event; and (3) refinements in ways to measure exposure, proximity, target attractiveness, and guardianship.

For decades criminologists have been intrigued with the effects that social structural factors might have on crime rates. Many factors, from urbanization to the percentage of female-headed households in an area, have been considered as potential contributors to area crime and delinquency. In 1987, Robert Sampson and John Wooldredge were among the first researchers to apply this idea to explaining opportunities for victimization. They argued that while the characteristics of individuals and their lifestyles generate opportunities for victimization, community characteristics also create opportunities for victimization. These dual effects are often described as micro (individual) and macro (aggregate) influences on opportunities for victimization. For example, an individual's lifestyle, age, and sex are micro-level influences on victimization, whereas the poverty rate and percentage of single-resident households in a neighborhood are examples of macro-level factors.

Sampson and Wooldredge's research was pioneering because it was the first to consider both micro *and* macro dimensions of opportunities and how they influenced victimization risk simultaneously. For example, in explaining burglary victimization, they found that individual-level factors such as age, whether the dwelling was a single-person household, and how often the house was left empty during the day were significantly related to the likelihood of burglary victimization. The environmental context in which the household was located was also an important consideration in explaining burglary. Variables such as the percentage of apartments in the area's housing stock, the percentage of unemployed persons in the area, and the percentage of residents who owned videocassette recorders (VCRs) (remember, this study was conducted in the 1980s!) were significantly related to victimization.

Subsequent research continues to bridge the gap between micro- and macro-level explanations of opportunities for victimization. Collectively, this research has revealed that the larger environment is an important consideration in explaining victimization, but also that there are opportunity factors unique to different types of environments, such as neighborhoods, schools, and college campuses. For example, a study by Bonnie Fisher and colleagues (1998) examined victimization among college students and considered factors such as Greek presence on campus, the campus violence rate, and the existence of a campus-wide crime watch as macro-level influences on student violent and theft victimization. Building on this body of research, Pamela Wilcox, Kenneth Land, and Scott Hunt (2003) developed a ***multilevel opportunity theory*** that fully articulated the roles of micro- and macro-level factors of opportunity within a lifestyle–routine activities framework.

Multilevel Opportunity Theory

Multilevel opportunity theory explains how motivated offenders, suitable targets, and capable guardianship have both *individual-* and *aggregate-*level effects on opportunities for victimization. At the individual level, exposure, target suitability, and guardianship influence opportunities in the same manner as lifestyle–routine activities theory would suggest. At the aggregate level (e.g., within neighborhoods, within schools), these concepts alter or moderate the effects of individual-level factors on criminal opportunities. For example, an individual may pose an attractive target for robbery victimization, but if the aggregate supply of motivated offenders is small, the probability that a robbery will occur is reduced.

Figure 2-3 depicts multilevel opportunity theory's hypothesis that aggregate-level opportunity factors influence or alter the relationships between the individual-level lifestyle–routine activities concepts and victimization. The solid lines in the figure denote a direct effect on the likelihood of victimization. The dashed lines signify a conditioning effect of aggregate-level opportunity on the effects of individual-level motivated offenders, target suitability, and guardianship.

While Figure 2-3 communicates the idea that aggregate-level opportunity modifies the impact on victimization opportunities of individual-level motivated offenders, target suitability, and guardianship, the figure does not illustrate that these concepts also exist at the aggregate level. In other words, individuals or objects may be exposed to risk, be attractive targets, or lack guardianship, but the macro environment may also possess these characteristics.

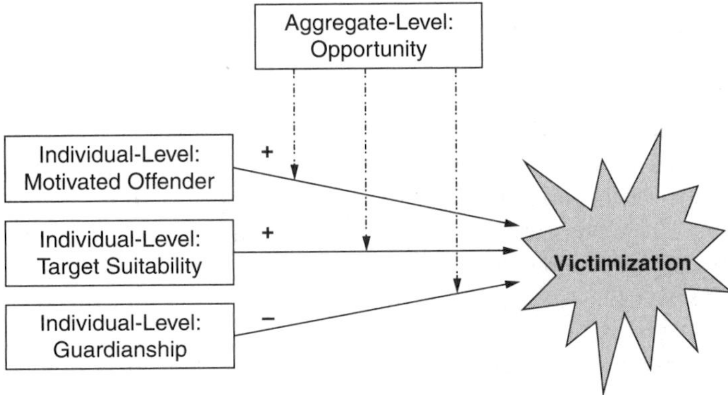

Figure 2-3 The Effects of Aggregate-Level and Individual-Level Opportunity Factors in Victimization
+ increases risk of victimization; - reduces risk of victimization.
Source: Wilcox, Land, and Hunt (2003).

Table 2-2 illustrates the multilevel nature of criminal opportunities according to multilevel opportunity theory. The concepts of motivated offenders, suitable targets, and capable guardians exist at both the individual and aggregate level. These two levels of opportunity have direct effects, but they also interact to either increase or decrease victimization risk. For example, at the individual level, a person who spends a lot of time out in public at night has an enhanced exposure to

Table 2-2: Multilevel Opportunity Theory: Interactions Among Individual- and Aggregate-Level Lifestyle–Routine Activities Concepts

	Aggregate-Level Motivated Offenders	Aggregate-Level Target Suitability	Aggregate-Level Guardianship
Individual-Level Exposure	1. A large supply of offenders at the aggregate level (+) makes individual exposure even more risky (+).	2. A large supply of suitable targets at the aggregate level (+) increases the importance of exposure (+).	3. More guardianship at the aggregate level (+) deters crime, which decreases the importance of individual exposure (−).
Individual-Level Suitability	4. A large supply of offenders at the aggregate-level (+) increases the importance of target suitability (+).	5. A large supply of suitable targets at the aggregate level (+) makes any one suitable target less likely to be victimized (−).	6. More guardianship at the aggregate level (+) deters crime, which decreases the importance of individual target suitability (−).
Individual-Level Guardianship	7. A large supply of offenders at the aggregate level (+) creates a demand for opportunities, making individual guardianship less important (−).	8. A large supply of suitable targets at the aggregate level (+) makes more-guarded targets less likely to be victimized (−).	9. More guardianship at the aggregate level (+) makes individual-level guardianship even more effective (+).

\+ increases victimization; - reduces victimization.

Source: Wilcox, Land, and Hunt (2003).

victimization. When considering the context, if this same exposed person is also in an environment with a large supply of motivated offenders, such as a neighborhood with a high crime rate, the effect of exposure is intensified and the person is even more likely to become a crime victim (see cell 1 of Table 2-2).

Multilevel opportunity theory also contends that the additive effects (sum of individual effects) of the three main concepts—motivated offenders, target suitability, and guardianship—ultimately influence the nature of environmental opportunities. To explore this idea, Wilcox and colleagues noted that at the macro level, the supply of motivated offenders, suitable targets, and capable guardians varies across contexts. In other words, each street, neighborhood, school, or city (or other environmental context) will theoretically vary in the number of motivated offenders, suitable targets, and capable guardians present. They identified nine ideal types of these environmental contexts and provided hypotheses predicting the amount of crime in each context. Remember, though, that these are just ideal types, and in reality the supply of each of the core theoretical concepts will vary.

Beyond presenting the field with a dynamic and complex theory of criminal opportunities, Wilcox and associates also raised a critical question about the lifestyle–routine activities perspective that has yet to be fully addressed: Which of the theory's core concepts—exposure, proximity, target attractiveness, or guardianship—is the *most important* in explaining why victimization occurs? Further, to what extent do "different levels" of these concepts predict who (e.g., which kinds of people) or what (e.g., which types of property) will be a victim of crime? These ideas are discussed in further detail later in the chapter.

Structural-Choice Theory

While not explicitly an explanation for victimization, structural-choice theory can be considered a descendant of the earlier lifestyle–routine activities theory. Terrance Miethe and Robert Meier's goal was to explain criminal events in their entirety. They argued that to do so required integrating existing theories of criminal behavior with opportunity theory—the leading theory of victimization. ***Structural-choice theory*** argues that crime cannot be adequately explained without considering the following three components: (1) offenders, (2) victims, and (3) the social context in which they meet (Miethe & Meier, 1994).

Figure 2-4 presents the structural-choice theoretical model proposed by Miethe and Meier (1994). Since the purpose of the theory is to explain criminal events, it necessarily takes into account sources of offender motivation, the first box in the model. In essence, these are some of the reasons that criminologists have proposed for why people commit crime, including economic disadvantage, weak social bonds, pro-crime values, psychological or biological attributes, generalized needs, and lack of noncriminal alternatives. The previous research that identifies these conditions as sources of offender motivation is too voluminous to review here; interested readers are encouraged to review a criminological theory textbook for more details (see, e.g., Cullen, Agnew, & Wilcox, 2013).

The second component of the theory is criminal opportunities—specifically, opportunities that have been generated by victim characteristics or behaviors such as lifestyles and daily routines. Once again, the key concepts accounting for victimization opportunities are proximity, exposure, target attractiveness, and guardianship.

Located in the middle of the model is the social context in which victimizations occur, a central focus of structural-choice theory. In the theoretical model, the primary effects (solid lines) of offender motivation and victimization opportunities are filtered through the social context before their effects are complete. The dashed arrows in their model indicate that these concepts exert direct effects on crime, but of a lesser strength. According to Miethe and Meier (1994, p. 66): "Factors that enhance offender motivation and factors that increase victim risk do not exist in a vacuum. Rather, each operates in a social context that brings them together and enhances their effects."

Simply put, an adequate explanation of crime must take into account the social context of the crime. By social context, Miethe and Meier are referring to three features of what they call the "micro-environment" in which crimes transpire: (1) physical location, (2) interpersonal relationships, and (3) behavioral setting (1994, p. 66). ***Physical locations*** can either facilitate or deter crimes depending on the crime and the characteristics of the location, which include physical space, darkness, tempo/pace/rhythm, and history. The amount of ***physical space*** in a crowded subway platform provides an ideal physical space for pickpockets because these small congested spaces allow offenders to get close to targets' pockets or purses without arousing too much suspicion. ***Darkness*** also may factor into the occurrence of criminal events by providing concealment to offenders, whereas well-lit areas are less hospitable environments

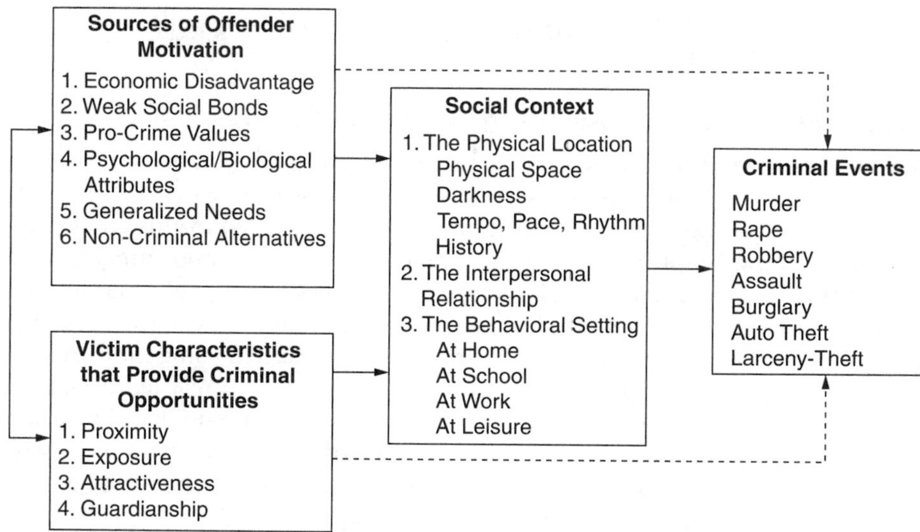

Figure 2-4 The Structural-Choice Model of Criminal Events
Source: Miethe and Meier (1994).

for crime. ***Tempo, pace, and rhythm*** refer to the timing, speed, and coordination of events within a location (see Hawley, 1950). For instance, a bustling city street may be an ideal environment for a purse-snatcher to target and victimize a pedestrian and disappear into the crowd. The ***history*** of an area refers to its criminal history. For example, most cities have one or more areas where crime concentrates, and these areas may be facilitating environments for offenders to flourish.

Interpersonal relationships are an aspect of the social context that refers to the nature of the association between the victim and the offender. In any type of crime, the victim and offender may be complete strangers, acquaintances, friends, intimate partners, or members of the same family. Miethe and Meier argued that the relationship between the victim and offender affects the dynamics of criminal events by shaping the offender's motivations and the victim's opportunity-inducing behaviors. For example, motivations for physical assault between strangers are usually quite different than assaults between intimate partners. Both of these examples may require an opportunity, but the nature of the opportunity would differ accordingly.

The ***behavioral setting*** is the final element of the social context that explains criminal events. Miethe and Meier maintained that most crimes would occur in one of four behavioral settings: the home, at school, at work, and at leisure. Further, the behavioral setting in which a crime takes place has unique properties, including its physical space, darkness, tempo, pace, rhythm, and history. All of these condition the suitability of the setting as a place that may facilitate crime. A large body of environmental criminology research emphasizes the importance of environmental characteristics in influencing offender decision making, victim behaviors, and opportunities for crime. These concepts are reviewed in Chapters 3 and 14. Further, the opportunity perspective suggests that opportunities for crime are domain-specific; that is, the circumstances converging to create victimization opportunities will be influenced by where they occur (see, e.g., Lynch, 1987). Different domains of victimization are discussed in greater detail in Chapter 8.

Measuring, Refining, and Assessing Theoretical Concepts

The idea that opportunities are a necessary but not sufficient condition for victimization is intuitively appealing—in fact, to some it may seem obvious. However, the theoretical propositions of the opportunity theories presented in this chapter underscore just how complicated a seemingly simple idea can be. Opportunity theories agree that motivated offenders, suitable targets, and a lack of capable guardianship are *necessary* conditions for victimization opportunities, but they may not be *sufficient* conditions—their impact can vary dramatically. Research using these theories to explain victimization has often disagreed when it comes to creating variables to represent these key theoretical concepts. Not only are there no universal measures of exposure, proximity, target attractiveness, or guardianship, but conceptually the concepts differ depending on the type of victimization that is being studied. Consider residential burglary. Locking doors and leaving house lights on may be forms of guardianship against that type of crime, whereas these two measures would have no protective effect against online identity theft. Further, decades of research have resulted in many refinements to the core theoretical concepts of the theories, particularly the lifestyle–routine activities perspective. The measurement, refinement, and effects of these concepts are reviewed next.

Exposure to Risk

Researchers have measured the concept of exposure to risk in diverse ways. Recall that exposure entails the degree to which potential targets are visible and accessible to motivated offenders. Early researchers who considered the effects of exposure on victimization often relied on demographic characteristics such as marital status or used somewhat crude indicators, such as time spent outside the home or number of evenings spent out (see, e.g., Cohen et al., 1981; Sampson & Wooldredge, 1987). Eventually, more detailed measures of exposure were developed to reflect the types of activities that potential victims may engage in while outside the home, rather than simply whether or how often they left their homes. Examples of these activities may include, among others, going to bars, going to the gym, or going to the shopping mall (e.g., Kennedy & Forde, 1990; Mustaine & Tewksbury, 1998).

Among the most important findings related to exposure from the victimization research is the connection between delinquency, criminal behavior, and victimization. In other words, participating in delinquent (e.g., underage drinking) or criminal activities (e.g., drug use) has been identified as a type of lifestyle—one that significantly increases one's exposure to victimization risk. These risky lifestyles often place individuals in situations that are conducive to victimization for three reasons. First, participation in risky lifestyles can make one an attractive target for victimization. For example, belonging to a gang can make members the targets of rival gangs or objects of retaliation. Second, these types of activities also increase proximity to motivated offenders. As Hindelang and colleagues' (1978) principle of homogamy described, people are likely to share lifestyles with others of similar lifestyles. Greater proximity to motivated offenders increases victimization risk. Third, these lifestyles create an absence of capable or willing guardians. Overall, risky lifestyles expose individuals to risk and alter the dynamics of victimization opportunities through proximity to motivated offenders, target attractiveness, and guardianship.

Proximity to Motivated Offenders

Researchers have generally considered proximity to motivated offenders to be an indicator of the physical distance between victims and offenders. Studies examining the effects of proximity on victimization have relied on indicators such as whether victims live in an urban area, whether they live in an area with a high crime rate, and whether they perceive their neighborhood to be dangerous (e.g., Hough, 1987; Lynch, 1987; Stahura & Sloan, 1988). The assumption behind using these indicators as measures of proximity is that the victimization occurred at or near victims' homes. The problem is, this may not actually be the case because theoretically individuals should be safer at home, since guardianship should be greater there than elsewhere. Regardless, these sorts of aggregate-level characteristics, such as neighborhood characteristics, tend to significantly affect the risk of victimization (e.g., Sampson, 1987; Smith & Jarjoura, 1989).

Target Attractiveness

Researchers have devised a variety of ways to study target attractiveness in the context of victimization. Yet, there appears to be no consensus among researchers about how to measure this core concept. Cohen and Felson's (1979) concept of VIVA suggests that target attractiveness is a function of value, inertia, visibility, and access. However, the applicability of these characteristics depends on the type of victimization under consideration. In the context of property victimization (e.g., theft, burglary), VIVA may help to identify attractive targets. Items that are valuable, easy to target, and exposed offer tempting opportunities. For personal crimes (e.g., sexual offenses, homicide), however, the VIVA classification may be less useful, especially since notions of value and inertia take on different meanings in the context of these types of victimization. Overall, most research has used monetary value as a measure of target attractiveness and examined variables such as household income or the amount of money individuals spend on nonessential items (e.g., Fisher et al., 1998; Miethe, Stafford, & Long, 1987).

Researchers also have expanded the notion of target suitability beyond the lifestyle and daily routine behaviors of potential victims. For example, David Finkelhor and Nancy Asdigian (1996) argued that for certain types of crimes and victims (e.g., crimes against children), personal attributes, such as gender or emotional vulnerability, make victims more attractive targets irrespective of lifestyle or routines. They labeled the increased vulnerability faced by victims because of their characteristics as ***target congruence***. Target congruence can further be divided into three unique categories: target vulnerability, target gratifiability, and target antagonism. ***Target vulnerability*** makes potential victims more attractive because they are easier targets for the offender. For example, an elderly nursing home patient may be an attractive and vulnerable target for theft because she is frail, physically weak, incapacitated, or having problems with memory recall. ***Target gratifiability*** increases victimization risk because the victim possesses an attribute or quality that the offender wants. An example of target gratifiability may be gender—either male or female—or the intersection of youth with gender, such as child molesters who are attracted to young boys or girls. ***Target antagonism*** refers to victim characteristics that provoke certain individuals to act out criminally. For instance, hate crime victims are targeted because of some personal characteristic that provokes the offender, such as race, sexual orientation, or disability. Overall, findings support the notion that aspects of target congruence contribute to individuals' victimization risk net of lifestyles and routine activities (e.g., Finkelhor & Asdigian, 1996; Tillyer, Tillyer, Miller, & Pangrac, 2011). For example, in examining the victimization of youth between 10 and 16 years old in the United States, Finkelhor and Asdigian reported that aspects of target congruence (e.g., psychological distress, physical limitations, age, and gender) increased the risk of different types of victimization (nonfamily, sexual, and parental assault), even after taking into account the effects of lifestyles (e.g., risky behavior).

Guardianship

The presence of guardianship is hypothesized to eliminate or at least reduce opportunities for victimization by making criminal action by the offender riskier, more difficult, or less rewarding. Therefore, an absence of guardianship contributes to victimization opportunities. Studies investigating the effects of guardianship on victimization have mostly examined this concept by considering behaviors such as target hardening (e.g., locking doors) or the degree of home occupancy (e.g., Massey, Krohn, & Bonati, 1989; Miethe & McDowall, 1993) as types of guardianship. More recent research has begun to explore the varied dimensions of guardianship within a multilevel opportunity theory framework. These researchers have simultaneously considered individual- and aggregate-level measures of guardianship, such as physical (target hardening), personal (home occupancy), social (ties between neighbors), and defensible space (aspects of the physical location that discourage crime) dimensions of guardianship (Wilcox, Madensen, & Tillyer, 2007).

The guardianship aspect of opportunity also has been further refined, as represented by the expanded crime triangle in Figure 2-5. The traditional crime triangle appears in the center of the figure, with the three sides representing the intersection in time and space of motivated offenders, suitable targets, and (places) lacking capable guardianship. The outer triangle represents three forms of guardianship that can prevent crime—these are referred to as the ***triplets of guardianship***. First, potential targets or victims can be protected by ***guardians***. For example, walking home from a night class with a fellow student provides a guardian against potential victimization. Family, neighbors, friends, and even police also are examples of guardians. Second, crime can be discouraged at places by using ***place managers***, individuals who have control over the activities that transpire within certain locations. Landlords, maintenance workers, or store managers are examples of place managers. The presence and effective place management of these individuals has the potential to reduce crime and victimization at the place level.

Figure 2-5 The Triplets of Guardianship
Source: Clarke and Eck (2005).

Third, ***handlers*** are people who have influence over the behavior of offenders and can potentially prevent them from behaving criminally. Depending on the offender, examples of handlers could be parents, family members, friends, or intimate partners (Felson, 1995).

Following up the triplets of guardianship conceptual modification to the crime triangle, Sampson, Eck, and Dunham (2010) imposed another layer of guardianship on the opportunity triad of offenders, targets, and places. Referring to managers, guardians, and handlers as "controllers," Sampson and her colleagues (2010, p. 39) pointed out that victimization occurs when motivated offenders meet suitable targets in places where these ***controllers*** are ineffective. In other words, even in circumstances where controllers are present, often they fail and victimization still occurs. This is because the controllers have not been properly motivated to fulfill their crime prevention potential by ***super controllers***. According to Sampson and colleagues (2010, p. 40), "super controllers control the controllers." They are the people, organizations, or institutions that provide incentives to controllers to prevent victimization. Courts, regulatory agencies, legislatures, the media, and even families are just a few examples of the wide variety of super controllers.

Critiques of the Opportunity Perspective: Concepts Matter

The opportunity perspective, and specifically lifestyle–routine activities theory, has demonstrated its usefulness in explaining a wide variety of personal and property victimization types (e.g., burglary, stalking) among different populations (e.g., adolescents, adults) and across different contexts (e.g., workplaces, college campuses).

The effects of the main theoretical concepts—exposure, proximity, target attractiveness, and guardianship—on victimization, when evaluated across research studies, mostly exhibit the effects the theory would predict (e.g., Madero-Hernandez & Fisher, 2012; Spano & Freilich, 2009). Further, the theory has been successfully used to account for victimization at different levels of analysis, including the individual and aggregate levels, as well as combined perspectives simultaneously considering both levels. The research findings that consistently and repeatedly link lifestyles and daily routines to victimization risk have solidified lifestyle–routine activities theory as the leading theory of victimization in the field of victimology. However, this does not mean that the theories are immune to criticism. Despite the popularity and utility of the theories, four main issues related to the validity of the theory remain open for the theories' proponents to address.

Influence of the Concepts

The theories hypothesize that opportunities for victimization are generated by the intersection of motivated offenders, suitable targets, and an absence of guardianship. The theory does not address which of the concepts is the most important in creating opportunities, or to what degree each of the concepts must be represented. Research using lifestyle–routine activities theory has not consistently identified any of the main elements of the theory as having a greater influence on victimization risk than any other. For example, perhaps exposure to motivated offenders has a more substantial impact on one's likelihood of victimization than does proximity, target attractiveness, or guardianship. Or perhaps some combination of factors, such as increased proximity and reduced guardianship, has the highest predictive power, while exposure and target attractiveness have only minimal effects on victimization opportunities.

At present, it appears that the effects of the individual elements on explaining victimization vary depending on the ways in which researchers conduct their studies (e.g., characteristics of the sample, measurement of the concepts) and the type of victimization they are trying to explain (e.g., personal, property). For example, Richard Spano and Joshua Freilich (2009) examined the collective body of research studies using routine activities theory to explain individual victimization published between 1995 and 2005. They concluded that exposure to motivated offenders, target attractiveness, and guardianship usually performed as lifestyle–routine activities theory would predict. However, certain methodological choices made by researchers also influenced these results. To illustrate, they reported that for samples including individuals from the United States, target attractiveness was fairly consistent across studies in its prediction of victimization, but its effects were much less reliable in studies using respondents from countries other than the United States. This suggests the possibility of a cultural effect on victimization.

Measuring the Concepts

There is an absence of universal or accepted ways of measuring the theoretical concepts in studies of victimization. If the core opportunity concepts of exposure, proximity, target suitability, and guardianship are represented differently across studies of victimization, identifying patterns and improving our understanding of the dynamics of victimization becomes more difficult. Further, the concepts have been defined and operationalized differently from study to study, making it hard to compare results across studies and further obscuring the true dynamics of victimization. Consider what makes a person a suitable target for robbery victimization. Is it that she is elderly and presumably less likely to resist an attack? Is it that he is traveling alone? Is it that she is carrying a large amount of cash?

Each of these behaviors, by itself, could be considered a possible indicator of target attractiveness in the context of robbery victimization. On the other hand, an argument could be made that they represent some other aspect of opportunity. For example, those who are traveling alone may seem to be attractive targets, yet this habit of traveling alone may also represent a lack or guardianship or exposure to risk. Carrying or displaying large sums of cash could also represent a lack of self-guardianship or care in preventing oneself from presenting an attractive target. These are just a few examples, but they do illustrate the point that operationalization of opportunity is a key aspect of understanding victimization risk.

Applying the Concepts

Sampson (1987) and others have observed that the opportunity perspective implicitly assumes that offenders and victims will be strangers to each other. However, for many crime types (e.g., sexual victimizations, stalking, homicide), it is more likely that the offender will be known to the victim than that the parties will be strangers. The concepts of proximity, exposure, target attractiveness, and guardianship vary depending on the relationship between victims and offenders (e.g., intimate partners, family members, friends, and strangers). Further, depending on the victim–offender relationship and the type of victimization, these characteristics may not be a product of the victim's lifestyle or routine activities. For example, Finkelhor and Asdigian (1996) argued that for certain types of victimization, particularly victimization by intimates (e.g., intimate partners, family members), the lifestyle–routine activities concepts of exposure, proximity, and guardianship should not be thought of as victim behaviors that either increase or decrease victimization risk. Rather, they argued that these factors should be thought of as environmental conditions, giving the example of a child who is placed at risk for sexual abuse because her parents are careless in their protective duties as parents (Finkelhor & Asdigian, 1996). This lack of guardianship is not an aspect of that child's lifestyle or daily routines but a feature of her environment. These arguments call into question the types of victimization the opportunity perspective is capable of explaining, but more research is needed before any conclusions can be made.

Breadth of the Concepts

Both lifestyle-exposure theory and routine activities theory were originally devised to explain direct-contact predatory offenses (e.g., forcible rape, robbery, and burglary). In other words, Hindelang and colleagues as well as Cohen and Felson assumed that the victim (or victim's property) and the offender would physically be in the same place at the same time. Yet, a number of types of victimization do not require this direct contact and are instead characterized by the physical and temporal separation of the victim and the offender. For example, crimes in which the victim and offender interact over the phone (e.g., texting), through the mail, or online (e.g., e-mail, Facebook) do not necessarily involve an immediate intersection in time or space. For this reason, some theorists have questioned the validity of the theory as an explanation for certain types of victimization, such as online victimization (e.g., Yar, 2005). Researchers recently have begun to explore whether lifestyle–routine activities theory can be successfully used to explain online victimization (e.g., Reyns, 2013), a topic that will be discussed further in Chapter 3.

Summary

The second and third generations of victimology theories advanced the field of victimology away from the idea that victims are responsible for their victimization toward a perspective focused on opportunities as the key focal point to understanding why and how victimization occurs. The four theories reviewed in this chapter, which are summarized in Table 2-3, explain the circumstances under which opportunities for victimization arise.

The lifestyle–routine activities perspective focuses on four main influences on opportunity: (1) exposure to risk, (2) proximity to motivated offenders, (3) target attractiveness, and (4) guardianship. Multilevel opportunity theory describes opportunity as a consequence of these factors operating at both the individual and aggregate levels, with opportunity structures changing with the context. Structural-choice theory similarly focuses on the context in which crimes take place, arguing that to fully explain why crime occurs requires understanding offender motivation, victimization opportunities, and the social context.

Over time, the propositions of the opportunity perspective, and especially the lifestyle–routine activities concepts of exposure, proximity, target attractiveness, and guardianship, have been measured in a variety of ways by researchers examining

Table 2-3: Summary of Oppertunity Theories of Victimization

Theory	Key Concepts
1. Lifestyle-Exposure Theory	Personal victimizations are the result of lifestyles that expose potential victims to victimization risk.
2. Routine Activities Theory	Direct-contact victimizations are the result of an intersection in time and space of motivated offenders, suitable targets, and an absence of capable guardianship.
3. Multilevel Opportunity Theory	Victimization is best explained by examining individual- and aggregate-level routine activities that together increase or decrease victimization risk.
4. Structural-Choice Theory	Criminal events cannot be adequately understood without taking into account offender motivation, victimization opportunities, and the social context in which crime occurs (physical location, interpersonal relationship, behavioral setting).

different types of victimization. Generally, their findings support the usefulness of the theory in explaining victimization. The theory and research findings surrounding the opportunity perspective have also influenced the ways in which the criminal justice system responds to crime. The "Spotlight on Policy: Problem-Oriented Policing" box explains how problem-oriented policing has emerged in part due to the contributions of criminological and victimological research based on the concept of opportunity.

The opportunity perspective is not the only theoretical framework victimologists have used to probe into why individuals and their property are victimized. Chapter 3 reviews the fourth generation of victimization theories: the application of criminological theories to explain victimization through the victim–offender overlap and updates to contemporary opportunity theory.

Spotlight on Policy: Problem-Oriented Policing

The idea that opportunities are a major reason why crime and victimization occur has directly affected police practices in countries all over the world, including the United States. This is one of the foundations of problem-oriented policing. Problem-oriented policing differs from other police philosophies because it takes a problem-specific approach to preventing crime that addresses its underlying causes. Contrast this idea with random patrolling strategies or simply responding to calls for service, and it is clear that the problem-oriented approach is quite different.

The philosophy behind problem-oriented policing is that police are tasked with responding to a number of diverse problems that often recur, and addressing or solving these problems requires an approach specifically designed for that problem. Police officers solve problems by defining the problem, analyzing its causes, devising initiatives to address the problem, and evaluating the impact of their efforts. In the language of problem-oriented policing, this process is referred to as SARA: Scanning, Analysis, Response, and Assessment.

Key to addressing recurring police problems is identifying the circumstances under which opportunities for crime and victimization occur. By defining problems specifically, and understanding the nature of criminal opportunities, officers are able to disrupt these opportunities, thereby preventing crime and victimization. Problem-oriented policing is one example of how the theoretical ideas presented in this chapter have been put into practice in the real world. Another example, situational crime prevention, will be discussed in Chapter 14.

See Clarke and Eck (2005) for more information about problem-oriented policing, or visit the Center for Problem-Oriented Policing at www.popcenter.org.

KEYWORDS

Opportunity perspective
Lifestyle-exposure theory
Role expectations
Routine activity theory
Crime triangle
Exposure
Physical guardianship
Social guardianship
Lifestyle-routine activities theory

Structural constraints	Proximity	Multilevel opportunity theory
Lifestyles	VIVA	Structural-choice theory
Principle of homogamy	CRAVED	Physical locations
Routine activities	Hot products	Physical space
Household activity ratio	Guardianship	Darkness
Tempo, pace, rhythm	Target vulnerability	Place managers
History	Target gratifiability	Handlers
Interpersonal relationships	Target antagonism	Controllers
Behavioral setting	Triplets of guardianship	Super controllers
Target congruence	Guardians	

DISCUSSION QUESTIONS

1. Can you think of any types of victimization in which opportunity does *not* play a role? Explain and provide an example.
2. What types of lifestyles do you think expose people to the greatest risk of victimization? Explain and provide an example.
3. What are key differences between lifestyle-exposure theory and routine activities theory?
4. What *types* of routine activities might increase individuals' likelihood of criminal victimization? Explain and provide an example.
5. How does the concept of target suitability differ depending on the type of victimization?
6. How do environmental contexts shape victimization opportunities for individuals within those specific contexts?
7. Which of the four theories from this chapter (lifestyle-exposure theory, routine activities theory, multilevel opportunity theory, and structural-choice theory) provides the "best" explanation of criminal victimization in your opinion? Justify your choice.

REFERENCES

Clarke, R. V. (1999). *Hot products: Understanding, anticipating and reducing demand for stolen goods.* Police Research Series, Paper 112. London: Home Office.

Clarke, R. V., & Eck, J. E. (2005). *Crime analysis for problem solvers in 60 small steps.* Washington, DC: Office of Community Oriented Policing.

Cohen, L. E., & Felson, M. (1979). Social change and crime rate trends: A routine activity approach. *American Sociological Review, 44,* 588–608.

Cohen, L. E., Kluegel, J. R., & Land, K. C. (1981). Social inequality and predatory criminal victimization: An exposition and test of a formal theory. *American Sociological Review, 46,* 505–524.

Cullen, F. T., Agnew, R., & Wilcox, P. (2013). *Criminological theory: Past to present* (5th Ed.). New York: Oxford University Press.

Felson, M. (1995). Those who discourage crime. In J. E. Eck & D. Weisburd (Eds.), *Crime and place* (pp. 53–66). Monsey, NY: Criminal Justice Press.

Felson, M., & Boba, R. (2010). *Crime and everyday life* (4th Ed.). Thousand Oaks, CA: Sage Publications, Inc.

Felson, M., & Clarke, R. V. (1998). *Opportunity makes the thief: Practical theory for crime prevention.* Police Research Series, Paper 98. London: Home Office.

Finkelhor, D., & Asdigian, N. L. (1996). Risk factors for youth victimization: Beyond a lifestyles/routine activities theory approach. *Violence and Victims, 11,* 3–19.

Fisher, B. S., Sloan, J. J., Cullen, F. T., & Lu, C. (1998). Crime in the ivory tower: The level and sources of student victimization. *Criminology, 36,* 671–710.

Garofalo, J. (1987). Reassessing the lifestyle model of criminal victimization. In M. R. Gottfredson, & T. Hirschi (Eds.), *Positive criminology* (pp. 23–42). Newbury Park, CA: Sage Publications, Inc.

Hawley, A. H. (1950). *Human ecology: A theory of community structure.* New York: Ronald Press Co.

Hindelang, M. J., Gottfredson M. R., & Garofalo, J. (1978). *Victims of personal crime: An empirical foundation for a theory of personal victimization.* Cambridge, MA: Ballinger Publishing Company.

Hollis, M. E., Felson, M., & Welsh, B. C. (2013). The capable guardian in routine activities theory: A theoretical and conceptual reappraisal. *Crime Prevention and Community Safety, 35,* 65–79.

Hough, M. (1987). Offenders' choice of target: Findings from victim surveys. *Journal of Quantitative Criminology, 3,* 355–369.

Kennedy, L. W., & Forde, D. R. (1990). Routine activities and crime: An analysis of victimization in Canada. *Criminology, 28,* 137–152.

Lynch, J. P. (1987). Routine activity and victimization at work. *Journal of Quantitative Criminology, 3,* 283–300.

Madero-Hernandez, A., & Fisher, B. S. (2012). Routine activity theory. In F. T. Cullen & P. Wilcox (Eds.), *The Oxford handbook of criminological theory* (pp. 513–534). New York: Oxford University Press.

Massey, J. L., Krohn, M. D., & Bonati, L. M. (1989). Property crime and the routine activities of individuals. *Journal of Research in Crime and Delinquency, 26,* 378–400.

Miethe, T. D., & McDowall, D. (1993). Contextual effects in models of criminal victimization. *Social Forces, 71*, 741–759.

Miethe, T. D., & Meier, R. F. (1990). Opportunity, choice, and criminal victimization: A test of a theoretical model. *Journal of Research in Crime and Delinquency, 27*, 243–266.

Miethe, T. D., & Meier, R. F. (1994). *Crime and its social context: Toward an integrated theory of offenders, victims, and situations.* Albany, NY: SUNY Press.

Miethe, T. D., Stafford, M. C., & Long, J. S. (1987). Social differentiation in criminal victimization: A test of routine activities/lifestyle theories. *American Sociological Review, 52*, 184–194.

Mustaine, E. E., & Tewksbury, R. (1998). Predicting risks of larceny theft victimization: A routine activity analysis using refined lifestyles measures. *Criminology, 36*, 829–858.

Pires, S., & Clarke, R. V. (2011). Are parrots CRAVED? An analysis of parrot poaching in Mexico. *Journal of Research in Crime and Delinquency, 49*, 122–146.

Reyns, B. W. (2013). Online routines and identity theft victimization: Further expanding routine activity theory beyond direct contact offenses. *Journal of Research in Crime and Delinquency, 50*, 216–238.

Sampson, R. J. (1987). Personal violence by strangers: An extension and test of the opportunity model of predatory victimization. *Journal of Criminal Law & Criminology, 78*, 327–356.

Sampson, R., Eck, J. E., & Dunham, J. (2010). Super controllers and crime prevention: A routine activity explanation of crime prevention success and failure. *Security Journal, 23*, 37–51.

Sampson, R.J., & Wooldredge, J. (1987). Linking the micro- and macro-level dimensions of lifestyle-routine activity and opportunity models of predatory victimization. *Journal of Quantitative Criminology, 3*, 371–393.

Smith, D. A., & Jarjoura, G. R. (1989). Household characteristics, neighborhood composition and victimization risk. *Social Forces, 68*, 621–640.

Spano, R., & Freilich, J. D. (2009). An assessment of the empirical validity and conceptualization of individual level multivariate studies of lifestyle/routine activities theory published from 1995 to 2005. *Journal of Criminal Justice, 37*, 305–314.

Stahura, J. M., & Sloan, J. J. (1988). Urban stratification of places, routine activities and suburban crime rates. *Social Forces, 66*, 1102–1118.

Tillyer, M. S., Tillyer, R., Miller, H. V., & Pangrac, R. (2011). Reexamining the correlates of adolescent violent victimization: The importance of exposure, guardianship, and target characteristics. *Journal of Interpersonal Violence, 26*, 2908–2928.

Wilcox, P., Land, K. C., & Hunt, S. A. (2003). *Criminal circumstance: A dynamic multicontextual criminal opportunity theory.* New York: Aldine de Gruyter.

Wilcox, P., Madensen, T. D., & Tillyer, M. S. (2007). Guardianship in context: Implications for burglary victimization risk and prevention. *Criminology, 45*, 401–433.

Yar, M. (2005). The novelty of 'cybercrime': An assessment in light of routine activity theory. *European Journal of Criminology, 2*, 407–427.

CHAPTER 3

Contemporary Theories of Victimization

CHAPTER OUTLINE

LEARNING OBJECTIVES

- Explain how opportunity theory has been revised from its origins in lifestyle-exposure theory and routine activities theory.
- Describe the assumptions underlying gendered routine activities theory and how it is used to explain victimization.
- Summarize the points underlying feminist routine activities theory and describe how it can be used to explain the victimization of women.
- Review the main concepts of age-graded routine activities theory and describe its usefulness in explaining victimization.
- Identify the ways in which cyberlifestyle–routine activities theory adapted the opportunity perspective to account for cybercrimes.
- Explain the notion of "victim–offender overlap" and how it enhances explanations of victimization.
- Describe the general theory of crime and explain how it can be reinterpreted to also explain victimization.
- Discuss control balance theory as a theory of crime and as a theory of victimization.
- Summarize the core ideas in environmental criminology and explain how it can be applied to victimization.
- Explain how life course criminology contributes to better understanding criminal victimization.

> *If offenders and victims are frequently drawn from the same group of individuals, and they seem to be, then insights borrowed from criminological theory should advance our understanding of victimization.*
>
> **Schreck, Stewart, and Osgood, 2008, p. 873**

Introduction

Chapter 2 reviewed the origins and development of the opportunity perspective, which defined the second and third generations of victimology theories. Recall that opportunity theories focus on how and why victims' daily activities—most of which are relatively mundane—create chances for individuals or their property to be victimized. The fourth or contemporary generation of victimization theories and theorists advanced the field of victimology with two additional approaches to explaining criminal victimization. First, researchers continued to build on the foundation of opportunity theory to explain victimization. Their additions to the opportunity perspective include: (1) gender-based opportunity frameworks, (2) a feminist opportunity perspective, (3) an age-graded opportunity theory, and (4) an adaptation of the opportunity perspective to account for the physical and temporal separation of offenders and victims. Once again, the purpose of these contemporary theories is to identify factors that create opportunities for victimization to occur.

Second, contemporary victimologists also have considered factors beyond opportunity to explain how and why victimization occurs, including general theories that may account for both criminal offending and criminal victimization (Schreck, Stewart, & Osgood, 2008). This line of research focuses on the shared characteristics of victims and offenders and uses criminological theories, especially Gottfredson and Hirschi's (1990) general theory of crime, to explain why victims and offenders are often one and the same. Other notable examples of this orientation include applications of control balance theory, environmental criminology, and life course criminology as explanations of victimization. Similarly, contemporary victimology theories have integrated the opportunity perspective with theories of crime and delinquency to explore how victim traits that have been identified as predictors of criminal behavior, such as low self-control, can affect opportunities for victimization. This chapter reviews these theoretical arguments and other contributions of the fourth generation of victimology theorists and their theories.

Contemporary Revisions to Opportunity Theory

Like the arguments put forth by Michael Hindelang, Michael Gottfredson, and James Garofalo (1978) in their description of lifestyle-exposure theory, contemporary opportunity theorists have explored how lifestyles and routine activities *differ* for certain groups of people. Recall that according to lifestyle-exposure theory, individuals' demographic characteristics indirectly affect lifestyles through role expectations, structural constraints, and adaptations to those societal forces (Hindelang et al., 1978). Likewise, the fourth generation of victimization theories focused, in part, on how lifestyles and routine activities vary by gender and across age groups. In other words, these theorists have concentrated on the extent to which lifestyles and daily routines differ for males and females, as well as across different stages of life (e.g., childhood, adolescence, young adulthood), and how these differences may enhance or diminish the risk of victimization.

Feminist scholars also have recognized the important role that gender plays in explaining why victimization occurs. This research focuses on how women's victimizations, especially sexual victimizations such as rape, are the consequence of a patriarchal culture—where men dominate and women are submissive to men. In such a culture, the lifestyle–routine activities concepts of motivated offenders, target suitability, and guardianship take on modified meanings. For instance, certain female lifestyle behaviors, such as drinking alcohol, may inadvertently make women suitable targets for motivated male offenders who believe it is socially acceptable to use physical and psychological violence to obtain sex (Schwartz & Pitts, 1995).

Finally, the fourth generation of victimologists has applied the lifestyle–routine activities perspective to "long-distance" victimizations. The original opportunity theories—lifestyle-exposure and routine activities—were mostly developed to explain direct-contact victimizations in which the victim, or the victim's property, and the offender came together in time and space and thus created an opportunity for a criminal victimization to occur. With the advent of the Internet and the long-distance connections it makes possible (e.g., to communicate, to remotely purchase goods and services), crimes as diverse as identity theft and stalking can now transpire between victims and offenders in cyberspace. In these instances, victims and offenders may be many miles apart, and thus not in the same physical location, or even not in the same temporal space (e.g., not online at the same time). Therefore, a recent contribution by theorists has been to adapt and apply the opportunity perspective to these long-distance crimes. Each of these contemporary revisions to opportunity theory is presented in subsequent sections.

Gendered Routine Activities Theory

Compared to women, men are far more often the victims of homicide, robbery, aggravated assault, and other personal crimes. However, with certain offenses, such as sexual victimization and stalking, women are disproportionately the victims. These examples illustrate that for some types of victimization there is a ***gender gap*** in which victimization risk is not equally distributed for males and females. Such a gap is illustrated in Figure 3-1, which shows that since the early 1990s, while closing somewhat, the rate of intimate partner violence for women is greater than the rate for men. Other crimes, such as simple assault, seem to be gender-neutral, occurring at similar rates to both males and females (Truman, 2011).

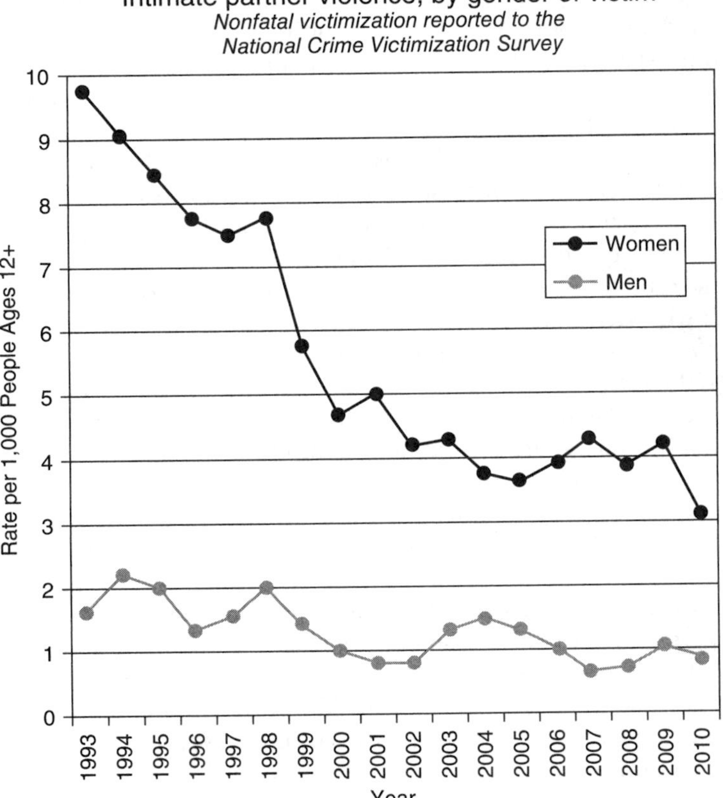

Figure 3-1 Recent Trends (1993–2010) in Intimate Partner Violence by Gender of Victim
Source: Catalano (2010).

Victimologists have used the opportunity perspective, particularly lifestyle–routine activities theory, to explain gender-based victimization patterns. According to opportunity theory, victim characteristics, such as age, race, and gender, should *not* predict who experiences victimization once lifestyle behaviors are considered. In essence, lifestyles and routine activities facilitate crime opportunities, not whether the victim is a male or female. Further, regardless of a potential gender gap in victimization, it appears that risk factors for certain types of victimization are different for males and females. Researchers have found that indicators of opportunity—exposure, target suitability, and guardianship—differ by gender and type of victimization (Wilcox, Tillyer, & Fisher, 2009). For example, Wilcox and colleagues (2009) reported that among students in their study, involvement in sports decreased the likelihood that male adolescents would experience assault victimization, while among girls involvement in sports increased these risks.

Gendered routine activities research has developed three approaches to explaining why victimization occurs. The first approach, gender-based theories, considers whether gender gaps in victimization patterns are actually driven by differences in the lifestyles and routine activities of men and women. For example, perhaps men's lifestyles or routine activities are more likely to expose them to a high risk of robbery victimization, while women do not generally participate in these activities to the same degree and therefore are not as likely to be targets for robbery. In this case, lifestyles and routine activities are actually structured by gender, as Hindelang and colleagues (1978) suggested, and gendered lifestyles and routine activities, in turn, explain differences in male and female victimization patterns.

Regarding support for this idea, researchers have not arrived at a firm conclusion. On the one hand, some research suggests that routine activities–based factors for victimization are different for males and females. As an example, Elizabeth Ehrhardt Mustaine and Richard Tewksbury's (1998) study of college students revealed that behaviors such as playing team sports, spending evenings out for leisure, and marijuana use increased victimization risks for males, but not females. Likewise, activities such as eating out often, the amount of time spent in social activities, and the frequency of alcohol consumption were positively related to female but not male victimization. On the other hand, victimization studies also have revealed that gender remains an important influence on victimization, even after the effects of lifestyles and routines are considered (Henson, Wilcox, Reyns, & Cullen, 2010). For example, in their study of adolescent victimization, Billy Henson and his colleagues reported that males were more likely to experience violent victimization than females after accounting for the effects of lifestyles and routine activities such as commuting to work, participating in sports, or attending church.

The second gender-based lifestyle–routine activities approach to explaining victimization stresses the possible interaction effects that gender has with certain lifestyles and routines. In other words, it is possible that gender, in combination with specific lifestyles and routine activities, exposes males and females to differing levels of victimization risk. For example, perhaps among adolescents, alcohol use, tobacco use, and drug use increase risks of victimization, but only among females. This effect was reported in a recent study of sexual assault and sexual harassment victimization of middle- and high-school students by Tillyer, Wilcox, and Gialopsos

(2010). Ann Marie Popp and Anthony Peguero (2011) also explored these types of interaction effects in their study of violent and property victimization experienced by 10th-grade students. Results of the study revealed that certain extracurricular routine activities affected students' likelihood of victimization, but the nature of these effects depended on the students' gender. For example, Popp and Peguero reported that female students who participated in intramural sports were at an increased risk of both violent and property victimization compared to male students, but participating in clubs (e.g., hobby clubs, service clubs) significantly decreased risks of violent victimization for females compared to males.

The third gender-based opportunity approach to victimization conceptualizes gender as an element of target attractiveness. Consider a scenario in which two college students, one male and one female, separately walk home alone to their respective off-campus apartments after attending evening classes. They take the same route and live in the same residential complex. Yet, the female is robbed, while the male makes his way home safely. Both students were exposed to risk, in comparable proximity to motivated offenders, and equally unguarded, yet the female was targeted. According to gender-based revisions to opportunity theory, the female student was targeted *because* her gender signaled to motivated offenders that she is vulnerable. In describing this process Wilcox and colleagues (2009, p. 263) remarked that "gender exacerbates indicators of opportunity because it also provides cues (perhaps misguided) to offenders about opportunity." Put differently, gender alters perceptions of opportunity for offenders, in which case being female can *itself* be considered one element of target attractiveness. This idea is comparable to feminist theorists' arguments in their adaptation of opportunity theory to explain sexual victimization against women.

Overall, these three gender-based approaches to opportunity theory suggest that gender is an important consideration in understanding opportunities for victimization. Gender may structure lifestyles and routine activities; have interaction effects with certain lifestyles and routines; represent a dimension of target attractiveness; or perhaps produce all of these effects. More research into the intersection of gender, opportunity, and criminal victimization is needed to continue to explore these relationships and better understand the role gender plays in explaining how and why individuals become crime victims.

Feminist Routine Activities Theory

Another conceptual extension of the opportunity framework that focuses on gender is feminist routine activities theory. More broadly, a central concept in feminist theory is ***patriarchy***. In patriarchal societies, men control a disproportionate share of the power in all domains of social life (e.g., the home, the workplace), and this power imbalance between men and women ensures that men retain their positions of dominance while women are relegated to second-class status. ***Feminist routine activities*** research has focused mostly on the sexual victimization of women, and how opportunities for victimization are aggravated by the backdrop of a patriarchal society. Martin Schwartz and Victoria Pitts (1995) were the first victimologists to integrate feminist perspectives with the lifestyle–routine activities approach. In their study, Schwartz and Pitts revised the core theoretical concepts of lifestyle–routine activities theory—motivated offenders, suitable targets, and a lack of guardianship—into a feminist explanation for the sexual victimization of college women.

Schwartz and Pitts (1995) explained that a feminist routine activities theory could examine motivated offenders in two ways. First, while routine activities theory does not attempt to address the issue of *why* individuals are motivated to offend, Schwartz and Pitts (1995, p. 628) argued that, at least on college campuses, there are male peer groups that "perpetuate and legitimate the sexual exploitation of women, especially intoxicated females." A second element representing the presence of motivated offenders is the assertion that the United States has a "rape-supportive culture," which means that there are a variety of excuses found in U.S. culture that allow motivated offenders to commit sexual crimes without thinking of themselves as "rapists" or "criminals" (Schwartz, DeKeseredy, Tait, & Alvi, 2001). Overall, then, a patriarchal, "rape-supportive" culture produces a large supply of potentially motivated sexual offenders, especially on college campuses.

Second, in considering the suitability of college women as targets for sexual victimization, Schwartz and Pitts explained that two lifestyle behaviors—alcohol abuse and friendships with men who perpetrate sexual crimes—represent feminist conceptions of this theoretical concept (i.e., target suitability). They hypothesized that women who consume more alcohol in a single sitting and who drink on more days of the week than other women would be more likely to be targeted by motivated offenders due to their increased vulnerability. They also argued that women whose male friends use alcohol to get women intoxicated to have sex with them will be likely targets of sexual victimization. Although Schwartz and Pitts viewed these friendships as a reflection of target suitability, an argument also could be made that these friendships create proximity to motivated offenders. Schwartz and Pitts's conception of target suitability also implies that because of their gender, women are targets of sexual aggression by men.

The third component of lifestyle–routine activities theory that researchers have modified to be congruent with a feminist perspective is guardianship. Schwartz and Pitts (1995) presented two examples of feminist conceptions of how guardianship would relate to the sexual victimization of college women. First, college campuses generally have ineffective guardianship against sexual victimization because offenders are rarely brought to the attention of campus disciplinary hearings or the criminal justice system, and therefore escape punishment for their crimes (Schwartz et al., 2001). They argued that institutional responses to sexual victimization occurring on college campuses mirror the responses found in the larger population—namely that rape and sexual victimization are not treated as seriously as they should be. Second, the "rape-supportive culture" Schwartz and Pitts described enables social support among male peers (i.e., motivated offenders) and perpetuates "rape myths" that neutralize and legitimize behaviors such as getting a woman drunk with the intent to have sex with her. We discuss rape myths further in Chapter 6, but briefly, they are stereotypical perceptions about the nature of rape victimization, such as the belief that "real rapes" are only perpetrated by strangers to the victim, that women who dress in a certain fashion "ask" to be raped, and that when a woman says "no" to sexual relations she actually means "yes."

A small body of research has applied the above arguments to the study of the sexual victimization of college women. Study results for the most part suggest that a feminist interpretation of routine activities theory can be useful in understanding sexual victimization. Schwartz and Pitts's (1995) original article that reframed routine activities theory in the feminist perspective reported that college women who go out drinking often and who have male friends who get women drunk in order to have sex with them (i.e., they are motivated offenders) are at an increased likelihood of sexual victimization. Schwartz and colleagues (2001) built upon this earlier research and examined both opportunities for and sources of offender motivation for sexual victimization. They reported that drinking alcohol, especially drinking with dating partners, increased both women's likelihood of victimization and men's likelihood of perpetrating sexual abuse. Further, men who indicated they had friends who advocated the use of violence against women under certain circumstances were more likely to engage in sexually abusive behavior. Schwartz and colleagues also pointed out that the combination of these two behaviors was an especially powerful predictor of sexual offending. Men who consumed alcohol two or more times per week and had male peers who supported and advocated sexual violence against women were *nine times* more likely to admit to having engaged in sexual violence than men who did not drink or have friends who supported violence against women (Schwartz et al., 2001).

In another feminist routine activities study of sexual assault victimization among college women, Mustaine and Tewksbury (2002) reported that alcohol consumption was not a significant predictor of victimization risk. Instead, lifestyle behaviors such as frequently going out at night for leisure, using illegal drugs, and having membership in many school groups or organizations (including athletic teams but not Greek organizations), increased women's risk of sexual assault victimization.

To date, feminist routine activities theory has been limited to examining the sexual victimization of college women. It is not clear to what extent the perspective has utility in explaining other types of victimization (e.g., stalking, assault) among other groups of victims, such as women in the general population. As was the case with the gendered routine activities perspective discussed previously, it appears that more research is needed to develop and explore the usefulness of a feminist interpretation of lifestyle–routine activities theory.

Age-Graded Routine Activities Theory

Trends in victimization rates reveal that age is a strong predictor of victimization, with younger individuals usually being more at risk for victimization than older people (Truman, 2011). And, similar to the gendered routine activities emphasis on lifestyle and routine activity differences across males and females, the ***age-graded routine activities*** perspective highlights differences in these behaviors across developmental stages in the life course. Broadly speaking, a life course perspective studies various aspects of people's lives (e.g., criminal behavior, victimization) by integrating knowledge from many disciplines, such as sociology, psychology, history, economics, biology, and criminology, and emphasizes that these aspects of life differ with age. For instance, life course criminologists study the development, continuance, and desistance of offending over time, as well as the reasons for these changes (see, e.g., Sampson & Laub, 1993; Wright, Tibbetts, & Daigle, 2008).

Within an opportunity framework, differences in lifestyles and routine activities also are seen as dynamic and changing over the course of life. For example, adolescents participate in school-based routine activities and spend more time with friends because of their developmental stage in the life course. Adults engage in home- and work-based lifestyles to a higher degree than adolescents, and spend their time with spouses, children, and coworkers. Consequently, the differences in adolescent and adult behaviors converge to create victimization opportunities. Once again, however, these lifestyles and routines will differ across age groups and stages of life.

One of the early studies to focus on adolescent lifestyles was conducted by Gary Jensen and David Brownfield (1986). In this study, adolescent victimization was examined in light of routine activities such as dating, going to the movies, driving around for fun, and most importantly, engaging in delinquent/criminal behaviors, which included using a weapon on someone, setting fire to someone's property, and damaging school property on purpose. Jensen and Brownfield reported that activities associated with "pursuing fun" such as dating or going to parties were also related to criminal victimization, presumably because these activities exposed adolescents to risk for victimization. Jensen and Brownfield also found that engaging in delinquent/criminal activities were more strongly related to victimization than were the noncriminal routines. Their study was the first of many that identified delinquency as a risky activity that often precedes adolescent victimization.

In a more recent study, Marie Tillyer and colleagues (2011) explored the effects of exposure, target characteristics, and guardianship on the violent victimization of adolescent middle- and high-school students using multiple measures of the concepts. They reported that each of these concepts was significantly related to victimization, but that self-reported involvement with violent criminal behavior was by far the strongest predictor of victimization, increasing the risk of violence over 12 times. Given the reality that a large portion of crime is committed by adolescents, research showing strong links between engaging in delinquent and criminal behaviors and increased victimization risk is significant for explaining the age–victimization relationship.

Age-graded routine activities theory also emphasizes that the theoretical concepts of opportunity theory have different effects at different life stages. Henson and colleagues (2010, p. 322) explained that an age-graded routine activities theory "stresses the importance of criminal opportunity as a predictor of victimization at all ages, but it recognizes that opportunity is not equally tied to routine activities at all stages of the life course." This argument implies that exposure, proximity, target attractiveness, and guardianship have differential effects on the likelihood of victimization depending on the age of the potential victim.

In their study, Henson and colleagues (2010) identified several lifestyles of, and activities by, members of a sample of adolescents, and examined the effects of those lifestyles on both minor and serious violent victimization. Among the different lifestyles and routine activities they considered, including spending time with boy/girlfriend, spending time online in electronic activities, church activities, and playing sports, only engaging in delinquent activities was consistently related to an increased risk for victimization. In interpreting these findings, the authors suggested that adolescent lifestyles do not vary as much as adult lifestyles because of the presence of parental supervision. This explains why activities that might otherwise expose adolescents to risk, such as dating or spending time unsupervised with friends, did not increase victimization. Instead, being an adolescent conferred a level of guardianship through parental supervision that reduced the effects of exposure, thereby reducing the likelihood that victimization would occur.

Overall, research testing opportunity theory from an age-graded perspective is still in its early stages of development. Victimologists continue to study the lifestyles and routine activities of individuals at different stages of the life course and identify lifestyle and routine activity behaviors that lead to victimization opportunities. One of the major findings of this body of research is that delinquent and criminal offending increase victimization risk, highlighting an area of overlap between offenders and victims where proximity to motivated offenders may be of importance to opportunities for victimization. Criminologists and victimologists have recognized that if offenders and victims are often one and the same, then theories that have traditionally been used to explain criminal behaviors may provide insights into victimization as well. The practice of applying and testing criminological theories to explain victimization is discussed later in this chapter.

Cyberlifestyle–Routine Activities Theory

When lifestyle-exposure theory and routine activities theory were developed in the late 1970s, implicit in the theories was an assumption that most criminal victimizations would involve the intersection in space and time of motivated offenders and suitable targets. In Cohen and Felson's (1979, p. 589) words, routine activities theory applied to "those predatory violations involving direct physical contact between at least one offender and at least one person or object which that offender attempts to take or damage." Since that time, the number and scope of crimes in which offenders and potential targets do *not* have direct physical contact have grown dramatically because of technological progress (e.g., mail, phone, and online frauds). For example, con artists have used deceit and trickery to commit fraud since antiquity, and throughout history these frauds were mostly carried out face to face. As technologies and services were created to allow individuals to communicate and interact with each other across many miles, long-distance frauds became very common. Today, the Internet connects billions of individuals worldwide and a variety of online frauds are becoming a growing concern by the public, law enforcement, and public officials.

As the previous example suggests, technology has facilitated the expansion of criminal opportunities, allowing motivated offenders to target potential victims regardless of the physical distance between them (see, e.g., Clarke, 2004). For instance, online frauds often use techniques called *phishing* and *spoofing* to persuade Internet users to divulge sensitive personal information, such as passwords or bank account numbers, to motivated offenders. The victim's information is then used for criminal purposes or sold to other criminals who use it to procure loans, apply for government benefits, or engage in other fraudulent activities. These frauds originate all over the world and often target individuals in the United States. Hence, physical contact is not a necessary condition for a victimization to occur. Figure 3-2 provides an example of a phishing attempt in which e-mail recipients were instructed to visit a web link and enter their personal information.

From: US Airways - Reservations
[mailto: reservations@myusairways.com]
Sent: Wednesday, April 04, 2012 9:51 AM
Subject: [BULK] Confirm your US airways online reservation.
Importance: Low

You can check in from 24 hours and up to 60 minutes before your flight (2 hours if you're flying internationally). Then, all you have to do is print your boarding pass and go to the gate.

We are committed to protecting your privacy. Your information is kept private and confidential. For nformation about our privacy policy visit usairways.com.

US Airways, 111 W. Rio Salado Pkwy, Tempe, AZ 85281, Copyright US Airways, All rights reserved.

Figure 3-2 US Airways Phishing E-mail
Source: Internet Crime Complaint Center (2012).

Phishing and spoofing often occur in tandem, as the example in Figure 3-2 illustrates. In cases of spoofing, communications are sent that have been forged so they appear to be from a legitimate business, in this example US Airways. Phishing is the act of posing as a business or organization for the purpose of deceiving e-mail recipients into disclosing personal information. Figure 3-3 includes the Better Business Bureau's response to this phishing attempt, which instructs recipients how to tell if their flight confirmation e-mail is genuine, and further demonstrates the point that for many cybercrimes offenders and victims are physically separate. Or, in other words, the parties are interacting from physically separate locations.

New Phishing Scam Contains Fake US Airways Itinerary

There's a new phishing scam flooding email inboxes; this time it's an itinerary for a fake US Airways flight.

The scam involves an e-mail containing a phony itinerary for a flight reservation the recipient never actually made. The email contains a link to "check-in" online for the flight, a fake confirmation code, and flight details. The phishing scam is deceiving because it looks authentic, even including the US Airways logo.

US Airways reminds customers that official e-mails often include personal information such as their name and Dividend Miles number. However their Web Check-in e-mails will not contain a name, but will have a valid confirmation code that will either be alphanumeric or all letters.

If you receive the e-mail:

- Check any links by hovering your mouse pointer over the link to identify the URL. A legitimate link will have a URL with "usairways.com."
- Do not click on any links or download any attachments.
- Delete the e-mail.

Figure 3-3 Better Business Bureau Alert to Consumers About US Airways Phishing E-mail
Source: Internet Crime Complaint Center (2012).

These distal opportunities also alter the condition of an intersection in time between the offender and the target because electronic communications between the parties are not necessarily instantaneous. In direct-contact victimizations, such as a physical assault, the offender and the victim are obviously interacting in real time because they are physically engaged with one another. However, in the above example, it is likely that there was a potentially long lag between the time the offender ("fraudster") sent the phishing e-mail(s) and the time the target(s) received the message. Regardless of the length of this time lag, the temporal overlap between offenders and victims as originally articulated by the theory also can be considered indirect.

Most of the research into opportunities for distal victimizations has focused on cybercrimes, such as the fraud attempt depicted in the US Airways phishing example, and used lifestyle–routine activities theory to differentiate victims from nonvictims. Given the spatial and temporal disconnect between victims and offenders, the applicability of lifestyle–routine activities theory to cybercrimes is not firmly established (Yar, 2005). However, ***cyberlifestyle–routine activities theory*** explains how the opportunity perspective, specifically lifestyle–routine activities theory, can be adapted to explain victimizations in which the contact between victims and offenders is indirect, and they connect neither in physical space nor in real time.

Bradford Reyns, Billy Henson, and Bonnie Fisher (2011) presented theoretical arguments that attempted to resolve the conceptual limitations of the theory relating to space and time with their cyberlifestyle–routine activities theory. In their research examining stalking victimization occurring in cyberspace ("cyberstalking"), Reyns and colleagues explained that although cyberstalkers and their victims were not meeting at a physical location, they *were* coming together within the confines of a computer network. Networks can connect individuals and allow them to interact even if they never meet face to face or are present in the same physical location. For instance, the Internet, telephones, and even the postal service are networks that connect those who are physically separated. In this way, it is often within a network rather than a physical place that victims and offenders interact.

As Figure 3-4 illustrates, the traditional crime triangle includes motivated offenders and suitable targets coming together at a place or physical location. The adapted conceptualization of the crime triangle to account for indirect or long-distance crimes shifts the environment or context in which victimization occurs

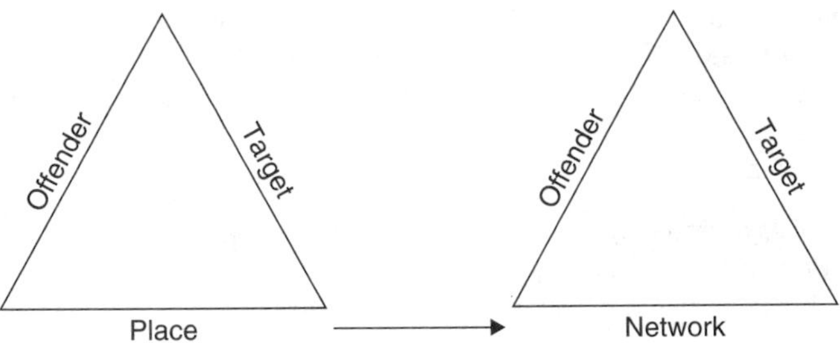

Figure 3-4 Network Crime Triangle
Source: Adapted from Eck and Clarke (2003).

from a place to a network (see also Eck & Clarke, 2003). In the case of cyberstalking, much of this interaction takes place by e-mail or instant messages, through social networking websites, or by some other electronic means (e.g., use of global positioning systems, computer programs).

Reyns and colleagues (2011) also addressed the apparent lack of *direct* interaction between offenders and victims during cyberstalking. The authors reasoned that most of the time these interactions would be lagged in time to some degree. In the US Airways example, this time lag between when the offender sent the e-mail and when the target received it could have been very short (e.g., the target opened the e-mail a few minutes after it was sent), very long (e.g., the target opened the e-mail days or weeks after it was sent), or some time in between. Despite the time lag, Reyns and colleagues explained that eventually there *is* a temporal overlap between the offender's act and the victim's receipt of that act. In other words, although victims and offenders may never interact in real time, the offender's actions eventually reach the victim, at which point there is an overlap in time. Figure 3-5 depicts this indirect and asynchronous interaction of victims and offenders within a network. In the figure, the eventual asynchronous time overlap between the two parties (i.e., time 1, time 2) and their convergence within a network represent the circumstances under which opportunities for cybercrime victimization are created.

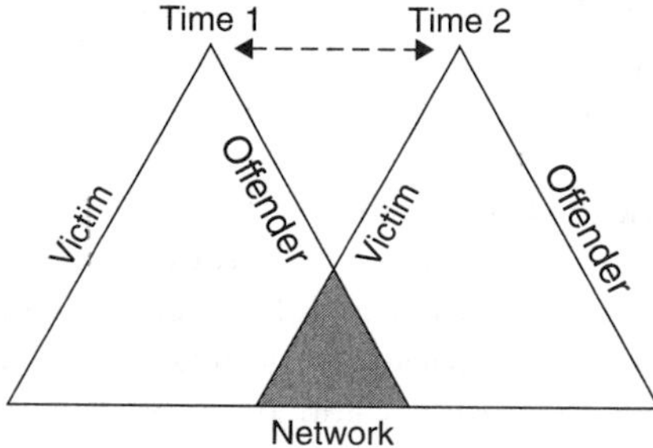

Figure 3-5 Indirect and Asynchronous Intersection of Cybercrime Offenders and Victims
Source: Reyns (2012).

With these theoretical adaptations to lifestyle–routine activities theory in mind, Reyns and colleagues (2011) examined the effects of online-specific exposure, proximity, target attractiveness, and guardianship on cyberstalking victimization using various measures of these four concepts. Their research revealed that each of these theoretical concepts set cyberstalking victims apart from nonvictims. In other words, exposure, proximity, target attractiveness, and guardianship significantly influenced the likelihood of cyberstalking victimization, but the effect differed depending on the cyberstalking behavior under consideration. For instance, the number of social network accounts (e.g., Facebook) belonging to participants—a measure of exposure—significantly increased the odds of receiving repeated and unwanted sexual advances online (a form of cyberstalking). Similarly, adding strangers as friends to social network accounts (a measure of proximity to prospective offenders), thereby granting them access to user profile information, increased the likelihood of receiving unwanted contacts, harassment, sexual advances, and overall cyberstalking victimizations.

Additional research, while not specifically framed in the language of cyberlifestyle–routine activities theory, has also explored the usefulness of opportunity theory as an explanation of cybervictimization. For example, Adam Bossler, Thomas Holt, and David May (2012) used the routine activities perspective to examine online harassment victimization among adolescent Internet users. In their study, they used "having an online social network" as a measure for motivated offenders, along with "having peers who harass others online" as their measure of proximity to motivated offenders. They also used "having software on my computer that restricted access to certain websites" as a measure of guardianship and "involvement with risky information sharing" as a measure of lack of personal guardianship. Their results showed all of these factors predicted online harassment victimization.

For the most part, these effects suggest that routine activities theory is useful in explaining online harassment victimization, although the effects of guardianship were opposite what the theory would predict. Also, none of the authors' measures of target attractiveness were related to victimization. Other research studies using lifestyle–routine activities theory to explain online forms of victimization also have reported that the theory is useful in identifying behaviors that place individuals at risk for victimization (Marcum, Higgins, & Ricketts, 2010; Pratt, Holtfreter, & Reisig, 2010; Van Wilsem, 2011). For example, Pratt and colleagues (2010) reported that among residents of Florida, making Internet website purchases significantly increased the likelihood that these individuals would be targets of fraud.

Technological innovations, particularly the Internet, have permeated nearly every aspect of social life. Given the lifestyle–routine activities theory's emphasis on behaviors that facilitate opportunities for victimization, it is not surprising that Internet-based routine activities also contribute to criminal opportunities. Cyberlifestyle–routine activities theory and an increasing number of research studies have concentrated on bridging the gap between a theory that was originally developed to explain direct-contact offenses and the changing nature of opportunities created through individuals' online routines and Internet use. So far, the results of this research are encouraging, but as always, more research is needed to test cyberlifestyle–routine activities theory's usefulness to predicting different types of online and long-distance victimization.

Criminological Theories of Victimization

Early victimologists suggested that victims play a pivotal role in criminal events, and that to understand offending, it is also necessary to understand victimization (e.g., Wolfgang, 1957; see also Lauritsen & Laub, 2007). Some of this early research also revealed that criminal behavior is a strong predictor of victimization—that is, those who offend often become victims too. Researchers have also reported that those who are victimized later commit crimes. This link between victimization and offending is known as the ***victim–offender overlap.*** The victim–offender overlap implies that victims and offenders often behave similarly, such as in their daily routines or lifestyles, and possess similar characteristics, including age and gender. Both victimologists and criminologists have recently "rediscovered" the victim–offender overlap and begun to consider explanations of victimization beyond the victimization opportunity approaches. In view of the commonalities that appear to exist between victims and offenders, contemporary victimologists are exploring the possibility that there may be an underlying "cause" of both offending *and* victimization. In turn, this research has begun investigating the utility of criminological theories in explaining criminal victimization. In particular, Gottfredson and Hirschi's (1990) general theory of crime has been a key focus. Other theories, such as Tittle's (1995) control balance theory, as well as environmental criminology, and even life course–based explanations, have also been the focus of recent research. The remainder of this chapter reviews criminological theories and perspectives that researchers have begun to use as explanations for victimization.

A General Theory of Crime

In 1990, criminologists Michael Gottfredson and Travis Hirschi published their book, *A General Theory of Crime*. Gottfredson and Hirschi presented a general theory meant to explain criminal and other analogous behaviors such as delinquency and deviance. According to ***a general theory of crime***, the reason some people offend while others do not is that offenders have a propensity or tendency to take advantage of opportunities for criminal behavior. This propensity is established early in life through a lack of direct control by parents and caregivers and remains fairly stable thereafter throughout the life course. The propensity to offend is best thought of as a person's level of ***self-control***, which theoretically consists of six dimensions (Grasmick et al., 1993):

1. *Impulsivity*: Individuals with low self-control are said to be impulsive. They often react immediately to situational inducements and do not delay gratification as someone with high self-control would.
2. *Simple tasks*: Those with low self-control are said to lack persistence or diligence, which means that these people prefer simple to complex tasks because they provide quick and easy opportunities for gratification.
3. *Risk seeking*: Low self-control is also related to risk-seeking behaviors and the pursuit of excitement, adventure, and thrills.
4. *Physical activity*: Those with low self-control prefer physical rather than mental activities. These people may be less likely to act rationally or think their way through situations, instead preferring more immediate physical solutions in certain situations.
5. *Self-centered*: People who have low self-control are said to be self-centered in that they do not consider how their behavior may affect others.
6. *Temper*: Low self-control is associated with impatience or a low tolerance for frustration. People with quick tempers may respond to frustrating problems with aggression or through other physical means rather than thinking through the problem and its consequences.

Describing why individuals with low self-control would be more likely than those with high self-control to engage in criminal behaviors is fairly straightforward: An impulsive, risk-seeking, self-centered person who is quick to anger, prefers to take the easy route, and uses his or her physical abilities to get what he or she wants is probably going to take advantage of criminal opportunities when presented. Those with greater self-control will think twice about taking such risks, consider the possible consequences of their actions for themselves and others, and most likely refrain from offending (see Hirschi, 1969). Since the victim–offender overlap suggests that victims and offenders possess many of the same characteristics, low self-control should be able to explain not only why individuals *offend*, but why they are *victimized*.

Christopher Schreck (1999) was among the first criminologists to recognize that Gottfredson and Hirschi's theory also could be used to explain victimization, not just offending. In his pioneering study, Schreck reformulated Gottfredson and Hirschi's general theory of crime and explained that people with low self-control are especially vulnerable to victimization. Whereas Gottfredson and Hirschi labeled the first dimension of low self-control as *impulsivity*, Schreck referred to it as *future orientation*, and explained that people with low self-control live in the "here and now" and as a result do not consider how their behavior might put them or their property at risk for victimization. Having low self-control, therefore, increases the tendency for individuals to be in situations that enhance their vulnerability to victimization.

The second dimension of low self-control is *simple tasks*, which Schreck discussed as a lack of *diligence* or persistence on the part of victims. Schreck argued that those who are not diligent will not consistently use security measures or ensure adequate guardianship of themselves or their property, even when such measures are readily available. According to the opportunity perspective, reduced, ineffective, or absent guardianship creates criminal opportunities, so individuals with low self-control may inadvertently increase their likelihood of being targeted by offenders through a lack of diligence. The third component of low self-control, *risk seeking*, also creates vulnerability in victims. Activities such as driving around late looking for excitement, bar hopping, or going home with a stranger after meeting him or her at a social gathering, club, or bar place individuals in positions where they have an increased likelihood of being victimized. Those who prefer *physical activities*, the fourth component of low self-control, are theoretically less able to assess the risk in situations and respond in a nonphysical manner. For someone with low self-control, perhaps being insulted by someone in a bar evokes a physical response such as starting a fight, whereas someone with high self-control who prefers mental solutions to situations would determine the risk of getting into a fight to be too great and shrug off the insult without incident.

Gottfredson and Hirschi asserted that those with low self-control are *self-centered*. Schreck, however, explained that the fifth aspect of self-control also could be thought of as a person's level of *empathy*. This means that people low in self-control are insensitive and do not empathize very well with others. A lack of empathy can increase one's likelihood of being victimized in several ways. For example, a person who is insensitive may not be able to assess the intentions of others, which in conjunction with other aspects of low self-control may lead to misunderstandings and altercations, resulting in being victimized. Schreck also noted that those who lack empathy have fewer close relationships with others, which theoretically reduces guardianship against victimization.

The final element of low self-control is temper, or what Schreck described as *low tolerance for frustration*. Those who are easy to anger, hostile, or argumentative are more likely to be antagonistic toward others and create situations that ultimately result in victimization. As Schreck (1999, p. 636) noted, "the difference between offending and being victimized depends on who wins the fight." The "Spotlight on Theory: Low Self-Control as an Explanation of Offending and Victimization" box highlights the theoretical arguments for using low self-control to explain offending and victimization.

Spotlight on Theory: Low Self-Control as an Explanation of Offending and Victimization

Offending	Victimization
Impulsivity: Impulsive people are more likely to seek out and exploit criminal opportunities.	*Future orientation*: Living in the moment and not considering the consequences of one's actions places individuals in risky or vulnerable situations.
Simple tasks: Simple tasks provide quick gratification while more complex tasks require delayed gratification. Many crimes are relatively simple.	*Diligence*: Those who are inconsistent in their use of security and protective measures present attractive targets for offenders.
Risk seeking: Crime, delinquency, and deviance can be exciting, so risk seekers may engage in these behaviors for the thrills.	*Risk seeking*: The pursuit of excitement can unintentionally put individuals into dangerous situations in which they are victimized.
Physical activity: Many problems can be solved by thinking them through, and physical responses often result in criminal behaviors.	*Physical activity*: Solutions are overlooked when the initial reaction to a problem is physical, and physical responses can lead to altercations and victimization.
Self-centered: Disregarding how others are affected by behavior eliminates controls on criminal activities, such as conscience and guilt.	*Empathy*: Indifference to others leads to fewer social relationships and a decreased ability to evaluate their intentions. The result is reduced guardianship and avoidance of dangerous situations.
Temper: Frustration and anger escalate situations and lead to law-breaking behaviors.	*Tolerance for frustration*: Confrontational or belligerent individuals are more likely to create or find themselves in high-risk situations.

Source: Schreck (1999).

Besides describing how low self-control could be extended to account for victimization, Schreck examined the violent and property victimization of undergraduate students at the University of Arizona. In his test of the theory, Schreck reported that both low self-control and having engaged in criminal behaviors predicted violent and property victimizations. These findings reiterate the importance of the victim–offender overlap. This study was the first to establish the utility of the general theory of crime in predicting victimization.

Research based on Schreck's interpretation of the general theory has continued to investigate the connection between low self-control and victimization. For example, Alex Piquero and colleagues (2005) used self-control to explain violent offending and homicide victimization among a sample of parolees from the California Youth Authority. The results indicated that those with low self-control were more likely not only to be violent offenders, but also to become homicide victims. A study by Schreck, Wright, and Miller (2002) integrated the general theory of crime with the lifestyle–routine activities perspective. The authors argued that opportunity factors, such as routine activities, are important precursors to victimization, but low self-control influences the kinds of routines in which individuals engage. As Figure 3-6 illustrates, Schreck and colleagues suggested that self-control affects associations with delinquent peers, as well as the quality of bonds to family and school. These routines, in turn, predict both the likelihood of violent victimization and the likelihood of participation in risky lifestyles, which also increases violent victimization risks. Their results suggested that individuals with low self-control are more likely to become victims of violence. At the same time, routine activities were also related to victimization, regardless of whether the victim had high or low self-control. These findings imply that self-control and opportunity influence victimization risk, and that a comprehensive explanation of victimization requires both theoretical perspectives.

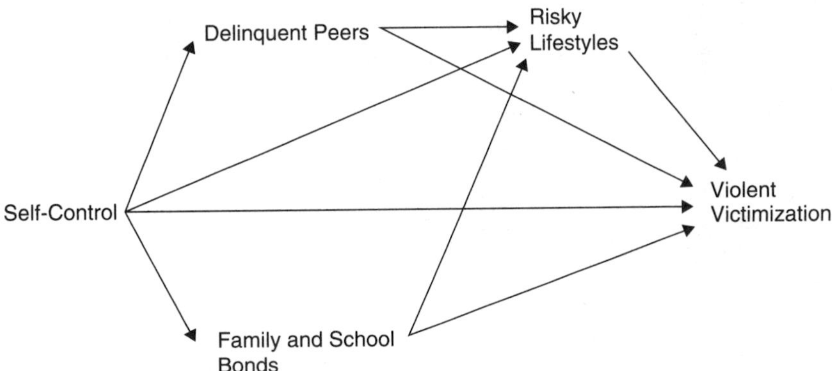

Figure 3-6 The Effects of Self-Control on Lifestyles, Routine Activities, and Victimization
Source: Schreck et al. (2002).

Gottfredson and Hirschi's a general theory of crime and its central concept—self-control—have emerged as prominent explanations of both offending and victimization. The theory is so popular that it has been described as "The *Tyrannosaurus rex* of criminology" (DeLisi, 2011, p. 103). Recognizing its usefulness and acknowledging the overlap between victims and offenders, the victimization research, notably Schreck's studies, supports this statement. And, when coupled with the concept of opportunity, low self-control appears to be a strong predictor of several different types of victimization. However, the potential flaw in using self-control as an explanation of victimization vis-à-vis the victim–offender overlap is that many victims are not offenders. Yet, the finding that low self-control brings with it an added vulnerability to victimization continues to drive much victimization research. The next section describes how another criminology theory—control balance theory—can be used to explain not just offending but also victimization.

Control Balance Theory

Charles Tittle's (1995) ***control balance theory*** integrates key principles from several criminological theories, including Sutherland's (1947) differential association, Hirschi's (1969) control theory, Cohen and Felson's (1979) routine activities theory, and labeling theory (e.g., Becker, 1963; Lemert, 1951) to explain deviant behavior. By *deviance*, Tittle is referring to any behavior that the majority views unfavorably and that invokes a negative reaction from the group in the form of social control. Although many criminal acts also are considered deviant (e.g., gambling), not all deviance is necessarily criminal (e.g., passing gas in public; Tittle, 1995). The label applied depends on the context and how those with the power to label the behavior feel about it. Of course, there are also behaviors that are considered to be both deviant and criminal, such as rape and murder. To the extent certain deviant behaviors also are criminal, Tittle's theory should apply.

As the name suggests, *control* is one of two key elements to control balance theory. Like other popular criminological theories based on the notion of control (including the previously discussed a general theory of crime), control balance theory views deviant acts as a consequence of weak or absent constraints on behavior (see also Hirschi, 1969). In other words, people behave in these ways because there is no one to stop them from doing so. Similar to the concept of power, Tittle (2004, p. 397) explained that "Control means the ability of an individual or other kind of social entity to manipulate or block social or other actions and circumstances." The *balance* in control balance theory refers to one's control ratio. The ***control ratio*** is the amount of control an individual can *employ* relative to the amount of control he or she *experiences*. When an individual's control ratio is in balance, he or she is not likely to engage in deviant behaviors. When the ratio is unbalanced in either direction, then a person will be more likely to participate in deviant acts. Depending on the degree and direction of the imbalance, Tittle (1995) discussed different types of deviance that would be likely, including submission, defiance, predation, conformity, exploitation, plunder, and decadence.

Figure 3-7 depicts the concept of the control ratio and indicates the expected effect of control balance and imbalance. Those who have a ***control deficit*** are *being* controlled (more than they are controlling others), and the greater the deficit, the higher the probability of deviance. Those who have a ***control surplus*** are *exerting* control (more than they are being controlled by others), and the greater the surplus, the more likely it is the person will engage in deviance. Control deficits and control surpluses explain different types of deviance, with deficits leading to repressive forms of deviance (i.e., submission, defiance, predation) and surpluses resulting in autonomous forms of deviance (i.e., decadence, plunder, exploitation).

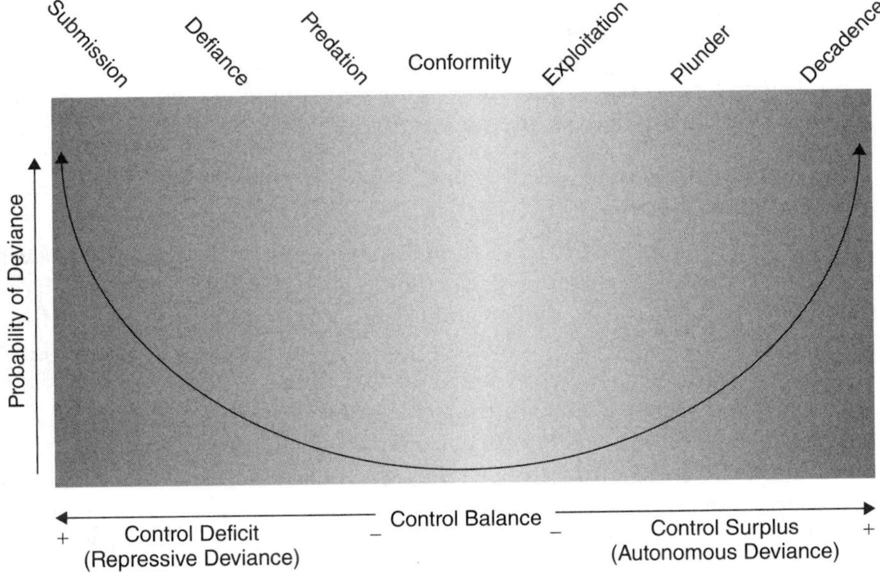

Figure 3-7 The Control Ratio and its Effects
Source: Nobles and Fox (2013).

Control balance theory is complex. Further review of its application in explaining deviance is not necessary to illustrate how it can be adapted to explain victimization. Alex Piquero and Matthew Hickman (2003) were the first scholars to adapt and extend control balance theory as a theory of victimization. They explained that individuals with control imbalances should theoretically be at greatest risk for victimization, and those with a balanced control ratio should be at the lowest risk. First, consider the extreme left side of Figure 3-7: individuals with control deficits. Since those on the control deficit side of the spectrum are in weaker positions as a result of their control shortfall, they are theoretically more likely to become passive, removed, or submissive and therefore lack the convictions to effectively defend themselves and resist victimization. In Piquero and Hickman's (2003, p. 285) words: "The key point is that those individuals with control deficits have a less-than-normal capacity to overcome individuals with control surpluses and as such are less likely to engage in protective behaviors." Further, given their relatively weak positions, those with control deficits appear to be vulnerable and consequently make attractive targets for offenders. Overall, as control deficits become more pronounced (moving away from balance), vulnerability to victimization becomes greater and the probability of victimization increases.

Now, consider those on the farthest right side of Figure 3-7: those with control surpluses. According to Piquero and Hickman, control surpluses also are linked with victimization, but for different reasons than control deficits. Whereas those with control deficits are downtrodden and less likely to resist victimization, people with control surpluses are brazen and self-assured; they know that they have a superior position, especially compared to those with control deficits, and they act the part.

A fictitious example from a workplace illustrates this point since there are inherent control imbalances in workplaces: Supervisors often have control surpluses and subordinates have control deficits. Imagine a scenario in which a supervisor continuously pushes employees hard, makes unfair decisions, and provides few rewards for those he supervises. An employee arrives at work two minutes late. This upsets the supervisor, who calls the employee into his office. In an effort to extend even more control over this employee, the supervisor demands the employee perform extra work off the clock (this demand may be considered a form of deviance according to Tittle's theory) and threatens to fire him if he does not agree. Having a control deficit in this situation, the employee can either apologize profusely and agree to complete the extra work (again, possibly a form of deviance) or, feeling pushed to his breaking point, he can lash out and physically assault his boss (a much stronger form of deviance!). Let's assume he chooses to assault his boss. Control balance theory would predict that the supervisor's attempt to build on his control surplus by further exploiting an employee backfired, and in an effort to overcome his control deficit, the employee assaulted his boss (this scenario should sound somewhat familiar to those of you who have seen the movie *Horrible Bosses*).

Piquero and Hickman tested their ideas about the applicability of control balance theory to victimization on a sample of college students. Interestingly, they reported that those with control surpluses and those with control deficits had significantly higher risks of experiencing victimization than did those with balanced control ratios. In other words, their findings suggest that the control ratio is a risk factor for victimization. Unfortunately, given the relative newness of control balance theory, and the even more recent extension of the theory to explain victimization, there are few victimization studies that have tested Piquero and Hickman's reformulation of the theory. Only further tests applied to victimization will assess the usefulness of their idea.

Environmental Criminology

Environmental criminology is a perspective that draws from rational choice theory, crime pattern theory, and routine activities theory to explain criminal events and the circumstances under which they occur, including criminal victimization. Although these theories are not necessarily new, ideas from environmental criminology have informed the development of the opportunity perspective. Environmental criminology also represents another source of traditional criminological theory that aids contemporary victimologists in understanding victimization. According to Richard Wortley and Lorraine Mazerolle (2008, p. 1), "Environmental criminologists look for crime patterns and seek to explain them in terms of environmental influences." This perspective is important for victimologists because identifying environmental factors that influence criminal victimization can be helpful in devising strategies for preventing victimization from occurring, a topic that is discussed in Chapter 14.

Additional theories of crime prevention from environmental criminology, such as crime prevention through environmental design (CPTED), defensible space, and situational crime prevention, also are discussed in Chapter 14.

Spotlight on Policy: CPTED and Reducing Robberies at Automatic Teller Machines

Photo Credit: © Bryan Mullennix/Alamy

A common problem in many areas is robberies occurring at or near automatic teller machines (ATMs). These machines are sometimes located in poorly lighted areas, do not have much surveillance around them which enhances the risk for victimization. Police departments, bank and credit union branches, and neighborhood groups have begun tackling this problem using various strategies, some of which involve CPTED.

ATMs were introduced in the mid-1960s in the United Kingdom and later in the United States. The number of ATMs has increased dramatically since then, to the point where their presence is almost ubiquitous. Billions of financial transactions now occur with these machines, most of which are cash withdrawals. With the spread of these machines, people have, to a degree, traded safety for convenience. ATM services are highly profitable for banks, which aggressively market use of ATM cards. Further, machines off bank premises are usually more profitable because they attract a higher volume of non-bank customers who must pay service fees. Unfortunately, customers using off-premise ATMs are those most vulnerable to robbery.

Contributing to Robbery at ATMs

Understanding the factors contributing to ATM robberies would help identify and select appropriate responses. A few studies, although they are becoming dated, have provided data on common ATM robbery patterns. Their general conclusions are as follows:

- Drive-up machines are more secure.
- Most robberies are committed by a lone offender—using some type of weapon—against a lone victim.
- Most occur at night, with the highest risk between midnight and 4 a.m.
- Most involve robbing people of cash after they have made a withdrawal.

- Robberies are somewhat more likely to occur at walk-up ATMs than at drive-through ATMs.
- About 15% of victims are injured.
- The average loss is between $100 and $200.

Responses to the Problem: Altering Lighting, Landscaping, and Location

The following response strategies are drawn from a variety of research studies and police reports. Several may apply to addressing ATM robberies at a particular location. In most cases, an effective strategy will involve implementing several different responses. Law enforcement responses alone are seldom effective in reducing or solving the problem.

ATM operators should consider security as well as marketing in deciding where to install ATMs. The most commonly mentioned ATM robbery prevention measures in the literature are those that will be familiar to CPTED practitioners—*lighting, landscaping, and location.* ATM sites should be inspected regularly to ensure that safety features have not become compromised. ATM operators, police, and bank regulators all should share responsibility for monitoring compliance.

Photo Credit: Sunpix Travel/Alamy

Adequate lighting. Adequate lighting at and around ATMs allows users to see suspicious people near the ATM and allows potential witnesses, including police, to see a crime in progress and get a good look at the offender. Good lighting can deter people from robbing ATM users in the first place. There should be adequate light around all building corners adjacent to the ATM, as well as for nearby parking places. Most ATM lighting standards, including some mandated by law, call for minimum light levels at and around ATMs.

Ensuring the landscaping around ATMs allows for good visibility. Trees and shrubbery should be trimmed routinely to remove potential hiding places for offenders and to ensure the ATM is visible to passersby. Slow-growing shrubbery that does not need trimming as often is preferable. Obstacles such as dumpsters, benches, or walls that obstruct clear views of the ATM should be removed.

Installing mirrors on ATMs. Rearview mirrors on ATMs and adjacent building corners allow ATM users to detect suspicious people and behavior.

Installing ATMs where there is a lot of natural surveillance. ATMs should be placed in areas where there is a lot of routine vehicle and pedestrian traffic. The potential for witnesses deters offenders, and heavy traffic increases the probability of victim assistance when a robbery occurs. ATMs are increasingly being placed inside businesses such as grocery and convenience stores, where there is a lot of natural surveillance; this should help prevent ATM robberies. Some security experts recommend that ATMs have high visibility and activity on all three adjacent sides—ideally, with high-speed traffic on one side, slow-speed traffic on another, and relatively permanent observers (e.g., residents) on the third. Indoor ATMs should be free of sight obstructions like plants and blinds and should be visible from the street through transparent windows and doors. Tinted glass should not be used.

Installing ATMs in police stations. Some jurisdictions have installed publicly accessible ATMs in police stations to attract ATM users to a safe place to conduct their business. While the idea has merit, many police stations might not be able to accommodate the added vehicle and pedestrian traffic generated by an ATM. Where this is a problem, ATM

(Continued)

Spotlight on Policy: CPTED and Reducing Robberies at Automatic Teller Machines – *Continued*

Photo Credit: david pearson/Alamy

use might be limited to nighttime hours, when the risk of robbery is greatest and when the police business being conducted at the station is at a minimum. ATMs might also be installed in or near other government buildings such as post offices or fire stations, where there is at least some natural surveillance.

Source: Adapted from Scott, M. (2001). *Robbery at automated teller machines*. Guide No. 8. Center for Problem Oriented Policing. http://www.popcenter.org/problems/robbery_atms/

Rational choice theory is not a theory of victimization. Instead, rational choice theory provides insights into offender decision making that also are helpful in explaining how and why victimization occurs. The assumption of a rational offender is shared with other theories in environmental criminology, notably crime pattern theory and routine activities theory. The contemporary version of ***rational choice theory*** as it applies to criminal behavior was introduced by Ronald Clarke and Derek Cornish in 1985. They explained that decisions to offend are based on environmental factors, such as whether there are potential witnesses around or the difficulty in accessing a target. Further, according to the rational choice theory, offenders are, like everyone else, rational actors whose decisions are preceded by a calculation of the costs (e.g., possibly getting caught and punished) and benefits (e.g., money, revenge, thrills) associated with criminal activity. In other words, offenders take into account characteristics of the situation, what the payoff might be, and how likely it is that they will be seen or apprehended. These calculations are made at many points in the crime process, including the initial decision to commit the crime, decisions to continue offending behaviors (e.g., continue to burglarize homes), and decisions to desist or abstain from future criminal behaviors. However, Clarke and Cornish also pointed out that in trying to meet their needs and fulfill goals, offenders make choices based on the information they have, which does not always produce the best possible decision (Cornish & Clarke, 2008). This latter idea is known as ***bounded rationality***, in which individuals make decisions based on limited information, possible impairments to their thinking (e.g., alcohol), and time constraints.

From a victimization standpoint, knowing that offenders consider environmental factors and make their decisions based on a rational cost/benefit calculus helps to explain why crime and victimization are patterned in certain ways (e.g., within neighborhoods, on certain streets). ***Crime pattern theory*** accounts for geographic crime patterns by proposing that there are aspects about certain parts of neighborhoods or cities that attract potential offenders. Patricia and Paul Brantingham (1993) have done considerable research into crime patterns. They have explained that, like victims, offenders have routine daily activities that structure their "search for crime." Given that offenders search for suitable crime targets along their routes of daily activity, crime pattern theory hypothesizes that victimization should be most concentrated in areas adjacent to offender activity spaces.

According to Brantingham and Brantingham, features of the environment called nodes, paths, and edges account for spatial patterns of crime and victimization (e.g., in cities, neighborhoods, campuses). ***Nodes*** are places of primary activities for offenders, such as their homes, workplaces, schools, and shopping or entertainment areas. Since nodes essentially anchor daily routines, crime pattern theory suggests that crime and victimization should concentrate spatially around offenders' nodes of activity. There should be more crime in areas where offenders live, work, shop, and so on. There will also be a supply of targets or victims at most of these locations, such as coworkers, fellow students, or shoppers. ***Paths*** are the routes that connect nodes and that also provide opportunities and awareness of potential targets for offenders. Streets, sidewalks, alleys, and the like that connect offenders' nodes tend to have more crimes than routes that are less frequently used and less familiar to offenders. ***Edges*** are the spaces that form boundaries around nodes and paths and also serve as transitions from one space to another. For example, a residential neighborhood (a node) may have been developed close to a highway (a path), but on the other side of the highway, the space is primarily industrial. Therefore, offenders' awareness of the industrial area probably does not extend much past the edge space of the highway.

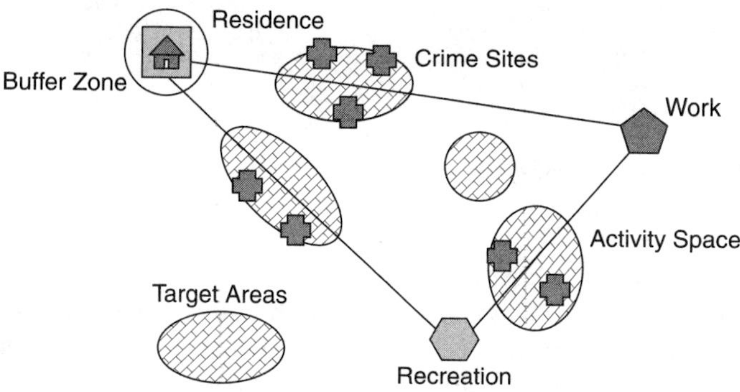

Figure 3-8 Crime Pattern Theory
Source: Rossmo (2000).

Figure 3-8 presents a diagram by Kim Rossmo (2000) depicting crime pattern theory. The figure shows a particular offender's activity space (his residence, work, recreation, and travel routes), the buffer zone that is close to his home (where the offender does not usually commit crimes), and five potential target areas (e.g., parking lots). Crimes happen where the offender's activity space intersects a target area. Note that in this example no crimes occur around the offender's workplace, because there are no suitable targets there. Also, there are two target areas with no crimes in them because the offender is not aware of those places. Considering the position that offenders rationally weigh the costs and benefits of criminal behavior before acting, it makes sense that offenders would choose targets within their "awareness spaces" rather than those that are unfamiliar and probably riskier in terms of being caught.

Brantingham and Brantingham (1995) also explained that these environmental features can themselves either attract or generate crime and victimization. ***Crime attractors*** are places to which offenders are drawn because of the criminal opportunities they offer. For instance, busy subway stations attract panhandlers, pickpockets, and thieves because large supplies of suitable targets congregate regularly and opportunities for crime are plentiful. ***Crime generators*** are locations in which crime transpires because opportunities are presented, and not necessarily because offenders are drawn to those opportunities. For example, spectator violence during or after sporting events occurs because the interaction of offenders, targets, and guardianship lack thereof is suitable to crime and victimization—in most cases, people do not attend sporting events just so they can fight afterwards. Overall, then, risks of victimization are higher in places that become crime attractors or crime generators.

Low-cost motel: The risk of crime varies a great deal among facilities of the same type.
Photo Credit: John Eck.

As previously explained, routine activities theory has mostly been used as a theory of individual victimization, even though it was originally developed as a theory to explain rising crime rates over time. This theory has also been used to explain how risks for victimization vary across geographic areas. Coupled with crime pattern theory, routine activities theory also illustrates how hot spots of crime form, and the types of locations in which victimization repeatedly occurs.

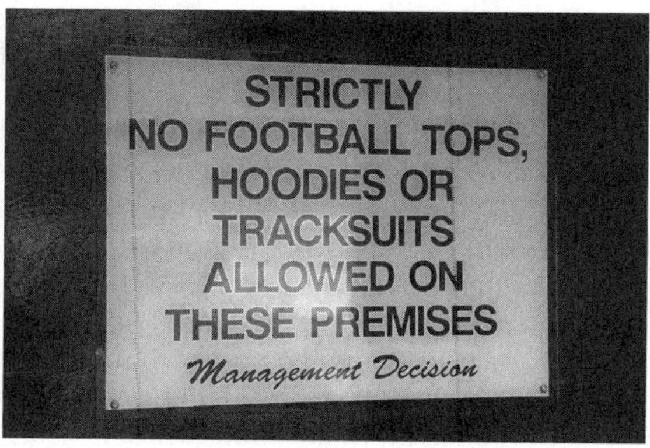

A sign outside a bar—How managers regulate patron conduct can have a big influence on crime risk.
Photo Credit: John Eck.

Geographic ***hot spots*** are physical locations or places where crime and victimization concentrate. Most readers will be able to identify the "bad neighborhoods" in their hometown, or the areas of their city that they avoid if possible because of high crime. Many times, these areas will be hot spots for crime, because as routine activities theory suggests, they facilitate the convergence in space and time of motivated offenders, suitable targets, and ineffective or absent guardianship.

A seminal study by Lawrence Sherman, Patrick Gartin, and Michael Buerger (1989) used routine activity theory to examine hot spots in Minneapolis, Minnesota, from 1985 to 1986. Using police calls for service data, they found that about 3% of addresses and intersections in the city accounted for over 50% of all police calls. A number of subsequent studies have replicated their findings. For example, David Weisburd and colleagues (2004) focused on street segments in Seattle, Washington, over a 14-year period (1989–2002) and found that over time about 5% of the street segments contained nearly 50% of the total crime reported to police. There were also fluctuations in hot spots over time, with a small portion of places experiencing either rising or declining crime rates. The finding that a small portion of the addresses required so much police attention suggests that these places have crime-inducing qualities that increase victimization risks for targets at and around these hot spots. According to routine activity theory, this is because these places have characteristics that converge to create opportunities for victimization.

Research examining the land use patterns of areas has revealed that the routine activities of places are also a good indicator of area crime and victimization. Put differently, the way land is used draws people into areas for different reasons and alters the convergence of offenders, targets, and guardianship. A study by Dennis Roncek and Antoinette Lobosco (1983) explored the effects of a particular kind of land use—having high schools in a neighborhood—on neighborhood burglaries and auto thefts in San Diego, California. After taking into account the effects of other possible explanations for crime (e.g., density of the neighborhood, demographics of residents), the results showed that residential city blocks next to public high schools had more crime, but private high schools did not increase area crime. Roncek and Pamela Maier (1991) also examined the routine activities of places through land usage. In this study, the authors studied the effects of taverns and lounges on residential city blocks in Cleveland, Ohio. They reported that every type of index crime (e.g., murder, rape, robbery) was higher on blocks with taverns or lounges than those without. The results of these two studies suggest that the way land is used influences the routine activities of the area. Nonresidential land use can affect crime by (1) drawing offenders into an area, (2) expanding their awareness spaces, (3) bringing potential targets into proximity to offenders, or (4) exposing targets to risk. In essence, land use can determine where hot spots form.

Table 3-1 summarizes the main points of the three previously discussed theories of environmental criminology: rational choice theory, crime pattern theory, and routine activity theory. These theories highlight the importance of the environment in which crimes take place in understanding victimization trends. The environmental context of crime is important because it influences offender decision making, the ways in which crime is patterned, and the routine activities of places through land use. The next section discusses the recent trend in victimology in which the principles of life course criminology are used to understand victimization.

Life Course Criminology

The life course perspective was discussed previously in the context of age-graded routine activities theory, but by way of review, ***life course criminology*** focuses on the nature of offending over time and reasons for beginning, continuing, and ending offending behaviors. There are two opposing viewpoints in life course criminology: (1) the criminal propensity position, which argues that propensities or tendencies to offend are stable over the life course (i.e., low self-control) and (2) the criminal careers position, which says that different factors influence offending at different stages of life. Aside from a general theory of crime, which was reviewed earlier in this chapter, most of the research surrounding life course explanations of victimization

Table 3-1: Summary of Environmental Criminology Theories

Theory	Summary
1. Rational Choice Theory	Decisions to offend are based on a rational calculation of the costs and benefits. Environmental factors, especially those affecting whether a crime seems "worth it," factor into this decision.
2. Crime Pattern Theory	Crime and victimization are patterned in nonrandom ways. These concentrations of crime are explained by offenders' search patterns along their nodes, paths, and edges, and by crime attractors and crime generators.
3. Routine Activity Theory	Like people, places have routine activities. Land use can affect opportunities for victimization in an environment by altering the supply of motivated offenders and suitable targets, and levels of guardianship.

has concentrated on the latter position, namely that factors influencing victimization differ across developmental stages. Life course researchers also have begun to study how genes and gene–environment interactions might influence a person's likelihood of victimization. In the sections that follow, the importance of social bonds, family, peers, and genes are discussed as influences on victimization.

Working from a criminal careers perspective, Robert Sampson and John Laub (1993) developed their ***age-graded theory of social control***, theorizing that reasons for delinquent and criminal behaviors vary across developmental life stages. In general, control theories hypothesize that criminal behavior occurs when individuals' social bonds are weak (Hirschi, 1969). For example, a juvenile who is strongly attached to his parents (a bond) is less likely to offend than someone with weak parental attachments. Sampson and Laub's theory identified social ties or bonds as among the important influences on participation in crime for adults, especially bonds of marriage and employment. Theoretically, those who have previously been involved in delinquency or crime will discontinue these behaviors when strong bonds of marriage and employment are established. Since offending threatens to jeopardize these ties, offenders cease their illegal activities. Table 3-2 summarizes the criminal propensity position as exemplified by a general theory of crime and the age-graded theory of social control as each applies to explaining the occurrence of victimization.

Considering the link between offending and victimization, research has recently begun to explore the possibility of applying Sampson and Laub's arguments about social bonds to explaining victimization. In theory, strong social bonds may act as protective forces against victimization in the same way they do against criminal behavior. For example, juveniles with strong parental bonds spend more time with family participating in safe activities (i.e., at home or with family), thereby reducing their exposure to risk. At the same time, weak bonds or bonds to deviant peers increase victimization risk through exposure to dangerous situations and motivated offenders. Much of the research estimating the effects of social bonds on victimization has been based on information collected from the National Longitudinal Study of

Table 3-2: Summary of Life Course Theories

Theory	Summary
1. A General Theory of Crime	Behaviors such as deviance, delinquency, and crime can be explained by an individual's level of self-control. Self-control is a propensity, or a static trait that does not change over the life course once it has been established in early life. This underlying trait also is an important predictor of criminal victimization across stages of the life course.
2. Age-Graded Theory of Social Control	The influences on crime and analogous behaviors are dynamic and change throughout one's life. In particular, life events such as marriage and employment counteract impulses to engage in crime. The strength of one's bonds (e.g., to family, to one's beliefs) explain whether one will conform to social norms or engage in crime and delinquency. Likewise, social bonds also explain criminal victimization, with individuals lacking strong bonds being more susceptible to victimization.

Adolescent Health (Add Health). This study began to collect information from a sample of seventh- through 12th-graders in the United States during the 1994–1995 school year, and researchers have been interviewing this group of participants over time ever since. Study participants provide information on a variety of topics, including their physical and psychological well-being, social environment, relationships, and much more.

One study to use the Add Health data to examine how social bonds affect personal victimization (e.g., being stabbed, threatened) was conducted by Leah Daigle, Kevin Beaver, and Jennifer Hartman (2008). This study was based on Sampson and Laub's theory and focused on the bonds of marriage and employment as possible influences on desistence from victimization (when people stop being victimized). Daigle and colleagues reported that those who were employed were more likely to continue being victimized than those who were unemployed. However, those who were married were more likely to stop being victimized than those who were not married. Interestingly, they also found that changes in their level of delinquent involvement did not influence the likelihood of victimization.

Although not explicitly testing Sampson and Laub's theory, other victimization studies have examined the effects of family and peers on the probability of victimization. For instance, a study by Christopher Schreck and Bonnie Fisher (2004) indicated that having delinquent peers and uncaring parents increased violent victimization risk, while living in a positive or nurturing family climate decreased victimization risks. A study by Xiaojin Chen (2009) also used data collected from the Add Health survey and reported that school bonds (e.g., whether students are happy at school, whether they feel teachers treat students fairly) protected students from different types of personal victimization, such as being threatened, being shot or stabbed, and being "jumped." Overall, research indicates that social bonds, especially those related to family and peers, influence the risk of personal victimization.

One limitation of this body of research is that most of the studies that have been conducted have been based on data from the Add Health survey. Therefore, one shortcoming of this research is that it has thus far been limited to adolescents. Future research examining stages in the life course beyond adolescence is needed to better understand and explain the relationships among family, peers, and victimization across the life course.

Life course researchers also have investigated possible genetic influences on experiencing victimization. This research extends findings in life course criminology that have centered on whether specific genes are related to antisocial behaviors, such as aggression and other maladaptive traits. The logic for applying these findings to victimization relies on the overlap between victims and offenders, hypothesizing that the same genetic polymorphisms, or gene variants, that affect offending also affect victimization. In essence, individuals with these genetic variants will behave in ways such that they provoke their victimization. For example, someone with a foul temper may react aggressively in a situation, thereby starting a fight. Research by Kevin Beaver and colleagues (2007) explored the possibility of gene–environment interactions as an explanation of victimization. Their results revealed that an interaction between DRD2 (a dopamine receptor gene that can affect violence and aggression) and having a low number of delinquent peers (an environmental factor) predicted victimization, but only among white males. Jamie Vaske, John Wright, and Kevin Beaver (2011) also analyzed the effects of a dopamine gene (DRD2) on victimization, and compared offenders who had been violently victimized with those who had not been victims of violence. This research reported that offenders who are violently victimized are more likely to possess this genetic characteristic than offenders who had not been violently victimized. Other research reinforces the connections between genetic factors and victimization risk (see Daigle, 2010). Life course research will likely continue to explore the effects of genes and gene–environment interactions as sources of victimization, but for now, this area of research is still in its infancy. Many unanswered questions underlying why and how genes influence victimization risk remain.

Summary

The fourth or contemporary generation of victimology theories and theorists continued to build on the foundation of opportunity theory as an explanation for criminal victimization. Extensions to the opportunity perspective based on gendered, feminist, age-graded, and long-distance modifications to lifestyle–routine activities theory expanded and refined the concept of opportunity. While these developments in refining opportunity theory are still relatively new and not thoroughly tested by examining different types of criminal victimization, the studies that have been published support the continued exploration and elaboration of opportunity as a predictor of victimization.

At the same time, important contributions have been made to explain victimization based on the victim–offender overlap. Because offenders are often victimized, a current trend in victimology has been to adapt and apply criminological theories to explain victimization. A general theory of crime, control balance theory, environmental criminology, and life course criminology each have provided varying degrees of support for factors that increase the risk of victimization. The theoretical sources of victimization reviewed in Chapters 2 and 3 offer a backdrop for thinking about different types of criminal victimization in the chapters that follow, and how and why they occur, and to whom. Throughout the remainder of the text, references to these theories appear as a means of discussing predictors of different types of victimization. Chapter 4 discusses the national sources of data used to estimate the amount of criminal victimization in the United States, including the Uniform Crime Reports, the National Crime Victimization Survey, and the National Incident-Based Reporting System, as well as critical issues in conceptualizing and measuring victimization.

KEYWORDS

Gender gap	Age-graded routine activities	A general theory of crime
Patriarchy	Cyberlifestyle–routine activities theory	Self-control
Feminist routine activities	Victim–offender overlap	Control balance theory

Control ratio	Bounded rationality	Crime attractors
Control deficit	Crime pattern theory	Crime generators
Control surplus	Nodes	Hot spots
Environmental criminology	Paths	Life course criminology
Rational choice theory	Edges	Age-graded theory of social control

DISCUSSION QUESTIONS

1. Are lifestyles and routine activities gendered? Provide examples of gender-specific behaviors that might influence victimization risks.
2. Do you think that feminist routine activities theory can explain other types of victimization that are primarily committed against females (e.g., stalking)?
3. Provide examples of age-graded lifestyle and routine activity behaviors. Discuss how and why these behaviors affect victimization risk for different age groups.
4. Could the opportunity perspective described in cyberlifestyle–routine activities theory apply to other forms of victimization besides cybercrimes? Provide examples and explain your answer.
5. Can criminological theories explain victimization of individuals who are not offenders?
6. Does applying self-control theory to explain victimization blame victims? If so, how so? If not, why not?
7. Is control balance theory more useful for understanding certain forms of victimization over others? Provide examples and explain your answer.
8. Think about your college campus and the environmental features that might influence offender decision making either positively or negatively. Explain why you chose the features you did and how these might influence offender decision making.
9. Do you think that your genes can influence your likelihood of becoming a victim of crime? Explain your thinking, especially about different types of crime.

REFERENCES

Beaver, K. M., Wright, J. P., DeLisi, M., Daigle, L. E., Swatt, M. L., & Gibson, C. L. (2007). Evidence of a gene × environment interaction in the creation of victimization: Results from a longitudinal sample of adolescents. *International Journal of Offender Therapy and Comparative Criminology, 51,* 620–645.

Becker, H. (1963). *Outsider: Studies in the sociology of deviance.* New York: The Free Press.

Bossler, A. M., Holt, T. J., & May, D. C. (2012). Predicting online harassment victimization among a juvenile population. *Youth & Society, 44,* 500–523.

Brantingham, P., & Brantingham, P. (1993). Nodes, paths, and edges: Considerations on the complexity of crime and the physical environment. *Journal of Environmental Psychology, 13,* 3–28.

Brantingham, P., & Brantingham, P. (1995). Criminality of place: Crime attractors and crime generators. *European Journal of Criminal Policy and Research, 3,* 5–26.

Catalano, S. (2010). *Intimate partner violence, 1993–2010.* (NCJ239203). Washington, DC: Bureau of Justice Statistics. Retrieved March 12, 2015 from: http://www.bjs.gov/ content/pub/pdf/ipv9310.pdf

Chen, X. (2009). The link between juvenile offending and victimization: The influence of risky lifestyles, social bonding, and individual characteristics. *Youth Violence and Juvenile Justice, 7,* 119–135.

Clarke, R. V. (2004). Technology, criminology and crime science. *European Journal on Criminal Policy and Research, 10,* 55–63.

Clarke, R. V., & Cornish, D. (1985). Modeling offender's decisions: A framework for research and policy. In M. Tonry & N. Morris (Eds.), *Crime & justice: An annual review of research* (Vol. 6, pp. 147–185). Chicago, IL: University of Chicago Press.

Cohen, L. E., & Felson, M. (1979). Social change and crime rate trends: A routine activity approach. *American Sociological Review, 44,* 588–608.

Cornish, D. B., & Clarke, R. V. (2008). The rational choice perspective. In R. Wortely & L. Mazerolle (Eds.), *Environmental criminology and crime analysis* (pp. 21–47). Portland, OR: Willan Publishing.

Daigle, L. E. (2010). Risk heterogeneity and recurrent violent victimization: The role of DRD4. *Biodemography and Social Biology, 56,* 137–149.

Daigle, L. E., Beaver, K. M., & Hartman, J. L. (2008). A life-course approach to the study of victimization and offending behaviors. *Victims and Offenders, 3,* 365–390.

DeLisi, M. (2011). Self-control theory: The Tyrannosaurus rex of criminology is poised to devour criminal justice. *Journal of Criminal Justice, 39,* 103–105.

Eck, J. E., & Clarke, R. V. (2003). Classifying common police problems: A routine activity approach. *Crime Prevention Studies* (Vol. 16, pp. 7–39). Monsey, NY: Criminal Justice Press.

Gottfredson, M. R., & Hirschi, T. (1990). *A general theory of crime.* Stanford, CA: Stanford University Press.

Grasmick, H. G., Tittle, C. R., Bursik, R. J., & Arneklev, B. J. (1993). Testing the core empirical implications of Gottfredson and Hirschi's general theory of crime. *Journal of Research in Crime and Delinquency, 30,* 5–29.

Henson, B., Wilcox, P., Reyns, B. W., & Cullen, F. T. (2010). Gender, adolescent lifestyles, and violent victimization: Implications for routine activities theory. *Victims & Offenders, 5,* 303–328.

Hindelang, M. J., Gottfredson M. R., & Garofalo, J. (1978). *Victims of personal crime: An empirical foundation for a theory of personal victimization.* Cambridge, MA: Ballinger Publishing Company.

Hirschi, T. (1969). *Causes of delinquency.* Berkeley: University of California Press.

Internet Crime Complaint Center (2012). *Internet Crime Complaint Center's (IC3) Scam Alerts May 23, 2012.* Retrieved July 15, 2012, from http://www.ic3.gov/media/2012/120523.aspx

Jensen, G. F., & Brownfield, D. (1986). Gender, lifestyles, and victimization: Beyond routine activity. *Violence and Victims, 1,* 85–99.

Lauritsen, J. L., & Laub, J. H. (2007). Understanding the link between victimization and offending: New reflections on an old idea. *Crime Prevention Studies, 22,* 55–75.

Lemert, E. (1951). *Social pathology.* New York: McGraw Hill.

Marcum, C. D., Higgins, G. E., & Ricketts, M. L. (2010). Potential factors of online victimization of youth: An examination of adolescent online behaviors utilizing routine activities theory. *Deviant Behavior, 31,* 381–410.

Mustaine, E. E., & Tewksbury, R. (1998). Victimization risks at leisure: A gender-specific analysis. *Violence and Victims, 13,* 231–249.

Mustaine, E. E., & Tewksbury, R. (2002). Sexual assault of college women: A feminist interpretation of a routine activities analysis. *Criminal Justice Review, 27,* 89–123.

Nobles, M. R., & Fox, K. A. (2013). Assessing stalking behaviors in a control balance theory framework. *Criminal Justice and Behavior, 40,* 737–762.

Piquero, A. R., & Hickman, M. (2003). Extending Tittle's control balance theory to account for victimization. *Criminal Justice and Behavior, 30,* 282–301.

Piquero, A. R., MacDonald, J., Dobrin, A., Daigle, L. E., & Cullen, F. T. (2005). Self-control, violent offending, and homicide victimization: Assessing the general theory of crime. *Journal of Quantitative Criminology, 21,* 55–71.

Popp, A. M., & Peguero, A. A. (2011). Routine activities and victimization at school: The significance of gender. *Journal of Interpersonal Violence, 26,* 2413–2436.

Pratt, T. C., Holtfreter, K., & Reisig, M. D. (2010). Routine online activity and Internet fraud targeting: Extending the generality of routine activities theory. *Journal of Research in Crime and Delinquency, 47,* 267–296.

Reyns, B. W. (2012). *The anti-social network: Cyberstalking victimization among college students.* El Paso, TX: LFB Scholarly Publishing, LLC.

Reyns, B. W., Henson, B., & Fisher, B. S. (2011). Being pursued online: Applying cyberlifestyle–routine activities theory to cyberstalking victimization. *Criminal Justice and Behavior, 38,* 1149–1169.

Roncek, D. W., & Lobosco, A. (1983). The effect of high schools on crime in their neighborhoods. *Social Science Quarterly, 64,* 598–613.

Roncek, D. W., & Maier, P. A. (1991). Bars, blocks, and crimes revisited: Linking the theory of routine activities to the empiricism of "hot spots." *Criminology, 29,* 725–753.

Rossmo, D. K. (2000). *Geographic profiling.* Boca Raton, FL: CRC Press.

Sampson, R. J., & Laub, J. H. (1993). *Crime in the making: Pathways and turning points through life.* Cambridge, MA: Harvard University Press.

Schreck, C. J. (1999). Criminal victimization and low self-control: An extension and test of a general theory of crime. *Justice Quarterly, 16,* 633–654.

Schreck, C. J., & Fisher, B. S. (2004). Specifying the influence of family and peers on violent victimization. *Journal of Interpersonal Violence, 19,* 1021–1041.

Schreck, C. J., Stewart, E. A., & Osgood, D. W. (2008). A reappraisal of the overlap of violent offenders and victims. *Criminology, 46,* 871–906.

Schreck, C. J., Wright, R. A., & Miller, J. M. (2002). A study of individual and situational antecedents of violent victimization. *Justice Quarterly, 19,* 159–180.

Schwartz, M. D., DeKeseredy, W. S., Tait, D., & Alvi, S. (2001). Male peer support and a feminist routine activities theory: Understanding sexual assault on the college campus. *Justice Quarterly, 18,* 623–649.

Schwartz, M. D., & Pitts, V. L. (1995). Exploring a feminist routine activities approach to explaining sexual assault. *Justice Quarterly, 12,* 9–31.

Sherman, L. W., Gartin, P. R., & Buerger, M. E. (1989). Hot spots of predatory crime: Routine activities and the criminology of place. *Criminology, 27,* 27–55.

Sutherland, E. H. (1947). *Criminology* (4th Ed.). Philadelphia: Lippincott.

Tillyer, M. S., Tillyer, R., Miller, H. V., & Pangrac, R. (2011). Reexamining the correlates of adolescent violent victimization: The importance of exposure, guardianship, and target characteristics. *Journal of Interpersonal Violence, 26,* 2908–2928.

Tillyer, M. S., Wilcox, P., & Gialopsos, B. M. (2010). Adolescent school-based sexual victimization: Exploring the role of opportunity in a gender-specific multilevel analysis. *Journal of Criminal Justice, 38,* 1071–1081.

Tittle, C. R. (1995). *Control balance: Toward a general theory of deviance.* Boulder, CO: Westview Press.

Tittle, C. R. (2004). Refining control balance theory. *Theoretical Criminology, 8,* 395–428.

Truman, J. L. (2011). *Criminal victimization, 2010.* Washington, DC: Bureau of Justice Statistics.

Van Wilsem, J. (2011). Worlds tied together? Online and non-domestic routine activities and their impact on digital and traditional threat victimization. *European Journal of Criminology, 8,* 115–127.

Vaske, J., Wright, J. P., & Beaver, K. M. (2011). A dopamine gene (*DRD2*) distinguishes between offenders who have and have not been violently victimized. *International Journal of Offender Therapy and Comparative Criminology, 55,* 251–267.

Weisburd, D., Bushway, S., Lum, C., & Yang, S. (2004). Trajectories of crime at places: A longitudinal study of street segments in the city of Seattle. *Criminology, 42,* 283–321.

Wilcox, P., Tillyer, M. S., & Fisher, B. S. (2009). Gendered opportunity? School-based adolescent victimization. *Journal of Research in Crime and Delinquency, 46,* 245–269.

Wolfgang, M. E. (1957). Victim-precipitated criminal homicide. *Journal of Criminal Law, Criminology, & Police Science, 48,* 1–11.

Wortley, R., & Mazerolle, L. (2008). Environmental criminology and crime analysis: Situating the theory, analytic approach and application. In R. Wortely & L. Mazerolle (Eds.), *Environmental criminology and crime analysis* (pp. 1–18). Portland, OR: Willan Publishing.

Wright, J. P., Tibbetts, S. G., & Daigle, L. E. (2008). *Criminals in the making: Criminality across the life course.* Thousand Oaks, CA: Sage Publications, Inc.

Yar, M. (2005). The novelty of 'cybercrime': An assessment in light of routine activity theory. *European Journal of Criminology, 2,* 407–427.

PART II

Sources, Trends, and Types of Victimization

Answering the question "What causes victimization?" is at once seemingly straightforward and extremely complex. The theories presented in Part I of this textbook provide useful frameworks for victimologists and others to consider in answering this deceptively simple question, but without data and hypothesis testing it is not possible to determine whether the theories are valuable or useful for answering victimization-related research questions. Thus, victimologists collect empirical data about the myriad types of criminal victimization and, with these data, seek to identify trends and patterns describing victimization experiences. Those data also help to either generate theoretical explanations of victimization or test the utility of various theories.

Part II of the textbook provides an overview and critique of research that has identified risk factors for different types of victimization. Not every type of victimization is included in these chapters, or indeed in this textbook; the varieties of victimization far exceed the scope of this textbook. Victims of crimes such as terrorism, hate crimes, or kidnapping, for example, are better left to specialty books or edited volumes devoted solely to those topics. The reason for this is primarily because within the field of victimology, the research needed to address the above question related to the causes of these types of victimization and their associated risk factors has only just begun in earnest.

Part II is divided into six chapters, beginning with Chapter 4, which provides an overview of the many sources of victimization data that are collected both in the United States and internationally. Official sources of data, general and specific victimization surveys, and measurement issues inherent to victimization research are discussed. This provides readers with a well-informed background into the different sources that generate criminal victimization data.

Chapter 5 discusses five types of personal victimization: homicide, rape, stalking, assault, and robbery. Chapter 6 addresses personal victimization of specific populations: women, children, and elders. A reasonable question might be "Why isn't there a chapter on male victimization?" Overall, males are at greater risk for violent victimization than are females. Thus, with the exceptions noted in Chapter 6 and in specific instances stated in Chapter 5 (you'll have to read the chapters to find out), the victimization of males is a salient theme throughout this textbook. Together, these two chapters provide a comprehensive summary of crimes perpetrated against persons rather than against property.

Chapter 7 elaborates the nature of criminal victimization with an emphasis on victimizations involving property and white-collar victimization. Several major types of property offenses, including larceny-theft, identity theft, motor vehicle theft, burglary, and arson, are reviewed, followed by an introduction to white-collar victimization. Although white-collar offenses are omnipresent in our society and have the potential of harming many more victims than other types of crime, they are rarely discussed from a victimological perspective. Thus, Chapter 7 highlights the prominent place of white-collar victimization in 21st-century victimology.

Chapters 8 and 9 extend the discussion of patterns in criminal victimization. Specifically, Chapter 8 focuses on the domains in which criminal victimization occurs. Although crimes transpire virtually everywhere (e.g., streets, neighborhoods), there are certain environments that create domain-specific opportunities for victimization. Therefore, this chapter describes the nature of victimization within specific domains (e.g., educational institutions, cyberspace) as well as the types of victimization that most commonly occur within these domains (e.g., bullying, sexual violence). Chapter 9 rounds out Part II with respect to patterns in victimization, while also providing a bridge to the topics covered in Part III. The topic of this chapter is recurring victimization, which occurs when individuals or their property are victimized two or more times. Recurring victimization also can be viewed as a consequence of victimization, because it appears that people who experience an initial victimization are at increased risk for experiencing more victimizations in the future. The chapter also provides a natural transition into Part III of the book, which describes responses to, and consequences of, victimization.

CASE STUDY #2

Measuring Victimization: Not as Easy as You Thought!

In Part II, we examine several important topics in victimology: what is known about crime victims (who they are and what they experience); the different contexts in which victimization can happen; and what sources of data on victimization are commonly used to reach conclusions about the "who, what, where, and when" of criminal victimization.

While one might imagine that answering such questions as "How many rapes occurred in the United States during 2016?" or "Are men more likely to be victims of violence than women?" is rather easy, the reality is this: Answering those questions accurately is a function of *measurement*, and different measures lead to different answers. To think about this another way, consider the question "How much does Brad Pitt weigh?" How might one answer that question? One could "eyeball" Mr. Pitt, considering his height and body build, and provide an estimate. One also could have Mr. Pitt stand on a scale, which would provide another estimate of his weight. Note that both measures provide estimates and have a margin of error associated with them (with the "eyeball" measure likely having a much greater margin than the scale).

Criminologists and victimologists are keenly aware of how the measure used affects the estimate of how many victimizations occur or how much crime there is. While each measure of victimization has a margin of error associated with it, that error actually can be calculated (but that discussion is for your statistics class!), which makes it manageable. The point here is this: Depending on the measure used, the estimate you calculate to answer your question can vary quite dramatically (i.e., have a much larger margin of error).

Let's say that you are interested in determining how many students at your college or university experienced a robbery victimization during academic year 2016–2017. How might you go about answering that question? One way might be for you to check statistics published by your school as required by the *Clery Act*, a federal law that mandates colleges and universities receiving federal financial aid to report their crime statistics each year. *Clery Act* statistics are compiled by your school's police or security department and consist of the number of crimes reported to those agencies from among a list of offenses required by the law to be included. Pretty straightforward, right? Well, maybe not. For example, let's say you came home from a party and found your dormitory room had been broken into and your laptop computer and DVD player had been stolen. Many students might call the police and claim, "I've been robbed!" However, in reality, they have suffered a *burglary*—not the same thing. Further, what if, for any number of reasons, you chose *not* to notify the campus police. Your victimization would not show up in the statistics reported, would it? Thus, we've already identified two possible sources of error with the statistics reported: misclassification of the incident (robbery when in fact it was a burglary) and underreporting (the incident never came to the attention of the police, so it was not included in the crime totals provided by the campus police or security).

OK, so you're thinking, "there must be a better way." What about if you conducted a survey of a random sample of students at your college or university and *asked them* about their victimization experiences? In other words, you could just ask them: "Were you robbed during academic year 2016–2017?" One advantage to using a *victimization survey* is that you can capture those offenses that were not reported to the police. You could even ask your respondents why they chose not to report the incident and learn some interesting facts about nonreporting. Thus, you would overcome some of the problems that come with relying on data compiled by the police.

However, you're not out of the woods: Your survey has some issues of its own. For example, if you just asked people "Have you been robbed during academic year 2016–2017?" you run the following risks: (1) people may again misclassify what happened to them (e.g., confusing burglary with robbery) and (2) people may *misremember* when the event had actually occurred (called *telescoping*) and move the event forward in time (the incident had actually happened during the 2016–2017 academic year or even earlier). One way to handle the former issue is to use what are called *behaviorally specific* questions (Fisher, 2009), which leave no doubt in your respondents' minds about what it is you're trying to measure. Instead of asking "Were you robbed?" you might ask "Did anyone, using force or threat of force, take property from you without your permission?" You are no longer relying upon each respondent's own definition of robbery; you are using the same definition for each respondent. To address the telescoping issue, you might use what is called a *landmark event* (Gaskell, Wright, & O'Muircheartaigh, 2000) in your question to help your respondent anchor what happened in time. Here, you might ask, "*Since school began this fall term*, has anyone, using force or threat of force, taken property from you without your permission?" "Since school began this fall term" helps your respondent to anchor the robbery within the boundary of the current school year.

You also may need to determine whether the incident happened on campus or off, depending on your interest. If you're interested in whether college students have comparable robbery victimization rates to nonstudents, you wouldn't necessarily care where the incident occurred. However, if you are primarily interested in robberies occurring on campus, you would again need to narrow the boundaries for your respondents. So, in addition to adding a landmark event ("since school began this fall term"), you might also include a *contextual boundary* such as "Since school began this fall term and *while you have been on campus*—that is, on university-owned property such as a residence hall, classroom building, at the football stadium or basketball arena . . ." Here, you've not only anchored when the event occurred, but where the incident occurred to help respondents narrow their recollection of the location where the incident might have happened.

You also face the question of how many students you should survey, since the number you include directly affects how much confidence you have in the estimate you end up with (called the *confidence interval*, or the probability—your confidence—that the estimate you calculated is within a certain range of possible estimates that includes the unknown "true" amount. The smaller the range, the better). If you interviewed *all* the students at your school, your confidence in coming up with the "true" number of robberies would be very high, indeed. However, can you imagine how long it would take to do this? Instead, you would likely select a *sample* of students to complete your survey. You can even calculate how many students you'd need to interview to have a certain *margin of error* for your estimate. You can also calculate what your sample should include in terms of the number of men and women, ages, minority students, and so forth to have a *representative sample* of students at your school (the more your sample resembles the characteristics of the student body as a whole, the more confidence you have in your estimate of how many robberies occurred).

So, what seems at first glance like an easy question gets complicated in a hurry. Remember that how much of something there is depends on how you measure it!

References

Fisher, B. (2009). The effects of survey question wording on rape estimates: Evidence from a quasi-experimental design. *Violence Against Women, 15*, 133–147.

Gaskill, G.D., Wright, D.B., & O'Muircheartaigh, C.A. (2000). Telescoping of landmark events. *Public Opinion Quarterly, 64*, 77–89.

CHAPTER 4

Sources of Victimization Data

CHAPTER OUTLINE

Introduction

Official Sources of Victimization Data

- United States
  - Uniform Crime Reports
  - National Incident-Based Reporting System
- International

General Crime Victimization Surveys

- United States
- International
  - International Crime Victims Survey
  - European Crime and Safety Survey
  - Crime Survey for England and Wales

Specialized Crime Victimization Surveys

- United States
  - National Violence Against Women Survey
  - National College Women Sexual Victimization Survey
  - National Intimate Partner and Sexual Violence Survey
- International

Issues in Victimization Research

- Challenges in Victimization Survey Research
- Neglected Forms of Victimization and Victim Populations
- Innovations in Survey Administration and Data Collection

LEARNING OBJECTIVES

- Identify the sources and uses of official statistics in understanding criminal victimization.
- Describe the Uniform Crime Reports and National Incident-Based Reporting System.
- Identify the sources and uses of self-report victimization surveys in understanding criminal victimization.
- Explain the contributions of the United Nations as a source of crime and victimization data.
- Describe the National Crime Victimization Survey.
- Compare and contrast official sources of victimization data with self-report victimization surveys.
- Identify and describe international general victimization surveys, including the International Crime Victims Survey, the European Crime and Safety Survey, and the Crime Survey for England and Wales.
- Identify and describe specialized victimization surveys from the United States and abroad, including the National Violence Against Women Survey, the National College Women Sexual Victimization Survey, the National Intimate Partner and Sexual Violence Survey, and the International Violence Against Women Survey.
- Explain the limitations of surveys for studying victimization.

Routine activity, opportunity theory, and even rational choice theories of crime flourished in large part because of the availability of victim survey data.

Cantor and Lynch, 2000, p. 90

Adolphe Quetelet

Introduction

For almost 200 years, researchers have been interested in crime trends and patterns. Important questions related to the extent of crime generally or of certain types (e.g., murder) specifically, and whether crime rates fluctuate from year to year, were the focus of early efforts to understand and predict these trends and patterns. The first researchers to address these issues by examining national-level crime data were André-Michel Guerry and Adolphe Quetelet, who studied French crime statistics that were published in 1827. Guerry, a French lawyer, and Quetelet, a Belgian astronomer and mathematician, separately analyzed the crime statistics, but both arrived at the same conclusion: Crime incidents are not random events—they are *patterned* in certain ways. For example, Guerry discovered that the *wealthiest* area of France had the *highest* property crime rates. Interestingly, he attributed these high property crime rates to greater *opportunities* for victimization (see Chapter 2) that were present in the wealthy areas. Modern-day scholars have continued in Guerry's and Quetelet's footsteps by studying victimization trends and patterns and, based on this information, developing explanations for why and how victimization occurs.

This chapter reviews several key issues related to sources of victimization data in the United States and elsewhere in the world. Victimization data allow researchers to test hypotheses related to risk factors for victimization (e.g., opportunities) and examine issues such as consequences of crime for victims, victim decision making, and much more. The data sources reviewed in the chapter are grouped together according to the method of data collection used and the populations to which they apply. The first group of sources includes the Uniform Crime Reports (UCR) and the National Incident-Based Reporting System (NIBRS), both of which provide crime estimates for the United States and are based on crimes reported to the police. Following this, general victimization surveys are discussed as sources of information about crime victims and the circumstances surrounding their victimization.

In contrast to official sources of crime data like the UCR, which rely on victims reporting the incident to police, general victimization surveys collect information directly from crime victims regardless of whether their victimization had been officially reported to police. The National Crime Victimization Survey (NCVS) collects general information about criminal victimization in the United States, while internationally several general victimization surveys are conducted, including the International Crime Victims Survey (ICVS) and the European Crime and Safety Survey (ECSS), among others. Finally, there are victimization surveys that are designed to measure specific types of victimization. Examples of these specialized victimization surveys, including the National Intimate Partner and Sexual Violence Survey (NISVS) and the International Violence Against Women Survey (IVAWS), also are discussed in the chapter.

The chapter summarizes the goals, purpose, and history of each source of victimization data. For each data source, information also is presented on the type or types of victimization the source measures and the methods used to collect the victimization data. The chapter concludes with a discussion of victimization research issues, such as the challenges faced by researchers who collect data about criminal victimization, innovations in survey administration that allow victimologists to answer new research questions, and neglected areas of study in the field of victimology.

Official Sources of Victimization Data

Official sources of victimization data include offenses known to police. Accordingly, they are limited by the fact that not all crimes that occur are discovered by the police, let alone reported to them. These unreported and undiscovered offenses are known as the ***dark figure of crime***, because although they are crimes that have been committed, they do not come to the attention of the criminal justice system. Official data also tend to provide more information about offenders and offending than about victims and victimization, and are thus not ideal for answering questions in victimology. In the United States, the UCR and the NIBRS are the primary sources of official victimization data, including crime rates and other relevant national crime statistics (e.g., clearance rates). It is important to understand how crime rates are calculated so they can be properly interpreted throughout the remainder of the text. ***Crime rates*** are ratios that are calculated based on the number of known crimes. These raw numbers are then standardized by a measure of the population, which in the UCR is per 100,000 residents. The resulting statistic represents the number of crimes committed per 100,000 residents of the United States.

Figure 4-1 depicts how crime rates are calculated for two fictitious cities, Metropolis and Gotham City. In the scenario depicted in the figure, Metropolis experienced 500 murders in the course of year, while 250 murders were committed in Gotham City. Also notice that the population of Metropolis outnumbers the population of Gotham City by 3 million residents. Although it is tempting to assume that Metropolis is the more dangerous city because it has twice the number of murders, calculating crime rates for each allows for a comparison that tells a different story. To do this, the number of murders is first divided by the city's population. The resulting figure is then multiplied by 100,000, the unit of standardization used by the UCR, which removes differences in population size for the two cities. Once the rates for murder are calculated for both cities, it is then possible to compare them and determine which city is really the more dangerous for homicide victimization. Metropolis's murder rate was 10 per 100,000 residents, which means that for every 100,000 residents 10 murders were committed that year. Meanwhile, Gotham's murder rate was 12.5 per 100,000. Clearly, of the two cities, Gotham is the most crime-ridden, at least with respect to homicide.

Metropolis
Number of murders: 500
Population: 5,000,000

Calculation of murder rate:
500/5,000,000 =
0.0001 * 100,000 =
10 murders per 100,000 residents

Gotham City
Number of murders: 250
Population: 2,000,000

Calculation of murder rate:
250/2,000,000 =
0.000125 * 100,000 =
12.5 murders per 100,000 residents

Figure 4-1 Calculating Crime Rates

Criminologists and victimologists calculate crime rates for purpose of comparison. Crime rates published in the UCR can be compared across cities, counties, and states. For example, imagine that a victimologist wanted to know how Texas compared to Alaska with respect to burglary victimization. Comparing the raw number of burglaries committed in Texas to the number of burglaries committed in Alaska would not be very informative because Texas has many more residents than Alaska, and should therefore have a higher raw number of burglaries. In addition, the two states may define burglary differently, making comparisons problematic. The UCR standardizes these definitions to allow for comparisons. In addition, by standardizing the raw number of burglaries with a measure of the population, such as per 100,000 individuals, Texas and Alaska can be compared despite their differences in population size. It is also important to point out that while the UCR standardizes by 100,000 individuals, this is not a universal base rate across all sources of victimization data. The NCVS, for example, reports victimization rates as per 1,000 individuals (for personal crimes) or per 1,000 households (for household crimes).

United States

Uniform Crime Reports

Created in 1929 by the International Association of Chiefs of Police with data collection formally begun in 1930, the ***Uniform Crime Reports*** (UCR) represent the oldest source for crime data in the United States. The UCR's purpose is to provide reliable crime data for use by those in the criminal justice system, but it is also a valuable resource for those who study crime, and the information found in the UCR is compiled and published annually by the Federal Bureau of Investigation (FBI) in a report called *Crime in the United States*. That report provides multiple pieces of useful information, including (1) the number of offenses known (reported) to the police; (2) the number of arrests made by the police for specific offenses and the characteristics of those arrested (e.g., age, race, and sex); (3) the distribution of crimes known and arrests by different geographic units (states, cities, suburbs, metropolitan areas); (4) employment information for police departments; and (5) the number of police officers killed annually in the line of duty. The UCR also provides data on the number of "hate" or "bias" crimes occurring in the United States each year, as well as detailed information on homicides through Supplemental Homicide Reports.

The UCR divides its data into two categories—Part I ("Index") offenses and Part II ("Other") offenses—and provides various estimates about how many of these offenses occur each year in the United States. Approximately 18,000 law enforcement agencies (e.g., municipal, county, state, federal, university) voluntarily contribute data to the UCR annually.

There are currently eight offenses that are considered Part I or ***index crimes***: criminal homicide, forcible rape, robbery, aggravated assault, burglary, larceny-theft, motor vehicle theft, and arson. Definitions of the eight index crimes are provided in Table 4-1. In addition to collecting arrest data on these eight offenses, the UCR also has information related to the gender, race, and age of those arrested for these crimes. Further, as part of the annual UCR, the FBI also publishes a "crime clock," which provides a standardized estimate of how frequently Index offenses happen as a function of time. The 2011 crime clock for Index offenses is shown in Figure 4-2.

Table 4-1: UCR Definitions of Index Crimes

Criminal Homicide	The willful (non-negligent) killing of one human being by another.
Forcible Rape	Penetration, no matter how slight, of the vagina or anus with any body part or object, or oral penetration by a sex organ of another person, without the consent of the victim.
Robbery	The taking or attempting to take anything of value from the care, custody, or control of a person or persons by force or threat of force or violence and/or by putting the victim in fear.
Aggravated Assault	An unlawful attack by one person upon another for the purpose of inflicting severe or aggravated bodily injury. Attempted aggravated assault that involves the display of—or threat to use—a gun, knife, or other weapon is included in this crime category because serious personal injury would likely result if the assault were completed.
Burglary	The unlawful entry of a structure to commit a felony or theft. The UCR definition of "structure" includes apartment, barn, house trailer or houseboat when used as a permanent dwelling, office, railroad car (but not automobile), stable, and vessel (i.e., ship).
Larceny-Theft	The unlawful taking, carrying, leading, or riding away of property from the possession or constructive possession of another. Examples are thefts of bicycles, motor vehicle parts and accessories, shoplifting, pocket-picking, or the stealing of any property or article that is not taken by force and violence or by fraud.
Motor Vehicle Theft	The theft or attempted theft of a motor vehicle. In the UCR Program, a motor vehicle is a self-propelled vehicle that runs on land surfaces and not on rails. Examples of motor vehicles include sport utility vehicles, automobiles, trucks, buses, motorcycles, motor scooters, all-terrain vehicles, and snowmobiles. Motor vehicle theft does not include farm equipment, bulldozers, airplanes, construction equipment, or water craft such as motorboats, sailboats, houseboats, or jet skis.
Arson	Any willful or malicious burning or attempting to burn, with or without intent to defraud, a dwelling house, public building, motor vehicle or aircraft, personal property of another, etc.

Source: Federal Bureau of Investigation (2013).

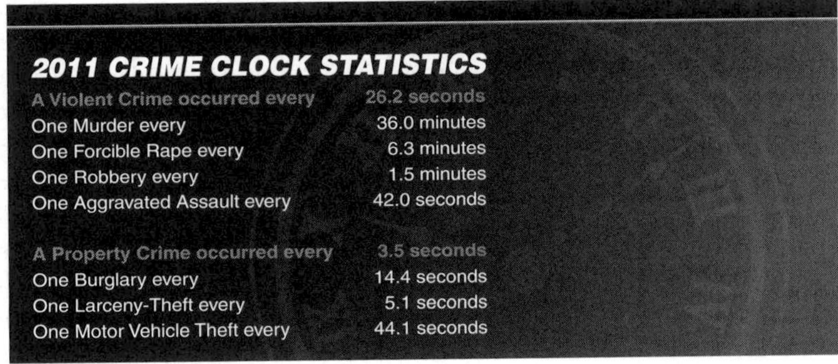

Figure 4-2 The FBI's Crime Clock

The Crime Clock presents crime statistic averages across time. In actuality, crime tends to cluster at certain times of the day, week, month, and year.

Source: Federal Bureau of Investigation (2012).

Part II, or "Other" offenses, are also tracked and reported by the FBI in the UCR but not in as much detail as is the case for Index offenses. For Part II offenses, only arrest data are available. Further, agencies that contribute data to the UCR are not required to submit information about Part II offenses. As a result, less information is available on the circumstances surrounding these types of offenses in the United States. UCR Part II offenses include

1. Other assaults (simple assaults)
2. Forgery and counterfeiting
3. Fraud
4. Embezzlement
5. Stolen property: buying, receiving, possessing
6. Vandalism
7. Weapons: carrying, possessing
8. Prostitution and commercialized vice
9. Sex offenses
10. Drug abuse violations
11. Gambling
12. Offenses against the family and children
13. Driving under the influence
14. Liquor law violations
15. Drunkenness
16. Disorderly conduct
17. Vagrancy
18. All other offenses (except traffic violations)
19. Suspicion (person arrested, but not charged)
20. Curfew and loitering (persons under age 18)
21. Runaway (persons under age 18)

In addition to the information provided in the UCR for Part I and Part II offenses, detailed information about homicides is collected and published annually in the FBI's ***Supplementary Homicide Report (SHR)***. Like the UCR, data about homicides are collected, recorded, and transmitted by law enforcement agencies from across the country to the FBI for the SHR. The SHR includes detailed information about homicide victims and offenders, such as their age, sex, and race, the victim–offender relationship, and the type of weapon that was used. The SHR is the primary source of homicide victimization data in the United States, since large-scale victimization surveys, which are discussed later in this chapter, do not include measures of homicide victimization. An example of the type of data provided by the SHR is included in Table 4-2. This table includes percentages and rates of homicide victimization and offending by demographic characteristics.

Although the UCR is a useful source of crime data, it also possesses several characteristics that limit its value for victimologists. First, law enforcement participation in the UCR is completely voluntary, and thus not every law enforcement agency provides crime data to the FBI for inclusion in the UCR. Further, the same agencies

Table 4-2: Homicide Victims and Offenders, 1980–2008

	Percent of—			Rate per 100,000 Inhabitants	
	Victims	Offenders	Population	Victims	Offenders
Total	100%	100%	100%	7.4	8.3
Age					
Under 14	4.8%	0.5%	20.0%	1.8	0.2
14–17	5.2	10.6	5.8	6.6	15.0
18–24	24.4	37.5	10.6	17.1	29.3
25–34	28.7	28.0	15.6	13.7	14.9
35–49	22.8	17.1	21.1	8.0	6.7
50–64	8.9	4.9	14.7	4.5	2.7
65 or older	5.1	1.6	12.3	3.1	1.1
Sex					
Male	76.8%	89.5%	48.9%	11.6	15.1
Female	23.2	10.5	51.1	3.4	1.7
Race					
White	50.3%	45.3%	82.9%	4.5	4.5
Black	47.4	52.5	12.6	27.8	34.4
Other*	2.3	2.2	4.4	3.8	4.1

*Other race includes American Indians, Native Alaskans, Asians, Native Hawaiians, and other Pacific Islanders.
Source: Cooper and Smith (2011).

may not participate each year, so the total number of agencies can vary from year to year. However, the vast majority of state, county, and municipal police agencies *do* participate, and they provide service to approximately 98% of the population of the United States.

Second, when more than one offense is committed during a single incident, what is known as a ***series event***, the UCR directs law enforcement agencies to report only the most serious offense to the FBI. Consider the following series event: During the course of an armed robbery of a convenience store, the offender not only takes money from the cash register while brandishing a gun at the attendant, but also hits the attendant in the mouth with the gun, causing injury to the attendant; while fleeing, the offender also shoots and wounds a customer who was entering the store. Thus, multiple crimes occurred during this single incident, making it a series event. However, only the most serious of the multiple crimes—shooting of the customer—would be included for UCR purposes. This method of counting crimes is known as the ***hierarchy rule*** because Index offenses are ranked hierarchically in terms of their seriousness and only the most serious offense in a series event appears in UCR crime statistics.

Third, criminologists have long questioned the accuracy of the information found in the UCR (e.g., McCleary, Nienstedt, & Erven, 1982). Most of the criticism has concentrated on differences that exist across police agencies and the ways in which they record offenses. For example, Police Department A may record an offense as a larceny-theft, whereas Police Department B classifies a similar crime as a burglary. If these types of differences exist, critics claim that UCR statistics cannot be compared across jurisdictions because they are not being classified in a uniform way.

Finally, and perhaps most importantly, UCR statistics do not illuminate the dark figure of crime—that is, they do not include crimes that are not reported to law enforcement. This limitation underscores the importance of using alternative sources of data, such as victimization surveys, which include victims who did not report what happened to them to law enforcement. Overall, despite these limitations, there are also compelling reasons to trust the information included in the UCR as useful measures of crime in the United States, at least insofar as they reflect crimes considered serious enough by citizens to be reported (Gove, Hughes, & Geerken, 1985).

National Incident-Based Reporting System

The ***National Incident-Based Reporting System*** (NIBRS) was officially created in 1988 as an incident-based revision to the UCR. NIBRS was created in an effort to overcome many of the previously discussed limitations of the UCR, particularly those related to the data quantity and quality collected by law enforcement. In many respects, NIBRS has been successful at improving the design of, and data found in, the UCR. One important aspect of NIBRS is that it collects data on more offenses than does the UCR. Like the UCR, NIBRS divides offenses into two categories, Group A and Group B offenses. Group A includes 22 crime categories consisting of 46 offenses. For instance, the Group A crime category "fraud offenses" contains the crimes of false pretenses/swindle/confidence games, credit card/automatic teller machine fraud, impersonation, welfare fraud, and wire fraud. Group B consists of 11 crime categories and includes all offenses that do not fall into Group A. Group A and Group B offenses are listed in Table 4-3.

Another advantage the NIBRS possesses in comparison to the UCR is that it is incident-based. In practical terms, this means that a more complete crime count is produced because the hierarchy rule from the UCR is eliminated. NIBRS incident reports include the 10 most serious offenses that transpired during any single incident. Thus, from the previous example of the armed robbery of the convenience store, the robbery, assault, and attempted murder would all be included in NIBRS data, not just the attempted murder, since the hierarchy rule would not be applied. In addition to recording multiple offenses in the incident report, NIBRS data also include a wealth of information related to the circumstances of the crime. For Group A offenses, this information is divided into segments, relating to:

1. The offense (e.g., type of offense, location, type of weapon involved)
2. Property (e.g., description, value, quantity)
3. Victim(s) (e.g., age, injury, relationship to offender)
4. Offender(s) (e.g., sex, age, race)
5. Arrestee(s) (e.g., race, ethnicity, resident status)

Table 4-3: Group A and Group B Offenses

Group A	
Arson	Kidnapping/abduction
Assault offenses	Larceny/theft offenses
Aggravated assault	Pocket-picking
Simple assault	Purse snatching
Intimidation	Shoplifting
Bribery	Theft from building
Burglary/breaking and entering	Theft from coin-operated machine or device
Counterfeiting/forgery	Theft from motor vehicle
Destruction/damage/vandalism of property	Theft of motor vehicle parts or accessories
Drug/narcotic offenses	All other larceny
Drug/narcotic violations	Motor vehicle theft
Drug equipment violations	Pornography/obscene material
Embezzlement	Prostitution offenses
Extortion/blackmail	Prostitution
Fraud offenses	Assisting or promoting prostitution
Credit card/automatic teller machine fraud	Robbery
Impersonation	Sex offenses, forcible
Welfare fraud	Forcible rape
Wire fraud	Forcible sodomy
Gambling offenses	Sexual assault with an object
Betting/wagering	Forcible fondling
Operating/promoting/assisting gambling	Sex offenses, nonforcible
Gambling equipment violations	Incest
Sports tampering	Statutory rape
Homicide offenses	Stolen property offenses
Murder and non-negligent manslaughter	Weapon law violations
Negligent manslaughter	
Justifiable homicide (not a crime)	

Group B	
Bad checks	Liquor law violations
Curfew/loitering/vagrancy violations	Peeping tom
Disorderly conduct	Runaway
Driving under the influence	Trespass of real property
Drunkenness	All other offenses
Family offenses, nonviolent	

Besides including incident reports and expanding the number of offenses for which data are collected, NIBRS has other strengths. First, states must be NIBRS-certified before data from state law enforcement agencies can be submitted to the FBI for the NIBRS. In turn, agencies across the state must submit their crime data through their state NIBRS-certified programs. This system of data submission is designed to minimize errors and variation across agencies that could influence the quality of the data submitted to the FBI. Second, the data are more useful for criminologists and victimologists interested in examining relationships between or among variables, since details related to crime incidents can be linked to specific victims, offenders, offenses, or arrestees (James & Council, 2008). Finally, NIBRS allows law enforcement agencies to identify shared crime patterns across their respective jurisdictions and work together toward solutions.

Although NIBRS has clear strengths as a data source, it is not without limitations. First among them relates to the incidents that are included in the database. Like the UCR, the crime information in NIBRS originates from law enforcement agencies from across the country. As a result, only crimes known to police are included in NIBRS, and therefore the dark figure of crime remains unexamined. Second, as was the case with the UCR, participation in NIBRS is voluntary, and not every state is NIBRS-certified. According to the Federal Bureau of Investigation (2015), in 2012, 6,115 law enforcement agencies contributed data to the program, which equates to about 33% of the U.S. population. To put this figure in context, recall that agencies participating in the UCR represent some 98% of the U.S. population. This low rate of participation is problematic because a large share of the nation's crime is not being included in the data. However, over time, as more states and agencies gain NIBRS certification, this issue will be less of a problem. Finally, although certain information from NIBRS is available to researchers interested in exploring the nature of crime and victimization, a nationally representative NIBRS dataset is not publicly available, which limits its utility in answering research questions in both criminology and victimology.

International

The ***United Nations Office on Drugs and Crime*** (UNODC) was formed in 1997 when the United Nations Drug Control Programme was merged with the Centre for International Crime Prevention. UNODC has many functions, one of which includes conducting research and producing estimates on the extent and nature of drug and crime problems among United Nations member nations. UNODC provides information on crimes such as corruption, drug trafficking, firearms crimes, crimes involving fraudulent medicines, human trafficking, migrant smuggling, money laundering, organized crime, piracy, terrorism, and wildlife and forest crimes.

The crime data collected by UNODC are obtained through available data sources, which vary depending on the type of crime under consideration. For example, in the UNODC global study on homicide, records generated by national and international agencies, such as Interpol, Eurostat, UNICEF, and the World Health Organization, were used in describing the volume and character of international homicide. In sum, data from 207 countries were used to produce the international homicide statistics included in the report. Figure 4-3 includes a map of homicide rates throughout the world for 2010. The report indicates that there were an estimated 468,000 international homicides in 2010, which equates to a homicide rate of 6.9 per 100,000 population; a third of them (36%) occurred in Africa (UNODC, 2011).

It is important to point out, however, that not all of the information compiled by UNODC is based on official crime data produced by law enforcement, and a

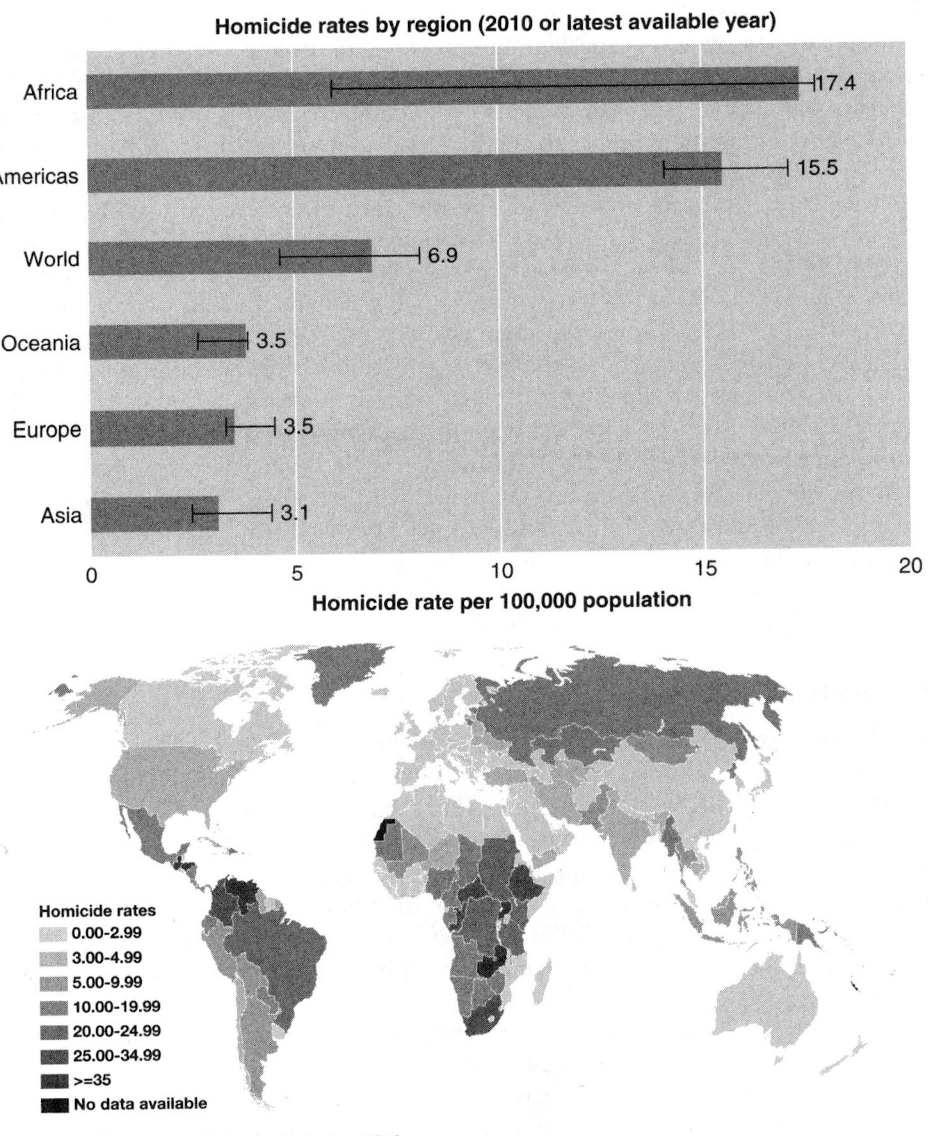

Figure 4-3 International Homicide Rates, 2010
Source: UNODC (2011).

significant component of the research wing of the organization involves surveys of offending, victimization, and criminal justice system operations. For example, a 2013 report on corruption in Afghanistan was based on a survey of a nationally representative sample of the adult population of the country. One of the key findings of the survey was that in 2012, half of Afghan citizens paid a bribe to obtain a public service. Further, those paying bribes for services paid an average of 5.6 bribes each at a cost of about $214 per incident. All told, the report estimated that bribes paid to public officials amounted to $3.9 billion in 2012 (UNODC, 2012a). Another UNODC project used several data sources (e.g., police agencies, surveys of governments) to describe the international state of human trafficking (UNDOC, 2012b). The UNODC report found that about 60% of trafficking victims are women and 27% are children (Fig. 4.4). Of the trafficking cases uncovered, 58% were for sexual exploitation, 36% were for forced labor, and 1.5% were for begging (see Fig. 4.4). Victims were found living in 118 countries between 2007 and 2010.

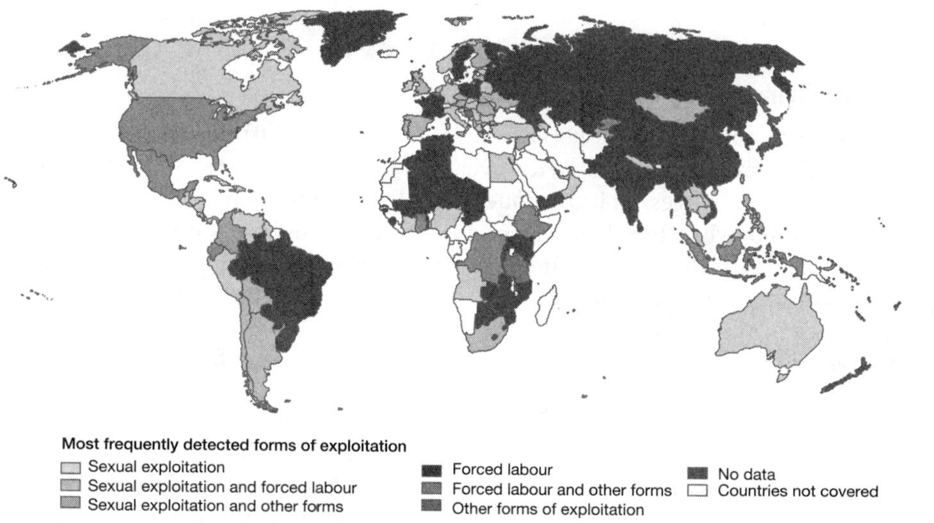

Figure 4-4 Forms of Exploitation by Country, 2007–2010
Source: UNODC (2012b).

UNODC also collects survey data on an annual basis with its ***United Nations Survey of Crime Trends and Operations of Criminal Justice Systems*** (UN-CTS). This survey has been administered 11 times to United Nations member nations' governments, most recently covering 2007–2008. The UN-CTS includes a main questionnaire (or survey), mostly focused on crime statistics and with the components of countries' criminal justice systems (e.g., police, prosecution, courts, and prisons). The survey also includes modules that collect information on selected crime issues. For instance, the most recent UN-CTS module topics were trafficking in persons and protection against illicit trafficking in cultural property.

The data produced by UNODC provide a barometer for crime throughout the world but have limited value for victimologists interested in identifying risk factors for victimization or developing and testing theories. There are many challenges associated with estimating the extent of world crime. First, universal definitions of crime do not exist across countries, which makes data collection and analysis difficult. Second, in some countries there is resistance to producing and publishing crime statistics. Third, like all official statistics, much of the data collected and published by UNODC are generated through law enforcement agencies, and citizen reporting behaviors will differ from country to country, affecting the official levels of crime recorded. Further, police agencies have different procedures for recording and reporting on crimes, not only within countries but across countries. This makes it difficult to compare crime rate estimates internationally.

There are several other sources of international crime data and data on criminal justice operations, such as Interpol, the Eurostat Division of the European Commission, and the European Institute for Crime Prevention and Control. While not all of these sources can be reviewed in this text, another important source of victimization data are general crime victimization surveys, which are discussed in forthcoming sections.

General Crime Victimization Surveys

Since the early 19th century, scholars have had an interest in collecting statistics related to criminal victimization. However, this area of scholarship was not without controversy or challenges, as it continues to be for contemporary victimologists. As previously noted, while the UCR is a potential source of information about crime in the United States, it does not include a great deal of information related to victims or victimization. Therefore, scholars interested in these issues were left to collect their own victimization data (e.g., Fitzpatrick & Kanin, 1957).

Recognizing the deficiencies in official crime statistics, combined with the need for more information about criminal victimization, the President's Commission on Law Enforcement and the Administration of Justice undertook three studies to better understand the scope of criminal victimization. The first of these was a self-report study of criminal victimization among individuals living in three police districts in Washington, DC. A ***self-report study*** is one in which research participants answer questions about their behaviors and experiences, often by taking a survey. In this case, participants answered questions about their victimization experiences. The second study focused on crimes occurring against businesses and organizations in high-crime areas of Washington, DC, Boston, and Chicago to gauge the extent of criminal victimization among participants. The largest of the three studies was a national-level self-report victimization survey conducted by the National Opinion Research Center that included respondents from 10,000 randomly selected households. The results from each of these studies suggested that statistics compiled by the UCR underrepresented the extent of crime in the United States. Specifically, the results indicated that twice as many incidents of personal violence and property victimization were occurring than were reported to police and, therefore, were included in the UCR (Mosher, Miethe, & Hart, 2011). Thus, the concerns expressed by criminologists and victimologists about the accuracy of official statistics as a measure of crime were confirmed.

The three studies underscored the importance of having independent sources of crime and victimization data that did not rely on whether victims reported their victimizations to the police. Consequently, a series of test studies was undertaken to identify and develop techniques for administering the ***National Crime Survey*** (NCS), the forerunner to today's ***National Crime Victimization Survey*** (NCVS), the primary source for victimization data and statistics in the United States. The NCVS and other large-scale general victimization surveys provide estimates of the extent and nature of victimization that do not rely on victim reporting behaviors or police recording practices, and thereby address the dark figure of crime. Similar to official sources of crime data, victimization surveys report the extent of victimization in terms of rates. The notable difference is that while official statistics describe rates of *offending* per a particular population unit (e.g., per 100,000 individuals), victimization rates describe how many *victimizations* occurred per a particular population unit (e.g., per 1,000 individuals). We will review the NCVS next, followed by discussion of similar general victimization surveys from other countries.

United States

Following the previously described test studies, the U.S. federal government reached a decision that there was a need for the permanent collection of victimization data in the United States that would supplement the UCR. Thus, the NCS was created for the purposes of providing estimates of victimization and related experiences in the United States, acting as a complementary measure of crime to the UCR, supplying information on other criminal justice issues not typically available from other sources (e.g., attitudes about police efficiency, victim reporting decisions), and more. The NCS was first administered in 1972, and at the time consisted of three components: (1) a national-level survey of households throughout the nation; (2) a household survey from 26 major cities; and (3) a survey of businesses. Each of these surveys was designed to provide estimates of the extent of criminal victimization throughout the United States. However, due to the enormous costs involved with completing three surveys and concerns over how efficiently the data were being collected, beginning in 1977 only the survey of households was retained (Rand, 2005). Over the years, the NCS continued to evolve (e.g., reduced sample size, changes to question wording) and in 1992 it underwent the first of several major redesigns.

As part of the 1992 redesign of the NCS, its name was changed to the National Crime Victimization Survey (NCVS) to more accurately reflect its emphasis on victimization rather than crime. Other changes to the survey included new strategies to aid respondents with comprehending and remembering incidents of victimization; adding questions relating to new types of victimization such as rape, sexual assault, and domestic violence; adding questions reflecting lifestyle and routine activity behaviors of victims; implementing new technologies to partially replace in-person interviews; and reducing the sample size from 72,000 households to 58,700 households (Rennison & Rand, 2007). Since the large-scale 1992 redesign of the NCVS, the survey has continued to undergo revisions, mostly aimed at further reducing costs (e.g., further reducing sample size) and expanding the survey to address emerging issues in victimology. Topical supplements to the standard NCVS survey have also been added, addressing such issues as hate crimes, victimization of individuals with disabilities, computer-related victimization, identity theft, stalking, school crime, and workplace victimizations.

Today, the NCVS reaches a nationally representative cross-section of the population of the United States, with two provisions. First, certain persons are not included, notably armed service personnel living in military barracks, U.S. citizens living abroad, and institutionalized persons (e.g., prison inmates). Second, those younger than 12 years old are not eligible to participate in the NCVS. These exceptions aside, most experts agree that the NCVS provides accurate estimates on the scope and nature of criminal victimization among residents of the United States.

NCVS data are collected through a self-report incident-based survey administered to household members over the age of 12 who have been selected for inclusion in the sample. The NCVS uses what is known as a stratified, multi-stage cluster sampling design to select households (and members of them) to participate. Despite its complexity, it is important to understand how victimization estimates are produced in the NCVS, so the sampling procedure is briefly described in the following sections.

First, ***primary sampling units*** consisting of counties, groups of counties, or other large metropolitan areas are stratified (grouped) according to shared geographic and demographic characteristics of their populations (e.g., age, race, and sex). Certain of these primary sampling units are automatically included, while others are randomly selected for inclusion. In the second stage of sampling, the automatically included and selected sampling units are further divided into what are referred to as ***sampling frames***, which are generated from the U.S. Census based on household addresses. From these frames, several ***clusters***, composed of up to four housing units, are then selected. From the selected housing units, all members of each household age 12 and older take the survey. Table 4-4 provides the number of households and persons interviewed in the NCVS from 1996 to 2007, along with corresponding response rates (i.e., rates of participation).

The very first time individuals participate in the NCVS, it is through face-to-face interviews in which an interviewer asks the respondent survey questions and records his or her answers using a paper-and-pencil questionnaire; subsequent administrations are conducted through ***computer-assisted telephone interviewing (CATI)***, which is essentially a "telemarketing method." With CATI, interviewers ask respondents questions over the telephone and enter their responses directly into a computerized questionnaire that exactly replicates the paper-and-pencil questionnaire. The survey itself consists of a basic screen questionnaire and an incident report.

For the ***basic screen questionnaire***, respondents provide various pieces of personal information (e.g., age, education, time at residence) as well as responses to questions related to whether the respondent had experienced a criminal victimization. The 2009–2011 NCVS-1 basic screen questionnaire included 12 pages and 80 questions (not including sub-questions). A sample of screen questions from the NCVS is presented in Figure 4-5.

Overall, the purpose of the screen questionnaire is to help respondents recall having experienced the victimization behaviors being measured. A separate ***incident report*** is then administered for each incident of criminal victimization uncovered in

Table 4-4: Number of Households and Persons Interviewed in the NCVS, 1996–2007

Number of Households and Persons Interviewed by Year				
Year	Household Response Rate	Response Rate for Persons	Number of Persons Interviewed	Response Rate for Persons
1996	45,000	93%	85,330	91%
1997	42,910	95%	79,470	90%
1998	43,000	94%	78,900	89%
1999	43,000	93%	77,750	89%
2000	43,000	93%	79,710	90%
2001	44,000	93%	79,950	89%
2002	42,000	92%	76,050	87%
2003	42,000	92%	74,520	86%
2004	42,000	91%	74,500	86%
2005	38,600	91%	67,000	84%
2006	38,000	91%	67,650	86%
2007	41,000	90%	73,650	86%

Source: Bureau of Justice Statistics (2013).

the basic screen questionnaire. These incident reports include questions on a range of issues related to the incident, including the victim, the offender, circumstances surrounding the crime, and the consequences for the respondent of each victimization. The 2009–2011 NCVS crime incident report consisted of 174 questions (not including sub-questions) and 37 pages.

The NCVS is administered every six months to participating households for a term of three years, at which time the household is replaced with another randomly selected household. The six-month survey interval is used for ***bounding***, which is a certain timeframe that respondents are asked to focus on when answering the questions. A six-month bounding period was selected because research suggests six months is the optimal amount of time in which respondents could accurately remember events while still ensuring the survey was cost-effective (Cantor & Lynch, 2000).

Based on information collected through the NCVS, it is possible to estimate the incidence of victimization in the United States, not the prevalence. ***Incidence*** refers to the proportion of respondents who have been victims of a given crime within a specified time period, which is usually one year. General victimization surveys sometimes collect data sufficient to estimate the prevalence of victimization as well. ***Prevalence*** is similar to incidence but reflects the proportion of individuals who have *ever* experienced a particular crime in their lives. In both cases, victimization estimates are expressed as rates, which are calculated in the same manner as was discussed in the section on the UCR and presented in Figure 4-1. Currently, the NCVS

OMB No. 1121-0111: Approval Expires 09/30/2012

NOTICE - We are conducting this survey under the authority of Title 13, United States Code, Section 8. Section 9 of this law requires us to keep all information about you and your household strictly **confidential**. We may use this information only for statistical purposes. Also, Title 42, **Section 3732,** United States Code, authorizes the Bureau of Justice Statistics, Department of Justice, to collect information using this survey. Title 42, Sections 3789g and 3735, United States Code, also requires us to keep all information about you and your household strictly confidential. According to the Paperwork Reduction Act of 1995, no persons are required to respond to a collection of information unless such collection displays a valid OMB number.

Control number

PSU	Segment/Suffix	Sample designation/Suffix	Serial/ Suffix	HH No.	Spinoff Indicator

1. Field representative identification
201 Code | Name

2. Unit status
202 1 ☐ Unit in sample the previous enumeration period - Fill 3
2 ☐ Unit in sample first time this period - SKIP to 4

3. Household status - Mark first box that applies.
203 1 ☐ Same household interviewed the previous enumeration
2 ☐ Replacement household since the previous enumeration
3 ☐ Noninterview the previous enumeration
4 ☐ Other - Specify ________

4. Line number of household respondent
204 ________ Go to page 2

5. Group Quarters [GQ] type code
205 ________

6. Tenure
206 1 ☐ Owned or being bought 2 ☐ Rented for cash 3 ☐ No cash rent

7. Land Use
207 1 ☐ Urban 2 ☐ Rural

8. Farm Sales
208 X ☐ Item blank 1 ☐ $1,000 or more 2 ☐ Less than $1,000

9. Type of living quarters
Housing unit
209 1 ☐ House, apartment, flat
2 ☐ HU in nontransient hotel, motel, etc.
3 ☐ HU permanent in transient hotel, motel, etc
4 ☐ HU in rooming house
5 ☐ Mobile home or trailer with no permanent room added
6 ☐ Mobile home or trailer with one or more permanent rooms added
7 ☐ HU not specified above - Describe ________

OTHER unit
8 ☐ Quarters not HU in rooming or boarding house
9 ☐ Unit not permanent in transient hotel, motel, etc.
10 ☐ Unoccupied site for mobile home, trailer, or tent
11 ☐ Student quarters in college dormitory
12 ☐ OTHER unit not specified above - Describe ________

10a. Use of telephone
Location of phone - Mark first box that applies.
210 1 ☐ Phone in unit ....
2 ☐ Phone in common area (hallway, etc.) ....
3 ☐ Phone in another unit (neighbor, friend, etc.)
4 ☐ Work/office phone .... } Fill 10b
5 ☐ No phone - SKIP to 11a

10b. Is phone interview acceptable?
211 1 ☐ Yes 2 ☐ No 3 ☐ Refused to give number

11a. Number of housing units in structure
212 1 ☐ 1 - SKIP to 11c 2 ☐ 2 3 ☐ 3 4 ☐ 4 5 ☐ 5-9 6 ☐ 10+ 7 ☐ Mobile home/trailer - SKIP to 11c 8 ☐ Only OTHER units

11b. Direct outside access
213 1 ☐ Yes 2 ☐ No 3 ☐ DK X ☐ Item blank

11c. Restricted access
222 Gated or walled community 1 ☐ Yes 2 ☐ No X ☐ Item blank
223 Building with restricted access 1 ☐ Yes 2 ☐ No X ☐ Item blank

USCENSUSBUREAU

FORM NCVS-1
Implementation Date: (07-01-2008)

U.S. DEPARTMENT OF COMMERCE
Economics and Statistics Administration
U.S. CENSUS BUREAU

ACTING AS COLLECTING AGENT FOR THE BUREAU OF JUSTICE STATISTICS
U.S. DEPARTMENT OF JUSTICE

NATIONAL CRIME VICTIMIZATION SURVEY
NCVS-1 BASIC SCREEN QUESTIONNAIRE

12a. Household Income
214 1 ☐ Less than $5,000 2 ☐ $5,000 - 7,499 3 ☐ 7,500 - 9,999 4 ☐ 10,000 - 12,499 5 ☐ 12,500 - 14,999 6 ☐ 15,000 - 17,499 7 ☐ 17,500 - 19,999 8 ☐ 20,000 - 24,999 9 ☐ 25,000 - 29,999 10 ☐ 30,000 - 34,999 11 ☐ 35,000 - 39,999 12 ☐ 40,000 - 49,999 13 ☐ 50,000 - 74,999 14 ☐ 75,000 and over

12b. College/University
218 1 ☐ Yes 2 ☐ No

12c. Public Housing
219 X ☐ Item blank 1 ☐ Yes (public housing) 2 ☐ No (not public housing)

12d. Manager Verification of Public Housing
220
Able to verify: 1 ☐ Public housing 2 ☐ Not public housing
Unable to verify: 3 ☐ Telephone 4 ☐ Other - Specify

12e. American Indian Reservation or American Indian Lands
221 1 ☐ Yes 2 ☐ No

13. Proxy information - Fill for all proxy interviews

a. Proxy interview obtained for Line No.	b. Proxy respondent Name	Line No.	c. Reason (Enter code)
301		302	303
304		305	306
307		308	309
310		311	312

Codes for item 13c
1-12-13 years old and parent refused permission for self interview
2- Physically/mentally unable to answer
3- TA and won't return before closeout

14. Type Z noninterview

a. Interview not obtained for Line No.	b. Reason (Enter code)
313	314
315	316
317	318
319	320

Codes for item 14b
1-Never available
2-Refused ....
3-Physically/ mentally unable to answer-no proxy available
4-TA and no proxy available ....
5-Other ......
6-Office use only

Complete 17-28 for each Line No. in 14a

15a. Household members 12 years of age and OVER
321 ________ Total number

15b. Household members UNDER 12 years of age
322 ________ Total number 0 ☐ None

15c. Number of Type Z noninterview household members 12 years of age and OVER
332 ________ Total number 0 ☐ None

15d. Crime Incident Reports filled
323 ________ Total number of NCVS-2s filled 0 ☐ None

16. Changes in Household Composition

a. Line No.	b. Reason (Enter code)
324	325
326	327
328	329
330	331

Only enter changes discovered during the current enumeration

Fill BOUNDING INFORMATION

N C V S 1

Figure 4-5 Excerpt from NCVS Basic Screen Questionnaire
Source: NCVS, 2009–2011; http://www.bjs.gov/index.cfm?ty=dcdetail&iid=245#Questionnaires.

collects data on violent crimes, which include rape and sexual assault, robbery, aggravated and simple assault, and domestic violence, as well as the property crimes of household burglary, motor vehicle theft, and theft.

The NCVS and other general victimization surveys provide essential information for victimologists to study the extent and nature of victimization. However, no research endeavor is perfect, and victimization surveys are not without their limitations. The shared limitations of victimization surveys are discussed later in the chapter. General victimization surveys also are used in other countries and are important sources of victimization data for researchers studying victimization outside the United States. Selected international surveys, including the International Crime Victims Survey, the European Crime and Safety Survey, and the Crime Survey for England and Wales, are reviewed in succeeding sections. Other countries, such as Canada, Australia, and Scotland, to name a few, also have general victimization surveys, which students are encouraged to read about independently.

International

International Crime Victims Survey

The ***International Crime Victims Survey*** (ICVS) is a self-report victimization survey that measures victimization in different countries across the world. The survey was designed and implemented by European criminologists, notably Jan Van Dijk, and has been administered five times: in 1989, 1992, 1996, 2000–2002, and 2004–2005. The ICVS was designed to provide information on criminal victimization internationally that is free of the many problems inherent in using official sources of crime data when making cross-country comparisons. Over the five administrations of the ICVS, over 320,000 individuals have been interviewed in 78 countries; however, the countries participating in the survey differed from round to round (van Dijk, 2008). For example, the first round of the ICVS in 1989 included 14 countries, whereas in 1996 48 countries were included in the survey.

Participants in the ICVS were chosen based on a random-digit dialing sample procedure, which involves a random selection of telephone numbers, rather than selection from a list (sampling frame), such as a telephone directory. Those selected for inclusion in the ICVS were usually administered the survey through CATI, in which case 2,000 residents of a particular country were interviewed. In countries without a sufficient distribution of landline telephones, the ICVS was administered face to face in the nation's capital city. In those instances, ICVS samples included 1,000 to 1,500 respondents. Among households selected for inclusion in the ICVS, one household member age 16 or above was interviewed regarding his or her victimization experiences as well as those of other household members. The ICVS questionnaire has been translated into the languages of all countries that have participated and measures different types of common crimes that have shared definitions across the countries.

Crimes contained in the ICVS included theft of car, theft from car, car vandalism, theft of motorcycle, theft of bicycle, burglary, attempted burglary, robbery, theft of personal property, sexual incidents, assault/threats, consumer fraud, and bribery/corruption. Figure 4-6 illustrates the extent of worldwide victimization, mapping out the percentage of a country's population that experienced any of the common crimes included in the ICVS. In addition to estimating the volume of world crime, the ICVS also asked respondents about related criminal justice issues, such as the causes of crime, victim reporting practices, satisfaction with police, and the consequences of crime for victims.

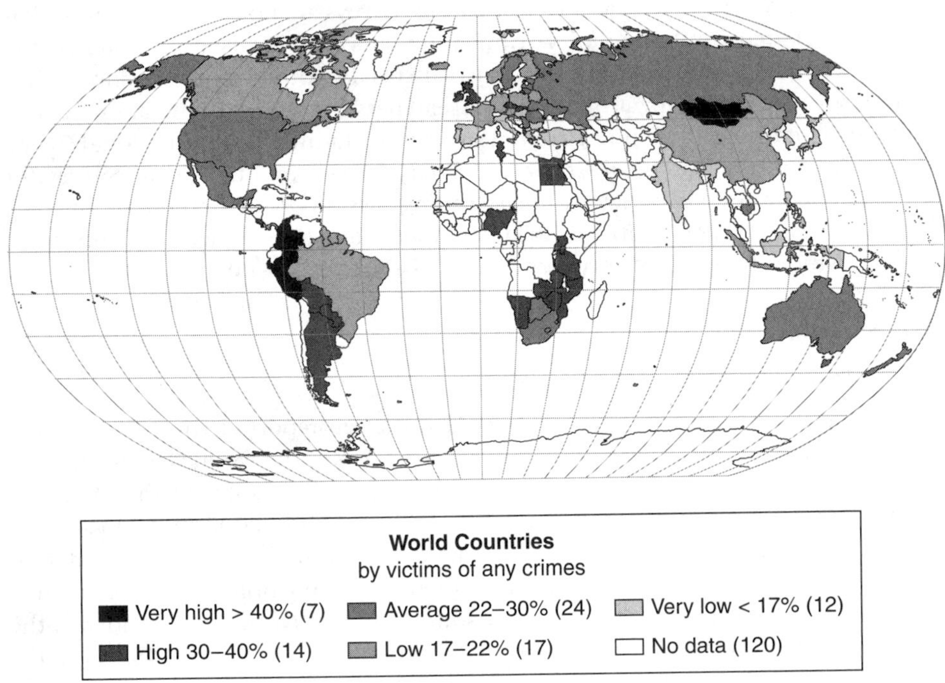

Figure 4-6 ICVS Estimates of Worldwide Victimization
Source: Van Dijk (2008).

European Crime and Safety Survey

The ***European Crime and Safety Survey*** (EU ICS) can be considered a successor to the ICVS but was aimed at estimating the extent and nature of victimization in Europe. The EU ICS was a self-report victimization survey administered in 2005 among the 15 member states of the European Union, as well as Poland, Hungary, and Estonia (the 18 participating countries in the EU ICS are listed in Box 4-1). Like the NCVS, the EU ICS interviewed participants using CATI and Internet-based CATI that allowed the survey to be translated and administered in several languages. The EU ICS was methodologically similar to the ICVS as well. For instance, EU ICS respondents were chosen through random-digit dialing, and for most countries, 2,000 residents over the age of 16 were selected and included in the survey. Response rates to the EU ICS ranged from 36% in Luxembourg to 57% in Finland, with an average of 47% for all countries except Poland, where the survey was administered face to face.

The victimization rates estimated by the EU ICS reflected rates for those over 16 years old who were victimized in 2004. Crimes included were categorized as

Box 4-1: Countries Included in the EU ICS

- Austria
- Belgium
- Denmark
- Estonia
- Finland
- France
- Germany
- Greece
- Ireland
- Italy
- Luxembourg
- The Netherlands
- Poland
- Portugal
- Spain
- Sweden
- United Kingdom (England, Wales, Scotland, and Northern Ireland)

vehicle-related (e.g., motor vehicle theft, bicycle theft, thefts from cars), theft and burglary (e.g., personal property, pickpocketing), contact crimes (e.g., robbery, sexual offenses), hate crimes, and nonconventional crimes (e.g., consumer fraud, corruption). The survey also asked respondents about their fear of crime, perceived risk of victimization, reporting practices, security precautions, and attitudes toward the police. Although the survey produced too many findings to review in their entirety in this textbook, a few of the highlights suggest that nearly 15% of the population of the 18 EU countries had been victims of crime in 2004. Figure 4-7 displays country victimization rates, with darker-colored countries having the highest victimization among their citizens. The countries with the highest victimization rates were Ireland, the United Kingdom, Estonia, the Netherlands, Denmark, and Belgium. The EU ICS also indicated that there were no relationships between a country's wealth or economic equality and its victimization rate, but victimization was associated with urbanization and the proportion of young adolescents in the populations (EU ICS Report, 2005).

Crime Survey for England and Wales

Although England has participated in both the ICVS and the EU ICS, it also has its own general victimization survey called the ***Crime Survey for England and Wales*** (CSEW). Formerly named the ***British Crime Survey*** (BCS), the CSEW is a general self-report victimization survey that is administered annually to residents of England and Wales. The BCS was first carried out in 1982 in England, Wales, and Scotland and was intended to provide estimates of the dark figure of crime in these countries. Besides producing victimization estimates, the BCS also was designed to identify

Figure 4-7 Victimization Across EU ICS Countries in 2004
Source: EU ICS Report (2005).

risk factors for victimization and measure residents' fear of criminal victimization, perceptions of victimization risk, and contact with the police (Jansson, 2006). After its introduction in 1982, the BCS was administered in 1984, 1988, 1992, 1994, 1996, 1998, 2000, 2001, and every year since.

Following the commission of the Scottish Crime and Victimization Survey, the BCS was renamed in 2012 to reflect its coverage of England and Wales exclusively. In Figure 4-8 victimization trends over the life of the BCS and CSEW are compared against crime recorded by police. As the figure clearly illustrates, the survey has captured a large volume of crime that otherwise would have remained in the dark.

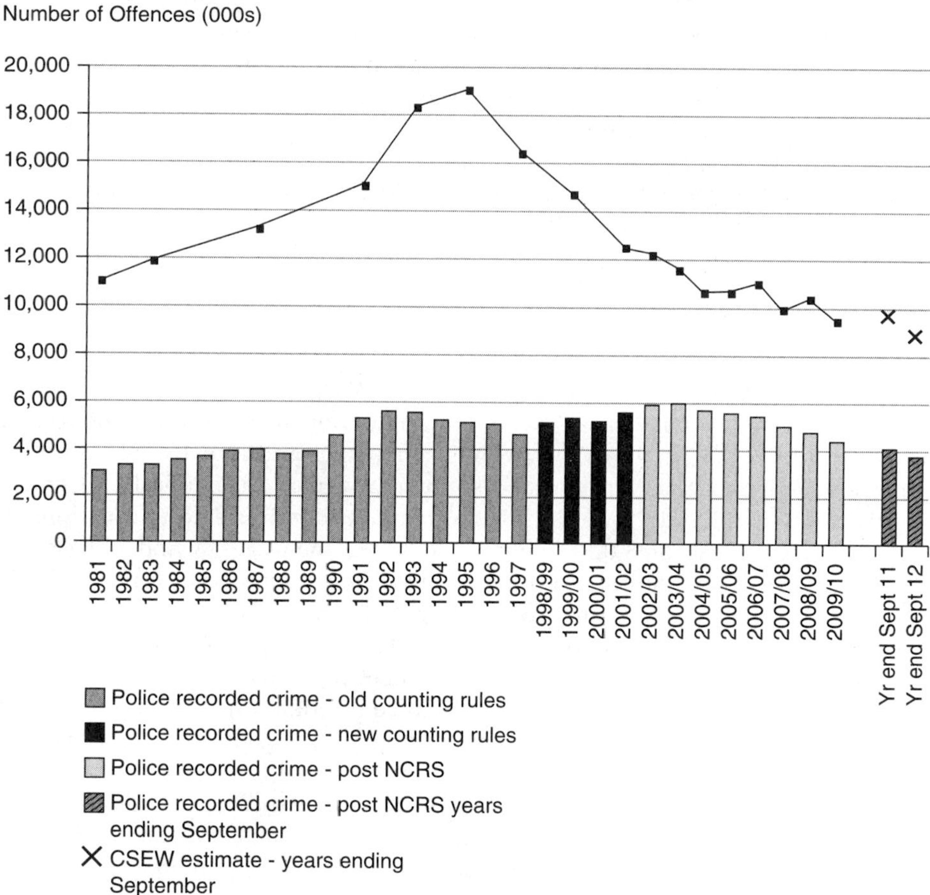

Figure 4-8 Comparison of CSEW Data and Police Recorded Crime, 1981–2001
Source: Crime Survey for England and Wales—Office for National Statistics, Home Office.

Similar to the NCVS, the CSEW uses a stratified cluster sampling design to obtain a representative sample of residents of England and Wales aged 16 or older to participate in the survey. The questionnaire includes modules, consisting of sets of questions. Some of these modules are asked of all members of the sample, while others are asked of sub-samples of the overall sample of respondents (e.g., young adults). Respondents are asked about their crime-related experiences in the year prior to the survey through face-to-face interviews and computer-assisted self-interviewing. Historically, the BCS has played an important part in the development of victimology. In particular, the BCS included questions reflecting respondents' lifestyles and routine activities, and the resulting data allowed criminologists and victimologists to conduct some of the earliest tests of the theories (e.g., Maxfield, 1987; Sampson & Wooldredge, 1987).

Specialized Crime Victimization Surveys

The previously described victimization surveys include many types of victimization, but there also are specialized surveys that are concerned only with specific types of crimes, or particular populations of victims not well represented in general victimization surveys (e.g., the elderly or the very young). These types of surveys have been administered in the United States (e.g., the National College Women Sexual Victimization Survey) and internationally (e.g., the International Violence Against Women Survey). Select examples of specialized victimization surveys for each group are reviewed in the following sections.

United States

National Violence Against Women Survey

The ***National Violence Against Women Survey*** (NVAWS) is a specialized self-report victimization survey that focused exclusively on the violent victimization of women in the United States. The NVAWS was conducted in 1995 and 1996 by the Center for Policy Research in partnership with the National Institute of Justice and the Centers for Disease Control and Prevention. The survey was administered to a nationally representative sample of 8,000 women and 8,000 men age 18 and older from throughout the nation. Similar to other victimization surveys, the NVAWS sample was generated through random-digit dialing of households in all 50 states and Washington, DC. Also, the survey was administered through CATI and had a participation (response) rate of 72% for females and 69% for males.

The NVAWS asked survey participants detailed information about rape, physical assault, and stalking victimization, including questions about the consequences victims suffered as a result of a specific offender's behavior. The NVAWS used behaviorally specific screen questions to ensure that respondents had no doubt about what they were being asked (Tjaden & Thoennes, 2000). Box 4-2 includes an example of a behaviorally specific screen question used in the survey to identify respondents as having experienced stalking. Notice that the question itself does *not* include the word "stalking." If respondents answered *yes* to any of the questions, they were asked follow-up questions about whether the behaviors occurred on more than one occasion, and whether they were very frightened or feared bodily harm as a result. Positive answers to each of these items meant the individual may have been a victim of stalking. Those who answered *no* to the initial screen question were skipped ahead to other survey questions. Similar procedures were followed for the rape and physical assault portions of the survey.

Box 4-2: Example of a Behaviorally Specific Screen Question from the NVAWS

Not including bill collectors, telephone solicitors, or other salespeople, has anyone, male or female, ever...

- Followed or spied on you?
- Sent you unsolicited letters or written correspondence?
- Made unsolicited phone calls to you?
- Stood outside your home, school, or workplace?
- Showed up at places you were even though he or she had no business being there?
- Left unwanted items for you to find?
- Tried to communicate in other ways against your will?
- Vandalized your property or destroyed something you loved?

Source: Tjaden and Thoennes (2000)

The NVAWS was designed to provide estimates of the annual incidence and lifetime prevalence of victimization that could be compared with other victimization surveys, such as the NCVS. The survey produced too much information to review here, but key findings from the NVAWS revealed that over 50% of women and over 65% of men surveyed had been physically assaulted at some time in their lives. Further, about 17% of women in the survey had been victims of attempted or completed rape during their lifetime, and approximately 54% of these were under 18 years old at the time of the incident (Tjaden & Thoennes, 2000). Regarding stalking, about 8% of women and 2% of men surveyed indicated they had been stalked during their lives. Findings from the NVAWS are highlighted in several upcoming chapters of the textbook.

National College Women Sexual Victimization Survey

The ***National College Women Sexual Victimization Survey*** (NCWSV) is a specialized self-report victimization survey covering the victimization of college women in the United States that was conducted by Bonnie Fisher, Francis Cullen, and Michael Turner in 1997. This study included a nationally representative sample of over 4,000 college women who were attending two- or four-year colleges or universities during the fall of 1996. The survey for the NCWSV study was administered through CATI by female interviewers in 1997 and had a response rate of about 85%. Similar to the NCVS, the NCWSV study included victimization screen questions and incident reports.

The NCWSV study was designed to measure the extent of sexual victimization and stalking among college women in the United States. The types of sexual victimization included in the NCWSV survey were attempted and/or completed rape, sexual coercion, unwanted sexual contact, noncontact verbal abuse, and noncontact visual abuse. Respondents were also asked if someone had threatened to rape or sexually victimize them in some other way. In addition to examining these types of victimization, the survey also included incident-level questions about offenders, the circumstances under which sexual victimizations against this population occur, protective behaviors taken by victims, and whether victims reported the incident to the police.

This study produced several important findings related to the criminal victimization of college women. First and foremost, 2.8% of the women were victims of either completed or attempted rape, which translates into a victimization rate of 27.7 rapes per 1,000 female college students (Fisher, Cullen, & Turner, 2000). Put differently, for every 1,000 female students on your campus, nearly 30 are at risk for rape each year. If your college or university has 5,000 female students, that translates to 150 completed or attempted rapes annually. Interestingly, of those women who were victims of a completed rape, less than half (46%) considered themselves to be victims of rape (the issue of victim acknowledgment of criminal victimization is discussed in detail in Chapter 10). Most of the rapes in the NCWSV study were perpetrated by classmates, followed by friends, and boyfriends/ex-boyfriends. Regarding stalking, 13.1% of the sample were victimized since the beginning of school the year the survey was administered. This estimate translates to a victimization rate of 156.5 per 1,000 female students. These stalking estimates are higher than those found in the NVAWS, but this study focused exclusively on college women, raising the question of whether this population is more at risk for being stalked than are women generally (stalking is discussed in greater depth in Chapter 5).

National Intimate Partner and Sexual Violence Survey

The ***National Intimate Partner and Sexual Violence Survey*** (NISVS) is a specialized self-report victimization survey that was conducted by the National Center for Injury Prevention and Control of the Centers for Disease Control and Prevention in 2010. Building upon the NVAWS, the NISVS estimated the prevalence and incidence of several types of sexual violence, stalking, and intimate partner violence in the United States. The NISVS used random-digit dialing to generate a sample of 18,049 U.S. men and women aged 18 or older from the 50 states and Washington, DC. In keeping with the rapid pace of technological advancement, about 45% of the interviews were conducted on landline telephones, whereas the other 55% were completed using the respondent's cellphone.

The NISVS includes some of the most methodologically rigorous and up-to-date information on intimate partner and sexual violence. For example, according to the survey results, in the United States 24 people per minute are victims of rape, stalking, or physical violence by an intimate partner (e.g., spouse, boyfriend). The survey found that nearly 1 in 5 women and 1 in 71 men have been raped at some time in their lives. Among women, over half of victims were raped by an intimate partner. For stalking victimization, 1 in 6 women and 1 in 19 men have been victimized during the course of their lives, and two thirds of female victims were stalked by a current or former intimate partner. Regarding other forms of intimate partner violence, the study reported that nearly 1 in 4 women and 1 in 7 men have experienced severe physical violence of some kind during their lives, such as being beaten or slammed against something. The data produced in the NISVS also allowed for calculations of recurring victimization, which occurs when an individual is victimized two or more times (recurring victimization is described in detail in Chapter 9). Although the majority of victims experienced physical violence only, according to Figure 4-9, 12.5% of female victims in the study experienced rape, physical violence, and stalking during their lifetime.

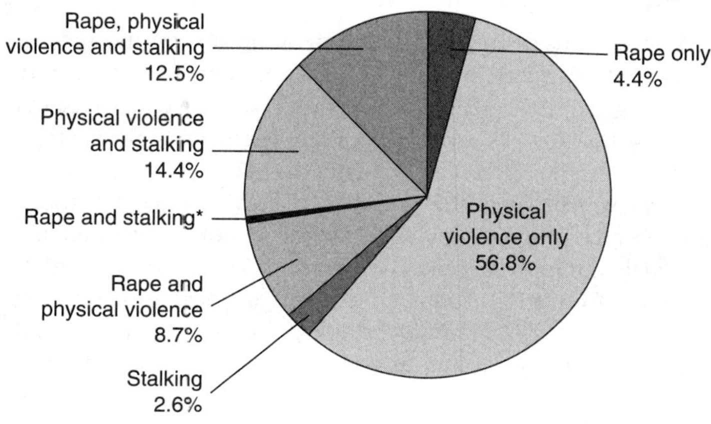

Figure 4-9 Overlap in Victimization Among Female Victims in NISVS
Source: Black et al. (2011).

International

The ***International Violence Against Women Survey*** (IVAWS) is an international self-report victimization survey that estimates violence perpetrated against women by men. The IVAWS has been administered in more than 30 countries, representing all continents, and across administrations of the survey, over 23,000 women have been interviewed. The IVAWS is coordinated by the European Institute for Crime Prevention and Control, which is affiliated with the United Nations, and relies on the existing networks, methodology, and infrastructure used in the ICVS. The most recent IVAWS data, which were published in 2008, were based on information from 11 countries: Australia, Costa Rica, the Czech Republic, Denmark, Greece, Hong Kong, Italy, Mozambique, the Philippines, Poland, and Switzerland (Johnson, Ollus, & Nevala, 2008).

Major findings from the 2008 publication of the IVAWS disclosed that violence against women by men affects between 24% and 73% of women in participating countries. Total violence against women, which entails having experienced at least one incident of physical or sexual violence, was most prevalent in Costa Rica (73%) and least prevalent in the Philippines (24%). On average, the lifetime prevalence of violence across all participating countries was over 35%. This means that approximately 35% of women in these countries have been criminally victimized by men. Similarly, rates of lifetime intimate partner violence from these countries ranged between 9% and 40%. Countries with the highest rates of intimate partner violence were Mozambique, Costa Rica, and the Czech Republic; countries with the lowest rates were Hong Kong, the Philippines, and Switzerland. Interestingly, among those who were victimized by intimate partners, victims in Mozambique had the lowest percentages of physical injuries, while those in the Czech Republic had the highest (Johnson et al., 2008).

Issues in Victimization Research

As the preceding sections demonstrate, victimization surveys, both general and specialized, are used extensively in the field of victimology to collect information on issues surrounding criminal victimization and to produce data that can examine its correlates and test theories. The previously reviewed surveys are a sampling of some of the well-known large-scale surveys that have been administered by victimologists, but many surveys were not included in the discussion. Noteworthy, too, is that much victimization research relies on smaller-scale surveys of single populations, such as students in a particular high school or college. Although the results of many of these surveys are limited to specific groups, they nevertheless address important research questions in victimology that cannot otherwise be answered. After all, not every survey can include every important question related to criminal victimization.

The previously described surveys, influential and important as they are, also have their limitations. These limitations are described in the following section, which addresses some of the challenges that are associated with survey research in victimology. Following this, innovations in victimization and survey research that have broadened victimologists' understanding of crime victims are discussed briefly.

Challenges in Victimization Survey Research

One of the perpetual challenges in conducting victimization research involves defining and then operationalizing criminal victimization. This issue is perhaps most apparent when considering the various definitions and measurement choices that have been used to study rape victimization. For most of its 80-year history, the UCR defined rape as the carnal knowledge of a female forcibly and against her will. This definition is problematic for several reasons. First, it assumes that the only people who experience rape are females. Second, it is not clear whether it includes both completed and attempted rapes. Third, it does not include statutory rapes (in which no force was used but the victim was under the legal age of consent), but this is not clear in the definition. Fourth, the language is not specific enough to determine which behaviors are considered to involve force. Does a verbal threat imply force? Fifth, the use of the phrase "carnal knowledge" implies penile–vaginal penetration, but rapes are also committed with objects or involve penetration of other orifices. The list of problems with this definition could go on, but the point is made: How a behavior is defined is a critically important stage in the research process.

Although the UCR does not include data collected through surveys, this example also applies to defining victimization in survey research. Namely, definitions directly affect how concepts will be measured in victimization surveys. In other words, questions are crafted based on definitions of certain behaviors. This makes survey question wording a crucial step in the research process.

In survey research, the form that questions take is how important research concepts are operationalized. This means that the quality of the data that are obtained from the survey hinges on how questions are worded, how they are asked (e.g., face to face, over the phone), and how they are interpreted by respondents. Consider the two survey questions in Box 4-3 that were used to measure rape victimization in two different surveys. Question number one allows the interviewee to determine for herself what constitutes a rape or an attempted rape and answer accordingly. Question number two does not use the word *rape* but instead describes the behavior. It is likely that if these two questions were asked of two different populations of women, they would produce two different estimates of the extent of rape victimization if for no other reason than the way they are worded. This example highlights the importance of question wording for measuring if someone has been a victim of rape, but these issues also apply to many other types of victimization that are measured in surveys (e.g., sexual assault, stalking, identity theft).

Another possible limitation of victimization survey research involves deciding who will be asked to take the survey—and therefore to whom the results will apply. Recall that the NCVS sampling design ensures that the survey is given to a representative cross-section of residents of the United States aged 12 and over. Since the sample is representative of the U.S. population generally, the resulting victimization estimates can be considered an accurate reflection of victimization nationally. But does the sampling design really generate a sample of research participants that is representative of the population to which the results should apply? For instance, imagine that for whatever reason the upcoming NCVS includes 80% females and 20% males. Since research consistently reports that males have higher victimization rates than females, the NCVS will most likely underestimate the true extent of victimization in the United States. As a further example, say one of the professors in the criminal justice department at your college or university surveys your class about students' experiences with theft on campus. Would you say that the results of this quick survey represent the experiences of all students at your university? Are they representative of all college students in your state, or across the nation? Overall, then, the quality of information gathered using surveys depends on the sample design, and whether those who participate in the survey truly represent the target population.

Box 4-3: Examples of Survey Questions Measuring Rape Victimization

1. "At any time in your life, have you ever been the victim of a rape or attempted rape?"
2. "Since school began in the Fall 1996, has anyone made you have sexual intercourse by using force or threatening to harm you or someone close to you? Just so there is no mistake, by intercourse I mean putting a penis in your vagina."

Sources: Fisher and Cullen (2000); Russell (1982).

As discussed, one of the potential weaknesses of surveys is that they are dependent on the researcher's definitions and question wording choices. The mode of data collection is also an element of survey research that affects results. As the earlier descriptions of various victimization surveys illustrated, there are many modes or methods for administering surveys, including through the mail, in person, over the telephone, and online. Even carefully constructed questionnaires will fail to produce useful data if the method of survey delivery is flawed, resulting in low rates of participation or questions that are not answered, what is called "missing data." It may be that when researching certain topics or surveying particular victim populations some modes of administration are more appropriate than others. For example, a victimologist interested in studying elder abuse may decide that an online survey is not an ideal method of reaching this population of victims due to their lack of computer proficiency or access. If individuals cannot or decide not to take the online survey, this would result in a low response rate, which can introduce bias into the study's results. A related issue involves the interviewers. For example, a female victim of intimate partner violence may be unwilling to discuss her victimization with a male interviewer, or vice versa. Therefore, researchers must also be mindful of how the choice of interviewers can affect survey results.

Using surveys to ask people about their experiences with criminal victimization can also raise ethical dilemmas. First, by asking victims to think about, acknowledge, and sometimes discuss their victimization, the survey research process may be intrusive and harmful to some victims because of the stress generated by remembering the event. Because of this, researchers will often include information at the beginning and/or end of the survey related to where respondents can seek victim services (e.g., health, legal). This is also one of many reasons why participation in research is voluntary. Second, if funds are available, some researchers provide incentives, such as money or a chance to win a prize in exchange for participation in a survey. The dilemma here is that an argument can be made that individuals are being coerced into participating, or made to feel an obligation to reveal personal information because they have been given an incentive. For example, imagine that you return home from school and find a survey from a well-known company in your mail. You also notice that there is a five-dollar bill offered as an incentive to complete and return the survey. Do you now feel as if you must take the survey out of a sense of responsibility for accepting the money? Third, some victimization surveys are confidential while others are anonymous. Confidentiality suggests that researchers will be able to associate survey responses with the specific individuals who provided them, whereas anonymity means that they cannot. In both cases, there is an expectation that the researcher not disclose participants' identities without permission. Researchers have an ethical obligation to ensure that if confidentiality or anonymity were promised to participants, this promise be honored.

Neglected Forms of Victimization and Victim Populations

This chapter has demonstrated that there are many data sources, both nationally and internationally, that provide information on the extent and nature of criminal victimization. In spite of this abundance of data, there are still many forms of victimization (e.g., human trafficking, bride burning, genital mutilation) for which reliable data are not available. As such, there is much that is not known about these types of victimization. There are also populations of victims that are not well represented in current sources of victimization data, such as the homeless and lesbian/gay/bisexual/transgender/queer (LGBTQ) individuals. Thus, the amount of victimization against these populations and the circumstances surrounding their victimization are not well documented. Further, although international sources of data such as the ICVS and IVAWS reach far and wide, there are many countries (e.g., Iran) that do not participate in these surveys or have their own victimization surveys. As a result, little is known about criminal victimizations against people who live in these nations.

There are many types of criminal victimization for which extensive data are not available. This section reviews a few of these, recognizing that the discussion of neglected forms of victimization is far from comprehensive. Global violence against women and children is an issue in victimology needing not only much research, but also prevention efforts. Violent acts such as bride burning, genital mutilation, and human trafficking disproportionately affect females throughout the world. For example, in India it is still a common practice for a bride's parents to pay a dowry to her new in-laws on the occasion of her marriage. In cases of bride burning, the husband or his family consider the dowry to be insufficient and douse the victim in gasoline or another flammable substance and set her on fire. According to India's National Crime Records Bureau (2013) there were nearly 8,600 reported cases of bride burning in India in 2011.

Another global crime committed against females is known as female genital mutilation. The World Health Organization (2014, p.1) defines this as "all procedures that involve partial or total removal of the external female genitalia, or other injury to the female genital organs for non-medical reasons." Female genital mutilation is considered a human rights violation that has no health benefits for victims and has been carried out on millions of girls and women worldwide. For instance, in Africa it is estimated that 101 million females age 10 and over have undergone it (World Health Organization, 2013).

Human trafficking is a term that is used to describe several forms of modern-day slavery. Victims of human trafficking are compelled into service through forced labor, sex trafficking, bonded labor, debt bondage, involuntary domestic servitude, forced child labor, child sex trafficking, or by using children as soldiers. According to the U.S. State Department's 2010 Trafficking in Persons report, there are 12.3 million children and adults in forced or bonded labor and forced prostitution around the world (U.S. State Department, 2010). Of these victims, 56% are women and girls. The report further estimates the prevalence of human trafficking to be 1.8 per 1,000 inhabitants, and nearly twice this—3 per 1,000 inhabitants—in Asia. More recent estimates from the State Department (2014) suggest that there are as many as 20 million victims of human trafficking in the world. To put these figures in context, the most recent NCVS report estimated the robbery victimization rate in the United States to be 2.2 per 1,000 residents (Truman & Planty, 2012). Although data on human trafficking are difficult to obtain, the State Department noted a 59% increase in trafficking victims from the previous year.

These neglected forms of victimization and many others (e.g., female infanticide, honor killings) are not included in victimization surveys, nor are they regularly reported to law enforcement. This leaves victimologists with the challenge of developing innovative methods to study and prevent these hidden forms of victimization. An additional challenge that victimologists face is studying the criminal victimization of individuals and populations with special characteristics. One such group is the homeless. Opportunity theories suggest that homeless individuals should be at high risk for criminal victimization because of their increased exposure and proximity to motivated offenders and an absence of guardianship. Yet, little is known about the circumstances surrounding the victimization of the homeless. These individuals are not included in the NCVS and are otherwise a difficult-to-reach population. Crimes against the homeless are included in official crime statistics such as the UCR, but information on the homeless status of victims is not collected, so it is not possible to distinguish their victimizations from those of the general population.

Another group of crime victims for which data are not readily available are LGBTQ victims. The *Hate Crimes Statistics Act of 1990* requires the U.S. Department of Justice to collect and publish hate crime statistics annually. As a result, the annual reports provide a glimpse of victimization against this group, but more data are needed for several reasons. First, not all hate crimes are reported to law enforcement, so not all hate crimes against LGBTQ individuals will be represented in hate crime statistics. Second, not all victimizations against LGBTQ persons are motivated by hate, and these, therefore, are excluded from the Department of Justice reports. Third, crimes that are reported to the police will appear in official statistics, but like victimization of the homeless, there is no way to separate LGBTQ victims from other victims to examine their unique victimization circumstances. Further, since the NCVS does not ask respondents about sexual orientation, national information on victimization of LGBTQ individuals is in short supply. Offender bias motivations for hate crimes, including sexual orientation, are depicted in Figure 4-10 for the years 2003–2006 and 2007–2011. Smaller-scale studies and surveys indicate that LGBTQ individuals have a higher risk of victimization than those who are not LGBTQ, but more research is needed to explain why this is the case (e.g., Pilkington & D'Augelli, 1995; Toomey & Russell, 2013).

Although not every understudied group of crime victims can be reviewed here, the brief discussion of these two groups reinforces the argument that more research is necessary on certain victim populations (e.g., persons with disabilities, prisoners). In the same way, there are many countries for which official statistics are not reliable and that have no victimization surveys. International victimization surveys such as the ICVS and IVAWS provide some information on criminal victimization in these countries, but their reach does not extend to every country and population in the world. Consequently, these nations' victimization rates are not known.

Innovations in Survey Administration and Data Collection

Since early political polling began in the 1930s, social scientists have learned a great deal about survey research. In the world of criminal justice, the 1960s and 1970s brought a wave of new surveys designed to collect data on criminal victimization in

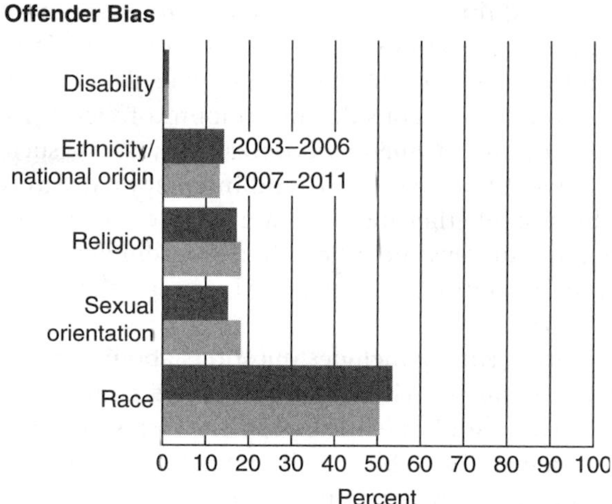

Figure 4-10 Hate Crime Victimization, 2003–2011
Source: Sandholtz, Langton, and Planty (2013).

the United States and internationally. Much like the early political pollsters, advancements have been made that allow victimologists to better understand who is victimized and why. One of these innovations is the behaviorally specific language that is now commonly used in victimization surveys. Boxes 4-2 and 4-3 provided examples of behaviorally specific victimization questions measuring stalking and sexual assault, respectively. Asking questions about victimization by describing the behavior rather than using the "crime label" not only helps victims recall details of their experience but also ensures that the respondent is not biased or put off by being labeled as a victim of stalking or a victim of rape.

Another innovation in victimization research has been the movement toward asking about a broader range of criminal victimizations. For example, the NCVS has fielded supplements on stalking and identity theft, two topics that until recently were not measured in the United States in either the NCVS or the UCR. A third innovation in victimization research has been including high-risk populations in surveys through targeted sampling. In other words, extra efforts are made to reach individuals who have a high risk for victimization. The CSEW, for example, now routinely includes a youth module to ensure that this group is well represented in the country's victimization estimates. These brief examples illustrate that improvements have been made over the years that result in more accurate and reliable victimization data. Future innovations will likely address many of the previously discussed challenges that are facing the field of victimology.

Summary

Victimologists scientifically study criminal victimization by collecting and examining data, identifying patterns in victimization, testing theories, developing victimization prevention strategies, and providing advocacy and services to those who have been victimized. Much of this would not be possible without the sources of victimization data reviewed throughout this chapter. Official sources of victimization data, such as the UCR and NIBRS, provide information on victimizations that are known to law enforcement, and can therefore be considered a baseline estimate of criminal victimization. Still, a considerable amount of victimization does not come to the attention of police. General victimization surveys, such as the NCVS and ICVS, are administered both nationally and internationally to collect data on victimization regardless of whether incidents are reported to the authorities. This way, general victimization surveys and official statistics complement each other and provide a broad portrait of criminal victimization by reporting crime and victimization rates.

Not every victimization survey includes questions about every type of victimization, which is why specialized victimization surveys such as the NVAWS and IVAWS are conducted. These studies focus on specific forms of victimization, such as violence against women, and are able to collect more in-depth and detailed information than is usually possible in generalized surveys.

Victimization data have greatly contributed to the growth and development of the field of victimology, but existing data sources have limits and more work is needed to overcome the challenges facing researchers in this area. These challenges include issues such as defining, measuring, and operationalizing victimization; sampling; ethical considerations; collecting data on neglected forms of victimization; reaching underserved populations; and obtaining victimization data on residents of countries without victimization surveys. Upcoming chapters use the data sources reviewed in this chapter to describe the extent and nature of victimization in the United States. Chapter 5 describes personal victimizations, such as homicide, assault, and robbery; Chapter 6 reviews the victimization of women, children, and the elderly; and Chapter 7 discusses property victimizations, such as burglary, theft, and identity theft. Keep in mind that without victimization data, there would be far more unanswered questions related to who is victimized, how and why they are victimized, and under what circumstances they become victims.

KEYWORDS

Official sources
Supplementary Homicide Report
United Nations Survey of Crime Trends and Operations of Criminal Justice Systems
Dark figure of crime
Series event
Self-report study
Crime rates
Hierarchy rule
National Crime Survey
Uniform Crime Reports
National Incident-Based Reporting System
National Crime Victimization Survey
Index crimes
United Nations Office on Drugs and Crime
Primary sampling units

Sampling frames	Incidence	National Violence Against Women Survey
Clusters	Prevalence	National College Women Sexual Victimization Survey
Computer-assisted telephone interviewing	International Crime Victims Survey	National Intimate Partner and Sexual Violence Survey
Basic screen questionnaire	European Crime and Safety Survey	International Violence Against Women Survey
Incident report	Crime Survey for England and Wales	
Bounding	British Crime Survey	

DISCUSSION QUESTIONS

1. Why is it a concern that the Uniform Crime Reports and National Incident-Based Reporting System only include data based on crimes that have come to the attention of law enforcement? How does this affect what is known about victimization?
2. How are self-report victimization surveys different than official sources of victimization data? Do they produce a different type of quality of information on victimization?
3. Can individuals' responses to surveys regarding their victimizations be regarded as valid and reliable? In other words, can they be trusted? Explain your answer.
4. Do you think the ICVS, which includes between 1,000 and 2,000 respondents from participating countries, can produce valid and reliable estimates of world crime? Explain your answer.
5. If you were designing a victimization survey, which types of victimization would you include? How would you define and measure victimization? Who would you administer your survey to, and how would you administer it? How would these decisions influence the findings that your survey ultimately generates?
6. Which of the two survey questions provided in Box 4-3 do you think would produce a more accurate estimate of rape victimization? How might you improve these two questions to produce a more accurate estimate of rape victimization? Explain your answer.
7. How can victimologists collect data on neglected forms of criminal victimization such as human trafficking or female genital mutilation?
8. How can victimologists collect data on special populations of victims such as the homeless or LGBTQ?

REFERENCES

Black, M. C., Basile, K. C., Breiding, M. J., Smith, S. G., Walters, M. L., Merrick, M. T., Chen, J., & Stevens, M. R. (2011). *The National Intimate Partner and Sexual Violence Survey: 2010 summary report.* Atlanta, GA: National Center for Injury Prevention and Control, Centers for Disease Control and Prevention.

Bureau of Justice Statistics. (2013). *Survey methodology for criminal victimization in the United States.* Retrieved April 24, 2013, from www.bjs.gov

Cantor, D., & Lynch, J.P. (2000). Self-report surveys as measures of crime and criminal victimization. In D. Duffee (Ed.), *Criminal justice 2000* (Vol. 4, pp. 85–138). Washington, DC: U.S. Department of Justice.

Cooper, A., & Smith, E. L. (2011). *Homicide trends in the United States, 1980–2008* (NCJ 236018). Washington, DC: Bureau of Justice Statistics.

EU ICS. (2005). *The burden of crime in the EU: A comparative analysis of the European Survey of Crime and Safety* (EU ICS) 2005. Retrieved April 29, 2013, from http://www.europeansafetyobservatory.eu/

Federal Bureau of Investigation. (2012). *2012 Crime clock statistics.* Retrieved March 12, 2015 from: http://www.fbi.gov/about-us/cjis/ucr/crime-in-the-u.s/2012/crime-in-the-u.s.-2012/offenses-known-to-law-enforcement/national-data

Federal Bureau of Investigation. (2013). *Crime in the United States.* Uniform Crime Reports. Retrieved April 29, 2013 from: http://www.fbi.gov/about-us/cjis/ucr/crime-in-the-u.s/2013/crime-in-the-u.s.-2013

Federal Bureau of Investigation. (2015). *NIBRS participation by population group.* Retrieved March 16, 2015 from: http://www.fbi.gov/about-us/cjis/ucr/nibrs/2012/resources/nibrs-participation-by-population-group

Fisher, B. S., & Cullen, F. T. (2000). Measuring the sexual victimization of women: Evolution, current controversies, and future research. In D, Duffee (Ed.), *Criminal justice 2000* (Vol. 4, pp. 317–390). Washington, DC: National Institute of Justice. Retrieved March 12, 2015 from: http://www.ncjrs.gov/criminal_justice2000/vol_4/04g.pdf

Fisher, B. S., Cullen, F. T., & Turner, M. G. (2000). *The sexual victimization of college women* (NCJ 182369). Washington, DC: U.S. Department of Justice.

Fitzpatrick, C., & Kanin, E. (1957). Male sex aggression on a university campus. *American Sociological Review, 22,* 52–58.

Gove, W. R., Hughes, M., & Geerken, M. (1985). Are Uniform Crime Reports a valid indicator of the index crimes? An affirmative answer with minor qualifications. *Criminology, 23,* 451–501.

James, N., & Council, L. R. (2008). *How crime in the United States is measured.* Washington, DC: Congressional Research Service.

Jansson, K. (2006). *British crime survey: Measuring crime for 25 years.* London: Research Development and Statistics, Home Office.

Johnson, H., Ollus, N., & Nevala, S. (2008). *Violence against women: An international perspective.* New York: Springer.

Maxfield, M. G. (1987). Lifestyle and routine activity theories of crime: Empirical studies of victimization, delinquency, and offender decision-making. *Journal of Quantitative Criminology, 3,* 275–282.

McCleary, R., Nienstedt, B. C., & Erven, J. M. (1982). Uniform Crime Reports as organizational outcomes: Three time series experiments. *Social Problems, 29,* 361–372.

Mosher, C. J., Miethe, T. D., & Hart, T. C. (2011). *The mismeasure of crime* (2nd ed.). Thousand Oaks, CA: Sage Publications, Inc.

National Crime Records Bureau. (2013). *Crime in India 2011.* Retrieved May 18, 2013, from http://ncrb.nic.in/

Pilkington, N. W., & D'Augelli, A. R. (1995). Victimization of lesbian, gay, and bisexual youth in community settings. *Journal of Community Psychology, 23,* 34–56.

Rand, M. R. (2005). *The National Crime Victimization Survey: 32 years of measuring crime in the United States.* Presented at the meeting of the Siena Group on Social Statistics, Helsinki, Finland.

Rennison, C., & Rand, M. (2007). Introduction to the National Crime Victimization Survey. In J. Lynch, & L. Addington (Eds.), *Understanding crime statistics: Revisiting the divergence of the NCVS and UCR* (pp. 17–54). New York: Cambridge University Press.

Russell, D. E. H. (1982). The prevalence and incidence of forcible rape and attempted rape of females. *Victimology: An International Journal, 7,* 81–91.

Sampson, R. J., & Wooldredge, J. (1987). Linking the micro- and macro-level dimensions of lifestyle-routine activity and opportunity models of predatory victimization. *Journal of Quantitative Criminology, 3,* 371–393.

Sandholtz, N., Langton, L., & Planty, M. (2013). *Hate crime victimization, 2003–2011* (NCJ241291). Washington, DC: U.S. Department of Justice.

Tjaden, P., & Thoennes, N. (2000). *Full report of the prevalence, incidence, and consequences of violence against women* (NCJ 183781). Washington, DC: U.S. Department of Justice.

Toomey, R. B., & Russell, S. T. (2013). The role of sexual orientation in school-based victimization: A meta-analysis. *Youth & Society.* DOI: 10.1177/0044118X13483778

Truman, J. L., & Planty, M. (2012). *Criminal victimization, 2011* (NCJ 239437). Washington, DC: U.S. Department of Justice.

United Nations Office on Drugs and Crime. (2011). *Global study on homicide: Trends, contexts, data.* Vienna, Austria: Vienna International Centre.

United Nations Office on Drugs and Crime. (2012a). *Corruption in Afghanistan: Recent patterns and trends.* Vienna, Austria: Vienna International Centre.

United Nations Office on Drugs and Crime. (2012b). *Global report on trafficking in persons 2012.* New York: United Nations.

U.S. State Department. (2010). *Trafficking in persons: Ten years of partnering to combat modern slavery.* Retrieved June 11, 2010, from www.state.gov

U.S. State Department. (2014). Trafficking in persons report 2014. Retrieved March 16, 2015 from www.state.gov

Van Dijk, J. (2008). *The world of crime: Breaking the silence on problems of security, justice, and development across the world.* Thousand Oaks, CA: Sage Publications, Inc.

World Health Organization. (2014). *Female genital mutilation, fact sheet No. 241.* Retrieved March 12, 2015 from: http://www.who.int/mediacentre/factsheets/fs241/en/

CHAPTER 5

Personal Victimization

CHAPTER OUTLINE

LEARNING OBJECTIVES

- Define personal victimization.
- Classify different types of personal victimization.
- Describe the extent of different types of personal victimization.
- Identify risk factors associated with different types of personal victimization.
- Explain how leading victimology theories can be used to account for experiencing different types of personal victimization.

You are not a victim. No matter what you have been through, you're still here. You may have been challenged, hurt, betrayed, beaten, and discouraged, but nothing has defeated you. You are still here! You have been delayed but not denied. You are not a victim, you are a victor. You have a history of victory.

Maraboli, 2013, p. 28

Introduction

Personal victimization involves interactions between a victim and an offender that result in some harm to the victim. In instances of personal victimization, the target of the offense is usually the victim himself or herself rather than the victim's property (offenses in which the victim's property is targeted are typically referred to as property victimization, and are reviewed in Chapter 7). Further, personal victimizations involve actual, attempted, or threatened violent behavior on the part of the offender. In addition, personal victimizations can be lethal (i.e., homicide) or nonlethal (e.g., assault, robbery); they can be sexual (e.g., rape); or they may be given different labels based on the characteristics of the victim (e.g., elder abuse) or the circumstances under which the victimization occurs (e.g., domestic violence).

Much of what victimologists know about personal victimizations has been uncovered through the Uniform Crime Reports (UCR) and the National Crime Victimization Survey (NCVS). Although these sources of victimization data do not estimate the extent and nature of all types of personal victimization, they do provide insights into those that are most common and/or more serious. Together, the UCR and NCVS regularly provide information on homicide, rape and sexual assault, assault (simple and aggravated), and robbery victimization. Trends in these offenses over time are illustrated in Figure 5-1, which shows that simple assault is the most common personal type of victimization in the United States. In addition, as part of the 2006 NCVS, a Supplemental Victimization Survey was administered to include one-time estimates of stalking victimization, another form of personal victimization.

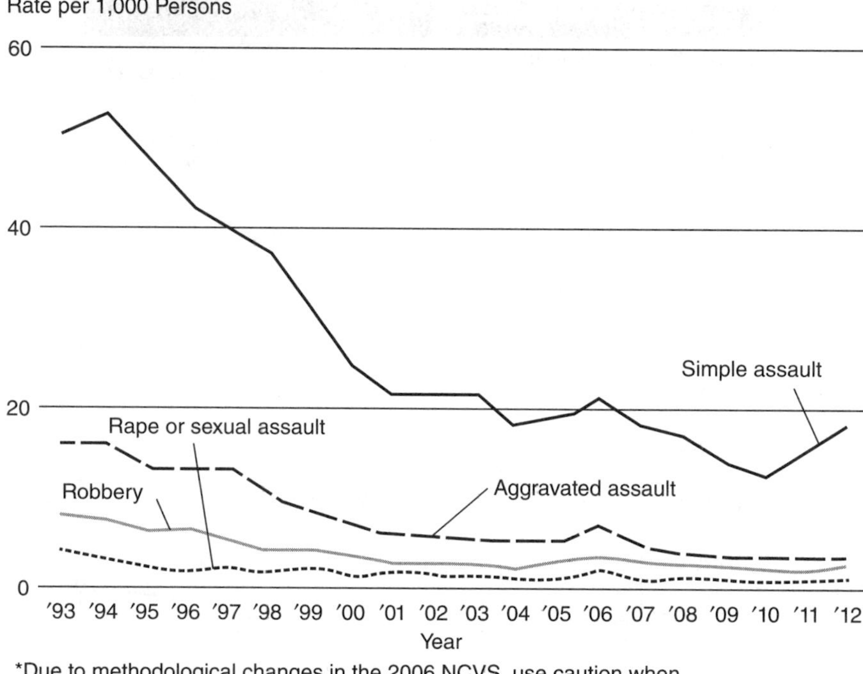

Figure 5-1 Trends in Personal Victimization Rates by Type of Crime, 1993–2012
Source: Truman, Langton, and Planty (2013).

The most recent UCR data from 2012 indicate that over 1.2 million personal crimes (i.e., murder and non-negligent manslaughter, forcible rape, robbery, and aggravated assault) were reported to law enforcement that year. Figure 5-2 shows a five-year trend (2008–2012) in personal (violent) crime based on UCR data. According to the figure, the number of personal crimes declined steadily between 2008 and 2011, but between 2011 and 2012 it increased slightly (by 0.7%). Recall that Chapter 4 explained that the extent of victimization is often reported as a rate, and that the UCR reports rates of crimes known to the police per 100,000 inhabitants of the United States. For 2012, the crime rate for personal offenses was 386.9 per 100,000 inhabitants, with aggravated assaults being the personal crime with the highest rate (242.3 per 100,000 inhabitants) and homicide having the lowest rate (4.7 per 100,000 inhabitants). The NCVS also reported a slight increase in personal victimization in its most recent administration, with an overall rate of personal victimization in 2012 of 26.1 per 1,000 persons age 12 and older (Truman, Langton, & Planty, 2013).

This chapter reviews five types of personal victimization: (1) homicide, (2) rape/sexual assault, (3) stalking, (4) assault, and (5) robbery. Assault and rape/sexual assault also are further discussed in Chapter 6, which reviews the victimization of women, children, and the elderly.

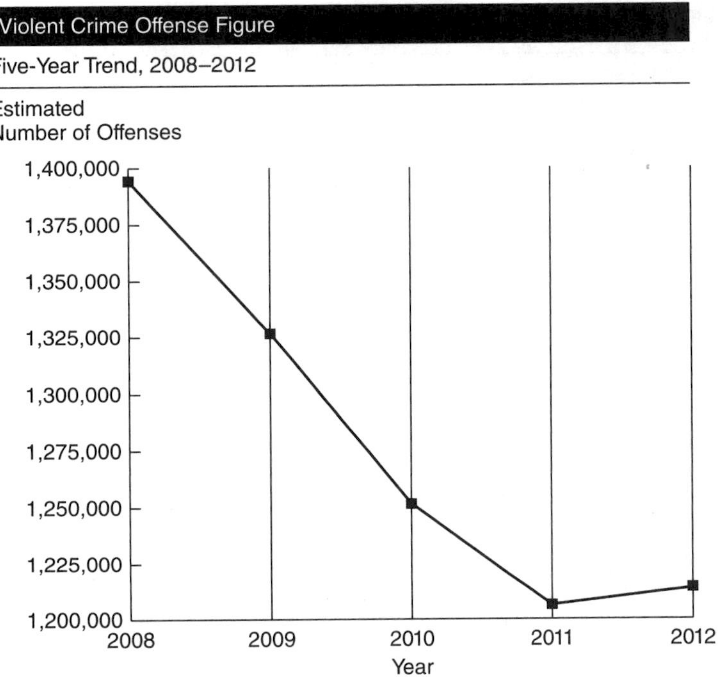

Figure 5-2 UCR Personal (Violent) Crime Trends
Source: Federal Bureau of Investigation (2013a).

Homicide Victimization

The UCR is the principal source of information on homicide victimization in the United States as it includes the ***Supplementary Homicide Report*** (SHR), which annually provide additional details related to ***homicide*** that are usually not collected for other UCR offenses (e.g., burglary). In general, homicide describes the killing of one human being by another (NOLO, n.d.); some homicides are legally justified (e.g., self-defense), while others are not (e.g., murder, manslaughter). The UCR includes counts of homicides that meet two criteria. The first are homicides that involve the willful (non-negligent) killing of another known as *murder* and *non-negligent manslaughter*. Deaths caused by negligence, attempts to kill, assaults to kill, suicides, and accidental deaths are excluded. Justifiable homicides are included provided they involve the killing of a felon by law enforcement in the line of duty or the killing of a felon during the commission of a felony by a private citizen. The second type of homicides included in the UCR are those identified as *manslaughter by negligence* which is the killing of another person through gross negligence (Federal Bureau of Investigation, 2009). The latest UCR data indicate that there were 14,827 homicide victims in 2012. This figure represents a homicide rate of 4.7 per 100,000 inhabitants, which is a very slight increase of 0.4% from 2011 (Federal Bureau of Investigation, 2013a).

With respect to homicide victims, the SHR indicate that 77.7% of homicide victims were males and 51.1% were African American. Further, the most victimized age group in 2012 included those aged 20 to 24. Trends in homicide victimization rates from 1980 to 2008 by age are presented in Figure 5-3. The figure clearly indicates that, overall, young people had greater risks of homicide victimization than other age groups over time.

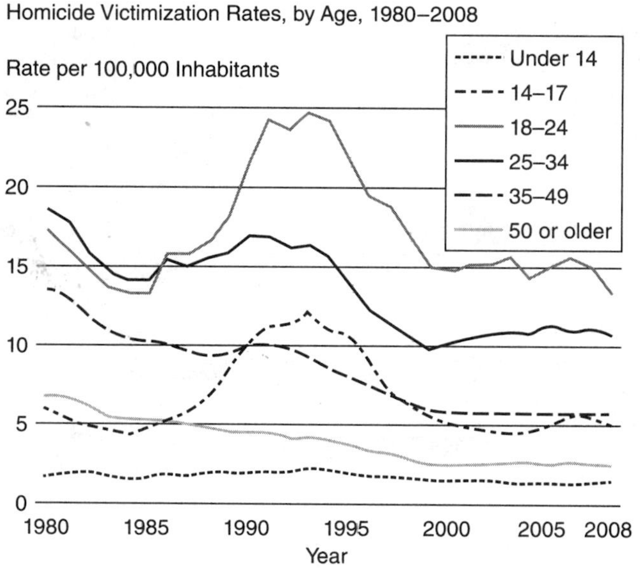

Figure 5-3 Homicide Victimization Rates by Age, 1980–2008
Source: Cooper and Smith (2011).

The SHR also publish information on the circumstances surrounding homicide victimization. For example, according to the SHR 3,085 (21%) of the homicides reported to police occurred during an argument between the victim and the offender. This finding is consistent with what Wolfgang (1957) reported in his classic study of victim-precipitated homicides in Philadelphia (see Chapter 1). UCR data also reveal that 1,841 (12%) homicides were perpetrated in conjunction with another felony, most notably robberies. In addition, of the homicides included in the SHR, 69% were committed using firearms, in particular handguns (Federal Bureau of Investigation, 2013a). SHR data are also available on the relationship between the homicide victim and the offender. Figure 5-4 illustrates those relationships using 2012 SHR data.

The figure shows that in a majority of cases law enforcement was able to determine the victim–offender relationship, but in 45% of homicides reported to the police this relationship is unknown. Of those offenses in which law enforcement can determine the victim–offender relationship, about 12% are perpetrated by a family member, 12% by a stranger, and 30% by other individuals known to the offender (e.g., a friend, an acquaintance). Overall, then, it appears that individuals are more likely to be murdered by someone they know rather than by a stranger. Within the larger context of homicide victimization, there are also particular terms used to identify the killing of specific types of victims or involving certain victim–offender relationships.

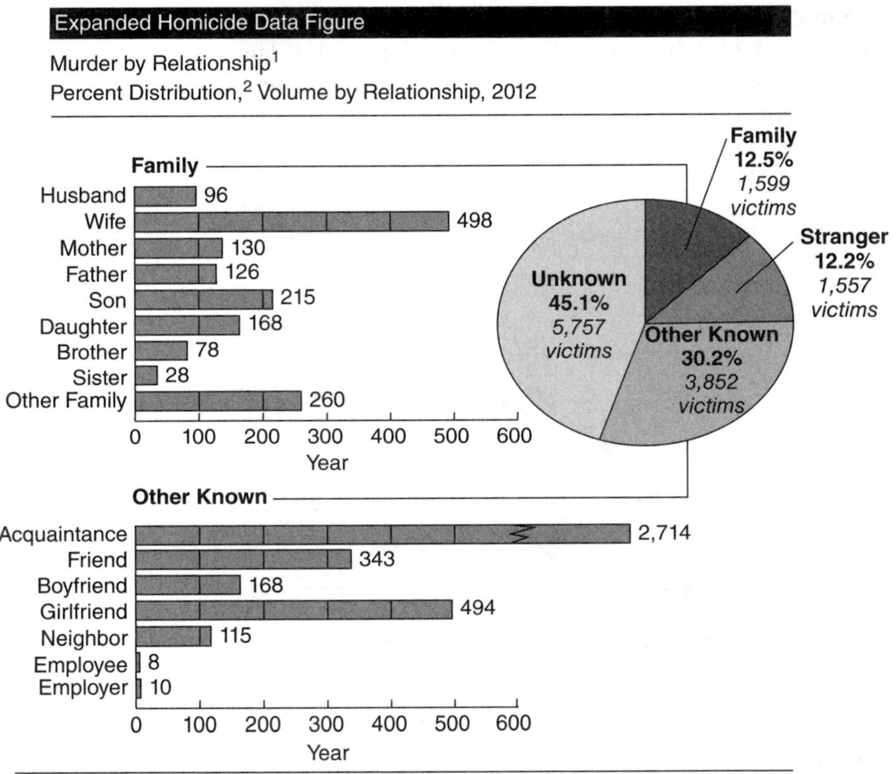

Figure 5-4 The Victim–Offender Relationship in Homicide Victimization, 2012
Source: Federal Bureau of Investigation (2013a).

Special labels are used for certain homicides based on the victim–offender relationship, such as spousal homicide, intimate partner homicide, and parricide. ***Spousal homicide*** involves killing one's legally married partner, whereas ***intimate partner homicide*** is a more general label that does not necessarily imply the victim and offender were legally married. To illustrate the prevalence of spousal and intimate partner homicide respectively, Figure 5-4 indicates that in 2012, a total of 498 homicide victims were wives murdered by their husbands, 96 victims were husbands murdered by their wives, 494 victims were killed by their male intimate partners, and 168 were killed by their female intimate partners. Importantly, although males have higher homicide victimization rates than females, they are much less likely to be murdered by their partners than are females. The term ***parricide*** is used to describe homicides in which parents are murdered by their children. SHR data suggest that 130 mothers and 126 fathers were murdered by their children in 2012.

Unique terms also are used to refer to homicide victims with certain characteristics, such as infanticide, neonaticide, eldercide, and femicide. Infanticide and neonaticide are related in that they both involve the killing of infants. However, the age of the victim differentiates the two. Infants who are murdered within 24 hours of being born are victims of ***neonaticide***, whereas ***infanticide*** is used to describe the murder of child victims up to 4 years of age. SHR statistics suggest that in 2012 there were 144 victims under the age of 1 and 261 between the ages of 1 and 4 (Federal Bureau of Investigation, 2013a). These data, however, do not specify the number of homicides involving babies within 24 hours of birth. Figure 5-5 further depicts the victimization of children 4 years and under by providing victimization rates of children in this age group from 1980 to 2008. Studies of child homicide have reported, as the figure illustrates, that children are at the greatest risk for homicide victimization during the first year of life, and that this risk decreases every year thereafter. Further, infanticide is most often committed by parents or caregivers, in the home, using opportunistic weapons (those in close proximity and easily accessible to the offender), and during winter months (Cooper & Smith, 2011; McCleary & Chew, 2002).

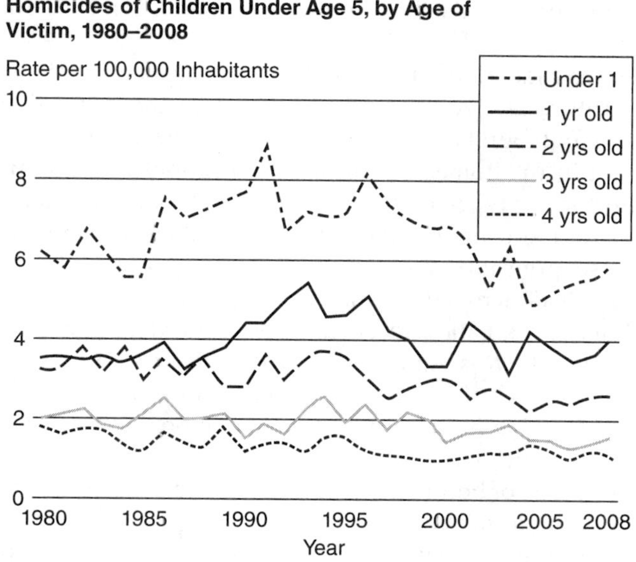

Figure 5-5 Homicide Victimization Rates for Children Aged 4 and Younger, 1980–2008
Source: Cooper and Smith (2011).

Another type of homicide that is defined according to the age of the victim is ***eldercide***, the killing of elderly persons. Overall, the elderly have lower homicide rates than younger persons. For example, in 2012 there were 612 homicide victims over the age of 65; by comparison, there were 2,362 homicides against those 20 to 24 years old (Federal Bureau of Investigation, 2013a). In terms of absolute numbers, though, it has been suggested that the number of eldercides may grow in the future as individuals live longer (Roberts & Willits, 2011). Although studies on eldercide are somewhat sparse, recent research suggests that at the macro level, eldercide may be explained by lifestyles and routine activities. Aki Roberts and Dale Willits (2011) examined elder-specific lifestyles and routine activities and felony-related eldercides in 195 American cities, concluding that areas with higher percentages of elderly persons living alone and with a disability were linked with higher eldercide rates.

Broadly speaking, ***femicide*** is the homicide victimization of women, but some definitions of femicide also stipulate that the killing takes place *because* the victim is female (Garcia-Moreno, Guedes, & Knerr, 2012). In general, femicide is typically perpetrated by males, especially current or former intimate partners. Under the larger umbrella of femicide, subtypes of female homicide have also been identified, such as intimate partner femicide. For example, the World Health Organization (WHO) and the London School of Hygiene and Tropical Medicine have examined femicide on a global scale, reporting that over 35% of femicides are perpetrated by intimate partners, while only 5% of male murder victims are killed by their intimate female partners (Garcia-Moreno et al., 2012; WHO, 2012). Femicide can also be committed by non-intimates; the city of Ciudad Juárez, Mexico, for instance, has been the site of over 400 violent murders of women in the last decade. These murders are believed to be connected to violence against women more generally, such as domestic violence and sexual assault, but some may also be gang-related. As discussed in Chapter 4, femicides can also be committed in connection with a dowry or in the name of honor.

Studies also have identified risk factors for intimate partner femicide. Jacquelyn Campbell and colleagues (2003) studied intimate partner femicide in 11 cities in the United States and found that factors such as offender's gun access, perpetrator's stepchild present in the home, and prior victimization (e.g., stalking, forced sex) were risk factors for this type of victimization. WHO (2012) also recognized unemployment, alcohol and drug use, mental health problems, gun ownership, forced sexual intercourse, prior intimate partner abuse, and societal gender inequality as risk factors for femicide across the world. Although the majority of homicide victims in the United States are males, in 2012, 22% of murder victims included in the SHR were females, which is equivalent to 2,834 victims. Further, 35% of female murder victims for which the victim–offender relationship was known were murdered by husbands or boyfriends, indicating a high prevalence of intimate partner femicide—and a statistic identical to that reported globally.

Assessing the scope of homicide victimization and patterns in its varied types is an important task undertaken by victimologists, but equally important is understanding the risk factors associated with this most serious of crimes. In other words, victimologists and researchers trained in other disciplines (e.g., public health) have worked toward understanding *why* individuals are murdered by developing and testing theories of homicide victimization. In criminology and victimology, the lifestyle–routine activities perspective, the general theory of crime, and the subculture of violence theory have been used as explanations of homicide victimization. With the exception of the subculture of violence theory, which is discussed subsequently, the other two theoretical perspectives have been reviewed elsewhere in the text. However, some readers may find a brief recap helpful. Recall that, in general, lifestyle–routine activities theory posits opportunities are necessary for victimization to occur (see Chapter 2). Further, victim lifestyles and routine activities contribute to such opportunities by bringing suitable targets into proximity with motivated offenders in the absence of guardianship. The general theory of crime argues that individuals with low self-control are at increased risk for victimization because possessing this trait affects victim decision making and behavior (see Chapter 3).

Therefore, individuals may place themselves in risky situations or perhaps act in ways that antagonize offenders.

Since its inception, lifestyle–routine activities theory has been applied to homicide victimization; even the original research study by Cohen and Felson (1979) that introduced the theory included homicide in the analyses. Successive research has continued to explore the theory as an explanation for homicide. For instance, Steven Messner and Kenneth Tardiff (1985) conducted one of the first studies to use routine activities to explain homicide patterns in Manhattan. They found that, consistent with the theory, males were more likely than females to be victimized away from home by strangers; this is because males spend more time away and therefore are exposed and in proximity to motivated offenders. Similarly, they reported that those who were unemployed were more likely to be killed at home. Again, this is due to how individuals spend their time and the routine activities they engage in. Recent research by Jesenia Pizarro, Nicholas Corsaro, and Sung-suck Yu (2011) affirmed these findings, reporting similar patterns in their study of homicides in Newark, New Jersey. Overall, they concluded that homicides occur near areas where victims and offenders carry out their daily routines.

Other studies have integrated lifestyle–routine activities theory with notions of victim precipitation to explain homicide victimization. Recall that victim precipitation suggests that victims are to some degree responsible or accountable for their criminal victimization (see Chapter 1). From a lifestyle–routine activities perspective, then, researchers have suggested that criminal lifestyles and routine activities can precipitate or contribute to homicide victimization through the victim–offender overlap. For example, Michael Ezell and Emily Tanner-Smith (2009) reported that factors such as gang membership, history of arrest for violence, and family criminality were positively and significantly related to homicide victimization among individuals released from the California Youth Authority. A study by Lisa Muftic' and Donald Hunt (2013) that was based on an examination of homicides in Dallas, Texas, found that victims with criminal histories were more likely to be victims of victim-precipitated homicides than those without criminal histories. Together, these two studies reinforce the importance of not only lifestyles and routine activities as providing opportunities for homicide victimization, but also the victim–offender overlap in increasing victimization risk. Yet, there are other approaches to explaining homicide victimization.

Researchers also have used the general theory of crime to account for homicide victimization. For example, Alex Piquero and his colleagues (2005) used the general theory of crime (Gottfredson & Hirschi, 1990), which emphasizes low self-control as a precursor to victimization, to examine homicide victimization among parolees from California. The research team reported that low self-control was positively and significantly related to homicide victimization, meaning that parolees with low self-control were more likely to be murdered than those with higher self-control. In addition to this, the study results indicated that low self-control was a significant predictor of violent offending behaviors as well. Thus, as the victim–offender overlap suggests, victims and offenders may have shared characteristics—such as low self-control—that explain both victimization and criminal behaviors. This finding is consistent with the two previously discussed studies that used lifestyles and routine activities to explain victimization as well.

Another potential explanation for homicide victimization is found in the subculture of violence theory. The ***subculture of violence*** theory was originally developed by Marvin Wolfgang and Franco Ferracuti (1967) to explain homicides and other violent offenses. Although it is not strictly a theory of homicide victimization, it certainly offers insights into homicide patterns. The theory explains that within the context of the larger culture, such as American culture in the United States, subcultures exist with unique values, attitudes, norms, and practices. In some of these subcultures, violence is viewed as an appropriate response in certain social situations. For example, Elijah Anderson's (1999) code of the street theory explains that violence is expected in inner-city subcultures in response to disrespectful behavior. These subcultures are learned and diffused throughout certain areas (e.g., neighborhoods) or regions (e.g., the South), where they take root and are essentially passed from generation to generation. Therefore, those who are a part of violent subcultures will be more likely to not only perpetrate violence, but also to become victims of violence.

Classical and contemporary research exploring the subculture of violence theory is supportive of the contention that subculture explains homicide rates and patterns. For example, an early study by Raymond Gastil (1971) examined the relationship between homicide rates and region of the country in the United States. Gastil concluded that even after considering factors such as income, education, age, and urbanization, homicides clustered in the South because of a "Southern subculture of violence." Figure 5-6 displays property and violent crime rates by region in the United States, clearly indicating the South has the highest rates of both property and

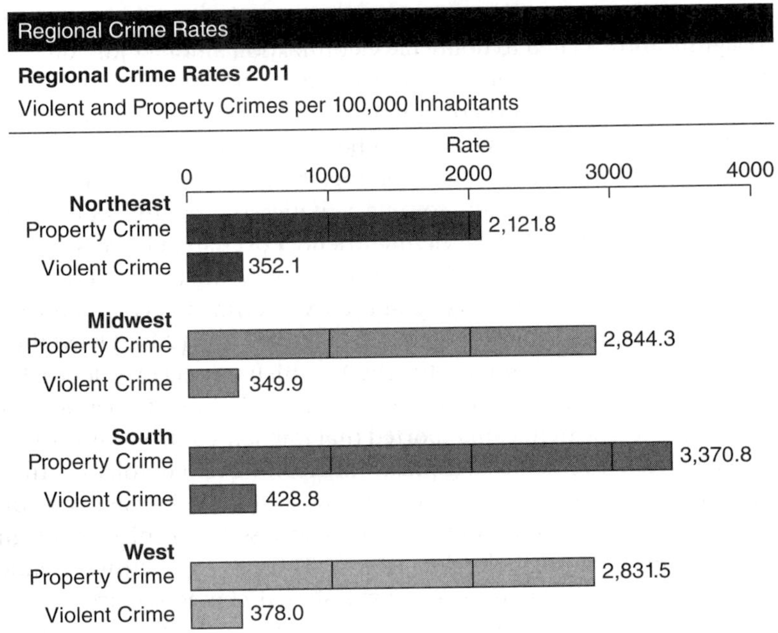

Figure 5-6 Regional Crime Rates, 2011
Source: Federal Bureau of Investigation (2012).

violent crimes, even today. The subculture of violence theory also has been used to explain lynching in the South. Further, recent research has found that areas in the South in which lynching was perpetrated historically (circa 1882–1930) have elevated homicide rates in contemporary times (Messner, Baller, & Zevenbergen, 2005). The subculture of violence theory offers a plausible explanation for this result in that the violent culture has been sustained over time.

Rape Victimization

The term ***sexual victimization*** encompasses many types of personal victimization of a sexual nature. Several of these offenses are discussed in Chapter 6 as they apply to specific types of victims, especially women, children, and the elderly. Rape is discussed in general terms in this chapter as an important type of personal victimization. Historically, rape has been a topic of considerable debate and controversy in the academic community and in other legal and advocacy circles.

For 80 years, the FBI defined rape as the "carnal knowledge of a female forcibly and against her will." This definition is antiquated for several reasons. First, the term "carnal knowledge" is outdated. Further, the definition is restrictive in that it only acknowledges female rapes. Finally, it implies that rape is always perpetrated through force. As discussed in Chapter 4, the reality of rape victimization does not completely square with this definition, since males are also victims of rape, and rape can be completed through the use of coercion and other tactics not constituting actual force. Acknowledging that it was time to revisit the definition of rape included in the UCR, in 2013 the definition of ***rape*** victimization was changed to "Penetration, no matter how slight, of the vagina or anus with any body part or object, or oral penetration by a sex organ of another person, without the consent of the victim" (Federal Bureau of Investigation, 2013b).

Rape victimization has been the topic of considerable research attention in the field of victimology, and much is known about its extent and nature. National-level estimates of victimization are provided by the UCR and the NCVS, along with other large-scale victimization surveys (e.g., National Violence Against Women Survey). As a starting point, UCR statistics for rape show that there were 84,376 forcible rapes reported to law enforcement in 2012, which is a rate of 52.9 per 100,000 female inhabitants (Federal Bureau of Investigation, 2013a). This is a very slight increase of 0.2% from 2011. However, UCR estimates of rape are generally regarded as unreliable due to low levels of victim reporting to law enforcement (upwards of 90% are unreported).

The NCVS uses a definition of rape similar to the new UCR definition and provides annual estimates of rape victimization. In general, NCVS estimates are considered to be more trustworthy than UCR estimates, but they must still be approached with caution because of difficulties in measuring and collecting information from rape victims (Kruttschnitt, Kalsbeek, & House, 2013). Further, NCVS estimates are a combination of rape and sexual assault victimization. ***Sexual assaults*** are sexual victimizations, either forceful or non-forceful, and involve attempted or completed unwanted sexual contact between the victim and the offender. Grabbing, fondling, or verbal threats are examples of sexual assault in the NCVS.

Since rape and sexual assault are grouped together in the NCVS, the estimates are not directly comparable to those reported in the UCR. Still, for 2012 the NCVS estimates there were 346,830 rapes and sexual assaults in the United States, which translates to a victimization rate of 1.3 per 1,000 persons age 12 or older (Truman et al., 2013). This too, is an increase over 2011 estimates, with over 100,000 more rapes and sexual assaults uncovered compared to the previous year. Because the NCVS collects detailed information about victimization incidents, it is also possible to distinguish between completed, attempted, and threatened rapes and sexual assaults. Figure 5-7 shows the extent of rape and sexual assault victimization against females from 1995 to 2010.

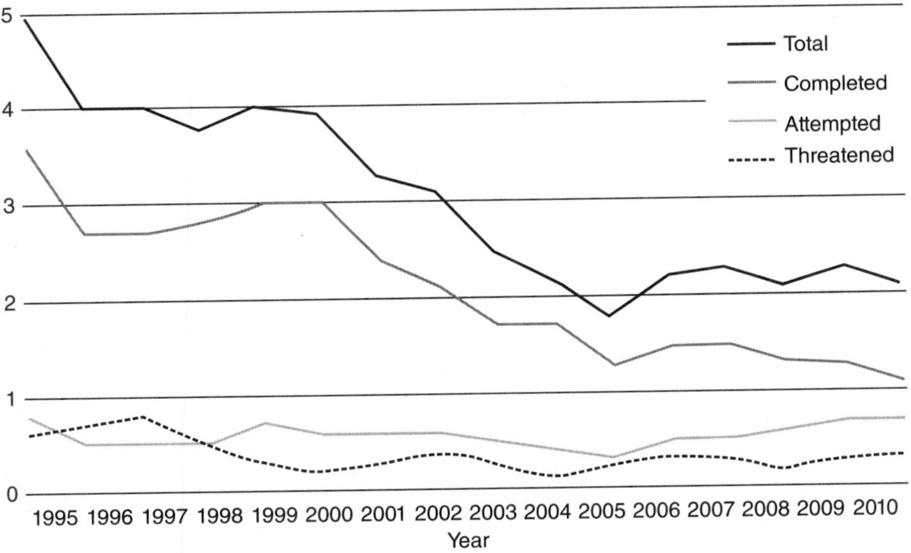

Figure 5-7 Completed, Attempted, and Threatened Rape and Sexual Assault Victimization Against Females, 1995–2010

Source: NCVS (Planty, Langton, Krebs, Berzofsky, & Smiley-McDonald, 2013).

Beyond the scope of rape, victimologists also have studied the demographic characteristics of rape victims. For example, most victims of rape are female, which may be why the original UCR definition was limited to female victims. However, the most recent NCVS estimates from 2012 suggest that victimization rates for rape/sexual assault are not all that disparate for males and females. The rate for females in the United States during 2012 was 1.6 per 1,000 females 12 or older compared to 1.0 per 1,000 for males age 12 and older. With respect to victims' age, young people overall have the highest victimization rates, with persons 18 to 20 years old being at greatest risk for rape/sexual assault. Age becomes a very important consideration in estimating victimization risks, because research shows that females who are raped as minors have a high likelihood of being raped again as adults (revictimized). According to one estimate, over one third (35.2%) of victims who were raped as minors were also raped as adults. This contrasts with a much smaller percentage (14%) of adult rape victims who were revictimized (Black, Basile, Breiding, Smith, Walters, Merrick, Chen, & Stevens, 2011).

In terms of race, while numerically there are more white rape *victims* than there are victims of other races, whites have lower victimization rates compared to other racial groups. Notably, American Indian and Alaska Natives, and individuals identifying with two or more races, had the highest victimization rates: 14.4 per 1,000 individuals 12 and older and 4.3 per 1,000, respectively. Other characteristics of victims are patterned less consistently across data sources, but the latest information from the NCVS suggests that those who are separated from their intimate partners, those with lower household incomes, and those living in urban areas had higher victimization rates than those without these characteristics (NCVS Victimization Analysis Tool, 2013).

These statistics represent the state of rape and sexual assault victimization at a single point in time based on annual victimization estimates. Other sources of information on these types of victimization take a more long-term view and ask study participants about their *lifetime* experiences with sexual victimization. For example, the National Intimate Partner and Sexual Violence Survey (NISVS, see Chapter 4) recently reported that nearly one in five women (18.3%) and 1 in 71 men (1.4%) in the United States have been raped at some point during their lives (Black et al., 2011). This translates to about 22 million women and 1.6 million men. Nearly the same prevalence of victimization was reported in the NVAWS, which estimated that 18% of women had experienced a completed or attempted rape in their lifetime. Of these victims, 22% were under 12 years old and 32% were 12 to 17 years old when they were first raped (Tjaden & Thoennes, 1998a).

The relationship between the victim and the offender is another important consideration in understanding the nature of rape victimization. In general, it appears that rape is perpetrated more often by someone the victim knows than by someone he or she does not know. Further, these types of offenses are frequently experienced at places familiar to the victim. For example, NCVS data since 1994 consistently reveal that among female victims of rape and sexual assault, over three in four are victimized by non-strangers (78%). Among offenders in this group, about 38% of offenses are committed by an acquaintance, 34% by an intimate partner, and about 6% by a relative (Planty, Langton, Krebs, Berzofsky, & Smiley-McDonald, 2013). The different terms for rape victimization based on the varied victim–offender relationships are presented in Box 5-1.

Regarding the location and the victim's activities at the time of the event, the same longitudinal NCVS data suggest that a majority of the time, the crime occurs at or near the victim's home (55%). Also, victims are frequently engaged in activities in the home or even sleeping when they are victimized. These are important situational characteristics to consider because they are contrary to the current victimological emphasis on using opportunity theory, and specifically lifestyle–routine activities theory, to explain victimization. After all, the home is theoretically a place where potential

Box 5-1: Types of Rape Victimization Based on the Victim–Offender Relationship

Type	Description	Lifetime Prevalence
Intimate Partner Rape (also known as *marital rape* if partners are married)	Rape perpetrated by an intimate partner or former intimate partner	34%
Acquaintance Rape (may also be referred to as *date rape)*	Rape perpetrated by a person known to the victim who is not an intimate partner or former intimate partner	38%
Stranger Rape	Rape perpetrated by a person who is not known to the victim	22%

Source: Planty et al. (2013).

victims are safe and protected, intimate partners and acquaintances are often thought to be effective guardians, and sleeping is by no means a "risky" activity.

Researchers have nonetheless explored possible connections between opportunities and rape and sexual assault victimization. Victim behaviors related to criminal opportunities are identified in the hopes of developing prevention strategies based on known risk factors rather than blaming victims for their role in the event. With this caveat in place, research has found certain lifestyles and routine activities as being conducive to a higher risk of rape and sexual assault victimization. A recent study by Cortney Franklin, Travis Franklin, Matt Nobles, and Glen Kercher (2012) found that specific routine activities were associated with sexual assault victimization among college students. In their study, students who spent more time on campus or partied during the week—elements of exposure—were significantly more likely to be victims. Those who came into proximity to motivated offenders by participating in drug sales were also at greater risk. Finally, the research team assessed the effects of low self-control on sexual assault victimization, reporting that individuals with low self-control were significantly more likely to become victims.

In a further exploration of the effects of lifestyles, routines, and self-control on sexual assault victimization, Marie Tillyer, Brooke Gialopsos, and Pamela Wilcox (2013) examined repeat sexual assault victimization involving seventh- to 10th-grade students in Kentucky. Tillyer and colleagues found that particular victim activities were associated with repeat sexual victimization. Specifically, students who participated in school sports or other school activities or had delinquent peers were significantly more likely to be repeat sexual assault victims (i.e., sexually victimized more than once). Those identified as having low self-control were also at significantly greater risk. They further noted that 95% of all the incidents uncovered in the study were experienced by repeat victims. Of these repeat victims, an often-victimized group of students called "chronic victims" who experienced 10 or more victimizations in a single school year accounted for nearly 50% of all the incidents. Repeat and recurrent victimization are discussed in Chapter 9.

Amy Cass (2007) also has studied sexual assault victimization from a routine activities perspective. Like Franklin and associates, Cass focused on victimization of college students but her study differed in that Cass considered the effects of both individuals' routine activities and the routine activities of the campus itself (e.g., availability of on-campus escorts) in explaining student victimization. Interestingly, none of the characteristics of the campus affected students' victimization risks (e.g., fenced campus perimeter or self-defense classes available on campus). Only students' gender and drug use were related to an increased probability of victimization, with females and drug users being more likely victims. In Chapter 3, the idea that gender may be an indicator of target attractiveness was discussed. Cass' study supports this idea, although overall support for lifestyle–routine activities theory in accounting for sexual assault victimization was modest at best. Further examples of theoretical tests of the lifestyle–routine activities perspective are given elsewhere in the text (e.g., Mustaine & Tewksbury, 1998; Schwartz & Pitts, 1995). The overall conclusion seems to be that opportunities play a partial role in explaining these types of victimization. However, theories related to rape also have concentrated on some alternatives to opportunity, although they mostly consider the crime from an offending rather than a victimization standpoint. These perspectives on explaining rape victimization are highlighted in the "Spotlight on Theory: Explanations for Rape Victimization" box.

Spotlight on Theory: Explanations for Rape Victimization

1. *Gender Inequality* Theoretical explanations of rape perpetration often focus on gender inequality within a society or culture as the cause of rape. These theories note that in patriarchal societies, men maintain their dominant position and assert their power and control over women through rape (see, e.g., Baron & Straus, 1987; Brownmiller, 1975).
2. *Socialization* Socialization theories of rape concentrate on processes by which individuals acclimate into society in ways that are conducive to rape perpetration or victimization. These explanations also may overlap with the gender inequality perspective in that socialization helps reinforce gender inequality. Socialization also can be related to rape myth acceptance, wherein only stereotypical conceptions of rape are accepted as "real rapes," while incidents that do not align with the stereotype are not recognized as rape.
3. *Biology and Psychology* Biological and psychological explanations of rape root its causes in the male instinctive drive to perpetuate the species, or in psychological disorders that may be shared by rapists. Currently, neither of these perspectives has gained widespread support as rape is thought to be motivated more by power and control than by sexual desire. Also, no specific mental illness has consistently been linked with rape perpetration.

Stalking Victimization

Stalking did not become a crime until 1990, when the state of California passed the first stalking law in the nation. Since then, all 50 states, the District of Columbia, the federal government, and several nations throughout the world have followed suit and criminalized stalking. Compared to other crimes, stalking is relatively "new" in a legal sense, but despite this, there has been much research focused on understanding stalking, especially stalking victimization. One of the ongoing issues in stalking research that scholars continue to debate is how best to define stalking victimization (Fox, Nobles, & Fisher, 2011). Legal definitions of stalking vary from state to state but usually require that three conditions be satisfied for an incident to be labeled as stalking. These three criteria are reflected in the Model Stalking Code, which was developed by the National Center for Victims of Crime (NCVC) in 1993 to assist states in crafting new stalking laws. The Model Stalking Code, which was revised in 2007 (NCVC, 2007, p. 31), explains that:

> Any person who purposefully engages in a course of conduct directed at a specific person and knows or should know that the course of conduct would cause a reasonable person to fear for his or her safety or the safety of a third person; or suffer other emotional distress is guilty of stalking.

The three legal criteria for stalking recommended in the Model Stalking Code are (1) a course of conduct, (2) criminal intent, and (3) harm to the victim in the form of emotional distress or fear. "Course of conduct" refers to the offender's pursuit behaviors. From the victim's point of view, these may include behaviors such as receiving unwanted phone calls, messages, letters, e-mails or being followed or spied on. This concept implies, although not explicitly included in this particular definition, that these behaviors be repeated. The Model Stalking Code also suggests that an element of criminal intent be established—that is, the offender should know that his or her actions are likely to cause the victim to be fearful or distressed. Finally, the NCVC definition stipulates that the victim suffer emotional distress or fear as a consequence of these pursuit behaviors.

The Model Stalking Code is a useful starting point for conceptualizing stalking, but it was written mostly to be used in legal contexts. This is why victimologists and other researchers have debated and explored alternative definitions of stalking victimization. For example, victimologists often exclude the element of criminal intent from definitions of stalking victimization because they are studying it from the victim's perspective and it may not be possible to assess the offender's intent. Therefore, most definitions of stalking victimization focus on the other two essential elements: a course of conduct and fear or emotional distress. These two behavioral and emotional criteria are included in Patricia Tjaden and Nancy Thoennes' (1998b, p. 2) definition of ***stalking*** victimization from their seminal study, the NVAWS. They defined stalking as "a course of conduct directed at a specific person that involves repeated visual or physical proximity, nonconsensual communication, or verbal, written or implied threats, or a combination thereof that would cause a reasonable person fear."

Box 5-2: Stalking Definition Scenarios

Scenario 1: Holly loves her criminology class, but she doesn't like how a certain male student sits next to her and tries to engage her in conversation. This happens every class period. Is Holly being stalked?

Scenario 2: Jesse and Jane's romantic relationship ends amicably, but after a while, Jesse starts getting strange phone calls. What began as abrupt hang-ups escalates into threats against him and his new girlfriend. Eventually, his car is vandalized. Is Jesse being stalked?

Scenario 3: Lydia has been receiving small presents and flowers at work. The notes on the gifts simply say "from an admirer." Over time, the anonymous gift giver gets more aggressive and starts sending her e-mails, leaving notes on her car, and even phoning her at home. Fearing for her safety, Lydia calls the police. Is Lydia being stalked?

Scenario 4: Walter receives a phone call the same time every day from a salesperson. Annoyed, he begins screening his calls. Is Walter being stalked?

Scenario 5: One of Marie's friends monitors her social network updates to keep tabs on her online. He also repeatedly checks her status updates and views her photos. Is Marie being stalked?

Scenario 6: Hank receives an obscene text message. Is Hank being stalked?

As previously noted, the course of conduct includes the offender's repeated pursuit behaviors (e.g., following, spying, showing up, e-mailing). It is important that these behaviors be experienced repeatedly (on two or more occasions) by victims in order for the encounter to be labeled stalking. Next, the harm that victims experience takes the form of fear or another form of emotional distress (e.g., anxiety, stress, anger). This fear criterion is often referred to as the ***fear standard*** and is sometimes a point of contention among stalking researchers because not all victims interpret or respond to the offender's pursuit in the same manner (Dietz & Martin, 2007). For instance, males and females may experience fear of crime differently (see Chapter 13). Considering all the issues previously raised in defining stalking, evaluate the scenarios presented in Box 5-2. Which of these situations involve stalking, and why?

Definitions aside, stalking researchers have extensively investigated its scope and nature. In terms of the extent of victimization, several studies have been undertaken since the 1990s that suggest a substantial portion of individuals experience stalking. The most recent national estimates in the United States were collected as part of the NISVS in 2010. The results of the report indicated that 16.2% of women and 5.2% of men in the United States have experienced stalking at some point during their lives (Black et al., 2011).

Another recent national-level survey of stalking victimization in the United States was administered as part of the 2006 N CVS. This supplement, called the Supplemental Victimization Survey (SVS), estimated the extent of stalking victimization against adults in the United States during a one-year period. According to the results of the survey, 1.5% of all adults were victims of stalking during the 12 months preceding the survey. Put differently, as estimated 3.3 million individuals age 18 or older were victims of stalking in a 12-month period (Catalano, 2012). A final example of a national study that estimated the extent of stalking victimization may be particularly interesting to college student readers. Bonnie Fisher, Francis Cullen, and Michael Turner (2002) reported that among a national sample of female college students, 13.1% had experienced stalking in the seven months prior to the study. A quick comparison of these two study estimates suggests that college women have substantially higher risks for stalking victimization than do adults in the general population.

These estimates show that stalking is somewhat widespread, and research also has found patterns in victim characteristics suggesting that certain individuals may be at higher risk of being stalked than others. The SVS, for example, reported that victimization rates for women in the United States were 20 per 1,000 persons 18 and older, while for men they were 7.4 per 1,000 persons 18 and older. This is consistent with other research that has found females to be at higher risk than males, but the SVS also revealed victimization risks across age, race, ethnicity, marital status, and household income characteristics. Complete statistics are presented in Table 5-1, but overall, the results identify young people, especially those 18 and 19 years, individuals of more than one race, non-Hispanic individuals, persons who are divorced or separated, and those with lower annual household incomes being at the greatest risk for stalking victimization (Baum, Catalano, Rand, & Rose, 2009).

Table 5-1: Stalking Victimization Rates by Victim Characteristics

	Rate per 1,000 Victims[a]
Gender	
Male	7.4
Female	20.0
Age	
18–19	29.7
20–24	28.4
25–34	20.2
35–49	17.3
50–64	10.4
65 or older	3.6
Race	
White	14.2
Black	12.2
American Indian/Alaska Native	19.6*
Asian/Pacific Islander	7.0
More than one race[b]	31.6

Hispanic origin	
Hispanic	10.6
Non-Hispanic	14.4
Marital status	
Never married	16.6
Married	8.7
Divorced or separated	34.0
Widowed	7.5
Household Income	
Less than $7,500	31.7
$7,500–14,999	27.4
$15,000–24,999	21.1
$25,000–34,999	15.8
$35,000–49,999	15.8
$50,000–74,999	12.6
$75,000 or more	9.6

*Based on 10 or fewer sample cases.
Note: Table excludes missing data.
[a]Victimization rates are per 1,000 persons age 18 or older.
[b]Includes all persons of any race, including persons who identify two or more races.
Source: Adapted from Baum et al. (2009).

Victimologists also have investigated the nature of stalking victimization, including the varied forms it takes. Some offenders persistently follow their victims in close physical proximity, while other victims may never see their stalker's face. Information on the pursuit experienced by stalking victims can be found in the stalking supplement to the NCVS. The survey asked victims about several offender pursuit behaviors, including receiving unwanted phone calls and messages, receiving unwanted letters and e-mails, having rumors spread about them, being followed or spied on, having the stalker show up at places he or she knew the victim would be, having the stalker wait for the victim, and receiving unwanted presents from the stalker. The results from the survey are provided in Table 5-2, which indicates that the most common pursuit behavior experienced by victims is receiving unwanted phone calls and messages, followed by spreading rumors, and following or spying.

This information is useful, but it is also somewhat dated given the spread of technologies since 2006 that could potentially be used by stalkers. Even so, the NCVS did include estimates of cyberstalking victimization in the survey. The results suggest that approximately 26% of victims of stalking also experienced some form of cyberstalking as part of the offender's course of conduct. ***Cyberstalking***, which involves repeated pursuit through digital or Internet-based devices, is discussed in

Table 5-2: Common Pursuit Behaviors Experienced by Stalking Victims

Pursuit Behavior	Percentage
Unwanted phone calls and messages	66.7%
Spreading rumors	36.3%
Following or spying	34.4%
Showing up at places	31.6%
Unwanted letters and e-mails	30.7%
Waiting for victim	29.3%
Leaving unwanted presents	12.5%

Source: Catalano (2012).

detail in Chapter 8. This finding from the NCVS implies that there is an overlap between physical stalking and cyberstalking, with some victims experiencing both. By the same token, it is also possible for victims to experience only physical pursuit or only online pursuit, although conceptually either experience qualifies as stalking victimization (Nobles, Reyns, Fox, & Fisher, 2014).

Further research has concentrated on other facets of the stalking encounter for victims, such as the victim–offender relationship, the number of stalkers who have pursued the victim, and the duration of stalking events. In general, stalking victims are most often pursued by someone they know rather than by a stranger. To some degree, the victim–offender relationship appears to vary depending on the victim's gender. For example, the NISVS found that females were stalked by intimate partners 66.2% of the time, but males were stalked by intimate partners 41.4% of the time (Black et al., 2011). The next most common victim–offender relationship for both genders was being stalked by an acquaintance (24% of females, 40% of males), followed by strangers (13.2% of females, 19% of males), and family members (6.8% of females, 5.3% of males) (Black et al., 2011). It also appears based on the existing research that most victims of stalking are victimized by a single stalker who pursues them repeatedly, although nearly a quarter of female stalking victims have had more than one stalker, compared to about 10% of male victims (Black et al., 2011). Finally, with respect to the length of time that victims are typically stalked, research studies indicate that most victims are pursued for 6 months or less, but some are targeted for longer periods. Figure 5-8 presents the results from the SVS related to stalking victimization duration.

As is the case with all types of victimization, researchers study stalking victimization to better understand what puts victims at risk and how victims and potential victims can be protected in the future. The previously identified patterns in victimization, such as those related to age, gender, and marital status, are a good starting point, but victimologists have also identified other factors, such as victims' lifestyles and routine activities that are related to stalking victimization. For example, in a study by Elizabeth Ehrhardt Mustaine and Richard Tewksbury (1999) that focused on explaining stalking victimization among college women, the authors concluded

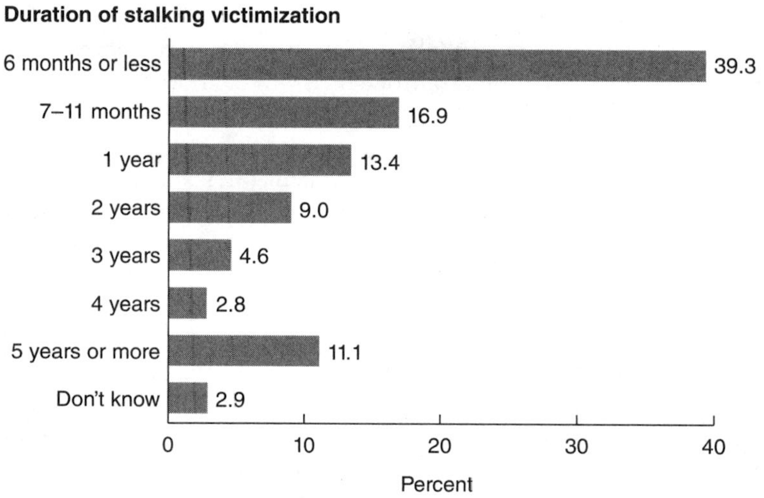

Figure 5-8 Duration of Stalking Victimization
Source: NCVS (Catalano, 2012).

that exposure to motivated offenders was a strong predictor of victimization. Victim behaviors such as going to the mall and being employed increased stalking victimization risks by 32% and 56%, respectively. They also found that drinking and drug use were related to victimization, with both behaviors increasing victimization risk for college women, and that women who lived off campus were at greater risk than women who lived on campus.

The study by Fisher and colleagues (2002) that found that 13.1% of college women in the United States were victims of stalking in a seven-month period also asked students about their lifestyles, routine activities, and other characteristics that could be related to victimization. They reported that women who were often at places with alcohol, who were in a committed relationship, who were dating, who lived alone, or who were previously victims of sexual offenses were at increased likelihood for being victims of stalking.

Much like homicide studies and empirical examinations of other types of victimization, stalking research also has identified low self-control as an explanation for stalking victimization. For example, Kathleen Fox, Angela Gover, and Catherine Kaukinen (2009) assessed the relationship between low self-control and victimization for male and female undergraduate college students at a large southeastern university. Their findings indicated that low self-control was significantly and positively related to victimization, but only for female students. In other words, according to these results, self-control is only a risk factor for females. Low self-control has also been linked to other types of personal victimization, such as alcohol-induced sexual assault victimization (e.g., Franklin, 2011), but thus far Fox and colleagues' study is one of the few to apply this theoretical framework to stalking victimization.

Another theoretical study by Matt Nobles and Kathleen Fox (2013), however, examined control balance theory as a potential explanation of stalking victimization. Control balance theory, which was reviewed in Chapter 3, is similar to the general theory of crime in that both theories focus on the importance of control in explaining victimization. However, control balance theory hypothesizes that individuals with a control surplus or a control deficit will be those most likely to experience criminal victimization. In a finding somewhat similar to Fox and colleagues' (2009) test of self-control, Nobles and Fox discovered that control deficits were related to stalking victimization, but only among women. Interestingly, control surpluses predicted stalking perpetration among both men and women. Notwithstanding the previously discussed research studies, there are few theoretically grounded examinations of stalking victimization.

Assault Victimization

The crime of ***assault*** involves a physical attack or a threat of an attack on another person. Assaults can be classified as either simple or aggravated. The distinction between them is usually whether a weapon was involved and/or the nature of physical injury suffered by the victim. In instances of ***simple assault***, the offender physically attacks or threatens to physically attack the victim without a weapon, resulting in only minor injuries such as bruises or scratches or no injuries at all. ***Aggravated assault*** is a more serious crime than is simple assault and entails the use, threatened use, or attempted use of a weapon by the offender. If injuries are sustained by the victim, they are usually quite serious, such as broken bones, lost teeth, or loss of consciousness. Guns, knives, and other objects such as clubs are typical weapons used by offenders during aggravated assaults.

Based on the primary sources of victimization data available, assault victimization appears to be the most common personal crime occurring in the United States. Simple assault is not one of the index crimes tracked in the UCR, but estimates suggest that there were 760,739 recorded aggravated assaults reported to law enforcement in the United States in 2012, a 1% increase over 2011 (Federal Bureau of Investigation, 2013a). Considered as a rate, this equates to 242.3 aggravated assaults per 100,000 inhabitants.

The NCVS offers a chance to examine the different types of assault victimization by providing estimates of simple assault, aggravated assault, and total assaults. Altogether there were at least 5,754,010 assault victimizations in the United States in 2012 according to the NCVS, (at a rate of 22 per 1,000 persons age 12 or older). Simple assault was nearly five times more common than aggravated assault, with 4,757,900 incidents of simple assault (18.2 per 1,000 persons age 12 or older) compared to 996,110 incidents of aggravated assault (3.8 per 1,000 persons age 12 and older).

Since the NCVS collects information on both simple assault and aggravated assault victimization, it is possible to consider risk factors for these offenses separately. However, for the most part, there are few differences in victimization patterns by victim characteristics for these two offenses. For example, in both cases, males have higher victimization rates than females. For simple assaults occurring in 2012, males were victimized at a rate of 19.7 per 1,000 persons age 12 or older, while for females this rate was 16.7 per 1,000 persons 12 or older. For aggravated assault, victimization rates were lower, but the gender-based pattern held, with males having a victimization rate of 4.5 per 1,000 persons age 12 or older and females having a rate of 3.1 per 1,000 persons age 12 or older (NCVS Victimization Analysis Tool, 2013).

With reference to victim race, there are differences in level of risk across types of assault. For simple assaults, persons of two or more races (35.8 per 1,000 persons age 12 or older) and African Americans (22.8 per 1,000 persons age 12 or older) had the highest victimization rates, while for aggravated assault the highest rates were experienced by American Indian/Alaskan Natives (9.7 per 1,000 persons age 12 or older) and African Americans (5.6 per 1,000 persons age 12 or older). Patterns in age are generally similar for simple and aggravated assault in that younger persons are more frequently victimized, although the age at which victimization risk is highest is slightly different across age groups. For simple assault, those aged 12 to 14 (48.9 per 1,000 persons age 12 or older) and 15 to 17 (28.0 per 1,000 persons age 12 or older) have the highest victimization rates, whereas for aggravated assault, the highest-risk groups are those aged 18 to 20 (9.8 per 1,000 persons age 12 or older) and 12 to 14 (7.0 per 1,000 persons age 12 or older) (NCVS Victimization Analysis Tool, 2013).

Other victim characteristics associated with assault victimization include relationship status (e.g., married), the victim–offender relationship, and the location of the victim's residence. Identifiable patterns across these characteristics suggest that persons who are separated from their intimate partners and those who have never been married are most at risk for both simple and aggravated assault. The relationship between the victim and the offender is also an important influence on assault victimization, with strangers being frequent offenders for both types of assault (although it is actually the case that those well known to the victim or casual acquaintances are more often perpetrators of simple assaults). Finally, individuals who live in urban areas have higher assault rates than those who do not live in these locales (NCVS Victimization Analysis Tool, 2013).

The victimization theories described in Chapters 2 and 3 provide additional depth related to potential reasons why individuals become victims of assault. One of the early studies among many to research the nature of assault victimization was conducted by Terance Miethe, Mark Stafford, and J. Scott Long (1987). Like many theoretical tests of the opportunity perspective, however, Miethe and his colleagues examined the effects of lifestyles and routine activities on multiple types of victimization, combining assault, robbery, and larceny into a single measure of victimization. While useful, this approach is also somewhat limited because potentially unique predictors of assault, robbery, or larceny cannot be identified. Nevertheless, they concluded that individuals who spend more time engaged in nighttime activities—and hence are more exposed to risk—are at heightened risk for victimization, including assault.

A succeeding study by Leslie Kennedy and David Forde (1990) specifically examined assault victimization against residents of Canada using the Canadian Urban Victimization Survey. This research is useful in understanding assault victimization not only because assault was treated as a unique form of victimization, but also because Kennedy and Forde included more detailed lifestyles and routines as influences on victimization (e.g., attending sporting events, playing bingo). They identified four routine activities that significantly increased one's likelihood of becoming an assault victim: Individuals who frequent bars, go to the movies, go to work, or spend time out of the house either walking or driving around were at added risk for victimization. Research conducted following Kennedy and Forde's study reiterates the importance of lifestyles, routines, and opportunities in explaining assault victimization specifically and violent victimization generally. For instance, Jackson Bunch, Jody Clay-Warner, and Man-Kit Lei's (2012) analysis of NCVS data found that individuals' nighttime activities and shopping behaviors were significantly related to their chances of violent and theft victimization.

In a break from traditional victimological explanations of violent victimization, Jillian Turanovic and Travis Pratt (2012) examined risky lifestyles and low self-control in light of their effects on repeat personal victimization. Repeat victimization is reviewed in detail in Chapter 9, but the concept denotes that an individual who is victimized (at time 1) is victimized again (at time 2). Assault was one of the types of victimization included in Turanovic and Pratt's analysis of repeat personal victimization. They concluded that self-control and lifestyles were both important considerations toward explaining victimization, and that low self-control was the determining factor in whether first-time victims changed their risky lifestyles after being victimized. These changes, in turn, influenced whether one-time victims became repeat victims. Thus, it appears based on this study that a continued effort to integrate these theories will bring victimologists closer to understanding the nature of not only assault victimization and personal victimization, but also repeat violent victimization as well.

Robbery Victimization

The final type of personal victimization to be reviewed in this chapter is robbery. ***Robbery*** involves the completed or attempted theft of property directly from a person using force or threat of force, irrespective of weapon use by the offender or physical injury to the victim. Although robbery is sometimes mistaken for a property offense, such as those discussed in Chapter 7, it is considered to be a form of personal victimization because it is a face-to-face crime in which the offender uses force or threat of force. Similar to other types of personal victimization, the UCR and NCVS provide slightly different information and insights regarding the extent and nature of robbery victimization. The UCR estimated that 354,520 robberies were perpetrated nationally in 2012, at a rate of 112.9 per 100,000 inhabitants (Federal Bureau of Investigation, 2013c). This is essentially the same rate at which they were reported in the previous year. Uncovering the dark figure of crime for robbery, the NCVS found that there were at least 741,756 victims of robbery in 2012, which translates to a robbery victimization rate of 2.8 per 1,000 persons age 12 or older (NCVS Victimization Analysis Tool, 2013).

Patterns in robbery victimization are evident upon examining the latest NCVS data. First, males have higher victimization rates than females: about 3.9 per 1,000 persons age 12 or older compared to 1.8 per 1,000 persons age 12 or older. Second, considering race patterns in victimization, African Americans have the highest victimization rates (5.2 per 1,000 persons age 12 or older), followed by individuals of two or more races (4.0 per 1,000 persons 12 and older). Third, age is a personal characteristic that seems to be linked to this type of personal victimization. Those aged 21 to 24 have the highest victimization rates (5.9 per 1,000 persons age 12 or older). Elderly persons (those 65 or older) have the lowest victimization rates (0.7 per 1,000 persons age 12 or older). Other personal characteristics may also be viewed as risk factors for victimization. Individuals who are separated from their intimate partners, those with household incomes less than $7,500, and those living in urban areas have the highest victimization rates compared to their counterparts without these characteristics (NCVS Victimization Analysis Tool, 2013).

It is also possible, drawing from various sources of information, to identify patterns in incident characteristics, such as where the crime took place, the relationship between the victim and the offender, or whether a weapon was involved. These factors most likely are important from a prevention perspective because they provide glimpses into the opportunities for robbery victimization and suggest possibilities for reducing those opportunities. For instance, according to the UCR, robberies reported to law enforcement were most often perpetrated on streets or highways. The next most frequent locations for robberies to be committed in 2012 were in a residence, followed by commercial houses, convenience stores, gas/service stations, and banks. These estimates of robbery by location are presented in Figure 5-9.

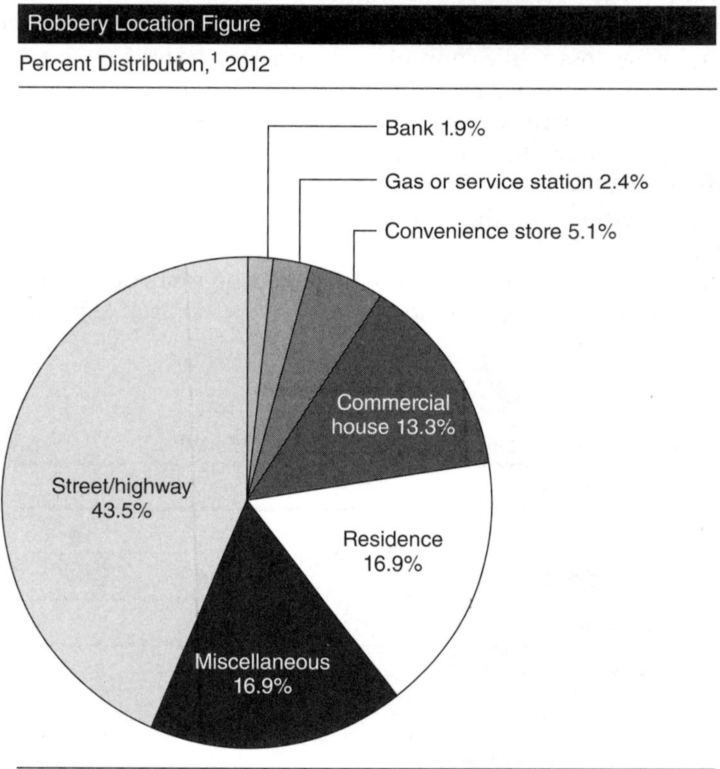

Figure 5-9 Robbery by Location, 2012

Source: Federal Bureau of Investigation (2013c). Note: Commercial houses are buildings of commerce, such as a liquor store or restaurant.

Studying the victim–offender relationship in robbery victimization reveals that most robberies are committed by strangers. However, it is interesting to assess robbery rates in conjunction with the victim–offender relationship and gender, because males have higher victimization rates by strangers than females (2.8 per 1,000 persons age 12 or older compared to 0.7 per 1,000 persons age 12 or older), yet females are victimized at similar rates by intimates (0.5 per 1,000 persons age 12 or older) (NCVS Victimization Analysis Tool, 2013). This suggests that these personal and incident characteristics should be studied collectively to truly understand the nature of risks of robbery victimization. A final incident characteristic to discuss is whether a weapon was used during the crime. Most of the time, this is the case, although some may be surprised to learn that the most frequently used weapons are strong-arm tactics (42.5%), firearms (41%), and knives or other cutting instruments (7.8%) (Federal Bureau of Investigation, 2013c).

Since robbery is a personal victimization that involves the loss of property, it is also possible to assess the financial cost of being a victim of robbery. Clearly the amount lost by victims will depend on whether the victim is an individual, a business, or some other type of organization, but all told, robberies collectively cost victims in the United States $414 million in 2012. Table 5-3 provides the average dollar loss based on the location of the robbery. As the table illustrates, banks had the highest average loss, while convenience stores lost the least on average.

The previously mentioned patterns in robbery victimization suggest target characteristics that place victims at risk for robbery. Richard Wright and Scott Decker (1997) wanted to find out how robbers selected their targets. The researchers used a referral-based sampling process known as snowball sampling to make contact with offenders, get referrals from them to other active robbers, and so on until they had generated a sample of 86 active offenders in St. Louis, Missouri. They asked their group of offenders many questions about committing robberies, such as how they chose their victims and other decisions related to the act itself (e.g., gaining victim compliance, getting away).

Table 5-3: Average Dollar Loss by Robbery Location, 2012

Robbery Location	Average Loss
Total	$1,167
Street/highway	$798
Commercial house	$1,754
Gas or service station	$943
Convenience store	$706
Residence	$1,631
Bank	$3,810
Miscellaneous	$1,071

Source: FBI (2013b).

Based on their offender interviews, Wright and Decker made several conclusions about the characteristics robbers look for in victims. First, a majority of offenders preyed on other criminals, especially small-time drug dealers or their customers. This finding underscores the importance of criminal and deviant behaviors as risk factors for criminal victimization. One active offender from the study was quoted as saying: "[I like robbing] them drug dealers [because] it satisfies two things for me: my thirst for drugs and the financial aspect. [I can] actually pay my rent, pay for my car, [and things like that too]" (Wright & Decker, 1997, p. 63).

Second, the active robbers considered the demographic characteristics of potential targets, with many preferring to rob the elderly, whites, and women. A common theme expressed by the offenders was that individuals with these characteristics were unlikely to offer much resistance. Third, dress and demeanor factored into the targeting decision, with those appearing to have a lot of cash and those who are not paying attention being attractive targets for the robbers. Finally, many of the offenders explained that they chose a familiar site, not far from their own neighborhoods, to look for victims. Although Wright and Decker did not test a victimization theory in their study, many of their findings align with what would be expected based on such theories, especially the lifestyle–routine activities perspective.

In a study of robbery victimization among adolescents, Richard Felson, Jukka Savolainen, Mark Berg, and Noora Ellonen (2013) examined many victim behaviors as they related to criminal opportunities. They concluded that victimization risk was greatest at night (after 6 p.m.), and therefore lifestyles including an active night life increased the likelihood that individuals would become victims of robbery. However, they also noted that this effect was strongest among boys, and that ultimately robbery risks were linked with alcohol use. This supports Wright and Decker's (1997) finding that robbers tend to select targets who are not aware of their surroundings. Finally, Felson and his colleagues found that these relationships held regardless of whether the offender was a stranger or a non-stranger. Although this study supports some of the ideas put forth by the opportunity perspective, the finding that exposure to strangers is not entirely consequential does not line up with theoretical expectations.

As a final example of a theoretically driven study of robbery victimization, Marie Tillyer and Rob Tillyer (2012) used multilevel opportunity theory developed by Pamela Wilcox, Kenneth Land and Scott Hunt (2003) to explain not the risks of victimization, but victim injuries. Tillyer and Tillyer argued that features of the micro- and macro-environment may affect how robberies unfold and consequently how severely victims are injured. Their results confirmed that victim injuries during robberies were affected by both incident-level as well as city-level characteristics. For example, the location of the robbery and the time of day were associated with victim injuries. Incidents that transpired in semipublic places were 37% less likely to result in injuries to the victim. Further, incidents occurring during "business hours" (between 7 a.m. and 7 p.m.) were less likely to end in injuries. At the city level, the authors reported that the tempering effects of location (i.e., semipublic) were reduced in cities with higher levels of concentrated disadvantage (e.g., higher unemployment, more vacant housing). In other words, being in public and potentially around a guardian or someone who would intervene to stop the crime was less effective in reducing the likelihood of injury during a robbery in cities with certain characteristics.

Summary

Personal victimization occurs when an offender targets a victim, resulting in some harm to the victim. This chapter reviewed five main types of personal victimization: (1) homicide, (2) rape, (3) stalking, (4) assault, and (5) robbery. While all of these offenses are quite different, resulting in differing degrees of harm to the victim, each involves an offense against a person rather than an offense against his or her property. These forms of personal victimization also vary in their prevalence, with homicide being relatively rare and simple assault being fairly common. Rape, stalking, and robbery occur at rates somewhere in between. However, considered collectively, trends in personal victimization suggest that such offenses have been declining for years. It was not until 2012 that both the NCVS and the UCR reported a slight increase in personal victimizations; until that time both had estimated declines for several years. Time will tell whether this is a sustained increase or simply a minor deviation from a downward trend.

General and crime-specific explanations for personal victimization have been offered, but victimologists have primarily focused on explaining these types of victimization from opportunity or self-control perspectives. Several examples of research studies that adopted these theoretical frameworks were reviewed, with the general conclusion being that lifestyles, routine activities, and opportunities affect personal victimization. Still, how these behavioral and situational factors affect victimization often varies depending on the type of personal victimization under study. For example, opportunity clearly played a role in the pedophile priest scandal that has now plagued the Catholic Church for more than a decade ("Spotlight on Policy: The Catholic Church's Sexual Abuse Scandal" box) and which has cost the church billions of dollars (Figure 5-10). Opportunity may also play a larger role in explaining robbery in comparison to homicide. In turn, perhaps homicide can be better understood by considering risky lifestyles, low self-control, and potential victim precipitation. Although this chapter reviewed the extent and nature of assault and rape victimization, distinctive types of assault and sexual violence are discussed in greater detail in the next chapter, which addresses the victimization of women, children, and the elderly.

Spotlight on Policy: The Catholic Church's Sexual Abuse Scandal

On June 20, 1985, the *New York Times'* Jon Nordheimer published a story about Father Gilbert Gauthe, a priest in rural Henry, Louisiana, who was facing 34 counts of child molestation for allegedly abusing altar boys and members of the local Boy Scout troop over a period of several years. Father Gauthe was apparently the first U.S. priest to face criminal charges for child molestation, but more importantly his case began a sexual abuse scandal involving priests, brothers, deacons, and seminarians that has rocked the Catholic Church, both in America and around the globe, for nearly 30 years. To get a sense of how much coverage has been devoted to the scandal, an October 10, 2014, search of the *New York Times* archives indicated that it has published over 2,200 stories on the scandal since 1985, or roughly 73 stories a year—more than one per week. And that's just one media source!

In a 2003 comprehensive examination of the scandal, the *New York* Times' Laurie Goodstein wrote that

> The data, together with extensive interviews with priests and former priests, abuse victims, church historians, psychologists and experts on sexual disorders, suggest that although the problem involved only a small percentage of priests, it was deeply embedded in the culture of the Catholic priesthood. Many priests began seminary training as young as [age] 13, and all of them spent years being groomed in an insular world in which sexual secrets and transgressions were considered a matter for the confessional, not the criminal courts (Goodstein, 2003, p.1).

The website www.bishopaccountability.org has gathered exhaustive information on the scandal from a huge array of sources, including print and electronic news outlets, the Catholic Church itself, law enforcement and prosecutors' offices, the courts, victims, and victims' advocacy groups. A cursory review of this information paints a very troubling picture of the scope of the problem over the past 30 years in the United States, with strong evidence that large-scale sexual abuse of children by Catholic clergy in this country extends as far back as the 1950s.

Table 5-4: Accused U.S. Catholic clerics whose names have been made public (as of May 2, 2014)

Bishops	24
Priests	3,536
Nuns	91
Brothers	245
Deacons	56
Seminarians	21
Total	3,973

Source: www.bishopaccountability.org

According to the website, the United States Conference of Catholic Bishops (USCCB) estimates that 17,259 children have been the victims of sexual abuse by priests and other members of the Catholic clergy in the U.S. since the 1980s (see Table 5-4). However, there is not a consensus on this figure; some estimates run as high as 100,000 victims (e.g., Greeley, 1993). A total of 6,427 priests have been identified and/or accused of sexual abuse, although only about half of them have had their names released to the public. The abusers and alleged abusers are disproportionately diocesan priests (77%) rather than members of religious orders such as Jesuits, Franciscans, or Dominicans (23%). In the few U.S. dioceses where investigations or disclosures have provided adequate data, the percentage of accused priests is about 10%; when translated to the national level, this would mean that 11,505 priests have been identified and accused. Approximately two thirds of sitting U.S. bishops have allegedly kept accused priests in ministry or moved accused priests to new assignments.

(Continued)

Spotlight on Policy: The Catholic Church's Sexual Abuse Scandal *(Continued)*

Costs of the scandal. The scandal has cost the Catholic Church billions of dollars in damages paid to victims, legal fees, court costs, and so forth. The scandal has also hurt the Catholic Church in terms of negatively affecting the attitudes of its members and generating negative press about the Church's handling of the scandal (including sometimes-substantiated charges of coverups and/or other efforts to bully, intimidate, or silence victims who have come forward) (*Frontline*, 2014).

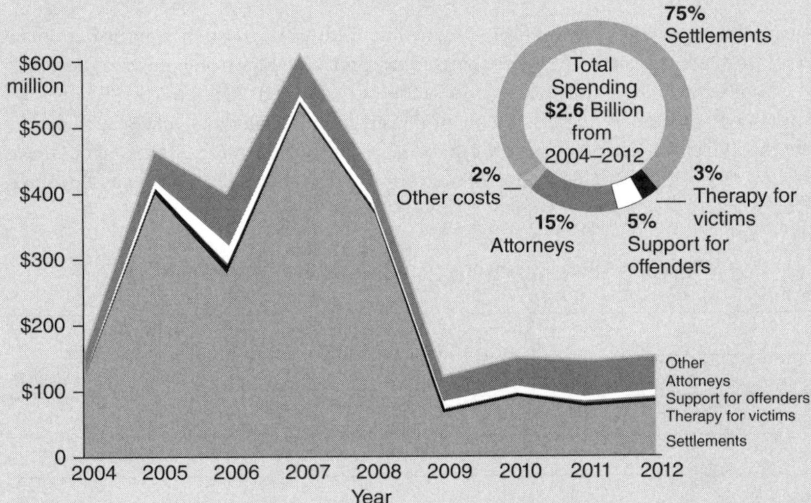

Figure 5-10 Costs to the Catholic Church of the Pedophile Priest Scandal
Source: *Frontline* (2014).

Responses to the scandal. In response to the scandal, the USCCB issued the *Charter for the Protection of Children and Young People* in 2002 and has revised it several times (e.g., United States Council of Catholic Bishops, 2013). The *Charter* is "a comprehensive set of procedures . . . for addressing allegations of sexual abuse of minors by Catholic clergy" (United States Council of Catholic Bishops, 2013, p. 1). The *Charter* also includes guidelines for reconciliation, healing, accountability, and prevention of future acts of abuse. Finally, the *Charter* directs action in the following matters:

- Creating a safe environment for children and young people
- Healing and reconciliation of victims and survivors
- Making prompt and effective response to allegations
- Cooperating with civil authorities
- Disciplining offenders
- Providing for means of accountability for the future to ensure the problem continues to be effectively dealt with through the Secretariat of Child and Youth Protection and the National Review Board.

The USCCB also established an annual audit process to assess compliance with the *Charter* and to collect data on allegations of abuse involving members of the Catholic clergy. Finally, in 2014, Pope Francis met with a group of survivors in Rome and asked each person individually for his or her forgiveness on behalf of the Church. The Pope promised to continue working to resolve the problem and to prevent future abuse of children by priests as well (Boghani, 2014).

KEYWORDS

Personal victimization	Infanticide	Stalking
Supplementary Homicide Report	Eldercide	Fear standard
Homicide	Femicide	Cyberstalking
Spousal homicide	Subculture of violence	Assault
Intimate partner homicide	Sexual victimization	Simple assault
Parricide	Rape	Aggravated assault
Neonaticide	Sexual assaults	Robbery

DISCUSSION QUESTIONS

1. Why are children at the highest risk for homicide in the first year of life? Why does risk of victimization decrease thereafter until the teenage years?
2. Studies discussed in this chapter found that lifestyles, routines, and low self-control were related to personal victimization, but there were differences across types of personal victimization. Why might such differences exist?
3. Should the fear standard be included in definitions of stalking victimization? Further, how many pursuit behaviors should a victim experience before being considered a stalking victim? Explain your answer.
4. Why are college women at a heightened risk for stalking victimization?
5. Why are the risk factors different between simple assault and aggravated assault?
6. Wright and Decker's study revealed that individuals who engage in criminal activities are often attractive victimization targets for robbers. Why do you think this is the case?
7. One of the consistent findings across many types of personal victimization is that the offender is often known to the victim. How does the victim–offender relationship create opportunities for victimization? Explain for different types of personal victimization.
8. What have current victimological theories overlooked in their explanation as to why individuals experience personal victimization? Provide your insights as to which factors are missing and how and why these factors might explain risk of personal victimization.
9. Why might rates of personal victimization be different for males and females?

REFERENCES

Anderson, E. (1999). *Code of the street: Decency, violence, and the moral life of the inner city.* New York: W.W. Norton and Company.

Baron, L., & Straus, M.A. (1987). Four theories of rape: A macrosociological analysis. *Social Problems, 34,* 467–489.

Baum, K., Catalano, S., Rand, M., & Rose, K. (2009). *Stalking victimization in the United States* (NCJ 224527). Washington, DC: Bureau of Justice Statistics.

Black, M. C., Basile, K. C., Breiding, M. J., Smith, S. G., Walters, M. L., Merrick, M. T., Chen, J., & Stevens, M. R. (2011). *The National Intimate Partner and Sexual Violence Survey: 2010 Summary Report.* Atlanta, GA: National Center for Injury Prevention and Control, Centers for Disease Control and Prevention.

Boghani, P. (2014). *What Pope Francis has done differently in tackling the sexual abuse scandal.* Retrieved October 10, 2014, from: http://www.pbs.org/wgbh/pages/frontline/ religion/secrets-of-the-vatican/what-pope-francis-has-done-differently-in-tackling-the-sexual-abuse-scandal

Brownmiller, S. (1975). *Against Our Will: Men, Women and Rape.* New York: Simon and Schuster.

Bunch, J., Clay-Warner, J., & Lei, M. K. (2012). Demographic characteristics and victimization risk: Testing the mediating effects of routine activities. *Crime and Delinquency.* DOI: 10.1177/0011128712466932

Campbell, J. C., Webster, D., Koziol-McLain, J., Block, C., Campbell, D., Curry, M. A., Gary, F., Glass, N., McFarlane, J., Sachs, C., Sharps, P., Ulrich, Y., Wilt, S. A., Manganello, J., Xu, X., Schollenberger, J., Frye, V., & Laughon, K. (2003). Risk factors for femicide in abusive relationships: Results from a multisite case control study. *American Journal of Public Health, 93,* 1089–1097.

Cass, A.L. (2007). Routine activities and sexual assault: An analysis of individual- and school-level factors. *Violence & Victims, 22,* 350–366.

Catalano, S. (2012). *Stalking victims in the United States—Revised* (NCJ 224527). Washington, DC: Bureau of Justice Statistics.

Cohen, L., & Felson, M. (1979). Social change and crime rate trends: A routine activity approach. *American Sociological Review, 44,* 588–608.

Cooper, A., & Smith, E. L. (2011). *Homicide trends in the United States, 1980–2008: Annual rates for 2009 and 2010* (NCJ 236018). Washington, DC: Bureau of Justice Statistics.

Dietz, N. A., & Martin, P. Y. (2007). Women who are stalked: Questioning the fear standard. *Violence Against Women, 13,* 750–776.

Ezell, M. E., & Tanner-Smith, E. E. (2009). Examining the role of lifestyle and criminal history variables on the risk of homicide victimization. *Homicide Studies, 13,* 144–173.

Federal Bureau of Investigation (2009). *UCR offense definitions.* Retrieved March 12, 2015 from: http://www.ucrdatatool.gov/offenses.cfm

Federal Bureau of Investigation (2012). *Crime in the United States.* FBI Uniform Crime Reports. Retrieved March 12, 2015 from: http://www.fbi.gov/about-us/cjis/ucr/crime-in-the-u.s/2012/crime-in-the-u.s.-2012/tables/4tabledatadecoverviewpdf

Federal Bureau of Investigation. (2013a). *Crime in the United States*. FBI Uniform Crime Reports. Retrieved November 5, 2013, from: http://www.fbi.gov/about-us/cjis/ucr/crime-in-the-u.s/2012/crime-in-the-u.s.-2012/cius_home.

Federal Bureau of Investigation. (2013b). *UCR Program Changes Definition of Rape*. FBI Uniform Crime Reports. Retrieved October 30, 2013, from: http://www.fbi.gov/about-us/cjis/cjis-link/march-2012/ucr-program-changes-definition-of-rape

Federal Bureau of Investigation. (2013c). *Robbery*. FBI Uniform Crime Reports. Retrieved November 5, 2013, from: http://www.fbi.gov/about-us/cjis/ucr/crime-in-the-u.s/2012/crime-in-the-u.s.-2012/violent-crime/robbery

Felson, R. B., Savolainen, J., Berg, M. T., & Ellonen, N. (2013). Does spending time in public settings contribute to the adolescent risk of violent victimization? *Journal of Quantitative Criminology, 29*, 273–293.

Fisher, B. S., Cullen, F. T., & Turner, M. G. (2002). Being pursued: Stalking victimization in a national study of college women. *Criminology and Public Policy, 1*, 257–308.

Fox, K. A., Gover, A. R., & Kaukinen, C. (2009). The effects of low self-control and childhood maltreatment on stalking victimization among men and women. *American Journal of Criminal Justice, 34*, 181–197.

Fox, K. A., Nobles, M. R., & Fisher, B. S. (2011). Method behind the madness: An examination of stalking measurements. *Aggression and Violent Behavior, 16*, 74–84.

Franklin, C. A. (2011). An investigation of the relationship between self-control and alcohol-induced sexual assault victimization. *Criminal Justice and Behavior, 38*, 263–285.

Franklin, C. A., Franklin, T. W., Nobles, M. R., & Kercher, G. A. (2012). Assessing the effect of routine activity theory and self-control on property, personal, and sexual assault victimization. *Criminal Justice and Behavior, 39*, 1296–1315.

Frontline. (2014). *What's the status of the Church's child abuse crisis*? Retrieved October 10, 2014, from: http://www.pbs.org/wgbh/pages/frontline/religion/secrets-of-the-vatican/whats-the-state-of-the-churchs-child-abuse-crisis

Garcia-Moreno, C., Guedes, A., & Knerr, W. (2012). *Understanding and addressing violence against women: Femicide*. New York: World Health Organization.

Gastil, R. D. (1971). Homicide and a regional culture of violence. *American Sociological Review, 36*, 412–427.

Goodstein, L. (2003). *Decades of damage: Trail of pain in Church crisis leads to nearly every diocese*. Retrieved October 10, 2014, from: http://www.nytimes.com/2003/01/12/us/decades-of-damage-trail-of-pain-in-church-crisis-leads-to-nearly-every-diocese.html

Gottfredson, M. R., & Hirschi, T. (1990). *A general theory of crime*. Stanford, CA: Stanford University Press.

Greeley, A. (1993). *How serious is the problem of sexual abuse by the clergy*? Retrieved October 10, 2014, from: http://www.bishop-accountability.org/resources/resource-files/ timeline/1993-03-20-Greeley-HowSerious-1.htm.

Kennedy, L. W., & Forde, D. R. (1990). Routine activities and crime: An analysis of victimization in Canada. *Criminology, 28*, 137–152.

Kruttschnitt, C., Kalsbeek, W. D., & House, C. C. (2013). *Estimating the incidence of rape and sexual assault*. Washington, DC: The National Academies Press.

Maraboli, S. (2013). *Unapologetically you: Reflections on life and the human experience*. Port Washington, NY: A Better Day Publishing.

McCleary, R., & Chew, K. S. Y. (2002). Winter is the infanticide season: Seasonal risk for child homicide. *Homicide Studies, 6*, 228–239.

Messner, S. F., Baller, R. D., & Zevenbergen, M. P. (2005). The legacy of lynching and Southern homicide. *American Sociological Review, 70*, 633–655.

Messner, S. F., & Tardiff, K. (1985). The social ecology of urban homicide: An application of the "routine activities" approach. *Criminology, 23*, 241–267.

Miethe, T. D., Stafford, M. C., & Long, J. S. (1987). Social differentiation in criminal victimization: A test of routine activities/ lifestyle theories. *American Sociological Review, 52,* 184–194.

Muftic', L. R., & Hunt, D. E. (2013). Victim precipitation: Further understanding the linkage between victimization and offending in homicide. *Homicide Studies, 17,* 239–254.

Mustaine, E. E., & Tewksbury, R. (1998). Victimization risks at leisure: A gender-specific analysis. *Violence and Victims, 13,* 231–249.

Mustaine, E. E., & Tewksbury, R. (1999). A routine activity theory explanation for women's stalking victimizations. *Violence Against Women, 5,* 43–62.

National Center for Victims of Crime. (2007). *The Model Stalking Code revisited: Responding to the new realities of stalking.* Washington, DC: National Center for Victims of Crime.

NCVS Victimization Analysis Tool. (2013). Accessed October 31, 2013, from: http://www.bjs.gov

Nobles, M. R., & Fox, K. A. (2013). Assessing stalking behaviors in a control balance theory framework. *Criminal Justice and Behavior, 40,* 737–762.

Nobles, M. R., Reyns, B. W., Fox, K. A., & Fisher, B. S. (2014). Protection against pursuit: A conceptual and empirical comparison of cyberstalking and stalking victimization among a national sample. *Justice Quarterly, 31,* 986–1014.

NOLO (n.d.). *Homicide.* Retrieved March 11, 2015 from http://www.nolo.com/legal-encyclopedia/homicide-murder-manslaughter-32637.html

Nordheimer, J. (1985). *Sex charges against priest embroil Louisiana parents.* Retrieved October 10, 2014, from: http://www. nytimes.com/1985/06/20/us/sex-charges-against-priest-embroil-louisiana-parents.html

Piquero, A. R., MacDonald, J., Dobrin, A., Daigle, L. E., & Cullen, F. T. (2005). Self-control, violent offending, and homicide victimization: Assessing the general theory of crime. *Journal of Quantitative Criminology, 21,* 55–71.

Pizaro, J. M., Corsaro, N., & Yu, S. V. (2011). Journey to crime and victimization: An application of routine activities theory and environmental criminology to homicide. *Victims and Offenders, 2,* 375–394.

Planty, M., Langton, L., Krebs, C., Berzofsky, M., & Smiley-McDonald, H. (2013). *Female victims of sexual violence, 1994–2010* (NCJ 240655). Washington, DC: Bureau of Justice Statistics.

Roberts, A., & Willits, D. (2011). Lifestyle, routine activities, and felony-related eldercide. *Homicide Studies, 17,* 184–203.

Schwartz, M. D., & Pitts, V. L. (1995). Exploring a feminist routine activities approach to explaining sexual assault. *Justice Quarterly, 12,* 9–31.

Tillyer, M. S., Gialopsos, B. M., & Wilcox, P. (2013). The short-term repeat sexual victimization of adolescents in school. *Crime and Delinquency.* DOI: 10.1177/0011128713501026

Tillyer, M. S., & Tillyer, R. (2012). Violence in context: A multilevel analysis of victim injury in robbery incidents. *Justice Quarterly.*DOI:10.1080/07418825.2012.696127

Tjaden, P., & Thoennes, N. (1998a). *Prevalence, incidence, and consequences of violence against women: Findings from the National Violence Against Women Survey.* Washington, DC: National Institute of Justice.

Tjaden, P., & Thoennes, N. (1998b). *Stalking in America: Findings from the National Violence Against Women Survey.* Washington, DC: National Institute of Justice.

Truman, J., Langton, L., & Planty, M. (2013). *Criminal victimization, 2012* (NCJ 243389). Washington, DC: Bureau of Justice Statistics.

Turanovic, J. J., & Pratt, T. C. (2012). "Can't stop, won't stop": Self-control, risky lifestyles, and repeat victimization. *Journal of Quantitative Criminology.* DOI 10.1007/s10940-012-9188-4

United States Council of Catholic Bishops, (2013). *Charter for the protection of children and young people.* Washington, DC: United States Council of Catholic Bishops. Retrieved October 10, 2014, from: http://www.usccb.

org/issues-and-action/child-and-youth-protection/upload/2011-Charter-booklet.pdf

Wilcox, P., Land, K. & Hunt, S. (2003). *Criminal circumstance: A dynamic, multi-contextual criminal opportunity theory.* New York: Aldine de Gruyter.

Wolfgang, M. (1957). Victim precipitated homicide. *Journal of Criminal Law, Criminology & Police Science, 48,* 1–11.

Wolfgang, M. E., & Ferracuti, F. (1967). *The subculture of violence: Towards an integrated theory in criminology.* London: Tavistock Publications.

World Health Organization. (2012). Femicide: Understanding and addressing violence against women. Retrieved October 15, 2013, from: http://apps.who.int/iris/bitstream/10665/77421/1/WHO_RHR_12.38_eng.pdf

Wright, R. T., & Decker, S. H. (1997). *Armed robbers in action: Stickups and street culture.* Boston, MA: Northeastern University Press.

CHAPTER 6

Victimization of Women, Children, and the Elderly

CHAPTER OUTLINE

LEARNING OBJECTIVES

- Define intimate partner violence and explain who is at risk for this form of victimization.
- Describe the extent and nature of intimate partner violence.
- Distinguish among forcible rape, drug- or alcohol-facilitated rape, and incapacitated rape.
- Identify and describe the different types of sexual victimization perpetrated against women.
- Describe the extent and nature of the sexual victimization of women.
- Explain the differences among child maltreatment, child abuse, and child neglect.
- Describe the extent and nature of child maltreatment.
- Differentiate among elder maltreatment, elder abuse, and elder neglect.
- Describe the extent and nature of elder maltreatment.

Violence against women is primarily intimate partner violence.

Tjaden and Thoennes, 2000, p. iv

Introduction

Certain types of criminal victimization are disproportionately perpetrated against and experienced by women, children, and the elderly. In considering these victim populations, a few clarifications are necessary. First, although by their nature these offenses are similar to those described in Chapter 5, they are ascribed specific labels because of the characteristics of the crime victim. For example, intimate partner violence shares attributes with assault victimization, but the act and its effects are recognized as a different type of crime because it is perpetrated by an intimate partner—someone who is trusted by and familiar to the victim. Second, women, children, and elderly victims are often targeted either *because* of these characteristics or the nature of their circumstances. For example, perhaps an elderly person depends on assistance from others to take care of his daily needs. If his caretaker ignores these needs, the elderly person is the victim of elder neglect. Absent this dependency, elder neglect would not have occurred because the would-be victim could have taken care of his own needs. Third, an additional consideration is the harm that is caused by offenses against these vulnerable populations. For instance, in the case of assault victimization, an adult man may recover relatively quickly from his injuries, whereas a child victim who is still developing physically could suffer greater harm, take longer to recuperate, and experience much longer-lasting effects. While several types of victimization against women, children, and the elderly are reviewed together in this chapter, these forms of victimization are nevertheless distinct. Just as assault victimization is different than intimate partner violence, so too are child abuse and elder abuse different in character from each other. They are discussed together in one chapter because they are all recognized as unique given the characteristics of the victim.

This chapter begins by reviewing the victimization of women, including discussions of intimate partner violence and sexual victimization. Rape victimization, which primarily affects females, was discussed in Chapter 5, but other types of sexual victimization experienced by women, such as sexual coercion and unwanted sexual contact, are presented in this chapter. Next, the victimization of children, specifically child abuse and child neglect, is discussed. Finally, elder victimization is reviewed; it is similarly divided into the categories of elder abuse and elder neglect.

Victimization of Women

A fairly consistent finding from victimization surveys is that men have higher rates of personal victimization than women (Truman, Langton, & Planty, 2013). For certain specific offenses, however, women are more often victimized than men. Notably, women are more likely than men to experience intimate partner violence and sexual victimization (Black, Basile, Breiding, Smith, Walters, Merrick, Chen, & Stevens, 2011). As a result, victimologists have concentrated on developing a better understanding of why this is the case. One of the keys to understanding these types of victimization is often, but not always, rooted in the relationship between the victim and the offender. This is particularly the case with respect to intimate partner violence, which by definition is committed by an intimate partner. And, as was discussed in Chapter 5, sexual victimizations such as rape are often perpetrated by those known to the victim—if not an intimate partner, then frequently a friend or an acquaintance. These two forms of violence against women are discussed with an emphasis on their extent and nature, while also noting the importance of the victim–offender relationship.

Intimate Partner Violence

Intimate partner violence (IPV) is a somewhat expansive term that includes violent acts perpetrated by current or former spouses, boyfriends, or girlfriends. IPV takes many forms, ranging from physical and sexual violence, to psychological aggression or emotional abuse, to stalking. IPV is sometimes referred to as ***domestic violence***, which is an even broader label applied to violent acts committed by intimate partners *and* other family members. Another frequently used term is ***wife battering***, but that is generally considered a historic relic and has been subsumed by the IPV term. Although IPV-related victimizations are diverse, they each entail intentional harm being inflicted on the victim by an intimate partner. Men may experience IPV at the hands of their intimate partners as well, but research shows that, as has been observed for sexual offenses, men are at a significantly reduced risk for such victimizations (Black et al., 2011; Tjaden & Thoennes, 2000). For example, Patricia Tjaden and Nancy Thoennes (2000) reported that 22.1% of women in the National Violence Against Women Survey (NVAWS) had experienced IPV during their lives compared to just 7.4% of men. Further, victimization rates for women who had been physically assaulted, raped, and/or stalked since the age of 18 were four times greater than rates for men (64% vs. 16%) (Tjaden & Thoennes, 2000). To illustrate this gender split in IPV victimization, Figure 6-1 provides IPV victimization rates for males and females from the NCVS. These data show trends in victimization rates from 1994 through 2011 and clearly indicate that violence against females by intimate partners is more common than is violence against males by their partners.

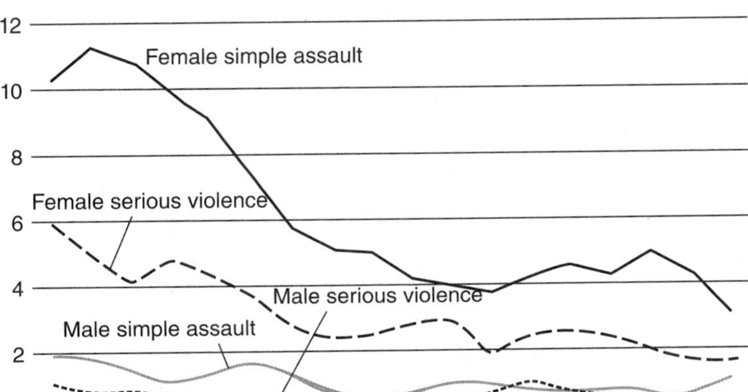

Note: Estimates based on 2-year rolling averages beginning in 1993. Serious violent crime includes rape or sexual assault, robbery, and aggravated assault. Intimates include current or former spouses, boyfriends, and girlfriends.

*Due to methodological changes, use caution when comparing 2006 NCVS criminal victimization estimates to other years. See *Criminal Victimization, 2007*, NCJ 224390, BJS website, December 2008, for more information.

Figure 6-1 IPV Rates by Sex, 1994–2011
Source: Catalano (2013).

IPV also occurs within same-sex relationships. A recent study by Adam Messinger (2011) reported that persons in same-sex relationships were more likely to experience IPV, including physical, verbal, sexual, and other controlling behaviors by intimate partners, than persons involved in heterosexual relationships. While research in the area of same-sex IPV has only recently begun, early work suggests that IPV in same-sex relationships is complex and more research is needed in this important area. For example, Naomi Goldberg and Ilan Meyer (2013) found that the prevalence of IPV was higher among same-sex couples in California (as compared to opposite-sex couples), but this finding applied only to bisexual women and gay men. Those who are victimized by same-sex intimate partners also may face hurdles in obtaining victim services or be reluctant to report the crime to law enforcement. As an example, many states do not have domestic violence shelters for male victims of IPV which means that gay men who are victims of IPV may have no safe place to go. Victims may also be concerned that law enforcement will not take their situation seriously and therefore will be unwilling to report what happened to them.

Victimologists have devoted research attention to studying the forms of IPV. The diversity of harmful behaviors perpetrated by intimate partners has been studied extensively, and although these studies differ in the method used for assessing intimate partner victimization, a few conclusions can be made regarding this form of violence against women. First, nonphysical abuse, or what has been referred to as "psychological abuse," is more common than physical abuse. Aggressive behaviors, such as being "put down," called names, insulted, or otherwise humiliated, are frequently uncovered by victimization surveys. Nonphysical abuse often involves controlling behaviors as well. Perpetrators may keep track of victims' activities, physically threaten them, destroy property they care about, make decisions they can make for themselves, or keep them from seeing others, such as friends or family. Second, among physical forms of IPV, slapping, pushing, shoving, being slammed against something, hit with something, hair pulling, beating, and choking are most commonly experienced by victims. Third, with respect to sexual victimization by an intimate, women also can be subjected to sexual coercion, rape, non-contact unwanted sexual experiences, and unwanted sexual contact. Further, these forms of IPV may overlap; that is, victims may experience more than one type of IPV. For example, 12.5% of victims in the National Intimate Partner and Sexual Violence Survey (NISVS; see Chapter 3 for details) experienced rape, physical violence, and stalking by their partners (Black et al., 2011).

The prevalence of IPV also has been the subject of a substantial amount of research by victimologists. Recent NCVS estimates suggest that there were 810,790 IPV incidents in the United States in 2012, which represents a victimization rate of 3.1 per 1,000 persons (Truman et al., 2013). More detailed information is provided by the NISVS, which reported the estimated percentage of U.S. women and men who experienced different types of IPV, including rape, physical violence, stalking, and/or any of the three types of victimization. Results from this survey are provided in Table 6-1, which highlights several key findings about IPV in the United States. First, women are more at risk for every form of IPV than men. Second, among both women and men, experiencing any form of IPV is common, with over 35% of women and 28% of men being victimized during their lives. Third, among physical forms of IPV, physical violence is the most common, followed by stalking, and rape, which is the least common. Finally, 5.9% of women and 5% of men are victimized annually, underscoring the widespread problem that IPV poses and the staggering number of people that are affected.

Besides the finding that females are at higher risk for IPV than males, victimologists also have found several other risk factors related to victimization by intimate partners. One such factor is an individual's race. Considering rape, physical violence, and/or stalking perpetrated by an intimate partner, the NISVS revealed that among women, multiracial individuals (i.e., two or more races) have the highest lifetime prevalence (53.8%) of IPV victimization, followed by American Indian or Alaska Natives (46%), African Americans (43.7%), Hispanics (37.1%), whites (34.1%), and Asian or Pacific Islanders (19.6%) (Black et al., 2011). Like many other types of victimization discussed throughout the text, age also is linked to IPV

Table 6-1: Lifetime and 12-Month Prevalence of Rape, Physical Violence, and/or Stalking Victimization by an Intimate Partner, 2010 for U.S. Women and Men NISVS

Women				
	Lifetime		12 Month	
	Weighted %	Estimated Number of Victims[1]	Weighted %	Estimated Number of Victims[1]
Rape	9.4	11,162,000	0.6	686,000
Physical violence	32.9	39,167,000	4.0	4,741,000
Stalking	10.7	12,786,000	2.8	3,353,000
Rape, physical violence, and/or stalking	35.6	42,420,000	5.9	6,982,000
With IPV-related impact[2,3,4]	28.8	34,273,000	–	–

Men				
	Lifetime		12 Month	
	Weighted %	Estimated Number of Victims[1]	Weighted %	Estimated Number of Victims[1]
Rape	*	*	*	*
Physical violence	28.2	31,893,000	4.7	5,365,000
Stalking	2.1	2,427,000	0.5	519,000
Rape, physical violence, and/or stalking	28.5	32,280,000	5.0	5,691,000
With IPV-related impact[2,3,4]	9.9	11,214,000	–	–

[1]Rounded to the nearest thousand.
[2]Includes experiencing any of the following: being fearful, concerned for safety, any PTSD symptoms, need for health care, injury, contracted a crisis hotline, need for housing services, need for victim's advocate services, need for legal services, missed at least one day of work or school. For those who reported being raped it also includes having contracted a sexually transmitted disease.
[3]IPV-related impact questions were assessed in relation to specific perpetrators, without regard to the time period in which they occurred, and asked in relation to any form of IPV experienced (sexual violence, physical violence, stalking, expressive aggression, coercive control, and reproductive control) in that relationship.
[4]By definition, all stalking incidents result in impact because the definition of stalking includes the impacts of fear and concern for safety.
*Estimate is not reported; relative standard error > 30% or cell size < 20.
– 12-month prevalence of IPV-related impact was not assessed.
Source: Black et al. (2011).

victimization. Although IPV is perpetrated against women of all ages, it appears that most victims experience some type of IPV for the first time when they are between 18 and 24 years old (47.1%). The next most frequent life stages for onset of IPV are 11 to 17 years (22.4%) and 25 to 34 years (21.1%) (Black et al., 2011). In general, then, young women are at greatest risk for IPV victimization.

Further risk factors for IPV have been derived from victimization theories, as well as theories from criminology, psychology, and other fields. Explanations of IPV span a range of perspectives on victimization and offending and include social learning theory, feminist theories, as well as evolutionary, ecological, social psychological, and integrated theoretical models (see DeKeseredy & Schwartz, 2011). Most of the theoretical developments in IPV research have focused on the causes and correlates of offending, but victimological explanations of IPV are emerging and also being tested by researchers. Although the opportunity perspective of lifestyle–routine activities theory features prominently in victimization research generally, it has not been widely used by researchers to examine IPV. However, a study by Kristin Carbone-Lopez and Candace Kruttschnitt (2010) examined IPV against female offenders using the opportunity perspective of lifestyle–routine activities theory. They argued that criminal offending could be regarded as a type of lifestyle, one in which victimization risks are heightened because of the victim–offender overlap. The results of the study supported the contention that having an intimate relationship with a partner who is criminally involved increased women's risk for experiencing IPV. Carbone-Lopez and Kruttschnitt's study is not a "full test" of lifestyle–routine activities theory, but it does suggest that certain types of lifestyles might affect IPV victimization risk.

In another study to explore factors related to IPV, Emily Wright (2012) assessed the effects of micro- and macro-level influences on victimization. She concluded that at the individual level, factors such as age, education, income, and cohabitation without marriage were related to either the prevalence or frequency of IPV. A primary purpose of Wright's study was also to assess the effect on IPV of having the social support of family or friends. Interestingly, the results showed that those with a supportive family were less likely to experience IPV, but those with supportive friends were more likely to be victimized. However, the effects of social support differed from neighborhood to neighborhood. In turn, neighborhood-level factors, specifically concentrated disadvantage within neighborhoods, were related to experiencing IPV, even after considering the effects of individual-level correlates of victimization. In other words, as other multilevel studies have shown, both micro- and macro-level factors elevate victimization risk. Findings from this study are consistent with other research on IPV, particularly the effects of age, education, income, nonmarital cohabitation, and concentrated disadvantage (e.g., Lauritsen & Schaum, 2004).

Victimologists also have viewed IPV as a consequence of large-scale social forces. For example, Min Xie, Karen Heimer, and Janet Lauritsen (2012) studied violence against women from a feminist routine activities perspective. They evaluated the effects of women's labor force participation, female voter participation, income, and education on violence perpetrated across victim–offender relationships. For violence by intimate partners, results indicated that as women made gains economically and politically, they were less vulnerable to, and more protected from, IPV. For other victim–offender relationships (strangers and non-intimates) female labor force participation increased violence against women. This finding is consistent with Cohen and Felson's (1979) original presentation of routine activities theory, which proposed that as more women entered the workforce, their personal victimization rates increased because of their greater exposure to motivated offenders.

Much of the research on the correlates of IPV also has focused on the offender and the reasons for his or her behavior. While these perspectives are more useful for explaining offending than victimization, they are nonetheless prominent pieces in the IPV puzzle. The ***intergenerational transmission of violence theory*** is one of the foremost of these explanations. Developed from a social psychological framework, the premise of this theory is that violent behaviors between intimates are learned by children as they watch how their parents interact (e.g., Straus, Gelles, & Steinmetz, 1980). Theoretically, then, children who have witnessed IPV among their parents are more likely to perpetrate IPV themselves when they are older and have intimate partners of their own—hence, the violence is perpetuated across generations. This argument is also compatible with some of the learning theories from criminology that point toward mechanisms such as observing the behaviors of others, developing attitudes or values from others, imitating behaviors, and having those behaviors either reinforced or punished (e.g., Akers, 1998). Overall, social learning–type theories have received moderate support in research examining the causes of IPV (e.g., Stith, Rosen, Middleton, Busch, Lundeberg, & Carlton, 2000; Wareham, Boots, & Chavez, 2009). Other frequently cited explanations for why offenders attack their partners include personal pathologies (e.g., personality disorders), stress, alcohol and drug abuse, and social and economic inequality between men and women.

IPV can have a negative toll on victims in many ways. The consequences of victimization depend on the nature of the victimization and, in some ways, how the victim responds. Nonphysical forms of violence often produce feelings of fear in victims, concern for their safety, or even posttraumatic stress disorder (PTSD). Those who are physically assaulted also incur injuries, may contract sexually transmitted diseases, or can potentially become pregnant by the offender. In extreme cases, the victim also can be killed by the partner, a specific type of homicide called *intimate partner homicide* (see Chapter 5). An additional concern is repeat victimization, wherein the victim is victimized in the future, sometimes repeatedly, by the intimate partner (see Chapter 9).

Many observers question why victims would stay in a situation in which they could be attacked in the future. While some victims seek services to escape the circumstances they are in, many do not. Lenore Walker (1979) explained that IPV represents a cycle of abuse that often repeats. Her ***cycle of violence theory*** (also known as battered woman syndrome) articulates three phases that battered women experience ("Spotlight on Theory: Walker's Cycle of Violence" box), and she notes that the cycle can be repeated. Walker described a battered woman who experiences the cycle of violence as one who "is repeatedly subjected to any forceful physical or psychological behavior by a man in order to coerce her to do something he wants her to do without any concern for her rights" (Walker, 1979, p. xv). She also explained that a victim of IPV is not considered a battered woman until she experiences the cycle of violence two or more times.

Spotlight on Theory: Walker's Cycle of Violence

Phase 1: The Build-Up Phase

During this phase, *tensions mount in the relationship* for any number of reasons (e.g., stress, alcohol, or money). The male partner begins to abuse the victim through minor assaultive behaviors or emotionally using threats or belittling comments. The victim often tries to de-escalate the situation or change her behavior to avoid triggering battering episodes. Both parties may rationalize the offender's behavior or find a way to excuse it. Eventually, the victim's coping mechanisms become ineffective and the acute battering phase begins. This phase can last days or weeks.

Phase 2: The Acute Battering Phase

This phase is characterized by the *most abusive violence*. With tensions having reached a "boiling point," the offender perpetrates extreme physical and emotional abuse upon the victim. During this time, which has a short duration of up to 24 hours, the victim is at risk for serious physical and emotional injury. This is the time at which the police are most likely to be called since the incident is undeniably serious.

Phase 3: The Respite (or Honeymoon) Phase

The "honeymoon phase" finds the *offender being very contrite, loving, and kind to the victim*. He may promise to change his ways, seek help, and/or apologize for his behavior. Many times, though, this is an attempt to keep the victim from ending the relationship. The perpetrator may also still be exerting some type of control over the victim (e.g., coercion) without physically assaulting her. For the victim's part, she may be hoping that the relationship has turned a corner and that this phase in their relationship is the new normal. As a consequence, this is a difficult time for victims to leave their abusers.

Source: Walker (1979).

Sexual Victimization

As discussed, one of the persistent findings related to IPV is that women are more likely to be victimized than men. This pattern also holds for sexual types of victimization, regardless of the relationship between the victim and the offender. For example, victimization rates for rape and sexual assault from the NCVS indicate that 1.6 per 1,000 women were victimized in 2012 compared to 1.0 per 1,000 men (NCVS Victimization Analysis Tool, 2013). It is also important to keep in mind that the estimates of these types of victimization reported in the NCVS are likely an underestimation of the true extent of rape and sexual assault in the United States. Data from the NVAWS revealed a larger gap between women and men with respect to sexual victimization, finding that 17.6% of women and 3.0% of men had experienced either an attempted or completed rape during their lives (Tjaden & Thoennes, 1998). In terms of lifetime prevalence, then, women have much higher victimization rates than men. Given the intensity of sexual victimization as a type of violence against women, victimologists have devoted special attention to understanding the many forms it takes.

Just as IPV is a broad label capturing many different behaviors, the term ***sexual victimization*** can describe different victimization experiences. Rape, sexual coercion, and unwanted sexual contact are all types of physical sexual victimization that are experienced by women. Even rape takes many forms, including forcible rape, drug- or alcohol-facilitated rape, incapacitated rape, and statutory rape. Then again, sexual victimization may be nonphysical in nature. These types of sexual victimization are referred to as ***non-contact unwanted sexual experiences*** and can be expressed as either visual or verbal victimization. The sexual victimization of women is discussed according to these types with a specific emphasis placed on their prevalence and the circumstances surrounding victimization.

In Chapter 5, ***rape*** was defined as penetration of the vagina or anus with any body part or object, or oral penetration by a sex organ of another person, without the victim's consent. The methods used by the rapist to carry out this act are what distinguish the various types of rape victimization. ***Forcible rapes***, which can be either attempted or completed, are those that involve the use of physical force or threats of physical force by the rapist. These are the offenses most often represented in ***rape myths***, which are stereotypes about the nature of rape that often are not supported by the facts. For example, rape myths suggest that rapes are violent encounters perpetrated by strangers. The reality, however, is that rape is often perpetrated by individuals the victim knows and may not involve physical force. Several rape myths are contrasted with rape facts in Box 6-1 to illustrate the concept of the rape myth. Further details on the extent and nature of forcible rape are provided in Chapter 5.

Box 6-1: Selected Rape Myths and Facts

Myth: Rape is caused by lust or uncontrollable sexual urges and the need for sexual gratification.

Fact: Rape is an act of physical violence and domination that is not motivated by sexual gratification.

Myth: Once a man gets sexually aroused, he can't just stop.

Fact: Men do not physically need to have sex after becoming sexually excited. Moreover, they are still able to control themselves after becoming aroused.

Myth: Women provoke sexual assault by their appearance. Sexual attractiveness is a primary reason why a rapist selects a victim.

Fact: Rapists do not select their victims by their appearance. They select victims who are vulnerable and accessible. Victims of sexual assault range in age from infants to the elderly; sexual attractiveness is not an issue.

Myth: If a woman really did not want to be raped, she could fight off her attacker.

Fact: Even if the rapist is not carrying a weapon, the element of surprise, shock, and fear or the threat of harm can overpower a victim.

Source: Roger Williams University (n.d.).

Many occurrences of rape do not involve physical force or threats of physical force; instead, drugs or alcohol can enable the offender to take advantage of the victim. Drugs and alcohol can assist the rapist in at least one of two ways. First, they can be used as a tool by the offender to facilitate the act. This type of rape is known as ***drug- or alcohol-facilitated rape***. Consider the following scenario. At a crowded party, a male college student gives a female whom he has just met a beer in a plastic cup and strikes up a conversation. She does not know that the beer has been spiked with flunitrazepam (Rohypnol; also known as "roofies" and the "date rape drug"), which has a number of physiological effects, including sleepiness, decreased blood pressure, and amnesia. A half-hour later, the offender has sex with the helpless victim. Here, the offender used drugs and alcohol to make it impossible for the victim to consent to having sex. Second, drugs or alcohol can debilitate would-be victims, allowing would-be rapists to take opportunistic advantage of intoxicated victims. To offer another scenario, a couple (Emma and Owen) go on their third date and start the evening at a bar. Emma gets drunk. When they get back to the car, Owen makes continued sexual advances, which Emma is too drunk to resist. They have sex. In this situation, Emma is a victim of ***incapacitated rape***, which means because of her self-induced use of alcohol (or drugs), she is unable to consent to having sexual relations with Owen. Notice that if Owen had *purposely* gotten Emma drunk so he could have sex with her, this would have been a drug- or alcohol-facilitated rape. The distinction between these two forms of rape hinges on whether the rapist deliberately used intoxicants as a tool to incapacitate the victim before having sexual relations with her, or whether the victim is incapacitated because of self-induced consumption. The victim is unable to consent to having sex in both forms of rape.

The extent of drug- or alcohol-facilitated rape and incapacitated rape is not tracked annually in the primary sources of victimization data in the United States (NCVS, UCR). However, a recent study by Dean Kilpatrick, Heidi Resnick, Kenneth Ruggiero, Lauren Conoscenti, and Jenna McCauley (2007) sheds some light on the scope of these forms of rape in both the general U.S. population and among college women more specifically. Kilpatrick and colleagues (2007) reported that for lifetime prevalence of drug- or alcohol-facilitated rape, 2.3% of their sample of women in the U.S. population had been victimized compared to 2.7% of college women. Further, their results suggest that alcohol is a more common intoxicant in these circumstances than are drugs. The research team also reported on the extent of incapacitated rape among these groups. In the general population, about 2.8% of women were victims of incapacitated rape during their lives, while among college women the estimates were about 4%.

In instances of drug- or alcohol-facilitated rape and incapacitated rape, the victim is unable to consent to sex because of her inebriated condition. The issue of consent is also of critical importance for another form of rape: statutory rape. ***Statutory rape*** occurs when a person who is under the legal age of consent engages in sexual activities with another person. In American law, ***age of consent*** refers to the age at which one is considered competent to give permission or agree to have sexual relations with another person. The age of consent differs slightly from state to state in the United States but generally falls between the ages of 16 and 18. Further, different states make exceptions under certain circumstances. For example, in Vermont the age of consent is 16. However, if the persons are married or if the child is at least 15, the other person is less than 19, and the child consents, in neither case would the sexual encounter be legally considered statutory rape. To continue this example forward, if these two conditions are not met—say, the child is 14 and the offender is 24—the offender could be charged with statutory rape. In Utah the age of consent is 18, but minors aged 16 or 17 can legally engage in sexual activity with partners 10 years older or less. This simple comparison suggests that in some circumstances what is considered statutory rape in one state (Vermont) is considered legal in another state (Utah). The point is that age of consent and the conditions under which statutory rape is defined are different across the United States. Age of consent also differs from country to country. For instance, in Canada, the age of consent is set at 16 years old, while in Mexico individuals as young as 12 may be able to consent (with some restrictions).

Additional types of sexual victimization, including sexual coercion, unwanted sexual contact, coerced sexual contact, and forced unwanted sexual contact, involve physical sexual contact between the victim and the offender, but not necessarily penetration of the victim. ***Sexual coercion*** occurs when victims are verbally coerced into unwanted sexual penetration (e.g., anal, vaginal, oral). For instance, the perpetrator may verbally threaten the victim with nonphysical punishment (e.g., ending the relationship), promise some type of reward, or pester or pressure the victim until he or she relents. To give some idea of the scope of sexual coercion, estimates from research by Bonnie Fisher, Francis Cullen, and Michael Turner (2000) indicated that 1.7% of a nationally representative sample of college women were victims of completed sexual coercion in about a seven-month period. Reflected as a victimization rate, about 16.6 per 1,000 female college students were victimized during this same time period. NISVS estimates suggest that 13% of women and 6% of men have been victims of sexual coercion at some time in their lives (Black et al., 2011).

Unwanted sexual contact is another form of sexual victimization that refers to intrusive sexual experiences involving physical contact (i.e., touching) but not sexual penetration. These unwanted sexual experiences might involve kissing, grabbing, fondling, or other types of sexual touching of the breasts, buttocks, or genitals. These experiences can be either forcefully perpetrated, in which case the offense is referred to as ***unwanted sexual contact with force***, or non-forceful, which is called ***coerced sexual contact***. The college-based study by Fisher and associates (2000) and the NISVS also provide victimization estimates for unwanted sexual contact victimizations. According to the former, nearly 2% of college women or 19.1 per 1,000 female students were victimized using force or threat of force in a seven-month period. Estimates from the latter source of victimization data suggest that 27.2% of women and 11.7% of men are victims of unwanted sexual contact at some point in their lifetime, without making distinctions between those that are forceful or coerced. Victims also are coerced into these forms of sexual contact using tactics similar to those described in relation to sexual coercion. Coerced sexual contact involves psychological or emotional coercion to touch, kiss, grab, fondle, lick, or otherwise sexually touch the victim. The study by Fisher and colleagues (2000) found similar rates and percentages of victimization to unwanted sexual contact, with 1.8% of female students being victims of coerced sexual contact.

The final type of sexual victimization to be discussed is non-contact unwanted sexual experiences. On the whole, these offenses do not involve touching or penetration but are still either visually or verbally sexually charged. For example, ***visual victimization*** may include unwanted experiences such as having someone masturbate in front of the victim, having someone expose his or her genitals (i.e., "flashing"), or making the victim view pornographic materials, either videos or pictures. Non-contact unwanted sexual experiences may also include having the victim participate in these activities, such as posing for sexual photos. ***Verbal victimization*** entails using harassing, degrading, or abusive language of a sexual nature. Sexual remarks, noises with sexual overtones, catcalls, whistles, obscene language, and other sexualized verbal behaviors are all examples of verbal victimization. These more "minor" forms of sexual victimization are common. For instance, the study by Fisher and her collaborators (2000) found that 6.1% of female students had been exposed to unwanted pornographic materials without their consent, and 4.8% had experienced "flashing." For verbal victimization, over half of students—54.3%—had sexist remarks made in their presence, and 48.2% were subjected to catcalls, whistles about their looks, or noises with sexual overtones. The NISVS did not separate visual and verbal victimization but overall found that 33.7% of women and 12.8% of men in the United States have been victims of non-contact unwanted sexual experiences during their lives.

Risk factors and theories of sexual victimization of women were reviewed in Chapter 5 as they apply to rape victimization, and thus are not repeated here. However, these risk factors and theories are useful in explaining the types of sexual victimization presented in this chapter as well. In sum, the sexual victimization of women is a prominent area of focus in the field of victimology. Sexual victimization is diverse, is experienced by a significant portion of women in the United States and abroad, and will continue to be an important subject for victimological research. For instance, a developing trend is to study recurring sexual victimization, in which victims are successively or repeatedly sexually victimized (e.g., Daigle, Fisher, & Cullen, 2008). The previously reviewed forms of sexual victimization also are experienced by other vulnerable populations, including children and the elderly, to whom we now turn our attention.

Victimization of Children

Many crimes against children are referred to as child maltreatment, which is a general term that includes both child abuse and child neglect. The Centers for Disease Control and Prevention (CDC) have advocated for a uniform definition of child maltreatment across academic disciplines and service sectors to allow for consistency and comparisons of child victimization rates and improved responses for victims. Therefore, we are adopting the CDC definition of ***child maltreatment***, which is "any act or series of acts of commission or omission by a parent or other caregiver resulting in harm, potential harm, or threat of harm to a child" (Leeb, Paulozzi, Melanson, Simon, & Arias, 2008). It is necessary to give special attention to a number of components of this definition to clearly elucidate the characteristics of child maltreatment. First, "caregivers" are persons who have custody of children and are entrusted with their care and control on either a temporary or permanent basis. Those who have permanent custodial roles are primary caregivers who live with the child, such as biological, adoptive, step-, or foster parents, or other legal guardians. Individuals with temporary custodial roles, or substitute caregivers, do not necessarily live with the child and include relatives, teachers, coaches, babysitters, members of the clergy, or others who do not fulfill primary caregiver roles. Second, the term "child" refers to persons who are age 17 or under at the time of the maltreatment (Leeb et al., 2008). Third, "harm" denotes any disruption to the child's physical (e.g., physical injuries, avoidable illnesses, inadequate nutrition) or emotional health (e.g., anxiety problems, eating disorders, disruption of social functioning) that occurs as a consequence of the acts, either actual or threatened (Leeb et al., 2008).

Child Abuse

The difference between acts of commission (overt actions) and omission (failing to act) is what distinguishes child abuse from child neglect. ***Child abuse*** occurs when parents or caregivers overtly or intentionally act in ways that are harmful to the child either physically or emotionally. Physical abuse, sexual abuse, and psychological abuse are different forms of maltreatment that are all considered to be child abuse. There are clear differences between each of these three types of child abuse. Deliberate and intentional use of physical force against a child that either results in injury or has the potential to result in physical injury is defined as ***physical child abuse*** (Leeb et al., 2008). A key element to defining child abuse is that the abusive act is deliberate or intentional, and thus accidental acts are usually not labeled as child abuse. To illustrate, a parent who strikes his child to punish him for spilling a glass of milk has committed child abuse, whereas a parent who accidently strikes his child while trying to tag him during playtime has not committed child abuse. A further obstacle to defining and identifying child abuse is that it is legal for parents (and guardians) to use ***corporal punishment*** in the home (e.g., spanking) to correct or control children's behavior, but the dividing line between corporal punishment and child abuse is not always clear.

Sexual child abuse is defined as any sexual acts, contact, or exploitation of a child by a caregiver. As is the case with sexual victimization of women, the nature of sexual abuse of children is very diverse. It can include sexual acts involving penetration, genital-on-genital contact, or mouth-on-genital contact. It can involve abusive sexual contact, including touching above or beneath the clothing, of the genitalia, anus, groin, breast, inner thigh, or buttocks. In each of these instances, the abuse may involve either the offender performing sexual acts upon the child or the offender forcing the child to perform sexual acts upon him or her. Sexual child abuse also involves non-contact acts in which there is no physical contact but rather exposure to sexual activities (e.g., filming or photographing a child in a sexual manner), materials (e.g., pornography), or language (e.g., sexual harassment). Further, prostitution of a child or sexual trafficking, which both involve forced sexual activity of the child, are considered serious forms of sexual child abuse (Leeb et al., 2008).

Psychological child abuse, like other forms of child maltreatment, occurs in a variety of circumstances. Overall, ***psychological child abuse*** consists of any caregiver behavior that is harmful or potentially harmful to a child psychologically, emotionally, or developmentally. Psychological child abuse can be episodic or continual and involve behaviors that are degrading, belittling, terrorizing (e.g., life-threatening), isolating (e.g., forbidding contact with others), intimidating, blaming, or otherwise expressing to the child that he or she is unwanted, unloved, worthless, in danger, or valued only for what he or she can do for others (Leeb et al., 2008). As an example, a mother who constantly tells her teenage son who suffers from acne breakouts on his face that he is "ugly" or that no one "wants to look at *that* face" may be psychologically abusing her child.

Determining the prevalence and characteristics of child maltreatment, and hence devising responses to it, are continuing challenges for victimologists. Currently, the NCVS and the UCR, which are primary sources of victimization data for other types of victimization, are limited in their use as sources of information on child maltreatment. Instead, alternative sources of information are used to describe the extent and nature of child maltreatment in the United States. For example, the U.S. Department of Health and Human Services (HHS) recently published a report on child maltreatment in 2012 based on data collected through the National Child Abuse and Neglect Data System (NCANDS). The NCANDS is a voluntary data collection system that includes information gathered from all 50 states, the District of Columbia, and Puerto Rico about reported cases of child abuse and neglect.

The HHS report includes information on a variety of aspects of child maltreatment, such as victimization rates and characteristics of child victims. According to data from 2012, the national victimization rate for children who suffered at least one form of maltreatment was 9.2 per 1,000 children. This translates to approximately 686,000 child victims in 2012, which was a modest decrease from 716,000 victims in 2008 (HHS, 2012). The report also provides information related to victims' age, sex, and race. For example, the report indicates that the youngest children are the most vulnerable to maltreatment, with over one quarter of victims being younger than 3 years old. Figure 6-2 illustrates child maltreatment victimization rates by the age of victim. Regarding victim sex, girls had slightly higher victimization rates (9.5 per 1,000 children) in 2012 than did boys (8.7 per 1,000 children) (HHS, 2012). In terms of victim race, African Americans (14.2), American Indian or Alaska Natives (12.4), and those of multiple races (10.3) had the highest rates of victimization, followed by Pacific Islanders (8.7), Hispanics (8.4), whites (8.0), and Asians (1.7) (HHS, 2012).

Noteworthy research into child maltreatment victimization has been undertaken by researchers such as David Finkelhor and his colleagues at the Crimes Against Children Research Center at the University of New Hampshire. A recent study by Finkelhor, Turner, Ormrod, and Hamby (2010) used telephone survey methods to assess the extent of childhood victimization among 4,046 children aged 2 to 17 years in the United States using the National Survey of Children's Exposure to Violence. With the resulting nationwide data, they were able to estimate the annual victimization rates for several types of child maltreatment, including physical abuse, sexual abuse, and psychological abuse. Several findings from the study are significant. First, results suggested that 11.1% of children surveyed experienced some type of maltreatment, including child neglect, which is discussed below. Second, psychological/emotional abuse was the most common form of child

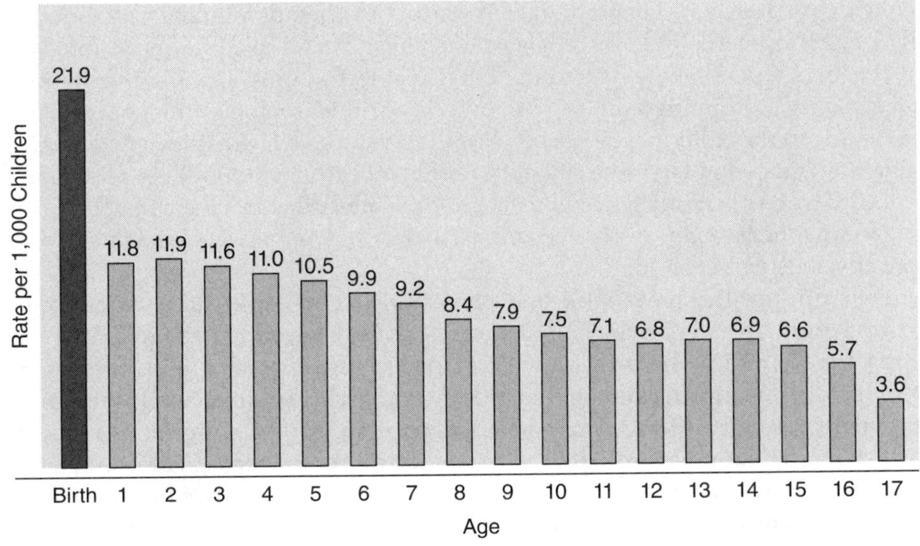

Figure 6-2 Child Victimization Rate by Age, 2012
Source: U.S. Department of Health and Human Services (2012).

maltreatment, with 7.1% of children in the study experiencing a victimization in 2008. Third, any type of sexual victimization was the next most common; this included victimizations such as sexual assaults, sexual exposure (being "flashed"), sexual harassment, and sexual misconduct. All told, 6.7% of children experienced one of these types of sexual victimization, but 2% of children were victims of sexual assault. Finally, 4.2% of children were victims of physical abuse by caregivers.

Further research by Finkelhor, Turner, Shattuck, and Hamby (2013), using a similar research methodology, indicates that children have a high lifetime prevalence of criminal victimization by caregivers. Data on the victimization experiences of 4,503 children age 1 month to 17 years revealed that 25.6% experienced any maltreatment, 9.6% were physically abused, 14.9% were psychologically/emotionally abused, and 0.5% were sexually abused at some point during their lives. Table 6-2 highlights the sex and age of child victims across four types of maltreatment. For example, males had higher rates of physical abuse than did females, but females had higher rates of psychological abuse.

This study also reported that children exposed to one type of victimization were at risk for being victims of other types of crime and/or maltreatment. This phenomenon, sometimes referred to as ***polyvictimization***, occurs when children are frequently victimized and is discussed in Chapter 9. Since much of the research into child maltreatment jointly examines both child abuse and child neglect, it is necessary to define child neglect before reviewing its prevalence as well as discussing explanations and risk factors for child maltreatment generally.

Child Neglect

If child abuse is considered an act of commission, or what has been done *to* a child, child neglect involves an act of omission—what has *not* been done for a child. ***Child***

Table 6-2: Percentage of Children Victimized in One Year by Sex and Age

	Sex		Years				
Type of Victimization	Male	Female	0–1	2–5	6–9	10–13	14–17
Any Maltreatment	13.4	14.2	6.2	9.5	11.5	16.8	20.6
Physical Abuse	4.5	2.9	0.6	1.8	3.8	5.2	5.5
Psychological Abuse	6.9	9.2	–	3.4	7.0	7.4	13.9
Sexual Abuse	0.0	0.3	0.0	0.2	0.1	0.2	0.1
Neglect	6.9	6.0	5.7	4.6	2.8	10.1	8.6

Source: Adapted from Finkelhor et al. (2013).

neglect occurs when caregivers fail to provide for the child's needs, or fail to protect a child from harm through proper supervision. Because a child's needs are physical, emotional, and educational, child neglect, like child abuse, occurs in many ways. Categories of "failure to provide" include physical neglect, emotional neglect, educational neglect, and medical or dental neglect. ***Physical neglect*** occurs when a child's needs related to nutrition, shelter, hygiene, or clothing are not met. ***Emotional neglect*** is similarly varied and involves inattention to the child's emotional needs, ignoring the child, or failure to provide mental health care if necessary (Leeb et al., 2008). ***Educational neglect*** happens when caregivers do not provide access to education for the child. Finally, ***medical or dental neglect*** takes place when caregivers fail to provide medical, dental, or vision care for the child. Examples of each of these types of child neglect are provided in Table 6-3.

Second, failure to protect a child from harm may be a consequence of either *inadequate supervision* or exposing the child to a *dangerous environment* (Leeb et al., 2008). In other words, caregivers are responsible not only for meeting the child's physical, emotional, educational, and medical or dental needs, but also for ensuring that the child is safe both inside and outside the home. Consider the first aspect of failure to protect a child, inadequate supervision. Imagine a scenario in which a father is washing his car with his 3-year-old son in the front yard of the family's residence. The father gets down on his hands to buff a smudge on the car's paint and the child walks into the street, where he is injured by an older child riding a bicycle. This is a fairly benign example, but it illustrates the point that caregivers are accountable for watching or supervising their children. Even though the injury was an accident, it would not have happened if the father had watched his son more closely. There are countless other examples of how momentary inattention by caregivers could lead to severe consequences for children. The second aspect of child protection involves exposing the child to dangerous environments. This is an element of child neglect that often intersects with the caregiver's criminal behaviors. For example, caregivers who manufacture or sell drugs in the child's home are exposing that child to a dangerous and possibly violent environment. As another example, if a caregiver allows a child to be victimized and does nothing to prevent it, this too constitutes child neglect through exposure to a dangerous environment (Leeb et al., 2008).

Table 6-3: Types, Definitions, and Examples of Child Neglect

Type of Neglect	Definition	Examples
Physical	Failure to provide adequate nutrition, shelter, hygiene, or clothing for the child	• Nutrition: A 9-year-old boy prepares food for himself because his caregiver does not cook him meals; the boy is malnourished. • Shelter: The child's living arrangements are not stable, lack heat in winter months, are unsanitary, or are transient for more than two weeks at a time. • Hygiene: The child goes to school wearing dirty clothing, is unbathed, or has unwashed/unkempt hair. • Clothing: A 7-year-old girl is not provided warm clothing or a coat to wear during winter months.
Emotional	Ignoring the child, being unresponsive to the child emotionally, or failing to provide mental health care	• An infant is perpetually ignored when she cries and is instead left in her crib. • A young girl is never hugged, given emotional support, or made to feel loved or valued. • A 6-year-old boy with autism is not provided therapy, counseling, medication, or available individualized education programs.
Educational	Failure to provide for the child's educational needs	• A 12-year-old boy has never attended school. • A young teenager is encouraged to drop out of school and get a job to support the family.
Medical or Dental	Failure to provide medical, dental, or vision care for the child	• Medical: While climbing a tree a young boy falls and breaks his wrist, and his caregiver fails to seek medical attention in a timely manner. • Dental: A young girl cracks her tooth, which becomes abscessed, and her caregiver fails to take her to the dentist. • Vision: A child's caregiver fails to provide the child with corrective lenses.

The previously reviewed HHS report, as well as Finkelhor and colleagues' research, is also valuable in shedding light on the state of knowledge on child neglect. Child neglect is perhaps less known to the general public, but the available information suggests that it is far more common than is child abuse. Illustrating this point, the HHS (2012) report found that nationally, four in five (78.3%) of victims of child maltreatment were neglected. The report found that physical abuse (18.3%) and sexual abuse (9.3%) were the next most common types of maltreatment. These figures do not necessarily align with those of Finkelhor and colleagues (2013), but that is due to methodological reasons. First, the HHS report is based on data collected through NCANDS, which means only cases involving child protective services (CPS) across the states are included in the victimization estimates.

Second, Finkelhor and colleagues' study was based on a national survey that included children ages 1 to 17, regardless of whether their victimization experiences were reported to their state's CPS. In essence, Finkelhor and colleagues' study captures the "dark figure" of child maltreatment, while the HHS report reflects only known cases. With that in mind, the most recent study by Finkelhor and his research team (2013) found that child neglect occurred in 6.5% of the nationally representative sample during the year prior to the study. Further, 14.6% of the sample had experienced neglect during their lifetime. Referring back to Table 6-2, the study also found that males had a slightly higher annual prevalence of neglect than females, and the age group with the highest percentage of victimization was children ages 10 to 13.

Besides assessing the prevalence of victimization and characteristics of victims, researchers studying child maltreatment, abuse, and neglect also have focused on trying to explain why these heinous acts occur. However, most of the research that has been done has concentrated on the behavior of caregivers as offenders rather than on factors that increase risk for victims. Along these lines, well-known theories include the intergenerational transmission of violence theory and ***social learning theory***. These theories were previously discussed as explanations for IPV, but they can also be useful for understanding why some individuals perpetrate child maltreatment. Jointly, these theories view child maltreatment as a behavior that is learned through observation and experience. Or, simply put, those who experience maltreatment as children are more likely to abuse or neglect their own children. The reasoning behind this theory is grounded in empirical research showing a relationship between maltreatment in childhood and delinquency or criminal offending later in life (Widom, 1989). For example, Widom and Maxfield (2001) reported that being abused or neglected as a child increased the likelihood of arrest as a juvenile by 59% and as an adult by 28%. In terms of child maltreatment specifically, research generally finds that there *is* an intergenerational transmission of violence, but study findings often depend on the research methods used to investigate the issue (Thornberry, Knight, & Lovegrove, 2012).

Research and theory also have developed around a more "victim-centric" approach and identified risk factors for child maltreatment victimization. Sandra Stith and colleagues (2009) conducted a meta-analysis on the topic of risk factors for child maltreatment by examining findings from over 155 studies that have investigated the issue. Across this large body of research, the authors noted several risk factors that have been linked to maltreatment victimization and categorized them as involving (1) parent–child interactions (e.g., stress over parenting, parent perceives child as a problem); (2) parent characteristics independent of the child (e.g., psychopathy, unemployment, depression); (3) child characteristics separate from parents (e.g., child social competence, child externalizing behaviors); and (4) family factors (e.g., family size, socioeconomic status). Although factors from each of their identified categories were statistically related to maltreatment, and can therefore be considered risk factors, a few stood out as strong predictors of childhood victimization. For physical child abuse, parent anger, family conflict, and family cohesion had robust effects on maltreatment across several studies. The relationship between the parent and the child, the parent's perception that the child is a problem, the parent's level of stress, parent anger/hyperreactivity, and parent self-esteem were related to child neglect victimization (Stith et al., 2009).

David Finkelhor and Nancy Asdigian (1996) advocated a different approach to explaining youth victimization, including abuse and neglect. Offering a critique of lifestyle–routine activities theory, Finkelhor and Asdigian pointed out that the theory was not very well suited to accounting for victimizations suffered by acquaintances or family members. Their reasoning was that the theory presumes that time away from home represents exposure to risk, while time at home signifies guardianship and/or protection from risk. Yet, in terms of abuse and neglect by caregivers, activities away from home actually serve a protective benefit, while being home increases a child's chance for victimization. Therefore, Finkelhor and Asdigian explained that youth victimization is mostly not a consequence of the victim's lifestyle or routine activities, but rather a consequence of his or her *target suitability*. For that reason, they adapted the concept of target suitability to better conform to youth victimization by integrating it with the previously discussed risk factors for child maltreatment victimization. Their revised conceptualization of target suitability, which was referenced briefly in Chapter 2, is based on the idea that children's characteristics make them targets because they "have some congruence with the needs, motives or reactivities of offenders" (Finkelhor & Asdigian, 1996, p. 6). Referring to this revised conception of target suitability as ***target congruence***, Finkelhor and Asdigian expanded the concept into three dimensions: target vulnerability, target gratifiability, and target antagonism. These three aspects of target congruence are defined, along with examples, in the "Spotlight on Theory: Target Congruence" box. It is important to point out that what constitutes target congruence will differ from crime to crime (e.g., hate crimes, child maltreatment, sexual victimization) and from offender to offender.

Finkelhor and Asdigian (1996) examined the effects of these dimensions of target congruence on parental assaults using data collected from a sample of youth between the ages of 10 and 16. They found only target antagonism—for example, children with physical limitations, children in step-parent families, and children who engaged in risky behavior (e.g., stealing, running away from home)—was significantly related to physical abuse by parents. Further analyses examining sexual abuse that occurred among members of the sample suggested that target vulnerability (psychological problems) and target gratifiability (age and being male) had positive and significant relationships with sexual abuse. Overall, this study supports a revision of lifestyle–routine activities theory to include target congruence to better explain child maltreatment victimization. Few studies, however, have replicated Finkelhor and Asdigian's research by including target congruence as a key variable.

While the consequences of, and responses to, victimization are fully discussed elsewhere, it is important to note that in severe cases, child abuse and/or neglect can lead to fatalities. For example, in 2012 in the United States, there were 1,640 deaths resulting from child abuse or neglect, a rate of 2.2 per 100,000 children in the population (HHS, 2012). What this means is that in a state with 100,000 children, at least two will die from abuse/neglect in a particular year. Further, of those children who died, nearly 70% suffered neglect and over 44% were victims of physical abuse. To explain the high prevalence of neglect in child fatalities, experts note that neglect is generally much less visible than is child abuse, making it harder to identify and

Spotlight on Theory: Target Congruence

Dimension	Definition	Examples
Target Vulnerability	The potential victim is less able to resist or deter victimization, which makes him or her an easier target for the offender.	• Small size • Physical weakness • Emotional deprivation • Psychological problems
Target Gratifiability	The potential victim has some characteristic, attribute, skill, or quality that the offender wants to have access to, use, or manipulate.	• Age • Sex • Physical appearance
Target Antagonism	The potential victim has some characteristic, attribute, skill, or quality that makes the offender angry, jealous, or act in a destructive manner.	• Race or ethnicity • Disability • Sexual orientation • Antagonistic behavior

Source: Adapted from Finkelhor and Asdigian (1996).

potentially allowing the behavior to occur over longer periods before being noticed. Further, child fatalities show distinct patterns. For example, in four of every five child fatalities parents were responsible for their child's death, and boys and children of certain races (e.g., Pacific Islanders, African Americans) had higher fatality rates than did girls and children of other races. Contributing factors to child fatalities in 2012 included having parents who abused drugs or alcohol or being exposed to domestic violence in the home (HHS, 2012).

Childhood victimization is common, and understanding and responding to child abuse and neglect are significant challenges for practitioners, law enforcement, academics, and others interested in helping this vulnerable population. As the previous sections demonstrate, victimologists are continuously working toward accurately estimating the scope of child maltreatment and pinpointing the circumstances under which it occurs to aid in the development of prevention and protective strategies. A similar approach is ongoing as it relates to victimization of the elderly.

Victimization of the Elderly

There are many parallels to be drawn between crimes against children and crimes against the elderly. First, for both types of victims, it is their status, as either younger or older, that facilitates their criminal victimization. These respective stages in the life course create victimization opportunities that otherwise would not exist. For example, in either case the victim may be physically unable to resist an attack. Second and relatedly, depending on the elderly person's circumstances, both children and the elderly are or may be dependent upon caregivers for their physical and emotional needs. Third, the terminology used to describe elder crimes is analogous to that used to describe the victimization of children. In other words, elder victimization is broadly referred to as elder maltreatment; elder abuse involves acts of commission; and elder neglect involves acts of omission.

Unlike the standardized definitions for child maltreatment, child abuse, and child neglect developed by the CDC, uniform definitions of elder maltreatment have *not* been developed or universally accepted in the field of victimology or other disciplines (e.g., sociology, gerontology). In part, this may be because research into elder victimization did not begin to take shape until the late 1970s and early 1980s in the United States. As a result, several issues related to defining and studying elder maltreatment have yet to be resolved. First, the age at which an individual is considered to be an "elder" is a point of some debate, but the National Center for Injury Prevention and Control (2013) suggests that persons aged 60 and older are considered "elders." However, across studies of elder maltreatment, the age criteria used to identify elderly persons has fluctuated, which makes it difficult to compare results across the studies. Second, the *context* in which elder maltreatment is recognized as taking place also has resulted in clouded definitions. Elder maltreatment can be perpetrated in domestic (i.e., the home) or institutional (e.g., long-term care) settings, but these parameters have not always been clearly defined in the elder victimization research. A third and related issue involves perpetrators of elder maltreatment, abuse, and neglect. Since these forms of victimization can be experienced in the home or in an institution, the perpetrator can be anyone fulfilling a caregiver role (e.g., family member, employee) in either setting.

As a starting point for discussion, we are defining ***elder maltreatment*** as any act or series of acts of commission or omission by a caregiver that results in harm, potential harm, or threat of harm to an elder. It is important to point out, however, that dozens of definitions of elder maltreatment, abuse, and neglect have been suggested by scholars in various fields of study (for a review, see Castle, Ferguson-Rome, & Teresi, 2013). Several recognized forms of elder maltreatment are discussed below and categorized as either elder abuse or elder neglect.

Elder Abuse

Elder abuse involves purposeful or intentional acts that are harmful to an elderly person. These acts primarily take one of four forms, several of which are analogous to behaviors involved in child abuse. In other words, elder abuse can involve physical abuse, sexual abuse, or psychological/emotional abuse. However, unlike child abuse, elder abuse also can include acts that cause financial harm to the victim.

Physical elder abuse occurs when physical force is used to cause injury, pain, or impairment to an elderly person through hitting, slapping, burning, kicking, or some other deliberate action. Other types of physical abuse that affect elderly persons are force feeding, unwarranted administration of drugs, and use of physical restraints.

Sexual elder abuse often involves forcing an elderly person to participate in a sexual act without his or her consent, but it also can involve any of the forms of sexual victimization previously discussed throughout this chapter (e.g., sexual exploitation). Emotional or ***psychological elder abuse*** consists of behaviors such as scaring or embarrassing the elderly person, destroying his or her property, or damaging his or her emotional or psychological well-being in some other manner. Isolating the elderly person from family or friends and needlessly disrupting his or her regular activities also are forms of psychological elder abuse. Finally, ***financial elder abuse***, which is also referred to as ***material exploitation***, occurs when an elderly person's money, property, or other assets are misused. Financial abuse can be relatively simple, such as the case of an elderly person whose caregiver takes money from his or her purse or wallet; or it can be complicated, such as a caregiver who deceives an elderly person into signing documents (e.g., a will) that provide financial gain to the caregiver, or a caregiver who improperly uses a power of attorney granted by the victim or a court.

The study of elder abuse has lagged behind research into other forms of violence, resulting in somewhat scant information concerning the extent and nature of this form of victimization. As was observed for child maltreatment, the UCR and NCVS are limited in the information they provide for elder maltreatment. For instance, a Bureau of Justice Statistics publication (Klaus, 2005) using the NCVS reported on the extent of elder victimization over the period 1993 to 2002. The report indicated that elderly persons experienced substantially less criminal victimization as a group than did younger persons. Specifically, the elderly experienced nonfatal violent crime at a rate one-twentieth that of younger persons and household crime at a rate one-fourth that of younger persons (Klaus, 2005). The most recent NCVS data also indicate that individuals 65 and older have the lowest violent victimization rates of any age group (NCVS Victimization Analysis Tool, 2013). The problem, however, is with determining whether the victimization experienced can be considered elder maltreatment, abuse, or neglect, as NCVS data are unclear in this respect.

Alternative sources of information on elder maltreatment are therefore necessary to shed light on the extent and nature of these forms of victimization. For instance, in the first large-scale survey of elder abuse and neglect in the United States, Karl Pillemer and David Finkelhor (1988) assessed the prevalence of victimization among 2,020 elderly persons in community settings in the Boston area. Their findings suggested that elder maltreatment occurred at a rate of 32 per 1,000 elderly persons, that men and women were equally at risk for victimization, and that spouses were the most likely offenders. Another fairly early study focused on the scope of elder maltreatment was conducted by the National Center on Elder Abuse (NCEA) in 1996. The results of the nationwide study suggested that 449,924 elderly persons experienced some form of elder maltreatment (i.e., abuse or neglect) in 1996. Of these, 70,942 were reported to and substantiated by Adult Protective Services, which suggests a very low rate of reporting for elder maltreatment. The NCEA study also found that older women had the highest victimization rates, and that most incidents were perpetrated by family members (e.g., spouses, adult children). Those over 80 years old were at the highest risk for maltreatment (NCEA, 1998).

In the years since these initial pieces of research were conducted, several studies have examined the extent of elder maltreatment. For example, Ron Acierno and colleagues (2010) conducted the National Elder Mistreatment Study, which estimated the extent of several types of elder maltreatment among a national sample of 5,777 adults over 60 years old in the United States. Their one-year prevalence estimates suggested that financial elder abuse was the most widespread, with 5.2% of the sample experiencing this type of elder victimization. The results also indicated that emotional abuse was experienced by 4.6% of those sampled, 1.6% were physically abused, and 0.6% were sexually abused. As with all types of victimization, the information gleaned from studies of elder maltreatment and abuse hinges upon how victimization is defined, who is included in the study, and where the study is conducted.

In another study, Rajini Sooryanarayana, Wan-Yuen Choo, and Noran Hairi (2013) assessed the state of the research on elder maltreatment in domestic settings by comparing 26 published articles that focused on elder maltreatment. Their conclusion was that elder maltreatment is a worldwide problem and that research has reported prevalence estimates as low as 1% in the United States to as high as 44% in Spain. They also found that across studies, older subgroups of elderly persons and older women had the highest rates of victimization. Finally, the results showed that psychological abuse was most prevalent, followed by neglect, financial abuse, physical abuse, and sexual abuse. The World Health Organization (WHO, 2011) notes that while some estimates of the scope of elder maltreatment exist for developed countries such as the United States, virtually nothing is known about maltreatment in developing countries. Despite this, the WHO (2011) estimates that approximately 4% to 6% of elderly people have experienced some form of maltreatment.

These studies are valuable in terms of illuminating the scope of domestic elder maltreatment, but for the most part they do not address abuse in institutional settings. For whatever reason, few studies have examined elder maltreatment in long-term care settings such as nursing homes or assisted-living situations. A study by Connie Page and colleagues (2009) using survey data from Michigan compared maltreatment against persons in different care settings and found that nursing homes—in comparison to home care or assisted-living settings—had the highest rates of abuse for all types of abuse. This study also suggested that the form of maltreatment varied with the type of setting, with psychological/emotional abuse being the most common problem for assisted living (10%) but neglect being more common in nursing homes (9.8%). In another research study to examine elder maltreatment in institutional settings, Nicholas Castle (2012) surveyed 3,433 nurse aides in Pennsylvania regarding abuses they had observed in prior nursing home employment. The results suggested that verbal forms of abuse were common (36% of staff observed argumentative behavior with residents) and that physical abuse (6%), financial abuse (10%), and sexual abuse (1%) were observed less frequently. Understanding abuse in institutions is a growing area of interest in the elder abuse research literature. Attention now turns to elder neglect, which can also occur in domestic or institutional settings.

Elder Neglect

Like child neglect, ***elder neglect*** involves failure or refusal by a caregiver to provide for an elder's needs, be they physical, emotional, or social. Further, the types of child neglect provided in Table 6-3 are comparable to these forms of elder neglect. For example, physical elder neglect happens when an elderly person's needs related to nutrition, hygiene, clothing, shelter, or health care are not satisfied by their caregiver. However, two distinctive types of neglect also affect elder victims: (1) abandonment and (2) self-neglect. ***Elder abandonment*** refers to situations in which caregivers willfully desert an elderly person for whom they are responsible. For example, if a family member gives the hospital incorrect contact information upon admission of an elderly patient, the hospital may be unable to reach him or her in the future. Elder neglect also can occur when elderly persons threaten their own health by failing to take care of themselves, which is called ***self-neglect***. Self-neglect can be related to physical, emotional, or medical needs, and examples of self-neglect include refusing medication or other medical care, inattention to personal hygiene (e.g., poor grooming), or unsafe living conditions (e.g., unclean living quarters, lack of utilities in the home). Signs and symptoms of elder neglect, abandonment, and self-neglect are provided in Box 6-2.

Box 6-2: Signs and Symptoms of Elder Neglect

Type of Elder Maltreatment	Examples of Signs and Symptoms
Neglect	• Dehydration, malnutrition, untreated bed sores, and poor personal hygiene • Unattended or untreated health problems • Hazardous or unsafe living condition/arrangements (e.g., improper wiring, no heat, or no running water) • Unsanitary and unclean living conditions (e.g., dirt, fleas, lice on person, soiled bedding, fecal/urine smell, inadequate clothing)
Abandonment	• The desertion of an elder at a hospital, a nursing facility, or other similar institution • The desertion of an elder at a shopping center or other public location • An elder's own report of being abandoned
Self-Neglect	• Dehydration, malnutrition, untreated or improperly attended medical conditions, and poor personal hygiene • Hazardous or unsafe living conditions/arrangements (e.g., improper wiring, no indoor plumbing, no heat, no running water) • Unsanitary or unclean living quarters (e.g., animal/insect infestation, no functioning toilet, fecal/urine smell) • Inappropriate and/or inadequate clothing, lack of necessary medical aids (e.g., eyeglasses, hearing aids, dentures) • Grossly inadequate housing or homelessness

Source: National Center on Elder Abuse (2014).

Victim characteristics for abuse and neglect have been identified in several studies of elder maltreatment. For example, the NCEA (1998) study previously referenced found that for all types of maltreatment except abandonment, females made up the largest percentage of victims experiencing abuse. Patterns related to race of the victim are also evident in the NCEA study, with whites representing the highest percentage of victims for all types of maltreatment except abandonment, for which African Americans were more often victimized. The study also provided estimates of victimization pertaining to age and income of victims. While all individuals identified as victims were 60 or older, those who were 80 or older were at substantially increased risks for victimization, experiencing the majority of victimization for every type of maltreatment, except abandonment, which primarily affected those 75 to 79 years old. Finally, those individuals with incomes of $5,000 to $9,999 made up the largest percentage of victims for every type of elder maltreatment. These patterns are valuable in terms of identifying those who may be at greatest risk for victimization, but they do not fully explain why elderly persons become victims. Further, although it is possible to identify these patterns, it is important to acknowledge that elder maltreatment affects individuals from all walks of life and demographic backgrounds.

Research that explains why elder maltreatment, abuse, and neglect occur has focused on developing theories and identifying risk factors for both offending and victimization. Explanations for perpetration are not dissimilar from the explanations previously reviewed related to the victimization of women or child maltreatment. For example, the intergenerational transmission of violence theory and social learning theory offer explanations for why caregivers might mistreat elderly persons. In other words, in the same way that children can learn to batter their partners or their own children later in life, caregivers may have learned to use violence against elderly parents or others for whom they have a caregiving responsibility.

Still other perspectives address elder maltreatment in its relation to factors such as stress on the caregiver, the caregiver's psychopathology, or the sociocultural climate or ecological context in which the mistreatment takes place (see Castle et al., 2013). From a victimization standpoint, most research has concentrated on correlates of victimization of elderly persons, such as the dependency of the elderly person and his or her situation. Together, research suggests that risk factors for perpetration and victimization occur at multiple levels, including the individual level, the relationship level, the community level, and the societal level. Factors in each of these areas can help account for why individuals perpetrate or become victims of elder maltreatment. Table 6-4 provides examples of risk factors for both perpetration and victimization at each of these levels of analysis.

Richard Bonnie and Robert Wallace (2003) synthesized existing research findings relating to elder maltreatment in domestic settings in their report for the National Research Council. Their resulting theoretical model emphasized that the interaction between characteristics of the potential victim and the potential offender must be considered for elder maltreatment to be understood and explained. The theoretical model, which is illustrated in Figure 6-3, integrates risk factors at the individual, relationship, and contextual levels. In the diagram, the left side of the model lists the characteristics of the elderly person at risk for maltreatment and

Table 6-4: Risk Factors for Perpetration and Victimization of Elder Maltreatment

	Risk Factors	
Level	Perpetration	Victimization
Individual	• Mental illness • Alcohol abuse • Poor training for caregiving responsibilities • Inadequate coping skills • Exposure to abuse as a child	• Dementia of the victim • Gender: women are at greater risk of persistent and severe forms of abuse
Relationship	• Lack of social support • Lack of emotional support • High financial and emotional dependence upon a vulnerable elderly person	• Shared living situation • History of poor family relationships
Community	• Formal services for those providing care to an elderly person are limited, inaccessible, or unavailable	• Social isolation • Lack of social support for the elderly person
Society	• Tolerance or acceptance of aggressive behavior • Cultural belief that family members are expected to care for elderly persons without seeking help from others	• Cultural depictions of elderly persons as frail, weak, or dependent • Erosion of bonds between generations of a family

Source: Adapted from National Research Council (2003).

the right side includes the characteristics of the caregiver (i.e., trusted other) who could potentially perpetrate the maltreatment. The interaction of these characteristics is depicted in the middle of the model, with status inequality (i.e., level of dependence), the type of relationship between the parties, and power and exchange dynamics (i.e., caregiving expectations based on exchanges between parties) playing important roles. The "social embeddedness" boxes at the top of the model represent the social networks of the elder and the caregiver. These social networks are hypothesized to be critical to preventing elder maltreatment from occurring. The outcomes in the model represent the possible maltreatment of the elderly person, as well as the health and happiness of the elderly person and the caregiver. Bonnie and Wallace also discussed that the model may be useful in understanding maltreatment in different settings (e.g., nursing homes), but it was primarily devised to account for outcomes in domestic care situations.

According to the WHO (2011), by the year 2025 the population of persons aged 60 and older in the world will more than double, reaching an estimated 1.2 billion. Elder maltreatment is hypothesized to increase correspondingly as elderly persons make up a greater share of the global population. This likelihood underscores the importance

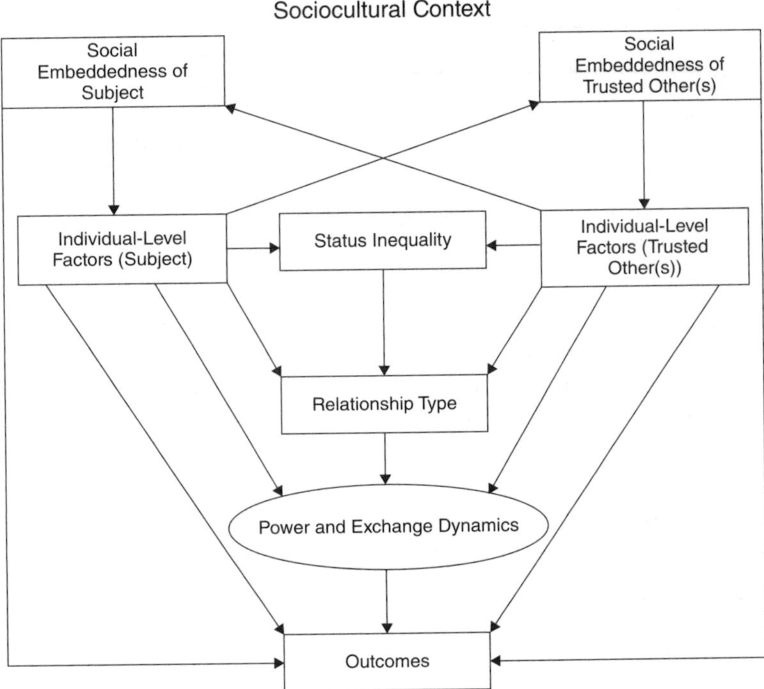

Figure 6-3 A Conceptual Model of Elder Maltreatment
Source: National Research Council (2003).

of a continued focus on the criminal victimization of the elderly, and particularly those crimes that are perpetrated by trusted caregivers. An added challenge may entail the ability of communities to handle the proper care of aging populations. Although much research has concentrated on identifying risk factors for victimization, less has focused on prevention and protective factors against victimization. Despite this, fostering ties among elderly persons, family members, community groups, agencies, and others appears to be one way to reduce the risk of maltreatment.

Summary

This chapter reviewed the criminal victimization of women, children, and the elderly, particularly those crimes that are perpetrated by individuals in positions of trust. Intimate partner violence and many forms of sexual victimization, including several types of rape, were discussed as they relate to the victimization of women. Several forms of abuse and neglect affecting children and elderly persons were also reviewed. Children and elderly victims experience physical, sexual, and psychological abuse and/or neglect of many kinds. Each group also experiences unique forms of victimization, such as educational neglect among children and self-neglect among the elderly. An especially troubling form of child victimization is the commercialized sex trade that involves children. The "Spotlight on Policy: Commercial Sexual Exploitation of Children" box discusses such cases.

Spotlight on Policy: Commercial Sexual Exploitation of Children

In recent years, governments, parents, schools, and law enforcement personnel have become aware of and increasingly concerned about the sexual exploitation of children for commercial gain. Such exploitation occurs when individuals buy, trade, or sell sexual acts with a child. Common illustrations of this include ***sex trafficking***, which involves recruiting, harboring, transporting, or so forth of a child for the purpose of commercial sexual activities (any sexual act for which something of value is given or received by any person). Children involved with these activities are considered to be the victims of severe forms of trafficking in persons.

Statistics on Commercial Sexual Exploitation of Children:

- Pimps prey on victims as young as 12 to 14.
- One study estimates that as many as 325,000 children in the United States, Canada, and Mexico are at risk each year for becoming victims of sexual exploitation.
- A history of physical and sexual abuse is often common among victims.
- One study estimates that 30% of shelter youth and 70% of street youth are victims of commercial sexual exploitation. They may engage or be coerced into prostitution for "survival sex" to meet daily needs for food, shelter, or drugs.
- Sex trafficking need not involve actual movement of the victim.
- Pimps may earn hundreds of thousands of dollars every year from selling minors.
- 75% of child victims engaged in prostitution are under the control of a pimp.

Children become victims of commercialized sexual exploitation through targeting by pimps and traffickers. These offenders often lure vulnerable children into prostitution or other forms of sexual exploitation (e.g., sexually explicit photographs or films) using psychological manipulation, drugs, and even violence. Offenders will often establish an online relationship, which then progresses to the point where an in-person meeting is arranged. They then create the illusion of a warm, loving, caring relationship with the child to create trust and dependence. It also helps to ensure the child will remain loyal to the offender even after suffering repeated victimizations. In short, victims are "targeted, tricked, and traumatized."

- Some potential indicators of trafficking and exploitation include the following:
- History of emotional, sexual, or other physical abuse
- Signs of current physical abuse and/or sexually transmitted diseases
- History of running away or current status as a runaway
- Inexplicable appearance of expensive gifts, clothing, or other costly items
- Presence of an older boyfriend or girlfriend
- Drug addiction
- Withdrawal or lack of interest in previous activities
- Gang involvement

Source: Adapted from the Innocence Lost Project (2010).

Although these populations share some characteristics that may be linked to victimization risk (e.g., vulnerability), the opportunity perspective that has been highlighted throughout the text suggests that there also may be distinctive features of these victim populations and their circumstances that facilitate opportunities for their victimization. As present, this theoretical perspective has been somewhat underdeveloped as it pertains to these offenses, and more research is needed. Further, the victimization of women, children, and the elderly represents an especially interdisciplinary area in the study of crime victims. This is a positive sign because it suggests that researchers from many disciplinary fields of study are interested in protecting these groups, but it also implies that it is often difficult to identify common threads and consistent findings across studies. As research in these areas progresses, it is likely that a more complete picture of the extent and nature of these types of victimization will emerge.

KEYWORDS

Intimate partner violence	Domestic violence	Wife battering
Intergenerational transmission of violence theory	Cycle of violence theory	Sexual victimization
Non-contact unwanted sexual experience	Rape	Forcible rapes
Rape myths	Drug- or alcohol-facilitated rape	Incapacitated rape
Statutory rape	Age of consent	Sexual coercion
Unwanted sexual contact	Unwanted sexual contact with force	Coerced sexual contact
Visual victimization	Verbal victimization	Child maltreatment
Child abuse	Physical child abuse	Corporal punishment
Sexual child abuse	Psychological child abuse	Polyvictimization
Child neglect	Physical neglect	Emotional neglect
Educational neglect	Medical or dental neglect	Social learning theory
Target congruence	Elder maltreatment	Elder abuse
Physical elder abuse	Sexual elder abuse	Psychological elder abuse
Financial elder abuse	Material exploitation	Elder neglect
Elder abandonment	Self-neglect	Sex trafficking

DISCUSSION QUESTIONS

1. Walker wrote about "battered *women*." Are there also "battered *men*"? Explain why or why not.
2. Can you think of reasons why IPV victims often stay in abusive relationships?
3. Explain the similarities and differences of the three forms of rape. Are the lifestyle–routine activities concepts useful in explaining how and why each type occurs? Provide a rationale for your answer.
4. Why does the prevalence of child maltreatment vary by victims' demographic characteristics, such as sex or race?
5. Can the intergenerational transmission of violence theory explain IPV, child maltreatment, *and* elder maltreatment? Is this theory better suited to explaining offending or victimization?
6. Compare and contrast child maltreatment with elder maltreatment. In what ways are they similar and in what ways are they different?
7. Why would elderly persons who have social support be *less* likely to experience maltreatment?
8. Apply Finkelhor and Asdigian's target congruence concepts to elder maltreatment. Is the adaptation of the lifestyle–routine activities concept also useful for understanding different forms of elder abuse and elder neglect? Explain how and why.

REFERENCES

Acierno, R., Hernandez, M. A., Amstadter, A. B., Resnick, H. S., Steve, K., Muzzy, W., & Kilpatrick, D. G. (2010). Prevalence and correlates of emotional, physical, sexual and financial abuse and potential neglect in the United States: The National Elder Mistreatment Study. *American Journal of Public Health, 100*, 292–297.

Akers, R. L. (1998). *Social learning and social structure: A general theory of crime and deviance*. Boston, MA: Northeastern University Press.

Black, M. C., Basile, K. C., Breiding, M. J., Smith, S. G., Walters, M. L., Merrick, M. T., Chen, J., & Stevens, M. R. (2011). *The National Intimate Partner and Sexual Violence Survey: 2010 summary report*. Atlanta, GA: National Center for Injury Prevention and Control, Centers for Disease Control and Prevention.

Bonnie, R. & Wallace, R. (2003). *Elder mistreatment*. Washington, DC: National Academies Press.

Carbone-Lopez, K., & Kruttschnitt, C. (2010). Risky relationships? Assortative mating and women's experiences of intimate partner violence. *Crime and Delinquency, 56*, 358–384.

Castle, N. (2012). Nurse aides' reports of resident abuse in nursing homes. *Journal of Applied Gerontology, 31*, 402–422.

Castle, N., Ferguson-Rome, J. C., & Teresi, J. A. (2013). Elder abuse in residential long-term care: An update to the 2003 National Research Council report. *Journal of Applied Gerontology, 32*, 1–37.

Catalano, S. (2013). *Intimate partner violence: Attributes of victimization, 1993–2011* (NCJ 243300). Washington, DC: Bureau of Justice Statistics.

Cohen, L., & Felson, M. (1979). Social change and crime rate trends: A routine activity approach. *American Sociological Review, 44*, 588-608.

Daigle, L. A., Fisher, B. S., & Cullen, F. T. (2008). The violent and sexual victimization of college women: Is repeat victimization a problem? *Journal of Interpersonal Violence, 23*, 1293–1316.

DeKeseredy, W. S., & Schwartz, M. D. (2011). Theoretical and definitional issues in violence against women. In C. M. Renzetti, J. L. Edleson, & R. K. Bergen (Eds.), *Sourcebook on violence against women* (2nd ed., pp. 3–22). Thousand Oaks, CA: Sage Publications, Inc.

Finkelhor, D., & Asdigian, N. L. (1996). Risk factors for youth victimization: Beyond a lifestyles/routine activities theory approach. *Violence and Victims, 11*, 3–19.

Finkelhor, D., Turner, H., Ormrod, R., & Hamby, S. L. (2010). Trends in childhood violence and abuse exposure: Evidence from 2 national surveys. *Archives of Pediatrics & Adolescent Medicine, 164*, 238–242.

Finkelhor, D., Turner, H. A., Shattuck, A., & Hamby, S. L. (2013). Violence, crime, and abuse exposure in a national sample of children and youth: An update. *JAMA Pediatrics, 167*, 614–621.

Fisher, B. S., Cullen, F. T., & Turner, M. G. (2000). *The sexual victimization of college women* (NCJ 182369). Washington, DC: U.S. Department of Justice.

Goldberg, N. G., & Meyer, I. H. (2013). Sexual orientation disparities in history of intimate partner violence: Results from the California Health Interview Survey. *Journal of Interpersonal Violence, 28,* 1109–1118.

Innocence Lost Project (2010). *Commercial sexual exploitation of children: A fact sheet.* Washington, DC: Federal Bureau of Investigation. Retrieved July 14, 2012 from: http://www.fbi.gov/about-us/investigate/vc_majorthefts/cac/innocencelost

Kilpatrick, D., Resnick, H. S., Ruggiero, K. J., Conoscenti, L. M., & McCauley, J. (2007). *Drug-facilitated, incapacitated, and forcible rape: A national study.* Charleston, SC: National Crime Victims Research and Treatment Center. Retrieved July 14, 2012, from www.ncjrs.gov

Klaus, P. (2005). *Crimes against persons age 65 or older, 1993–2002* (NCJ 206154). Washington, DC: Bureau of Justice Statistics.

Lauritsen, J. L., & Schaum, R. J. (2004). The social ecology of violence against women. *Criminology, 42,* 323–357.

Leeb, R. T., Paulozzi, L. J., Melanson, C., Simon, T. R., & Arias, I. (2008). *Child maltreatment surveillance: Uniform definitions for public health and recommended data elements.* Atlanta, GA: Centers for Disease Control and Prevention National Center for Injury Prevention and Control.

Messinger, A. M. (2011). Invisible victims: Same-sex IPV in the National Violence Against Women Survey. *Journal of Interpersonal Violence, 26,* 2228–2243.

National Center for Injury Prevention and Control. (2013). *Understanding elder abuse.* Retrieved January 18, 2014, from http://www.cdc.gov/violenceprevention/pdf/em-factsheet-a.pdf

National Center on Elder Abuse. (1998). *The national elder abuse incidence study.* Retrieved January 21, 2014, from http://aoa.gov/AoA_Programs/Elder_Rights/Elder_Abuse/docs/ABuseReport_Full.pdf

National Center on Elder Abuse. (2014). *Types of abuse.* Retrieved January 23, 2014, from http://www.ncea.aoa.gov/FAQ/Type_Abuse/index.aspx#self

National Research Council. (2003). *Elder mistreatment: Abuse, neglect, and exploitation in an aging America.* Washington, DC: National Academies Press.

NCVS Victimization Analysis Tool. (2013). Retrieved December 12, 2013, from http://www.bjs.gov/index.cfm?ty=nvat

Page, C., Conner, T., Prokhorov, A., Fang, Y., & Post, L. (2009). The effect of care setting on elder abuse: Results from a Michigan survey. *Journal of Elder Abuse & Neglect, 21,* 239–252.

Pillemer, K., & Finkelhor, D. (1988). The prevalence of elder abuse: A random sample survey. *The Gerontologist, 28,* 51–57.

Roger Williams University (n.d.). *Myths and facts.* Retrieved March 13, 2015 from: http://rwu.edu/campus-life/health-counseling/counseling-center/sexual-assault/rape-myths-and-fac

Sooryanarayana, R., Choo, W. Y., & Hairi, N. N. (2013). A review on the prevalence and measurement of elder abuse in the community. *Trauma, Violence, & Abuse, 14,* 316–325.

Stith, S. M., Liu, T., Davies, C., Boykin, E. L., Alder, M. C., Harris, J. M., Som, A., McPherson, M., & Dees, J. E. M. E. G. (2009). Risk factors in child maltreatment: A meta-analytic review of the literature. *Aggression and Violent Behavior, 14,* 13–29.

Stith, S. M., Rosen, K. H., Middleton, K. A., Busch, A. L., Lundeberg, K., & Carlton, R. P. (2000). The intergenerational transmission of spouse abuse: A meta-analysis. *Journal of Marriage and the Family, 62,* 640–654.

Straus, M. A., Gelles, R. J., & Steinmetz, S. K. (1980). *Behind closed doors: Violence in the American family.* Garden City, NY: Anchor Books.

Thornberry, T. P., Knight, K. E., & Lovegrove, P. (2012). Does maltreatment beget maltreatment? A systematic review of the intergenerational literature. *Trauma, Violence, and Abuse, 13,* 135–152.

Tjaden, P. & Thoennes, N. (1998). *Prevalence, incidence, and consequences of violence against women: Findings from the National Violence Against Women Survey* (NCJ 172837). Washington, DC: U.S. Department of Justice.

Tjaden, P., & Thoennes, N. (2000). *Full report of the prevalence, incidence, and consequences of violence against women: Findings from the National Violence Against Women*

Survey (NCJ 183781). Washington, DC: U.S. Department of Justice.

Truman, J., Langton, L., & Planty, M. (2013). *Criminal victimization, 2012* (NCJ 243389). Washington, DC: Bureau of Justice Statistics.

U.S. Department of Health and Human Services, Administration for Children and Families, Administration on Children, Youth and Families, Children's Bureau. (2012). *Child maltreatment 2012*. Retrieved January 2, 2014, from http://www.acf.hhs.gov/defaultfiles/cb/cm2012.pdf

Walker, L. (1979). *The battered woman*. New York: William Morrow.

Wareham, J., Boots, D. P., & Chavez, J. M. (2009). A test of social learning and intergenerational transmission among batterers. *Journal of Criminal Justice, 37,* 163–173.

Widom, C. S. (1989). Child abuse, neglect, and violent criminal behavior. *Criminology, 27,* 251–271.

Widom, C. S., & Maxfield, M. G. (2001). *An update on the "Cycle of Violence."* Washington, DC: National Institute of Justice.

World Health Organization. (2011). *Elder maltreatment, fact sheet 357.* Retrieved January 25, 2014, from http://www.who.int/mediacentre/factsheets/fs357/en/index.html

Wright, E. (2012). The relationship between social support and intimate partner violence in neighborhood context. *Crime & Delinquency.* doi:10.1177/0011128712466890

Xie, M., Heimer, K., & Lauritsen, J. L. (2012). Violence against women in U.S. metropolitan areas: Changes in women's status and risk, 1980–2004. *Criminology, 50,* 105–143.

CHAPTER 7

Property and White-Collar Victimization

CHAPTER OUTLINE

LEARNING OBJECTIVES

- Define property victimization.
- Identify different types of property victimization.
- Describe what distinguishes types of property victimization from each other.
- Define white-collar crime.
- Identity different types of white-collar victimization.
- Describe what distinguishes the types of white-collar victimization from each other.

Greed, for lack of a better word, is good. Greed is right. Greed works. Greed clarifies, cuts through, and captures, the essence of the evolutionary spirit. Greed, in all of its forms; greed for life, for money, for love, knowledge, has marked the upward surge of mankind and greed, you mark my words, will not only save Teldar Paper, but that other malfunctioning corporation called the U.S.A.

Gordon Gecko, *Wall Street*, **1987**

Introduction

Property victimization occurs when public or private possessions are taken, damaged, or destroyed without permission of the owner. These offenses can be perpetrated against individuals, places, objects, or institutions and represent the most common forms of criminal victimization experienced in the United States. Property victimizations by definition do not involve actual or threatened force to the victims, and consequently do not by themselves result in physical injuries to individuals. Yet, these offenses can nevertheless be quite distressing and cause psychological harm to their victims.

Information on the extent and nature of property victimizations comes in large part from the Uniform Crime Reports (UCR) and the National Crime Victimization Survey (NCVS), although, as discussed in Chapter 4, these sources of victimization data are limited in the types of victimization that are included. Together, the UCR and NCVS indicate that the most common forms of property victimization are larceny-theft, burglary, motor vehicle theft, and arson. UCR data show that over 9 million of these property offenses were reported to law enforcement in 2012, but as Figure 7-1 demonstrates, the property crime rate has declined steadily over a five-year period (FBI, 2013a). However, data from the NCVS suggest that there has recently been a slight increase in property offenses from 2011 to 2012 to 155.8 victimizations per 1,000 households in the United States. This equates to 19,622,977 total property victimizations captured by the NCVS for 2012 (NCVS Victimization Analysis Tool, 2014). Aside from the property offenses tracked by the UCR and presented in Figure 7-1, additional data sources suggest that other financially motivated offenses such as fraud, certain white-collar crimes, and property-based cybercrimes (see Chapter 8) also have high victimization rates.

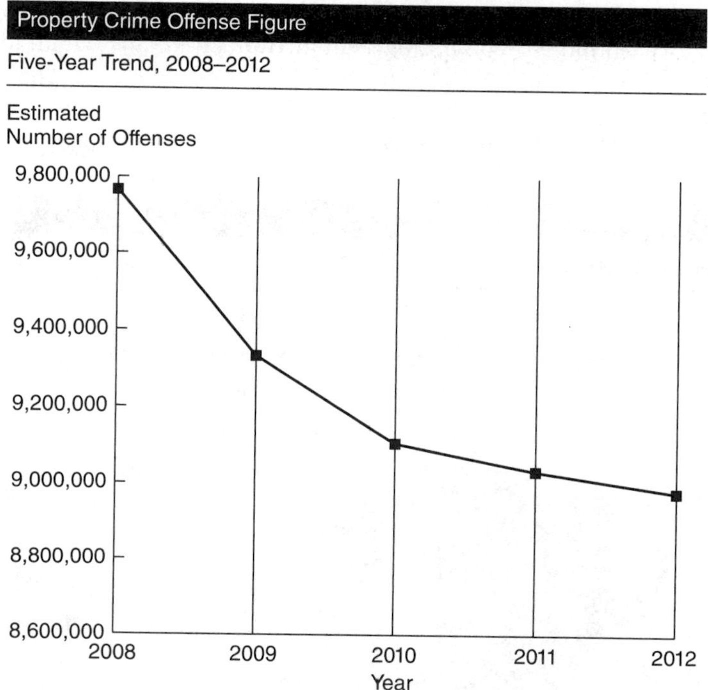

Figure 7-1 UCR Property Crime Trends
Source: FBI (2013a).

Frauds and white-collar crimes are interrelated property offenses. They involve loss, damage, destruction, or misuse of the victim's property without his or her permission, and often offenders will use deceit or deception to perpetrate the offense. In the case of fraud, offenders deceive victims into some course of action, usually into turning valuables (e.g., money, financial account numbers) over to the offender. White-collar crimes usually involve fraudulent behavior on the part of the offender resulting from some kind of business relationship between the victim and offender. In many cases, the offender simply violates the victim's trust and access to the victim's finances to perpetrate the crime. This chapter reviews the extent and nature of several types of property victimization, including larceny-theft, motor vehicle theft, burglary, arson, identity theft, and white-collar offenses.

Larceny-Theft Victimization

Larceny-theft is not only the most common form of *property* victimization but also the most frequently experienced criminal victimization of *any* type in the United States. The FBI categorizes any unlawful taking, carrying, leading, or riding away of property from the possession or constructive possession of another as a ***larceny-theft***. Put differently, when property (excluding motor vehicles) is taken by stealth, and without force or fraud, it is considered a larceny-theft. Therefore, larceny-theft involves the loss of many types of property and includes offending behaviors such as shoplifting, pocket-picking, and theft of motor vehicle parts, to name a few. Since the UCR is focused more on offending than victimization, it is not an ideal source to use to better understand larceny-theft victimization. However, Figure 7-2 provides information from the UCR on the distribution of larceny-thefts reported to law enforcement (UCR, 2013b).

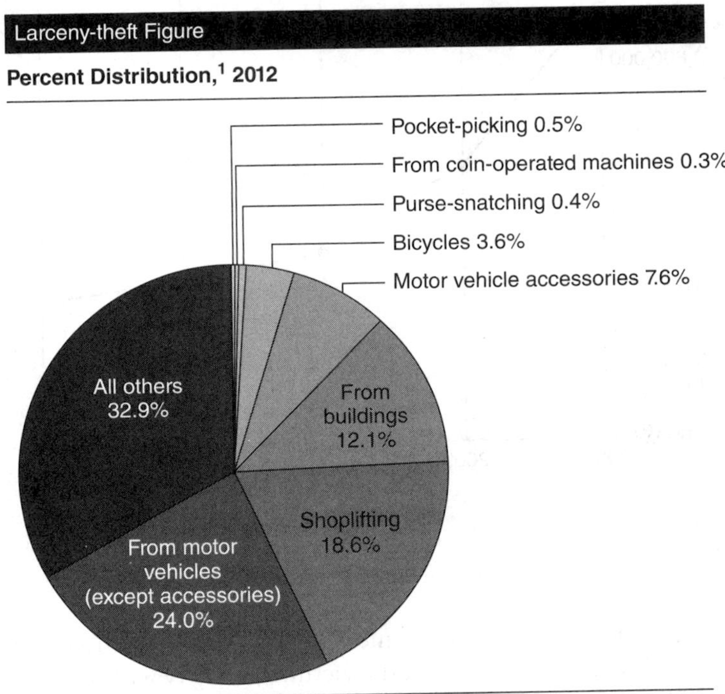

Figure 7-2 Larceny-Theft in the 2012 UCR
Source: FBI (2013d).

Official data published in the UCR show that there were 6,150,598 larceny-thefts perpetrated in 2012 that were reported to law enforcement, and although this is a decline from previous years, it still represents a significant number of offenses occurring nationwide. Since the NCVS produces data exclusively from crime victims, it also is a useful tool for understanding larceny-theft victimization. However, the NCVS departs from the UCR in how larceny-theft is defined, and for this reason, making comparisons between the two is difficult. The NCVS treats larceny and theft as two separate types of victimization. First, ***larcenies*** are considered personal crimes in the NCVS, not household crimes. Larcenies are offenses that involve personal contact between the victim and the offender such as pocket-picking, shoplifting, and thefts from motor vehicles. Second, ***thefts*** in the NCVS include property victimizations *without* personal contact. For example, if a guest in your home steals valuables from a dresser or nightstand when you are not looking, this would be considered a theft rather than a larceny.

The most recently published NCVS statistics show that in 2012 there were 15,224,695 thefts across the United States, while there were 153,583 larceny victimizations (NCVS Victimization Analysis Tool, 2014). Even though these figures are not directly comparable to those from the UCR, it is apparent that there is a large dark figure of larceny-theft victimization where a significant number of these offenses are never reported to law enforcement. These NCVS estimates translate into victimization rates of 120.9 per 1,000 households for thefts and 0.6 per 1,000 persons age 12 and older for larcenies. As a final point about the extent of thefts and larcenies, both types of victimization have decreased over the past several years, but have recently been on the rise.

The NCVS also helps to identify households and individuals who have the highest rates of theft and larceny victimization. In terms of theft, households that are headed by individuals 12 to 19 years of age, nonwhites, or females; those with lower household incomes; and those that consist of six or more individuals had higher victimization rates in 2012 than did households without these characteristics. Larceny victimization rates for 2012 tell a somewhat different story: individuals between 12 and 14 years of age, whites, females, and those with lower household incomes had higher victimization rates than persons without these traits (NCVS Victimization Analysis Tool, 2014).

Larceny and theft can be quite costly for victims. UCR statistics show that over 46% of victimizations resulted in a loss of over $200, with an average value of property taken of $987 and a total of $6 billion for all recorded larceny-theft offenses (FBI, 2013b). Despite these high costs, rates for reporting thefts and larcenies to law enforcement are fairly low; only about 32% of household thefts and 30% of larcenies were reported to law enforcement in 2012 according to the NCVS (NCVS Victimization Analysis Tool, 2014).

From a law enforcement perspective it is important to understand who is at highest risk for larceny-theft victimization. Research conducted using the opportunity perspective has identified several risk factors for theft victimization. In one of the first routine activity theory articles, Lawrence Cohen and David Cantor (1980) used the NCS to study the determinants of larceny victimization. They identified several correlates of victimization, such as age (younger persons), income (higher incomes), and race (whites), but pivotal to explaining larceny as a consequence of opportunity, unemployed persons and those who lived alone were at greater risk for victimization. Cohen and Cantor interpreted these findings as support for routine activity theory, which argues that victimization is the result of opportunity. First, young people spend more time outside the home than older people and also are more frequently in contact with potentially motivated offenders simply because young people are more likely to be involved in crime than older people. Second, the unemployed are exposed to potential offenders because their time is not as structured as someone who has a regular work schedule. Finally, people who live alone will be at increased risk for victimization because they have lower levels of guardianship.

Elizabeth Ehrhardt Mustaine and Richard Tewksbury (1998) also applied the opportunity perspective to explaining larceny victimization. They surveyed college students from nine universities in the United States and examined their routine activities and lifestyles as causes of larceny, identifying several behaviors related to victimization. For example, they reported that deviant and criminal behaviors (e.g., smoking marijuana, threatening other people), lifestyle behaviors (e.g., eating out frequently, leaving home to study), and environmental factors (e.g., neighborhood crime) increased students' risk of larceny victimization, while factors related to increased guardianship (e.g., a dog in the residence, extra locks installed) decreased students' likelihood of victimization. Overall, these findings support the premise that opportunities are linked with property victimization.

Identity Theft Victimization

Identity theft consists of criminal behaviors that involve the fraudulent use of another's personal information without consent and for criminal purposes. According to the *Identity Theft and Assumption Deterrence Act of 2003*, an identity thief is someone who "knowingly transfers, possesses or uses, without lawful authority, a means of identification of another person with the intent to commit, or to aid or abet, or in connection with, any unlawful activity that constitutes a violation of Federal law, or that constitutes a felony under any applicable State or local law." More simply, as Bert-Jaap Koops and Ronald Leenes (2006, p. 553) explained, "Identity criminals do not steal identities: they use identity as a tool to steal money." Identity theft is a specific type of ***identity fraud***, which has a broader definition and involves offenses in which an identity is used as a tool to commit some kind of fraud (Koops & Leenes, 2006).

The keys to distinguishing identity theft from the myriad other forms of identity fraud is that the identity (1) is being misused without the permission of its owner and (2) belongs to an actual person. For example, if an offender creates a fictitious name and personal history to go along with it and applies for a credit card, this would not be considered identity theft because the identity does not actually belong to anyone. Instead, this would be a case of identity fraud. Consider, though, an offender who intercepts the social security card of a newborn baby in the mail and misuses the baby's identity to apply for a home loan. This would be an example of identity theft, more specifically child identity theft, because the identity of an existing person (the baby) has been used without lawful authority.

Because identity theft is a relatively easy crime to perpetrate, would-be victims need to be vigilant in protecting valuable personal information such as their social security number or date of birth. For example, identity thieves "dumpster dive" and sift through dumpsters, trash cans, or garbage bags left for pickup, looking for discarded bills or preapproved credit card applications; they can watch or listen to victims disclose their information legitimately during transactions and use it themselves at a later time; or they can simply send victims fraudulent e-mail messages asking for personal information, a practice known as *phishing*.

Recent administrations of the NCVS in 2005, 2007, 2009, 2010, 2012 included questions designed to assess the extent and nature of identity theft victimization in the United States, and the results suggest it is both widespread and becoming more common over time. In fact, while not as prevalent as larceny-theft, identity theft is one of the most common forms of property victimization. A key finding from the 2010 NCVS is that identity theft victimization has grown since 2005, when it was first measured in the survey. As Figure 7-3 illustrates, about 6.4 million households, or 5.5% of the total, included a member who experienced identity theft victimization in 2005. By 2009, 7.3% of all households had a member who had been victimized, and in 2010, 7% of households had a member affected by identity theft (Langton, 2011). According to 2010 NCVS data, at least one household member over the age of 12 from 8.6 million households was a victim of one or more types of identity theft. The NCVS also tells us that identity theft most often takes the form of misuse of an existing credit card, which affected 64% of all victims. The next most frequent form of identity theft, which affected about 35% of victims, involved other accounts, such as bank checking or savings or PayPal accounts. The remaining pool of victims either had their personal information misused in some other way or experienced multiple types of identity theft (Langton, 2011).

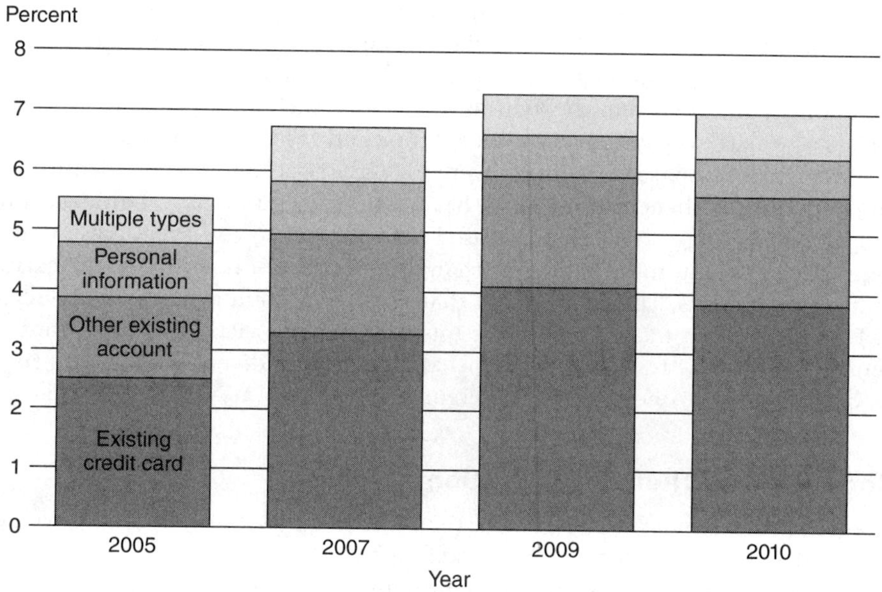

Figure 7-3 Percentage of U.S. Households that Experienced Identity Theft by Type
Source: Langton (2011).

Certain individuals appear to be at greater risk for identity theft victimization than others. Specifically, households headed by those under 24 years old, African American households, and those with an annual income of less than $24,999 had the lowest rates of identity theft victimization in 2012. Conversely, households headed by individuals between 35 and 49 years, those of two or more races, and earning over $75,000 annually had the highest victimization rates (Harrell & Langton, 2013). About two thirds of victims in 2012 suffered a direct financial loss as a result of their victimization, with the severity of the loss varying by type of identity theft. For example, victims who experienced misuse of their personal information reported an average loss of $9,650, victims of new-account fraud lost $7,135 on average, and victims of existing-account misuse incurred averages losses of $1,003 per incident (Harrell & Langton, 2013).

Besides victim characteristics such as age and race that are related to identity theft victimization, opportunity factors also differentiate victims from nonvictims. Fewer studies have used the opportunity perspective to explain identity theft, but those that have support the idea that identity theft victimization can partially be attributed to victims' lifestyles and routine activities. For example, Bradford Reyns (2013) used the British Crime Survey to identify online routine activities that were associated with identity theft victimization. His results revealed that victim characteristics such as sex, age, and income predicted victimization risk, but so did online routines, including banking, shopping, using e-mail or instant messaging, and downloading online content (e.g., music, games). Each of these online activities significantly increased the likelihood of identity theft victimization against residents in England and Wales.

In another study, Heith Copes and colleagues (2010) used data from the 2005 National Public Survey on White Collar Crime (Kane & Wall, 2006) to examine identity theft perpetrated against a nationally representative sample of victims. Their study concluded that the victims' behaviors, such as responding to solicitations (e.g., e-mail solicitations to work at home and earn a large amount of money) or giving out personal information, were higher for certain types of identity theft crimes than for others. Victims who had existing accounts (e.g., bank accounts) compromised or new credit cards misused were more likely to either occasionally or frequently engage in these behaviors than were victims of fraud involving existing credit card accounts. They also found that victims of fraud against existing credit card accounts spent more time on the Internet than did victims of other forms of identity theft. These results support the contention that diverse factors give rise to not only different crimes but also different types of the same crime.

Motor Vehicle Theft Victimization

Simply stated, ***motor vehicle theft*** is the theft (or attempted theft) of a motor vehicle. The FBI defines *motor vehicles* as being self-propelled and running on land surfaces but not on rails. Therefore, examples of motor vehicles included in the UCR are automobiles, trucks, motorcycles, sport utility vehicles, buses, all-terrain vehicles, and snowmobiles. Excluded from UCR motor vehicle thefts are watercraft, including boats or jet skis, airplanes, bulldozers, and farm equipment. In comparison to the other types of property victimization included in this chapter, motor vehicle theft victimization is quite uncommon. The latest NCVS estimates that the motor vehicle theft victimization rate in the United States in 2012 was 5.0 per 1,000 households. In other words, 5 of every 1,000 households experienced a motor vehicle theft that year, a very slight decrease from 2011 (5.1 per 1,000 households). In absolute numbers, the UCR reported that nationwide there were 721,053 motor vehicle thefts in 2012, which is an offense rate of 229.7 per 100,000 inhabitants. The majority of targets were automobiles (74%), with the remainder being trucks or other motor vehicles.

Since the NCVS considers motor vehicle theft to be a crime against the household, the survey also provides information on the characteristics of households that were victimized by motor vehicle theft. Specifically, households in which the head

Table 7-1: 10 Most Stolen Motor Vehicles, 2012

Rank	Model	Thefts
1	Honda Accord	58,596
2	Honda Civic	47,037
3	Ford Pickup (Full size)	26,770
4	Chevrolet Pickup (Full size)	23,745
5	Toyota Camry	16,251
6	Dodge Caravan	11,799
7	Dodge Pickup (Full size)	11,755
8	Acura Integra	9,555
9	Nissan Altima	9,169
10	Nissan Maxima	6,947

Note: Includes all model years for each vehicle.
Source: Insurance Information Institute (2013).

was younger than age 34, was nonwhite, and was male had higher victimization rates than households that were not headed by individuals with these characteristics. Further, households with six or more residents and those located in urban areas had higher victimization rates than did households not possessing these characteristics (NCVS Victimization Analysis Tool, 2014). Interestingly, the Insurance Information Institute (2013) annually releases a list, provided in Table 7-1, of the motor vehicles most frequently stolen. This list also illustrates the substantial financial cost of motor vehicle theft. UCR estimates place the total losses as a result of motor vehicle theft to be $4.3 billion for 2012. This works out to an average of $6,019 per theft.

A number of factors likely influence which motor vehicles are stolen, including appearance, value, accessibility, availability, and location, among others. Or, in the language of routine activities theory and the opportunity perspective, targets that are less guarded, more attractive/suitable, and in greater proximity to motivated offenders will provide greater opportunities for victimization. Along these lines, Heith Copes (1999) conducted a study to determine whether the theoretical concepts from routine activities theory helped to identify areas with high rates of motor vehicle theft. Using census tracts in Louisiana as the unit of analysis, he assessed the effects of offender, target, and guardianship factors on motor vehicle theft rates in these areas. Results suggested that census tracts with high percentages of people below the poverty line (representing larger pools of motivated offenders) and those with high road density (i.e., number of roads per square miles of the census tract, representing suitable targets) had higher rates of motor vehicle theft than did census tracts lacking these two features.

Another study integrated routine activity theory with social disorganization theory from criminology to examine the characteristics of face blocks (i.e., both

Table 7-2: U.S. States with the Most and Fewest Motor Vehicle Thefts in 2012

Most Motor Vehicle Thefts			Fewest Motor Vehicle Thefts		
Rank	State	Vehicles Stolen	Rank	State	Vehicles Stolen
1	California	168,608	1	Vermont	435
2	Texas	64,996	2	Wyoming	584
3	Florida	37,330	3	Maine	995
4	Georgia	28,536	4	New Hampshire	1,023
5	Washington	26,402	5	South Dakota	1,065
6	Illinois	25,690	6	North Dakota	1,151
7	Michigan	25,115	7	Idaho	1,364
8	Ohio	19,512	8	Delaware	1,436
9	Arizona	19,158	9	Alaska	1,522
10	New York	17,348	10	Montana	1,689

Source: Insurance Information Institute (2013).

sides of a street between two intersections) that were associated with motor vehicle theft. Kennon Rice and William Smith (2002) identified several routine activities of face blocks that significantly affected motor vehicle theft, such as the number of hotels/motels, the number of commercial places, the number of restaurants/gas stations/bars, and the number of stores/shops. At the macro level, blocks possessing these characteristics had different effects on levels of motivated offenders, suitable targets, and capable guardians on the block, thereby influencing the rate of motor vehicle theft. In a final example of opportunity-based motor vehicle theft research, Aki Roberts and Steven Block (2012) used several sources of data, including the UCR, to differentiate between the predictors of permanent (e.g., resale, export, dismantling) and temporary (e.g., joyriding, short-term transportation) motor vehicle theft. Their results suggested that different factors explained the two types of motor vehicle thefts. For instance, for temporary thefts, variables such as the size of the adult male population and the percentage of households without a motor vehicle were important, while in permanent motor vehicle thefts, factors such as the percentage of households with high disposable income, unemployment, and proximity to the United States–Mexico border were important factors.

It is interesting that the study by Roberts and Block (2012) found a relationship between proximity to the United States–Mexico border and motor vehicle theft rates. Clearly, the macro-environment in which potential targets for motor vehicle theft operate is a primary determinant of the likelihood they will be stolen. To illustrate, Table 7-2 lists the 10 states with the most motor vehicle thefts and the 10 states with the fewest motor vehicle thefts in 2012. In terms of macro-opportunities for victimization, the concentration of offenses in certain states and the scarcity of thefts in other states suggest that there are circumstances favorable to motor vehicle theft in certain locales within states but not others.

Burglary Victimization

There is a wide variety in the nature of experiences and behaviors that constitute burglary victimization. To illustrate, the FBI's definition of ***burglary*** includes offenses that involve the unlawful entry of a structure to commit a felony or theft, and it subdivides burglaries into those that involve forcible entry, unlawful entry but no force, and attempted forcible entry. Further, a *structure* includes houses, apartments, house trailers, house boats, offices, barns, railroad cars, stables, and vessels. Therefore, all burglaries involve the illegal entry or attempted entry of these structures and they may not involve forcible entry.

According to both the UCR and the NCVS, burglary is a fairly common crime: It accounts for nearly one quarter of the property victimizations occurring in the United States. These sources of victimization data are useful in understanding the prevalence and circumstances of burglary. The UCR, for instance, categorizes burglaries as either commercial or residential, and 2012 UCR data indicate that most of the 2,103,787 burglaries reported to law enforcement occurred against residences. In all, 1,381,122 of 2012 burglaries were residential while 473,045 were nonresidential (commercial establishments), occurring against stores, offices, or other commercial structures (e.g., restaurants, bars). An interesting difference between residential and commercial burglary revealed in the UCR is that most often residences are burglarized during the day, whereas nonresidential burglaries more frequently take place at night (FBI, 2013c).

Burglary victimization patterns also are reported annually in the NCVS, which indicates that the victimization rate for household burglary (attempted or completed) is about 29 in every 1,000 residences in the United States. Although this figure may appear somewhat high, it is important to point out that the burglary victimization rate has decreased by more than half between 1994 and 2011. These trends in burglary victimization in the NCVS are presented in Figure 7-4, which shows the total household burglaries, completed unlawful entries, completed forcible entries, and attempted forcible entries.

The NCVS is useful for understanding the extent of burglary victimization, but it also provides information regarding household characteristics, target selection, and dollar value of loss to victims. For example, in considering the characteristics of households that experienced a completed burglary, those headed by females, nonwhites, and young people had the highest victimization rates compared to households without these characteristics. Further, and as one might expect, items taken during completed burglaries are most frequently those with relatively high value or items that can be easily removed. Household appliances and portable electronics (e.g., TVs, Blu-ray players) were the most frequently taken items (34%), followed by personal portable objects (e.g., silver cutlery, china dining and serving plates, art) (31%), and cash/checks, credit/bank cards, and purses/wallets (17%). Interestingly, the value of items lost during burglaries has increased over time, with an average loss to victims in 2011 of $2,116 (with estimates adjusted for inflation) (Walters et al., 2013). Slightly

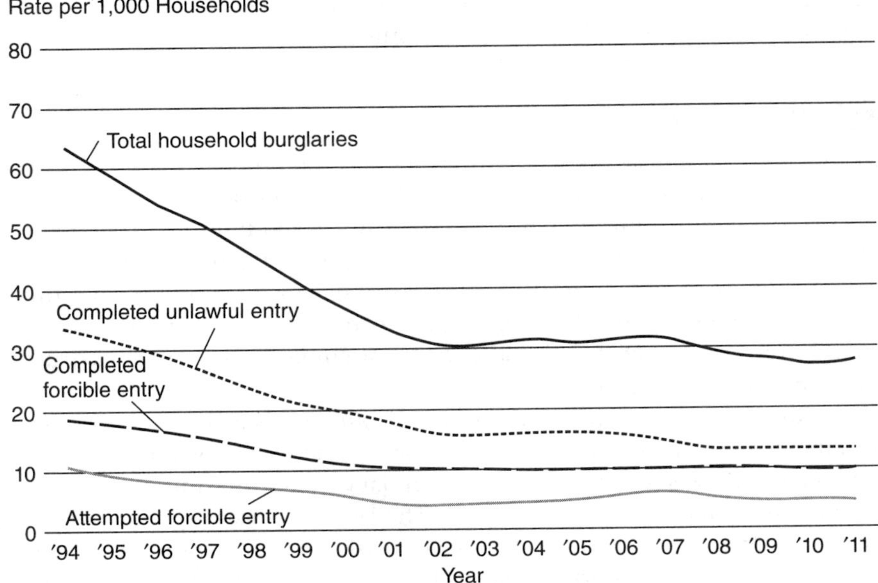

Figure 7-4 Rate of Household Burglary by Type, 1994–2011
Source: Walters, Moore, Berzofsky, and Langton (2013).

over half of burglary victims reported the crime to law enforcement (54%) in 2012 (NCVS Victimization Analysis Tool, 2014).

Burglary is a type of victimization that is aptly explained by the opportunity perspective. Indeed, many of the pioneering studies that developed and shaped the opportunity perspective, such as Cohen and Felson's (1979) original routine activity study and Sampson and Wooldredge's (1987) examination of the multilevel influences on victimization, incorporated burglary into their analyses. More recent work also illustrates the importance of opportunity in understanding burglary victimization. For example, a study of burglary in The Hague, Netherlands, by Wim Bernasco and Floor Luykx (2003) reported that target attractiveness, opportunity, and accessibility of the neighborhood to burglars all significantly influenced where burglaries occurred. Another comparative study of burglary victimization by Andromachi Tseloni and colleagues (2004) examined lifestyles and routine activities as indicators of burglary victimization for three countries—the United States, England and Wales, and the Netherlands. The results showed that households headed by younger persons or single parents, in urban areas, and with security measures were more likely to experience burglaries. This last effect may be due to victims acquiring security measures after the crime. These factors were significant predictors of victimization in all or in at least two of the three countries.

As a final example, consider a recent study by Lynn Addington and Callie Marie Rennison (2013) that used the NCVS to explore the nature of burglary victimization in gated versus nongated communities. In general, opportunity theory would suggest that residences in gated communities should have fewer burglaries because entry into these areas is restricted. In terms of routine activity theory, residences in gated communities have higher guardianship and/or lower target attractiveness as targets for burglars. Overall, the authors reported that households in gated communities have a 33% lower likelihood of being burglarized than comparable units in nongated communities.

Arson

Arson is defined by the FBI as "any willful or malicious burning or attempting to burn, with or without intent to defraud, a dwelling house, public building, motor vehicle or aircraft, personal property of another, etc." In short, arson involves completed (or attempted) burning of property with illegal intent. Despite being categorized as a Part I or Index crime in the UCR, information on arson victimization is fairly scarce. This is primarily for two reasons. First, the NCVS and other victimization surveys do not include questions about arson. Second, the UCR only collects limited information about the offense due to reporting practices of law enforcement agencies. However, the most recent available information from the UCR indicates that in 2012, 45,926 arsons were recorded by law enforcement (FBI, 2013d). This translates into a rate of approximately 18.7 offenses per 100,000 residents of the United States. Of the known arsons in 2012, about 46% involved structures (e.g., public buildings, residential dwellings), 23% involved mobile property (e.g., automobiles), and 30% involved other types of property (e.g., fences, crops) (FBI, 2013d). Property that was commonly the target of arson in 2012 is listed in Table 7-3, as well as the percentage of total arsons the property involves, the percentage not in use, and the average damage for each type of property burned.

Beyond the information presented in Table 7-3, little is known about risk factors associated with arson victimization. Indeed, most of the research that has been conducted with respect to arson has explored the perpetrator's psychological reasons behind arson perpetration. However, an opportunity-based interpretation of Table 7-3 suggests that opportunity may play a role in which targets are selected by arsonists. First, the majority of arsons are committed against physical structures, especially single-occupancy residential dwellings. Second, regardless of the type of structure, a large proportion of targets appear to be vacant or not being used at the time of the arson. This suggests that arsonists may select targets with reduced levels of guardianship, particularly those previously used for industrial or manufacturing purposes. Third, certain types of targets appear to be less attractive to motivated offenders, such as storage units and community/public buildings. Further, few arsonists target mobile properties besides motor vehicles.

While little can be definitively stated about victims of arson due to the lack of data on this type of criminal victimization, the UCR's damage estimates for property involved in arson show that it can be financially harmful for victims. As Table 7-3 illustrates, on average arson costs over $13,000, but the degree of the damage depends on the type of property that has been selected by the offender. Specifically, industrial, manufacturing, and other commercial targets stand out as having the highest average dollar losses.

Table 7-3: Arson by Property Type, 2012 UCR

Type of Property	Percent	Percent Not in Use	Average Damage
Total	100.0		$12,796
Structures	46.8	16.5	$22,477
Single-occupancy residential	22.7	18.4	$24,993
Other residential	7.7	11.6	$20,736
Storage	3.3	18.3	$12,890
Industrial/manufacturing	0.4	22.5	$42,133
Other commercial	3.8	14.4	$46,933
Community/public	4.3	16.8	$13,380
Other structure	4.8	15.6	$7,183
Mobile	23.1		$7,281
Motor vehicles	21.7		$6,849
Other mobile	1.4		$13,860
Other	30.1		$1,974

Source: Adapted from FBI (2013a).

White-Collar Victimization

White-collar crime and victimization are not easy to define. The term ***white-collar crime*** was coined by the American criminologist Edwin Sutherland, who emphasized that crimes are not only committed on the streets by persons in the lower classes. Sutherland explained that criminologists had for too long ignored crimes committed by professionals and businessmen in the corporate suites, and described white-collar offenses as those "committed by a person of high social status and respectability in the course of his occupation" (Sutherland, 1949, p. 9). Sutherland's classic definition of white-collar crime has been debated by criminologists and others ever since. It is controversial because it defines the offense based on the characteristics of the *offender* rather than the *behavior* in question. That is, Sutherland's conception of white-collar crime stresses that offenders are of "high social status" and "respectability." It also narrows the range of offenses that can be considered as white-collar crimes by stipulating that they occur in relation to the offender's occupation. Beyond the white-collar offender's characteristics or occupation, the nature of white-collar crime suggests that any person, business, or organization can, and probably will, become a victim of white-collar crime.

Alternative definitions of white-collar crime have emerged over the years. For instance, a definition that contrasts with Sutherland's was provided by Herbert Edelhertz (1970). He defined white-collar crime as "an illegal act or series of illegal acts committed by nonphysical means and by concealment or guile, to obtain money or property, to avoid the payment or loss of money or property, or to obtain business or personal advantage" (Edelhertz, 1970, p. 3). The stark contrasts between

Sutherland's and Edelhertz's definitions illustrate the difference between offender-based and offense-based definitions of white-collar crime. An ***offender-based definition*** of a particular form of crime stresses the characteristics of the offender (e.g., high social status, respectability), whereas an ***offense-based definition*** would emphasize the behaviors that are being perpetrated (e.g., non-physical means, concealment). Figure 7-5 depicts the relationship between offender-based and offense-based definitions of white-collar crime. This figure shows that defining a crime based on its characteristics provides complete coverage of all offenses that might be considered "white collar," while defining white-collar crime according to offender characteristics ensures that only those offenses committed by individuals with certain characteristics are identified as white-collar crimes.

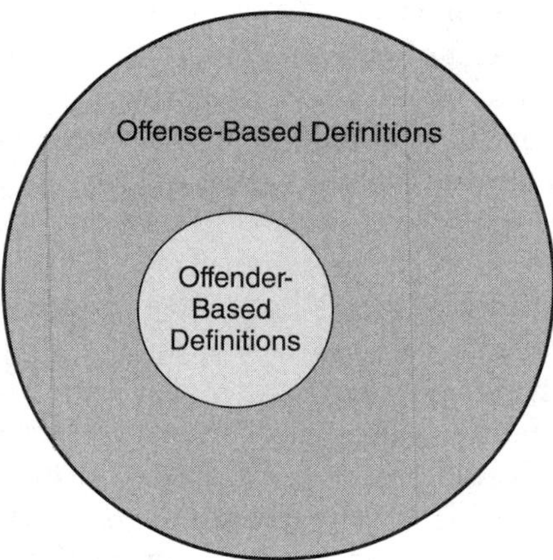

Figure 7-5 Offender-Based and Offense-Based Definitions of White-Collar Crime

For the purposes of understanding ***white-collar victimization*** within the context of this chapter, the FBI's (FBI, 2000) definition is useful:

> . . . [white collar crime includes] those illegal acts which are characterized by deceit, concealment, or violation of trust and which are not dependent upon the application or threat of physical force or violence. Individuals and organizations commit these acts to obtain money, property, or services; to avoid the payment or loss of money or services; or to secure personal or business advantage.

This definition is *offense*-based rather than *offender*-based and thus focuses on the behavior perpetrated rather than on the status of the offender. As a result, given our focus on *victimization* (rather than on offenders), the characteristics of offenders, especially their social status, are not as important to understanding this form of victimization as is the nature and type of the offense.

Having defined white-collar victimization, we can now discuss the forms it takes, its prevalence, , and how it affects victims. However, very little is known about the extent or nature of white-collar victimization because data on these offenses are not routinely collected or published by the federal government, and most of the white-collar research that has been undertaken has focused on offenders rather than on victims. An added hurdle for victimologists to overcome in studying white-collar victimization is that many victims either do not know they have been victimized or never report the crime to law enforcement.

There are two notable studies that provide information on white-collar victimization. First, as part of the Yale White-Collar Crime Project, which lasted for nearly a decade during the mid-1980s through the 1990s, David Weisburd and his colleagues (1991) examined white-collar crimes committed by a sample of federally convicted offenders. Eight specific offenses were included in the study: antitrust offenses, securities fraud, mail and wire fraud, lending- and credit-institution fraud, false claims, bribery, tax violations, and bank embezzlement. The study also included property-based common crimes ("street crimes") to allow for comparisons between white-collar and street offenses. Although the research mostly focused on such issues as characteristics of offenders and white-collar sentencing, Weisburd and colleagues reported useful information about white-collar victimization. For instance, they found that victims of these eight white-collar crimes were often organizations. In their study, nearly 95% of the victimizations were against some type of organization, whereas common crimes targeted organizations only about 28% of the time. Sixteen percent of white-collar crimes involved a loss of more than $100,000 (compared to only 3% of street crimes), and 5.7% had 100 or more victims (0% of common crimes had this many victims). The nature of white-collar victimization also differed depending on the type of offense under consideration. Table 7-4 compares the eight white-collar crimes from the Yale White-Collar Crime Project from a victimization perspective. Based on the findings presented in Table 7-4, there clearly are some white-collar offenses that affect more victims, result in higher losses for victims, and have more widespread effects than others.

The second, and more recent, study of white-collar victimization is the 2010 National Public Survey on White-Collar Crime administered by the National

Table 7-4: White-Collar Victimization

Type of Victimization	Percent with 100 or More Victims	Percent with $100,000 or Greater in Losses	Percent Reaching Statewide or Wider
Antitrust	85.7%	100.0%	68.6%
Securities Fraud	62.9%	85.9%	73.3%
Mail Fraud	11.9%	25.0%	28.0%
False Claims	1.5%	10.3%	7.4%
Credit Fraud	0.7%	20.2%	5.1%
Bribery	1.6%	7.3%	8.6%
Tax Fraud	1.5%	10.4%	1.0%
Bank Embezzlement	0.0%	7.6%	2.7%

Source: Weisburd et al. (1991).

White-Collar Crime Center. For this study, Rodney Huff, Christian Desilets, and John Kane (2010) used random-digit dialing to select a sample of 2,503 adults from throughout the United States and ask them about their experience with different types of white-collar victimizations during the previous 12 months. The study included mortgage fraud, credit card fraud, identity theft, unnecessary home or auto repairs, price misrepresentation, fraudulent business ventures, Internet scams, and losses occurring due to false stockbroker information as types of white-collar victimization. Overall, the results indicated that 24% of households and 17% of individuals were victims of at least one form of white-collar crime in the previous year. The extent of victimization for each type of white-collar victimization is included in Figure 7-6. The figure also illustrates one of the difficulties in estimating the extent of white-collar crime and victimization. Credit card fraud was found to be the most prevalent type of victimization, but whether credit card fraud is even a form of white-collar crime is debatable. It depends on one's definition of "white collar" and whether identity theft is considered to be a white-collar crime.

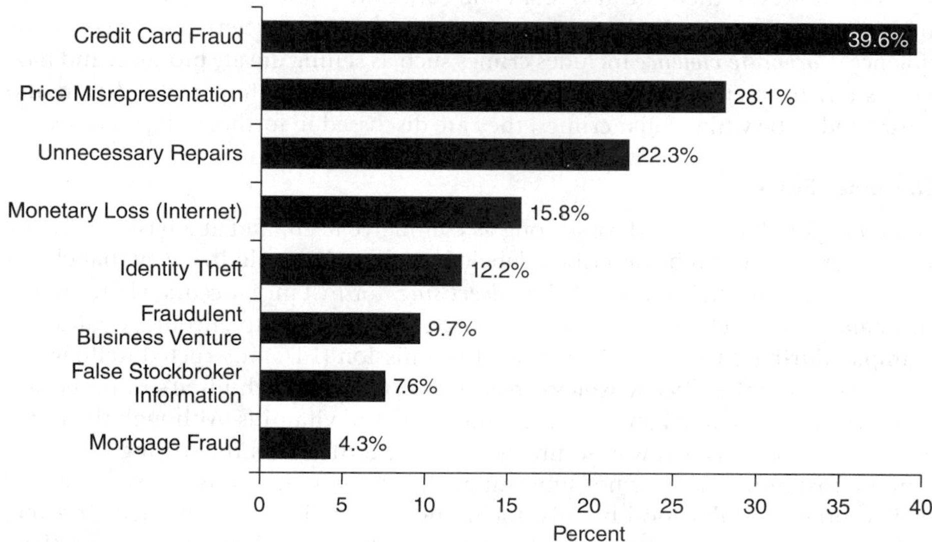

Figure 7-6 White-Collar Victimization Trends from the 2010 National Public Survey on White Collar Crime
Source: Adapted from Huff, Desilets, and Kane (2010).

Even though the extent of white-collar victimization remains elusive, several types of white-collar victimization are well known. One of the persistent elements across the many definitions of white-collar crime is that perpetrators use their occupational roles to commit these offenses, the very point Sutherland made in his classic definition. Therefore, occupational crimes committed by small businesses and corporations against consumers, crimes by professionals, and employee crime against employers are reviewed here, with emphasis placed on victimization as it relates to these occupational positions. Note there is a key difference between white-collar crime and corporate crime. While both can (and often do) occur within complex organizations, the former involves crimes mainly committed for personal gain (e.g., embezzlement, fraud), while the latter involves illegal behavior perpetrated to benefit the organization (e.g., price fixing, illegal monopolies). Further, corporate crime may involve violence (e.g., an unsafe product that kills or injures consumers), whereas white-collar crime generally does not. Subsequent sections examine these dynamics under the "umbrella" term of white-collar victimization.

Crimes Against Consumers

Many types of white-collar crime are perpetrated against consumers. Consistent with the FBI definition of white-collar crime, these offenses are financially motivated and committed through nonphysical means using deceit, concealment, and/or violation of trust. Although occurring in virtually every field, occupation, and industry, they generally involve some type of consumer fraud, such as false advertising or deceptive sales techniques. Other types of white-collar property crimes known as antitrust offenses seek to limit competition in the marketplace through tactics such as price fixing and bid rigging. The effects of these crimes against consumers are primarily financial; however, there are also retail and corporate crimes that inflict physical injuries on consumers and others. These types of offenses are referred to as corporate violence. ***Corporate violence*** includes crimes such as selling unsafe products and hazardous environmental practices. Because these offenses are financially driven and considered to be white-collar crimes, they are discussed in forthcoming sections.

Consumer Fraud

Consumer fraud has existed for as long as commerce itself, and at a basic level, any product or service can be described, labeled, packaged, or sold in a way that cheats consumers out of their money. ***False advertising***, for instance, occurs when inaccurate statements or claims are made about goods or services to encourage sales. For example, during 2010 the Federal Trade Commission (FTC) instructed Kellogg's to stop advertising that Rice Krispies cereal helped to support children's immune systems because it included antioxidants, nutrients, and vitamins. Although the nutritional value of the cereal was accurately described, the claim that eating the cereal would boost immunity was not substantiated. Similar accusations have been levied against other popular food brands, including Taco Bell, Kentucky Fried Chicken, and Activia yogurt, to name a few. As with many types of white-collar crime, there is no systematic collection of information on the prevalence or cost of false advertising victimization. There are, however, federal and state laws that create civil (and in some instances criminal) sanctions for false advertising. At the federal level, the *Lanham Act* (Public Law 79-489; 15 U.S.C. § 1051 *et seq.*) expressly forbids false or misleading claims concerning goods and services made in commerce.

Section 43(a)(1)(A) of the *Act* is typically used when a plaintiff claims that false or misleading statements hurt consumers. In such instances, the plaintiff has to prove the statement was false, was made in commerce, and created a strong likelihood of harming the plaintiff. Section 43(a)(1)(B) of the *Act* is usually invoked when claims are made that false or misleading statements harmed a business. Under this section, a plaintiff must prove there was a false or misleading statement made; the statement was used in advertising; and the statement created a high likelihood of harming the plaintiff. Remedies under the *Act* include injunctions and compensatory and punitive damages (e.g., *Clorox Co. Puerto Rico v. Procter & Gamble Commercial Co.*, 228 F.3d 24, 33 n.6 [1st Cir. 2000]; *Pizza Hut, Inc. v. Papa John's Int'l, Inc.*, 227 F.3d 489, 495 [5th Cir. 2000]).

Deceptive sales techniques are another popular method of consumer fraud in which employees use dishonest tactics to convince buyers to purchase products or services. These practices may be fostered by pressures created by commissions paid on sales or encouraged through company policies involving sales quotas for commissioned workers. In a sense, these techniques are similar to false advertising in that the salesperson is describing the product or service in a misleading way. One common tactic is to tell consumers that a particular price for an item (e.g., a new vehicle) is only good "today" and that they must make the purchase immediately. Car dealers may also mislead buyers when it comes to financing their new automobile purchase, hiding various add-ons in the paperwork so that buyers do not even know they are purchasing the add-ons. As another example, dishonest insurance agents may describe a worst-case scenario to scare their customers into buying certain products or higher levels of coverage. Finally, a practice that overlaps with false advertising and involves deceptive sales techniques is known as "bait-and-switch" advertising. Here, a retail business will advertise a product such as a computer or camera for a low price to entice shoppers to visit the store, at which point they are told the item is out of stock and are encouraged to buy a more expensive product.

Antitrust Offenses

Consumers also are victimized by what are called antitrust offenses. ***Antitrust offenses*** are perpetrated by businesses that violate the spirit of an open marketplace by trying to obtain an unfair advantage over their competition. Although there are many types of antitrust offenses, such as monopolization, conspiracies that restrain trade, bid rigging, and market allocation, from a victimization perspective two types of antitrust offenses that are most relatable to consumers are price fixing and price gouging. ***Price fixing*** happens when competitors collectively agree to price goods or services at a particular level. For example, if all the major airlines agreed to charge the same prices for flights to certain destinations, consumers would have no choice but to pay what would presumably be higher rates. The airlines would increase their profits, but consumers would lose because they are no longer benefiting from lower prices generated through competition among the airlines. ***Price gouging*** is a similar offense that involves unreasonably inflating prices on goods or services, especially goods that are considered to be essential, such as gasoline or milk. As an example, following Hurricane Sandy, which was particularly devastating in parts of New Jersey and New York, hotels and gas stations charged customers extra because of the high demand for their goods and services. In a press release, New Jersey's Acting Attorney General John J. Hoffman said, "We simply will not allow businesses to victimize vulnerable residents, who are already suffering hardships during a declared state of emergency" (New Jersey Division of Consumer Affairs, 2013). As is the case with most forms of white-collar victimization, its extent and harm are largely unknown because such offenses are underreported and data are not routinely collected.

Unsafe Products

Unfortunately, some businesses do not stop at simply misrepresenting their products or resorting to deception or manipulation to sell them. A related offense involves companies producing and selling unsafe products to consumers that cause sickness, physical injury, and even death. Harmful products take many shapes, including food, medical supplies and pharmaceuticals, construction materials, cars, toys, and various household items (e.g., appliances, clothing, cleaning products). Although some of these products prove harmful to consumers, in general, corporations do not purposely design their products to be dangerous; rather, during the course of design or production, they may make decisions that increase profits by cutting corners that would otherwise ensure consumer safety. For example, in 1980, Ford Motor Company was put on trial in Indiana for criminal reckless homicide following the deaths of three Indiana teenagers who were involved in a car crash in their Ford Pinto. The case was unprecedented because it was the first time criminal charges had been brought against a corporation for faulty product design. In its case, the prosecution argued that Ford executives and engineers *knew* the Pinto was dangerous—because of a design defect in its gas tank, the car could explode when involved in a rear-end collision at relatively low speeds—but the company's management decided it would be less expensive to settle civil lawsuits from injured drivers than it would be to recall and fix the car (see Cullen, Cavender, Maakestad, & Benson, 2006). Although Ford was ultimately acquitted on the charges, the case was highly influential because of the (then) novel idea that a corporation, like an individual, could be held criminally accountable for its actions (Becker, Jipson, & Bruce, 2002).

Since there are so many types of products, the dangers they pose vary widely and include choking hazards, fire risks, exposure to hazardous metals, shock hazards, danger of laceration, and violations of federal standards (e.g., flammability standards). It is difficult to estimate the extent or cost of unsafe products to consumers, but as a starting point, the U.S. Consumer Product Safety Commission issues recalls on hundreds of products every year. In fiscal year 2012, the Commission (2013) stopped more than 4.8 million units of imported products from entering the United States because they violated federal safety rules or were found to be hazardous.

Environmental Offenses

Environmental offenses are a related form of white-collar victimization—and corporate violence—because they result in physical harm not only to customers but also third parties and the natural world. There are many varieties of environmental crime (e.g., illegal logging, overfishing), but perhaps the most prevalent white-collar environmental offenses are those that involve polluting the environment, such as through illegal emissions or illegal disposal of hazardous waste. The dark figure of environmental crime looms large, and ultimately the extent of the problem is unknown. However, because opportunities to offend against the environment by polluting it are so pervasive and because regulatory agencies often have to rely on whistleblowers or self-reporting to discover that offenses have been committed, it is likely that most offenses do not come to light.

Michael Benson and Sally Simpson (2009) explained that there are two key features related to opportunities for illegally disposing of hazardous wastes. First, companies are expected (and trusted) to dispose of their hazardous wastes in environmentally responsible ways. Second, if they choose not to, their crimes may not be discovered for a considerable amount of time, if ever. Because there are thousands of businesses throughout the United States that legitimately produce hazardous waste as part of their normal business operations (e.g., dry cleaners, auto repair shops), it is not possible to monitor all of them continuously to ensure that their employees are fulfilling their responsibilities to properly dispose of their hazardous waste. Thus, a situation exists in which businesses can save money through illegal disposal or dumping of hazardous waste and a low risk that the crime will be detected. Further, the expense of legal waste disposal can be quite high relative to the fines that might be incurred if the offenses are detected, so businesses are nearly provided lucrative incentives to offend. Like practically all types of white-collar victimization, the dark figure of environmental victimization mostly remains hidden, but the toll it takes has repeatedly proven devastating for many. Box 7-1 summarizes some of the problems associated with illegal dumping of waste materials.

Box 7-1: Illegal Dumping of Hazardous Materials

Photo Credit: © Jim West/Alamy

According to the U.S. Environmental Protection Agency, illegal waste dumping is becoming an increasingly common and dangerous problem in many areas of the country. Known as "fly dumping," "midnight dumping," "open dumping," or "wildcat dumping," the practice involves illegally disposing of waste materials in unpermitted areas, including abandoned industrial, residential, or commercial facilities; in rural communities; or on vacant lots, either publicly or privately owned. Typically, waste such as used tires, construction debris, abandoned automobiles and auto parts, medical waste, and household appliances and trash will be dumped, partly because such waste is often banned from permitted sites or because proper management of the waste is difficult. If not addressed, illegal dump sites attract more waste, including hazardous waste such as asbestos, household chemicals, paint, automobile fluids (e.g., oil, antifreeze), and commercial and industrial waste. Illegal waste dumping is a problem for many reasons. These sites pose serious health hazards, as they attract vermin and cause physical injury to people from protruding nails or sharp edges. The sites also pose significant fire hazards, either through spontaneous combustion or arson. Such sites make surrounding areas more susceptible to flooding by blocking culverts, ravines, and drainage basins. In rural areas, burning that often occurs at these sites causes forest fires that lead to excessive erosion of topsoil as the fires burn away trees and underbrush. Runoff from these sites contains hazardous chemicals that contaminate wells, underground aquifers, and surface water used as sources for drinking water. Finally, these sites negatively affect property values in the community.

Source: U.S. Environmental Protection Agency (1998).

Crimes by Professionals

Generally speaking, a professional is someone who is paid to perform a specified activity, such as an accountant, lawyer, or physician. Further, because the definition of white-collar crime previously provided is offense-based, white-collar crimes can be perpetrated by those in virtually every industry, even those that may be considered "blue collar" or "pink collar." Overall, white-collar crimes are perpetrated by individuals in nearly every profession or occupation. The reasoning behind this more inclusive conceptualization of white-collar crime is that professionals enter into legitimate relationships with clients, and the resulting business transactions provide them with access to white-collar crime opportunities. From this point of view, anyone who enters into a business relationship with a professional could become a victim of white-collar crime (Benson & Simpson, 2009). Marcus Felson (2002) has pointed out that white-collar offenses involve *specialized access* to opportunities to victimize others. This specialized access provides professionals with opportunities to offend that, by definition, are not available to those outside of the profession or occupation.

Suppose you slipped, fell, and were injured in one of the aisles at the grocery store because a broken jar of pickles was not properly cleaned up by store personnel. Following the incident, you hire an attorney to handle a civil action involving a lawsuit you want to file against the store. Your attorney welcomes your case and tells you that have a "great chance of success." As it turns out, the attorney has a doctor on staff that conducts diagnoses of clients' injuries that inflate their severity in an effort to settle the case for more money. In effect, the attorney is presenting false evidence, which, although potentially beneficial to you, is nonetheless illegal and would harm the grocery store were the evidence ever admitted. Such a crime could not have been perpetrated without the specialized access provided through the attorney's profession and the relationship the attorney has entered into with his or her client. In the remainder of the discussion of white-collar crimes by professionals, we limit it to victimizations perpetrated by those within the health care, banking, and securities professions.

Crimes of Health Care Professionals

The massive health care industry in the United States provides medical professionals with many opportunities for white-collar crime, especially health care fraud. Health care fraud takes many forms because the nature of health care itself is so diverse. Consider all the different people who work in the health care field (doctors, nurses, pharmacists, medical supply providers) and the many domains in which they work (hospitals, clinics, laboratories, nursing homes). Further, there are specializations within these occupations (e.g., podiatrists, optometrists, dentists, psychiatrists). The combinations of circumstances under which medical professionals perform their work are staggering. It appears, however, that the majority of health care fraud is connected in some fashion to the medical insurance system, either through private insurance providers or the government programs of Medicare and Medicaid.

Health insurance, and specifically the way in which claims are processed, is the key factor in creating opportunities for ***health care fraud*** (Benson & Simpson, 2009). The way that insurance programs are supposed to work is that a patient visits a health care provider; the provider treats the patient; and the provider then submits a claim to the patient's insurance company to receive compensation. However, the party paying for the medical care is never on site to verify which services were, in fact, provided to the patient. In addition, because programs like Medicare and Medicaid process so many claims, this verification process is mostly automated. In effect, the health care provider has the opportunity to perpetrate fraud against the patient's insurance company as long as the claims have the *appearance* of legitimacy. These types of fraud might involve performing unnecessary services, overcharging patients, billing for services not provided, billing for more expensive services than those provided, and a whole host of other schemes. In this scenario, the victim may not be immediately apparent. Indeed, patients may never find out that their health care provider is using them as a means to commit white-collar crime. As such, health insurance providers and government programs are the direct victims of health care fraud. Indirectly, these white-collar offenses affect a much larger population because they add to the already high costs of providing health care and contribute to the increasing costs of health insurance for everyone.

A central question related to health care fraud concerns its scope. Unfortunately, there is no way of knowing precisely how many cases of health care fraud are perpetrated annually. Considering that in 2011 Medicare and Medicaid collectively served over 100 million people, the potential for fraud is incredible (Henry J. Kaiser Family Foundation, 2011). Frequently cited estimates of the possible extent of health care fraud suggest that as much as 10% or $100 billion is wasted on fraud annually (Sparrow, 1996). However, this figure may be high. Although current national health care spending exceeds $2.7 trillion annually, the FBI (2013) estimates that about $80 billion a year is lost to health care fraud. As Malcolm Sparrow (1996, p. 2) has pointed out, "The truth is, of course, that nobody knows the true figure, because nobody systematically measures it."

Crimes of Banking Professionals

Fraud also is perpetrated by professionals in the banking industry. In a manner analogous to health care fraud and even environmental offenses, it is the nature of the industry and its regulations that often facilitates opportunities for fraud. ***Financial institution fraud*** is a general label applied to crimes such as check fraud, check kiting (floating a check), frauds that contribute to the failure of financial institutions, and mortgage fraud. Presumably banking professionals could perpetrate all of these financial offenses, but fraud that can cause the collapse of financial institutions and mortgage fraud are two particularly important white-collar crimes involving the banking industry.

The regulations and protections that are in place to protect customers should the institution fail at least in part facilitate opportunities for white-collar criminals to perpetrate bank fraud. To illustrate, the Federal Deposit Insurance Company (FDIC) insures deposits in federally chartered banks up to $100,000, which means that if the bank fails, the depositors do not lose their money. As of October 2011, this amounted to nearly $9.8 trillion across 7,433 banking institutions (FBI, 2013f). Knowing this, motivated offenders within the bank, such as the owner, can make high-risk loans without worrying about the consequences since depositors will be protected up to $100,000 in losses. Some white-collar offenders in banking have even gone as far as to make loans to co-conspirators, taking a large portion or at least a kickback in the process. If this type of insider bank fraud is serious enough, it can lead to the outright collapse of the bank. However, if the bank is FDIC insured, the only victimized parties are the government and its taxpayers. Figure 7-7 shows the number of bank failures from 2007 to 2011. Although most of these failures were likely due to the financial crisis, inspection of records from failed banks usually uncovers some insider fraud.

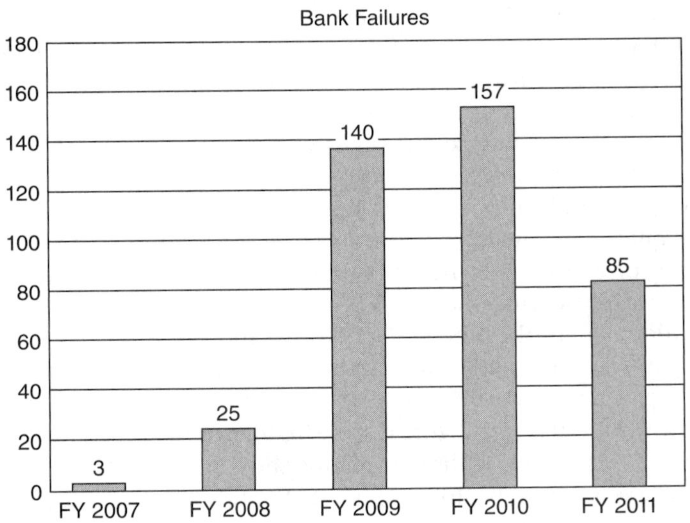

Figure 7-7 Bank Failures in the United States, 2007–2011
Source: FBI (2013f).

Mortgage fraud is a crime that is committed by professionals from many sectors of the economy, such as brokers, lenders, borrowers, agents, appraisers, and others, to defraud lending institutions throughout the mortgage loan process. A distinction can be made between mortgage frauds committed for *profit* and those committed for *housing*. Those committed for profit involve professionals who facilitate the fraud, while those committed for housing are perpetrated by borrowers who overstate their assets on loan applications. For-profit mortgage frauds are prime examples of white-collar crimes because professionals use their specialized knowledge and access to facilitate the fraud. Mortgage fraud can be experienced by lending institutions or consumers and represents a growing form of white-collar crime. While the cost of mortgage fraud is currently unknown, it can lead to individuals losing their homes, business failures, lowered property values in communities, and damage to local and state economies (Box 7-2).

Crimes of Securities Professionals

In the world of high finance, a security is a tradable asset, such as stocks, bonds, or promissory notes. Many types of securities frauds exist, but Susan Shapiro (1984)

Box 7-2: "Redlining" by Mortgage Companies

"Redlining" is the illegal, under both federal and many states' law, practice of "mortgage lenders figuratively drawing a red line around minority neighborhoods and refusing to make mortgage loans available inside the red lined area. Broadly defined, racial redlining encompasses not only the direct refusal to lend in minority neighborhoods, but also procedures that discourage the submission of mortgage loan applications from minority areas, and marketing policies that exclude such areas" (Brown & Bennington, 1993, p. 1).

In a major study of 16 metropolitan areas, Brown and Bennington (1993) used Geographic Information System (GIS) data to map lending patterns of 49 major mortgage lenders during 1990 and 1991 and found 62 separate instances where the lenders substantially excluded or underserved minority neighborhoods. Their study concluded that the 62 worst-case lending patterns were *prima facie* evidence of unlawful discrimination in mortgage lending in violation of the federal fair lending laws—the *Fair Housing Act* and the *Equal Credit Opportunity Act.*

Source: Brown and Bennington (1993).

has explained that there are five main types of securities offenses: (1) misrepresentations; (2) stock manipulation; (3) misappropriation; (4) insider trading; and (5) investment schemes. Shapiro's first type of securities fraud, misrepresentations, refers to manipulating or withholding information to encourage buying or selling of certain securities. Essentially, misrepresentations involve falsely describing the value of a security. For example, executives with Enron, among other things, regularly reported high profits on projects for which the company actually lost money. If the executives were doing so to mislead investors about the value of the company's stock, this can be considered an example of misrepresentation.

The second type of securities offense identified by Shapiro is stock manipulation, which is related to misrepresentation. The purpose of stock manipulation is to artificially manipulate the price of stock, to induce either buying or selling of that stock. In the Enron example, if the executives were misrepresenting the company's profitability to manipulate the stock and drive up the price, perhaps so they themselves could sell some of their stock, they were engaging in stock manipulation.

Misappropriation, Shapiro's third type of securities offense, is simply stealing money or property in the form of securities. It is similar to embezzlement in that funds that are entrusted to brokers by their clients are taken and used for other purposes. For example, a stockbroker who was instructed by a client to invest in a relatively safe (low-risk) fund but instead lost the money by investing it in a high-risk stock would be guilty of misappropriating the client's money.

The fourth type of securities offense described by Shapiro is insider trading. Insider trading, perhaps the best-known securities offense, involves trading securities based on information that is not publicly available. With this inside information, individuals have an unfair advantage over other traders in the market. As an example, Martha Stewart was indicted in 2003 on charges of securities fraud related to insider trading. Allegedly, she had sold stock in a friend's company after receiving inside information that the stock was about to lose some of its value. The loss avoided was purportedly around $45,000. After her conviction, she served five months in a federal correctional facility and two years of supervised release.

Finally, investment schemes are simply ways in which offenders convince individuals to invest their money in some venture for the purposes of stealing that money. Common investment schemes are called ***Ponzi schemes*** or ***pyramid schemes***. In general, both of these schemes involve a promise to investors that they can make a much higher than average rate of return on an initial investment. Also, in both cases investors are paid, at least initially, using money generated from subsequent investors. However, while pyramid schemes require investors to attract new recruits to perpetuate the growth of the pyramid, Ponzi schemes are sustained through the offender's efforts to increase investments. It is often the case that pyramid schemes require participants to sell a product of some sort, such as a membership in a club, even if the product does not actually exist. If participants recruit others to invest in the business and become distributors of the product themselves, the original investor may move up the hierarchy of the pyramid, with a corresponding increase in payment. In 2008, Bernard L. Madoff confessed to the largest Ponzi scheme in history (Box 7-3).

Box 7-3: Madoff's Ponzi Scheme

Bernard L. Madoff is the world's most famous white-collar criminal. The former stockbroker, financial adviser, and chairman of NASDAQ perpetrated the largest Ponzi scheme in history. Madoff began working in securities in 1960 when he founded Bernard L. Madoff Investment Securities LLC. By 2008, when he confessed, Madoff had cheated investors out of billions of dollars; he admitted the fraud had gone on for 20 years.

In general terms, Madoff's crime was an investment scheme in which his clients gave him their money to invest. He appeared to be a very savvy steward of their money because he made it appear that their investments were doing well. He would mail his clients statements showing how their money was invested and how much their accounts were growing. In reality, these transactions were completely fictitious. As the fraud grew, other investment firms began funneling their clients' money through Madoff to invest since he appeared to have a guaranteed method for getting high returns on investments. Yet, instead of investing the money and turning a profit for his clients, Madoff deposited the funds into a Chase bank account.

This fraud collapsed in 2008 when conditions in the U.S. economy resulted in too many clients asking for withdrawals from their investment accounts. Under normal circumstances, Madoff would simply have paid them out of his secret bank account, but when he could not meet the demand for withdrawals, the scheme was revealed. It is difficult to say exactly how much money his victims lost, but estimates suggest more than $17 billion was given to Madoff by investors. Of course, because he was telling them that their investments were growing, they thought their investments were worth much more. While serving his 150-year sentence, one of his fellow inmates pressed Madoff about the harm he caused to victims, to which he replied, "Fuck my victims. I carried them for twenty years, and now I'm doing 150 years" (Fishman, 2010).

Employee Crime Against Employers

Much of what is written about white-collar crime assumes that businesses, corporations, or professionals are the perpetrators and clients, customers, employees, or other individuals are the victims. However, white-collar victimization can also be experienced *by* businesses, corporations, and professionals in the form of employee crimes.

The primary crime perpetrated by employees against their employers involves employee theft, which fits most offense-based definitions of white-collar crime because it is committed as part of an occupational role, involves special access to opportunities, and is financially motivated. Such offenses can take place in virtually any field, industry, or occupation by those who are working on the front lines of the firm or organization, by those in the corporate suites, or any employee in between. For example, in retail sales occupations, employees can steal goods, money, or time from their employers through various methods, but perhaps the simplest way is to take money from the cash register or safe. Other common forms of retail employee theft include giving unauthorized discounts to friends, giving refunds to co-conspirators posing as customers for goods that were never purchased, or stealing wages by taking long breaks or lunches while still on the clock. Likewise, executives and managers have ample opportunities to engage in employee theft because of the nature of their positions and their greater access to larger pools of money (e.g., through performance bonuses or expense accounts).

The prime example of employee theft as a white-collar crime that can be perpetrated by employees at nearly any level of an organization is embezzlement. ***Embezzlement*** occurs when assets (e.g., money) that have been entrusted to a party are used for unauthorized purposes. Embezzlement is therefore different than larceny-theft because the victim has given the offender legitimate access to the victim's property and trusted the offender to act responsibly with it. The cult classic film *Office Space* provides an excellent example of embezzlement. In the movie, three friends conspire to embezzle funds from their company by writing a computer virus that will steal fractions of a cent from thousands of business transactions and put the money in a bank account for them. They believed that no one would notice such small amounts and that over time their bank account would grow. Of course, the scheme did not go as planned! Embezzlement schemes can be complex, as this example illustrates, or they can be simple and straightforward, such as an executive who uses company money for personal reasons.

Although neither the UCR nor the NCVS collects information on the extent of embezzlement in the United States, according to the National Incident Based Reporting System (NIBRS) there were 17,000 embezzlement offenses (incidents) reported by participating law enforcement agencies in 2012. These 17,000 incidents included 18,009 victims and 18,520 known offenders (FBI, 2014). As with all other types of white-collar victimization, there is a large dark figure of crime, and thus the actual number of incidents is probably much higher than this. However, Weisburd and the research team (1991) involved in the Yale White-Collar Crime Project did report that in more than half of the cases of bank embezzlement in the study, the loss to the bank was usually less than $5,000. This may sound like a lot of money, but such offenses were usually committed by line-level employees such as bank tellers and cashiers. However, antitrust offenses, which are often perpetrated by managers and executives, resulted in losses of over $1 million in 60% of cases. This underscores, like with many other types of victimization, the key role that opportunity plays. In these cases, employees often have easy opportunities to embezzle, but with low payoffs compared to those afforded to those with "high social status and respectability."

Summary

Property victimizations affect millions of individuals, businesses, organizations, and others every year in the United States. Primarily, the term *property victimization* refers to the offenses of larceny-theft, identity theft, motor vehicle theft, burglary, and arson, which target property rather than the owner of the targeted property. Although violent crimes usually receive more attention in the media, property victimizations are more widespread and thus an important area of research in the field of victimology.

White-collar victimizations also target property (e.g., money) but are distinct from these other property offenses. Often, researchers will adopt either an offender-based conceptualization of white-collar crime, which means the focus is placed on the characteristics of the offender (e.g., high social status), or an offense-based approach, in which certain offenses are labeled as white collar. Usually offense-based definitions of white-collar crime acknowledge that the specialized knowledge or access associated with certain occupations provides opportunities to offend. Hence, white-collar crime takes many forms. Several retail and corporate crimes, crimes by professionals, and employee crimes against employers were reviewed, although the magnitude of white-collar victimization is essentially unknown to practitioners and victimologists. The "Spotlight on Policy" box highlights instances of white-collar crimes perpetrated by corporations that affected millions of consumers.

Spotlight on Policy: They Knew and Failed To . . .

Recall Defective Tires in a Timely Manner: Defective Firestone tires on Ford Explorers took the lives of at least 271 people and seriously injured many more before the companies issued the largest tire recall in history. Internal company documents would later show that the two corporations had known of the deadly tire separation and associated rollover problems for years. Firestone knew by at least 1997 that there were serious problems with its tires. Vehicle owners began sending complaints of tire failures in a rate 100 times greater than normal. Firestone employees would later state that they punctured bubbles in tires to conceal flaws and that inspection of finished tires was nonexistent. In May 2000, at least three years after Firestone had learned of serious problems with its tires, the National Highway Traffic Safety Administration opened an investigation into the tread separations. In August 2000, Firestone recalled 6.5 million tires. The following month, the National Highway Traffic Safety Administration warned the company that over 1 million more tires had worse problems than the recalled tires. Firestone refused to order another recall.

Recall Automobiles That Did Not Properly Remain in Park: Between 1970 and 1979 the Ford Motor Company manufactured automobiles with a defective automatic transmission design. This defect produced an "illusory park" position, giving the driver the impression that the car was secured when in fact it was not. Vibration or slamming of a car door could cause the car's transmission to slip out of the "park" position and into reverse gear. About 90 injuries and deaths were reported as a result of this defect. A "smoking gun" interoffice memo discovered during litigation established that Ford engineers had been aware of the "illusory park" problem since 1971 but had taken no action to correct it. The trial jury found that the transmission design was defective and, critically, that Ford had failed to give drivers adequate warnings of the problem. Ford finally eliminated the "illusory park" position hazard after it lost two lawsuits filed by people injured as a result of the design.

Recall Automobiles With A Defective Fuel Tank: General Motors knew for several decades that the placement of the fuel tank in the Chevy Malibu created an unreasonable risk of exploding in the event of a rear collision. An internal GM memo obtained during litigation over injuries sustained from the defective design showed that the company estimated that deaths resulting from post-collision fuel-tank fires cost General Motors $2.40 per car. This calculation was based on an estimate that each life "has a value of $200,000." Internal memos also showed that the company had developed an improved design that would do a better job of protecting the gas tank in collisions. Improving the design would cost the company $8.59 per car. Yet, GM executives decided not to make this change. GM managed to hide the memo from civil justice attorneys and keep it out of court for decades until 1998, when a judge allowed it to be entered into the record as an internal GM analysis document evidence, saying, "This Court advised General Motors that it is not 'big enough to thumb its nose at the court,' and that it is not `big enough to interfere with the orderly administration of justice,' and that it is not `big enough to obstruct justice or conceal evidence'."

Source: American Association of Justice (2013).

KEYWORDS

Property victimization	White-collar crime	Price fixing
Larceny-theft	Offender-based definition	Price gouging
Larcenies	Offense-based definition	Environmental offenses
Thefts	White-collar victimization	Health care fraud
Identity theft	Corporate violence	Financial institution fraud
Identity fraud	Consumer fraud	Mortgage fraud
Motor vehicle theft	False advertising	Ponzi schemes
Burglary	Deceptive sales techniques	Pyramid schemes
Arson	Antitrust offenses	Embezzlement

DISCUSSION QUESTIONS

1. Apply the opportunity perspective to explaining burglaries of college students' living quarters located in residence halls. Consider the factors that facilitate these opportunities. Also, which types of items do you think burglars would choose to take in these types of offenses? Explain your answer.
2. Explain why residential burglaries mainly take place during the day, while commercial burglaries occur at night.
3. Why has identity theft victimization increased so rapidly over the last several years? What types of online activities do you engage in that might increase your chance of becoming a victim of identity theft? Provide an example.
4. What characteristics do the motor vehicles listed in Table 7-1 possess that would make them the most stolen models in 2012? Can you explain the distribution of motor vehicle thefts among the states listed in Table 7-2?
5. Which approach to defining white-collar crime better reflects the concept—offender-based or offense-based definitions? Explain your answer.
6. Why is it so difficult to gauge the extent of white-collar victimization? How might these difficulties be remedied?
7. Are white-collar victimizations *less* serious than other forms of property victimization? Why or why not?
8. Provide a list of risk factors for a specific type of white-collar victimization. Define your type of white-collar crime, explain why you chose these factors, and describe your rationale for reducing white-collar victimization risk.

REFERENCES

Addington, L. A., & Rennison, C. M. (2013). Keeping the barbarians outside the gate? Comparing burglary victimization in gated and non-gated communities. *Justice Quarterly*. DOI:10.1080/07418825.2012.760644

American Association of Justice. (2013). *They knew and failed to . . .* Retrieved October 10, 2013, from http://www.justice.org/clips/theyknewandfailedto.pdf

Becker, P. J., Jipson, A. J., & Bruce, A. S. (2002). *State of Indiana v. Ford Motor Company* Revisited. *American Journal of Criminal Justice, 26,* 181–202.

Benson, M. L., & Simpson, S. S. (2009). *White-collar crime: An opportunity perspective.* New York: Routledge.

Bernasco, W., & Luykx, F. (2003). Effects of attractiveness, opportunity and accessibility to burglars on residential burglary rates of urban neighborhoods. *Criminology, 41,* 981–1002.

Brown, J., & Bennington, C. (1993). *Racial redlining: A study of racial discrimination by banks and mortgage companies in the United States.* Washington, DC: Essential Information. Retrieved October 5, 2013, from http://www.public-gis.org/reports/redindex.html

Cohen, L. E., & Felson, M. (1979). Social change and crime rate trends: A routine activity approach. *American Sociological Review, 44,* 588–608.

Cohen, L. W., & Cantor, D. (1980). The determinants of larceny: An empirical and theoretical study. *Journal of Research in Crime and Delinquency, 17,* 140–159.

Copes, H. (1999). Routine activities and motor vehicle theft: A crime specific approach. *Journal of Crime and Justice, 22,* 125–146.

Copes, H., Kerley, K. R., Huff, R., & Kane, J. (2010). Differentiating identity theft: An exploratory study of victims using a national victimization survey. *Journal of Criminal Justice, 38,* 1045–1052.

Cullen, F. T., Cavender, G., Maakestad, W. J., & Benson, M. L. (2006). *Corporate crime under attack: The fight to criminalize business violence* (2nd ed.). Cincinnati, OH: Anderson Publishing.

Edelhertz, H. (1970). *The nature, impact, and prosecution of white-collar crime.* Washington, DC: National Institute of Justice.

Federal Bureau of Investigation. (2000). *The measurement of white-collar crime using Uniform Crime Reporting (UCR) data.* Washington, DC: U.S. Department of Justice. Retrieved August 26, 2013, from http://www.fbi.gov/about-us/cjis/ucr/nibrs/nibrs_wcc.pdf

Federal Bureau of Investigation. (2013a). *Property Crime.* Retrieved March 10, 2015 from http://www.fbi.gov/about-us/cjis/ucr/crime-in-the-u.s/2013/crime-in-the-u.s.-2013/property-crime/property-crime-topic-page/propertycrimemain_final

Federal Bureau of Investigation. (2013b). *Larceny-Theft.* Retrieved August 15, 2013, from http://www.fbi.gov/about-us/cjis/ucr/crime-in-the-u.s/2012/crime-in-the-u.s.-2012/property-crime/larceny-theft

Federal Bureau of Investigation. (2013c). *Burglary.* Retrieved March 10, 2015 from http://www.fbi.gov/about-us/cjis/ucr/crime-in-the-u.s/2013/crime-in-the-u.s.-2013/property-crime/burglary-topic-page

Federal Bureau of Investigation. (2013d). *Arson.* Retrieved August 21, 2013, from http://www.fbi.gov/about-us/cjjs/ucr/crime-in-the-u.s/2012/crime-in-the-u.s.-2012/property-crime/arson

Federal Bureau of Investigation. (2013e). *Health care fraud.* Retrieved August 31, 2013, from http://www.fbi.gov/about-us/investigate/white_collar/health-care-fraud

Federal Bureau of Investigation. (2013f). *Financial Crimes Report to the Public: Fiscal Years 2010–2011*. Retrieved September 7, 2013, from http://www.fbi.gov/stats-services/publications/financial-crimes-report-2010-2011

Federal Bureau of Investigation. (2014). *National incident-based reporting system 2012: Incidents, offenses, victims, and known offenders*. Retrieved July 15, 2014, from http://www.fbi.gov/about-us/cjis/ucr/us/ nibrs/2012

Felson, M. (2002). *Crime and everyday life* (3rd ed.). Thousand Oaks, CA: Sage Publications, Inc.

Fishman, S. (2010, June 6). Bernie Madoff: Free at last. *New York Magazine*. Retrieved September 10, 2013, from http://nymag.com/news/crimelaw/66468/

Harrell, E., & Langton, L. (2013). *Victims of identity theft, 2012* (NCJ 243779). Washington, DC: Bureau of Justice Statistics.

Henry J. Kaiser Family Foundation. (2011). *Pulling it together: Medicare, medicaid, and the multiplier effect*. Retrieved August 31, 2013, from http://kff.org/health-reform/perspective/pulling-it-together-medicare-medicaid-and-the-multiplier-effect/

Huff, R., Desilets, C., & Kane, J. (2010). *National public survey on white-collar crime*. Fremont, VA: National White-Collar Crime Center.

Insurance Information Institute. (2013). *Auto theft*. Available at http://www.iii.org/fact-statistic/auto-theft

Kane, J., & Wall, A. D. (2006). *The 2005 national public survey on white collar crime*. Fairmont, WV: National White Collar Crime Center.

Koops, B. J., & Leenes, R. (2006). Identity theft, identity fraud and/or identity-related crime. *Datenschutz und Datensicherheit, 30*, 553–556.

Langton, L. (2011). *Identity theft reported by households, 2005–2010* (NCJ 236245). Washington, DC: Bureau of Justice Statistics.

Mustaine, E. E., & Tewksbury, R. (1998). Predicting risks of larceny theft victimization: A routine activity analysis using refined lifestyle measures. *Criminology, 36*, 829–858.

NCVS Victimization Analysis Tool. (2014). Retrieved July 15, 2014, from http://www.bjs.gov

New Jersey Division of Consumer Affairs. (2013). Retrieved October 10, 2013, from http://www. njconsumeraffairs.gov/press/07232013.htm

Pressman, R., & Stone, O. (1987). *Wall Street* [Motion picture]. Twentieth Century Fox.

Reyns, B. W. (2013). Online routines and identity theft victimization: Further expanding routine activity theory beyond direct-contact offenses. *Journal of Research in Crime and Delinquency, 50*, 216–238.

Rice, K. J., & Smith, W. R. (2002). Socioecological models of automotive theft: Integrating routine activity and social disorganization approaches. *Journal of Research in Crime and Delinquency, 39*, 304–336.

Roberts, A., & Block, S. (2012). Explaining temporary and permanent motor vehicle theft rates in the United States: A crime-specific approach. *Journal of Research in Crime and Delinquency, 50*, 445–471.

Sampson, R. J., & Wooldredge, J. (1987). Linking the micro- and macro- level dimensions of lifestyle-routine activity and opportunity models of predatory victimization. *Journal of Quantitative Criminology, 3*, 371–393.

Shapiro, S. P. (1984). *Wayward capitalists: Target of the Securities and Exchange Commission*. New Haven, CT: Yale University Press.

Sparrow, M. K. (1996). *License to steal: Why fraud plagues America's health care system*. Boulder, CO: Westview Press.

Sutherland, E. H. (1949). *White collar crime*. New York: Dryden.

Tseloni, A., Wittebrood, K., Farrell, G. and Pease, K. (2004) Burglary victimization in England and Wales, the United States and the Netherlands: A cross-national comparative test of routine activities and lifestyle theories. *British Journal of Criminology*, 44, 66–91.

U.S. Consumer Product Safety Commission. (2013). *Port surveillance news: More than 4.8M units of violative imported products kept at bay during fiscal year 2012*. Retrieved September 2, 2013, from http://www.cpsc.gov

U.S. Environmental Protection Agency, Region 5 Waste, Pesticides, and Toxics Division. (1998). *Illegal dumping prevention guidebook*. Chicago: EPA.

Walters, J. H., Moore, A., Berzofsky, M., & Langton, L. (2013). *Household burglary, 1994–2011* (NCJ 241754). Washington, DC: Bureau of Justice Statistics.

Weisburd, D., Wheeler, S., Waring, E., & Bode, N. (1991). *Crimes of the middle classes: White-collar offenders in the federal courts*. New Haven, CT: Yale University Press.

CHAPTER 8

Domain-Specific Opportunities for Victimization

CHAPTER OUTLINE

Introduction

K–12 Schools

- Bullying Victimization
- Cyberbullying Victimization

Postsecondary Institutions

- Campus Climate
- College Students' Lifestyles and Routine Activities
- Motivated Offenders on Campus

Correctional Institutions

The Workplace

- Workplace Aggression
- Workplace Violence

The Military

Cyberspace

- Person-Based Cybercrime Victimization
- Property-Based Cybercrime Victimization

Summary

Keywords

Discussion Questions

References

LEARNING OBJECTIVES

- Describe how opportunities for victimization can be domain-specific.
- Identify the types of victimization that are associated with different domains.
- Explain why opportunities for specific types of victimization concentrate in certain domains.

Activity influences risk of victimization more in some spheres rather than others.

Lynch, 1987, p. 296

Introduction

Within the field of victimology, ***domains***, or areas of activity, are very important considerations for understanding victimization. Many victimologists have hypothesized that domains actually create opportunities for specific types of victimization. For example, K–12 schools are specific types of domains that facilitate opportunities for bullying victimization among students. While bullying could certainly occur outside school (e.g., at home between siblings), there are unique elements of the school domain that create opportunities for bullying, such as the convergence of motivated offenders and suitable targets in the same location at the same time. Likewise, colleges and universities possess characteristics that generate opportunities for particular types of victimization. For instance, thousands of emerging adults in their late teens and early twenties, many living away from their families for the first time, come together on campus and participate in the routines and lifestyles associated with college life. Some of these college-based routine activities and lifestyles are relatively safe (e.g., attending class), while others are inherently risky (e.g., binge drinking).

This chapter reviews several large domains of victimization and discusses how the routine activities and lifestyles associated with them create opportunities for criminal victimization. Bullying is discussed in light of two different domains, each with distinct opportunity-producing activities and characteristics that result in its occurrence: K–12 schools and the workplace. The workplace also is highlighted as a domain where workplace aggression and workplace violence occur. The chapter also reviews sexual violence victimizations that occur within postsecondary institutions, correctional institutions (i.e., jails and prisons), and the military. Again, while the offense is, by definition, legally the same across these different domains, the circumstances under which victimization occurs are quite different, and at least partially attributable to activities that individuals within the domain routinely engage. Several other types of victimization are discussed that take place within a unique and relatively new domain: cyberspace. Both person- and property-based cybervictimizations transpire in online domains. Some of these of victimizations are online extensions or variants of offline crimes, such as cyberbullying or online identity theft, whereas others are exclusive to the cyberspace domain, such as malware exposure.

The purpose of this chapter is to review domain-specific opportunities for victimization and the types of victimization associated with them. According to lifestyle-exposure theory and routine activities theory that were discussed in Chapters 2 and 3, opportunities for victimization are created through the intersection in time and space of motivated offenders, suitable targets, and absent or ineffective guardianship. Therefore, different domains produce opportunities for different types of victimization or unique circumstances under which victimizations can occur, based on differences in the quantities of offenders, targets, and guardianship present within them. Unfortunately, individuals whose activities bring them within the domains discussed in this chapter (e.g., schools, the workplace) sometimes become victims of other offenses not covered in this chapter. For instance, homicides occur within schools, on college campuses, and in correctional institutions, the military, and workplaces. The focus of this chapter is narrowed to highlight victimizations that are most often associated with a particular domain or are not discussed in other chapters.

K–12 Schools

In 2010 the U.S. Department of Education estimated that public secondary schools in the United States served about 55 million students in grades prekindergarten through 12th grade. Further, the Department of Education projects that this figure will grow by approximately a half-million students every year until at least 2020 (U.S. Department of Education, 2012). Clearly, K–12 schools are domains in which numerous potential victims congregate and spend a substantial portion of their day together for nine to 12 months a year. Rather than being safe places for intellectual and social development, for some children school is a place of worry, fear, and victimization. Diverse crimes are committed on school grounds, including drug-, hate-, gang-, and weapons-related offenses. In terms of victimization, the most recent available data indicate that there were 11 violent deaths of students (i.e., homicides) in schools between July 1, 2010, and June 30, 2011. In 2012, among students aged 12 through 18, there were over 1.3 million nonfatal victimizations at school, 749,200 of which were violent and 615,600 that involved theft (Robers, Kemp, Kemp, Rathbun, Morgan, & Snyder, 2014).

Figure 8-1 illustrates several important trends related to the victimization of K–12 students. First, since 1992, nonfatal victimization rates of K–12 students both at school and away from it declined steadily until 2010, when they increased slightly. Second, for most of this time, more students were victimized *at* school than *away* from it. This underscores the importance of studying and understanding the school as a unique domain of victimization. Third, the total victimization rate of students aged 12 to 18 at school was about 50 per 1,000 students. Comparing these data with those from the National Crime Victimization Survey (NCVS) for the same year indicates that students have slightly higher rates of violent victimization that does the general population aged 12 and older. For instance, for students the violent victimization rate in 2012 was 29 per 1,000 students, while the violent victimization rate in the general population was 26.1 per 1,000 residents (NCVS Victimization

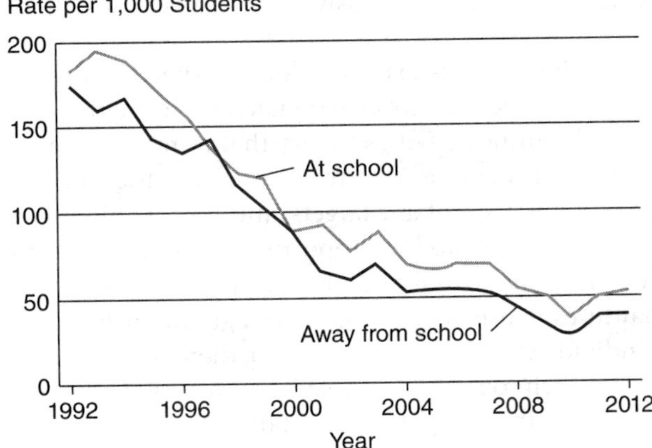

Figure 8-1 Total Nonfatal Victimization Rates at School Against Students Ages 12–18, 1992–2012
Note: Total victimizations include violent (serious violent crimes and simple assault) and theft (attempted or completed purse-snatching, completed pickpocketing, and all attempted and completed thefts) victimizations. At-school victimizations include those occurring in the school building, on school property, on the way to school, or on the way home from school.
Source: Robers, Kemp, Rathbun, Morgan, and Snyder (2014).

Analysis Tool, 2014; Robers et al., 2014). Many of the victimizations captured in the figure can be attributed to a type of victimization that until fairly recently did not receive much attention by researchers: bullying.

Bullying Victimization

Research into ***bullying*** has produced many definitions and typologies. One popular definition was provided by Dan Olweus (1993, p. 9):

> A person is bullied when he or she is exposed, repeatedly and over time, to negative actions on the part of one or more other persons, and he or she has difficulty defending himself or herself.

The three important components of bullying included in this definition are found in other definitions as well. First, the experience is *repeated*. For example, if a student is tripped and mocked by another student during lunch one day, the incident would not be considered bullying because it was a one-time event. However, if the student is targeted several times, such as over the course of a week, and repeatedly tripped and mocked, the student would be classified as a victim of bullying. Second, the victim is exposed to *unwanted negative actions*. Bullying takes many forms, but in the example previously described, the victim experienced physical and verbal bullying. Third, bullying definitions usually include a *power imbalance* between the victim and the perpetrator(s). Olweus's definition describes this in terms of the difficulty the victim has in defending himself or herself, but the nature of the power imbalance does not necessarily have to be physical.

Researchers have identified many types of behaviors that are considered to be bullying, including physical, verbal, relational, financial, racial, or sexual. ***Physical bullying***, as described in the previous example, involves hitting, kicking, pushing, spitting, and other similar negative and unwanted physical behaviors. ***Verbal bullying*** entails name calling, insults, and teasing. ***Relational bullying***, also referred to as indirect bullying, social exclusion, or social isolation, consists of behaviors such as telling lies or spreading (false) rumors about the victim. While bullying is typically done in person, it can be carried out behind the victim's back in an effort to make him or her feel isolated, exclude him or her from social activities, or tarnish his or her reputation in some way. ***Financial bullying*** involves the perpetrator taking money or damaging the property of the victim. For instance, in a particular school, if eighth-grade students repeatedly demand money from seventh-grade students to use a particular restroom, the eighth-graders would be engaging in financial bullying.

Other types of bullying are driven by demographic differences between bullies and victims and usually draw attention to the victim having a minority or "out-group" status. ***Racial bullying***, for example, can encompass other types of bullying behaviors, such as verbal threats, but the motive of the bully is based on the victim's race. Students who are not members of the majority race or "in-group" in a school may be singled out and targeted by bullies *because* they are of a different race or ethnicity. Similarly, ***sexual bullying*** may involve spreading rumors, teasing, or other previously described bullying behaviors, but underlying these tactics is a focus on the victim's sexual orientation. For instance, students who are homosexual may be made fun of because they are not heterosexual. In these two forms of bullying, race and sexual orientation are factors that put a student at added risk for bullying victimization.

Researchers from diverse fields who have studied bullying both within and outside the United States tend to agree that it is widespread in both primary and secondary schools. In the United States, for example, the School Crime Supplement (SCS) to the NCVS provides information on the extent of bullying and cyberbullying among students. These data indicate that the prevalence of bullying victimization varies considerably, and not all students are at equal risk for being bullied. For example, in 2012, about 28% of students ages 12 to 18 were victims of some form of bullying at school (Robers et al., 2014). The NCVS SCS indicated that 31% of female students experienced at least one episode of bullying at school, compared to 24% of males. Further, certain types of bullying were gender-specific: about 24% of females had rumors spread about them compared to just 13% of males. Conversely, males were physically bullied slightly more than females—9% compared to 7%. Figure 8-2 presents the percentage of students ages 12 to 18 who reported being bullied at school during 2012. The figure also displays percentages of bullying behaviors experienced by each gender.

Similar findings to the NCVS SCS have been reported in other studies of bullying victimization. For example, Jing Wang, Ronald Iannotti, and Tonja Nansel (2009) examined data from a nationally representative sample of sixth- to 10th-grade students in the United States. Using Olweus's bullying definition as a starting point, they divided bullying behaviors into four types—physical, verbal, relational, and cyberbullying—and estimated the extent of victimization among students in their sample. They found that males had a higher prevalence of physical bullying

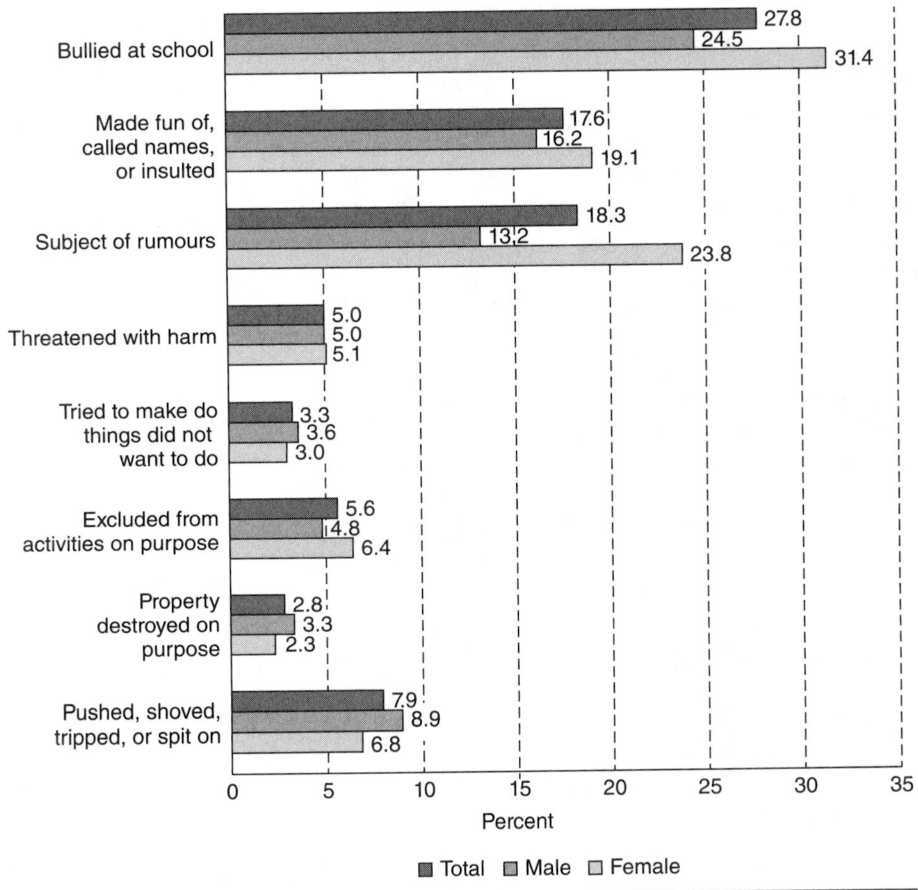

Note: "At school" includes the school building, on school property, on a school bus, or going to and from school. Bullying types do not sum to total "bullied at school" category because students could have experienced more than one type of bullying.

Figure 8-2 Bullying Victimization in the NCVS SCS by Gender of Victim
Source: Robers et al. (2014).

than females, with about 17% of males and 8% of females experiencing behaviors such as being hit, kicked, pushed or shoved by bullies. However, compared to males, females had a higher prevalence of relational bullying (45% vs. 36%), which included social isolation, being excluded from groups, or having rumors spread about them. Among the entire sample of both males and females, this study reported that, on average, relational bullying was most common (41%), followed by verbal (36%), physical (13%), and cyberbullying (10%) (Wang et al., 2009).

Cyberbullying is an interesting form of bullying victimization because it crosses domains, occurring at school and away from school, and its consequences can be felt both online and offline. Given its similarity to traditional bullying victimization, it is discussed as part of the school domain, recognizing that features of the cyberspace domain also contribute to its occurrence (Hinduja & Patchin, 2012a).

Cyberbullying Victimization

Cyberbullying has been defined and conceptualized in numerous ways by researchers and others interested in understanding this emerging form of bullying behavior. The debate regarding whether cyberbullying is a new form of victimization or essentially an extension of traditional or offline bullying into cyberspace is far from settled, but regardless, cyberbullying clearly shares characteristics with traditional or offline bullying. As is the case with offline bullying, cyberbullying victims are targets of negative or aggressive behaviors, such as teasing, insults, name calling, or threats. Further, the bullying behaviors are repeated, perhaps as often as hourly. However, cyberbullying possesses qualities that distinguish it from traditional bullying. For example, the methods used by the bully are electronic, including text messages, communications through online social networks, blogs, or other types of websites (e.g., sites with message boards). Cyberbullying also extends beyond school hours (e.g., evenings, weekends) and school grounds. While offline bullying victims usually get a reprieve after school, cyberbullies can harm their victims anytime and from virtually anywhere.

Many definitions of cyberbullying recognize the similarities and differences between offline and online bullying and often describe cyberbullying as "willful and repeated harm inflicted through the medium of electronic text" (Patchin & Hinduja, 2006, p. 152) or simply as "bullying via electronic communication tools" (Li, 2006, p. 157). The 2012 NCVS SCS provides estimates on the extent of cyberbullying victimization against students in the United States, as well as the types of bullying behaviors perpetrated against students. According to the report, 9% of students ages 12 to 18 were cyberbullied at some time during the school year. For most types of cyberbullying, it appears that females are victimized more than males. Figure 8-3 provides information on cyberbullying victimization for the total student sample as well as for males and females. The figure indicates that overall, about 11% of female students were victimized and that females experienced a higher prevalence of all forms of cyberbullying behaviors than males, with the exception of being harassed while gaming online (Robers et al., 2014).

Over the past decade, interest in cyberbullying has resulted in a growing body of research. Sameer Hinduja and Justin Patchin (2012b) summarized the results of 35 published cyberbullying studies and concluded that on average, 24% of students in the studies had been cyberbullied. They also noted that cyberbullying and bullying victims are often the same. According to Hinduja and Patchin (2012b, p. 3):

> We are often dealing with a population of targets who are doubly susceptible to victimization—both online and off—and a population of aggressors who do not discriminate when it comes to who they mistreat—and where.

If Hinduja and Patchin are correct, then the reach of bullies has extended beyond the schoolyard. While there is not much research into the consequences of being both bullied *and* cyberbullied, a good deal of scholarship has focused on the consequences of experiencing either offline or online bullying. Negative effects include,

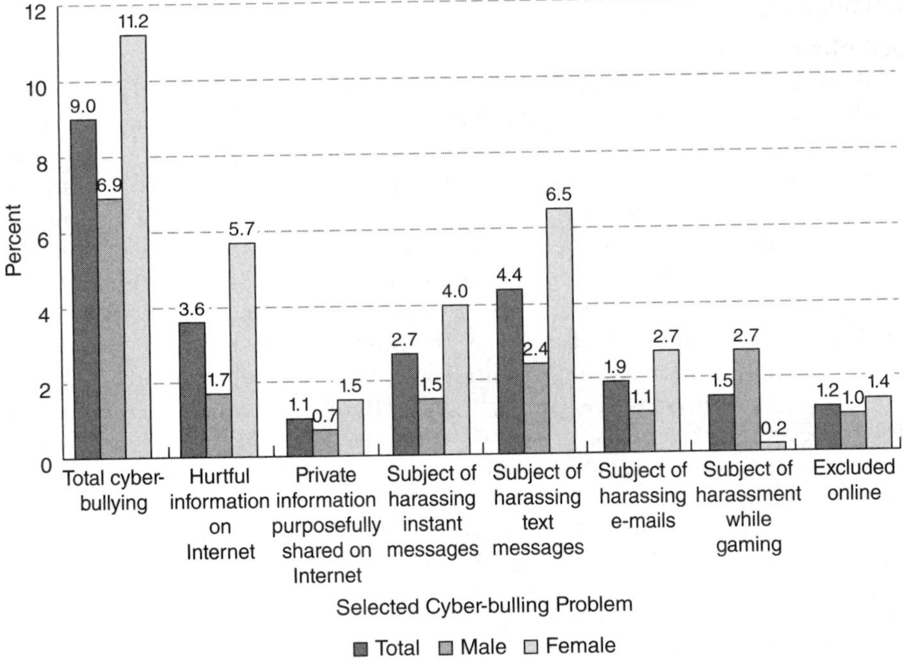

Figure 8-3 Cyberbullying Victimization in the NCVS SCS by Gender of Victim
Source: Robers et al. (2014).

but are not limited to, avoiding places at school or the school itself; emotional distress, such as depression or anxiety; reduced self-esteem; contemplated or actual self-harm; delinquent or deviant behavior; and decreased school performance (e.g., Esbensen & Carson, 2009; Hay, Meldrum, & Mann, 2010; Randa & Reyns, 2014). Given the personal costs of bullying on victims, a response by school administrators, researchers, parents, and victim advocates has been to develop prevention strategies that emphasize changing the school climate such that bullying is no longer tolerated (e.g., Hinduja & Patchin, 2012a, 2012b; Patchin & Hinduja, 2012). In other words, reducing bullying may occur through programs and interventions that alter opportunities for bullying within the school domain. As an example, a school environment that does not tolerate bullying would mean there are more willing guardians or bystanders around to stop, report, or diffuse bullying situations.

Domain-specific opportunities for victimization also can be found within postsecondary institutions, and while bullying of college students does occur, colleges and universities provide opportunities for another form of victimization—sexual violence.

Postsecondary Institutions

The college and university domain is sometimes referred to as an ivory tower that is set apart, out of touch, and sheltered from the problems of the real world (Sloan & Fisher, 2011). However, college students (and faculty) will likely be quick to dispute this claim, as has a voluminous body of research exploring the extent and nature of campus crime and the victimization of college students (e.g., Fisher & Sloan, 2013). The college domain, like the K–12 school domain, possesses characteristics enabling opportunities for specific types of victimization to occur. As an example, colleges and universities serve a fairly homogeneous population: emerging adults between 18 and 24 years of age. Concurrently, this age group is also at the highest risk for experiencing and perpetrating sexual violence. In the language of lifestyle–routine activities theory, college campuses bring together potential offenders in proximity to a large pool of suitable targets, often with little or no guardianship. Since enrollment in colleges and universities in the United States exceeded 21 million people in 2010, and with enrollment projected to reach 24 million by 2020 (U.S. Department of Education, 2012), postsecondary institutions are an important domain of victimization to consider.

Sexual violence victimization was discussed previously in Chapter 6 but is revisited in this chapter as it applies to college women. An alarming and often-cited victimization statistic first reported by Koss, Gidycz, and Wisniewski (1982) and replicated in other studies is that one in four college women has experienced a rape victimization in her lifetime. In Koss and associates' study, this figure represented a rape victimization rate among college women of 38 per 1,000 in the six months before the survey. Put differently, this means that on a campus of 10,000 students, about 380 college women will be raped every six months.

Fisher, Cullen, and Turner (2000) extended Koss and colleagues' research with a study examining the extent of sexual victimization among college women in the United States using a nationally representative sample. Their study reported that 2.8% of college women had experienced either a completed or attempted rape since school began (about seven months prior to the study), which equates to a victimization rate of about 27.7 rapes per 1,000 female students. Fisher and colleagues (2000) further explained that if the percentage is calculated for an entire year, the estimate of college women who are sexually victimized would rise to nearly 5%. Further, considering that the average student attends college for five years, over the course of a college career between 20% and 25% of female students face the possibility of experiencing an attempted or completed rape victimization.

Another study by Fisher and colleagues (1998) provides a means for comparing risks of on-campus versus off-campus sexual victimization. Making this type of comparison is important because it illustrates whether the college domain affects victimization risk or, alternatively, whether victimization risks are linked to other factors, such as students' lifestyles. Box 8-1 includes a comparison of several types of on-campus and off-campus victimization from the study by Fisher and colleagues. The picture that emerges from these results is that college students, especially college women, are more at risk for specific types of victimization *on campus* than they are *off campus*, suggesting that the campus domain *increases* victimization risk for these types of offenses. Reasons for this increased risk are discussed in the following sections. Further, most of the research on the sexual victimization of college women does not make the distinction between on and off campus but instead compares victimization risk among college students versus non-college students. Keep this in mind when considering the possible domain effects of college campuses on victimization risk.

Box 8-1: On-Campus and Off-Campus College Student Victimization

	Victimization Rate per 1,000 Male and Female Students	
Type of Victimization	On Campus	Off Campus
Rape	4.0	4.3
Sexual Assault	12.7	8.9
Robbery	0.3	2.6
Assault	14.7	30.0
Larceny with Contact	5.2	6.0
Larceny without Contact	109.5	49.3
Motor Vehicle Theft	0.6	0.3
Motor Vehicle Burglary	4.9	18.4
Burglary	37.2	27.6

Source: Adapted from Fisher, Sloan, Cullen, and Lu (1998).

An important question underlying the study of the sexual victimization of college women is whether this population is more at risk than are women in the general population. Dean Kilpatrick and his colleagues (2007) sought to answer this question by interviewing a nationally representative sample of 5,000 women in the United States regarding their rape victimization experiences. Of the 5,000 study participants, 2,000 were women attending colleges in the United States and the remaining 3,000 were representative of the general population. The study revealed that 20 million women (18%) in the United States have been raped during their lifetime and that 1 million (less than 1%) had been raped the previous year. When these national figures were compared to those for the sample of college women, Kilpatrick and colleagues found that lifetime estimates of rape for the general population sample were *higher* than those for the sample of college women (11.5%) but that experiencing a rape victimization in the past year was *five times higher* for college women than for women in the general population (Kilpatrick, Resnick, Ruggiero, Conoscenti, & McCauley, 2007). Aside from the fact that college women are younger (on average) than women more generally, something about the college domain, whether it is victims' lifestyles or routine activities, or the concentration of motivated offenders on campus, puts college women at a much higher risk for experiencing a sexual assault victimization in a given year than women in the general population. For instance, Kilpatrick and the research team (2007) reported that marijuana use was more prevalent among college student victims than among victims in the general population, indicating that drug use may be a risk factor for victimization.

Campus Climate

Colleges have historically been criticized as possessing a climate that is, at worst, tolerant of sexual violence against women and, at best, ineffective at protecting students from victimization. Three interrelated issues have contributed to this criticism. First, data indicate that the sexual victimization of college students by other students is fairly high, yet for a number of reasons, victim reporting of these crimes to law enforcement or campus administrators is low. Although institutions are mandated by the *Clery Act* (see Chapter 1) to publicly disclose campus crime statistics, they cannot do so if victims do not report their experiences to law enforcement or campus administration. It is therefore incumbent upon college administrators and policymakers to reduce barriers to reporting, to encourage students to report their victimizations to campus authorities, and to treat the incidents seriously and with care.

A second and related issue is that the campus climate acts as a mirror that both reflects and amplifies students' attitudes. For instance, if male college students possess attitudes that encourage violence against women, these beliefs can be diffused across campus via Greek or other organizations and become a part of the campus "culture." As an example, the Delta Kappa Epsilon fraternity at Yale University made headlines in 2010 when members and pledges assembled outside women's residence halls at night and repeated the slogan "No means yes, yes means anal!" While it should be noted that Yale University banned the fraternity from campus for five years and that such attitudes are not necessarily representative of members of all fraternities (nor are attitudes necessarily perfect predictors of behavior), research *has* reported a strong positive link between rape-supportive fraternity culture and practices and rape perpetration risk (e.g., Martin & Hummer, 1989). However, as Joanne Belknap and Edna Erez (2013, p. 222) pointed out, "rape is unheard of in some fraternities, happens occasionally in others, and . . . is [at] high risk of [happening] in still others." In sum, fraternity membership puts members at higher risk for violence against women when members are supportive of sexual violence against women.

Third, the acceptance by college students of "rape myths" contributes to a campus climate that is conducive to sexual violence. Rape myths have been discussed elsewhere (see Chapters 3 and 6), but briefly, ***rape myths*** are stereotypical and false beliefs about rape, rape victims, or rapists that serve to perpetuate or excuse sexual violence against women. The fraternity chant previously discussed is an example of a rape myth—that women who say "no" to sexual relations really means "yes" or that they just need "convincing." Other examples of rape myths include the belief that victims are only raped by strangers or that provocative clothing is an invitation for sex.

Research into rape myths and their acceptance among individuals has often involved study methodologies that ask respondents to interpret and assess rape scenarios or that use the ***Illinois Rape Myth Acceptance Scale*** (Burt, 1980; Payne, Lonsway, & Fitzgerald, 1999). This empirically validated psychometric scale consists of several items reflecting rape myths such as *she asked for it, it wasn't really rape, he didn't mean to,* and *she lied.* Using these four components of the scale, plus a subscale based on alcohol use, Sarah McMahon (2010) assessed rape myth acceptance among over 2,300 incoming undergraduate students at a large northeastern university.

McMahon reported that males, athletes, students pledging a fraternity or sorority, those who had not received prior rape education, and those who did not know someone who had been sexually assaulted accepted rape myths at higher levels than did students who did not have the described characteristics.

Acceptance of rape myths is a primary predictor of whether individuals, including victims, perceive and label situations as "real" rape (Basow & Minieri, 2011; Deming, Covan, Swan, & Billings, 2013). In the campus domain, rape myth acceptance takes on added importance for both potential perpetrators *and* victims. Students who accept rape myths may be more likely to perpetrate sexual violence against women and not label their behavior as rape. From the victim's perspective, rape myth acceptance affects victimization acknowledgment, which in turn stifles reporting the offense to authorities and seeking help to address the consequences of the victimization (see Chapter 10). If offenses are not reported, offenders may be emboldened to commit *more* crimes because they believe they will not get caught, thus providing increased campus-wide support for rape myths, resulting in a cycle of sexual violence.

College Students' Lifestyles and Routine Activities

The campus climate affects victimization risks among students, but research also has reported that students' activities put them at higher risk for victimization. As discussed in Chapters 2 and 3, opportunities for victimization arise through individuals' lifestyles and routine activities. Among college students, daily routines include attending class, spending time at the library or the gym, studying, or conducting research online—fairly safe routines. However, college students also engage in behaviors and routines that can produce or facilitate opportunities for victimization, such as binge drinking, taking illegal drugs, viewing pornography, being members of fraternities or sororities, and engaging in risky sexual activities, including having multiple intimate partners or engaging in unprotected sex. However, even though these behaviors *may* enable opportunities for offenders to victimize students, *offenders* are responsible for their behavior; victims are not responsible for their victimization. That being said, students' lifestyles and routine activities—especially those involving consumption of alcohol—have been identified as being significantly related to increased sexual victimization risk among college students.

Alcohol use and abuse is a routine activity often associated with college life, sexual offending, and criminal victimization on college campuses (Abbey, Clinton, McAuslan, Zawacki, & Buck, 2002). Henry Wechsler and his colleagues at the Harvard School of Public Health conducted a study of alcohol use at 144 college campuses throughout the United States and found that 84% of students drank alcohol during the school year (e.g., Wechsler & Nelson, 2008). Further, 44% of college students were classified as "binge drinkers" and 19% as "frequent" binge drinkers. ***Binge drinking***, which is defined by the National Institute on Alcohol Abuse and Alcoholism (2004) as "consuming 5 or more drinks (male), or 4 or more drinks (female), in about 2 hours," not only has been linked to an increased risk of rape victimization among college women, but has also been found to be increasing among this group (Grucza, Norberg, & Bierut, 2009). A recent study by Jenna McCauley, Karen Calhoun, and Christine Gidycz (2010) examined the relationship between binge drinking behaviors and rape victimization among a high-risk sample of college women from two different universities. The researchers reported three important findings: (1) binge drinking predicted subsequent binge drinking, (2) binge drinking significantly increased rape victimization risk, and (3) monthly binge drinkers were more likely to experience alcohol-facilitated rapes (i.e., rapes occurring when one or both parties had been drinking) than they were to experience forcible rapes.

In their test of the effects of college women's lifestyles and routine activities on experiencing sexual victimization, Elizabeth Ehrhardt Mustaine and Richard Tewksbury (2002) also reported a positive and significant relationship between alcohol use and risk for sexual victimization. Their results also indicated that college lifestyles, such as belonging to groups, clubs, or organizations; being a member of an athletic team; frequently going out at night for leisure activities; using alcohol at parties; and engaging in illegal behaviors such as buying and using illegal drugs were significant predictors of sexual victimization among college women. Similar results were uncovered in a study of rape victimization among a national sample of college women attending 119 postsecondary institutions conducted by Meichun Mohler-Kuo, George Dowdall, Mary Koss, and Henry Wechsler (2004). Their results showed that nearly 5% of women were raped, and over 70% of these victims were raped while intoxicated. Victims were also more likely to be white, reside in sorority houses, use illegal drugs, and attend institutions of higher education with high rates of alcohol use among students.

Motivated Offenders on Campus

Although aspects of the campus itself and opportunity-producing victim behaviors appear to contribute to sexual victimization in college domains, the importance of offender presence within these domains also cannot be overlooked. College campuses are populated with a potentially large pool of motivated offenders, with substantial portions of college men admitting that, under certain circumstances, they would force someone to have sex with them. For example, while somewhat dated, a finding from the previously discussed seminal study by Koss and colleagues (1982) also estimated the prevalence of sexual offending among college men. According to their results, 25% of men included in the study were identified as having used some sort of sexual aggression, such as coercion, to obtain sex. In a smaller-scale but more recent study of sexual offending among college men, Antonia Abbey and Pam McAuslan (2004) surveyed male college students about their self-reported sexual assault perpetration. Results showed that 35% of the men participating in the study admitted to having committed a sexual assault since the age of 14. A year later, they surveyed the same sample of male students and found that in the year between the initial and second surveys, 14% had committed a sexual assault. Apart from the presence of motivated offenders on campus, features of the campus, or college life more generally such as acceptance of rape myths, may provide male peer support for sexual offending (Schwartz & DeKeseredy, 1997).

Correctional Institutions

Correctional institutions are another domain in which certain types of criminal victimization are likely to occur. Jails and prisons are unique in terms of the opportunities they create for victimization, especially in comparison to the previously discussed K–12 and college campus domains. First, the population housed within these correctional domains is generally much smaller than those of schools or colleges, with jails nationwide collectively housing an average of 735,565 inmates between June 30, 2011, and June 30, 2012 (Minton, 2013) and prisons throughout the United States incarcerating 1,612,395 prisoners at the end of 2010 (Guerino, Harrison, & Sabol, 2011). From an opportunity standpoint, jails and prisons contain a substantial number of suitable targets (e.g., inmates, guards) available for criminal victimization. Second, correctional domains have no shortage of motivated offenders. Every prison resident and about half of all jail residents have been convicted of a crime, including serious felonies, which suggests that in these facilities potential victims (inmates and professional staff) are exposed daily to what would presumably be motivated offenders (inmates). Third, an interesting dynamic exists within correctional facilities related to the permanent presence of onsite guardians. Correctional officers and other staff are on site to ensure that inmates do not escape, but also to safeguard against other problems such as fights, the smuggling into prison or jail of contraband, and sexual violence. Yet, despite high levels of guardianship, criminal victimization within correctional institutions occurs, especially sexual victimization of inmates by other inmates and by staff members (who are actually responsible for a large portion of the crimes committed against inmates, according to survey data) (Beck, Berzofsky, Caspar, & Krebs, 2013).

Recall from Chapter 4 that the NCVS does not include institutionalized persons in its biannual survey of the criminal victimization experiences of U.S. residents. However, information on sexual violence against inmates *is* collected by the Bureau of Justice Statistics (BJS) through the National Inmate Survey, as mandated by the *Prison Rape Elimination Act of 2003*. The **Prison Rape Elimination Act** requires the BJS to annually compile a report on the incidence and effects of prison rape on inmates and staff from a scientifically drawn sample of at least 10% of facilities across the nation. The ***National Inmate Survey*** (NIS) has been administered three times, with the 2011–2012 NIS reaching inmates in 233 state and federal prisons, 358 jails, and 15 special facilities (i.e., military facilities, Immigration and Customs Enforcement facilities, and correctional institutions in Native American tribal land). Most of the NIS surveys were administered to inmates on a laptop with a touch screen and an audio feed that provides instructions to the respondent. This method of administering surveys ensures that inmate confidentiality is preserved while minimizing issues arising from inmate illiteracy. The 2011–2012 NIS included 92,449 inmates over the age of 18, plus smaller samples of incarcerated juveniles, ages 16 and 17, being held in state prisons and local jails. Inmates were asked about their experiences with sexual violence within the last 12 months at the facility, or since they arrived at the facility if they arrived less than 12 months ago.

The most recent NIS (2011–2012) estimated the prevalence of sexual violence against inmates purportedly perpetrated by other inmates and incidents that were allegedly perpetrated by staff in the correctional institution. These estimates are provided in Table 8-1. In total, 4% of prison inmates and 3.2% of jail inmates reported they had been sexually victimized either by other inmates or by correctional staff (Beck et al., 2013). Curiously, and perhaps counterintuitively, staff sexual misconduct against inmates was actually *more* prevalent than inmate-on-inmate sexual violence in both correctional domains. In addition to classifying incidents of sexual violence by the type of perpetrator, the NIS also makes it possible to examine the extent of two different types of inmate sexual violence: nonconsensual sexual acts and abusive sexual contacts only.

As Table 8-1 indicates, two types of inmate-perpetrated sexual violence were estimated: (1) nonconsensual sexual acts and (2) abusive sexual contacts only for prison and jail inmates separately. According to the NIS data, *nonconsensual sexual acts* are unwanted contacts involving oral, anal, or vaginal penetration, touching of genitals, and other sexual acts. For these types of offenses, which include rape, about 1% of prison inmates and less than 1% of jail inmates were sexually victimized. *Abusive sexual contacts* are offenses that involved unwanted touching of the inmate in a sexual way (e.g., touching of the penis, breasts, or vagina). About 1% of prison and jail inmates respectively experienced this type of sexual victimization by other inmates.

Table 8-1: Prevalence of Sexual Victimization in Prisons and Jails Across Administrations of the National Inmate Survey

	Percent of Prison Inmates			Percent of Jail Inmates		
Type of Incident	NIS-1 2007	NIS-2 2008–09	NIS-3 2011–12*	NIS-1 2007	NIS-2 2008–09	NIS-3 2011–12*
Total	4.5%	4.4%	4.0%	3.2%	3.1%	3.2%
Inmate-on-Inmate	2.1%	2.1%	2.0%	1.6%	1.5%	1.6%
Nonconsensual sexual acts	1.3	1.0	1.1	0.7	0.8	0.7
Abusive sexual contacts only	0.8	1.0	1.0	0.9	0.7**	0.9
Staff Sexual Misconduct	2.9%	2.8%	2.4%	2.0%	2.0%	1.8%
Unwilling activity	1.7	1.7	1.5	1.3	1.5	1.4
Excluding touching	1.3	1.3	1.1	1.1	1.1	1.0
Touching only	0.4	0.4	0.4	0.3	0.4	0.3
Willing activity	1.7	1.8**	1.4	1.1**	1.1**	0.9
Excluding touching	1.5**	1.5**	1.2	0.9**	0.9**	0.7
Touching only	0.2	0.3	0.2	0.2	0.2	0.1

Note: Detail may not sum to total because inmates may report more than one type of victimization. They may also report victimization by both other inmates and staff.
*Comparison group.
**Difference with comparison group is significant at the 95% confidence level.
Source: Beck et al. (2013).

Inmates and correctional staff are not permitted to engage in *any* type of sexual activity with inmates, regardless of whether it is consensual. Nevertheless, Table 8-1 provides estimates of offenses in which the inmate was either a willing participant or unwillingly subjected to sexual activities with facility staff. Approximately equal percentages of inmates (1.5%) were either unwillingly or willingly involved in sexual activities with staff within prison domains. Within jails, there were slightly higher percentages of unwilling sexual activities with staff than willing participation: 1.4% unwilling compared to 0.9% willing). Another piece of information provided in Table 8-1 relates to changes in sexual victimization of inmates over time. It appears that for the most part, the extent of sexual victimization of prison and jail inmates has not changed significantly since data collection via the NIS began in 2007. For example, the percentage of total prison inmates victimized changed only 0.5 percentage points between 2007 and 2011–2012.

Risks for sexual violence among inmates are not shared equally by those who are incarcerated; some inmates are at higher risk than others. The NIS results suggest that among prison and jail inmates, females, whites or those of two or more races, juveniles, those with some college or college degrees, individuals who are overweight or obese, non-heterosexuals, those who have previously been victimized, and sexual offenders have higher prevalence rates of sexual violence victimization compared to inmates without these characteristics (Beck et al., 2013).

Prior administrations of the NIS also collected information about the circumstances surrounding incidents of sexual victimization. The 2007 NIS report revealed when and where opportunities for victimization occurred, the type of coercion used, and other characteristics of the incident. Table 8-2 indicates, for example, that inmate-perpetrated sexual victimization in jails mostly occurred between 6 p.m. and midnight, whereas a majority of staff-perpetrated incidents occurred between midnight and 6 a.m. Patterns are also evident concerning where the victimization occurred. Inmate-on-inmate incidents most often occurred in the victim's cell/room or another inmate's cell/room. However, the most common locations for staff sexual misconduct included in a closet, office, or other locked room (Beck & Harrison, 2008).

Table 8-2: Circumstances and Opportunities for Inmate Sexual Victimization in Local Jails

	Inmate-on-Inmate		Staff-on-Inmate	
Circumstance	All Incidents	Nonconsensual Sexual Acts	All Incidents	Unwilling Activity
Number of victims	12,100	5,200	15,200	10,400
Time of Day[a]				
6 a.m. to noon	24.1%	32.4%	28.3%	32.2%
Noon to 6 p.m.	30.4	35.7	24.3	28.2
6 p.m. to midnight	48.4	50.8	28.0	32.4
Midnight to 6 p.m.	35.5	46.6	47.0	44.1

Where Occurred[a]				
Victim's cell/room	56.3%	63.7%	30.3%	30.0%
Another inmate's cell/room	37.2	50.0	14.5	17.3
Shower/bathroom	19.4	29.4	22.7	24.6
Yard/recreation area	14.2	14.7	9.2	10.3
Closet, office or other locked room	10.0	16.7	47.0	47.4
Workshop/kitchen	8.0	11.4	26.6	29.7
Classroom/library	5.6	9.0	20.5	24.9
Elsewhere in facility	5.9	3.7	5.4	5.6
Off facility grounds	5.8	10.8	14.4	15.3
Type of Ccoercion[a]				
Persuaded/talked into it	40.6%	56.3%	35.2%	42.0%
Given bribe/blackmailed	34.1	52.4	52.3	60.8
Given drugs/alcohol	16.7	29.1	24.7	32.6
Offered protection from other inmates	26.3	41.0	22.1	29.8
Threatened with harm or a weapon	43.7	54.3	24.6	32.1
Physically held down or restrained	34.1	41.8	15.0	18.7
Physically harmed/injured	25.6	32.5	11.4	14.3
Number of Perpetrators				
One	66.8%	57.8%	79.6%	73.4%
More than one	33.2	42.2	20.4	26.6
Number of Times				
1	:	50.8%	:	34.3%
2	:	13.8	:	24.4
3 to 10	:	21.3	:	26.3
11 or more	:	14.1	:	15.0
Reported at Least one Incident[b]				
Yes	23.9%	33.0%	14.4%	20.2%
No	76.1	67.0	85.6	79.8

: Not calculated.
[a]Detail may sum to more than 100% because multiple responses were allowed for each item.
[b]Indicated at least one incident was reported to facility staff (line staff-medical or mental health staff, teacher, counselor, volunteer, or chaplain), another inmate, or a family member or friend.
Source: Beck and Harrison (2008).

Not only are correctional facilities domains that possess many opportunities for sexual victimization, but findings related to victim (e.g., gender and weight) and incident characteristics (e.g., time of day and location in the facility) suggest that these opportunities concentrate in patterned ways. Perhaps inmates with certain characteristics are more attractive targets than others, or maybe guardianship is lower during certain times of day. Therefore, from a prevention perspective, it may be useful to target prevention efforts toward certain individuals, times, and places within correctional institutions. Of course, members of correctional staff are also at risk for experiencing victimization in the correctional domain. Thus, another prominent domain of victimization to consider is the workplace.

The Workplace

The workplace represents a domain in which opportunities for victimization occur and, depending on the nature of the work, facilitate different types of victimization. In other words, some occupations are more risky, in terms of workplace victimization, than others. Providing some sense of the vastness of the workplace domain, the Bureau of Labor Statistics reported that the percentage of working age-adults in the U.S. labor force was 63.4% in July 2013. Box 8-2 lists employment figures across different sectors of the economy to illustrate how opportunities for workplace victimizations are distributed.

Information on workplace victimization can be gleaned from different sources, and one important source is the Workplace Risk Supplement to the NCVS, which was administered in 2002. The Workplace Risk Supplement indicated that 4% of respondents experienced victimization while at work, and 7% worried about someone in their workplace attacking them (Jenkins, Fisher, & Hartley, 2012). Criminal victimizations occurring within workplace domains are usually categorized as either workplace aggression or workplace violence, but these categories are not mutually exclusive. ***Workplace aggression*** involves "behavior by an individual or individuals within or outside an organization that is intended to physically or psychologically harm a worker or workers and occurs in a work-related context" (Schat & Kelloway, 2004, p. 191). ***Workplace violence*** includes extreme forms of aggression,

Box 8-2: Employed Persons 16 and Older by Occupation, 2012

Occupation	Employed
Management, business, and financial operations	22,678,000
Professional and related occupations	31,365,000
Service occupations	25,459,000
Sales and office occupations	33,152,000
Natural resources, construction, and maintenance occupations	12,821,000
Production, transportation, and material moving occupations	16,994,000

Source: Bureau of Labor Statistics (2013).

usually intended to inflict severe physical harm to the victim (Baron & Neuman, 1996).

Workplace Aggression

Two common forms of workplace aggression are bullying and sexual harassment. Workplace bullying is not dramatically different in character than bullying at school; the distinguishing feature is that it occurs between adults while at work. Like bullying at school, ***workplace bullying*** involves regular and repeated unwanted behaviors (e.g., harassment, criticism, teasing) over time that make the victim feel inferior or powerless. Such behaviors may include threats to one's professional status (e.g., criticisms of work quality), threats to one's personal standing (e.g., comments about appearance), isolation (withholding information), overwork (e.g., unfeasible deadlines), and destabilization (e.g., not giving victim credit for work he or she did) (Rayner & Hoel, 1997).

Research shows that the type of workplace and its culture are important correlates of workplace bullying. Further, although estimates of the extent of victimization depend on how workplace bullying is measured, worldwide research has produced estimates showing that as many as 20% of workers have been bullied while at work, with an average of about 4% of workers being victimized across studies (Zapf, Escartín, Einarsen, Hoel, & Vartia, 2011). The accumulated body of research on workplace bullying suggests that it is influenced by many factors operating at different levels, including demographic and personality characteristics of victims; organizational factors; group/coworker characteristics; and perpetrator characteristics. Precursors to victimization that may be rooted in opportunities include factors such as group dynamics in which bullying perpetuates more of the behavior; organizations with weak (or no) policies outlining unacceptable behaviors; lack of workplace leadership; and the organization's culture. Workplace bullying negatively affects victims by reducing their productivity, job satisfaction, and psychological and physical well-being. Workplace bullying has also been linked to victim suicide, absenteeism, and intent to leave, and has repercussions for coworkers, organizations, and society (Samnani & Singh, 2012).

Sexual harassment in the workplace domain is also a serious form of victimization. Defining sexual harassment has proven to be a challenge because there are many behaviors that could constitute sexual harassment, and it occurs under varied circumstances. However, the U.S. Equal Employment Opportunity Commission (EEOC) provides a starting point for describing generally what this type of victimization entails. Overall, ***sexual harassment*** consists of any harassment of a sexual nature, such as unwelcome sexual advances, requests for sexual favors, or any other verbal or physical harassment of a sexual nature. Further, sexual harassment affects the victim's employment, interferes with his or her performance at work, or creates a hostile work environment. According to the EEOC's website (2013), sexual harassment occurs under the following circumstances:

- The victim as well as the harasser may be of either sex, while the victim does not have to be of the opposite sex.
- The harasser can be the victim's supervisor, an agent of the employer, a supervisor in another area, a coworker, or a non-employee.

- The victim does not have to be the target of the harassment but could be anyone affected by the offensive conduct.
- Unlawful sexual harassment may occur without economic injury to, or discharge of, the victim.
- The harasser's conduct must be unwelcome.

Although the circumstances surrounding sexual harassment victimization are quite varied, it is often conceptualized as either occurring as *quid pro quo* harassment or as creating a hostile work environment. *Quid pro quo* is a Latin term translated as "this for that." As a form of sexual harassment, *quid pro quo* harassment occurs when employment decisions (e.g., a promotion to a higher-paying position) are made based on the employee's willingness to submit to sexual advances from supervisors or coworkers. As an example, if a supervisor demands that her subordinate have sex with her in exchange for a promotion, a better work schedule, or anything else relevant to the employee's status at work, the supervisor has perpetrated *quid pro quo* harassment. When sexual harassment creates a work atmosphere that is persistently harmful, offensive, fearful, intimidating, or oppressive to the employee, the workplace can be considered a hostile work environment. For example, if male coworkers and/or supervisors continually subject female employees to sexually tinged remarks and sexually explicit jokes, their actions have created a hostile work environment for female employees. Box 8.3 presents highlights of a precedent-setting Supreme Court case involving the legal definition of sexual harassment.

Box 8-3: The Supreme Court and Sexual Harassment: Setting Precedent

Case	Facts	Issue	Decision	Held
Meritor Savings Bank v. Vinson (1986)	Mechelle Vinson was fired from her job of many years at Meritor Savings Bank and filed a lawsuit against her supervisor and the bank claiming she had been sexually harassed, including being raped, by the supervisor over a long period. She argued the harassment had created a "hostile work environment" that constituted a form of sex discrimination in violation of Title VII of the *Civil Rights Act of 1964*.	Does a "hostile work environment" constitute an illegal form of sex discrimination under the *Civil Rights Act of 1964*, or is the *Act* intended to only prohibit *tangible* economic discrimination in employment?	9–0 in favor of Vinson	The Court held that the *Civil Rights Act of 1964* was *not* limited to prohibiting "tangible" economic discrimination and that Congress intended the law to address *all* forms of unequal treatment in employment.

Source: *Meritor Savings Bank v. Vinson*, 477 US 57 (1986).

Estimating the extent of workplace sexual harassment is challenging for two reasons. First, there is no universal definition of sexual harassment. Second, national sources of victimization data (e.g., UCR, NCVS) do not routinely collect that information. However, in 2011 the EEOC reported that it received 11,364 sexual harassment complaints, 84% of which were filed by females (U.S. Equal Employment Opportunity Commission, 2013). Further documentation about the prevalence of sexual harassment in the workplace comes from survey research of employees' experiences, which suggests that levels of workplace sexual harassment are fairly high. In summarizing the research on sexual harassment, Paula McDonald (2012) explained that in the United States up to 75% of women and 31% of men have been victims of sexual harassment at work, while European studies have reported that between 17% and 81% of women have experienced such harassment. Research also has revealed that opportunities for sexual harassment are facilitated by workplace culture, climate, or tolerance of harassment, and discouraged through supervisor or coworker support, harmony, or solidarity. Like workplace bullying, sexual harassment in the workplace also has serious consequences for victims, physically, mentally, and financially. Research has linked sexual harassment with increased stress, depression, anxiety, and other mental and physical conditions; and in the workplace with lower job satisfaction, commitment, and productivity (McDonald, 2012).

Workplace Violence

In addition to these common forms of workplace aggression, serious violence also occurs in workplace domains. These extreme forms of workplace aggression affect employees in all occupations and job settings and are usually conceptualized as falling into one of four categories first identified by the State of California's Department of Industrial Relations (1995). These categories are presented along with examples in Table 8-3 and are based on the victim–offender relationship, rather than on the type of victimization or offense. First, incidents of workplace violence can be based on *criminal intent*, meaning that the perpetrator has no legitimate relationship with the workplace or employees. Second, *customer/client violence* involves situations where the perpetrator has a legitimate reason for interacting with the workplace and commits acts of violence during the course of this relationship. Third, *worker-on-worker violence* occurs when perpetrators have a relationship with the workplace (e.g., as an employee or former employee) and act violently in the victim's workplace setting. Fourth, *personal relationship violence* in the workplace occurs when violence spills over from one domain of victimization into the workplace domain, as would be the case if an abusive intimate partner goes to the victim's workplace to target him or her.

Workplace violence has the potential to physically injure victims and, according to recent NCVS reports, accounts for 15% of all nonfatal violence experienced by employed persons in the United States over the age of 16. Put differently, 15% of all nonfatal violent crime against those who are employed occurs in the workplace domain.

Table 8-3: Typology of Workplace Violence

Type of Workplace Violence	Description	Example
1. *Criminal Intent*	• The perpetrator has no legitimate relationship with the workplace or employees.	• Convenience store robbery • Bank robbery
2. *Customer/Client*	• The perpetrator has a legitimate relationship with the workplace or its employees and perpetrates violence during the course of this relationship.	• Patient who attacks doctor or nurse in an emergency department
3. *Worker-on-Worker*	• The perpetrator is an employee or former employee and targets a coworker. Usually involves a series of disputes at work.	• Former employee who shoots supervisor after a bad evaluation
4. *Personal Relationship*	• The perpetrator is usually not employed at the workplace and targets the victim at his or her place of work.	• Domestic violence at home carries over into the workplace

Source: Adapted from State of California Department of Industrial Relations (1995).

A primary interest of victimologists has been to identify those occupations linked with a high risk of experiencing workplace violence. In considering workplace violence to include the crimes of rape/sexual assault, robbery, aggravated assault, and simple assault, data from the NCVS reveal that those working in the medical, mental health, teaching, law enforcement, retail sales, and transportation fields are at high risk for experiencing workplace violence. Of these occupational categories, law enforcement is clearly the most risky in terms of workplace violence victimization. Table 8-4 presents workplace violence rates for specific occupations. For example, according to the NCVS findings in the table, within the retail sales domain bartenders have the highest likelihood of experiencing workplace violence, whereas within the teaching field, preschool teachers have lower victimization rates for workplace violence compared to other teachers.

Table 8-4: Workplace Violence by Occupation, 2005–2009

Occupation	Rate of Workplace Violence per 1,000 Employed Persons Age 16 or Older	Non-Workplace Violence Rate per 1,000 Employed Persons Age 16 or Older	Percentage of Workplace Violence	Percentage of Employed Population Age 16 or Older
Total	5.1	16.4	100.0%	100.0%
Medical	6.5	15.0	10.2%	8.2%
Physician	10.1	7.7*	1.1	0.6
Nurse	8.1	13.8	3.9	2.5
Technician	11.1	12.2	2.3	1.1
Other/medical occupations	3.7	17.5	2.9	4.1

Mental Health	20.5	17.2	3.9%	1.0%
Professional	17.0	12.8	1.4	0.4
Custodial case	37.6*	4.4*	0.7*	0.1
Other mental health occupations	20.3	24.1	1.8	0.5
Teaching	6.5	8.8	9.0%	7.2%
Preschool	0.9*	9.8	0.1*	0.5
Elementary	4.3	4.7	1.5	1.9
Jr. high/middle	8.6	5.0*	1.3	0.8
High school	13.5	7.4	2.6	1.0
College/university	1.9*	14.1	0.7*	1.9
Technical/industrial school	54.9*	–*	0.7*	0.1
Special education facility	17.8*	8.0*	0.5*	0.2
Other teaching occupations	8.9	11.4	1.6	0.9
Law Enforcement	47.7	13.7	18.9%	2.1%
Law enforcement officer	77.8	3.5*	9.1	0.6
Connections officer	33.0	13.0*	1.8	0.3
Security guard	65.0	23.1	5.6	0.5
Other law enforcement occupations	17.5	16.7	2.4	0.7
Retail Sales	7.7	24.3	13.2%	9.0%
Convenience or liquor store clerk	7.1*	25.1	0.7*	0.5
Gas station attendant	30.2*	25.9*	0.8*	0.1
Bartender	79.9	38.7*	1.9	0.1
Other retail sales occupations	6.3	24.0	9.8	8.2
Transportation	12.2	12.9	7.4%	3.2%
Bus driver	10.0*	3.1*	0.6*	0.3
Taxi cab driver	9.0*	33.3*	0.2*	0.1
Other transportation occupations	12.6	13.4	6.6	2.7
Other/unspecified	2.8	16.6	37.3%	69.3%

Note: The National Crime Victimization Survey and Census of Fatal Occupational Injuries use different categories of occupations. Includes 2006 data.
*Based on 10 or fewer sample cases.
-Less than 0.05.
Source: Harrell (2011).

Victimologists seeking to explain workplace violence and aggression have pointed to the differential opportunities for victimization that exist across occupational fields. That is, simply going to work does not necessarily increase one's victimization risk, but rather the duties or tasks performed *while at work* are what affect one's risk. In answering the question of "why," for example, take police officers. They have the highest risk for workplace violence of any occupation included in the NCVS. A plausible explanation for this is that they are exposed to, and tasked with, interacting with motivated offenders during the course of their work. In general, occupations requiring a high level of public interaction, those that involve handling money, and those that require mobility rather than working at a single site are riskier, in terms of being targets of workplace violence, than are jobs without these routines (Lynch, 1987).

The Military

For many, the military is both a workplace and a unique domain of victimization. Active military figures change continuously, but as of February 2013 Department of Defense reports indicate that there are over 1.4 million individuals total in the U.S. armed services (Army, Navy, Marine Corps, Air Force, and Coast Guard), which gives some indication of the size of this victimization domain. As is the case with all domains of victimization, the majority of individuals within the military never experience any form of criminal victimization. Yet studies of sexual assault victimizations among members of the military indicate that in some instances, the prevalence of victimization may be higher among those serving in the military than among those in the general U.S. population (Turchik & Wilson, 2010).

Although few studies have investigated this issue, existing research suggests that between 9.5% and 33% of women have experienced an attempted or completed rape during their military service, while as many as 12% of men in the military have been sexually assaulted (Turchik & Wilson, 2010). For example, based on data from the VA Women's Health Project, a national study to assess the health of female veterans, Katherine Skinner and colleagues (2000) reported that 23% of female veterans had been sexually assaulted while in the military. Sexual harassment also occurs in the military, with 55% of women in Skinner and associates' study reporting they had been sexually harassed. Further, a more recent study using a broad-based sample of active-duty service members found that 10.5% of women reported they had been victims of either attempted or completed rape while serving (Murdoch, Pryor, Polusny, & Gackstetter, 2007). Aside from findings that suggest sexual assault occurs at high rates in the military, data also indicate that rates of sexual assault among military personnel have increased over time and vary depending on the branch of the military in which one serves, with personnel in the Army experiencing the highest rates of victimization (Turchik & Wilson, 2010).

Researchers have also studied sexual assault victimization in military academies. Jamie Snyder, Bonnie Fisher, Heidi Scherer, and Leah Daigle (2012) used self-report victimization data from 5,220 cadets and midshipmen at three U.S. military academies to assess the extent of several types of sexual victimization in these military domains. The findings revealed that 60% of cadets and midshipmen were

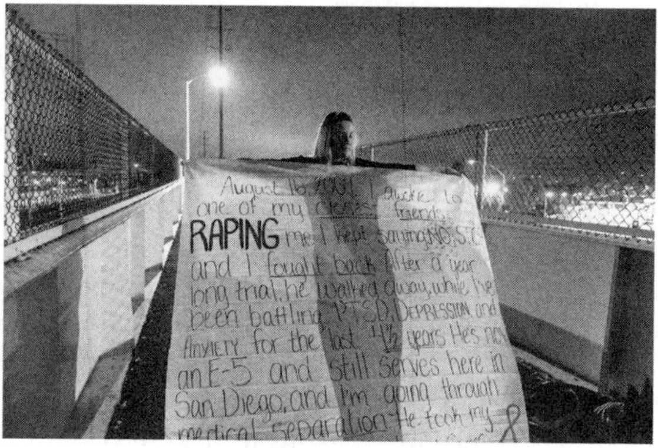

Sexual Assault in the Military
Source: Mary F. Calvert/ZUMA/Corbis.X
Photo Credit: © Mary F. Calvert/ZUMAPress.com

victims of unwanted sexual contact, unwanted sexual attention, sexual harassment, sexual coercion, and rape. Further, a quarter of these individuals experienced more than one type of sexual victimization. The study also revealed important gender differences in sexual victimization. Notably, 86% of females had been victimized compared to 42% of males.

As a domain of victimization, it is unlikely that there is any factor about the military *per se* that can be singled out as the cause of the high prevalence of sexual assault occurring against its members. More likely, several factors work in tandem to create situations and circumstances favorable to sexual assault victimization. Research studies have identified factors such demographic characteristics of service personnel; features of the military domain, such as its culture; low rates of reporting; high rates of prior sexual victimization against personnel; high rates of prior perpetration among its members; and substance use. In particular, the military's culture is male-dominated, normalizes violence, and adheres to a strict chain of command, and these characteristics are favorable to allowing sexual assault perpetrations to both occur and remain unreported. An additional influence may be the demographic profile of many members of the military, who volunteer for service and are at high risk for both perpetration and victimization because of their age. Like all victims of sexual assault, military members who are victimized suffer physically as well as psychologically, experiencing negative consequences such as depression, anger, posttraumatic stress disorder, substance use, and sexual and relationship difficulties. In addition, those victimized at military academies generally have more negative views of their leadership's morality and their tolerance for sexual victimization. Not only do these views discourage reporting, but they may undermine the functionality of the military chain of command (Synder et al., 2012).

Cyberspace

The online domain (not to be confused with online Domain Name Systems [DNS]) of cyberspace has become an arena for seemingly countless forms of victimization. Two primary features of this domain distinguish it from the other domains of victimization reviewed in this chapter. First, crimes occurring in cyberspace do not require that the victim and the offender be physically present in the same location at the same time for there to be an opportunity for victimization. For example, prior to the advent of the Internet, many identity thieves relied on fairly low-tech methods for gaining others' personal information: They would often sift through trash or steal purses or wallets from their victims. These tactics required that the offender connect with the victim or the victim's property to acquire the identity information for later misuse. In contrast, online identity theft requires no such physical contact, and savvy identity thieves can reach their victims from anywhere in the world at any hour.

Second, since individuals can interact in cyberspace 24 hours a day, seven days a week, from anywhere across the globe as long as they have an Internet connection, opportunities for online victimization have become ubiquitous. For example, opportunities for sexual harassment in the workplace are limited by practical considerations, such as the number of coworkers in the workplace, but opportunities for online sexual harassment are omnipresent, limited only by the offender's desire and tenacity to seek them out. Consider the popular online social network Facebook as an example. As of March 2014, Facebook (2014) reported an average of 802 million daily active users and 1.28 billion monthly active users. Depending on the nature of the offense, those motivated to find victims within this online domain do not have an exhaustive search ahead of them. Considering this, victimologists have begun to investigate not only online domains but also online social networks as environments in which victimization occurs. While these Facebook usage figures will likely change, the overall point is that there are essentially limitless supplies of suitable online targets and motivated offenders. However, online domains do vary in level of guardianship, and increasingly it appears that guardianship determines whether online victimization opportunities exist.

Cybercrime victimization takes many forms, but all online victimizations can broadly be categorized as either person-based or property-based, depending on the target. For example, cyberbullying is a behavior meant to assert power or domination over an individual, whereas identity theft has little to do with the individual and everything to do with the individual's property or personal information. The chapter's remaining pages review several types of person- and property-based forms of cybercrime victimization.

Person-Based Cybercrime Victimization

Earlier chapters discussed offline forms of person-based victimization such as homicide, rape, and physical assault. Person-based offenses often result in physical injuries to the victim, including death, as well as psychological and/or emotional harm. Yet, person-based offenses transpiring in cyberspace are necessarily different because of the physical separation between the perpetrator and the victim. As a consequence, person-based victimizations occurring in cyberspace primarily result in psychological rather than physical harm to the victim. Most person-based forms of online victimization involve some variation of harassing behavior. The nature of these behaviors is quite diverse, but all forms of ***online harassment*** generally involve a perpetrator behaving in a manner that is meant to annoy, torment, or terrorize the victim. Victimologists have studied harassment as a general type of person-based cybercrime victimization as well as specific types of online harassment, including cyberbullying (see school domain), sexual exploitation, and cyberstalking.

The Internet provides ample means for offenders to select and then harass victims. For instance, instant messaging systems, which facilitate online chatting in real time, can be used by online offenders to send hurtful comments, threats, or annoying messages to victims. Instant messaging is now integrated into many popular online social networks, supported by video messaging, and has mobile applications that allow users to communicate with each other "on the go." Depending on the digital connectedness of motivated offenders and suitable targets, instant messaging has made online harassment relatively easy to perpetrate. Barriers to offending are removed, since some of these communications can remain anonymous or individuals can assume a false identity or alias. Besides instant messaging, tools for online harassment may include online forums, social networking sites, message boards, video or photo sharing sites, or any other website to which users can post text, photos, or videos. In sum, nearly unlimited opportunities, combined with available technology facilitating it, make online harassment extremely common and difficult to address.

Neither the NCVS nor the UCR records incidents of online harassment occurring in the United States. Several studies, however, have examined the problem and estimated its prevalence, described its predictors, and documented the consequences of online harassment. For example, a study of online harassment among college students by Megan Lindsay and Judy Krysik (2012) found that 43% of students in the study had experienced some form of online harassment. Notably, the authors found that the more time individuals spent with online social networking, the more likely they were to be victims of online harassment. In a similar study, Billy Henson and colleagues (2011) examined online interpersonal victimization, which includes harassment, committed against college students and across different online social networks (e.g., Facebook, MySpace, Twitter, LiveJournal). They found that, overall, the number of social network accounts individuals had, how often they updated their account(s), and whether they added strangers as friends to their online social networks were significant predictors of online interpersonal victimization. Examining a different population of Internet users, Janis Wolak, Kimberly Mitchell, and David Finkelhor (2006) estimated the prevalence of online harassment against youth ages 10 to 17 to be about 9%. They also reported the prevalence of another type of online person-based victimization against this age group: sexual exploitation.

Online sexual exploitation usually takes the form of solicitations for sex or exposure to unwanted sexual materials within an online domain. Wolak and colleagues (2006) found that 13% of youth had been solicited while online, presumably by offenders who wanted to take the next step and meet them for a physical sexual encounter. The study also found that 34% had been exposed to unwanted sexual materials, such as links leading to pornographic photos or videos. Of course, these victimization experiences also may overlap, with offenders sending unwanted materials as an invitation for a face-to-face meeting. Data also suggest that unwanted exposure to sexual materials may increase with age and is particularly prevalent among college students. For example, Jerry Finn (2004) undertook one of the earliest studies of online harassment and found that nearly 60% of students in his sample received unwanted pornography, which he explained could be considered a form of harassment. A related behavior that may or may not constitute a person-based type of online victimization is sexting.

Sexting involves sharing nude or partially nude images, often of oneself, with another person using digital technology, usually a cellphone and through text messaging. The classification of sexting as a form of online victimization, however, depends on the circumstances under which it occurs. If the behavior is consensual, not coerced, and engaged in by adults, it can at worst be labeled as a deviant behavior, but this depends on one's attitudes about sexual behavior. If, on the other hand, either the sender or recipient does not want to participate, sexting may be considered a form of online harassment or sexual exploitation. In other words, some may only participate (and send images) because they have been repeatedly harassed, begged, or coerced into doing so. On the other hand, some sexters will send unsolicited images in the hopes of beginning a romantic relationship or asking for sex. To the recipient, the images may be offensive or at least unwanted.

Regardless of how it is viewed, sexting research indicates the behavior is fairly common, especially as youth transition into adulthood. Another consistent finding across studies is that receiving sexts is more common than sending them. For example, research from a national sample of Internet users ages 10 to 17 found that among this age group, 2.5% admitted to sending sexts while about 7% said they had received them (Mitchell, Finkelhor, Jones, & Wolak, 2012). MTV (2009) conducted an online survey using randomly selected telephone numbers and addresses across the United States and reported that 13% of individuals contacted who were between the ages of 14 and 24 admitted to sending sexually oriented text messages (sexts) while 21% had received such messages. Further, a study of sexting among college students reported that 20% had sent sexts and 36% had received them (Reyns, Burek, Henson, & Fisher, 2013). Hence, sexting appears to be more popular as individuals enter young adulthood and begin their college careers. Besides sometimes being considered a form of unwanted exposure to sexual materials or a kind of sexual coercion, early research also indicates that it is a routine activity that increases one's likelihood of personal victimization while online. Reyns and colleagues (2013) reported that sexting increased the likelihood of experiencing not only online personal victimization (e.g., harassment) but also repeat occurrences of online victimization.

Online harassment and sexual exploitation have shared characteristics and may also be mutually experienced. Another type of person-based cybercrime victimization with which they may overlap is cyberstalking. ***Cyberstalking*** occurs when individuals are repeatedly pursued through digital or Internet-based devices, such as tablets, smartphones, computers, or global positioning systems (GPS). This pursuit may involve repeated attempts at contacting the victim, threatening the victim, sexually propositioning the victim, monitoring the victim, or otherwise harassing the victim in the online domain. Current legal definitions of stalking (see Chapter 5) and cyberstalking do not separate them as distinct forms of victimization, which is why conceptually cyberstalking can be thought of as a "subset or special circumstance of generalized stalking" (Nobles, Reyns, Fox, & Fisher, 2012, p. 5).

Research into the extent and nature of cyberstalking began in the late 1990s when U.S. Attorney General Janet Reno identified cyberstalking as an emerging online social problem (U.S. Attorney General, 1999). Since this early report was published, several cyberstalking studies have been undertaken and identified its prevalence as well as patterns associated with it. First, although questions about cyberstalking victimization are not included in the annual NCVS, in 2006 a special stalking supplement was administered to a subsample of respondents 18 or older. These data provided an indication of the extent of cyberstalking nationally and suggest a victimization rate in the United States of approximately 14 per 1,000 individuals. Of those who were stalked, 26% were also cyberstalked by their pursuer and 7% were monitored electronically by their stalkers (Baum, Catalano, Rand, & Rose, 2009). The NCVS report also included information on the types of cyberstalking victims experienced and divided them into two categories: cyberstalking and cybermonitoring. Table 8-5 shows the types of cyberstalking behaviors that victims experienced, with most incidents at least including e-mail contact from stalker to victim.

Besides the estimates of cyberstalking provided by the NCVS report, most studies of cyberstalking have relied on college student samples to estimate its prevalence and nature. While estimates produced by these studies differ widely depending on how the respective researchers defined cyberstalking, some studies estimate that as many as 40% of college students have been cyberstalked at some point (Reyns, Henson, & Fisher, 2012). Victimologists also have begun exploring what puts individuals at risk for cyberstalking victimization, and whether opportunity plays a role in such events. Reyns, Henson, and Fisher (2011) answered this question by

Table 8-5: Types of Cyberstalking and Electronic Monitoring Against Stalking Victims

Percent of Stalking Victims also Cyberstalked:	26.1%
Percent of cyberstalking involving:	
E-mail	82.5%
Instant messaging	35.1%
Blogs or bulletin boards	12.3%
Internet sites about victim	9.4%
Chat rooms	4.4%
Percent of Stalking Victims also Electronically Monitored:	7.8%
Percent of Electronic Monitoring Involving:	
Computer spyware	33.6%
Video/digital cameras	46.3%
Listening devices/bugs	41.8%
GPS	10.9%

Source: Baum et al. (2009).

surveying college students at a large Midwestern university about their online experiences. The researchers reported that their adaptation of lifestyle–routine activities theory (see Chapter 3) to cyberspace domains was useful for explaining cyberstalking victimization, and that aspects of online exposure, online proximity, online guardianship, online target attractiveness, and online deviance were significantly related to victimization.

Online harassment, online sexual exploitation, and cyberstalking appear to be quite prevalent and have the potential, given the widespread use of online domains, to grow in scope. The same can be said for property-based forms of cybercrime victimization, such as online theft, digital piracy, and online fraud. Property-based victimizations occurring within online domains are discussed in the next section.

Property-Based Cybercrime Victimization

Property-based offenses committed in cyberspace involve the loss or destruction of property and can target individuals, businesses, institutions, organizations, or governments. The distinction between whether the property is destroyed or lost is an important one and determines whether the offense is labeled a cyberattack or a cybertheft. ***Cyberattacks*** are offenses that target the computer system or equipment and not necessarily any valuable information that it may contain; they include offenses such as malware exposure, denial of service attacks, and online vandalism or sabotage. These three types of cybercrime victimization each involve malicious disruption, defacement, or destruction of the victim's software, hardware, information flow, files, data, or programs. ***Malware*** involves software and/or programming codes that spread by infecting or modifying other programs. ***Denial of service attacks*** affect the victim's Internet connection, slowing or stopping normal operations. Like its offline counterpart, ***online vandalism/sabotage*** alters online content in some way. For example, a government website's server may be accessed and changes made to the site's appearance as a form of protest or to spread a message. As an example, see the accompanying screen shot, which shows the vandalism by hackers of the University of La Salette website in March 2013. Once again, opportunities for property-based cybercrime victimization seem endless when considering the number of individuals, businesses, organizations, and other potential suitable targets that have an online presence.

The National Computer Security Survey (NCSS), which was administered by BJS to a random sample of businesses located in the U.S., estimated the extent to which these types of cybercrimes occurred in 2005. The BJS reported that 67% of businesses detected at least one cybercrime, with 58% of these being victims of cyberattacks (Rantala, 2008). Table 8-6 shows the scope of cybercrimes against U.S. businesses as estimated by the NCSS. For example, a majority of victimized businesses detected computer viruses, such as worms or Trojan horses. Of course, there is likely a substantial dark figure when it comes to estimates for these types of offenses, because many victims may not know that their computers or devices have been exposed to malware. Malware infections such as these do not only affect businesses, with one study of victimization among college students finding that 30% had found malware on their computers (Bossler & Holt, 2009).

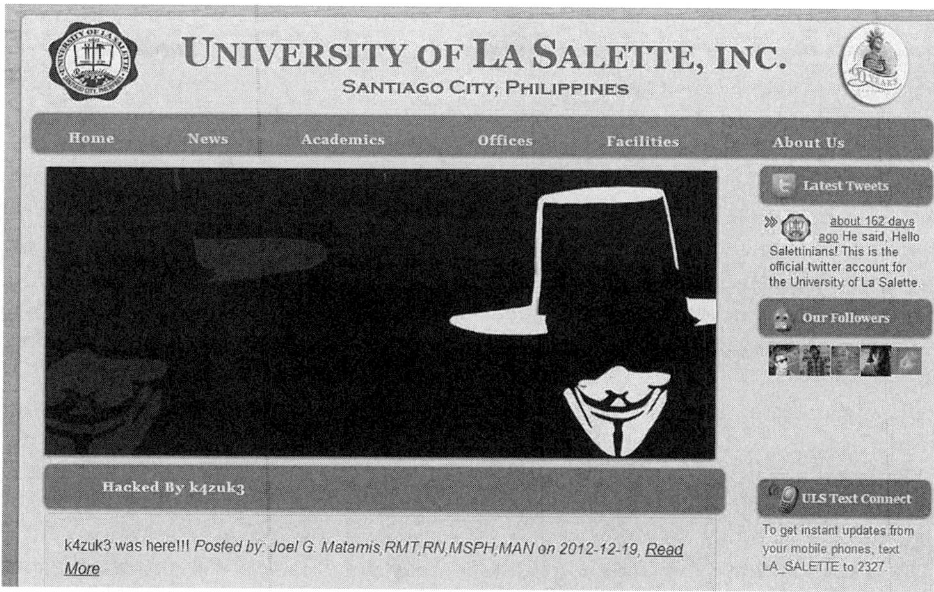

Online Vandalism of the University of La Salette Website

Source: http://www.pinoyhacknews.com/wp-content/uploads/2013/05/university-of-la-salette-defaced.jpg. Photo Credit: Pinoy Hack News

Table 8-6: Cybercrime Against Businesses from the NCVS

Type of Incident	All Businesses*	Businesses Detecting Incidents	
		Number	Percent
All incidents	7,636	5,081	67%
Cyber Attack	7,626	4,398	58%
Computer virus	7,538	3,937	52
Denial of service	7,517	1,215	16
Vandalism or sabotage	7,500	350	5
Cyber Theft	7,561	839	11%
Embezzlement	7,492	251	3
Fraud	7,488	364	5
Theft of intellectual property	7,492	227	3
Theft of personal or financial data	7,476	249	3
Other Computer Security Incidents	7,492	1,792	24%

Note: Number of businesses and detail may sum to more than total because respondents could answer questions about more than one type of incident.
*Based on businesses that indicated whether they detected an incident.
Source: Rantala (2008).

Cyberthefts, including those of intellectual property and personal or financial data, as well as fraud, also target businesses, individuals, and institutions (e.g., colleges and universities). They involve circumstances where the victim's property is taken or used without permission. Cyberthefts are qualitatively different from thefts in the physical world because in many cases the victim's property is not permanently taken from him or her. For example, a burglar may enter a victim's home and remove valuables such as jewelry, cash, or electronics, whereas a cyberthief remotely accesses a victim's computer and *copies* files or other data without the victim actually losing his or her computer. In such cases, the valuable property is not the computer itself but rather the *information* stored on it. For instance, the crime of ***intellectual property theft*** occurs when the victim's ideas, inventions, or creative works are taken or used without his or her permission. These ideas can be in the form of books, photos, software, music, films, designs, symbols, or other intangible intellectual creations. ***Digital piracy*** is a form of intellectual property theft where the offender illegally downloads from the Internet or shares peer-to-peer (p2p) copyrighted material (most commonly videos and music), and either uses the material or sells it. For example, say that you legally purchase and download a video from Amazon.com. You then share that video with a friend (p2p). You and your friend have engaged in digital piracy because the copyright holder (the entity that made the video) has not been compensated for the shared file. According to Richter (2012), Americans are the heaviest file sharers, downloading almost 97 million music albums and singles from BitTorrent between January and June 2012. The Recording Industry Association of America (RIAA), a trade organization that supports and promotes the creative and financial vitality of the major music companies, indicates the following trends in digital piracy in the music industry:

- Since the p2p file-sharing site Napster emerged in 1999, music sales in the United States dropped 47%, from $14.6 billion to $7.7 billion.
- From 2004 through 2009, approximately 30 billion songs were illegally downloaded on file-sharing networks.
- Only 37% of music acquired by U.S. consumers in 2009 was paid for.
- U.S. Internet users annually consume between $7 and $20 billion worth of digitally pirated recorded music.
- The digital theft of music, movies, and copyrighted content takes up huge amounts of Internet bandwidth—24% globally, and 17.5% in the United States.
- Digital storage locker downloads constitute 7% of all Internet traffic, while 91% of the links found on them were for copyrighted material, and 10% of those links were to music specifically (RIAA, 2014).

Digital piracy is reportedly perpetrated at high rates by college students (Hinduja & Higgins, 2011).

The NCSS reported that 11% of businesses in the United States were victims of cyberthefts in 2005. However, as is also the case with cyberattacks, the actual extent of these cybercrimes is likely higher because victims often do not know they have been victimized. Among cybertheft victims, 3% of businesses were victims of intellectual property theft. The widespread availability of Internet file-sharing networks in the online domain has created limitless opportunities for these offenses, and the true prevalence is actually much higher. Online identity theft is another growing and serious type of cybertheft. As explained in Chapter 7, ***identity theft*** is a label applied to offenses in which an individual's personal information is used without his or her consent for criminal purposes. Although the NCSS results indicate that 3% of businesses were affected by this crime, more recent figures from the NCVS suggest higher rates of victimization against individuals. In 2012, it is estimated that 16.6 million persons in the United States, or 5% of the population 16 or older, were victims of some kind of identity theft (Harrell & Langton, 2013). Unfortunately, the NCVS did not gather data regarding whether victims' identities were stolen online, but a majority of victims had an existing credit card misused, and of those who knew how their information was stolen, 30% believed it was during a purchase they had made. Presumably, both of these findings indicate that online purchases made with credit cards were targeted by identity thieves.

Online frauds of various types also are common forms of cybertheft that are perpetrated in online domains. In general, ***fraud*** involves an offender contacting the victim and convincing him or her, usually through deception, to provide money or information. The NCSS reported that 5% of businesses were victims of fraud in 2005. According to the Internet Crime Complaint Center (IC3), and in partnership with the FBI and the National White-Collar Crime Center, frequently reported online frauds in 2012 included hit man scams, real estate frauds, romance scams, auto frauds, FBI impersonation e-mail scams, and various extortion scams (e.g., process server scams, grandparent scams) (IC3, 2012). As an example, in hit man scams, the fraudster contacts the victim via e-mail and says that he or she has been hired to kill the victim. However, if the victim pays the amount of the contract instead, he or she will refrain from carrying out the hit. IC3 (2012) notes that some savvy fraudsters have even investigated victims through online social media to learn details of their lives and make the hit man scam seem more credible. While the IC3 only receives complaints from a small portion of cybertheft victims, the volume of complaints received in 2012 reached over 289,000 and amounted to over $525 million in loss to the victims.

Embezzlement, the final cybertheft to be discussed, is a type of financial fraud wherein assets such as money that have been entrusted to a party are used for other purposes without the victim's consent. Like many other cyberthefts, embezzlement can be carried out offline or online but is perhaps made easier with online communications tools. For example, the illegal activity may be perpetrated remotely rather than onsite, possibly minimizing risks of being observed (and caught).

Opportunities for cyberspace victimization seem to be unlimited, with different types of online domains from social networks to auction websites providing facilitating environments for many types of online victimization in the United States and abroad. As these domains become even more central and integrated features of individuals' personal and professional daily lives, the potential for online victimization will become even greater. Yet, there is reason to remain optimistic. As with all of the domains of victimization discussed in this chapter, efforts to reduce opportunities for victimization in domain-specific ways are likely to reduce the risk of victimization.

Summary

Domains of activity create opportunities for various types of victimization to occur. This chapter reviewed six specific domains of victimization and explained how each creates distinct opportunities for specific types of victimization. First, K–12 schools were discussed in light of bullying and cyberbullying victimization because of the concentration of these offenses in this domain and the features of the domain that contribute to victimization. Second, colleges and universities were examined as domains in which high rates of sexual assault victimization occur, with the campus climate, students' lifestyles and routines, and concentrations of motivated offenders on campus contributing to opportunities for victimization. Third, correctional institutions were explored as domains of victimization, highlighting the circumstances under which sexual victimizations occur in jails and prisons. Fourth, the workplace domain was revealed to be one in which bullying and sexual harassment occur as forms of workplace aggression, and in which workplace violence is perpetrated. Fifth, the military was examined as a domain for sexual assault victimization. Finally, several types of online victimization were described that occur within the cyberspace domain. With a few exceptions, the types of victimization reviewed throughout this chapter are not exclusively experienced within these six domains. However, a domain-specific approach to examining victimization reveals that crimes concentrate, in part, because opportunities for different types of criminal behavior are more prevalent in certain domains than others. This implies that strategies to reduce victimization should consider the context in which victimization occurs and how this context influences opportunities for victimization.

KEYWORDS

Domains
Bullying
Physical bullying
Verbal bullying
Relational bullying
Financial bullying
Racial bullying
Sexual bullying
Rape myths
Illinois Rape Myth Acceptance Scale
Binge drinking
Prison Rape Elimination Act
National Inmate Survey
Workplace aggression
Workplace bullying
Sexual harassment
Online harassment
Online sexual exploitation
Sexting
Cyberstalking
Cyberattacks
Malware
Denial of service attacks
Online vandalism/sabotage
Cyberthefts
Intellectual property theft
Digital piracy
Identity theft
Fraud
Embezzlement

DISCUSSION QUESTIONS

1. Is bullying a minor annoyance and a normal part of growing up or is it a serious form of victimization? Explain your rationale for your answer.
2. How common do you think binge drinking is among students at your college or university? Do you think this level of alcohol consumption by students (male or female) increases students' risks for sexual victimization? Explain your answer.
3. Do you think that the estimates of prison rape victimization provided by the National Inmate Survey are accurate? Explain your answer.
4. Consider the circumstances under which inmate sexual victimization occurs in correctional domains. Why might opportunities for sexual victimization occur within certain locations and at certain times?
5. Correctional staff members are facility guardians, but many incidents of sexual victimization are reportedly perpetrated by these individuals. What are the implications of this finding for routine activity theory's assumption as to the importance of guardianship?
6. Besides those occupations listed in Table 8-4, what other workplace characteristics pose high risks for workplace aggression or workplace violence? Explain your answer.
7. List the ways in which online social networks could be used as domains of online victimization and the types of victimization they might facilitate. What features do these networks possess that enable these crimes to occur? Do they possess features that protect users against victimization? Draw from your experiences or those of someone you know to provide examples to support your answer.
8. Do college students commonly engage in sexting? How would you characterize sexting—as part of a sexual relationship, as a form of deviance, or as a form of online criminal victimization? Explain your answer and provide examples.
9. How has the Internet and the availability of online domains changed the ways that identity thieves operate? Explain your answer.

REFERENCES

Abbey, A., Clinton, A. M., McAuslan, P., Zawacki, T., & Buck, P. O. (2002). Alcohol-involved rapes: Are they more violent? *Psychology of Women Quarterly, 26*, 99–109.

Abbey, A., & McAuslan, P. (2004). A longitudinal examination of male college students' perpetration of sexual assault. *Journal of Consulting and Clinical Psychology, 72*, 747–756.

Baron, R.A. & Neuman, J.H. (1996). Workplace violence and workplace aggression; Evidence on their relative frequency and potential causes. *Aggressive Behavior, 22*, 161–173.

Basow, S. A., & Minieri, A. (2011). "You owe me": Effects of date cost, who pays, participant gender, and rape myth beliefs on perceptions of rape. *Journal of Interpersonal Violence, 26*, 479–497.

Baum, K., Catalano, S., Rand, M., & Rose, K. (2009). *Stalking victimization in the United States* (NCJ 224527). Washington, DC: Bureau of Justice Statistics.

Beck, A. J., Berzofsky, M., Caspar, R., & Krebs, C. (2013). *Sexual victimization in prisons and jails reported by inmates, 2011–12: National Inmate Survey, 2011–12* (NCJ 241399). Washington, DC: Bureau of Justice Statistics.

Beck, A. J., & Harrison, P. M. (2008). *Sexual victimization in local jails reported by inmates, 2007* (NCJ 221946). Washington, DC: Bureau of Justice Statistics.

Belknap, J., & Erez, E. (2013). Violence against women on college campuses: Rape, intimate partner abuse, and sexual harassment. In B. S. Fisher & J. J. Sloan (Eds.), *Campus crime: Legal, social, and policy perspectives* (3rd ed., pp. 211–235). Springfield, IL: Charles C. Thomas Publisher, Ltd.

Bossler, A. M., & Holt, T.J. (2009). On-line activities, guardianship, and malware infection: An examination of routine activities theory. *International Journal of Cyber Criminology, 3*, 400–420.

Bureau of Labor Statistics. (2013). *Labor force statistics from the current population survey*. Retrieved September 1, 2013, from http://www.bls.gov/cps/cpsaat09.htm

Burt, M. R. (1980). Cultural myths and supports for rape. *Journal of Personality and Social Psychology, 38*, 217–230.

Deming, M. E., Covan, E. K., Swan, S. C., & Billings, D. L. (2013). Exploring rape myths, gendered norms, group processing, and the social context of rape among college women: A qualitative analysis. *Violence Against Women, 19*, 465–485.

Esbensen, F. A., & Carson, D. C. (2009). Consequences of being bullied: Results from a longitudinal assessment of bullying victimization in a multisite sample of American students. *Youth & Society, 41*, 209–233.

Facebook. (2014). *Facebook reports first quarter 2014 results*. Retrieved July 22, 2014, from http://investor.fb.com/releasedetail.cfm?ReleaseID=842071

Finn, J. (2004). A survey of online harassment at a university campus. *Journal of Interpersonal Violence, 19*, 468–483.

Fisher, B. S., Cullen, F. T., & Turner, M. G. (2000). *The sexual victimization of college women* (NCJ 182369). Washington, DC: National Institute of Justice.

Fisher, B. S., & Sloan, J. J. (2013). *Campus crime: Legal, social, and policy perspectives* (3rd ed.). Springfield, IL: Charles C. Thomas Publisher, Ltd.

Fisher, B. S., Sloan, J. J., Cullen, F. T., & Lu, C. (1998). Crime in the ivory tower: The level and sources of student victimization. *Criminology, 36*, 671–710.

Grucza, R. A., Norberg, K. E., & Bierut, L. J. (2009). Binge drinking among youths and young adults in the United States: 1979–2006. *Journal of the American Academy of Child and Adolescent Psychiatry, 48*, 692–702.

Guerino, P., Harrison, P. M., & Sabol, W. J. (2011). *Prisoners in 2010* (NCJ 236096). Washington, DC: Bureau of Justice Statistics.

Harrell, E. (2011). *Workplace violence, 1993–2009* (NCJ233231). Washington, DC: Bureau of Justice Statistics.

Harrell, E., & Langton, L. (2013). *Victims of identity theft, 2012* (NCJ 243779). Washington, DC: Bureau of Justice Statistics.

Hay, C., Meldrum, R., & Mann, K. (2010). Traditional bullying, cyberbullying, and deviance: A general strain theory approach. *Journal of Contemporary Criminal Justice, 26*, 130–147.

Henson, B., Reyns, B. W., & Fisher, B. S. (2011). Security in the 21st century: Examining the link between online social network activity, privacy, and interpersonal victimization. *Criminal Justice Review, 36*, 253–268.

Hinduja, S., & Higgins, G. E. (2011). Trends and patterns among music pirates. *Deviant Behavior, 32*, 563–588.

Hinduja, S., & Patchin, J. W. (2012a). *School climate 2.0: Preventing cyberbullying and sexting one classroom at a time.* Thousand Oaks, CA: Corwin.

Hinduja, S., & Patchin, J. W. (2012b). Cyberbullying: Neither an epidemic nor a rarity. *European Journal of Developmental Psychology, 9*, 539–543.

Internet Crime Complaint Center. (2012). *2012 Internet crime report.* Fairmont, WV: National White-Collar Crime Center.

Jenkins, E. L., Fisher, B. S., & Hartley, D. (2012). Safe and secure at work? Findings from the 2002 workplace risk supplement. *Work, 42*, 57–66.

Kilpatrick, D., Resnick, H. S., Ruggiero, K. J., Conoscenti, L. M., & McCauley, J. (2007) *Drug-facilitated, incapacitated, and forcible rape: A national study.* Charleston, SC: National Crime Victims Research and Treatment Center. Retrieved July 14, 2012, from https://www.ncjrs.gov/pdffiles1/nij/grants/219181.pdf

Koss, M. P., Gidycz, C. A., & Wisniewski, N. (1982). The scope of rape: Incidence and prevalence of sexual aggression and victimization in a national sample of higher education students. *Journal of Consulting and Clinical Psychology, 55*, 162–170.

Li, Q. (2006). Cyberbullying in schools: A research of gender differences. *School Psychology International, 27*, 157–170.

Lindsay, M., & Krysik, J. (2012). Online harassment among college students: A replication incorporating new Internet trends. *Information, Communication & Society, 15*, 703–719.

Lynch, J. P. (1987). Routine activity and victimization at work. *Journal of Quantitative Criminology, 3*, 283–300.

Martin, P. Y., & Hummer, R. A. (1989). Fraternities and rape on campus. *Gender & Society, 3*, 457–473.

McCauley, J. L., Calhoun, K. S., & Gidycz, C. A. (2010). Binge drinking and rape: A prospective examination of college women with a history of previous sexual victimization. *Journal of Interpersonal Violence, 25*, 1655–1668.

McDonald, P. (2012). Workplace sexual harassment 30 years on: A review of the literature. *International Journal of Management Reviews, 14*, 1–17.

McMahon, S. (2010). Rape myth beliefs and bystander attitudes among incoming college students. *Journal of American College Health, 59*, 3–11.

Meritor Savings Bank v Vinson, 477 US 57 (1986).

Minton, T. D. (2013). *Jail inmates at midyear 2012—Statistical Tables* (NCJ 241264). Washington, DC: Bureau of Justice Statistics.

Mitchell, K. J., Finkelhor, D., Jones, L. M., & Wolak, J. (2012). Prevalence and characteristics of youth sexting: A national study. *Pediatrics, 129*, 13–20.

Mohler-Kuo, M., Dowdall, G. W., Koss, M. P., & Wechsler, H. (2004). Correlates of rape while intoxicated in a national sample of college women. *Journal of Studies on Alcohol and Drugs, 65*, 37–45.

Murdoch, M., Pryor, J. B., Polusny, M. A., & Gackstetter, G. D. (2007). Functioning and psychiatric symptoms among military men and women exposed to sexual stressors. *Military Medicine, 172*, 718–725.

MTV (2009). A thin line: 2009 MTV/AP digital abuse study. Retrieved March 13, from http://www.athinline.org/MTV-AP_Digital_Abuse_Study_Executive_Summary.pdf

Mustaine, E. E., & Tewksbury, R. (2002). Sexual assault of college women: A feminist interpretation of a routine activities analysis. *Criminal Justice Review, 27*, 89–123.

National Institute on Alcohol Abuse and Alcoholism. (2004). NIAAA council approves definition of binge drinking. *NIAAA Newsletter, 3*, 3.

NCVS Victimization Analysis Tool (2014). Retrieved March 13, 2015, from http://www.bjs.gov/index.cfm?ty=nvat

Nobles, M. R., Reyns, B. W., Fox, K. A., & Fisher, B. S. (2012). Protection against pursuit: A conceptual and empirical comparison of cyberstalking and stalking victimization among a national sample. *Justice Quarterly*. DOI: 10.1080/07418825.2012.723030

Olweus, D. (1993). *Bullying at school*. Malden, MA: Blackwell Publishing.

Patchin, J. W., & Hinduja, S. (2006). Bullies move beyond the schoolyard: A preliminary look at cyberbullying. *Youth Violence and Juvenile Justice, 4*, 148–169.

Patchin, J. W., & Hinduja, S. (2012). *Preventing and responding to cyberbullying: Expert perspectives*. Thousand Oaks, CA: Routledge.

Payne, D.L., Lonsway, K.A., & Fitzgerald, L.F. (1999). Rape myth acceptance: Exploration of its structure and its measurement using the *Illinois Rape Myth Acceptance Scale*. *Journal of Research in Personality, 33*, 27–68.

Randa, R., & Reyns, B. W. (2014). Cyberbullying victimization and adaptive avoidance behaviors at school. *Victims and Offenders, 9*, 255-275.

Rantala, R. R. (2008). *Cybercrime against businesses, 2005* (NCJ 221943). Washington, DC: Bureau of Justice Statistics.

Rayner, C., & Hoel, H. (1997). A summary review of literature relating to workplace bullying. *Journal of Community & Applied Social Psychology, 7*, 181–191.

Reyns, B. W., Burek, M. W., Henson, B., & Fisher, B. S. (2013). The unintended consequences of digital technology: Exploring the relationship between sexting and cybervictimization. *Journal of Crime and Justice, 36*, 1–17.

Reyns, B. W., Henson, B., & Fisher, B. S. (2011). Being pursued online: Applying cyberlifestyle–routine activities theory to cyberstalking victimization. *Criminal Justice and Behavior*, 38, 1149–1169.

Reyns, B. W., Henson, B., & Fisher, B. S. (2012). Stalking in the twilight zone: Extent of cyberstalking victimization and offending among college students. *Deviant Behavior, 33*, 1–25.

RIAA. (2014). *Representing music*. Retrieved October 30, 2014, from http://www.riaa.com/faq.php

Richter, F. (2012). *United States top music piracy ranking*. Retrieved October 29, 2014, from http://www.statista.com/chart/614/music-downloads-via-bittorrent-in-the-first-half-of-2012/

Robers, S., Kemp, J., Rathbun, A., Morgan, R. E., & Snyder, T. D. (2014). *Indicators of school crime and safety: 2013*. National Center for Education Statistics, U.S. Department of Education, and Bureau of Justice Statistics, Office of Justice Programs, U.S. Department of Justice. Washington, DC.

Samnani, A. K., & Singh, P. (2012). 20 years of workplace bullying research: A review of the antecedents and consequences of bullying in the workplace. *Aggression and Violent Behavior, 17*, 581–589.

Schat, A., & Kelloway, E. K. (2004). Workplace violence. In J. Barling, E. K. Kelloway, & M. Frone (Eds.), *Handbook of work stress* (pp. 189–218). Thousand Oaks, CA: Sage.

Schwartz, M. D., & DeKeseredy, W. S. (1997). *Sexual assault on the college campus: The role of male peer support*. Thousand Oaks, CA: Sage Publications, Inc.

Skinner, K. M., Kressin, N., Frayne, S., Tripp, T. J., Hankin, C. S., Miller, D. R., & Sullivan, L. M. (2000). The prevalence of military sexual assault among female Veterans' Administration outpatients. *Journal of Interpersonal Violence, 15*, 291–310.

Sloan, J. J., & Fisher, B. S. (2011). *The dark side of the ivory tower: Campus crime as a social problem*. New York: Cambridge University Press.

Snyder, J. A., Fisher, B. S., Scherer, H. L., & Daigle, L. E. (2012). Unsafe in the camouflage tower: Sexual victimization and perceptions of military academy leadership. *Journal of Interpersonal Violence, 27*, 171–173, 194.

State of California Department of Industrial Relations (1995). *Cal/OSHA guidelines for workplace security*. Retrieved March 13, 2015 from: http://www.dir.ca.gov/dosh/dosh_ publications/worksecurity.html

Turchik, J. A., & Wilson, S. M. (2010). Sexual assault in the U.S. military: A review of the literature and recommendations for the future. *Aggression and Violent Behavior, 15*, 267–277.

U.S. Attorney General. (1999). *Cyberstalking: A new challenge for law enforcement and industry, report from the Attorney General to the Vice President*. Retrieved April 23, 2012, from http://www.usdoj.gov/ag/cyberstalkingreport.htm

U.S. Department of Education. (2012). *Digest of education statistics, 2011* (NCES 2012-001). Washington, DC: National Center for Education Statistics.

U.S. Equal Employment Opportunity Commission. (2013). *Sexual harassment charges EEOC & FEPAs combined: FY 1997–FY 2011*. Retrieved July 29, 2013, from http://www.eeoc.gov/eeoc/statistics/enforcement/sexual_harassment.cfm

Wang, J., Iannotti, R. J., & Nansel, T. R. (2009). School bullying among adolescents in the United States: Physical, verbal, relational, and cyber. *Journal of Adolescent Health, 45*, 368–375.

Wechsler, H. & Nelson, T. (2008). What we have learned from the Harvard School of Public Health College Alcohol Study: Focusing attention on college student alcohol consumption and the environmental conditions that promote it. *Journal of Studies on Alcohol and Drugs, 69*, 481–490.

Wolak, J., Mitchell, K., & Finkelhor, D. (2006). *Online victimization of youth: Five years later*. Washington, DC: National Center for Missing and Exploited Children.

Zapf, D., Escartín, J., Einarsen, S., Hoel, H., & Vartia, M. (2011). Empirical findings on prevalence and risk groups of bullying in the workplace. In S. Einarsen, H. Hoel, D. Zapf, & C. L. Cooper (Eds.), *Bullying and harassment in the workplace: developments in theory, research, and practice* (2nd ed., pp. 75–107). Boca Raton, FL: CRC Press.

CHAPTER 9

Recurring Victimization

CHAPTER OUTLINE

LEARNING OBJECTIVES

- Identify and distinguish among the different types of recurring victimization.
- Explain key research findings related to the extent of recurring victimization.
- Define and explain the key findings related to the time course of recurring victimization.
- Describe the state dependence and risk heterogeneity perspectives of recurring victimization.
- Describe how the lifestyle–routine activities and rational choice perspectives can be used to explain recurring victimization.
- Explain how recurring victimization research can inform crime prevention strategies.

One thing leads to another. Not always. Sometimes one thing leads to the same thing.Ask an addict.

George Carlin, 1997, p. 130

Introduction

Crime concentrates in many interesting and often predictable ways—those individuals who commit many offenses are called *repeat offenders;* areas in which crime incidents cluster are known as *hot spots* of crime; facilities such as convenience stores or apartment buildings in which many crimes take place are labeled *risky facilities;* and high-theft items are referred to as *hot products*. Even though criminologists and victimologists alike have long known about these patterns, it was not until the 1990s that a significant amount of researchers' attention was focused on another type of crime concentration—recurring victimization.

Recurring victimization happens when the same individual or his or her property is victimized two or more times. Fortunately, most individuals are not recurrent victims. In fact, most people are never victimized in their lifetime, and the majority of those who are experience only a single victimization. However, the unfortunate reality is that a small portion of victims are targeted for victimization multiple times (i.e., two or more times) in their lives—these are ***recurring victims***. For example, it is not uncommon for victims of bullying to experience these behaviors many times throughout their lives.

What is interesting is that recurring victims, while making up a small portion of individuals who are victimized, experience a large proportion of all victimization incidents. In other words, these people experience more than their share of victimization! Importantly, these trends have been consistently reported over the years by researchers who have studied the recurrence of different types of victimization (e.g., Ellingworth, Farrell, & Pease, 1995; Hindelang, Gottfredson, & Garofalo, 1978; Pease, 1998; Sparks, 1981).

Despite the relative newness of recurring victimization as a topic of study in victimology, important advances have been achieved in a relatively short period of time. This chapter reviews the current state of knowledge on recurring criminal victimization, including how it is identified and defined; types of recurring victimization; its extent and nature; theoretical explanations for its occurrence; factors associated with recurring victimization; and strategies for preventing initial victims from becoming recurring victims.

Types of Recurring Victimization

Conceptually, recurring victimization is an umbrella term under which different types of victimization are categorized. While *all* recurring victims experience two or more victimizations, the *type* of victimization suffered by the victim and the *time elapsed* between incidents are characteristics that distinguish among different types of recurring victimization. For instance, two types of recurring victimization that have been the subject of much research—*repeat victimization* and *revictimization*—are differentiated by both of these characteristics. Other types of recurring victimization include *multiple victimization*, *polyvictimization*, *series victimization*, *near repeat victimization*, and *virtual repeat victimization*. Although these are all types of recurring victimization, it is not possible to directly compare estimates of their occurrence because of differences in the way researchers have defined and measured these types of victimization.

A common finding in the victimization research is that most targets, be they individuals, their property, businesses, or households, do not experience any criminal victimization. For example, the most recent National Crime Victimization Survey (NCVS) indicates that the majority of individuals surveyed were not victims of violence in the year prior to the survey (Truman, Langton, & Planty, 2013). In actuality, in 2012 the total violent victimization rate in the United States was 26.1 per 1,000 individuals age 12 and over, while the serious violent victimization (rape or sexual assault, robbery, and aggravated assault) rate was 8.0 per 1,000 individuals age 12 and over. Property crime victimization rates for this same year indicated that 155.8 per 1,000 households experienced property victimizations in 2012 (Truman et al., 2013).

Although the majority of individuals and households do not experience criminal victimization, most of those who do are only victimized once. Yet, another key finding from victimization research is that a smaller group of victims are victimized more than once. These trends are generally supported by research studies of victimization regardless of the type of victimization under consideration (e.g., burglary, assault) or the country in which the victimization occurs (Farrell & Bouloukos, 2001). The nature of recurring victimization takes many forms. For instance, some targets experience the *same type* of victimization repeatedly within a short period of time, while others have longer periods between victimization incidents. Still others are victims of *different types* of crime.

Table 9-1 illustrates the concept of recurring victimization by highlighting results from the National College Women Sexual Victimization Study. Leah Daigle, Bonnie Fisher, and Francis Cullen (2008) analyzed recurring sexual victimization, and according to their results, most (84.5%) college women were not sexually victimized during the study's reference frame (a period of about seven months). However, 8.2% of women were sexually victimized once during this time and just over

Table 9-1: An Example of Recurring Victimization*

Number of Times Victimized	Percent of College Women	Percent of Victimization Incidents
0	84.5	0.0
1	8.2	27.6
2	4.0	27.2
3 or more	3.3	45.2

* A total of 4,446 college women participated and collectively experienced 1,318 sexual victimization incidents.

Source: Adapted from Daigle, Fisher, and Cullen (2008).

7% of victims were sexually victimized two or more times. In total, this small group experienced 72% of *all* of the sexual victimizations that were measured (e.g., rape, sexual coercion).

The different types of recurring victimization are discussed in the sections that follow. Students are encouraged to periodically refer to Figure 9-1 after reading about each type of recurring victimization. If you will note, the design of Figure 9-1 emulates the structure of a tree, with recurring victimization representing the "trunk" and the characteristics of the different types of recurring victimization representing its "branches." As an illustration of how to read Figure 9-1, consider an individual who has been a victim of crime across a long period of time spanning developmental life stages, such as childhood and adulthood. In this scenario, the characteristics of the victimization incident indicate a path that follows the lower branch because the initial and subsequent incident occurred over a long period of time. The next decision point among the tree branches is whether or not the victimization occurred across developmental life stages. Since in this example the victimization did occur across developmental stages, the apparent path leads to the label of revictimization. Hence, the circumstances described for the fictional victim in the example fit the definition of a revictimization. Each type of recurring victimization presented in this chapter can be identified in a similar manner by using the trunk and branches depicted in Figure 9-1. Overall, Figure 9-1 provides a useful diagram for identifying the characteristics of each type of recurring victimization and distinguishing it from the other types.

Repeat Victimization

Repeat victimization occurs when a victim experiences the same type of victimization two or more times within a specified, usually relatively short, time period (e.g., within a few days, weeks, or months). Using Figure 9-1, it is possible to identify repeat victimization based on these characteristics. That is, there is a short time between the initial and subsequent incidents and two or more instances of the same type of victimization (e.g., a robbery is followed by a robbery). It also is possible that a repeat victimization takes place over a longer period, as long as the incidents do not occur across developmental time periods, include the same types of offenses,

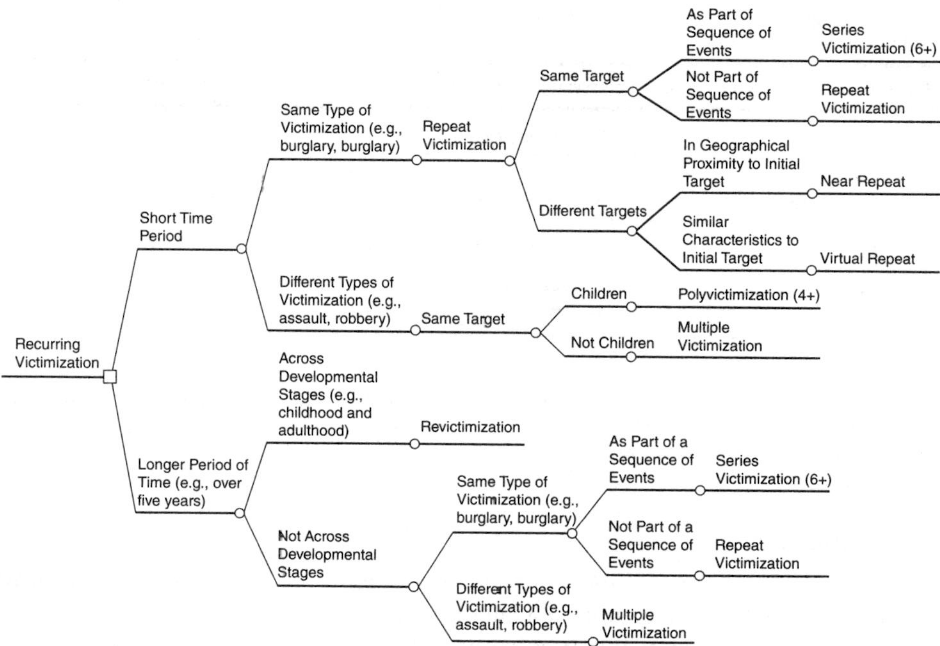

Figure 9-1 Diagram for Identifying Types of Recurring Victimization

and are not considered part of a sequence of events. As an example of repeat victimization, if a home on your street was burglarized, and two weeks later it was burglarized again, the homeowners would be considered repeat victims. Repeat burglary victimization is a common occurrence, and much of the recurring victimization research has focused on burglary. For instance, Shane Johnson, Kate Bowers, and Alex Hirschfield (1997) investigated repeat burglary victimization in Merseyside, England. Using police data on reported crimes in Merseyside, Johnson and colleagues reported that 7% of the burglaries were committed against previously burgled targets. Further, most of these repeat victims were burglarized twice (85%), while a smaller group of victims were burglarized three or more times (15%).

Another example of repeat victimization is provided in Table 9-2, which displays repeat assault victimization among adolescents and young adults ages 11 to 17 in the United States. Similar to Daigle and colleagues' (2008) study of sexual victimization among college women described above, Janet Lauritsen and Kenna Quinet (1995) reported that most youth were not victims of assault (68.9%). Of those who were assault victims, 12.9% were victimized one time, 8.2% were victimized twice, 2.9% were victimized three times, 2% were victimized four times, and 5.2% were assaulted five or more times. Interestingly, this last group represented only 5% of the respondents, but they experienced over 60% of the assaults recorded. These same general patterns were also observed by Lauritsen and Quinet with respect to larceny, vandalism, and robbery victims in the study.

Table 9-2: Repeat Assault Victimization Among Adolescents and Young Adults*

Number of Times Victimized	Percent of Respondents	Percent of Victimization Incidents
0	68.9	0.0
1	12.9	10.4
2	8.2	13.2
3	2.9	6.9
4	2.0	6.4
5 or more	5.2	63.2

* There were 1,718 youths participating in the assault portion of this study; collectively, they experienced 2,134 assault victimization incidents.
Source: Adapted from Lauritsen and Quinet (1995).

Revictimization

When victims experience some type of victimization (e.g., rape) and are victimized again (e.g., rape, sexual assault) at a later time in life, this is referred to as ***revictimization***. The types of crime involved in revictimization are not necessarily the same, but most revictimization research has focused on violent types of victimization, such as intimate partner violence, child abuse, and sexual assault. Usually revictimization is studied in the context of victims experiencing the same category of violence (e.g., sexual violence, intimate partner violence). There can also be a substantial length of time elapsed between victimization incidents since revictimization usually occurs, and is typically examined by researchers, across developmental periods (e.g., from childhood to adolescence or young adulthood to old age). For example, someone who has been a victim of child abuse and later in life is a victim of intimate partner violence has been revictimized. Referring back to Figure 9-1, it is possible to chart a path involving revictimization by following the branch indicating that the victimization took place over a long period of time. If the victimization also spanned developmental stages of life, such as childhood to adolescence, the victim has experienced revictimization.

Much of the research on revictimization has focused specifically on sexual revictimization occurring across the life course. For example, a study by Catherine Classen, Oxana Palesh, and Rashi Aggarwal (2005, p. 124) summarized previous research surrounding sexual revictimization and concluded that "The majority of findings on the prevalence of sexual revictimization suggest that approximately two of three individuals who are sexually victimized are revictimized." They further pointed out that across studies of revictimization, between 10% and 69% of victims are revictimized. There may have been some differences in the ways that these studies defined revictimization or in the individuals included in the various studies, which may explain the wide range in estimated prevalence of revictimization across studies. For example, some of the studies were based on community samples, some on clinical samples, and some on college student samples.

The accumulated body of research on sexual revictimization suggests that not only is it prevalent, but also that those who are victimized in childhood, adolescence, or adulthood have a high risk of being victimized again later in life (Classen et al., 2005; Roodman & Clum, 2001). Researchers Allison Roodman and George Clum studied 19 articles that examined the topic of sexual revictimization against adult females, with a focus on the effects of childhood victimization on adult victimization. Considering the studies' results collectively, Roodman and Clum concluded that there is a moderately strong relationship between childhood sexual victimization and adult sexual victimization (see also Desai, Arias, Thompson, & Basile, 2002).

Multiple Victimization

Another distinct concept in the study of recurrent victimization is ***multiple victimization***, in which victims experience two or more types of crime within a specific period of time (e.g., a year). Similar to repeat victimizations, multiple victimization is usually, but not always, restricted to having occurred within a relatively short timeframe. Unlike repeat victimization, multiple victimization does not involve the *same* type of crime. For example, if a victim experiences stalking and assault—two different crimes—this would be an instance of multiple victimization.

There are two paths to identifying a recurring victimization as a multiple victimization using Figure 9-1. First, if the victimization occurred over a short period of time, following the upper branch of the diagram, but involved different types of victimization against the same target, the victimizations may be considered multiple victimization. According to Figure 9-1, if the victimizations were not experienced by a minor, this is an example of multiple victimization (e.g., stalking and assault). Had the victimization been against a minor, this scenario would have described polyvictimization, a type of recurring victimization discussed below. The second path to identifying multiple victimization follows the bottom branch, representing victimizations that occurred over a longer period of time, but not across developmental stages, and involved different types of crimes.

In one of the few studies to focus on multiple victimizations, Maureen Outlaw, Barry Ruback, and Chester Britt (2002) considered individuals to be multiple victims if they had experienced at least one violent crime *and* one property crime in the last two years. Using data collected through telephone surveys of Seattle residents, these researchers reported that 44% of study participants had been the victims of some type of crime in the last two years. Within this group, about 13% were repeat property crime victims, and 4% were identified as multiple victims. In another study of multiple victimization, Tim Hope and his colleagues (2001) studied data from the 1992 British Crime Survey. Similar to the study by Outlaw and associates, they considered multiple victimization to have occurred if a victim experienced both a property victimization *and* a personal victimization within a five-year period. Their study found that these two victimization experiences—property and personal—were significantly related to each other. About 33% of victimized individuals were multiple victims while 17% of households experienced multiple victimization.

Polyvictimization

Another type of recurring victimization, ***polyvictimization***, occurs when a *minor* is frequently targeted for a variety of types of victimization within a reference period (e.g., a year). Thus, the concept of polyvictimization is similar to multiple victimization, except that it is applied to the victimization of *children*. With respect to Figure 9-1, recurring victimizations transpiring over a short period of time that involve different types of victimization against the same target are labeled polyvictimization as long as the crimes are committed against children.

The term polyvictimization was introduced by David Finkelhor, Richard Ormrod, and Heather Turner (2007). They conducted research examining the victimization of children (defined as those between the age of 2 and 17) living in the United States, and identified children as polyvictims if they had suffered *four* or more types of victimization (e.g., sexual victimization, maltreatment, property victimization, physical assault) in the year prior to the study. Finkelhor and his fellow researchers reported that 18% of children were polyvictims—they experienced at least four different types of victimization within a year's time. Another study of polyvictimization found that across a two-year period, 24% of children were victims of five or more types of victimization (Finkelhor, Ormrod, Turner, & Holt, 2009). This study also reported that the onset of polyvictimization (when it started) was somewhat variable across the sample, but the first incident most commonly occurred at age 15. Figure 9-2 shows the age of onset for polyvictimization amongst Finkelhor and colleagues' sample of 112 child victims. The authors suggested that the spikes at ages 7 and 15 roughly coincided with the beginning of elementary and high school respectively for these children.

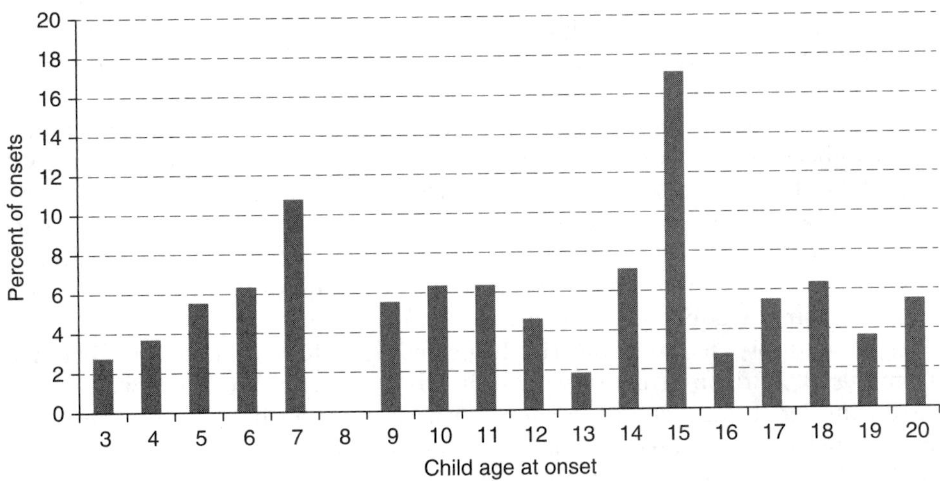

Figure 9-2 Polyvictimization Age of Onset

Although polyvictimization is defined as frequent repeat victimization against minors, this study included 18-, 19-, and 20-year-old victims as well.

Source: Adapted from Finkelhor et al. (2009).

Series Victimization

Another way of defining recurring victimization is to examine those instances of repeat victimization that occur as part of a chain or sequence of criminal events. In ***series victimization***, victims experience similar types of crimes repeatedly as part of a related sequence of incidents within a specified period of time, such as six months or a year. For instance, according to Janet Lauritsen and her fellow researchers (2012, p. iii), "the NCVS records a series victimization when the respondent reported experiencing six or more similar crimes during a six-month reference period and was unable to recall or describe each event in detail." Although any type of crime could occur as a series victimization given this definition, intimate partner violence, sexual violence, stalking, child abuse, and elder abuse often occur as series victimizations.

Figure 9-1 provides two ways of identifying series victimizations by following paths in the diagram. First, if the victimizations occur over a short time, involve the same (or similar) types of victimization, occur against the same target, and occur as part of a sequence of events, the victim has suffered a series victimization. The second route to experiencing a series victimization involves a longer period of time (but not across developmental stages), with the same (or similar) types of crime occurring as part of a sequence of incidents.

In 2012, Lauritsen and colleagues published a report for the Bureau of Justice Statistics discussing methods for using the NCVS to study series victimizations in the United States. This report also provided estimates on the prevalence of series victimizations in the United States between 1993 and 2009. As Table 9-3 indicates,

Table 9-3: Percent of Victimizations Reported as Series Victimizations, 1993–2009

Year	Violent	Property and Personal Larceny
1993	6.7%	1.3%
1994	6.2	1.2
1995	5.7	1.1
1996	6.0	1.1
1997	6.3	1.0
1998	5.5	1.1
1999	4.9	0.8
2000	3.9	0.9
2001	3.6	0.8
2002	4.4	0.8
2003	4.8	0.8
2004	3.6	0.5

(Continued)

Table 9-3: Percent of Victimizations Reported as Series Victimizations, 1993–2009 (*Continued*)

Year	Violent	Property and Personal Larceny
2005	4.1	0.5
2006*	4.4	0.7
2007	3.4	0.8
2008	3.7	0.7
2009	3.3	0.5

* Due to methodological changes in the 2006 NCVS, use caution when comparing 2006 criminal victimization estimates to other years. See *Criminal Victimization, 2007*, BJS Web, NCJ 224390, December 2008, for more information.
Source: Lauritsen et al. (2012).

Table 9-4: Types of Series Victimizations in the NCVS, 1993–2009

	1993–1999	2000–2009
Rape/sexual assault	6.3%	5.7%
Robbery	2.9	2.5
Aggravated assault	4.6	3.1
Simple assault	6.9	4.3
Personal larceny	0.3!	0.7!
Burglary	1.4	1.0
Motor vehicle theft	0.3	0.2!
Theft	1.1	0.7

! Interpret with caution; estimate based on 10 or fewer sample cases, or coefficient of variation is greater than 50%.
Source: Lauritsen et al. (2012).

series victimizations are most often violent crimes, with violent series victimizations exceeding property/personal larceny victimizations every year for 16 years. Further, both violent and property/personal larceny series victimizations have been steadily declining since 1993.

Table 9-4 separates the violent and property/personal larceny categories into specific types of victimization for 1993–1999 and 2000–2009. As the findings clearly show, violent series victimizations occur more often than do property/personal larceny victimizations. For example,. across the two time periods, rape/sexual assault was among the most common types of series victimizations, with about 6% of victims of these crimes being series victims. Similarly, simple assault, another violent crime, commonly occurs as part of a series of incidents. Conversely, property/personal larceny victimizations consistently represent the smallest percentage of series victimizations. For instance, as the table shows, only about 1% of thefts occur as part of a series.

Near Repeat Victimization

Studied mostly in the context of burglary victimization, ***near repeat victimization*** involves offenders selecting nearby targets for subsequent victimization rather than the previously victimized targets, based on the similarity of the target or the situation. For example, if a house on a quiet street is burglarized on a weekday afternoon when activity on the street is relatively light, the burglar may decide to return to the street the following day and choose a target four houses up the block from the original target. The idea behind near repeat victimization is that *proximity to victimized targets* increases victimization risks for nearby targets. It is possible to identify a recurring victimization as a near repeat by using Figure 9-1 and tracing the branches of the diagram from short time period, same type of victimization, against different targets, and in geographic proximity.

In a study of near repeat victimization, Shane Johnson and his coauthors (2007) employed a strategy similar to one used in studying disease contagion to better understand the risks for near repeat residential burglary victimization. The research revealed that across five different countries, houses within 200 meters of previously burglarized homes were at an increased risk of suffering a burglary for at least two weeks following the initial incident. Studies of near repeat victimization have also focused on other types of victimization. For example, research by Jerry Ratcliffe and George Rengert (2008) uncovered elevated risks of shooting victimizations occurring in Philadelphia within one block and two weeks of previous shootings. Near repeat victimizations are distinguished from virtual repeat victimizations (discussed below) by the geographic proximity of the targets.

Virtual Repeat Victimization

In ***virtual repeat victimization***, targets are chosen by offenders because they have characteristics similar to those of previously victimized targets. Once again, Figure 9-1 proves useful for identifying a recurring victimization as a virtual repeat victimization. Following the paths from short time period, same type of victimization, against different targets, and with shared characteristics, results in the virtual repeat victimization classification.

An interesting example of virtual repeat victimization can be found in 19th-century London. In 1888, the serial killer Jack the Ripper murdered at least five women in the Whitechapel neighborhood of London by slitting their throats and mutilating the corpses. By selecting female prostitutes from primarily poor areas of the city, Jack the Ripper was committing not only serial murder but also virtual repeat victimization. In a more contemporary example, a car thief who targets a specific make, model, and year of automobile, in locations all across town, may be doing so because this make, model, and year of car is particularly easy to steal.

Research into repeat, near repeat, and virtual repeat victimization suggests that many times it is the same offender who has targeted previously victimized, nearby, or similar targets. A study by Wim Bernasco (2008) examined the extent to which residential burglaries perpetrated in The Hague and nearby cities and towns were committed by the same offender between 1996 and 2004. Select results are presented in Table 9-5. As the results indicate, a significant portion of repeat burglaries were perpetrated by the same offender. For example, of those burglaries occurring at the same address and less than seven days after a previous burglary (i.e., repeat burglaries), 98% were committed by the same offender. Comparably, of those burglaries occurring eight to 15 days apart and within 101 to 200 meters of a previous burglary (i.e., near repeats), 55% were committed by the same burglar. It is difficult to determine the degree to which targets shared similar characteristics (i.e., virtual repeats) beyond their location, but research into offender decision making suggests that offenders choose their targets rationally with an eye toward likelihood and ease of success. For example, Julie Ashton and colleagues (1998) interviewed burglars about their target choices. One of the burglars disclosed that he targeted gas stations owned by the same retail chain because the floor plans were identical, making illegal entry easier than having to navigate an unfamiliar floor plan.

The study of recurring victimization is fairly new compared to other areas of study in the field of victimology and criminology. In a relatively short period of time victimologists have made much progress explaining and predicting recurring victimization. Table 9-6 summarizes the previous sections by listing the terms, defining them, and providing examples of the different types of recurring victimization. The

Table 9-5: Percentages of Burglaries Involving the Same Offender in The Hague and Surrounding Locales, 1996–2004*

	Distance (in meters) Between Incidents						
Time between incidents	Same address	1–100 m	101–200 m	201–300 m	301–400 m	401–1000 m	1001 + m
0–7 days	98	89	71	63	50	27	2
8–15 days	83	57	55	35	36	18	1
16–31 days	93	48	33	20	23	12	1
32–62 days	92	23	13	9	7	4	0
63–92 days	70	14	5	4	4	2	0
93+ days	31	3	2	1	1	1	0

* The authors analyzed 3,624 burglaries.
Source: Bernasco (2008).

Table 9-6: Summary of Terms, Definitions, and Examples of Recurring Victimization

Type of Recurring Victimization	Definition	Example
Recurring Victimization	Victimization two or more times (e.g., a first-time victimization followed by a subsequent one)	A young adult male's car is vandalized twice in the same month.
Repeat Victimization	The same type of victimization two or more times within a reference period (e.g., two years)	A fifth-grade student is bullied at school on and off for the first few weeks of the new academic year.

Revictimization	Initial victimization and subsequent victimization happen across periods of time (e.g., developmental stages) regardless of victimization type	An individual is a victim of child abuse early in life and a victim of elder abuse later in life.
Multiple Victimization	Victimization by two or more different types of crime within a reference period (e.g., a year)	A disabled man is a victim of a personal theft and a robbery within a year's time.
Polyvictimization	Children who experience a number of different types of victimization	A 13-year-old is the victim of parental abuse, maltreatment, neglect, and sibling victimization in the course of a year.
Series Victimization	High frequency of same type of victimization within a reference period (e.g., a year); the incidents are indistinguishable to victims	A young mother is the victim of intimate partner violence several times a month during the course of a year.
Near Repeat Victimization	Nearby targets are chosen for victimization rather than the initial target	A college student's residence hall room is burglarized; the next week, the residence hall room next door is burglarized.
Virtual Repeat Victimization	Targets with similar characteristics are chosen by offender for victimization rather than the initial target	A serial killer targets red-haired prostitutes from varied locations across the city.

remainder of the chapter focuses on reviewing the nature of recurring victimization, with particular emphasis on the time course of recurring victimization, crime switching, theories of recurring victimization, and preventing recurring victimization.

The Time Course of Repeat Victimization

As the previous review of the many types of recurring victimization illustrates, there are numerous ways in which targets can be victimized more than once. One of the key distinctions between these types of recurring victimization is the nature of the victimization. Another key distinction is the length of time between incidents. The length of time between incidents is the focus of research into the ***time course of repeat victimization***. This work explains (1) the length of time between incidents of repeat victimization and (2) how long the victim is at increased risk for a repeat victimization (Polvi, Looman, Humphries, & Pease, 1991). Irrespective of the type of victimization (e.g., rape, assault, and burglary), two primary research findings consistently have been reported regarding the time course of repeat victimization:

1. When a repeat victimization occurs, it is likely to be soon after the first incident of victimization.
2. The period of heightened risk of subsequent victimization dissipates over time.

Pioneering research into the time course of repeat victimization was conducted by Natalie Polvi and colleagues (1991) using data provided by the Saskatoon City

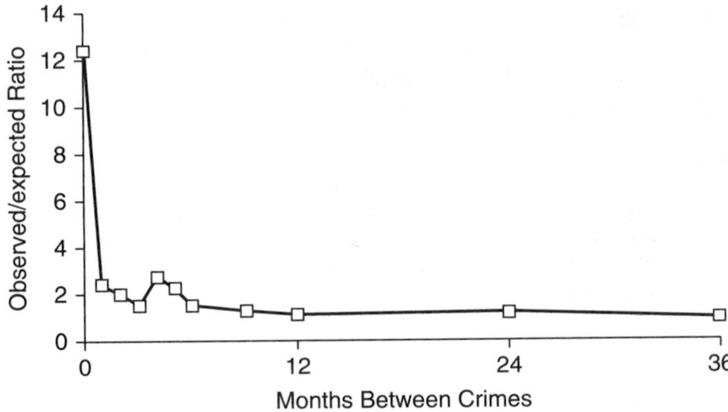

Figure 9-3 Time Course of Repeat Burglary Victimization
Source: Polvi et al. (1991).

Police in Saskatchewan, Canada. This research examined repeat burglary victimization in the city from 1984 to 1987 and focused on the issue of length of time between these repeats. Their analyses of these data revealed the risk for repeat burglary victimization was elevated by 12 times within one month of the initial burglary victimization. In other words, there is an immediate period of heightened risk, lasting about one month, following an initial burglary victimization incident. Further, half of the repeat burglaries occurred within seven days of the first incident. As depicted in Figure 9-3, Polvi and her fellow researchers carried their analysis of the time course out for three years and reported that after the first month, repeat victimization risk dissipated quickly and returned to a previctimization level of risk. The "Spotlight on Theory" box highlights the possible reasons for the time course of burglary according to Polvi and colleagues.

Like most of the recurring victimization research, many of the studies into the time course of repeat victimization have been directed at property victimizations, such as burglaries. However, repeat victimization involving sexual and violent victimization also has been studied with respect to the time course. In the previously referenced study by Daigle and colleagues (see Table 9-1), the authors estimated the time course of repeat victimization for six types of sexual and violent victimization: (1) rape, (2) unwanted sexual contact with force, (3) threats, (4) sexual coercion, (5) unwanted sexual contact without force, and (6) simple assault. The same general pattern of heightened repeat victimization risk immediately succeeding the incident, followed by a steady decline in likelihood of repeat victimization observed by Polvi and associates, was also reported by Daigle and colleagues. Put differently, similar to burglary victims, sexual and violent crime victims are at high risk for repeat victimization, but this risk decreases over time. Daigle and colleagues' findings are provided in Figure 9-4, which displays the percentage of incidents of repeat victimization and how much time had passed since the first victimization. The majority of repeat victimizations occurred within a month of the original offense.

Spotlight on Theory: Hypothesized Reasons for Heightened Risk of Subsequent Burglary Victimization Following an Initial Incident

1. ***The same offenders return to their previous target.*** There are several reasons why burglars would decide to return to the scene of the crime. First, offenders may return to burgle items they left the first time. Perhaps they took the victim's television and had to return for the remote control! Second, offenders may wait for the victims to contact their insurance company and replace their stolen property, and then return to target these items.
2. ***The initial offenders share information with their criminal associates about remaining crime opportunities at the previously victimized household.*** For whatever reason, burglars may decide to share information about their heist with other active burglars, who decide to target the house. This information could include the availability of valuables, easy ways to enter and exit the home, or the homeowner's routine activities.
3. ***The house possesses characteristics that make it an attractive target for victimization.*** If a house makes for an especially alluring target for burglary, there may be many motivated offenders who take notice and act. For example, the home may be on a quiet street with few neighbors to notice something out of the ordinary, or the homeowners could be away for long periods of time. Both of characteristics represent a lack of guardianship in the language of routine activity theory.

Source: Polvi et al. (1991).

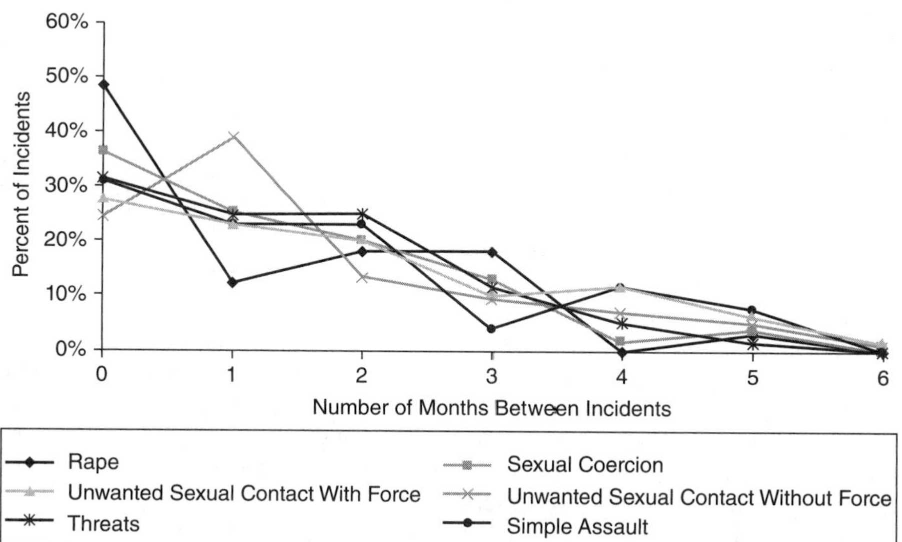

Figure 9-4 Time Course of Sexual and Violent Victimization
Source: Daigle et al. (2008).

For instance, 49% of repeat rapes happened within the same month of the initial rape. The exception to this pattern is the crime of unwanted sexual contact without force, in which 25% of repeats occurred the same month, while 39% took place the following month (Daigle et al., 2008).

These two studies by Polvi and colleagues (1991) and Daigle and colleagues (2008) investigated different types of victimization, at different times, and among different populations of victims. Yet, they are representative of the larger body of research that has explored the time course of repeat victimization. Generally, researchers have uncovered the same patterns consistently—that is, if a subsequent crime incident is going to occur, it will be soon after the initial incident.

Crime Switching

The time course of repeat victimization suggests that if a target is going to experience more than one crime victimization incident, the incident that follows will occur soon after the first one. Anticipating which type of victimization this subsequent incident will be remains a challenge. It is possible that the victim will experience the same type of victimization, such as a burglary followed by another burglary. Another possibility is that subsequent victimizations may be of a different type than the initial type of victimization, such as a sexual assault followed by a theft. The primary method that researchers have developed to examine these changes in type of victimization involves identifying and analyzing *crime-switch* patterns.

Albert Reiss (1980) devised a method for studying crime switching that involves constructing a ***crime-switch matrix***, a table that shows patterns of initial and subsequent victimization incidents (Daigle & Fisher, 2013). Table 9-7 provides an example of a crime-switch matrix in which the rows represent first-time victimization and the columns represent recurring victimization.

Reiss (1980, p. 43) described these tools as "a cross-classification of pairs of crimes in the order of their occurrence in a sequence of victimizations over time." He used this method, as seen in Table 9-7, to identify victims in the National Crime Survey (NCS; the precursor to the NCVS) who experienced the same type of victimization two or more times (i.e., a repeat victimization) or two different types of victimization (i.e., a crime switch indicating multiple victimization). For example, Table 9-7 shows that 9.5% of rape victims experienced a subsequent rape (repeat victimization) whereas 18.3% were later victims of assault (a crime switch).

Reiss' rationale in constructing crime-switch matrixes was that if victimization recurred against previously victimized targets, then victimizations may not be random occurrences. This means that targets that were repeatedly victimized could be more prone to victimization for some reason. In the theories of victimization section of this chapter, the theory of risk heterogeneity and the lifestyle-routine activities theory provide explanations of recurring victimization that could be considered victim vulnerability arguments.

Reiss reported that for many victims, there was a high likelihood that they would experience the same type of victimization again. This victim vulnerability was uncovered for the crimes of assault, household larceny, personal larceny without contact, and burglary. Reiss also reported that crime switching, although less common,

Table 9-7: Percent Distribution by Next Reported Type of Crime for Major Preceding Types of Crime Reported by Households with Two or More Victimizations of the Household and Its Members: All Household and Person Victimizations, July 1, 1972, to December 31, 1975

	Next reported type of crime[1]								Total	
Type of crime[1] preceding next reported crime	Rape	Assault	Robbery	Purse-snatch, pocket-picking	Personal larceny	Burglary	Household larceny	Motor vehicle theft	Percent	Number
Rape	9.5	18.3	4.0	2.2	30.0	14.3	17.6	4.0	99.9	273
Assault	0.8	34.9	2.8	1.0	29.7	12.6	15.7	2.5	100.0	8,586
Robbery	0.8	19.3	13.6	2.5	31.7	13.6	15.3	3.2	100.0	1,448
Purse-snatching, pocket-picking	0.4	14.5	5.7	8.7	34.6	16.4	14.4	6.4	100.1	703
Personal larceny	0.3	11.7	1.8	1.0	53.9	11.8	16.4	3.1	100.0	22,516
Burglary	0.5	11.6	2.0	1.1	27.6	33.5	20.6	3.1	100.0	9,595
Household larceny	0.3	10.1	1.7	1.0	30.4	15.9	37.6	3.2	100.1	12,372
Motor vehicle theft	0.2	11.6	2.7	1.2	35.4	15.7	19.2	14.0	100.0	1,914
Total	0.5	15.1	2.3	1.1	39.3	16.7	21.6	3.4	100.0	57,407

[1] All types of crime include both actual and attempted crimes.
Source: Reiss (1980).

did occur in cases of motor vehicle theft, robbery, purse-snatching/pick-pocketing, and rape. About 30% of victims of these crimes subsequently experienced a personal larceny without contact (Reiss, 1980). A crime-switch matrix was also used in a study by Daigle and colleagues (2008), discussed elsewhere in this chapter, to identify instances of crime switching among sexual violence victims. Like Reiss (1980), their results suggested that recurrent victims most often experienced the same type of sexual victimization in consecutive incidents, rather than switching to another type of sexual victimization. Overall, research using crime-switch matrixes indicates two patterns:

1. Most recurrent victims experience the same type of victimization in the subsequent incident.
2. Crime switching does occur, but it is a relatively rare phenomenon.

Theories of Recurring Victimization

Several theoretical perspectives have developed to explain why certain targets are victimized two or more times. Much of the theoretical progress to explain recurring victimization has been focused on repeat victimization. The leading theories include state dependence theory, risk heterogeneity theory, lifestyle–routine activities theory, and rational choice theory. Although these theories have different origins and have been applied to a variety of types of recurring victimization, many of the theoretical concepts discussed below have applicability across the different types of recurring victimization.

State Dependence: "Boost Theory"

The basic premise of the ***state dependence theory*** or event dependence theory of recurring victimization is that being victimized once increases a target's chances of being victimized a subsequent time. In other words, one future state or event (e.g., a subsequent victimization) depends on a previous state or event— the initial victimization. In support of this theory, Andromachi Tseloni and Ken Pease contend that "Victimization is a good, arguably the best readily available, predictor of future victimization" (2003, p. 196). This theory also has been described as the "***boost theory***" of recurring victimization, because having been a victim one time "boosts" an individual's likelihood of being a victim again in the future (Pease, 1998). At the core of this argument is the idea that for some victims, experiencing a victimization makes the individual either a more vulnerable or attractive target for future victimization.

As an example of state dependence as an explanation for recurring victimization, recall the college student, Sarah, described in Chapter 2. Sarah is 19 years old, lives on campus, goes out frequently during the week, and to parties on the weekend. Imagine that Sarah is attending a party sponsored by a fraternity. Sarah knows some of the people at the party, but many of the partygoers are strangers to her. The music is loud, the fraternity house is crowded with other partygoers, and there is a seemingly limitless supply of alcohol. Since she is there to have a good time, Sarah spends some time meeting new people and having a few beers (of course, Sarah should not be drinking at all since she is only 19 and hence under the legal drinking age). Someone she does not know offers her a beer in a plastic cup and invites her to find a private place where they can talk, and she accepts the beer and the invitation. In this more private setting, Sarah talks with her new friend and finishes her beer. Unknown to her, the beer contained a sedative that made her fall asleep, impairing her for over eight hours. During this time, she is raped by the man whom she thought was a new friend. The rapist's friend also has sex with Sarah while she is incapacitated. There are many ways a single victimization ultimately leads to another, but Sarah's story illustrates how repeat sexual victimization can be driven by state dependence. In this example, being victimized by the initial offender created a state that allowed for subsequent victimization by the other offender.

"Boost theory" has consistently been supported in the recurring victimization research. Many victimization studies find that previous victimization is a strong predictor of later victimization (see, e.g., Bowers & Johnson, 2004; Johnson, Summers, & Pease, 2009; Osborn & Tseloni, 1998). For example, in their study of repeat victimization, Denise Osborn and Andromachi Tseloni (1998) examined data collected as part of the 1992 British Crime Survey. They concluded that prior victimization influenced one's likelihood of experiencing a later victimization. Osborn and Tseloni also found that having experienced a car theft, a burglary, or an assault translated to increased odds of being a victim of any property crime, of burglary, and of theft. In another study testing the "boost" hypothesis, Kate Bowers and Shane Johnson examined police data from Merseyside, England, on near repeat burglaries. They reported that near repeats were dependent upon each other, noting that "there is a dependency between events that occur close together in both space and time" (Bowers & Johnson, 2004, p. 21). These and other studies generally support the state dependence argument that one victimization leads to future victimizations, or to paraphrase George Carlin from the beginning of this chapter, "sometimes one thing leads to the same thing."

Risk Heterogeneity: "Flag Theory"

Risk heterogeneity theory, or ***"flag theory,"*** is complementary to state dependence theory in explaining recurrent victimization. While state dependence asserts that victimization is a risk factor for more victimization to happen, ***risk heterogeneity*** argues that certain victims possess characteristics that make them likely targets for both an initial victimization *and* recurring subsequent victimization. That is to say, recurring victims may have certain attributes that "flag" them as particularly attractive or vulnerable targets for future victimization. Of course, the nature of this "flag effect" depends on the situation and type of crime. Consider a typical convenience store robbery. Certain characteristics of convenience stores may set them apart from other potential retail targets and thereby increase their chances of being repeatedly victimized, even by different offenders. For instance, a store may be repeatedly targeted because it is *conveniently located* near a freeway on/off ramp; has few customers during late night hours; or is staffed with a single employee. These characteristics raise flags or signals to potential offenders that this store is an "easy" target for robbery. Ken Pease (1998, p. 9) distinguished between the concepts of state dependence and risk heterogeneity with a sports analogy:

> A sports team loses the first two matches of the season. Why did it lose the second one? Was it because the first result reflected the fact that it was a poor team, and it was still a poor team at the time of the second match? This is a flag account. Alternatively, did the first result destroy its confidence so that it played tentatively in the second match? This is a boost account.

Tseloni and Pease (2003) reported support for both state dependence theory and risk heterogeneity theory in predicting recurring victimization. Using data from the 1994 NCVS, they examined the effects of prior victimization—a boost—and individual (e.g., race, educational level, length at residence) and household characteristics (e.g., annual household income, number of cars)—which may act as flags—on the likelihood of experiencing a repeat personal victimization. They concluded that both boosts and flags had a role in explaining repeat personal victimization, and that the two concepts were actually intertwined. That is, prior victimization explained repeat victimization, but the effect depended upon individual and household differences. For example, repeat victimizations were more likely to occur against males, young people, and those with lower household incomes.

The previously referenced study by Lauritsen and Quinet (1995) also investigated the boost and flag theories of recurring victimization. Upon examining data from the National Youth Survey, these researchers concluded that state dependence and risk heterogeneity were both influential in explaining a number of types of youth victimization, including assault, robbery, larceny, and vandalism. For example, the likelihood of robbery victimization among youth was associated with being male, being young, and engaging in delinquent activities, measures of risk heterogeneity; and previous victimization, a measure of state dependence. These two studies provide empirical support for state dependence and risk heterogeneity explanations of recurring victimization. However, these are not the only theories that scholars have used to explain recurring victimization. Lifestyle–routine activities theory, which emphasizes the importance of opportunities in the occurrence of victimization, also has been tested to explain and predict recurring victimization. The application of lifestyle–routine activities theory to recurring victimization is discussed below.

Lifestyle–Routine Activities Theory

Chapter 2 introduced lifestyle-exposure and routine activities theories, explaining the premise that opportunities are the primary cause of victimization. Over time the theories have been combined into the lifestyle–routine activities perspective. Chapter 3 reviewed the various contemporary refinements to the theory, such as gendered routine activities and age-graded routine activities, as further developments in using opportunity as an explanation of crime. The theoretical perspective has also been used to explain different forms of recurring victimization (e.g., Fisher, Daigle, & Cullen, 2010; Turanovic & Pratt, 2014; Wittebrood & Nieuwbeerta, 2000). The argument behind doing so is that victims who are targeted two or more times may participate in lifestyles and/or routine activities that create opportunities for their recurrent victimization. This is essentially a *risk heterogeneity* perspective to explaining recurring victimization. ***Lifestyle–routine activities theory*** provides a useful framework for studying how and why repeatedly victimized targets may signal offenders that they are susceptible or vulnerable to victimization.

In one of the pioneering studies to take this approach, Karin Wittebrood and Paul Nieuwbeerta (2000) used lifestyle–routine activities theory to explain seven types of victimization, including bicycle theft, automobile theft, sexual assault, and threats. In addition to exploring the effects that lifestyles and routines had on recurring victimization, Wittebrood and Nieuwbeerta examined how state dependence or previous victimization affected the likelihood of recurring victimization. Adding further depth to this study, Wittebrood and Nieuwbeerta also considered the links between previous and subsequent victimization across participants' life course. They examined life history data from nearly 2,000 individuals in the Netherlands, including such information as their lifestyles, routines, previous victimizations, employment and marriage history, and more.

Regarding the effects of prior victimization on recurring victimization, the authors reported that having been victimized once significantly affected one's likelihood of being victimized again. This pattern persisted for six of the seven types of victimization under study: burglary, personal larceny, car theft, bicycle theft, assault, and receiving a threat. For example, an individual who experienced any property crime in the past (e.g., bicycle theft, personal larceny) was at nearly double the risk for burglary victimization.

Wittebrood and Nieuwbeerta also reported that patterns in routine activities (e.g., target attractiveness, proximity, exposure, guardianship) and changes in those patterns across the life course substantially influenced victimization risks. In the authors' words: "For all types of crime, when persons are young, studying, and unmarried, their risk of victimization is clearly higher than when they are married, have started working, and had children" (Wittebrood & Nieuwbeerta, 2000, p. 112).

A study of the effects of lifestyles and routine activities on recurring victimization was conducted by Bonnie Fisher, Leah Daigle, and Francis Cullen (2010). This research investigated how close proximity to motivated offenders, exposure to crime, target suitability, capable guardianship, all dimensions of risk heterogeneity, and characteristics of the initial victimization incident (e.g., victim–perpetrator relationship, reporting behaviors of victims), or state dependence, influenced the risks for recurring sexual victimization against college women. Their analysis included over 4,000 female students enrolled at colleges and universities from across the United States. Similar to Wittebrood and Nieuwbeerta's study, their findings revealed support for both lifestyle–routine activities theory and state dependence as explanations of recurring victimization. In addition, the authors also compared risk factors for single-incident victimization (i.e., being a victim only once) to risk factors for recurring incidents. From this comparison, the authors concluded that lifestyles and routine activities did not distinguish one-time victims from recurrent victims. This finding suggests that victims who are put at risk through their lifestyles and routines will continue to be at higher risk if these are not altered after the initial incident.

Rational Choice Theory

The final theoretical framework that researchers have used to understand why and how recurring victimization occurs is rational choice theory. This theory was introduced in Chapter 3 in the context of the environmental criminology perspective. Its usefulness is in explaining why some individuals and targets are victimized while others are not. By way of a brief review, ***rational choice theory*** argues that when offenders are deciding whether or not to take advantage of criminal opportunities, they think about the potential costs (e.g., getting caught, getting punished) and the potential benefits (e.g., successfully completing the crime). This theory also is related to the lifestyle–routine activities perspective, because it is rational for offenders to want to choose targets that are proximate to their location, exposed, attractive or suitable, and unguarded.

As an explanation for recurring victimization, rational choice theorists consider recurring victimization from the viewpoint of the offender and the factors that influence offenders' decisions to act (Clarke & Cornish, 1985). The argument is that rational offenders will be likely to reoffend against targets that previously brought them benefits. For example, say a savvy identity thief finds a way to steal a victim's credit card number over the Internet, completely unbeknownst to the victim. From the standpoint of rational choice theory, it is likely that the offender will not only use the credit card information to make fraudulent purchases, but continue to use it until the card has been reported as stolen and no longer is valid to make purchases. For this reason, repeated identity theft victimization is rational on the part of the offender when compared to the alternative, which is to use the credit card information only a single time. Graham Farrell, Coretta Phillips, and Ken Pease (1995) discussed several crimes that recur because of a rational decision made by offenders. Select crimes are presented in the "Spotlight on Theory" box to illustrate the ways in

Spotlight on Theory: Recurring Victimization as a Rational Choice

Recurring Crime	Rational Choice Explanation
Domestic Violence	Unless offenders are discouraged after seeing the consequences of their actions, future incidents are likely to occur. Effort and risks (both costs) decline with repeated offenses, and "rewards" may increase with repetition.
Household Burglary	Targeting the same or similar households after an initial burglary requires less effort (e.g., points of entry are known), less risk (e.g., offenders know how to avoid detection), and comparable rewards (e.g., new items to steal).
Bank Robbery	Offenders know what the risks will be following their first successful robberies. Further, the effort required may be reduced if employees are more cooperative on successive attempts, and the rewards will be equivalent to the first time because the money has been replaced.
Racial Attacks	If an offender chooses to carry out multiple race-based attacks (hate crimes), additional offenses should involve little effort in finding a target since logically one target is just as acceptable as the next. Having succeeded once, offenders may perceive their risks to be lower in future attacks, and the rewards remain unchanged.
Abuse of Children	After completion of an initial "successful" victimization, be it sexual or physical, the offender may reason that future crimes will take less effort, involve less risk, and bring similar "rewards."

Source: Farrell et al. (1995).

Table 9-8: Summary of Recurring Victimization Theories

Theory	Summary
State Dependence	An initial victimization incident increases or "boosts" the likelihood of a future incident by making targets appear attractive or vulnerable to potential offenders.
Risk Heterogeneity	Certain target characteristics act as signals or "flags" to offenders that the target is suitable for victimization. Unless these characteristics change, they continue to flag targets as susceptible for victimization and the target is victimized again.
Lifestyle-Routine Activities	Lifestyles and routine activities of individuals facilitate opportunities for their victimization. As is the case with risk heterogeneity, continuing in these lifestyles and routines perpetuates victimization risk, resulting in recurring victimization.
Rational Choice	Decisions to offend are based on a consideration of the costs and benefits of criminal behavior. Therefore, it is rational for successful offenders to decide to reoffend against the same (or similar) targets that previously provided these benefits.

which rational choice theory is helpful in understanding recurring victimization. For instance, "Spotlight on Theory: Recurring Victimization as a Rational Choice" box explains that it is rational for a burglar to choose the same household after an initial burglary because it theoretically requires less effort, involves less risk, and provides similar rewards to the initial burglary.

This section has presented four theories that theorists have used to explain recurring victimization. Table 9-8 summarizes the main points of each of these four theories. This chapter concludes with a discussion of preventing recurring victimization.

Preventing Recurring Victimization

One of the practical implications of studying recurring victimization and identifying the factors that increase the risk of subsequent victimizations is that prevention efforts can be directed at these frequently targeted individuals or households. Research has revealed that focusing on recurrent victims has two important effects. First, if recurring victimizations can be prevented, a large portion of all crime would be prevented. As was demonstrated earlier in this chapter, although these victims typically represent only a small proportion of those victimized, they experience a disproportionate amount of overall victimization incidents. Logically, then, if future victimizations are prevented, crime rates should decline. Second, focusing preventive efforts on recurring victims, or those likely to be recurring victims, is an effective way to allocate valuable (and limited) law enforcement resources. And, since the time course of repeat victimization suggests that the subsequent offenses will be committed shortly after the initial victimization, these resources may only need to be in place for a short time following the first incident.

Most of the research devoted to the prevention of recurring victimization has focused on property crimes. However, a recent study by Fisher, Daigle, and Cullen (2010) examined the prevention of recurring sexual victimization (i.e., rape, sexual coercion, unwanted sexual touching) among college women. They focused on how victims' behaviors during an initial incident affected their likelihood of suffering a subsequent incident. Fisher and colleagues reported that self-protection during an initial incident of victimization significantly reduced subsequent victimization risk. In particular, women who resisted their offender during the first encounter by using non-forceful verbal actions, such as telling the offender to stop, reduced their likelihood of suffering a subsequent victimization. Other preventive behaviors, such as reporting the incident to the police, did not significantly reduce the likelihood that victims would become recurrent victims.

Aside from this study by Fisher and colleagues (2010), much of the crime prevention effort directed at reducing crime through a focus on recurrent or likely recurrent victims has taken place outside the United States (Daigle & Fisher, 2013). This research, conducted primarily in the United Kingdom, has often involved responses to preventing residential burglary, with a prime example being the ***Kirkholt Burglary Prevention Project***. This initiative was undertaken in the 1980s in Kirkholt, England. At the time, Kirkholt included approximately 2,280 dwellings, and prior to the project, residential burglary rates in Kirkholt were double those of all other high-risk areas identified by the 1984 British Crime Survey (Pease, 1992). Perhaps even more telling of the serious burglary problem Kirkholt residents were experiencing, in 1985 approximately 25% of the dwellings in Kirkholt were burglarized (Forrester, Frenz, O'Connell, & Pease, 1990; Pease, 1992). In collecting information prior to designing a prevention strategy (e.g., through interviews with victims, interviews with burglars), the project team identified repeat burglaries as one of the driving forces behind Kirkholt's overall high burglary rates. This finding suggested to project designers that a focus on repeat victimizations was of primary importance. Since repeat victimizations are more predictable than first-time victimizations (lightning can strike twice), attention could be directed at the dwellings previously victimized.

The Kirkholt Project included a variety of crime prevention techniques aimed at reducing or eliminating repeat burglary. For instance, based on information provided by victims and burglars, households that were previously targeted were given security upgrades to reduce their vulnerability and attractiveness to potential offenders. Another important element in the Kirkholt Project was the cocoon neighborhood watch. A ***cocoon neighborhood watch*** operates by insulating a victimized household. Residents of dwellings in the immediate area, such as the five or six closest houses, watch for and report any suspicious activity around the victimized household. Cooperating residents in the Kirkholt Project also were supplied with additional security for their homes. Project workers for the Kirkholt Project also provided community support, information for victims, and assistance in establishing and maintaining the cocoons (Forrester et al., 1990).

Overall, the Kirkholt Project was considered a success. Within five months of implementing the project, burglary rates in Kirkholt fell to 40% of what they were prior to the intervention. During that same time, repeat burglaries dropped to zero and remained consistently low thereafter (Forrester et al., 1990; Pease, 1992). Subsequent efforts in Kirkholt indicated a 75% drop in burglary over the next three years. Replications of the Kirkholt Project in other areas indicate that such measures are not always successful, however (Tilley, 1993). Efforts designed to address specific area problems, as was the case in Kirkholt, can be effective ways to reduce victimization (e.g., Budz, Pegnall, & Townsley, 2001; Chenery, Holt, & Pease, 1997; Tilley, 1993). For instance, a similarly successful prevention project was undertaken in the 1990s in Huddersfield, England. This project used prevention measures similar to those in Kirkholt (e.g., cocoon neighborhood watch) but also devised new prevention strategies specific to recurring victims in Huddersfield. For example, one of these strategies made use of temporary burglar alarms to protect previously victimized targets (Chenery et al., 1997). Since repeat victimization risk dissipates quickly, these devices could be relocated after the period of heightened risk. By focusing on these initial victims, the project was able to reduce overall burglary victimizations by 30%. Temporary security equipment also was used to reduce incidents of repeat vehicle crimes, but their effectiveness was less clear. Still, overall vehicle crimes declined by 20% in Huddersfield during the study period.

Summary

One of the most important areas of study in the field of victimology is recurring criminal victimization. Recurring victimization occurs when targets are victimized two or more times, with the nature of these subsequent victimizations, such as the length of time that has passed between incidents and the types of victimization suffered by victims, determining the type of recurring victimization that has occurred. Findings from studies of recurring victimization indicate that most targets are only victimized once. However, a smaller group, those identified as recurring victims, experiences a disproportionate amount of the overall victimization incidents.

The nature of recurring victimization is illuminated by the time course of repeat victimization, which reveals that the passage of time diminishes the likelihood of a subsequent victimization. Studies of crime switching that focus on which crimes are likely to follow initial victimization also contribute to understanding the larger issue of recurring victimization. The study of recurring victimization is further informed by four theoretical perspectives: state dependence, risk heterogeneity, lifestyle–routine activities, and rational choice. These theories explain that recurring victimization is a consequence of the initial victimization ("boost"), persistent characteristics of targets ("flags"), lifestyles and routines of recurrent victims, or a rational calculation by offenders that prior targets make good future targets. The importance of recurring victimization is reinforced by the significant policy implications surrounding it. Namely, if crime prevention efforts are concentrated on previously victimized targets, a substantial portion of overall crime can be prevented. Preventing victimization is discussed in detail in Chapter 14.

KEYWORDS

Recurring victimization	Near repeat victimization	Risk heterogeneity
Recurring victims	Virtual repeat victimization	Lifestyle–routine activities theory
Repeat victimization	Time course of repeat victimization	Rational choice theory
Revictimization	Crime-switch matrix	Kirkholt Burglary Prevention Project
Multiple victimization	State dependence	Cocoon neighborhood watch
Polyvictimization	Boost theory	
Series victimization	Flag theory	

DISCUSSION QUESTIONS

1. Do you think that the factors that increase risk of recurring victimization are the same for different types of crime (e.g., assault, cyberstalking, auto theft)? Explain your answer.
2. Consider Daigle and colleagues' analysis of repeat sexual and violent victimization among college women. Why do you think a subsequent incident occurred so soon after the first sexual or violent incident was committed?
3. Why does the risk for repeat victimization decrease so quickly, while those who experience revictimization remain at risk for long periods of time that cross developmental stages (e.g., childhood to adulthood)?
4. Can recurring victimization be explained in terms of both state dependence and risk heterogeneity concurrently? In other words, can both boosts and flags be operating simultaneously or are these concepts mutually exclusive? Explain your answer.
5. Consider Wittebrood and Nieuwbeerta's research on the effects of state dependence and lifestyle–routine activities/risk heterogeneity on recurring victimization. Why do you think changes in lifestyles and routines over the life course influence risks for recurring victimization?
6. Can the prevention lessons learned from the Kirkholt Project, with its emphasis on recurring burglary, be used to address other types of recurring victimization, such as sexual victimization, robbery, or simple assault? Explain your answer.

REFERENCES

Ashton, J., Brown, I., Senior, B., & Pease, K. (1998). Repeat victimization: Offender accounts. *International Journal of Risk, Security and Crime Prevention, 3*, 269–279.

Bernasco, W. (2008). Them again? Same-offender involvement in repeat and near repeat burglaries. *European Journal of Criminology, 5*, 411–431.

Bowers, K. J., & Johnson, S. D. (2004). Who commits near repeats? A test of the boost explanation. *Western Criminology Review, 5*, 12–24.

Budz, D., Pegnall, N., & Townsley, M. (2001). *Lightning strikes twice: Preventing repeat home burglary*. Queensland, Australia: Criminal Justice Commission.

Carlin, G. (1997). *Braindroppings*. New York: Hyperion.

Chenery, S., Holt, J., & Pease, K. (1997). *Biting back II: Reducing repeat victimisation in Huddersfield*. Crime Detection and Prevention Series, Paper 82. London: Home Office.

Clarke, R .V., & Cornish, D. (1985). Modeling offender's decisions: A framework for research & policy. In M. Tonry & N. Morris (Eds.), *Crime & Justice: An Annual Review of Research*, Vol. 6 (pp. 147–185). Chicago, IL: University of Chicago Press.

Classen, C. C., Palesh, O. G., & Aggarwal, R. (2005). Sexual revictimization: A review of the empirical literature. *Trauma, Violence, & Abuse, 6*, 103–129.

Daigle, L. E., & Fisher, B. S. (2013). The recurrence of victimization: Terminology, extent, characteristics, correlates, and prevention. In R. C. Davis, A. J. Lurigio, & S. Herman (Eds.), *Victims of crime* (4th ed., pp. 371–400). Thousand Oaks, CA: Sage Publications, Inc.

Daigle, L. E., Fisher, B. S., & Cullen, F. T. (2008). The violent and sexual victimization of college women: Is repeat victimization a problem? *Journal of Interpersonal Violence, 23*, 1296–1313.

Desai, S., Arias, I., Thompson, M. P., & Basile, K. C. (2002). Childhood victimization and subsequent adult revictimization assessed in a nationally representative sample of women and men. *Violence and Victims, 17*, 639–653.

Ellingworth, D., Farrell, G., & Pease, K. (1995). A victim is a victim is a victim? Chronic victimization in four sweeps of the British Crime Survey. *British Journal of Criminology, 35*, 360–365.

Farrell, G., & Bouloukos, A. C. (2001). International overview: A cross-national comparison of rates of repeat victimization. In G. Farrell & K. Pease (Eds.), *Repeat victimization* (pp. 5–25). Monsey, NY: Criminal Justice Press.

Farrell, G., Phillips, C., & Pease, K. (1995). Like taking candy: Why does repeat victimization occur? *British Journal of Criminology, 35*, 384–399.

Finkelhor, D., Ormrod, R. K., & Turner, H. A. (2007). Polyvictimization and trauma in a national longitudinal cohort. *Development and Psychopathology, 19*, 149–166.

Finkelhor, D., Ormrod, R., Turner, H., & Holt, M. (2009). Pathways to poly-victimization. *Child Maltreatment, 14*, 316–329.

Fisher, B. S., Daigle, L. E., & Cullen, F. T. (2010). What distinguishes single from recurrent sexual victims? The role of lifestyle-routine activities and first-incident characteristics. *Justice Quarterly, 27,* 102–129.

Forrester, D., Frenz, S., O'Connell, M., & Pease, K. (1990). *The Kirkholt burglary prevention project: Phase II.* Crime Prevention Unit, Paper 23. London: Home Office.

Hindelang, M. J., Gottfredson M. R., & Garofalo, J. (1978). *Victims of personal crime: An empirical foundation for a theory of personal victimization.* Cambridge, MA: Ballinger Publishing Company.

Hope, T., Bryan, J., Trickett, A., & Osborn, D. R. (2001). The phenomena of multiple victimization: The relationship between personal and property crime risk. *British Journal of Criminology, 41,* 595–617.

Johnson, S. D., Bernasco, W., Bowers, K. J., Elffers, H., Ratcliffe, J., Rengert, G., & Townsley, M. (2007). Space-time patterns of risk: A cross national assessment of residential burglary victimization. *Journal of Quantitative Criminology, 23,* 201–219.

Johnson, S. D., Bowers, K., & Hirschfield, A. (1997). New insights into the spatial and temporal distribution of repeat victimization. *British Journal of Criminology 37,* 224–241.

Johnson, S. D., Summers, L., & Pease, K. (2009). Offender as forager? A direct test of the boost account of victimization. *Journal of Quantitative Criminology, 25,* 181–200.

Lauritsen, J. L., Owens, J. G., Planty, M., Rand, M. R., & Truman, J. L. (2012). *Methods for counting high-frequency repeat victimizations in the National Crime Victimization Survey.* Washington, DC: Bureau of Justice Statistics.

Lauritsen, J. L., & Quinet, K. F. D. (1995). Repeat victimization among adolescents and young adults. *Journal of Quantitative Criminology, 11,* 143–166.

Osborn, D. R., & Tseloni, A. (1998). The distribution of household property crimes. *Journal of Quantitative Criminology, 14,* 307–330.

Outlaw, M., Ruback, B., & Britt, C. (2002). Repeat and multiple victimizations: The role of individual and contextual factors. *Violence and Victims, 17,* 187–204.

Pease, K. (1992). The Kirkholt Project: Preventing burglary on a British public housing estate. *Security Journal, 2,* 73–77.

Pease, K. (1998). *Repeat victimization: Taking stock.* Crime Detection and Prevention Series, Paper 90. London: Home Office.

Polvi, N., Looman, T., Humphries, C., & Pease, K. (1991). The time course of repeat burglary victimization. *British Journal of Criminology, 31,* 411–414.

Ratcliffe, J. H., & Rengert, G. F. (2008). Near-repeat patterns in Philadelphia shootings. *Security Journal, 21,* 58–76.

Reiss, A. J. (1980). Victim proneness in repeat victimization by type of crime. In S.E. Fienberg & A. J. Reiss (Eds.), *Indicators of crime and criminal justice: Quantitative studies* (pp. 41–53). Washington, DC: U.S. Department of Justice.

Roodman, A. A., & Clum, G. A. (2001). Revictimization rates and method variance: A meta-analysis. *Clinical Psychology Review, 21,* 183–204.

Sparks, R. F. (1981). Multiple victimization: Evidence, theory, and future research. *Journal of Criminal Law & Criminology, 72,* 762–778.

Tilley, N. (1993). *After Kirkholt—Theory, method, and results of replication evaluations.* Crime Prevention Unit Series, Paper 47. London: Home Office.

Truman, J., Langton, L., & Planty, M. (2013). *Criminal victimization, 2012* (NCJ 243389). Washington, DC: Bureau of Justice Statistics.

Tseloni, A., & Pease, K. (2003). Repeat personal victimization: 'Boosts' or 'flags'? *British Journal of Criminology, 43,* 196–212.

Turanovic, J. J., & Pratt, T. C. (2014). "Can't stop, won't stop": Self-control, risky lifestyles, and repeat victimization. *Journal of Quantitative Criminology, 30,* 29–56.

Wittebrood, K., & Nieuwbeerta, P. (2000). Criminal victimization during one's life course: The effects of previous victimization and patterns of routine activities. *Journal of Research in Crime and Delinquency, 37,* 91–122.

PART III

Responses to and Consequences of Victimization

Parts I and II of the textbook presented theoretical explanations for criminal victimization and reviewed the empirical evidence that provides a basis for identifying predictors of victimization. Part III marks a transition to a different set of research questions posed by victimologists, particularly those related to victims' experiences *after* the crime. Across four chapters, responses to, and the consequences of, criminal victimization are discussed along with highlights of the most up-to-date research on these topics.

Chapter 10 explores decisions made by victims following their victimization. This is an often overlooked yet very important topic in victimology. Decisions made by victims, such as whether to report the crime to law enforcement, have significant ramifications. These decisions affect not only the victim, and his or her ability to recover, but also ultimately the operations of the criminal justice system. The chapter includes topics such as acknowledgment of criminal victimization and decisions concerning reporting, self-protection, help seeking, and bystander intervention.

Chapter 11 examines the consequences of victimization and describes the harm victims experience in the aftermath of the crime. The chapter is divided into five sections that introduce readers to the physical, psychological and mental health, financial and economic, and social and behavioral consequences of victimization for victims. Recognizing that different consequences are associated with particular types of victimization, the chapter also includes an examination of selected types of victimization and their consequences (e.g., the consequences of child maltreatment for its victims). While each of these topics could by themselves fill an entire chapter or even a book, "the essentials" are collected and presented in this chapter.

Chapter 12 examines societal responses to victimization. An overview is provided of issues such as the victim's role in the criminal justice process, civil justice remedies, victims' rights, and victim assistance and services. These topics, out of necessity, are discussed in general terms because of the nature of the U.S. criminal justice system. Each state has its own criminal and civil justice systems, as well as its own victims' rights laws. Further, victim assistance and services available for victims differ, sometimes widely, from state to state and even community to community within a state. Therefore, the chapter discusses these issues in broad terms, while also providing examples of unique responses to criminal victimization that may not exist throughout the United States.

Part III concludes with Chapter 13, which addresses the topic of fear of criminal victimization. Fear can be a consequence not only for those actually experiencing victimization but also for those who have never been victimized. Nonetheless, fear of victimization is an important social problem and has been the subject of hundreds of research studies, as well as several textbooks and research monographs. Chapter 13 summarizes this body of research by discussing issues related to fear of criminal victimization, including defining, measuring, and estimating its extent; identifying patterns and elucidating theories of fear of crime; and discussing the consequences of fear and why fear can be healthy under some circumstances while damaging in others.

CASE STUDY #3

The Consequences of Victimization

In Part III of the textbook, we examine societal responses to, and the consequences of, criminal victimization. Over four chapters, we consider such issues as victims' decision making, including how they respond to their own victimizations; the physical, emotional, and psychological consequences suffered by crime victims, as well as how victimization affects people's fear and perceived risk of further victimization; and what victims encounter when pursuing formal charges against offenders in the criminal justice system. The short version of the story is this: Crime victims suffer—sometimes a great deal and sometimes not very much. The trauma they suffer can last for years, if not decades, and can have both a short- and a long-term negative impact on their quality of life. Sadly, at least some of the trauma that victims suffer—despite the best intentions of law enforcement officers, prosecutors, and judges coming into contact with them—can be traced to those involved with victims once their case comes into the system.

Male Victims of Sexual Assault: The Case of Military Sexual Trauma

> *The rape of a male soldier has a particular symbolism. In a hypermasculine culture, what's the worst thing you can do to another man? Force him into what the culture perceives as a "feminine" role. (Penn, n.d.)*

Recently, various news outlets, including the *New York Times*, Fox News, and CNN, have reported that sexual assaults of women in the armed forces are at epidemic levels, which has forced all branches of the military to develop policies and programs to address the scourge. These assaults have included wide-ranging behaviors, from unwanted sexual touching to outright rape.

Less often reported are instances of sexual victimization perpetrated against males both inside and outside the military (Tewksbury, 2007). This lack of attention is not surprising given that more generally, male victims of sexual assault, sexual harassment, and rape have been well hidden; if they did come to light, they were mocked, joked with, or ignored. Let's look a bit more closely at the problem of sexual victimization against males in the armed forces, including instances of rape, forced oral sex with an offender, and related behaviors.

> *One of the doctors said to me afterward, "Son, men don't get raped."* (Penn, n.d.)

> *The doctor would say, "You enjoyed it, didn't you? Come on, tell me the truth."* (Penn, n.d.)

In a recent *GQ* article, journalist Nathaniel Penn (n.d.) interviewed some three dozen victims of rape and sexual assault that occurred while the victims were serving their country in the military. According to Penn (n.d.):

- Once he enlists, a man's risk for sexual assault increases by a factor of 10.
- In raw numbers, more military men are sexually assaulted each year than women—nearly 14,000 of them in 2012 alone from all branches of the service.
- Prior to the repeal of "Don't ask, don't tell" male-on-male rape victims could be dishonorably discharged for having engaged in "homosexual conduct."
- "One of the myths is that perpetrators identify as gay, which is by and large not the case," says James Asbrand, a psychologist with the Salt Lake City VA's PTSD clinical team. "It's not about the . . . sex. It's about power and control."

> *The part that I remember before I passed out was somebody saying they were going to* teach me a lesson. (Penn, n.d.; emphasis added)

Indeed, Penn's interviews with victims reveal startling patterns associated with these assaults. Most of the incidents included severe beatings of the victims in addition to the actual sexual assault or rape, which often involved forced anal intercourse with a broomstick (or similar device). Prior to their assault, many victims had been singled out for various reasons and were openly ridiculed, had their lockers broken into or rearranged (to get them into trouble), or suffered physical assaults by members of their unit. Also interesting was that many of the victims Penn interviewed expressed great sadness at having to leave the service. They genuinely loved being in the armed forces and serving their country.

> *Above all, military sexual trauma (MST) victims keep quiet because they do not believe their attackers will be punished. And they're almost certainly right. The conviction rate in MST cases that go to trial is just 7 percent. An estimated 81 percent of male MST victims never report being attacked. Perhaps it should astonish us that any of them do. (Penn, n.d.; emphasis added)*

Penn (n.d.) concludes:

> *[S]exual assault is alarmingly common in the U.S. military, and more than half of the victims are men. According to the Pentagon, thirty-eight military men are sexually assaulted every single day. These are the stories you never hear—because the culprits almost always go free, the survivors rarely speak,* and no one in the military or Congress has done enough to stop it. (emphasis added)

References

Penn, N. (n.d.). *Son, men don't get raped.* Retrieved August 14, 2014, from http://www.gq.com/long-form/male-military-rape.

Tewksbury, R. (2007). Effects of sexual assault on men: Physical, mental, and sexual consequences. *International Journal of Men's Health, 6,* 22–35.

CHAPTER 10

Victim Decision Making

CHAPTER OUTLINE

- Introduction
- Acknowledgment of Criminal Victimization
- Reporting Decisions
  - Decisions to Report Victimization
    - The Seriousness of the Offense
    - The Relationship Between the Victim and the Offender
    - The Offender's Criminal History
  - Decisions to Not Report Victimization
- Self-Protection Decisions
- Help-Seeking Decisions
- Bystander Intervention Decisions
- Summary
- Keywords
- Discussion Questions
- References

LEARNING OBJECTIVES

- Explain the concept "acknowledgment of criminal victimization" and describe its importance.
- Describe the circumstances surrounding victims' decisions to either report or not report their victimization to law enforcement.
- Define victim self-protection and describe its different forms.
- Describe how victims seek help and explain what influences these decisions.
- Explain the concept of bystander intervention and how bystanders make decisions to intervene (or not).

> *The victim of criminal behavior may be the most influential of all criminal justice decision makers. By virtue of the decision as to whether or not to report a criminal victimization to the police, the victim is a principal "gate-keeper" of the entire criminal justice process.*
>
> **Gottfredson and Gottfredson, 1990, pp. 15–16**

Introduction

Victims are faced with several decisions during and after criminal events, such as whether to resist the offender during the crime by using self-protection, whether to contact law enforcement, and whether to seek help to overcome the harm they have suffered. Decisions made by crime victims have significant consequences, both for the individual and for the criminal justice system. Martin Greenberg and Barry Ruback (1992) conducted one of the most comprehensive studies of crime victim decision making and explained that there are three important stages in the decision-making process: (1) acknowledging or labeling the event as a crime; (2) determining the seriousness of the crime; and (3) deciding what to do next. Greenberg and Ruback's *stages of victim decision making*, which do not necessarily proceed in this order, provide a starting point for thinking about the decisions that are discussed throughout this chapter.

Victim acknowledgment refers to the recognition on the part of a crime victim that his or her experience constitutes a criminal victimization. Victimization acknowledgment is important for many reasons. Paramount among these reasons is that those who do not recognize or acknowledge their victimization as a crime must bear the consequences of their victimization alone. Another concern is that unacknowledged victimizations are never formally or legally addressed by the criminal justice system. Along these lines, those who consider themselves to be crime victims must decide what, if any, action they should take. For this reason, Michael and Don Gottfredson (1990) described victims as the "gatekeepers" of the criminal justice system. Victim reporting decisions determine whether the criminal justice system, starting with law enforcement, will be invoked to respond to a crime. This decision is consequential because in most cases, an event will not be processed as a crime unless or until it is first reported to police by victims or third parties. In addition, as Chapter 4 discussed, non-reporting of victimizations affects how crimes are counted in official crime statistics. Other decisions facing crime victims following a criminal event involve what measures to take to prevent future victimizations and recover from the harm they have recently suffered as a result of crime.

This chapter focuses on four important victim decisions: (1) acknowledging an experience as a criminal victimization; (2) reporting the victimization to the law enforcement (or not); (3) adopting self-protection measures either in response to victimization or fear of victimization; and (4) obtaining assistance or services to help overcome the effects of the crime. A fifth decision also is discussed in this chapter: intervention decisions on the part of bystanders who witness or hear about the criminal incident. These are choices made by third parties to intervene on behalf of crime victims.

None of these choices is made in a vacuum. Each decision influences each other, often determining whether and how subsequent decisions are made. They also are informed by a number of factors, especially the victim's judgment of the seriousness of the offense. This chapter discusses the importance of these influential victim decisions based on victimology research that has identified patterns in victim decision making and the factors that influence these decisions.

Acknowledgment of Criminal Victimization

As noted above, victim acknowledgment describes the decision made by a victim to recognize or label an experience as a crime and identity himself or herself as a crime victim. Conversely, those who do not acknowledge that they have been victimized are referred to as ***unacknowledged victims*** (Koss & Oros, 1980). According to Greenberg and Ruback (1992), acknowledging victimization and labeling the event as a crime is one of three major stages in victim decision making. They explain that "In order for individuals to label themselves as victims of a crime, they must perceive that they are or have been the target of a criminal action" (Greenberg & Ruback, 1992, p. 185). To do so, victims' own definitions of crime must match their experience. For example, imagine that you return home from class and find that your door has been forced open and many of your valuables are missing. More than likely you would conclude that you have been the victim of a burglary. This is because your experience fits your definition of what a burglary entails. Now consider a different scenario: You are receiving repeated unwanted and threatening phone calls from an ex-boyfriend or ex-girlfriend that make you fear for your safety. In legal terms, you are a victim of stalking, but if you do not recognize or label your pursuer's behavior as such, you are an unacknowledged victim.

Victim acknowledgment has been studied extensively as it relates to victims of sexual crimes, and other offenses, such as stalking, to a lesser degree. The stimulus for studying victim acknowledgment can be traced in part to the pioneering work of Mary Koss and colleagues' ***Sexual Experiences Survey*** (SES). The SES investigated the extent, nature, and measurement of rape victimization among college women in the United States. In one influential study using the SES, Koss and her co-researchers

Christine Gidycz, and Nadine Wisniewski (1987) reported that seven in 10 women who met the criteria for being labeled rape victims did not define their experience as a rape. This raised questions about both the prevalence of rape, as well as why those who had been raped did not see themselves as victims or their experience as a rape. Researchers have since reported levels of unacknowledged rape victimization similar to those found by Koss and colleagues (e.g., Pitts & Schwartz, 1993), but other sexual victimization research has reported much higher levels of acknowledgment among victims (e.g., Bondurant, 2001), which could be due in part to decades of efforts to raise awareness.

Victimization acknowledgment research has concentrated on identifying the characteristics of individuals as well as the circumstances surrounding the victimization that influence victim acknowledgment. This research suggests that victims are more likely to acknowledge their criminal victimization if it meets certain criteria, which are often stereotypical or even based in myths. To illustrate, take a moment to think of the "typical" rape. You likely considered a scenario referred to as the ***classic rape paradigm*** in which a young female is violently attacked by a stranger in a public place (e.g., an empty street or parking lot) at night (e.g., Williams, 1984). Research has found that victims whose experience is similar to the classic rape paradigm are more likely to acknowledge their rape, whereas a victim raped by a friend after a party, for example, will not necessarily label the experience as a rape because it falls outside the classic rape paradigm. Some researchers have suggested that the classic rape paradigm reflects individuals' commonly held definitions of rape, which makes it easier for the victim to label the experience as rape when it occurs under these circumstances. When the characteristics of the event fall outside that paradigm, victims are not reminded of their definition and are therefore less likely to label the event as a rape (Greenberg & Ruback, 1992).

Researchers studying rape victimization have identified several characteristics that influence whether a victim sees herself as a rape victim. While males can certainly be victims of rape, the remaining discussion focuses on female victims because they constitute the vast majority of rape victims. Characteristics of the victim, of the offender, of their respective behavior during the incident, and of the situation all can influence the victim's assessment of the experience. As an example, a study by Bonnie Fisher, Leah Daigle, Francis Cullen, and Michael Turner (2003a) identified factors that significantly influenced whether female rape victims considered an incident to be rape. The research team reported that if the offender actually used or threatened to use physical force, or penetrated the victim, she was more likely to consider the event as a rape. The researchers also found other important influences on acknowledgment, including injury to the victim (beyond penetration), presence of a weapon, prior sexual victimization, victim use of forceful verbal resistance, how recently the incident occurred, and the victim's age. Many of these characteristics are factors commonly associated with rape, making them somewhat stereotypical. Interestingly, the relationship between the victim and offender did not influence acknowledgment as predicted by the classic rape paradigm. This may reflect the effects of educating individuals about date and acquaintance rape.

Recent research also has explored the extent of, and influences on, acknowledgment among victims of stalking. For example, a study by Carol Jordan, Pamela Wilcox, and Adam Pritchard (2007) reported that less than half (42%) of college student stalking victims in their study acknowledged their incidents as stalking. A study by Christine Englebrecht and Bradford Reyns (2011) used the National Crime Victimization Survey (NCVS) stalking supplement to explore victim acknowledgment among adult victims of stalking in the United States. They found that approximately 40% of victims viewed the event as stalking, which suggests a similarly high percentage of unacknowledged victims when compared to rape victimization. In these two studies, stereotypical stalking criteria—what Jordan and associates (2007, p. 565) referred to as a "classic stalking paradigm"— also were reported to influence victimization acknowledgment. Jordan and colleagues reported that a victim who was fearful and experienced multiple pursuit behaviors was more likely to view the situation as stalking. Englebrecht and Reyns (2011) also found that fear affected acknowledgment, but only among women. Other characteristics, such as being attacked, losing time at work, and different types of pursuit behaviors employed by the offender (e.g., cyberstalking, phone calls, being spied on), positively influenced victim acknowledgment. For example, those who were cyberstalked in addition to being physically stalked were twice as likely to acknowledge their victimization compared to those who were not cyberstalked.

Victims' decisions to acknowledge that they have been criminally victimized are important for several reasons. First, unacknowledged victims may be more likely to be revictimized. As Chapter 9 explained, past victimization is a consistent predictor of future victimization, and those who do not acknowledge their own victimization or report the incident may be more attractive targets for offenders. Second, acknowledgment is the first link in the chain of events leading to reporting the crime to law enforcement (Greenberg & Ruback, 1992). For many crimes, such as rape and stalking, it is unlikely the police will make contact with the offender or investigate the crime without the victim first reporting it to them. Third, not all victims who label their experience as a crime will report crime to the law enforcement. Many will keep the matter private, seek help from friends or family, or find another method of coping with their victimization. It is to the reporting decision that our attention now turns.

Reporting Decisions

The ***reporting decisions*** of crime victims determine whether the criminal justice system will be invoked to respond to the crime. These decisions have been studied from two perspectives: the decision *to* report the victimization to law enforcement and the decision to *not* report the victimization. Researchers have identified patterns in these two decisions and developed explanations for why the patterns both exist and persist. In other words, the crux of much of this research is seeking to explain why victims either do or do not contact the authorities. As is the case with the research surrounding victimization acknowledgment, many but not all of these studies have concentrated on reporting decisions by victims of personal crime, notably rape and sexual assault.

Decisions to Report Victimization

Victim reporting decisions have been studied fairly extensively using victimization surveys such as the NCVS, which ask respondents whether their victimization was reported to the police, as well as about the factors that influenced this decision. Based on the NCVS, it appears that at most 50% of the crimes that are committed in the United States are reported to the police. However, whether a crime is reported depends on several factors, especially the type of crime. For example, in the 2012 NCVS approximately 44% of all violent victimizations and 33% of property victimizations were reported to police (NCVS Data Analysis Tool, 2014). The percentage of crimes reported by crime type is presented in Table 10-1. The findings presented in the table make clear that aggravated assault is the offense with the highest reporting percentage. Theft has the lowest, yet still close to one third of thefts were reported to the police.

To further illustrate the prevalence of the decision to report crimes to the police, Figure 10-1 depicts the reporting behaviors of crime victims from 1973 to 2000, comparing the total number of serious violent crimes found in the NCVS, to those reported to the police, and those recorded in the UCR. The figure indicates that there is substantially more serious violence committed than is either reported to the police or recorded by them. The figure also suggests that while serious violent crime declined steeply throughout the 1990s, a corresponding decline in reporting also occurred. Using NCS and NCVS data, criminologists Eric Baumer and Janet Lauritsen (2010) examined victim reporting in the United States from 1973 to 2005. They found that during this period, reporting rates for sexual assaults, other forms of violence, and property victimization, which are traditionally lower compared to other crimes, significantly increased over time.

Table 10-1: Violent and Property Victimizations Reported to the Police, 2012

Type of Crime	Percent Reported
Violent Crime	44.2%
Serious Violent Crime	54.4%
Rape/Sexual Assault	28.2%
Robbery	55.9%
Aggravated Assault	62.4%
Simple Assault	39.7%
Personal Theft/Larceny	46.2%
Property Crime	33.5%
Burglary	54.8%
Motor Vehicle Theft	78.6%
Theft	26.4%

Generated using the NCVS Victimization Analysis Tool at http://www.bjs.gov, July 16, 2014.
Source: NCVS Victimization Analysis Tool (2014).

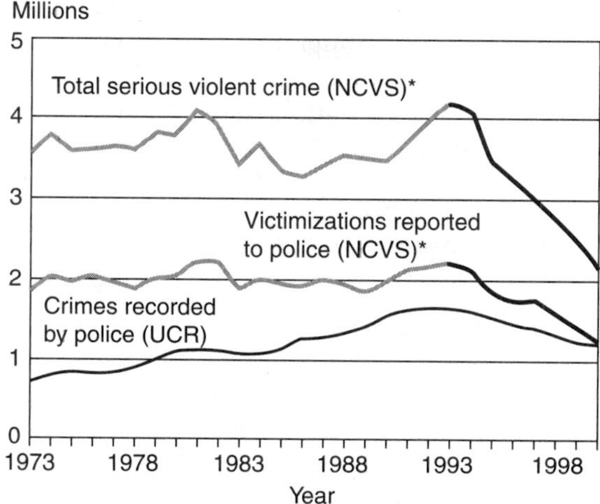

Figure 10-1 A Comparison of NCVS Serious Violent Crime Estimates to Victimizations Reported to Crimes Recorded by Police
Source: Hart and Rennison (2003).

Beyond the extent of victim reporting, certain patterns also are evident in the circumstances under which crimes are reported to law enforcement. First, as discussed, violent crime is more likely to be reported than is property crime. Second, victim characteristics play a role in determining whether violence is reported. For example, violence perpetrated against females and the elderly is more likely to be reported than is violence against males or young people. Third, victim reporting also is influenced by the situational characteristics of the criminal event. For instance, offenses are more often reported if the victim perceived the offender to be under the influence of drugs or alcohol, if the offender was armed, or if the victim was injured. Fourth, offender characteristics affect reporting as well, particularly the relationship between the victim and offender. Crimes committed by strangers are more often reported to the police than are crimes committed by nonstrangers. Explaining these patterns is crucial for both victimologists and criminologists, and they have conducted a great deal of research aimed at doing so.

Gottfredson and Gottfredson (1990), for example, developed a theory to explain what they referred to as rational decision making throughout the criminal justice process. Their ***theory of criminal justice decision making*** recognizes that many discretionary decisions are made throughout the criminal justice process, including those by victims, police officers, prosecutors, and so on. Their theory contends that regardless of the decision point in the system—from initial reporting, to arrest, to charging, to sentencing, to release—the same three factors persistently influence how decisions are made: the offense's seriousness, the victim–offender relationship, and the offender's prior criminal history.

According to the theory, these three factors heavily influence *all* criminal justice decisions, although depending on the stage in the process other factors also may be at work. While this theory was not developed exclusively to explain victim reporting decisions, it provides a useful framework for interpreting the results of studies of victim reporting. The theory is also compatible with the idea behind the classic rape paradigm and the labeling process described previously: Victims are more likely to acknowledge and report their victimization(s) to law enforcement if they see themselves as victims (Greenberg & Ruback, 1992; Williams, 1984).

The Seriousness of the Offense

Offense seriousness also was identified by Greenberg and Ruback (1992) as the second of their three major stages in victim decision making. They argued that seriousness is primarily determined by (1) the extent victims feel wronged and (2) the degree they consider themselves vulnerable to future victimization(s). In other words, victims who feel a greater sense of injustice or unfairness and/or think they might be victimized again are more likely to consider the incident to be serious and therefore report it. Greenberg and Ruback explained that victims who are unexpectedly victimized (i.e., victimized by someone they know and trust), who perceive their suffering to be great (e.g., a burglar steals valuables *and* destroys other items not stolen), and who, in retrospect, can imagine how they might have easily avoided the victimization (rather than feeling grateful that the injury was not worse) see themselves as having suffered a greater wrong and view the event as more serious (Greenberg & Ruback, 1992).

Consistent with Gottfredson and Gottfredson (1990) and Greenberg and Ruback (1992), studies of victim reporting decisions collectively suggest that one of the primary influences on reporting decisions is the seriousness of the offense. For instance, in one of the earliest studies of victim reporting, Michael Hindelang (1974) examined whether grocery store and drugstore management reported internal theft by employees to the police. Using data collected in 1963, 1965, and 1968, Hindelang reported that the value of the stolen items was the most important factor in explaining this decision, with higher-value items representing a more serious loss to the company (see also Gottfredson & Hindelang, 1979; Skogan, 1976).

More recent studies have uncovered similar findings with respect to offense seriousness. In one of these studies, Ronet Bachman (1998) used the NCVS to examine factors related to the likelihood that adult female victims of rape reported their victimization to the police. The study found that two dimensions of offense seriousness were significantly related to the rape being reported: if the victim suffered physical injuries (beyond penetration) and if the offender used a weapon during the event. The presence of either of these factors increased the probability that the crime would be reported to the police by over two times. Studies of victim reporting conducted outside the United States also find that offense seriousness is a major determinant of victim reporting. For example, Lening Zhang, Steven Messner, and Jianhong Liu (2007) analyzed victimization data collected in Tianjin, China. They found that for victims of robbery, assault, personal theft, and burglary, the most consistent predictor of victim reporting was the seriousness of the offense. In a study of victim reporting in Canada, Caroline Akers and Catherine Kaukinen (2009) analyzed data from the General Social Survey to identify the factors that influenced the reporting decisions of victims of intimate partner violence (IPV). They reported that victim and situational characteristics influenced reporting, notably the presence of children, spousal drinking, use of a weapon, damage or destruction of property, and injury to the victim. These situational characteristics arguably make the offense more severe or serious, adding further support to Gottfredson and Gottfredson's (1990) theory (see also Reyns & Englebrecht, 2010; Tarling & Morris, 2010).

The Relationship Between the Victim and the Offender

As predicted by the theory of criminal justice decision making, the relationship between the victim and the offender also has been identified as an important influence on the decision to report. Specifically, victims are more likely to contact the law enforcement if they were victimized by strangers. For example, Richard Felson and Paul-Philippe Paré (2005) used the NCVS to examine the factors that influenced reporting decisions of victims of IPV and sexual assault. They found that victims were less likely to report if the offender was a partner, other family member, or someone they knew, as compared to their likelihood of reporting victimization by strangers. This study also underscores the importance of offense seriousness in explaining the decision to report. In another study to investigate this issue, Bonnie Fisher, Leah Daigle, Francis Cullen, and Michael Turner (2003b) examined data from the National College Women Sexual Victimization Study. They reported that college students who had been victims of sexual assault were significantly more likely to contact the police when the offender was a stranger. This relationship also held true in victims' decisions to contact campus authorities, reinforcing the importance of the victim–offender relationship in victim decision making (see also Gartner & Macmillan, 1995). Fisher and colleagues also identified offense seriousness (primarily the presence of a weapon) and whether victims considered the incident to be a rape (victim acknowledgment) as significant predictors of reporting.

The Offender's Criminal History

The third and final component of Gottfredson and Gottfredson's (1990) theory that explains criminal justice decision making is the offender's criminal history. While this factor may be more influential at some stages of the criminal process (e.g., sentencing) than others (e.g., reporting), it still has been shown to influence the victim's decision to contact the police. For instance, victims who know their offender and know that he or she has a criminal record may view the offender as more threatening or dangerous, increasing the likelihood of reporting (e.g., Felson, Messner, Hoskin, & Deane, 2002). Reyns and Englebrecht (2010) tested this theoretical hypothesis by using data from the stalking supplement to the NCVS. They reported that victims who knew the offender had a prior criminal record were more than twice as likely to contact the police. Besides this study, little research has examined this component of Gottfredson and Gottfredson's theory as it applies to victims. Overall, however, in explaining why victims decide to contact law enforcement, the seriousness of the offense, characterized by presence of a weapon and/or injury to the victim, appears to be the most influential predictor of victim reporting.

Decisions to Not Report Victimization

It is just as important to explain why some victims do not report their victimizations to law enforcement as it is to explain why they do. The majority of crimes committed are *not* reported to the police according to the NCVS. A recent NCVS report examining victim non-reporting between 2006 and 2010 indicates that 58% of all victimizations, 52% of all violent victimizations, and 60% of all household property victimizations were *not* reported to the police. This means that an average of over 3.3 million violent victimizations went unreported annually during this period (Langton, Berzofsky, Krebs, & Smiley-McDonald, 2012). The reasons for non-reporting are varied and differ by crime type.

The same NCVS report also provides insights into why those who were criminally victimized decided not to contact law enforcement. Figure 10-2 displays the most important reasons uncovered by the NCVS concerning why crime victims did not report their victimization(s) to police. The most common response given by victims was that they considered the incident to be a "personal matter" and dealt with it in some other way (34%). In other words, victims did not want to involve the police. The second most frequently given reason for not contacting the police was that it was "not important enough" to the victim to do so (18%). Another frequent response was that the victim believed the police "would not or could not help them" (16%). Finally, many victims did not report because they "feared reprisal" from the offender or "getting the offender into trouble" (13%).

The reasons for victims not reporting their victimization to police differ depending on the type of victimization that has occurred. For example, a victim's decision to not report rape victimization to the police is likely very different than another victim's decision to not report robbery victimization, an argument supported by the information presented in Table 10-2. Table 10-2 includes NCVS data on victimizations not reported to the police for several types of crime as well as the most

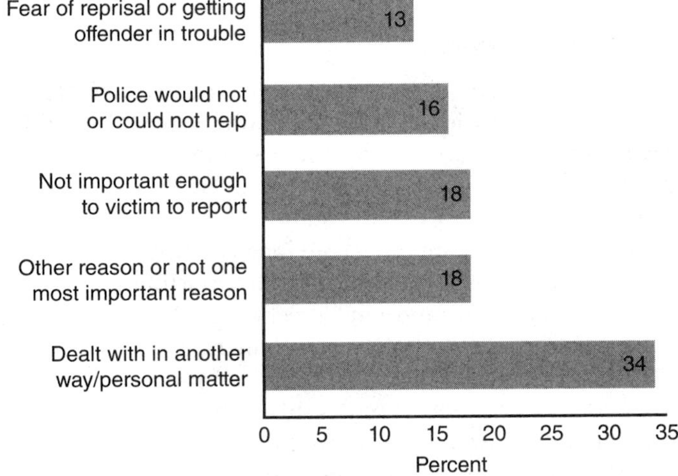

Figure 10-2 Most Important Reasons for Not Reporting Violent Victimization to the Police
Source: Langton et al. (2012).

Table 10-2: Reasons for Not Reporting by Crime Type

			Most Important Reason Victimizations Went Unreported				
Type of Crime	Average Annual Number Not Reported*	Percent Not Reported	Dealt with in Another Way/ Personal Matter	Not Important Enough to Victim to Report	Police Would Not or Could Not Help	Fear of Reprisal or Getting Offender in Trouble	Other Reason or Not one Most Important Reason
Total crime	13,998,600	58%	20%	27%	31%	5%	17%
Violent	3,382,200	52%	34%	18%	16%	13%	18%
Serious violent	1,016,000	46	25	13	21	19	21
Rape/sexual assault	211,200	65	20	6	13	28	33
Robbery	297,100	41	20	13	34	10	23
Aggravated assault	507,700	44	31	16	17	22	15
Simple assault	2,366,200	56	38	21	14	11	17
Personal larceny	69,200	41%	17%	24%	43%	2%!	14%
Household property	10,547,200	60%	15%	30%	36%	3%	16%
Burglary	1,584,700	45	12	27	40	4	17
Motor vehicle theft	140,600	17	16	26	30	7	21
Theft	8,821,900	67	16	31	35	3	16

*Rounded to the nearest hundred.
! Interpret with caution; estimate based on 10 or fewer sample cases, or coefficient of variation is greater than 50%.
Source: Langton et al. (2012).

important reason victims gave for why they did not report. Among the important points presented in the table is the finding that rapes and sexual assaults are *the* most unreported crimes. For this reason, much of the research into victim non-reporting decisions has focused on not reporting sexual victimization.

One of the most common responses victims gave for not reporting sexual victimizations was that they feared reprisal or getting the offender into trouble (28%). This finding reinforces the effect that the victim–offender relationship has on reporting. On the other hand, about 40% of victims of robbery decided not to contact the police, providing as the primary reason that the police either would not or could not help them (34%).

As previously noted, much of the research into non-reporting of criminal victimization comes from studies of rape and sexual assault. In Fisher and colleagues' (2003b) study of sexual victimization among college women, only 5% of victims of a completed rape reported the crime to the police. The most common reason given for not reporting was that it was "not serious enough" to report. Other frequently chosen reasons included the following: the victim was not sure that harm was intended; the victim did not want other people to know; the victim lacked proof that the incident happened; and the victim was afraid of reprisal. Similar findings have been replicated in other studies of non-reporting among victims of sexual offenses, but research by Amy Cohn and colleagues (2013) indicates that reasons for not reporting sexual victimization may depend on the tactics used by offenders. Their study considered two types of rape: forcible rape and drug- or alcohol-facilitated/incapacitated rape. They found that *criminal justice–related concerns*, such as lack of proof, not knowing how to report, and fear of being treated badly by criminal justice officials, predicted non-reporting of both forcible rape and drug- or alcohol-facilitated/incapacitated rape. However, among victims of the latter type of offense, unacknowledged victimization was a significant factor in not contacting the police. This suggests victims who had been drinking or were incapacitated viewed the experience differently than those who were forcibly raped, and that view affects reporting behaviors.

Research also has examined victim non-reporting decisions among victims of nonsexual crimes. One such study found very different reasons why these offenses went unreported. Recent work by Mark Berg, Lee Ann Slocum, and Rolf Loeber (2013) used data from the Pittsburgh Youth Survey, a long-term study into the causes and consequences of delinquency and mental health problems among juveniles, to determine the circumstances under which victims of robbery or assault notified the police of their victimization. Similar to the findings of previous research, offenses in which the victim was injured or a weapon was involved were more likely to result in police notification. Yet, interestingly enough, one of the strongest predictors of non-reporting was that the *victim* was involved in criminal offending in some manner. Victims who self-reported they had committed crimes in the past year were less likely to notify the police of their own victimization. Recall from Chapter 3 that the victim–offender overlap explains that there is a link between criminal behavior and subsequent victimization. While further research is needed, evidence suggests that the victim–offender overlap also affects victims' decisions on whether to report the crime to the police.

Whether victims decide to report or not report their victimization to the police has important collateral consequences. For example, scholars and practitioners alike have expressed concern that the criminal justice system is less effective when victims decide not to report crimes to the police. One of the principles of modern policing is that the police and the community work together to prevent and respond to crime. This philosophy is undercut when victims decide not to contact the police, leaving the possibility that many crimes will go unsolved and, hence, offenders are not held responsible for their criminal behaviors. Relatedly, modern criminal justice systems throughout the world are premised on the assumption that crime can be deterred. ***Deterrence theory*** states that the greater the probability of offenders receiving certain, severe, and swift punishment, the more likely they are to abstain from criminal behavior in the future. Therefore, if victims decide not to invoke the criminal justice system by calling the police, the possibility of deterring offenders is lost. For example, if a victim of IPV does not report her victimization to the police, the offender may reason that he can safely assault her again because he will not be punished for his criminal behavior. For the victim's part, she may fear reprisals from the offender or feel that the police will not believe her. Research by Richard Felson, Jeffrey Ackerman, and Catherine Gallagher (2005), however, indicates that reporting domestic assaults has a moderately strong deterrent effect against future domestic violence. It is also possible that victims will not obtain much-needed services to help them recover from their victimization if the offense is not reported to the police.

The previously reviewed material demonstrates that many victims of crime decide not to report their victimization to the police because they dealt with the matter in some other way. It may be that these victims adopted some form of self-protection during or after the criminal event and therefore did not think it was necessary to report the crime. These self-protection decisions are discussed in the next section.

Self-Protection Decisions

During and following a criminal victimization, victims often engage in self-protective behaviors. ***Self-protection*** refers to behaviors that victims take to stop or prevent victimization or avoid injury during the course of a crime. Depending on the circumstances and the crime in question, victims may resist the offender in a variety of ways. For example, the self-protective behaviors included in the NCVS range from offering no resistance to threatening or attacking the offender with a firearm. Based on recent NCVS data, a slight majority (56%) of crime victims indicated they offered resistance to the offender in some form, although about 44% of victims did not resist. Table 10-3 provides the percentages for different types of victim self-protection and whether the offense was a violent crime or a property crime. The table indicates that for both violent and property crimes included in the NCVS between 2007 and 2011, the most common reaction was for victims to offer no resistance; however, of those who did resist, the most often used method of resistance involved nonconfrontational tactics, such as yelling, running, or arguing. Victims of violent crimes threatened or attacked their offender without a weapon in about 22% of incidents. Although less often adopted, victims also threatened or attacked them with a firearm or with some other weapon, or resisted in some other way.

During a crime, victims must make split-second decisions not only whether to try to thwart the offender, but also as to which tactic has the greatest likelihood of succeeding. Depending on the type of crime and what the victim decides to do, offering resistance to an offender could be a dangerous proposition. The concern here is that resistance could prompt an attack that otherwise would not have occurred or lead to greater injury to the victim. Much of the research that has explored these issues has used data from the NCVS and considered different types of victim resistance in terms of its effects on crime completion and victim injury. Broadly

Table 10-3: Self-Protective Behaviors by Crime Type

	Violent Crime		Property Crime	
Self-protective Behavior	Number	Percent	Number	Percent
Total	29,618,300	100%	84,495,500	100%
Offered no resistance	12,987,300	43.8	10,162,000	12.0
Threatened or attacked with a firearm	235,700	0.8	103,000	0.1
Threatened or attacked with other weapon	391,100	1.3	38,200	–
Threatened or attacked without a weapon	6,552,900	22.1	421,300	0.5
Nonconfrontational tactics[a]	7,768,700	26.2	1,187,100	1.4
Other	1,641,300	5.5	223,400	0.3
Unknown	41,300	0.1	12,200!	–
Victim was not present[b]	~	~	72,348,200	85.6

! Interpret with caution. Estimate based on 10 or fewer sample cases, or coefficient of variation is greater than 50%.
~ Not applicable.
– Less than 0.05%.
[a] Includes yelling, running, or arguing.
[b] Includes property crime where the victim was not present.
Source: Planty and Truman (2013).

speaking, self-protection behaviors have been categorized as *forceful physical* (e.g., struggling, fighting back), *forceful verbal* (e.g., shouting for help, screaming), *non-forceful physical* (e.g., running, hiding), and *non-forceful verbal* (e.g., crying, pleading) or simply as physical or verbal (e.g., Santana, 2007). The results on the effectiveness of these self-protection behaviors have not been uniform across studies because researchers have used data from different time periods, different populations, and for different types of crimes. This has led to some controversy as to the best course of action for would-be crime victims.

Early research often found that victim self-protection through resistance, either physical or verbal, increased the likelihood that victims would suffer injuries (e.g., Lizotte, 1986; Skogan & Block, 1983). So, too, recent research has found that self-protection can result in victim injury, depending on the crime and how the victim resists. A recent study that did not use the NCVS examined the relationship between the use of self-protection and victim injuries sustained in domestic violence crimes among a sample of women who were incarcerated at the time of their participation in the study. Ráchael Powers and Sally Simpson (2012) reported that 80% of the incidents in their study involved victim self-protective behaviors of some kind, 55% of which were forceful verbal in nature. Their results also indicated that forceful physical resistance increased the likelihood of victim injury; however, non-forceful verbal self-protection decreased the odds of injury by 65%. These findings suggest that the form the victim's resistance takes affects victim injury, but the type of victimization is also an important factor to consider.

A study by Fisher and colleagues (2007) examined the effects of victim self-protection tactics on different types of sexual victimization, including rape, sexual coercion, unwanted sexual contact with force, and unwanted sexual contact without force. They found that any form of resistance decreased the likelihood of the victimization being completed, but that some types of resistance were more effective than others. For instance, forceful physical resistance to rape decreased the probability that the rape would be completed to 50%, whereas non-forceful physical resistance lowered the likelihood by 58%; using both tactics was most effective, with only 23% of rapes being completed. However, these tactics were generally less effective in unwanted sexual contact with force offenses.

One of the problematic issues with this research is that it is difficult to take into account whether injuries were sustained by victims *during* or *after* victims offered resistance to the offender's attack. An influential study that was able to make this distinction was conducted by Jongyeon Tark and Gary Kleck (2004). They examined NCVS data from 1992 to 2001 and found that self-protection behaviors by crime victims, both forceful and non-forceful, were effective at reducing the likelihood of injury and property loss. For example, they reported that only 3% of victims who resisted in personal contact crimes were injured after offering that resistance. Tark and Kleck also found that in instances where victims were injured after resisting, it was usually something minor such as scrapes or bruises. Overall, they concluded that "victim resistance is usually either successful or inconsequential, and on the rare occasions that it is harmful, it is rarely seriously so" (Tark & Kleck, 2004, p. 902). There is certainly evidence from other studies to the contrary (e.g., Bachman, Saltzman, Thompson, & Carmody, 2002), but the results of Tark and Kleck's study suggest that in general victims should resist an offender's assault (see also Kleck & Tark, 2004; Ullman, 2007).

Although there is not necessarily a theory of victim self-protection decisions, an underlying theoretical idea from the opportunity theories discussed in Chapters 2 and 3 is that self-protection behaviors reduce opportunities for criminal victimization and should therefore reduce crime. Rob Guerette and Shannon Santana (2010) used NCVS data spanning the period 1992 to 2004 to investigate whether victim resistance decreased the likelihood that the crime would be completed, using opportunity theory as their framework to test hypotheses. They explained that three opportunity theories are useful in anticipating the effects of victim resistance: routine activities theory, rational choice theory, and situational crime prevention. These three theories are discussed in detail elsewhere in the text, but they are briefly addressed here with respect to victim resistance.

First, routine activities theory indicates that three elements culminate to create opportunities for victimization: motivated offenders, suitable targets, and absent or ineffective guardianship. Interpreting self-protective behaviors through this lens suggests that victim resistance should make targets less suitable or attractive in addition to being more guarded. Second, rational choice theory argues that individuals consider the possible risks and rewards of their behaviors before acting. Victim resistance potentially makes the risks greater while simultaneously reducing the rewards, or making them no longer worth the effort. Third and relatedly, situational crime prevention, which is presented in Chapter 14, provides crime- and situation-specific means for reducing criminal opportunities. According to situational crime prevention, increasing the effort and the risk involved in committing a particular offense, while also reducing the expected rewards, eliminates opportunities for crime and makes victimization less likely. Therefore, victims who resist are effectively increasing the effort required of the offender and the risk to the offender while also making the crime less rewarding. Guerette and Santana found support for this theoretical rationale, reporting that victims who resisted reduced the likelihood that the crime would be completed by up to 93%. All victim resistance was effective at reducing opportunities, but threatening to use a weapon against the offender had the most significant impact on preventing the crime (see also Kleck & Gertz, 1995).

The preceding discussion makes clear that most of the research that has been conducted into victim self-protection decisions has examined the extent of victim resistance and the effectiveness of the decision rather than explaining why victims resist. After all, the assumption is that victims resist because they do not want the offender to complete the crime. The final victim decision to consider is victim help seeking.

Help-Seeking Decisions

Many crime victims engage in ***help-seeking decisions*** by soliciting advice or assistance in response to their victimization as a means of coping with and overcoming the event. The help that is sought can be from a formal or informal source. The formal aspects of help seeking involve contacting law enforcement to report that a crime has occurred. As was previously discussed, only about half of crimes are reported to the police, although the prevalence of reporting varies by crime type. Just as frequently or sometimes more frequently, victims seek help from more informal sources, especially their family and friends.

Research into victims' informal help-seeking decisions has concentrated on describing its prevalence, as well as identifying factors that determine whether victims will seek help. For example, in a study using data from the National Violence Against Women Survey (NVAWS, see Chapter 4), Kaukinen (2004) reported that about 52% of female victims of sexual assault, physical assault, stalking, and threats of violence sought help from family or friends. This same study found that victims also contacted psychiatrists or doctors (20%), social service agencies (5%), or the police (30%) for help. Recall that Fisher and colleagues (2003b) reported that only 5% of rape victims in their study contacted the police, and considering all types of sexual victimization in the study, victims reported the crime to the police for only 2% of incidents and only 3% reported their victimization to campus authorities. Yet, a substantial portion of victims—close to 70%—told someone else about the event, such as a family member or close friend.

In another study that estimated the prevalence of help seeking, Ann Coker and her colleagues (2000) found that 87% of female victims of IPV sought help from a source other than the police. The most frequent resources for these victims to turn to were friends (74%), family members (69%), therapists (45%), doctors or nurses (36%), support groups (16%), domestic violence shelter staff (11%), or someone at the health department (7%). Interestingly, on average over 80% of victims found the source to be helpful. Coker and her fellow researchers also reported that the prevalence of help-seeking behaviors was different for victims of IPV in comparison to rape victims, and that help seeking was significantly more common for female than male victims. Other research has also reported that gender is a predictor of help-seeking behaviors among crime victims (e.g., Kaukinen, 2004). Age, ethnicity, and marital status also have been found to influence these help-seeking decisions, with older, white, and single or divorced persons being more likely to seek mental health services compared to others (McCart, Smith, & Sawyer, 2010).

Other important influences on help seeking include the seriousness or severity of the crime, the type of crime, the psychological response of the victim, and whether victims receive support from family and friends. Regarding these relationships, those who judge the injury they have incurred as a result of the crime to be serious are more apt to decide that they need assistance in dealing with their victimization. Similarly, individuals who suffer psychological consequences as a result of their victimization, such as posttraumatic stress disorder, are also more likely to seek help (McCart et al., 2010). For instance, Betty Jo Barrett and Melissa St. Pierre (2011) used data from the General Social Survey to study help-seeking decisions among female victims of IPV in Canada. They reported that women who feared for their lives were significantly more likely to seek help from formal *and* informal sources. Finally, Greenberg and Ruback (1992) explained that talking with someone (e.g., a friend) may help victims to sort out the experience, leading to a higher likelihood of acknowledgment of victimization, and further help seeking. For example, victims of IPV may be more likely to consult a therapist or attend a support group if a family member has advised them to do so.

The importance of informal social networks in helping victims extends beyond listening and providing some sort of support. An emerging development in victimology has been to advocate that third parties get involved and intervene to prevent crimes, especially violent crimes. This approach to victimization prevention, called ***bystander intervention***, suggests that even strangers should intervene on behalf of those who are being or may become crime victims. The decisions of these individuals to intervene to prevent victimization are discussed in the chapter's final pages.

Bystander Intervention Decisions

One of the primary reasons that victimologists study the circumstances under which victimization occurs is so that evidence-based prevention strategies can be developed and implemented. Recently, research has shown that bystander intervention can be an effective means for preventing victimization. However, the challenge is in fostering a sense of responsibility to stop others from becoming victims and prompting bystanders to act. Therefore, to prevent victimization, bystander intervention studies have focused on understanding *why* some individuals act while others do not. Much of this research was prompted by the stabbing murder of Catherine Susan "Kitty" Genovese in New York City in 1964. Following the murder, the *New York*

Times published a story about the case indicating that there were 38 witnesses to the attack, but none intervened to stop the crime (Darley & Latané, 1968)—although there has been considerable debate over the veracity of this claim. Regardless of what exactly happened that day in 1964, social psychologists and other researchers became intrigued with studying why people might not help in such a situation.

The consensus among researchers is that ***bystander intervention decisions*** are influenced by many factors that can be generally divided into five conceptual categories (Box 10-1). First, bystanders feel less of an obligation to help when there are more people present. This situation, referred to as *diffusion of responsibility*, proposes that when there are more people present the responsibility to act is shared. In other words, "Someone else will shoulder the responsibility to help, so why should I?" Second, *evaluation apprehension* implies that bystanders do not act because they are afraid of how they will be viewed by others. For example, if your professor asks the class a question to which you know the answer, but you do not want to raise your hand and be "in the spotlight" and potentially be viewed by peers as "sucking up" to the professor, you may be feeling evaluation apprehension. Third, bystanders may not act because of *pluralistic ignorance.* With pluralistic ignorance in bystander intervention situations, the bystander may feel that intervening is the right thing to do, but decides it must not be appropriate because no one else is helping. Fourth, bystanders may not be confident in their ability to render assistance, or with their *confidence in their skills* to successfully intervene. For example, a diner in a restaurant may not try to help someone close by who is choking because he is unsure of how to perform the Heimlich maneuver. Fifth and finally, individuals are more likely to intervene if they have previously observed intervention behaviors that can be

Box 10-1: Influences on Bystander Intervention Decisions

Influential Factors	Explanation
1. *Diffusion of Responsibility*	• Individuals are less likely to intervene if there are more bystanders present, because they feel less of a sense of responsibility.
2. *Evaluation Apprehension*	• Individuals are less likely to intervene if they believe they will be judged or appear foolish if they make a mistake.
3. *Pluralistic Ignorance*	• Individuals will look for cues from other bystanders as to the appropriate course of action and decide whether to respond based on those cues.
4. *Confidence in Skills*	• Individuals are more likely to respond if they possess skills that are appropriate to the situation and believe they can help.
5. *Modeling*	• Individuals are more likely to intervene if someone models appropriate bystander behaviors first.

Sources: Coker et al. (2011); Darley and Latané (1968).

modeled. *Modeling* is one of the premises of bystander intervention programs that teach individuals how to diffuse high-risk situations to prevent victimization.

The prevention of sexual victimization has been a major focus of bystander intervention research, especially recent approaches that advocate bystander intervention to prevent sexual victimization among college women. Programs designed to address this specific type of victimization have looked beyond individual-level correlates of victimization, such as alcohol use by the victim and/or offender, and focused on more community-level contributors to the problem (Banyard, Plante, & Moynihan, 2004). Research indicates that sexual victimization is more likely to occur in college campus communities in which social norms are tolerant of sexual victimization or violence against women. For example, acceptance of rape myths, tolerance of violence against women, and patriarchal attitudes may foster an environment that is conducive to sexual victimization (Schwartz & DeKeseredy, 1997). From this perspective, bystander intervention strategies should focus on changing attitudes and creating new social norms that do not condone victimization. Although the bystander approach to prevention has been applied to sexual victimization, it also could be effective for preventing other types of personal victimization, such as bullying, IPV, and child abuse.

Research on bystander intervention programs suggests that these programs increase bystanders' willingness to intervene. For example, Ann Coker and colleagues (2011) evaluated the effects of a program called Green Dot designed to address issues that inhibit bystanders from intervening while also teaching students to evaluate situations and risk factors for violence. They (2011, p. 5) summed up the Green Dot philosophy by explaining that "Understanding how perpetrators target victims allows the bystander to assess the situation, view their options for action, and select safe active bystander behaviors that they are willing to carry out." Green Dot consisted of a motivational speech explaining the nature of sexual violence on college campuses, with elements designed to persuade students to take an active role in preventing such incidents. The program also contained a training component called Students Educating and Empowering to Develop Safety (SEEDS), which taught students how to effectively and safely intervene to prevent violence. Coker and associates concluded that among their sample of University of Kentucky undergraduates, those exposed to Green Dot reported that they engaged in more active bystander behaviors than students who were not exposed to the program. The study could not determine whether Green Dot reduced sexual victimization on campus among students, but if bystander intervention reduces violence as expected, then this may be the case.

Summary

Victims play an important role in the criminal justice process. Their decisions relating to victimization acknowledgment, reporting their victimization to police, choosing whether to resist, the self-protection actions taken to do so, and seeking help after the victimization have implications not only for the victims themselves, but the criminal justice process. According to Gottfredson and Gottfredson's (1990) theory of criminal justice decision making, victim decisions on how to respond to a victimization are heavily influenced by the seriousness of the offense, the relationship between victim and offender, and the offender's criminal history. The research reviewed throughout this chapter indicates that the theory is especially useful in understanding victims' decisions to report or not report the crime to law enforcement.

Victims also make important decisions during and after the criminal event, notably those involving self-protection and whether to seek help. Research surrounding self-protection decisions suggests that victims' efforts to disrupt the crime are often successful at either preventing the crime from occurring or reducing the damage caused by the offender. Further, similar to influences on other victim decisions, studies into informal help-seeking also suggest that in many instances, acknowledgment of victimization, the seriousness of the offense, the relationship between the victim and the offender, and other situational factors influence help-seeking. These four decisions potentially influence each other in many ways. For example, victimization acknowledgment and self-protection affect reporting decisions. Also, victims may decide to informally seek help even if they have decided not to contact the police. Similarly, those who do not acknowledge their victimization may take no further action and may not confront any of these decisions. In the future, victim decision making and its consequences will likely occupy a prominent place in the discipline of victimology.

Decisions made by third parties also influence the criminal justice response to victimization. Bystander decision making research indicates that individuals are more likely to intervene and prevent victimization if they are given the proper training and are convinced that they can and should act in this capacity.

KEYWORDS

Victim acknowledgment	Reporting decisions	Help-seeking decisions
Unacknowledged victims	Theory of criminal justice decision making	Bystander intervention
Sexual Experiences Survey	Deterrence theory	Bystander intervention decisions
Classic rape paradigm	Self-protection	

DISCUSSION QUESTIONS

1. Why is it important to understand victim decision making and the factors affecting such decisions?
2. Under what circumstances might one *not* recognize that one has been victimized? Explain your answer and provide examples.
3. Do you think that Gottfredson and Gottfredson's (1990) theory of criminal justice decision making can explain all of the victims' decisions reviewed in this chapter? Why or why not?

4. Imagine that you were the victim of a violent crime. Would you contact the police? Why or why not? Describe the circumstances that would influence your decision.
5. Would your answer to Question 4 change if you were a victim of a property crime?
6. What can the police and/or elected officials do to increase rates of reporting crimes to the police?
7. When and how should victims resist offenders to prevent or reduce their loss during a crime? Justify your answer and provide examples.
8. Why do you think a majority of crime victims decide to seek out an informal source for help, such as a friend or family member, rather than a formal criminal justice source? Explain your reasoning.
9. What is your school doing to prevent different types of crimes that college students frequently experience? What types of services and support (e.g., legal, medical, mental health) does your school provide students who are crime victims?
10. Apply the principles of bystander intervention to preventing bullying victimization in schools. How would you convince other students to intervene in a safe and effective way if someone was being bullied?

REFERENCES

Akers, C., & Kaukinen, C. (2009). The police reporting behavior of intimate partner violence victims. *Journal of Family Violence, 24*, 159–171.

Bachman, R. (1998). The factors related to rape reporting behavior and arrest: New evidence from the National Crime Victimization Survey. *Criminal Justice and Behavior, 25*, 8–29.

Bachman, R., Saltzman, L. E., Thompson, M. P., & Carmody, D. C. (2002). Disentangling the effects of self-protective behaviors on the risk of injury in assaults against women. *Journal of Quantitative Criminology, 18*, 135–157.

Banyard, V. L., Plante, E. G., & Moynihan, M. M. (2004). Bystander education: Bringing a broader community perspective to sexual violence prevention. *Journal of Community Psychology, 32*, 61–79.

Barrett, B. J., & St. Pierre, M. (2011). Variations in women's help seeking in response to intimate partner violence: Findings from a Canadian population-based survey. *Violence Against Women, 17*, 47–70.

Baumer, E. P., & Lauritsen, J. L. (2010). Reporting crime to the police, 1973–2005: A multivariate analysis of long-term trends in the National Crime Survey (NCS) and National Crime Victimization Survey (NCVS). *Criminology, 48*, 131–185.

Berg, M. T., Slocum, L. A., & Loeber, R. (2013). Illegal behavior, neighborhood context, and police reporting by victims of violence. *Journal of Research in Crime and Delinquency, 50*, 75–103.

Bondurant, B. (2001). University women's acknowledgement of rape: Individual, situational and social factors. *Violence Against Women, 7*, 294–314.

Cohn, A. M., Zinzow, H. M., Resnick, H. S., & Kilpatrick, D. G. (2013). Correlates of reasons for not reporting rape to police: Results from a national telephone household probability sample of women with forcible or drug- or alcohol-facilitated/incapacitated rape. *Journal of Interpersonal Violence, 28*, 455–473.

Coker, A. L., Cook-Craig, P. G., Williams, C. M., Fisher, B. S., Clear, E. R., Garcia, L. S., & Hegge, L. M. (2011). Evaluation of Green Dot: An active bystander intervention to reduce sexual violence on college campuses. *Violence Against Women, 17*, 777–796.

Coker, A. L., Derrick, C., Lumpkin, J. L., Aldrich, T. E., & Oldendick, R. (2000). Help-seeking for intimate partner violence and forced sex in South Carolina. *American Journal of Preventive Medicine, 19*, 316–320.

Darley, J. M., & Latané, D. (1968). Bystander intervention in emergencies: Diffusion of responsibility. *Journal of Personality and Social Psychology, 8*, 377–383.

Englebrecht, C. M., & Reyns, B. W. (2011). Gender differences in acknowledgment of stalking victimization: Results from the NCVS stalking supplement. *Violence and Victims, 26*, 560–579.

Felson, R. B., Ackerman, J. M., & Gallagher, C. A. (2005). Police intervention and the repeat of domestic assault. *Criminology, 43*, 563–588.

Felson, R. B., Messner, S. F., Hoskin, A. W., & Deane, G. (2002). Reasons for reporting and not reporting domestic violence to the police. *Criminology, 40*, 617–647.

Felson, R. B., & Paré, P. P. (2005). The reporting of domestic violence and sexual assault by nonstrangers to the police. *Journal of Marriage and Family, 67*, 597–610.

Fisher, B. S., Daigle, L. E., Cullen, F. T., & Santana, S. A. (2007). Assessing the efficacy of the protective action–completion nexus for sexual victimizations. *Violence and Victims, 22*, 18–42.

Fisher, B. S., Daigle, L. E., Cullen, F. T., & Turner, M. G. (2003a). Acknowledging sexual victimization as rape: Results from a national-level study. *Justice Quarterly, 20*, 535–574.

Fisher, B. S., Daigle, L. E., Cullen, F. T., & Turner, M. G. (2003b). Reporting sexual victimization to the police and others: Results from a national-level study of college women. *Criminal Justice and Behavior, 30*, 6–38.

Gartner, R., & Macmillan, R. (1995). The effect of victim–offender relationship on reporting crimes of violence against women. *Canadian Journal of Criminology, 37*, 393–429.

Gottfredson, M. R., & Gottfredson, D. (1990). *Decision making in criminal justice: toward the rational exercise of discretion* (2nd ed.). New York: Plenum.

Gottfredson, M. R., & Hindelang, M. J. (1979). A study of the behavior of law. *American Sociological Review, 44*, 3–18.

Greenberg, M. S., & Ruback, R. B. (1992). *After the crime: Victim decision making.* New York: Plenum Press.

Guerette, R. T., & Santana, S. A. (2010). Explaining victim self-protective behavior effects on crime incident outcomes: A test of opportunity theory. *Crime and Delinquency, 56*, 198–226.

Hart, T. C., & Rennison, C. (2003). *Reporting crime to the police, 1992–2000* (NCJ 195710). Washington, DC: Bureau of Justice Statistics.

Hindelang, M. J. (1974). Decisions of shoplifting victims to invoke the criminal justice process. *Social Problems, 21*, 580–593.

Jordan, C. E., Wilcox, P., & Pritchard, A. J. (2007). Stalking acknowledgement and reporting among college women experiencing intrusive behaviors: Implications for the emergence of a "classic stalking case." *Journal of Criminal Justice, 35*, 556–569.

Kaukinen, C. (2004). The help-seeking strategies of female violent-crime victims: The direct and conditional effects of race and the victim-offender relationship. *Journal of Interpersonal Violence, 19*, 967–990.

Kleck, G., & Gertz, M. (1995). Armed resistance to crime: The prevalence and nature of self-defense with a gun. *Journal of Criminal Law & Criminology, 86*, 150–187.

Kleck, G., & Tark, J. (2004). *Draft final technical report: The impact of victim self-protection on rape completion and injury.* Retrieved June 12, 2013, from https://www.ncjrs.gov/pdffiles1/nij/grants/211201.pdf

Koss, M. P., Gidycz, C. A., & Wisniewski, N. (1987). The scope of rape: Incidence and prevalence of sexual aggression and victimization in a national sample of higher education students. *Journal of Counseling and Clinical Psychology, 55*, 162–170.

Koss, M. P., & Oros, C. J. (1980). *The "unacknowledged" rape victim.* Paper presented at the annual meeting of the American Psychological Association, Montreal, Canada.

Langton, L., Berzofsky, M., Krebs, C., & Smiley-McDonald, H. (2012). *Victimizations not reported to the police, 2006–2010* (NCJ 238536). Washington, DC: Bureau of Justice Statistics.

Lizotte, A. J. (1986). Determinants of completing rape and assault. *Journal of Quantitative Criminology, 2*, 203–217.

McCart, M. R., Smith, D. W., & Sawyer, G. K. (2010). Help seeking among victims of crime: A review of the empirical literature. *Journal of Traumatic Stress, 23*, 198–206.

NCVS Victimization Analysis Tool. (2014). Retrieved July 16, 2014, from http://www.bjs.gov/index.cfm?ty=nvat

Pitts, V. L., & Schwartz, M. D. (1993). Promoting self-blame in hidden rape cases. *Humanity and Society, 17*, 383–398.

Planty, M., & Truman, J. L. (2013). *Firearm violence, 1993–2011* (NCJ 241730). Washington, DC: Bureau of Justice Statistics.

Powers, R. A., & Simpson, S. S. (2012). Self-protective behaviors and injury in domestic violence situations: Does it hurt to fight back? *Journal of Interpersonal Violence, 27*, 3345–3365.

Reyns, B. W., & Englebrecht, C. M. (2010). The stalking victim's decision to contact the police: A test of Gottfredson and Gottfredson's theory of criminal justice decision making. *Journal of Criminal Justice, 38*, 998–1005.

Santana, S. A. (2007). *Self-protective behavior and violent victimization*. New York: LFB Scholarly Publishing.

Schwartz, M. D., & DeKeseredy, W. S. (1997). *Sexual assault on the college campus: The role of male peer support*. Thousand Oaks, CA: Sage Publications.

Skogan, W. G. (1976). Citizen reporting of crime: Same national panel data. *Criminology, 13*, 535–549.

Skogan, W. G., & Block, R. (1983). Resistance and injury in non-fatal assaultive violence. *Victimology, 8*, 215–226.

Tark, J., & Kleck, G. (2004). Resisting crime: The effects of victim action on the outcomes of crimes. *Criminology, 42*, 861–909.

Tarling, R., & Morris, K. (2010). Reporting crime to the police. *British Journal of Criminology, 50*, 474–490.

Ullman, S. E. (2007). A 10-year update of "Review and Critique of Empirical Studies of Rape Avoidance." *Criminal Justice and Behavior, 34*, 411–429.

Williams, L. S. (1984). The classic rape: When do victims report? *Social Problems, 31*, 459–467.

Zhang, L., Messner, S. F., & Liu, J. (2007). An exploration of the determinants of reporting crime to the police in the city of Tianjin, China. *Criminology, 45*, 959–984.

CHAPTER 11

Consequences of Victimization

CHAPTER OUTLINE

LEARNING OBJECTIVES

- Identify and describe the different consequences of criminal victimization.
- Explain how victims are physically affected by victimization and the circumstances under which physical consequences occur.
- Describe the psychological and mental health consequences of victimization and the circumstances under which these consequences occur.
- Explain the financial effects of victimization and the circumstances under which these consequences occur.
- Describe the social and behavioral consequences of victimization and whether and how victims change their behavior as a result of their victimization.
- Explain how the consequences of victimization may vary by type of victimization experienced and identify the consequences for the specific types of victimization reviewed in this chapter.

> ***It is little wonder that rape is one of the least reported crimes. Perhaps, it is the only crime in which the victim becomes the accused and in reality it is she who must prove her good reputation, her mental soundness, and her impeccable propriety.***
>
> Adler, 1975, p. 215

Introduction

After a crime has occurred, victims are left to cope with the aftermath of the event. Potentially the most serious consequences of criminal victimization are physical injuries victims suffer as a result of the offender's actions. Yet, the exact nature of the harm suffered by victims largely depends on the type of crime they have experienced. As a simple illustration, personal crimes have the capacity to result in physical injuries, while the harm suffered by victims of property offenses is more likely to be financial. In addition, the consequences of victimization differ based on the varied circumstances under which the incident occurs. For example, physical injuries may be less severe if the victim and the offender know each other, whereas crimes occurring between strangers may be more likely to result in physical injury to the victim.

Most crime victims do *not* suffer physical injuries, and instead experience any number of other negative consequences, such as psychological or mental health harm, financial costs, or negative social consequences. Unfortunately, it is also possible for these consequences co-occur. In other words, victims may have to concurrently deal with some or all of these consequences. For example, those who are physically injured also sustain financial burdens, such as medical expenses or through lost time from work. Even those who are not physically harmed might suffer psychological harm following a crime, including depression, anxiety, or damaged self-esteem, to name a few. Further, the severity of the harm that victims experience often depends on the crime. For instance, a residential burglary will likely result in a greater financial loss than will a simple theft from a person.

In addition to the physical, psychological, and financial consequences of crime, negative social consequences often follow criminal victimization, particularly for certain types of crimes. Most notably, victims find themselves blamed, stigmatized, or persecuted for what happened to them. Victims also may behave differently after the victimization by changing their lifestyles or routine activities (e.g., to reduce their victimization risks, to cope).

As a whole, the myriad consequences for those experiencing criminal victimization often reduce their quality of life and, as a result, are an important area of study in the field of victimology. This chapter's focus is thus on the consequences of victimization. First, we review the general consequences of victimization, including physical, psychological, financial/economic, social, and behavioral. The chapter also includes discussion of the consequences associated with particular types of victimization, such as intimate partner violence (IPV) and child maltreatment. Understanding the consequences of victimization is essential because the after-effects of crime extend well beyond the criminal justice system and have implications for health care, prevention, and services for victims.

Physical Consequences

Personal victimizations, such as rape, robbery, and assault, are those in which the person himself or herself is the target of the offense (see Chapter 5). The nature of these crimes makes it possible for the victim to be injured during the incident. The ***physical consequences*** of victimization, however, may be more widespread than only physical injuries (e.g., elevated blood pressure, insomnia).

The likelihood of suffering a physical injury as a consequence of personal victimization depends on the type of crime involved, which also generally determines the extent and nature of the injury. For example, an assault may result in ***physical trauma*** such as bruises, lacerations, broken bones, sprains, or a host of other physical injuries. Further, victims of sexual assault could incur these types of injuries and also be at risk for exposure to sexually transmitted diseases or unwanted pregnancies. Figure 11-1 illustrates this point by showing the types of injuries sustained by female rape victims based on data collected by the National Violence Against Women Survey (NVAWS).

Fortunately, most individuals who are victimized do not incur any physical injuries, but the likelihood of this depends on the crime (Shapland & Hall, 2007). Table 11-1 provides numbers and rates of injuries across personal types of victimization based on the 2012 National Crime Victimization Survey (NCVS), which defines injury as bodily harm or damage sustained to the victim as a result of the victimization. As the table illustrates, the violent victimization rate, which includes all the categories of personal victimization measured in the NCVS, was 26.1 per 1,000 persons 12 and older. Of these victims, over 20% suffered an injury of some kind as a consequence of the criminal event. Further, the highest rate of injury is found for victims of assault.

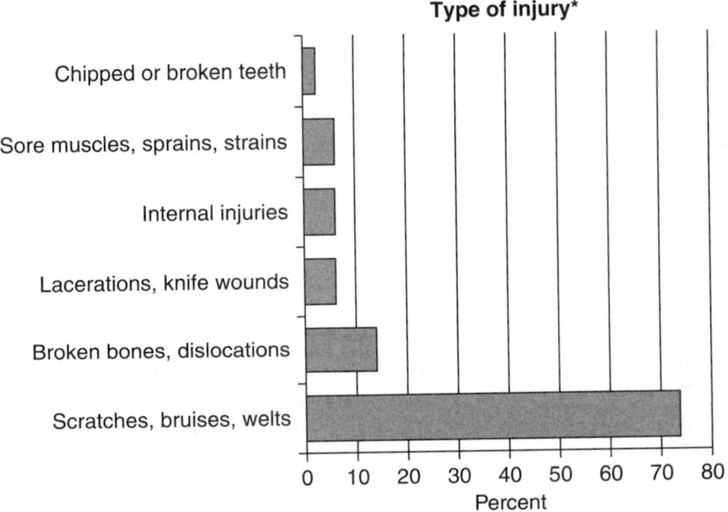

Figure 11-1 Injuries Sustained by Female Rape Victims
Source: Tjaden and Thoennes (2006).

Physical consequences of victimization may be immediate, such as losing a tooth, or it may take time for the toll of the experience to be felt by the victim. In addition, physical injuries can sometimes lead to other health conditions that otherwise would not have affected the victim. For example, victims can suffer cardiac distress, heart attacks, strokes, chronic pain, or fatigue that does not manifest immediately following the crime. Further, depending on the injury and its severity, victims may face a long road to recovery, or even sustain injuries that last the rest of their lives, such as disfigurement, permanent disability, or diseases. Beyond these direct injuries, victims can also experience other physiological impacts, such as stomach distress, lethargy, loss of appetite, excessive appetite, decreased libido, inability to work, or other factors that diminish the victim's quality of life. Health conditions also may develop as a consequence of risky coping behaviors, such as alcohol or drug use.

Unfortunately, not all victims who are injured receive the needed medical attention to recover from their injuries. Whether a victim receives medical treatment depends to some extent on the type of victimization he or she experienced. Table 11-2 provides numbers and rates of medical treatment after injury across types of personal victimization. For some offenses, such as rape and sexual assault, a majority of victims are not treated for their injuries, whereas for others, such as aggravated assault, it is more common for victims to receive treatment of some kind.

Research regarding the physical consequences of criminal victimization has mostly focused on identifying circumstances under which victims sustain injuries. This research has examined different types of victimization (e.g., rape, robbery) and different aspects of the criminal event, such as victim or offender characteristics or

Table 11-1: Number and Rate of Victim Injury by Type of Personal Victimization, 2012

Victimization Type	Number	Rate
Violent Victimization	6,842,593	26.1
Not injured	5,269,135	20.1
Injured	1,573,458	6.0
Rape/Sexual Assault	346,830	1.3
Not injured	201,812	0.8
Injured	145,018	0.6
Robbery	741,756	2.8
Not injured	458,574	1.8
Injured	283,182	1.1
Aggravated Assault	996,106	3.8
Not injured	662,132	2.5
Injured	333,974	1.3
Simple Assault	4,757,902	18.2
Not injured	3,946,617	15.1
Injured	811,284	3.1

Source: NCVS Victimization Analysis Tool (2014).

the context in which the victimization took place. However, clear patterns in the likelihood of victim injury are difficult to identify because studies often report conflicting results. For example, some research has found that African American victims are more likely to be injured during crimes than victims belonging to other races (e.g., Schnebly, 2002), while other studies report the opposite (e.g., Kleck & DeLone, 1993). Still other studies report that race does not affect the likelihood of being injured (Melde & Rennison, 2008). Similarly mixed results also have been reported regarding the effects of victim age and gender on injury risk during personal victimizations (e.g., Melde & Rennison, 2008; Schnebly, 2002; Tillyer, Miller, & Tillyer, 2011). Explaining victim injury by examining offender characteristics, such as age, gender, and race, produces a similarly muddled picture.

The relationship between victim and offender also has been viewed as a potential influence on the victim's likelihood of being injured during the crime. Once again, research in this area reports mixed results, with some studies reporting that victims are more likely to be injured if the perpetrator is known to them (e.g., Melde & Rennison, 2008), while others have reported the opposite (Messner, McHugh, & Felson, 2004) or that there is no effect of victim–offender relationship on risk of injury during personal victimizations (Brecklin & Ullman, 2001). Other important influences on the probability of experiencing an injury include drug and alcohol

Table 11-2: Number and Rate of Medical Treatments for Physical Injuries by Type of Personal Victimization, 2012

Victimization Type	Number	Rate
Violent Victimization	6,842,593	26.1
Not injured	5,269,135	20.1
Not treated for injury	878,070	3.4
Treated at scene, home, medical office, or other location	688,901	2.6
Serious Violent Victimization	2,084,691	8.0
Not injured	1,322,518	5.0
Not treated for injury	369,085	1.4
Treated at scene, home, medical office, or other location	386,601	1.5
Rape/Sexual Assault	346,830	1.3
Not injured	201,812	0.8
Not treated for injury	77,770	0.3
Treated at scene, home, medical office, or other location	67,247	0.3
Robbery	741,756	2.8
Not injured	458,574	1.8
Not treated for injury	157,931	0.6
Treated at scene, home, medical office, or other location	125,251	0.5
Aggravated Assault	996,106	3.8
Not injured	662,132	2.5
Not treated for injury	133,384	0.5
Treated at scene, home, medical office, or other location	194,103	0.7
Simple Assault	4,757,902	18.2
Not injured	3,946,617	15.1
Not treated for injury	508,985	1.9
Treated at scene, home, medical office, or other location	302,300	1.2

Note: Detail may not sum to total due to rounding and/or missing data.
Source: NCVS Victimization Analysis Tool (2014).

use, the location and time of the incident, weapon use by the offender, the type of weapon involved, and area crime rates.

In all likelihood, whether a victim is injured and the severity of that injury probably depend on the type of crime and the circumstances under which it occurs. A recent study by Marie Tillyer, J. Mitchell Miller, and Rob Tillyer (2011) addressed this issue using NIBRS data. They explored the risks for victim injury among victims of robbery, sexual offenses, and assaults. Their results confirmed that the predictors of physical injury differed by type of victimization. For example, older victims were more likely to experience injuries during sexual offenses and assaults, but age did not influence the chances of being injured during a robbery. However, certain factors affected injury risk for all types of victimization. If the offender was under the influence of alcohol or drugs, the victim was more likely to be physically injured regardless of the crime type. Characteristics of the event also affected victims' chances of being injured. For instance, sexual offenses in which a knife was used as a weapon were likely to result in victim injury, but robberies and assaults involving knives were less likely to result in injuries. As another example, victims who were assaulted during the daytime (7 a.m. to 7 p.m.) were significantly less likely to be physically injured, but the time of day did not affect victim injury for the other crimes.

The physical consequences of victimization, including their treatment and study, are an important focus in victimology and one of the more interdisciplinary areas of the field. Researchers from the health services professions, public health, and the social sciences continue to develop methods for treating, preventing, and better understanding physical harm that occurs as a result of criminal victimization. Furthermore, not only is this an interdisciplinary area, but physical injuries may also cause psychological and mental health problems in victims. For example, certain physical injuries, particularly head trauma, may hinder brain development in children. Such traumas also can lead to psychological and physiological disorders in adult brains. The psychological and mental health consequences of criminal victimization are reviewed in the next section of the chapter.

Psychological and Mental Health Consequences

Victims of any type of crime can suffer psychological disorders following the event, but the mental health effects of crime on victims have mostly been studied among victims of physical violence such as rape, stalking, and IPV. While some psychological consequences are associated with specific types of crime, there are also commonalities that cut across all types of victimization. As Barry Ruback and Martie Thompson (2001, p. 87) have said, "Although we generally think of violent crime in terms of specific types of crime (e.g., rape, physical assault, or partner violence), research suggests that the psychological consequences of crime are fairly consistent regardless of the type of crime."

Crime affects victims in many ways, and researchers and practitioners often divide ***psychological and mental health consequences*** of victimization into those that are either short term or long term. ***Short-term consequences*** that affect victims are usually experienced immediately by victims and only last a short time. Examples of these consequences include shock or emotional numbness, denial, disbelief, anger, fear (see Chapter 13), surprise, confusion, shame, and reduced self-esteem. Joanna Shapland and Matthew Hall (2007) explained that according to estimates from the British Crime Survey, over 80% of crime victims report experiencing emotional effects from their victimization, with the most common being anger and shock. Other common symptoms include depression and anxiety. Some of these outcomes also may become chronic or ***long-term consequences*** for victims.

While ***depression*** can be a normal part of life, especially when dealing with a loss, it is also a common response to being victimized. According to the *Diagnostic and Statistical Manual of Mental Disorders* (DSM-5) (American Psychiatric Society, 2013), which is used by psychiatrists, clinicians, and others to identify mental disorders, clinical depression occurs when individuals simultaneously experience five or more of the following symptoms:

- A depressed mood during most of the day, particularly in the morning
- Fatigue or loss of energy almost every day
- Feelings of worthlessness or guilt almost every day
- Impaired concentration, indecisiveness
- Insomnia (an inability to sleep) or hypersomnia (excessive sleeping) almost every day
- Markedly diminished interest or pleasure in almost all activities nearly every day
- Recurring thoughts of death or suicide (not just fearing death)
- A sense of restlessness or being slowed down
- Significant weight loss or weight gain

The DSM-5 indicates that symptoms should be present for most of the day, nearly every day, for at least two weeks, and result in some impairment of daily activities. Further, these symptoms may not represent clinical depression if they occur within two months of the loss of a loved one.

Like depression, ***anxiety*** is a normal human emotion and is synonymous with feeling worried, nervous, or uneasy. Those with anxiety disorders experience these feelings at exaggerated levels. For example, ***acute stress disorder*** (ASD) is an anxiety disorder that is frequently experienced by individuals following traumatic events (e.g., criminal victimization, the threat of death). In the case of crime victims, symptoms of ASD usually occur within one month of the victimization and may last for between two days and one month. Individuals with ASD experience a number of symptoms, such as re-experiencing the event (e.g., recurring nightmares, flashbacks), avoidance (e.g., of people, activities, places), increased arousal (e.g., irritability, difficulty concentrating, trouble sleeping), and general distress that disrupts the victim's everyday life.

A similar but longer-term anxiety disorder experienced by crime victims is known as ***posttraumatic stress disorder*** (PTSD). PTSD develops after a traumatic event such as a violent criminal victimization or other life-threatening experience and includes symptoms that are similar to ASD. In fact, it is not uncommon for those experiencing ASD to later be diagnosed with PTSD. DSM-5 revised the diagnostic criteria for PTSD and also introduced a preschool subtype for children six years old or younger. For a person over six years old to be diagnosed with PTSD, he or she must be experiencing the symptoms detailed in Box 11-1.

Box 11-1: DSM-V Diagnostic Criteria for Posttraumatic Stress Disorder

Criterion A: Stressor

The person was exposed to: death, threatened death, actual or threatened serious injury, or actual or threatened sexual violence, as follows: (one required)

1. Direct exposure.
2. Witnessing, in person.
3. Indirectly, by learning that a close relative or close friend was exposed to trauma. If the event involved actual or threatened death, it must have been violent or accidental.
4. Repeated or extreme indirect exposure to aversive details of the event(s), usually in the course of professional duties (e.g., first responders, collecting body parts; professionals repeatedly exposed to details of child abuse). This does not include indirect non-professional exposure through electronic media, television, movies, or pictures.

Criterion B: Intrusion Symptoms

The traumatic event is persistently re-experienced in the following way(s): (one required)

1. Recurrent, involuntary, and intrusive memories. Note: Children older than six may express this symptom in repetitive play.
2. Traumatic nightmares. Note: Children may have frightening dreams without content related to the trauma(s).
3. Dissociative reactions (e.g., flashbacks) which may occur on a continuum from brief episodes to complete loss of consciousness. Note: Children may reenact the event in play.
4. Intense or prolonged distress after exposure to traumatic reminders.
5. Marked physiologic reactivity after exposure to trauma-related stimuli.

Criterion C: Avoidance

Persistent effortful avoidance of distressing trauma-related stimuli after the event: (one required)

1. Trauma-related thoughts or feelings.
2. Trauma-related external reminders (e.g., people, places, conversations, activities, objects, or situations).

Criterion D: Negative Alterations in Cognitions and Mood

Negative alterations in cognitions and mood that began or worsened after the traumatic event: (two required)

1. Inability to recall key features of the traumatic event (usually dissociative amnesia; not due to head injury, alcohol, or drugs).
2. Persistent (and often distorted) negative beliefs and expectations about oneself or the world (e.g., "I am bad," "The world is completely dangerous").
3. Persistent distorted blame of self or others for causing the traumatic event or for resulting consequences.
4. Persistent negative trauma-related emotions (e.g., fear, horror, anger, guilt, or shame).
5. Markedly diminished interest in (pre-traumatic) significant activities.
6. Feeling alienated from others (e.g., detachment or estrangement).
7. Constricted affect: persistent inability to experience positive emotions.

(Continued)

Box 11-1: DSM-V Diagnostic Criteria for Posttraumatic Stress Disorder (*Continued*)

Criterion E: Alterations in Arousal and Reactivity
Trauma-related alterations in arousal and reactivity that began or worsened after the traumatic event: (two required)

1. Irritable or aggressive behavior
2. Self-destructive or reckless behavior
3. Hypervigilance
4. Exaggerated startle response
5. Problems in concentration
6. Sleep disturbance

Criterion F: Duration
Persistence of symptoms (in Criteria B, C, D, and E) for more than one month.

Criterion G: Functional Significance
Significant symptom-related distress or functional impairment (e.g., social, occupational).

Criterion H: Exclusion
Disturbance is not due to medication, substance use, or other illness.

Source: American Psychiatric Association (2013).

In addition to these psychological conditions that affect crime victims, Morton Bard and Dawn Sangrey (1979) have described the response to victimization as a "crisis reaction." Although there are obviously a number of authorities knowledgeable about how individuals respond to crises, Bard and Sangrey have explained how crises related to crime affect victims. According to these two scholars, a ***crisis reaction*** consists of three stages and is brought on by the stress of being victimized, but they also note that "The severity of the victim's crisis is in direct proportion to the degree of violation of the self" (Bard & Sangrey, 1979, p. 32). In other words, victims experience stress dependent on the nature of the victimization, with more intrusive acts eliciting a deeper crisis reaction. For example, experiencing a violent crime is probably a greater violation than experiencing a theft for most crime victims. While the severity of the crisis differs from victim to victim, Bard and Sangrey contend that victims tend to experience the reaction in similar ways. That is, crime victims usually experience three stages of crisis reaction (Fig. 11-2). However, these stages are not necessarily linear, and victims might move ahead or move back throughout the process.

The first stage of crisis reaction is the ***impact stage***. During this stage, victims are in shock, experiencing feelings of numbness, disorientation, disbelief, vulnerability and helplessness. They may have trouble sleeping and eating and feel physically immobilized, thinking, "I can't believe that this has happened." Bard and Sangrey explain that victims will become dependent on others and have trouble making decisions; social support and help for victims is thus crucial during the impact stage, which can last hours or days. The second stage of crisis reaction is the ***recoil stage***, which involves the victim beginning to adapt and recover from the victimization.

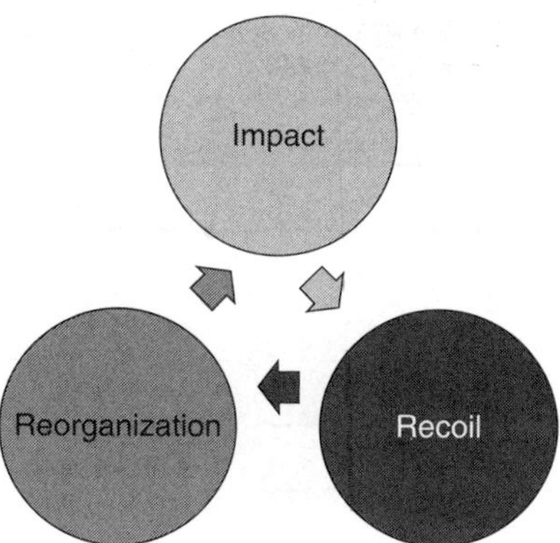

Figure 11-2 The Three Stages of Crisis Reaction to Criminal Victimization
Source: Adapted from Bard and Sangrey (1979).

One of the primary emotions that victims experience during this phase is denial, to which victims respond in different ways such as keeping busy as if everything were fine. However, between these periods of denial victims also will begin to reflect on the crime and experience the feelings and emotions associated with the event, especially fear and anger. Bard and Sangrey (1979, p. 40) note that "Family and friends can be most helpful in this phase by being nurturing and comforting, allowing the victim to find his or her own recuperative rhythm, and thus supporting the struggle." In the third stage of crisis reaction, the ***reorganization stage***, the victim comes to terms with the victimization. While the previously described feelings and emotions are still present, they are typically less intense, and the victim is able to return to some of his or her daily routines. At this point, some victims will emerge from the experience stronger, or they will undergo some of the long-term psychological and mental health consequences of victimization discussed previously.

Estimates of the extent of psychological and mental health consequences of victimization have only intermittently been included in large victimization surveys. For example, results from the NVAWS indicated that 33% of female rape victims and approximately 20% of male victims from the study received counseling from a mental health professional following the incident (Tjaden & Thoennes, 2006). More recent information regarding how crime affects victims was included in the National Intimate Partner and Sexual Violence Survey (NISVS). Some of the findings from the survey related to mental health effects of victimization are provided in Table 11-3. The table compares women with no history of rape, stalking, or IPV victimization to victims of at least one of these crimes on several physical and mental health outcomes. The main takeaway point from the table is that women who have been victimized have a significantly higher prevalence of all of the outcomes listed, as compared to nonvictims. The exception to this pattern is high blood pressure. Among men in the United States, victims had a higher prevalence of certain physical and mental health problems, including frequent headaches, chronic pain, difficulty sleeping, activity limitations, poor physical health, and poor mental health (Black, Basile, Breiding, Smith, Walters, Merrick, Chen, & Stevens, 2011).

Table 11-3: Prevalence of Physical and Mental Health Outcomes of U.S. Women, National Intimate Partner and Sexual Violence Survey 2010

	Weighted %		
Health Outcome	History	No History[1]	p value[2]
Asthma	23.7	14.3	<0.001
Irritable Bowel Syndrome	12.4	6.9	<0.001
Diabetes	12.6	10.2	<0.001
High Blood Pressure	27.3	27.5	n.s.[3]
Frequent Headaches	28.7	16.5	<0.001
Chronic Pain	29.8	16.5	<0.001
Difficulty Sleeping	37.7	21.0	<0.001
Activity Limitations	35.0	19.7	<0.001
Poor Physical Health	6.4	2.4	<0.001
Poor Mental Health	3.4	1.1	<0.001

[1]No history of rape, stalking, or intimate partner physical violence
[2]p-value determined using chi-square test of independence in SUDAAN™
[3]Non-significant difference
Source: Black et al. (2011).

The circumstances under which crime victims incur psychological injuries have mostly been researched within specific victimizations. For example, Matthew Johnson and Glen Kercher (2009) investigated the negative psychological reactions of stalking for victims. Using data from the Texas Crime Victimization Survey, they found that females, those who had a prior relationship with their stalker, and those who experienced multiple stalking behaviors had greater chances of experiencing multiple negative psychological outcomes (e.g., loss of sleep, depression, fear of being alone). In another study of the effects of victimization on mental health, Christine Kuehner, Peter Gass, and Harald Dressing (2012) reported that in a survey of residents of Germany, those who were victims of stalking were more likely to have poorer self-reported mental health.

Alfred Demaris and Catherine Kaukinen (2005) explored how violent victimizations such as physical and sexual assaults affected U.S. women's mental and physical health. Their results suggested that the severity of the violence had a significant impact on victims' physical health and that the victim–offender relationship was the most important explanation for victims' depression. That is, when the offender was known to the victim, the victim was more likely to exhibit signs of depression. As a final example, Matt DeLisi and his colleagues (2014) assessed the impact of robbery and burglary on victims' mental health. They reported that the effects of victimization were dependent on the victim's race, and the results indicated that

Box 11-2: Tips for Coping with Crime

These are some ideas that may help you cope with the trauma or loss:

- Find someone to talk with about how you feel and what you are going through. Keep the phone number of a good friend nearby to call when you feel overwhelmed or panicked.
- Allow yourself to feel pain. It will not last forever.
- Spend time with others, but make time to spend time alone.
- Take care of your mind and body. Rest, sleep, and eat regular, healthy meals.
- Re-establish a normal routine as soon as possible, but don't over-do.
- Make daily decisions, which will help to bring back a feeling of control over your life.
- Exercise, though not excessively, and alternate with periods of relaxation.
- Undertake daily tasks with care. Accidents are more likely to happen after severe stress.
- Recall the things that helped you cope during trying times and loss in the past and think about the things that give you hope. Turn to them on bad days.

Source: National Center for Victims of Crime (2014).

victimization reduced self-esteem and self-efficacy (sense of control over one's life), but only among African American victims.

Although an in-depth account of all of the psychological and mental health harms experienced by crime victims is beyond the scope of this chapter, it is clear these consequences can be quite debilitating. Box 11-2 provides some general tips from the National Center for Victims of Crime for coping with victimization and easing the psychological and emotional effects that it may have on victims. In addition to these consequences, victims will often sustain financial costs that can increase feelings of anxiety, stress, and depression. The financial and economic consequences of victimization are reviewed in the next section of the chapter.

Financial and Economic Consequences

Regardless of the crime, victimization can carry with it financial and economic consequences for victims. However, for victims of property offenses these costs are easier to estimate based on the value of the property that was lost, damaged, or destroyed. Thus, while recognizing that all victims can suffer financially to some degree, primary emphasis here is placed on property offenses, such as burglary, theft, and motor vehicle theft. The UCR and NCVS both provide information on the financial costs individuals incur after being victims of these offenses. The UCR, for example, estimated that property offenses resulted in losses of approximately $15.5 billion in 2012 alone.

Table 11-4 includes estimates of financial losses to victims, both individually and as a whole, using UCR and NCVS data. While NCVS estimates are slightly higher due to victim reporting (see Chapter 4), both data sources agree that the economic

Table 11-4: Estimated Financial Costs to Victims of Property Offenses

	Uniform Crime Reports (2012)		National Crime Victimization Survey (2008)*	
Victimization Type	Total Loss	Average Loss	Total Loss	Average Loss
Robbery	$414 million	$1,167	$644 million	$1,167
Burglary	$4.7 billion	$2,230	$4.9 billion	$1,539
Larceny-Theft	$6 billion	$987	$6.4 billion	$524
Motor Vehicle Theft	$4.3 billion	$6,019	$4.8 billion	$6,077

*Note: The statistical tables from the NCVS are published years after the initial report, and estimates for the year 2008 are the most recent that are available.
Source: Adapted from Federal Bureau of Investigation (2014) and the Bureau of Justice Statistics (2010).

impact of property victimization is enormous. It appears that the total amount lost to larceny-theft is the highest but that individually victims of motor vehicle theft suffer the greatest financial loss. This is interesting because larceny-thefts usually involve smaller economic losses at the individual level, but more of them are perpetrated, whereas motor vehicle theft is less common, but motor vehicles are usually of a much higher value. In their analysis of BCS results, Shapland and Hall (2007) reported that it is not uncommon for burglary victims to lose over £1,000 ($1,506), but approximately 45% lost less than £50 (about $75). Importantly, many individuals lose more or less money than the figures provided in the table, which provides estimates of the average amount lost.

The NCVS also includes information about losses to victims of identity theft, which, according to the NCVS, includes unauthorized use or attempted use of an existing account, unauthorized use or attempted use of personal information to open a new account, and misuse of personal information for a fraudulent purpose. In 2012, NCVS data showed that two thirds of identity theft victims experienced some direct financial loss as a result of their victimization. In the NCVS, *direct losses* represent the amount the offender obtained as a result of the crime and *indirect losses* are costs that are caused by the identity theft, such as overdraft fees charged by a bank or legal fees. Keep in mind, however, that victims of identity theft are often reimbursed for their direct losses, depending on how the theft was perpetrated, so the figures do not necessarily reflect true costs to victims. Nevertheless, when considered collectively, the NCVS estimated that the total direct and indirect losses as a result of identity theft were $24.7 billion and the average cost to victims was $2,183 (Harrell & Langton, 2013). Out-of-pocket losses aside, frauds such as identity theft result in other financial costs, such as losing inheritances, homes, college savings accounts, pensions, and life savings (Deem, Nerenberg, & Titus, 2014). Further, the amount of the loss varied according to the type of identity theft perpetrated. For instance, victims who had their personal information misused (e.g., social security number) had an average direct loss of $9,650, compared to those who had an existing account misused, who lost an average of $1,003. This is also true for other offenses. For example, among larceny-thefts, the average loss from pocket-picking is $627 compared to $468 for purse-snatching (FBI, 2014).

Besides determining the cost of financial crimes, researchers have also investigated patterns in financial costs to victims. For example, Fay Cook and her colleagues (1978) used national survey data collected for the Law Enforcement Assistance Administration to study the economic and physical consequences of elder victimization. They reported that the elderly were no more likely than persons of other ages to experience financial losses or severe physical injuries, but that elderly persons might be hurt more financially because of a greater need for medical care. This was particularly the case among low-income elderly persons.

Individuals are not the only victims of financial crimes. Indeed, businesses, organizations, and even governments are frequent targets of financial offenses and thus face financial consequences of victimization. Considering the assets of these potential victims, the economic consequences of victimization can be substantial. For example, a special report by the Bureau of Justice Statistics based on data from the National Computer Security Survey estimated the extent and consequences of cybercrime (crimes perpetrated using the Internet or computer networks) against businesses in the United States for 2005. National Computer Security Survey calculations of monetary losses suggested that businesses lost a total of $857 million to cybercrimes, including cybertheft ($450 million), cyberattacks ($314 million), and other cybersecurity incidents that year (Rantala, 2008). While not specifically focusing on cybercrimes, Kristy Holtfreter (2008) studied the factors that affect fraud victimization and financial loss among nonprofit organizations and reported that losses to the 128 organizations included in the study ranged from less than $100 to $3.5 million. Further, the results showed that individual and organizational characteristics explained the amount of financial losses to victims. For example, smaller organizations were more likely to incur larger losses. In addition, organizations that had an anonymous hotline experienced smaller losses than those without, suggesting that mechanisms for internal reporting of fraud reduced the financial losses from victimization. This study also highlights the potentially high losses associated with white-collar victimization (crimes perpetrated by business and government professionals that are nonviolent and financially motivated). One study in Canada that focused on explaining financial losses to the victims of white-collar occupational fraud found that the average loss to victims was $1,142,494 (Canadian) and that the perpetrator's position as an executive or owner and the presence of accomplices to the perpetrator were the most important influences on the level of financial loss suffered by the business (Peltier-Rivest & Lanoue, 2012).

Beyond the burdens placed on victims, financial crimes also impose a heavy burden on the larger society. White-collar offenses, in particular, can significantly harm governments, economies, and taxpayers as a whole. For example, financial losses from health care fraud (e.g., against Medicare) are estimated to range between $70 billion and $234 billion annually (National Health Care Anti-Fraud Association, 2010), which Debbie Deem, Lisa Nerenberg, and Richard Titus (2014, p. 195) point out is "roughly equivalent to the gross domestic product of a country the size of Colombia or Finland."

Crime affects victims physically, psychologically, and financially, but these consequences of victimization can sometimes have effects of their own. In some cases, the consequences of victimization can affect victims' social interactions and the ways they behave following criminal victimization. Social and behavioral consequences can also be independently caused by the criminal event.

Social and Behavioral Consequences

Research suggests that in addition to the physical, psychological and mental health, and financial consequences borne by crime victims, criminal victimization also affects victims' social interactions and their behavior. That is, victimization can affect the way others treat the victim following the event. Victimization also has been found to influence future behavior by victims, including changes to their routine activities to avoid further victimization.

A common reaction by others to certain types of victimization people suffer is social stigma, which is conceptually similar to "victim-blaming"—holding the victim primarily responsible for his or her own victimization. A ***social stigma*** is a condition that carries with it disapproval or shame owing to stereotypes or perceptions associated with certain characteristics or attributes. Noted sociologist Erving Goffman (1963, p. 3) defined stigma as "an attribute that is deeply discrediting" and for which the individual is rejected as a result of the attribute. Although social stigma may be associated with any number of characteristics, such as race, ethnicity, disability, or nationality, in this case the label *crime victim* often brings stigma with it.

Victimologists and other social scientists have studied the stigmatization process and its effects with respect to victims of particular crimes, especially sexual victimization and IPV. For example, research by Heather Littleton, Amie Grills-Taquechel, and Danny Axsom (2009) found that the type of rape the victim experienced resulted in differences in feelings of stigma, with victims of incapacitated rape reporting greater feelings of stigma than victims who were not impaired at the time of the rape. Significant predictors of feelings of stigma among rape victims included binge drinking by the victim, incapacitation, and having a relationship with the assailant. It thus appears that the perceived level of involvement by the victim in the incident greatly affected the level of stigma that victims experienced. The higher the perceived "facilitation" of the victimization through the victims' behavior, the greater the stigma others assign to the victim.

Victimologists also have examined how being victimized affects victims' subsequent behavior, specifically whether changes occur in their lifestyles and routine activities. The presumption here is that those who are victimized will change their behavior in an effort to prevent any subsequent victimization. For example, while in high school, one of the authors was robbed at gunpoint while walking home after school. After the robbery, he began riding the bus home after school. There are, however, methodological challenges confronting researchers when trying to determine whether actual changes occurred in behaviors after the victimization. One of these challenges is known as "social desirability bias," where victims *say* they changed their behavior so as not to appear irresponsible (and possibly avoid social stigma), when in truth they had not. Another difficulty in assessing behavioral change following victimization involves the data used. Since many studies rely on large cross-sectional datasets like the NCVS, it is impossible to determine chronology and therefore to determine whether a victimization incident occurred before or after the victim engaged in certain activities or lifestyles, especially "risky" ones.

Research in this area paints a complicated picture of the relationship between victimization and behavioral changes to victims' lifestyles and routines. Underscoring the complex nature of this type of research, some studies have reported that crime victims *do* behave differently after their experience, while other studies report no changes. For example, in an early effort using data collected in personal interviews of residents of Newark, New Jersey, and Houston, Texas, Wesley Skogan (1987) reported that victims of violent crimes and victims of property crimes were more likely to engage in avoidance behaviors (e.g., staying away from certain areas or people) than they were to engage in other crime prevention behaviors. Further, Skogan (1987) also found that victims of property crimes were more likely than other victims to take precautions involving target hardening, such as installing locks on doors and lights in their yards. Julie-Anne Gale and Timothy Coupe (2005) also support the hypothesized connection between victimization and subsequent changes in behavior. In their study of robbery victims in the United Kingdom, Gale and Coupe reported that three quarters of victims made some changes to their behaviors following victimization, either by taking added precautions or avoiding certain places or people. They also noted differences in these responses by gender, with women restricting their routines, avoiding risks (e.g., changing selected modes of transportation), taking security precautions (e.g., not carrying a handbag), and making attempts to appear a less attractive target (e.g., not wearing jewelry).

Research studies also have found a relationship between being victimized and households' decision to move. For example, two studies, both using the NCVS, have reported that households in which members are victimized have a higher probability of moving. Laura Dugan's (1999) study, for instance, reported that individuals who were victimized near their homes were significantly more likely to move than individuals victimized elsewhere. Min Xie and David McDowall's (2008) study found relationships between moving and both direct and indirect victimization experiences. That is, both direct violent or property victimizations—those experienced by someone in the household—increased the chances that individuals would decide to relocate. However, indirect property victimizations—those reported by households in neighboring dwellings—also increased the likelihood that individuals would decide to move. The effect of victimization on moving decisions is important because moving is an expensive enterprise that imposes additional financial costs on victims. Further, criminologists have identified high levels of residential mobility as facilitating neighborhood decline, disorder, and crime (e.g., Bursik & Grasmick, 1993).

In contrast to the studies that find victims change their behaviors after the crime, recent research reports that victimization either only marginally affects victims' subsequent behaviors and routines or has no effect. In one such study, Margit Averdijk (2011) used four years of NCVS data to assess the effects of victimization on subsequent behaviors, including how often victims went shopping, how often they spent the evening away from home, and whether they have a household crime prevention device (e.g., security system). Although the results suggested a limited impact of victimization on subsequent behavior, Averdijk was able to identify characteristics of the crime most associated with behavioral change. For example, violent victimization in public places reduced the frequency of shopping for victims, and being injured during the crime was associated with a reduction in evenings spent away from home.

Similarly, Jackson Bunch, Jody Clay-Warner, and Jennifer McMahon-Howard (2014) used longitudinal data from the NCVS to evaluate the effects of victimization on victims' subsequent routine activities. Their analysis also focused on frequency of nighttime activities and shopping, but the study differed from Averdijk's in two ways: Different years of the NCVS were examined and a different statistical technique was used to analyze the data. Results showed that compared to nonvictims, victims were out at night more often and shopped more often. Bunch and colleagues explained their results as follows: "Taking into account the propensity for victimization, we found that victimization itself has no influence on either of these activities. The reasons that victims spend more time away from home at night and shop more frequently are rooted in their underlying differences from nonvictims, not the experience of victimization" (Bunch et al., 2014, p. 588). In other words, Bunch and colleagues concluded that there *are* behavioral differences between victims and nonvictims, but they do not result from victimization.

There is not an unequivocal answer as to whether crime victims change their behavior following victimization. Most likely, this decision depends on the type of crime and its overall impact on the victim. Perhaps victims who are severely injured or sustain large financial losses are more likely to alter their behavior. Or, it may be that those who experience negative emotions or social consequences (i.e., stigma) are more likely to alter their behavior. On a related note, victimologists have devoted considerable research attention to studying the effects of fear of crime upon avoidance and protective behaviors (see Chapter 13). This research generally supports the contention that there is a link between emotional responses to crime and subsequent behavioral adaptations.

Specific Types of Victimization and Their Consequences

The preceding review of the consequences of victimization provided a general overview of how crime affects victims. The majority of research into the consequences of victimization, however, has had a specific rather than a general focus. In other words, studies investigating the effects of crime have usually focused on specific types of crime, such as bullying or IPV. Therefore, the remainder of the chapter takes this same approach and highlights the effects that crime has on victims of particular types of crimes, including child maltreatment and peer victimization, IPV and sexual victimization, elder maltreatment, and the effects of homicide on survivors.

Child Maltreatment and Childhood Peer Victimization

One of the most researched areas relating to the consequences of victimization involves child maltreatment, including how victimization by caregivers, peers, and others affects children and adolescents. The vast body of research on these topics suggests that there are both short- and long-term physical and mental health consequences for children and adolescents. Immediate physical consequences of child abuse include physical injuries such as fractures, bruises, burns, subdural hematomas, and traumatic brain injuries. Neglect can lead to vitamin deficiencies, obesity, untreated medical conditions, and injuries incurred due to a lack of supervision (Leeb, Lewis, & Zolotor, 2011).

In terms of mental health, child maltreatment is associated with lack of attachment, acting-out behavior, and mood disorders, among other negative consequences (Leeb et al., 2011). In addition, child maltreatment has been linked to physical and social problems, including drug and alcohol abuse, criminal behavior, risky sexual behavior, and other conditions affecting the child's quality of life into his or her adult years (Gilbert, Widom, Browne, Fergusson, Webb, & Janson, 2009). Sexual victimization of children likewise results in significant negative consequences, including stress, depression, delinquency, age-inappropriate sexual behaviors, aggression, and suicidal ideation; other consequences may materialize in adulthood (e.g., alcohol abuse, eating disorders) (O'Sullivan, 2014; Ruback & Thompson, 2001).

Although there are many published applicable studies of the consequences of childhood victimization on victims, for the sake of brevity only a few will be highlighted. The first of these was conducted by Heather Turner, David Finkelhor, and Richard Ormrod (2006), who used data from the Developmental Victimization Survey. These data included information from a representative sample of 2,030 children between the ages of 2 and 17 in the United States and allowed for an assessment of the effects of childhood victimization on childhood mental health. The results indicated that compared to children who had not been victimized, child victims of sexual assault or child maltreatment had significantly higher levels of depression, anger, and aggression. Significant relationships also were identified between these types of victimization and the likelihood of reporting depression or anger/aggression.

For students of criminology and sociology, it may be of particular interest that childhood victimization has been linked with a higher likelihood of juvenile delinquency and arrest. Once again, many rigorous studies have investigated this issue, but we will review a study by Jeanne Kaufman and Cathy Widom (1999) that explored relationships among childhood victimization, running away, and juvenile delinquency. Kaufman and Widom used a sophisticated research design that involved comparing cases of abuse and neglect to matched controls (cases that had no such victimization). This allowed the researchers to assess the predictors of delinquency for victims as well as nonvictims while controlling for other possible factors such as race, gender, age, and so forth. Most importantly here, results showed that juveniles who had experienced childhood victimization were twice as likely as nonvictims to be arrested for delinquency. Victimization also increased victims' likelihood of running away, which was a strong predictor of arrest, regardless of whether the juvenile had previously been victimized. However, victimized children who also ran way were found to be about 3.5 times more likely to be arrested for delinquency.

As previously stated, childhood victimization also affects victims in their adult years. Research by Scott Menard (2002) examined data from the National Youth

Survey and considered the effects of victimization in adolescence on experiences and behaviors in adulthood. Menard's research found a statistically significant relationship between adolescent violent victimization and several problems in adulthood, including violent crime victimization, domestic violence victimization and perpetration, violent and property crime perpetration, drug use, and PTSD. For example, those who were violently victimized as adolescents were 3.5 times more likely to perpetrate assault as adults. Adolescent property victimization also appeared to have a negative influence in later life, with property crime victims being 1.8 times more likely to use marijuana as adults.

Several studies also have examined the relationships between childhood peer victimization in the form of bullying and different types of consequences. For example, David Hawker and Michael Boulton (2000) reviewed 20 years of published research on the consequences of bullying victimization and found that, across studies, bullying was consistently associated with depression, loneliness, lower self-esteem, and anxiety among victims. In one such study, Finn-Aage Esbensen and Dena Carson (2009) estimated how school bullying affected victims across 15 schools in four U.S. states. The results showed significant relationships between bullying and several negative outcomes. However, the nature of the bullying victimization, especially whether the bullying was intermittent or repeated, determined how the experience affected victims. For example, repeat bullying victims showed significantly lower self-esteem than either intermittent victims or nonvictims. Victimization also was associated with greater fear and perceived risk of victimization, lower self-esteem, greater empathy, greater commitment to negative peers, lower school commitment, and less use of conflict resolution skills.

In another study of the consequences of early victimization experiences, Leana Bouffard and Maria Koeppel (2014) used long-term data from the National Longitudinal Survey of Youth to study the health risks of bullying and adolescent victimization. Specifically, because of the longitudinal nature of these data, the authors were able to consider how victimization at one period of time (when the study participants were between 12 and 14 years old) affected victims later in their lives (when the participants were between 18 and 21 years old). Like Esbensen and Carson, they found that victims of repeated bullying suffered severe effects after victimization. Notably, victims of repeated bullying (at time 1) were significantly more likely to have indicated (at time 2) their health as being only fair or poor, to have smoked in the last year, to have been a victim of a crime in the past five years, and to have been homeless in the past five years. Early victimization experiences were also related to negative mental health.

As a final example of the effects of bullying victimization on victims, Francis Cullen and his colleagues (2008) examined the relationship between being bullied and engaging in delinquent acts. After analyzing data from nearly 2,500 sixth-, seventh-, and eighth-graders in Virginia, they reported that experiencing victimization was a significant predictor of juvenile delinquency, including such offenses as damaging/destroying property, setting fires, and seriously hurting someone. The authors interpreted their findings according to general strain theory (Agnew, 2006) and argued that bullying victimization represents a form of strain, which then leads to negative emotional states (e.g., depression) and consequently to a higher likelihood of delinquent behavior.

Box 11-3: The Economic Toll of Nonfatal Child Maltreatment

Cost Category	Cost in 2010 Dollars per Victim
Child Health Care Costs	$32,648
Adult Medical Costs	$10,530
Lost Productivity	$144,360
Child Welfare Costs	$7,728
Criminal Justice Costs	$6,747
Special Education Costs	$7,999
Lifetime Cost Per Victim	$210,012

Source: Adapted from Fang, Brown, Florence, and Mercy (2012).

Given the point in the life course in which childhood victimization occurs, the long-term effects are potentially all the more devastating. Since research suggests that early victimization experiences have a negative impact on victims in both the short and long terms, victims may be dealing with the consequences for the rest of their lives. Further, if victimization increases the likelihood of delinquency and criminal behaviors, these experiences too will likely have long-term effects on victims' lives. Understanding the toll of victimization is necessary in developing more effective responses to help childhood victims of crime, which reportedly cost the United States $124 billion in 2008 (Centers for Disease Control and Prevention [CDC], 2014a). Estimates of the costs of child maltreatment in the United States are provided in Box 11-3.

Intimate Partner Violence and Sexual Violence Against Women

IPV has been identified as a pressing public health issue by the CDC, one that has physical, psychological, social, and behavioral consequences for victims. According to the NISVS, approximately 15% of women and 4% of men in the United States have been injured in their lifetime as a result of IPV (Black et al., 2011). These injuries can be an immediate result of the violence (e.g., bruises, back pain), or the physical consequences of IPV can be health related (see Table 11-3). Further, these health consequences can affect many systems throughout the body (e.g., brain and nervous system, cardiovascular system, gastrointestinal system) and have long-term effects (Black, 2011). For example, according to the CDC (2014c), common health conditions related to IPV include

- Asthma
- Bladder/kidney infections
- Circulatory conditions
- Cardiovascular disease

- Fibromyalgia
- Irritable bowel syndrome
- Chronic pain syndromes
- Central nervous system disorders
- Gastrointestinal disorders
- Joint disease
- Migraines/headaches

Being a victim of IPV is also associated with reproductive problems, such as gynecological disorders, pelvic inflammatory disease, sexual dysfunction, sexually transmitted infections, delayed prenatal care, preterm delivery, unintended pregnancy, and pregnancy difficulties, including low birth weight (CDC, 2014c).

IPV often takes the form of psychological or emotional abuse (see Chapter 6), which causes victims to suffer various mental health consequences. Like victims of other types of crime, IPV victims experience depression, anxiety, PTSD, and reduced self-esteem after victimization, but other common consequences are flashbacks (e.g., reliving the assault in the mind), insomnia, fear of intimacy, difficulty trusting others, and emotional detachment (Black, 2011). A victim of IPV described some of the psychological effects of abuse in the following way:

> *But the feeling like, um for the PTSD is . . . when I hear fire trucks or ambulances, a fire drill in a building, if there's too much yelling in a room, you know or . . . just somebody comes up and scares me, it immediately sets me into a panic mode and I have like these little episodes I call 'em. And . . . I get like a sharp pain in my head and I just I start crying and I can actually sometimes if it's a bad one I can go back and feel, re-feel what was done to me.* (Cerulli, Poleshuck, Raimondi, Veale, & Chin, 2012, p. 796)

Victims are also affected socially and behaviorally by IPV. Socially, IPV has been reported to be related to isolation from the victim's social networks (e.g., family and friends) and with homelessness. Behaviorally, researchers have found connections between victimization and suicidal behaviors, high-risk sexual behaviors (e.g., multiple sex partners, unprotected sex), using harmful substances (e.g., illicit drug use, drinking alcohol), and unhealthy diet-related behaviors (e.g., overeating, abusing diet pills) (CDC, 2014c). IPV in the home is also reportedly linked with child abuse (Appel & Holden, 1998).

As was the case for research investigating the consequences of childhood victimization, there are many excellent studies of the consequences of IPV, so only a few notable examples are discussed. First, Ann Coker and her colleagues (2002) analyzed the NVAWS data with a focus on victims of IPV and the health consequences, both physical and mental, incurred by victims of this crime. The results suggested that victims of IPV were at heightened risks for developing chronic health conditions. For instance, male and female victims experiencing psychological forms of

IPV were found to be at greater risks of developing depressive symptoms; women also were found to be at greater risks for developing a chronic disease. In a somewhat similar study examining a large sample of adolescents (age 11 to 21) from the National Longitudinal Study of Adolescent Health, Timothy Roberts, Jonathan Klein, and Susan Fisher (2003) reported that victimization by an intimate partner was associated with significantly higher levels of illicit substance use, antisocial behavior, violent behavior, suicidal behavior, and depression among victims.

Studies also have reported that IPV affects women financially. For example, research by Susan Lloyd and Nina Taluc (1999) found that among women in Chicago, those who were victims of IPV were more likely to have been unemployed in the past and to have higher rates of government assistance, such as being on food stamps. In addition, research by Wendy Max and colleagues (2004) explained that victimization carries significant costs, including medical care, mental health care, lost productivity, and loss of life. These costs translated nationally to roughly $6.2 billion for physical assaults and $1.2 billion for loss of life. (These estimates are based on health care costs in 2003 dollars and are likely significantly higher today given rising health care costs.)

The sexual victimization of women likewise results in physical, psychological, social, and health-related consequences for victims. Figure 11-1 provides information on the immediate types of physical injuries (e.g., scratches, welts, bruises) that female rape victims sustained based on data collected as part of the NVAWS. However, sexual victimization as a category is quite diverse, with offenses ranging from unwanted touching to rape, so the nature of injury is also quite varied. Further, the victim's reaction to the offense may also affect the type of injury sustained. For example, if the victim attempts to fight the attacker off and fails, the attacker may respond with even greater physical force.

The World Health Organization reported that the health implications of sexual violence are related to several long-term physical consequences, including pregnancy, gynecological complications, and sexually transmitted diseases (see Jewkes, Sen, & Garcia-Moreno, 2002). In terms of immediate psychological and mental health consequences, victims of sexual violence often experience feelings of shock, fear, guilt, denial, anxiety, withdrawal, nervousness, distrust, and symptoms of PTSD (CDC, 2014d). Like victims of IPV, long-term consequences for victims of sexual offenses include PTSD, depression, suicidal thoughts or attempts, and alienation (CDC, 2014d; Jewkes et al., 2002).

Sexual violence also has social and behavioral implications for victims. Socially, sexual victimization often strains victims' relationships with family and friends, leading to less frequent contact and reduced emotional support. Victimization is also related to risky behaviors, many of which can affect not only the victim's health but also the likelihood of subsequent victimization. Some of these include high-risk sexual behaviors (e.g., early sexual initiation, trading sex for food or money), using harmful substances (e.g., drugs, alcohol, cigarettes), and eating disorders (e.g., vomiting, fasting) (CDC, 2014d).

Many of the studies investigating how victims are affected by sexual violence have been undertaken within a public health framework. For example, research by

Ariel Lang and colleagues (2003) examined the relationship between sexual assault victimization, PTSD, and other risks to health. This study used a survey methodology that involved contacting women through the mail who had visited a Veterans Administration primary care clinic in San Diego. The results suggested that women actively or formerly serving in the armed forces with a history of sexual assault had significantly more symptoms of PTSD. Further, victims were significantly more likely to be regular smokers and engage in high-risk sexual behaviors, such as consenting to sex at a young age, having more lifetime sexual partners, and having sex with partners before knowing their sexual history.

Research by Melody Slashinski, Ann Coker, and Keith Davis (2003) has applicability for several types of victimization highlighted in this chapter, including IPV, sexual violence, and stalking. This study, based on the NVAWS, assessed how violence by a dating partner affected victims' health. With respect to sexual victimization, as compared to nonvictims, victims were twice as likely (or nearly) to report current poor health, depression, antidepressant use, pain medication use, recreational drug use, and heavy alcohol use for incidents occurring in the last five years. For physical aggression by a date, victims were twice as likely to report current recreational drug use and heavy alcohol use; victims of stalking were also at double the odds for these outcomes, as well as antidepressant usage.

In reference to the financial consequences of sexual victimization, the previously discussed study by Max and colleagues (2004) is again illustrative. The study estimated that in the United States the economic toll of rape victimization perpetrated by intimate partners totaled over $319 million (in 2003 dollars). Medical care costs were the largest contributor to this figure ($166 million), but mental health costs were also substantial ($104 million). The study also found that 20% of victims of IPV rapes lost time from paid work ($557 per woman on average) and 14% lost time from household work ($252 per woman on average).

In keeping with the emphasis on victimization across the life course, the consequences of elder maltreatment are discussed in the next section of the chapter. Although elderly persons are victims of the same crimes discussed throughout the chapter, the effects of elder victimization may be more severe due to advanced age or existing health conditions.

Elder Maltreatment

It is difficult to estimate the extent of elder maltreatment owing to a lack of research on the topic using national-level data (see Chapter 6). Given this fact, information on the consequences of elder maltreatment is also scarce. Clearly, however, there are substantial physical and psychological effects of criminal victimization for elderly persons, many of which could be exacerbated by the aging process. Like child maltreatment, IPV, and sexual victimization, the CDC has identified elder maltreatment as a serious public health concern, and as such, the agency provides some information on the consequences of victimization. Physical effects of elder maltreatment, as identified by the CDC (2014b), can be immediate injuries (e.g., broken bones, bruises, head injuries), other physical outcomes (e.g., susceptibility to new illnesses, worsening of existing health problems, hydration issues), or even an increased likelihood of premature death.

Although research in this area is still evolving, a few studies illuminate the nature of the consequences of elder maltreatment. For instance, a study by Bonnie Fisher and Saundra Regan (2006) examined the effects of elder abuse on the health of victims through the Women's Health and Relationship Survey. Their study included a sample of women over the age of 60 and asked them to disclose their health status/conditions, as well as any history of abuse since the age of 55. The results indicated that women who were abused were significantly more likely to report a higher number of health conditions than women who were not abused, as well as digestive problems and chronic pain. Women who reported being victims of psychological/emotional abuse were significantly more likely than nonvictims to report a range of health problems, including high blood pressure or other heart troubles, depression or anxiety, digestive issues, and joint or bone problems.

Psychologically, victims of elder maltreatment suffer in ways comparable to other adult crime victims. Victims are susceptible to depression, stress, anxiety, fear, and PTSD. Karl Pillemer and Demise Prescott (1989) were among the first to study the consequences of elder maltreatment. Their research included a random sample of participants from the Boston, Massachusetts, metropolitan area and found a strong relationship between victimization and psychological well-being. That is, victims of maltreatment had significantly higher levels of depression compared to nonvictims. Similar research also has been undertaken outside the United States. For example, a study by Hannie Comijs and colleagues (1998) focused on the prevalence and consequences of elder abuse in The Netherlands. The study found that one-year prevalence for abuse was 5.6%. Further, most victims had an emotional reaction to being victimized that included anger, grief, or disappointment. However, only a few victims incurred physical injuries (e.g., bruises) or financial losses due to their mistreatment.

As the discussion thus far illustrates, individuals experiencing a criminal victimization suffer significant consequences. However, victimization also affects those who care about the victim, even if they did not directly experience the event. Although this is many times the case (e.g., child maltreatment, elder maltreatment), the following discussion highlights the effects of crime on a previously unaddressed victimization type: homicide.

Homicide and Its Effects on Survivors

For homicide victims, the experience, by definition, is fatal. These victims are sometimes referred to as ***direct or primary victims*** because they experience the crime first hand. Yet, there are also ***indirect or secondary victims*** of this crime who continue to suffer long after the criminal event. For victimologists, these individuals are ***homicide survivors***—family, friends, and others (e.g., coworkers) who experience consequences (e.g., distress, anxiety, PTSD) similar to those affecting direct crime victims. That is, survivors experience psychological, mental health, social, and behavioral consequences of homicide victimization. In part, this is because losing a loved one is painful, regardless of the circumstances, but even more so if the loss is the result of sudden, violent, malicious, and fatal criminal behavior.

Most of the victimological research surrounding homicide survivorship and its consequences has focused on psychological and mental health effects suffered by survivors, which, among others, include PTSD, suicide, extreme grief, and fear (Zinzow, Thompson, & Rheingold, 2014). For instance, Heidi Zinzow and colleagues (2009) surveyed a national sample of young adults to investigate the prevalence and mental health correlates of losing a loved one to fatal violence. Among members of the sample, 15% were homicide survivors, and of these the largest proportion was African American. The results also suggested that being a homicide survivor was significantly related to PTSD, depression, and drug/alcohol abuse and dependence.

Being a homicide survivor also has been found to have more severe consequences than directly experiencing other forms of violence. For example, Zinzow and colleagues (2011) reported nearly double the prevalence of PTSD symptoms among homicide survivors in comparison to victims of other violent crimes (see also Freedy et al., 1994). They hypothesized that the reason for this is that survivors are dealing with multiple stressors simultaneously, such as financial hardship resulting from the loss, interactions with the criminal justice system and the media, and bereavement. It is also likely that the relationship between the direct victim and the homicide survivor influences how survivors respond to the criminal event. Whether the victim was a child, parent, sibling, other family member, or friend, survivorship will bring different constellations of additional stressors (e.g., financial loss, loss of companionship) that have differential effects on survivors.

Summary

Criminal victimization has general and crime-specific consequences for victims. Overall, personal forms of victimization can yield physical consequences (e.g., injuries), whereas all forms of victimization can affect victims physiologically, psychologically, emotionally, financially, socially, and behaviorally. Some of these consequences are commonly experienced by victims of all types of crime, whereas others have a greater frequency among victims of particular crimes. Common psychological and mental health consequences of criminal victimization include depression, anxiety, and PTSD and can affect victims of all crimes to varying degrees. The financial, social, and behavioral consequences of victimization depend on the type of crime and the other ways in which victims are affected after victimization. Along these lines, researchers have investigated how certain offenses affect victims. In particular, emphasis has been placed on child maltreatment and peer victimization, IPV and sexual violence, and elder maltreatment. Criminal victimization also has consequences for indirect victims of crime. Homicide survivors experience many of the same consequences of crime as direct victims of crime, even though they did not have first-hand involvement in the offense (Box "Spotlight on Policy: Coping with Media after a Homicide"). Understanding how individuals are affected by criminal victimization provides much-needed evidence for more effective responses to victims by the criminal justice system, service providers, and health care professionals.

Spotlight on Policy: Coping with Media after a Homicide

Americans do not readily understand that "the news" is a profit-making enterprise, whether we are talking about electronic or print media. Unbiased and straightforward reporting of the facts about an event or of a local or national issue is becoming increasingly rare. Instead, the focus is on ratings and the advertising dollars they generate. Indeed, "watching the news can be a psychologically risky pursuit, which could undermine [viewers'] mental . . . health" (Serani, 2011).

Over the past few decades, both electronic and print media are guilty of focusing on what some call "fear-based news" explicitly intended to prey on consumers' anxieties and keep them "glued" to the television. In the decades preceding the development of 24-hour news cycles, the generally agreed-upon mission of journalists was to report the news as it was actually happening or had happened with fairness, balance, and respect. However, with the rise of the 24-hour news cycle and the need to fill programming, much electronic and print journalism looks to the spectacular, the rare, and the violent to capture audiences and increase ratings. According to Serani (2011), "It's no longer a race to break the story first or get the facts right. Instead, it's to acquire good ratings in order to get advertisers, so that profits soar."

Because homicide is relatively rare, especially when multiple victims are involved, it is "newsworthy" and likely to generate coverage that can range from local to international in scope, depending on the circumstances. For homicide survivors, dealing with the media can be a major stressor. Part of the reason for this is because homicide survivors are unlikely to be able to grieve in private. As a result, the death of their loved one or friend and their grief over the loss become a very public event via coverage by local media, through stories posted on the Internet, and as a result of postings to social media (e.g., Facebook, Twitter). Anyone from any of these sources may contact friends and families to comment on what is taking place and the attention may become intrusive: Reporters may follow survivors home, may establish a "base of operation" outside the survivor's home, and so forth. Ultimately, members of the media may not have the best interests of survivors in mind.

Because of this new reality, victim advocacy groups offer assistance to homicide survivors in dealing with the media. Below are some of the tips for dealing with the media one victims' group provides to homicide survivors in New Zealand:

- Nominate someone you trust to speak on behalf of the family.
- Use an answering machine to filter calls.
- Decide with the family and friends what information will be shared with the public, including information shared on social media.
- Discuss with the police and the family liaison what photos you want to give to media.
- Remember that footage of photos/videos you allow the media to use can be used in the future.
- When possible, ask police to notify you of media releases they are making before they release them.
- If you choose to speak with the media, ask for questions in advance and ask if you are being recorded.
- If you choose not to speak to the media, then you can simply say "no comment."
- Be aware of incorrect information that may be provided by friends or others, and if necessary, issue a correction.
- Remember, there is no such thing as "off the record": Media will use anything you say at any time.

Source: Adapted from Serani (2011) and Victim Support of New Zealand (n.d.).

KEYWORDS

Physical consequences
Physical trauma
Psychological and mental health consequences
Short-term consequences
Long-term consequences
Depression
Anxiety
Acute stress disorder
Posttraumatic stress disorder
Crisis reaction
Impact stage
Recoil stage
Reorganization stage
Social stigma
Direct or primary victims
Indirect or secondary victims
Homicide survivors

DISCUSSION QUESTIONS

1. Why might the consequences of victimization differ depending on the characteristics of the victim?
2. Describe the consequences of victimization and how they depend on the type of crime.
3. Explain why studies such as those discussed in this chapter find a relationship between childhood victimization and juvenile delinquency among victims. Which consequences may be more severe?
4. Describe why being a homicide survivor may have more severe consequences than being a direct victim of crime.
5. What can the criminal justice system do to help crime victims overcome the damaging consequences of criminal victimization?
6. Explain why consequences differ by type of crime. Provide relevant examples for each type of crime,
7. Which type of consequence is the "worst" to experience after being victimized? Provide a rationale for your answer.
8. Other than the consequences identified in this chapter, what other types of consequences do crime victims experience? Describe using examples.

REFERENCES

Adler, F. S. (1975). *Sisters in crime: The rise of the new female criminal*. New York: McGraw-Hill.

Agnew, R. (2006). *Pressured into crime: An overview of general strain theory*. Los Angeles, CA: Roxbury.

American Psychiatric Association. (2013). *Diagnostic and statistical manual* (5th ed.). Arlington, VA: American Psychiatric Publishing.

Appel, A. E., & Holden, G. W. (1998). The co-occurrence of spouse and physical child abuse: A review and appraisal. *Journal of Family Psychology, 12*, 578–599.

Averdijk, M. (2011). Reciprocal effects of victimization and routine activities. *Journal of Quantitative Criminology, 27*, 125–149.

Bard, M., & Sangrey, D. (1979). *The crime victim's book*. New York: Basic Books.

Black, M. C. (2011). Intimate partner violence and adverse health consequences: Implications for clinicians. *American Journal of Lifestyle Medicine, 5*, 428–439.

Black, M. C., Basile, K. C., Breiding, M. J., Smith, S. G., Walters, M. L., Merrick, M. T., Chen, J., & Stevens, M. R. (2011). *The National Intimate Partner and Sexual Violence Survey: 2010 summary report*. Atlanta, GA: National Center for Injury Prevention and Control, Centers for Disease Control and Prevention.

Bouffard, L. A., & Koeppel, M. D. H. (2014). Understanding the potential long-term physical and mental health consequences of early experiences of victimization. *Justice Quarterly, 31*, 568–587.

Brecklin, L. R., & Ullman, S. E. (2001). The role of offender alcohol use in rape attacks: An analysis of National Crime Victimization survey data. *Journal of Interpersonal Violence, 16*, 3–21.

Bunch, J., Clay-Warner, J., & McMahon-Howard, J. (2014). The effects of victimization on routine activities. *Criminal Justice and Behavior, 41*, 574–592.

Bureau of Justice Statistics. *Criminal victimization in the United States, 2008: Statistical tables*. Retrieved April 25, 2014, from http://www.bjs.gov/content/pub/pdf/cvus08.pdf

Bureau of Justice Statistics. *Number and rate of victim injury by type of personal victimization, 2012*. Generated using the NCVS Victimization Analysis Tool at www.bjs.gov, April 15, 2014.

Bursik, R. J., & Grasmick, H. G. (1993). *Neighborhoods and crime: The dimensions of effective community control*. New York: Lexington Books.

Centers for Disease Control and Prevention. (2014a). *Child maltreatment: Consequences*. Retrieved May 11, 2014, from http://www.cdc.gov/violenceprevention/childmaltreatment/consequences.html

Centers for Disease Control and Prevention. (2014b). *Elder abuse: Consequences*. Retrieved May 11, 2014, from http://www.cdc.gov/violenceprevention/elderabuse/consequences.html

Centers for Disease Control and Prevention. (2014c). *Intimate partner violence: Consequences*. Retrieved May 11, 2014, from http://www.cdc.gov/violenceprevention/intimatepartnerviolence/consequences.html

Centers for Disease Control and Prevention. (2014d). *Sexual violence: Consequences*.

Retrieved May 11, 2014, from http://www.cdc.gov/violenceprevention/sexualviolence/consequences.html

Cerulli, C., Poleshuck, E., Raimondi, C., Veale, S., & Chin, N. (2012). "What fresh hell is this?" Victims of intimate partner violence describe their experiences of abuse, pain, and depression. *Journal of Family Violence, 27,* 773–781.

Coker, A. L., Davis, K. E., Arias, I., Desai, S., Sanderson, M., Brandt, H. M., & Smith, P. H. (2002). Physical and mental health effects of intimate partner violence for men and women. *American Journal of Preventive Medicine, 23,* 260–268.

Comijs, H. C., Pot, A. M., Smit, J. H., Bouter, L. M., & Jonker, C. (1998). Elder abuse in the community: Prevalence and consequences. *Journal of the American Geriatrics Society, 46,* 885–888.

Cook, F. L., Skogan, W. G., Cook, T. D., & Antunes, G. E. (1978). Criminal victimization of the elderly: The physical and economic consequences. *The Gerontologist, 18,* 338–349.

Cullen, F. T., Unnever, J. D., Hartman, J. L., Turner, M. G., & Agnew, R. (2008). Gender, bullying victimization, and juvenile delinquency: A test of general strain theory. *Victims and Offenders, 3,* 331–349.

Deem, D., Nerenberg, L., & Titus, R. M. (2014). Victims of financial crime. In R. C. Davis, A. J. Lurigio, & S. Herman (Eds.), *Victims of crime* (4th ed., pp. 185–210). Thousand Oaks, CA: Sage.

DeLisi, M., Jones-Johnson, G., Johnson, W. R., & Hochstetler, A. (2014). The aftermath of criminal victimization: Race, self-esteem, and self-efficacy. *Crime and Delinquency, 60,* 85–105.

Demaris, A., & Kaukinen, C. (2005). Violent victimization and women's mental and physical health: Evidence from a national sample. *Journal of Research in Crime and Delinquency, 42,* 384–411.

Dugan, L. (1999). The effect of criminal victimization on a household's moving decision. *Criminology, 37,* 903–930.

Esbensen, F. A., & Carson, D. C. (2009). Consequences of being bullied: Results from a longitudinal assessment of bullying victimization in a multisite sample of American students. *Youth & Society, 41,* 209–233.

Fang, X., Brown, D. S., Florence, C. S., & Mercy, J. A. (2012). The economic burden of child maltreatment in the United States and implications for prevention. *Child Abuse & Neglect, 36,* 156–165.

Federal Bureau of Investigation. (2014). *Uniform Crime Reports.* Retrieved April 25, 2014, from http://www.fbi.gov/about-us/cjis/ucr/crime-in-the-u.s/2012/crime-in-the-u.s.-2012/cius_home

Fisher, B. S., & Regan, S. L. (2006). The extent and frequency of abuse in the lives of older women and their relationship with health outcomes. *The Gerontologist, 46,* 200–209.

Freedy, J. R., Resnick, H. S., Kilpatrick, D. G., Dansky, B. S., & Tidwell, R. P. (1994). The psychological adjustment of recent crime victims in the criminal justice system. *Journal of Interpersonal Violence, 9,* 450–468.

Gale, J. A., & Coupe, T. (2005). The behavioural, emotional and psychological effects of street robbery on victims. *International Review of Victimology, 12,* 1–22.

Gilbert, R., Widom, C. S., Browne, K., Fergusson, D., Webb, E., & Janson, S. (2009). Burden and consequences of child maltreatment in high-income countries. *The Lancet, 373 (9657),* 68–81.

Goffman, E. (1963). *Stigma: Notes on the management of spoiled identity.* Englewood Cliffs, NJ: Prentice-Hall.

Harrell, E., & Langton, L. (2013). *Victims of identity theft, 2012* (NCJ 243779). Washington, DC: Bureau of Justice Statistics.

Hawker, D. S. J., & Boulton, M. J. (2000). Twenty years' research on peer victimization and psychosocial maladjustment: A meta-analytic review of cross-sectional studies. *Journal of Child Psychology and Psychiatry, 41,* 441–455.

Holtfreter, K. (2008). Determinants of fraud losses in nonprofit organizations. *Nonprofit Management and Leadership. 19,* 45–63.

Jewkes, R., Sen, P., & Garcia-Moreno, C. (2002). In E. Krug, L. L. Dahlberg, J. A.

Mercy, A. B. Zwi, & R. Lozano (Eds.), *World report on violence and health* (pp. 213–239). Geneva, Switzerland: World Health Organization.

Johnson, M. C., & Kercher, G. A. (2009). Identifying predictors of negative psychological reactions to stalking victimization. *Journal of Interpersonal Violence, 24*, 866–882.

Kaufman, J. G., & Widom, C. S. (1999). Childhood victimization, running away, and delinquency. *Journal of Research in Crime and Delinquency, 36*, 347–370.

Kleck, G., & DeLone, M. A. (1993). Victim resistance and offender weapon effects in robbery. *Journal of Quantitative Criminology, 9*, 55–81.

Kuehner, C., Gass, P., & Dressing, H. (2012). Mediating effects of stalking victimization on gender differences in mental health. *Journal of Interpersonal Violence, 27*, 199–221.

Lang, A. J., Rodgers, C. S., Laffaye, C., Satz, L. E., Desselhaus, T. R., & Stein, M. B. (2003). Sexual trauma, posttraumatic stress disorder, and health behavior. *Behavioral Medicine, 28*, 150–158.

Leeb, R. T., Lewis, T., & Zolotor, A. J. (2011). A review of physical and mental health consequences of child abuse and neglect and implications for practice. *American Journal of Lifestyle Medicine, 5*, 454–468.

Littleton, H., Grills-Taquechel, A., & Axsom, D. (2009). Impaired and incapacitated rape victims: Assault characteristics and post-assault experiences. *Violence and Victims, 24*, 439–457.

Lloyd, S., & Taluc, N. (1999). The effects of male violence on female unemployment. *Violence Against Women, 5*, 370–392.

Max, W., Rice, D. P., Finkelstein, E., Bardwell, R. A., & Leadbetter, S. (2004). The economic toll of intimate partner violence against women in the United States. *Violence and Victims, 19*, 259–272.

Melde, C., & Rennison, C. M. (2008). The effect of gang perpetrated crime on the likelihood of non-lethal victim injury. *American Journal of Criminal Justice, 33*, 234–251.

Menard, S. (2002). *Short- and long-term consequences of adolescent victimization.* Washington, DC: Office of Juvenile Justice and Delinquency Prevention.

Messner, S. F., McHugh, S., & Felson, R. B. (2004). Distinctive characteristics of assaults motivated by bias. *Criminology, 42*, 585–618.

National Center for Victims of Crime. (2014). *The trauma of victimization.* Retrieved April 25, 2014, from http://www.victimsofcrime.org

National Health Care Anti-Fraud Association. (2010). *Combating health care fraud in a post-reform world: Seven guiding principles for policymakers.* Retrieved May 10, 2014, from http://www.sas.com/resources/asset/health-insurance-third-party-white-paper-nhcaa.pdf

O'Sullivan, C. S. (2014). Sexual violence victimization of women, men, youth, and children. In R. C. Davis, A. J. Lurigio, & S. Herman (Eds.), *Victims of crime* (4th ed., pp. 3–28). Thousand Oaks, CA: Sage.

Peltier-Rivest, D., & Lanoue, N. (2012). Thieves from within: Occupational fraud in Canada. *Journal of Financial Crime, 19*, 54–64.

Pillemer, K., & Prescott, D. (1989). Psychological effects of elder abuse: A research note. *Journal of Elder Abuse & Neglect, 1*, 65–73.

Rantala, R. R. (2008). *Cybercrime against businesses, 2005* (NCJ 221943). Washington, DC: Bureau of Justice Statistics.

Roberts, T. A., Klein, J. D., & Fisher, S. (2003). Longitudinal effect of intimate partner abuse on high-risk behavior among adolescents. *Archives of Pediatrics and Adolescent Medicine, 157*, 875–881.

Ruback, R. B., & Thompson, M. P. (2001). *Social and psychological consequences of violent victimization.* Thousand Oaks, CA: Sage Publications.

Schnebly, S. M. (2002). An examination of the impact of victim, offender, and situational attributes on the deterrent effect of defensive gun use: A research note. *Justice Quarterly, 19*, 377–398.

Serani, D. (2011). If it bleeds, it leads: Understanding fear-based media. *Psychology Today*, June 7, 2011. Retrieved May 14, 2014, from http://www.psychologytoday

.com/blog/two-takes-depression/201106/if-it-bleeds-it-leads-understanding-fear-based-media

Shapland, J., & Hall, M. (2007). What do we know about the effects of crime on victims? *International Review of Victimology, 14*, 175–217.

Skogan, W. G. (1987). The impact of victimization on fear. *Crime and Delinquency, 33*, 135–154.

Slashinski, M. J., Coker, A. L., & Davis, K. E. (2003). Physical aggression, forced sex, and stalking victimization by a dating partner: An analysis of the National Violence Against Women Survey. *Violence and Victims, 18*, 595–617.

Tillyer, M. S., Miller, J. M., & Tillyer, R. (2011). The environmental and situational correlates of victim injury in nonfatal violent incidents. *Criminal Justice and Behavior, 38*, 433–452.

Tjaden, P., & Thoennes, N. (2006). *Extent, nature, and consequences of rape victimization: Findings from the National Violence Against Women Survey* (NCJ 210346). Washington, DC: National Institute of Justice.

Turner, H. A., Finkelhor, D., & Ormrod, R. (2006). The effect of lifetime victimization on the mental health of children and adolescents. *Social Science and Medicine, 62*, 13–27.

Victim Support of New Zealand (n.d.). *Coping with homicide.* Retrieved May 10, 2014, from http://www.victimsupport.org.nz/wp-content/uploads/2014/12/CopingWithMediaAfterHomicide.pdf

Xie, M., & McDowall, D. (2008). Escaping crime: The effects of direct and indirect victimization on moving. *Criminology, 46*, 809–840.

Zinzow, H. M., Rheingold, A. A., Byczkiewicz, M., Saunders, B. E., & Kilpatrick, D. G. (2011). Examining posttraumatic stress symptoms in a national sample of homicide survivors: Prevalence and comparison to other violence victims. *Journal of Traumatic Stress, 24*, 743–746.

Zinzow, H. M., Rheingold, A. A., Hawkins, A. O., Saunders, B. E., & Kilpatrick, D. G. (2009). Losing a loved one to homicide: Prevalence and mental health correlates in a national sample of young adults. *Journal of Traumatic Stress, 22*, 20–27.

Zinzow, H. M., Thompson, M. P., & Rheingold, A. A. (2014). Homicide survivors: A summary of the research. In R. C. Davis, A. J. Lurigio, & S. Herman (Eds.), *Victims of crime* (4th ed., pp. 133–160). Thousand Oaks, CA: Sage.

CHAPTER 12

Responding to Victimization

CHAPTER OUTLINE

LEARNING OBJECTIVES

- Describe the crime victim's role in the criminal justice process.
- Explain how individuals can use the civil justice system in response to criminal victimization.
- Identify crime victims' rights.
- Distinguish between victim *compensation* and victim *restitution*.
- Define victim advocacy and describe the types of assistance and services that are available to crime victims

---

> *Everyone is affected by crime, either as a direct victim or a friend or family member of a victim.*
>
> **Wasserman and Ellis, 2007, p. VI-3**

Introduction

The victims' rights movement of the 1980s dramatically affected how victims, justice system personnel, and legislators responded to crime. In general, responses to victims can be divided into three broad categories: (1) justice system responses, (2) legal rights of victims, and (3) victim assistance and services. First, the criminal justice system responds by investigating the alleged crime, arresting a suspect, charging him or her with a crime, trying the defendant in a court of law, and, if convicted, punishing the guilty party. Apart from the criminal justice system, there are also civil justice remedies available to victims which involve defendants paying damages to the victim. In both systems victims participate in varying degrees and ultimately may receive money that can be used to help them recover from the harm they suffered. Second, victims have certain legal rights, and they constitute another important response to victimization. In the United States, crime victims have the right to compensation and, depending on how the criminal justice system disposes of the case against the offender, perhaps restitution. In general, victims have the right to be notified of various proceedings, including those relating to the pretrial, trial, sentencing, and posttrial (e.g., parole hearings) stages of the process. Victims also have the right to participate in the criminal justice process, the right to protection from the defendant, the right to a speedy trial, and the right to be treated with dignity and respect by the system. Third, various types of assistance and services are available to victims of crime to help them recover from being victimized. Importantly, the type of assistance and services that victims may need differs according to the type of crime with which they were involved. This chapter reviews these three categories of responses to criminal victimization.

Justice System Responses

As Chapter 10 discussed, one of the most important decisions facing crime victims is whether to report the crime to law enforcement. If a victim does decide to contact law enforcement, the wheels of the criminal justice system officially begin to turn. Once the victim has reported the crime, his or her role in this process is of particular note—besides reporting the crime, victims often provide crucial evidence that informs the way law enforcement and prosecutors handle the case going forward. Assuming the case goes to trial rather than reaching a disposition through a plea arrangement, as most do, the victim may be called upon to testify in court, and if the defendant is found guilty, the victim has the right to submit a statement to the judge relating to the sentence the defendant should receive prior to formal sentencing. In the correctional system, parole boards may rely on victim statements in making their decisions on whether offenders may be released from prison prior to serving their full sentence.

In addition to responding to criminal victimization by pursuing a case against the offender in the criminal courts, the legal system offers victims an alternative for holding the offender accountable for their actions—through civil actions (lawsuits). The courts allow victims to sue those responsible for their victimization, such as offenders or other parties, for monetary damages. If the victim wins his or her case, the judge will order the offender(s) to pay the victim, and although money cannot fully restore the victim to how there were before the victimization, it can prove valuable in the recovery process.

Criminal Justice Responses

Law Enforcement

Crime victims are important to the functioning of the criminal justice system, which is divided into three segments: (1) law enforcement, (2) the courts, and (3) corrections, including institutional (jails and prisons) and community-based (e.g., probation or house arrest) corrections. The role of law enforcement in the criminal justice process is to receive crime reports from victims, witnesses, or others and make a report; reported crimes are then investigated and, with enough evidence, an arrest is made or a citation issued. A victim's initial contact with the criminal justice system is usually through law enforcement, which gives responding officers tremendous influence over how the victim perceives the situation, as well as how the victim views the criminal justice system. For example, if an officer is unsympathetic to the victim, he or she may view the experience with the system in a negative light and feel that law enforcement or the criminal justice system did not care about him or her. Law enforcement officers also may influence whether victims take advantage of available services by providing them information on the scope and nature of services available and by informing victims of their rights.

Perhaps the most important law enforcement response to criminal victimization, however, is identifying, apprehending, and arresting the offender. This function has been the subject of much research and debate, especially as it applies to domestic violence (see Chapter 6). Several states have enacted what are referred to as "mandatory arrest" laws in cases of domestic violence. ***Mandatory arrest laws*** require officers responding to domestic violence calls to arrest the offender if there is probable cause to believe an assault has occurred, *regardless of the victim's wishes.*

Mandatory arrest laws proliferated in the 1980s and 1990s following an influential study by Lawrence Sherman and Rickard Berk (1984) often referred to as the ***Minneapolis Domestic Violence Experiment*** (MDVE). That study used an experimental design where officers responding to calls for simple (misdemeanor) domestic assaults in Minneapolis, Minnesota, were randomly assigned to one of three responses: (1) arrest the perpetrator, (2) separate the victim and offender for eight hours, and (3) provide some form of advice (e.g., informal mediation) to the couple. For ethical reasons, aggravated (felony) assaults were not included in the random assignment scheme. The study's purpose was to determine if arrest deterred future offending, which would in turn reduce recurring victimization. To do so, Sherman and Berk tracked the behavior of offenders for six months after initial police contact using official data and victim surveys to determine whether there had been any further domestic assault incidents. The findings from this study were influential because they indicated that the most effective response to domestic assault, at least in terms of reducing offender recidivism, was arresting the perpetrator.

The MDVE has been criticized on several grounds, and replications of the study in other cities did not always find that arrest was the most successful response to domestic violence (Garner, Fagan, & Maxwell, 1995). To assess the validity of the study's findings, the National Institute of Justice sponsored five replications of MDVE (called the Spouse Assault Replication Program) at police departments in Charlotte, North Carolina; Colorado Springs, Colorado; Miami-Dade County, Florida; Milwaukee, Wisconsin; and Omaha, Nebraska. None of these studies was an exact replication of the MDVE, as there were differences in sample sizes, measurement of key variables, and available police responses across the studies, but all of them included an experimental design with arrest as one of the possible responses. Table 12-1 summarizes the findings from the Spouse Assault Replication Program and shows that two of the five studies found that arresting perpetrators reduced recidivism, two studies found arrest made no difference in whether the perpetrator

Table 12-1: Spouse Assault Replication Program Findings

Location of Study	Effect of Arrest on Reoffending
Charlotte, NC	No difference between arrest and other outcomes
Colorado Springs, CO	Arrest appeared to deter future offending under some circumstances
Miami-Dade County, FL	Arrest deterred future offending but only when perpetrator was married
Milwaukee, WI	Initial deterrent effects of arrest, but no long-term effects
Omaha, NE	No difference between arrest and other outcomes
Minneapolis, MN	Arrest deterred future offending

Source: Garner, Fagan, and Maxwell (1995).

reoffended, and one suggested that arrest reduced recidivism but only according to victim data, not official data.

In the time between MDVE and the replications, several states had enacted mandatory arrest laws, and today 22 states and the District of Colombia have mandatory arrest statutes. Despite the importance of determining whether arrest deters future intimate partner violence (IPV), there is no clear-cut answer. If arrest does cause offenders to change their behavior and deters them from reoffending, then the victim, the offender, and the criminal justice system will ultimately benefit. If, however, mandatory arrest laws simply discourage victims from reporting their victimization to the police for fear their partner will be arrested, then it is likely the victim will continue to be victimized by their partner. Of course, IPV is not the only crime for which police officers arrest suspects; in some cases, an arrest warrant is required (e.g., in most misdemeanors), while other times, particularly in felonies, officers are allowed to make warrantless arrests based on probable cause. However, prior to passage of mandatory arrest statutes, when the crime was misdemeanor assault, the offense had to occur in the officer's presence before he or she could legally execute an arrest. Mandatory arrest laws broadened police powers and allowed them to arrest perpetrators without a warrant or without having witnessed the incident in less serious, or misdemeanor, IPV situations.

Mandatory arrest laws require law enforcement to act in certain ways following IPV. Similarly, ***mandatory reporting laws*** require certain individuals to contact law enforcement or another appropriate agency (e.g., child protective services) regarding cases of suspected child maltreatment. All states and the District of Columbia have mandatory reporting laws, but to whom the laws apply varies from state to state. In general, those responsible for reporting suspected child maltreatment are individuals coming into frequent contact with children, such as teachers and other school personnel, child health care providers, and social workers, among others. In certain states, such as New Jersey and Wyoming, any person who suspects child maltreatment is supposed to report those suspicions to the police (Child Welfare Information Gateway, 2014). Most states have anonymous toll-free numbers that individuals can use to report suspected victimization, but some state laws require the individual reporting the suspected victimization to provide his or her name and contact information. In states that require reporting parties to disclose their contact information, there are statutory provisions to ensure confidentiality. Overall, the information obtained through mandatory reporting laws is used by social service and criminal justice agencies to investigate and respond to child maltreatment.

The Courts

Victims also are involved in the court process in the criminal justice system. Once law enforcement has arrested a suspect, a prosecutor reviews the evidence provided by law enforcement and decides whether to charge the suspect with a crime. There is a very strong possibility the accused will be offered—and will accept—a plea bargain, which negates the need for a trial and results in a conviction. For the most part, victims are not involved in these stages of the criminal process, but victims *do* have the right to be present at these proceedings, and may even consult with the prosecutor (depending on the state). Usually, however, victims are only involved at the trial and sentencing phases of the process, assuming the defendant is convicted.

In cases that go to trial, the victim may be called as a witness, which means that he or she will provide sworn testimony that will be used as evidence against the defendant. Witnesses are essential to the justice process, because this evidence will be used to help determine the guilt or innocence of the accused. This process can also be intimidating, and many victims experience strong feelings of frustration, confusion, anger, or fear before, during, and after the trial. This is why every state and the federal government have enacted ***victims' rights legislation*** that ensures victims are treated with dignity and respect during the criminal justice process (these rights are discussed in detail later in the chapter). Based on the evidence presented at trial, the judge (bench or waiver trial) or jury (jury trial) decides whether the defendant is guilty of the crime in question beyond a reasonable doubt. If the defendant is found guilty at trial or accepts a plea bargain from the prosecutor, the judge will schedule a sentencing hearing.

Crime victims are often involved in the sentencing phase of the court process. At the sentencing hearing, the victim has the right to submit a ***victim impact statement*** (VIS). A VIS is an account by the victim, either written or verbal, explaining how the crime affected him or her. First and foremost, the VIS is used during sentencing to help determine the offender's punishment. However, depending on the state these statements also may be used to make decisions relating to bail, pretrial release, plea bargains, and even parole. As part of a VIS, victims might describe the physical, emotional, psychological, financial, or medical consequences they experienced as a result of the crime. Some states also allow the victim to comment on the offender and what he or she believes an appropriate sentence should be.

The first known VIS was given in Fresno, California, in 1976 in court proceedings related to the so-called Manson Family murders (Manson Family Murders Facts, 2014), and the introduction of VIS became law in California in 1982. Since then, admission of these statements in the court process has been met with some resistance. Proponents argue that they provide valuable ways for victims to participate in the criminal justice process, in addition to the therapeutic effects they may have for victims. Opponents claim that their use unfairly disadvantages defendants and may result in more severe sentences than would otherwise have been given (e.g., Erez & Roberts, 2014). Regardless, in 1991 the Supreme Court ruled in the case of *Payne v. Tennessee* (501 U.S. 808) that VISs are admissible during the sentencing phase of criminal trials.

Researchers have examined the effects of VISs, both for victims and in the functioning of the criminal justice system. Studies have found that not all victims choose to submit statements to the court; that participation in generally low; and that submission varies by jurisdiction and by victim. For example, Julian Roberts and Allen Edgar (2006) reported that judges in Canada recalled VIS usage in only 11% of the criminal cases over which they presided. In many instances, victims may not even know they have the option to submit a VIS. In others, victims may decide against it for a number of reasons, such as not wanting to reveal personal information in court. Julian Roberts and Marie Manikis (2011) reported that among victims in

England and Wales, only 42% recalled being informed that they had the option to submit a VIS.

With regard to how VISs affect courtroom outcomes, research suggests they have no significant effects on the severity of the offender's sentence. For example, Robert Davis and Barbara Smith (1994) used an experimental design to determine whether the admission of a VIS affected sentencing outcomes in courts in the Bronx, New York. They found no significant differences in sentences received in cases that included a VIS and cases that did not. However, some studies have reported harsher or lighter sentences when VISs are used (e.g., Roberts & Manikis, 2011). In the United States, many jurisdictions have determinate sentencing laws that stipulate narrow ranges of terms of incarceration for crimes, in which case the judge would base the sentence on legal considerations related to the offender's prior record and the seriousness of the crime.

Victimologists have also examined how submitting a VIS affected the victim's satisfaction with the criminal justice process. Overall, the evidence suggests that greater victim participation translates to greater satisfaction with the outcome of the case (e.g., Cattaneo & Goodman, 2010). However, studies have also reported that submitting a VIS has no effect on victim satisfaction (Davis & Smith, 1994) and that other considerations, such as the offender's admission of guilt and considerations such as victim restitution, have a greater impact on satisfaction (see Erez & Roberts, 2014).

Corrections

Many times an offender's sentence will involve incarceration. In the United States, victims may also have input into the correctional process, especially at parole hearings. Parole hearings are proceedings in which a board reviews an offender's case history and determines whether he or she is eligible for early release from a correctional facility. In exchange, the parolee agrees to certain conditions, including continued supervision in the community. Parole boards base their decisions on a number of factors, such as sentence length and amount of sentence that has already been served, type and severity of the offense, and the individual's behavior while incarcerated. Another key piece of information in the decision-making process is the impact of the crime on the victim. Although the methods by which victim evidence is admitted vary across jurisdictions, ranging from a written statement read by the prosecutor in the case to the victim himself or herself appearing at the hearing, all jurisdictions in the United States now allow victims to submit a statement and be present at parole hearings. In some jurisdictions, victims might comment on whether an offender should be released on parole, while in other jurisdictions they may only be allowed to provide input into the conditions of parole (Erez & Roberts, 2014).

In considering victim participation in parole proceedings, researchers have investigated the extent to which victim input affects parole outcomes, but firm conclusions are difficult to make. In some of the most recent research to explore the topic, Joel Caplan (2010) used data from the New Jersey State Parole Board to assess whether and how victim input affected the parole release decisions of 805 inmates.

Caplan considered factors such as whether the parole board was provided with input from either victims or nonvictims into the decision, whether the input was positive or negative, and whether the input was written or verbal. Interestingly, only 22% of inmates received any input at their parole hearings; most of this input was negative (58%), coming from victims (53%), and in written form (69%). Study results suggested that ultimately victim input, regardless of its type or nature, did not affect parole outcomes. Instead, the most significant predictors of parole release were the offender's criminal record and institutional behavior and the severity of the crime. In other research, victim participation of this kind was found to have an effect on parole outcomes. For instance, Kathryn Morgan and Brent Smith (2005) reported that victim participation in parole proceedings in Montgomery, Alabama, was significantly associated with a higher likelihood that parole would be denied. It seems that the effect of victim participation on parole may vary by jurisdiction, and future research should examine whether this is the case.

Parole proceedings are the point in the correctional process at which victims can have the greatest participation and influence. However, victims might also participate in various correctional programs aligned with restorative justice philosophies. ***Restorative justice*** is an approach to justice that emphasizes repairing the harms caused by crime by involving all parties, or stakeholders, in the process. Such an approach requires addressing not only the needs of the victim following the crime, but also the needs of the offender and those of the community. Although the concept of restorative justice has roots dating back thousands of years, there are several contemporary practices that are based in the theory of restorative justice, such as victim–offender mediation, circle sentencing, and family group conferencing.

In brief, ***victim–offender mediation*** is a postconviction opportunity for victims and offenders to meet face to face in the presence of a mediator to discuss the crime and devise a plan for restitution. These programs originated in Canada but have since been adopted in countries all over the world, especially those in Europe and North America. ***Sentencing circles*** are formed after an offender has been found guilty, and at the discretion of the judge. Their purpose is to bring members of the community together to determine an appropriate sentence for the offender. This correctional philosophy also was developed and used in Canada and has been used in select jurisdictions in the United States. ***Family group conferencing*** originated in New Zealand as a means of addressing growing concerns related to the processing of Māori children through the formal criminal justice system. This practice is similar to victim–offender mediation but heavily involves family members in the process of deciding the best interests of the child. Since being legislated in New Zealand in 1989, family group conferencing has spread to several other countries, including the United States.

Research into the effects of restorative justice programs finds that, in general, both victims *and* offenders are more satisfied with outcomes than are either victims or offenders who did not participate in such programs (Latimer, Dowden, & Muise, 2005). Jeff Latimer, Craig Dowden, and Danielle Muise (2005) reported that offenders who participated in restorative justice programs were also more likely to comply with restitution orders and to have lower rates of recidivism.

In sum, the influence of crime victims in the criminal justice process cannot be overstated. Victims provide essential information to law enforcement, the courts,

Table 12-2: Summary of the Victim's Role in the Criminal Justice System

Law Enforcement	Courts	Corrections
Report the crime to law enforcement	Provide testimony during court proceedings	Restorative justice
Provide evidence related to the crime	Submit victim impact statement prior to sentencing	Victim impact statement used in deciding probation or parole

and correctional officials, and without this information the criminal justice system could not function properly. Table 12-2 summarizes the victim's role at these three stages within the criminal justice system. Furthermore, research has found that such participation benefits victims and is viewed by both victims and criminal justice system actors as valuable in the justice process (Englebrecht, 2011).

Civil Justice Responses

The ***civil justice system*** provides legal means by which victims and their families can take direct action against the offender. Civil procedures exist to hold offending parties responsible for the harm they caused as a result of their illegal behavior. In this process, it is not the innocence or guilt of the offender that is in question, but rather whether the offender or someone else (a third party) is liable for the harm sustained by the victim in wake of the crime. If it is determined that the defendant is liable for the injury caused to the victim, he or she will be ordered to pay the victim monetary damages that the victim or victim's family can use to help recover from the harm they have suffered. This system of justice also offers victims a means of attaining justice that may have eluded them in the criminal justice system, since offenders are held directly accountable to the victim rather than to the state.

The civil justice system is complex and the person initiating the action (the plaintiff) will likely require the assistance of an attorney in pursuing a lawsuit against the offender (the defendant). The process involved in filing a civil claim or lawsuit is outlined in Figure 12-1. As this figure indicates, civil lawsuits begin when the plaintiff (i.e., the victim) files a claim or complaint with the court. This is one of the distinctions between the criminal justice system and the civil justice system: In a civil case the victim initiates the proceedings instead of the state. Next, a summons is issued and served to the defendant, along with the complaint, informing the defendant that he or she is being sued, by whom, and that he or she must respond within a specified period of time (e.g., 30 days). At this point, the defendant either files a response to the complaint or neglects to do so. In case of the latter, the plaintiff can request a default judgment, which means that the plaintiff automatically wins the case. To make an analogy to sports, this is similar to winning because the other team forfeits. However, if the plaintiff responds, he or she will answer either by formally denying or admitting to the allegations. After the plaintiff answers, the case moves to the discovery stage.

Discovery is a pretrial phase in which the parties on each side in the lawsuit are able to obtain evidence from the opposing parties that will help them determine the

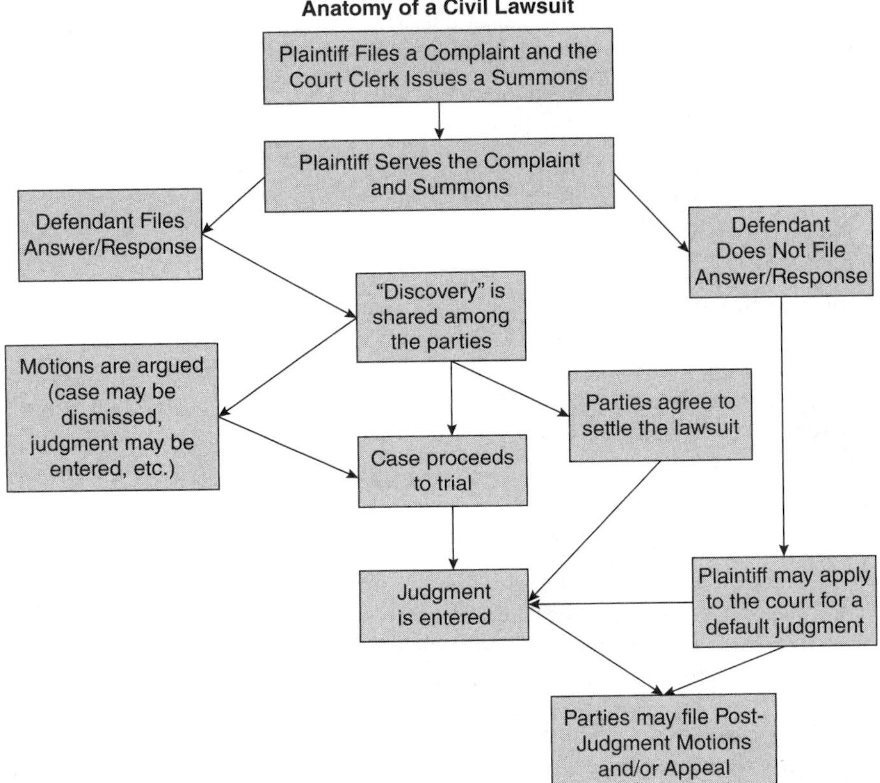

Figure 12-1 Process for a Civil Claim
Source: Clark County (NV) Courts (2014).

strength of the opponent's case and devise an effective response. Following discovery, the parties may agree to settle the lawsuit and avoid a trial, which is often the case. Under these circumstances, a judgment in the case is entered. If, however, a settlement is not reached between the parties, then it is likely one or both sides will submit motions, which are essentially requests that the court act in a certain way. For example, upon reviewing the plaintiff's case, the defendant may submit a motion that the case be dismissed and the lawsuit ended. Assuming that the judge does not grant such motions, the case will go to trial.

Civil trials unfold in a manner similar to criminal trials, in which both sides make opening statements, present evidence (e.g., testimony, documents), and then submit closing arguments. The burden of proof in civil trials requires that liability on the part of the defendant be proven by a preponderance of the evidence by the plaintiff, whereas in criminal trials the burden of proof rests with the state and must be shown beyond a reasonable doubt. After each side has presented its case, either a judge or jury will reach a decision as to whether the defendant is responsible for the plaintiff's injuries. However, this does not necessarily end the case. Following the judgment, either side may also make posttrial motions, such as a motion for a new trial, or an appeal, which is a request for the judgment to be changed or reversed on some specified grounds. Civil justice awards received by victims will then provide resources to pay for costs that were incurred because of the crime, such as medical care or counseling.

Victims' Rights

Historically, crime victims were pivotal in the administration of justice. For example, in colonial times, victims were responsible for paying the sheriff to apprehend the offender, as well as hiring the prosecutor to pursue a case (Howley & Dorris, 2014). Yet, following the adoption of the U.S. Constitution (which does not include specific rights for crime victims), a shift occurred in which the government became responsible for prosecuting offenders and ensuring the administration of justice. This dramatically reduced the role of victims in the justice process, and this more limited role lasted for nearly 200 years. Thus, until the 1960s, victims had a limited part to play in the administration of criminal justice—usually either by reporting crimes to law enforcement or acting as witnesses in criminal cases.

As Chapter 1 discussed, the 1960s were a time of significant social change and a greater recognition of the needs and plight of crime victims in the United States. Important events in victimology relating to victims' rights occurred as a result of several social movements (e.g., the civil rights movement, the "law and order" movement) during this time. The first crime victim compensation programs were created in the 1960s; the first victim impact statement was used in Fresno County, California, in 1976; the first crime victims' bill of rights was enacted in Wisconsin in 1980; and the first victims' rights amendment to a state constitution was enacted in California in 1982. Victims' rights, therefore, are a relatively recent legal development and are still evolving and expanding. Today, the federal government and every state have identified statutory rights for crime victims and 32 states have included such rights in their state constitutions. Internationally, there also has been a recognition and expansion of victims' rights.

While the federal government and all of the states have passed laws in the interests of victims' rights, the rights provided by these laws vary across jurisdictions. In addition, there are also differences by jurisdiction in who may exercise these rights. For example, some, but certainly not all, laws apply only to victims of specific offenses, such as victims of felonies, and do not extend rights to victims of misdemeanors. Further, some states allow individuals (e.g., family members) to act on the victim's behalf. Again, who is able to exercise victims' rights will be determined by the law in the jurisdiction in which the crime is investigated and/or prosecuted. For example, Connecticut law defines a crime victim as "an individual who suffers direct or threatened physical, emotional or financial harm as a result of a crime and includes immediate family members of a minor, incompetent individual or homicide victim and a person designated by a homicide victim in accordance with section 1-56r" (CT Gen Stat § 1-1k, 2012). Despite differences across states, there are common themes in victims' rights laws that broadly involve victims' rights as they apply to engagement and participation in the criminal justice process, or relate to restitution and compensation following the crime.

Engagement and Participation

The federal ***Crime Victims' Rights Act*** (18 U.S.C. § 3771) is part of the *Justice for All Act of 2004* and gives victims of crimes certain rights in federal criminal cases. Many states also have adopted these rights and enacted victims' rights legislation in the form of a ***victims' bill of rights***. While there is variation from state to state in the language used to describe these rights, those provided by the *Crime Victims' Rights Act* are listed below as a framework for discussing victims' rights generally. The eight rights named under the law are:

1. The right to be reasonably protected from the accused
2. The right to reasonable, accurate, and timely notice of any public court proceeding, or any parole proceeding, involving the crime or of any release or escape of the accused
3. The right not to be excluded from any such public court proceeding, unless the court, after receiving clear and convincing evidence, determines that testimony by the victim would be materially altered if the victim heard other testimony in that proceeding
4. The right to be reasonably heard at any public proceeding in the district court involving release, plea, sentencing, or any parole proceeding
5. The reasonable right to confer with the attorney for the government in the case
6. The right to full and timely restitution as provided in law
7. The right to proceedings free from unreasonable delay
8. The right to be treated with fairness and with respect for the victim's dignity and privacy

The first of these rights—the right to protection—also is given to victims in many states throughout the United States depending on their circumstances. On the whole, the right to protection refers to protecting victims from threats to their safety (e.g., retaliation) during criminal proceedings. To that end, victims might receive police escorts, have restraining orders issued against the perpetrator, or receive assistance in relocating, perhaps through a witness protection program. For instance, the California Witness Relocation and Assistance Program provides protection to witnesses, who are often victims of crimes, as well as their family, friends, or associates who may be in danger as a consequence of their participation in the criminal justice process. Specifically, the law affords protections in cases related to gangs, organized crime, or drug trafficking cases that involve risk to the witness' safety.

The second right listed in the *Crime Victims' Rights Act* is the right to be informed. This right also is provided to crime victims in several states. In general, the intent is that victims receive information related to their rights and are made aware of the resources available to them. In many states, the victim's right to be informed involves notification related to the case (e.g., bail proceedings, plea negotiations, parole hearings). For instance, Georgia specifies that victims be notified of events such as the inmate's release from custody, any judicial proceeding at which the release of the accused will be considered, an escape by and subsequent arrest of the accused, and release of the accused to community corrections (e.g., electronic monitoring). In some states (e.g., Oklahoma), victims must submit a request to be notified of these developments in the case, while in others (e.g., Illinois), automated systems will automatically notify victims. The right to notification is somewhat related to the seventh right listed in the *Crime Victims' Right Act*—the right to proceedings free from unreasonable delay. This is analogous to the speedy trial clause provided to defendants in criminal cases found in the Sixth Amendment to the U.S. Constitution. Such a right is important not only to accused persons but also to crime victims, who may feel that their ability to fully recover from the crime is on hold until the case against the offender has been resolved.

The third, fourth, fifth, and eighth rights enumerated by the *Crime Victims' Rights Act* broadly refer to the engagement, participation, and treatment of victims in the criminal justice process. Most states have extended these rights to victims as a means of increasing participation in the criminal justice system and ensuring that crime victims are not further wronged for their participation in the criminal justice process. For example, many state laws protect victims' rights to privacy and confidentiality by limiting disclosure of personally identifying information (e.g., phone number, address, place of work) as they participate in the criminal justice process or seek victim services. A majority of states also give victims the right to employment protection. This right prevents victims who have to miss work in order to participate in the criminal justice process, such as responding to a subpoena, from being penalized or discharged by their employers. The extensiveness of these protections, however, differs with state law. Many legislatures have recognized that victims must be treated fairly and encouraged to participate in the criminal justice process; otherwise they are less likely to exercise their rights and contribute to the functioning of the criminal justice system.

As discussed previously, VISs are the primary means of victim participation in the court process, but they are not the only way in which victims are engaged. Victims also may have the right to confer with the prosecutor before he or she makes decisions about the case—another form of participation. However, the *Crime Victims' Rights Act* only provides this right to victims in federal cases, and how far this right extends is not made entirely clear. While some states also may include this right in a victims' bill of rights or other law, in all cases the prosecutor ultimately makes decisions regarding the case, and not the victim. For example, a victim may wish to express his or her preference that the offender not be offered a plea bargain. However, the prosecutor may still elect to do so against the victim's wishes. While this is the prerogative of the prosecutor, victims' rights legislation also specifies that victims are treated with dignity, respect, and sensitivity. So, in continuing this example, the prosecutor and victim may disagree on how decisions be made, but the victim must be heard and respected throughout this process. This right also applies to victim interactions with law enforcement and other criminal justice officials.

Restitution and Compensation

Under the *Crime Victims' Rights Act*, victims in federal cases are also granted the right to restitution. ***Restitution*** is money that is paid by the offender as part of his or her court-ordered sentence. This is also a right afforded to victims across the United States, and depending on the jurisdiction and the type of crime, courts may be required by law to order restitution for the offender. The purpose of restitution is to help the victim recover from the harm he or she has experienced following the crime. Thus, restitution helps victims pay for provable out-of-pocket costs related to the crime, such as lost wages, medical expenses, or lost or damaged property. Restitution cannot be awarded for emotional distress or pain and suffering. The method by which restitution is paid differs from state to state. In many cases, the offender will make a direct payment to the victim, whereas other times offenders are ordered to pay restitution to a state agency, which then pays the victim. Paying fines and doing community service are other means by which the offender can make amends for the damage that he or she caused, with funds often being deposited into victim compensation programs.

Victim compensation programs are government-administered programs at the federal, state, and local levels designed to provide financial assistance to crime victims. Like restitution, compensation programs exist to alleviate some of the financial burdens created by criminal victimization, through assisting victims with expenses related to medical care, mental health treatment, lost wages, or funerals. Victim compensation differs from restitution in a few key ways. First, restitution is usually a direct payment to the victim from the offender; with compensation programs, agencies are responsible for paying victims. Second, restitution is entirely provided by the offender, whereas compensation programs receive funds from several sources such as criminal fines, payments of fees by offenders on probation or parole, or federal grants. Notably, a major source of funding for compensation programs across the United States is provided through grant funds from the *Victims of Crime Act of 1984* (VOCA). VOCA established the ***Crime Victims Fund***, which receives deposits from many sources, such as offenders convicted of federal crimes, forfeited bail bonds, penalties, and private donations. These funds are then distributed to victim service programs throughout the nation. Figure 12-2 depicts the process involved in victim compensation as it applies to VOCA. Third, and importantly, restitution requires that the offender be arrested, charged, and sentenced to restitution. Compensation is not contingent upon any of these events occurring, and victims may be eligible to receive compensation regardless of the offender's status. However, there are also several eligibility requirements that must be satisfied before victims can receive compensation funds, some of which are federally mandated.

Although victim compensation programs operate within the parameters of the state laws in which they are located, there are four basic criteria shared by all programs. First, to be eligible for compensation, victims *must* report the crime to law enforcement. The timeframe within which the crime must be reported is not the same in every state, but many states require the crime to be reported within 72 hours. Some states allow exceptions to such requirements as long as there is good cause for not reporting the crime within the designated time period, such as that the victim was a child. Eligibility is also contingent upon the victim cooperating with law enforcement and the prosecutor in the case. Second, victims must submit their applications for compensation in a timely manner. Whether an application is considered "timely" is determined by state law, but in many states the time limit is within one year of the date of the offense. Again, there may be flexibility with respect to time limits. For example, Mississippi law takes compensation applications for 36 months and gives program directors the discretion to extend the filing period if necessary. Third, victims must incur costs that are not already covered by insurance or another

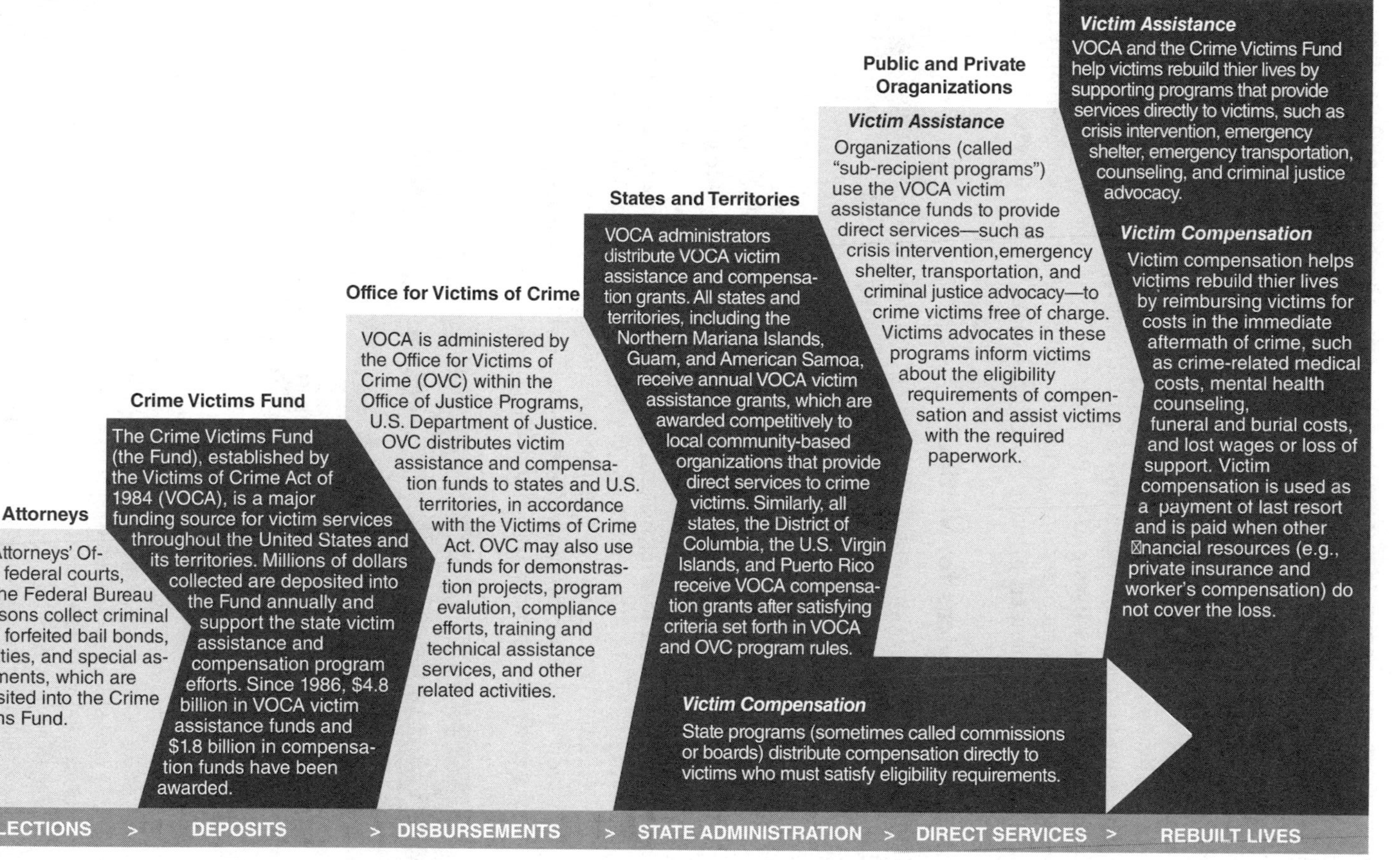

U.S. Attorneys
U.S Attorneys' Offices, federal courts, and the Federal Bureau of Prisons collect criminal fines, forfeited bail bonds, penalties, and special assessments, which are deposited into the Crime Victims Fund.
Crime Victims Fund
The Crime Victims Fund (the Fund), established by the Victims of Crime Act of 1984 (VOCA), is a major funding source for victim services throughout the United States and its territories. Millions of dollars collected are deposited into the Fund annually and support the state victim assistance and compensation program efforts. Since 1986, $4.8 billion in VOCA victim assistance funds and $1.8 billion in compensation funds have been awarded.
Office for Victims of Crime
VOCA is administered by the Office for Victims of Crime (OVC) within the Office of Justice Programs, U.S. Department of Justice. OVC distributes victim assistance and compensation funds to states and U.S. territories, in accordance with the Victims of Crime Act. OVC may also use funds for demonstration projects, program evalution, compliance efforts, training and technical assistance services, and other related activities.
States and Territories
VOCA administrators distribute VOCA victim assistance and compensation grants. All states and territories, including the Northern Mariana Islands, Guam, and American Samoa, receive annual VOCA victim assistance grants, which are awarded competitively to local community-based organizations that provide direct services to crime victims. Similarly, all states, the District of Columbia, the U.S. Virgin Islands, and Puerto Rico receive VOCA compensation grants after satisfying criteria set forth in VOCA and OVC program rules.
Victim Compensation
State programs (sometimes called commissions or boards) distribute compensation directly to victims who must satisfy eligibility requirements.
Public and Private Oraganizations
Victim Assistance
Organizations (called "sub-recipient programs") use the VOCA victim assistance funds to provide direct services—such as crisis intervention,emergency shelter, transportation, and criminal justice advocacy—to crime victims free of charge. Victims advocates in these programs inform victims about the eligibility requirements of compensation and assist victims with the required paperwork.
Crime Victims
Victim Assistance
VOCA and the Crime Victims Fund help victims rebuild thier lives by supporting programs that provide services directly to victims, such as crisis intervention, emergency shelter, emergency transportation, counseling, and criminal justice advocacy.
Victim Compensation
Victim compensation helps victims rebuild thier lives by reimbursing victims for costs in the immediate aftermath of crime, such as crime-related medical costs, mental health counseling, funeral and burial costs, and lost wages or loss of support. Victim compensation is used as a payment of last resort and is paid when other financial resources (e.g., private insurance and worker's compensation) do not cover the loss.
COLLECTIONS > DEPOSITS > DISBURSEMENTS > STATE ADMINISTRATION > DIRECT SERVICES > REBUILT LIVES

Figure 12-2 The Victims of Crime Act
Source: Office for Victims of Crime (2014).

government benefit program (e.g., Medicaid, Veterans Administration). For example, if the victim's health insurance pays for his or her medical treatment following an injury sustained during the crime, the victim would not be eligible to also receive compensation for these expenses. Fourth, the victim must be free of contributory misconduct, which is in many ways similar to the concept of victim precipitation discussed in Chapter 1. This means that if the victim was involved in criminal activity or his or her actions substantially contributed to the crime in some way, the victim would be exempted from receiving compensation benefits.

Restitution and compensation are important tools that help crime victims and their families rebuild their lives and ideally return to their previctimization status. They also serve the interests of restorative justice, which was discussed previously in the chapter, by forcing offenders to make reparations for the damage they have caused.

Assistance and Services for Victims

Criminal justice, civil justice, and victims' rights are essential instruments in responding to criminal victimization. Against these backdrops, however, are victim advocates and victim services that also help crime victims recover from their experiences. A ***victim advocate*** is a trained professional who provides support for crime victims. Advocates work in many locations and in different capacities. Some advocates are employed by a criminal justice agency, such as a police department or prosecutor's office, or they may work for nonprofit organizations (e.g., rape crisis centers) in either paid or volunteer positions. Following a crime, victim advocates are often pivotal resources for victims and their families as they navigate the criminal justice system and plan their recovery. The National Center for Victims of Crime (2008) has explained that advocates' responsibilities will be different depending on where they work and their job description. Box 12-1 lists the activities that victim advocates typically engage in as they provide services for crime victims.

Box 12-1: The Work of Victim Advocates

- Providing information on victimization
- Providing information on crime prevention
- Providing information on victims' legal rights and protections
- Providing information on the criminal justice process
- Providing emotional support to victims
- Helping victims with safety planning
- Helping victims with victim compensation applications
- Helping victims submit comments to courts and parole boards
- Intervening with creditors, landlords, and employers on behalf of victims
- Helping victims find shelter and transportation
- Providing referrals for other services for victims
- Helping to arrange funerals
- Notifying victims of inmates' release or escape

Source: National Center for Victims of Crime (2008).

Victims will require different services and assistance depending on the type of victimization they have experienced. For example, victims of IPV many need temporary housing after victimization, while victims of sexual violence or homicide survivors may have a need for emotional support and counseling. Box 12-2 provides information on unique responses to sexual assault victimization: sexual assault response teams (SART) and sexual assault nurse examiner (SANE) programs.

Box 12-2: SART and SANE

Sexual Assault Response Teams (SART)	Sexual Assault Nurse Examiners (SANE) Programs
The first SARTs were created in the 1970s in communities across the United States to provide a coordinated response to victims of sexual assault. Previously, responses were somewhat piecemeal, wherein a victim would seek services in isolation of each other. These teams comprise individuals from diverse backgrounds who can help victims recover from sexual assaults. A SART is usually activated when the victim makes contact with either the health care system or the criminal justice system. Although SARTs differ from community to community (see Greeson & Campbell, 2014), they commonly include a victim advocate, a law enforcement officer, a prosecutor, and a health care provider, such as a sexual assault nurse examiner (see adjacent side box). SARTs provide victims of sexual assault a compassionate, comprehensive recovery response. They work toward ensuring that victims receive services, collect evidence that can be used in court, and encourage that sexual assaults come to the attention of and are processed by the criminal justice system. The effectiveness of SARTs in attaining these goals is relatively unknown; however, research suggests that those with more stakeholder participation and more formalized implementation are perceived to be more effective by SART leaders (Campbell, Greeson, Bybee, & Neal, 2013).	SANE programs emerged nationwide throughout the 1990s in recognition of a need for specialized evidence collection following sexual assaults beyond what was being provided in hospital emergency departments. SANEs are registered nurses who have been trained to identify injuries (e.g., genital, anal) and document their prevalence and location. They provide 24-hour-a-day, first-response medical care and crisis intervention to sexual assault victims in either hospitals or clinic settings. SANEs carefully collect and document forensic evidence using a sexual assault evidence collection kit, commonly referred to as a "rape kit." In addition to collecting evidence, SANE programs also provide medical care, crisis intervention, and other services (e.g., psychological) following a sexual assault. Research has investigated the effects of SANE programs, especially as they relate to criminal justice processing of sexual assault cases. Studies by Rebecca Campbell and colleagues (2009, 2014) suggest that SANE programs and the forensic evidence collected by SANEs have a positive effect on criminal justice officials' decisions to investigate a complaint and pursue prosecutions in sexual assault cases.

Although the type and amount of help needed may vary, victim services can normally be divided into general categories. The precise form that services take may vary some from jurisdiction to jurisdiction across the United States, but Janine Zweig and Jennifer Yahner's (2014) typology of victim services provides a useful framework for a general discussion. Zweig and Yahner explained that there are six general types of service responses to criminal victimization: (1) safety and crisis intervention, (2) individual advocacy, (3) emotional support, (4) legal advocacy, (5) child advocacy, and (6) financial compensation. First, safety and crisis intervention services are available from service agencies to provide victims with safety and security immediately following a crime as well as planning and assistance for the long term. Such services might include protection from the offender, assistance with home security, relocation to a different area, or education and planning to prevent recurrent victimization (Zweig & Yahner, 2014).

Second, service providers assist with victims' individual needs. After a criminal victimization the victim's regular daily schedule and routines may be disrupted, especially if he or she moved to temporary housing to get away from the offender. For example, women's shelters across the United States provide safe, temporary, and transitional housing for victims of IPV and their children to rebuild their lives. Part of the recovery process will involve planning for the future (e.g., living arrangements, education, finances, and/or employment); service providers will assist victims with managing these goals. Third, emotional support helps victims in the recovery process, particularly for victims of family violence or sexual violence and survivors of homicide. Emotional support may come from family and friends but is also available in the forms of hotlines, support groups, and individualized and group counseling from victim advocates and organizations.

Fourth, victims may need legal services as they enter the criminal justice system, and these needs can be wide-ranging. Legal advocacy involves assisting victims in the legal process in their interactions with criminal justice personnel (e.g., law enforcement, prosecutors) by accompanying the victim to court, providing legal advice, and offering help in obtaining protective orders. ***Protective orders*** are meant to protect the victim by prohibiting the offender from approaching or contacting him or her. Protective orders are civil actions available to IPV victims and usually apply to family members (e.g., married spouses, domestic partners). However, eligibility criteria are somewhat different from state to state. Services also may be available that eliminate barriers to victim participation in the legal process, such as transportation to court, child care during court proceedings, and separate and private waiting areas in the courthouse.

Fifth, child advocacy serves the needs of both child victims and children of victims. In either case, services are available for children who have been victimized or witnessed victimization that focus on the overall well-being of the child, especially his or her physical and mental health needs. Governmental agencies, which are often referred to as child protective services, also exist to prevent, investigate, and respond to crimes against children, such as abuse and neglect. For children involved in legal proceedings, special victim advocates called ***guardians ad litem*** also may be appointed to represent the child in court and speak on the child's behalf. For example, if a child is removed from a dangerous environment by a state agency, a guardian ad litem will advise the court on what is in the child's best interests.

Sixth, financial compensation in the form of victim compensation and restitution has already been discussed, but it is notable that victim advocates are often involved in helping victims to determine if they are eligible for compensation, providing information related to compensation, and assisting victims with the paperwork involved.

The discussion thus far has demonstrated that there are many services available to victims of crime. Yet, research suggests that victim services are underused and do not always meet all victim needs. Research by Barbara Sims, Berwood Yost, and Christina Abbott (2005) sheds light on why some victims take advantage of available services while others do not. The research team used a quasi-experimental research design that compared users of victim services to non-users in Pennsylvania. The results suggested that only the type of crime and the age of the victim differentiated victims who used services from those who did not. Specifically, those who suffered violent crimes and older individuals were more likely to seek out and use victim services. The study also assessed the types of services that agencies in Pennsylvania provided for crime victims (Table 12-3). This is an important consideration, because it may be that victim services are underused because needed services are not being offered.

Table 12-3: Services Provided to Crime Victims in Pennsylvania

Type of Service	Percent of Agencies Offering the Service
Court Accompaniment	95
Justice Support/Advocacy	89
Follow-up Services	87
Crisis Intervention/Counseling	86
Community Outreach	85
Crime Victims' Compensation	81
Transportation	79
Victim Impact Statement	77
Hotline	61
Peer Counseling	61
Hospital Accompaniment	60
Notification Services	58
Bilingual Services	53
Emergency/Legal Advocacy	52
Victim Restitution	39
Shelter Services	36

(Continued)

Table 12-3: (*Continued*)

Type of Service	Percent of Agencies Offering the Service
Victim Impact Panels	35
Parenting Classes	28
Medical Services	27
Child Care	19
Therapy, Family or Victim	18
Transitional Housing	15
Death Notification	13
Employment Services	11
Substance Abuse Services	10
Spiritual/Religious Counseling	5

Source: Sims, Yost, and Abbott (2005).

A study by Robert Davis, Arthur Lurigio, and Wesley Skogan (1999) addressed this issue by surveying victims of robbery, assault, and burglary about their needs and satisfaction with victim services following their victimization. The results suggested that victims needed assistance relating to victimization prevention (52%), household logistical support (52%; e.g., repair broken lock or door, ride to police station), counseling, advice, or advocacy (47%), and property replacement (22%). The study also found that most of the victims' needs were addressed by family, friends, and neighbors, but about one third of victims were at least in contact with their local victim assistance programs. Interestingly, of those in need of counseling-related services, only about 24% were served, whereas of those needing help with crime prevention, household logistical support, and property replacement, only 4% to 5% were served. Of the two thirds who did not use victim services, many indicated that they took care of the problem themselves, did not need help, got help elsewhere, or did not have time to contact the victim program. The studies by Sims and colleagues (2005) and Davis and colleagues (1999) both seem to suggest that the reasons that services are underused may be parallel to the reasons why many victims do not report their victimization to the police following the crime: They view it as something they can handle on their own, with help from family and friends, or that it is not worth the trouble. However, more research is needed to address this possibility.

Summary

Society's response to criminal victimization was a primary impetus for the victims' rights movement. This chapter discussed present-day responses to victimization within the context of justice system responses, victims' rights, and assistance and services for victims. Victims have taken a more prominent place in the administration of justice, especially within the courts through the delivery of victim impact statements. Victims can also pursue justice on their own in the civil courts by seeking monetary damages for the harm they have suffered. Legislators have likewise acknowledged the importance of giving crime victims a voice by enacting legislation that provides specific rights for victims who are participating in the criminal justice process. These rights are designed to encourage victim participation and improve the functioning of the criminal justice system. Society has responded to victimization by creating state funded and nonprofit agencies that provide a variety of services and assistance to victims who need help following the crime. However, the amount and type of help that is available to crime victims varies considerably across the United States as well as across countries around the world.

KEYWORDS

Mandatory arrest laws	Victim–offender mediation	Restitution
Minneapolis Domestic Violence Experiment	Sentencing circles	Victim compensation programs
Mandatory reporting laws	Family group conferencing	Crime Victims Fund
Victims' rights legislation	Civil justice system	Victim advocate
Victim impact statement	*Crime Victims' Rights Act*	Protective orders
Restorative justice	Victims' bill of rights	*Guardians ad litem*

DISCUSSION QUESTIONS

1. Discuss the merits of mandatory arrest laws and mandatory reporting statutes.
2. Compare the victim's role in the criminal justice system to his or her role in the civil justice system.
3. Do victim impact statements have the potential to compromise offenders' due process rights in any way? Explain your position.
4. Why is it important to protect the privacy of crime victims by keeping some of their personal information confidential?
5. What are the benefits and potential problems with forcing offenders to pay restitution to victims as part of their sentence?
6. Review the criteria for victim compensation presented earlier in the chapter. Do you think that these eligibility requirements are fair? Explain your thinking.
7. Which of the responses to victimization discussed in this chapter is the most valuable to crime victims in the recovery process? Is there variation in responses across types of crime? Provide examples to support your argument.
8. What responses, if any, are missing from the range of responses to victimization presented in this chapter? Explain what is missing and how and why it is important to victims' and their families' recovery.

REFERENCES

Campbell, R., Bybee, D., Townsend, S. M., Shaw, J., Karim, N., & Markowitz, J. (2014). The impact of sexual assault nurse examiner programs on criminal justice case outcomes: A multisite replication study. *Violence Against Women, 20*, 607–625.

Campbell, R., Greeson, M., Bybee, D., & Neal, J.W. (2013). *Sexual assault response team (SART) implementation and collaborative process: What works best for the criminal justice system?* Retrieved October 25, 2014, from https://www. ncjrs.gov/pdffiles1/nij/grants/243829.pdf

Campbell, R., Patterson, D., Bybee, D., & Dworkin, E. R. (2009). Predicting sexual assault prosecution outcomes: The role of medical forensic evidence collected by sexual assault nurse examiners. *Criminal Justice and Behavior, 36*, 712–727.

Caplan, J. M. (2010). Parole release decisions: Impact of positive and negative victim and nonvictim input on a representative sample of parole-eligible inmates. *Violence and Victims, 25*, 224–242.

Cattaneo, L. B., & Goodman, L. A. (2010). The relationship between empowerment in the court system and well-being for intimate partner violence victims. *Journal of Interpersonal Violence, 25*, 481–502.

Child Welfare Information Gateway. (2014). *Mandatory reporters of child abuse and neglect*. Washington, DC: U.S. Department of Health and Human Services, Children's Bureau. Retrieved June 29, 2014, from https://www.childwelfare.gov/systemwide/laws_policies/statutes/manda.cfm

Clark County Courts (2014). *Anatomy of a civil lawsuit*. Retrieved March 15, 2015, from http://www.clarkcountycourts.us/CivilSHC/images/civil-lawsuit.gif

Davis, R. C., Lurigio, A. J., & Skogan, W. G. (1999). Services for victims: A market research study. *International Review of Victimology, 6*, 101–115.

Davis, R. C., & Smith, B. E. (1994). The effects of victim impact statements on sentencing decisions: A test in an urban setting. *Justice Quarterly, 11*, 453–469.

Englebrecht, C. M. (2011). The struggle for "ownership of conflict": An exploration of victim participation and voice in the criminal justice system. *Criminal Justice Review, 36*, 129–151.

Erez, E., & Roberts, J. (2014). Victim participation in the criminal justice system. In R. C. Davis, A. J. Lurigio, & S. Herman (Eds.), *Victims of crime* (4th ed., pp.251–270). Thousand Oaks, CA: Sage.

Garner, J., Fagan, J., & Maxwell, C. (1995). Published findings from the spouse assault replication program: A critical review. *Journal of Quantitative Criminology, 11*, 3–28.

Greeson, M. R., & Campbell, R. (2014). Coordinated community efforts to respond to sexual assault: A national study of sexual assault response team implementation. *Journal of Interpersonal Violence*. DOI: 10.1177/0886260514553119

Howley, S., & Dorris, C. F. (2014). Legal rights for crime victims in the criminal justice system. In R. C. Davis, A. J. Lurigio, & S. Herman (Eds.), *Victims of crime* (4th ed., pp. 271–292). Thousand Oaks, CA: Sage.

Latimer, J., Dowden, C., & Muise, D. (2005). The effectiveness of restorative justice practices: A meta-analysis. *Prison Journal, 85*, 127–144.

Manson Family Murders Fast Facts. (2014). Retrieved October 29, 2014, from http://www.cnn.com/2013/09/30/us/manson-family-murders-fast-facts/

Morgan, K., & Smith, B. L. (2005). Victims, punishment, and parole: The effect of victim participation on parole hearings. *Criminology and Public Policy, 4*, 333–360.

National Center for Victims of Crime. (2008). *What is a victim advocate?* Retrieved June 28, 2014, from http://www.victimsofcrime.org/help-for-crime-victims/get-help-bulletins-for-crime-victims/what-is-a-victim-advocate-

Office for Victims of Crime. (2014). *VOCA chart*. Retrieved June 11, 2014, from http://www.ovc.gov/about/victimsfund.html

Roberts, J. V., & Edgar, A. (2006). *Judicial perceptions of victim input at sentencing: findings from surveys in Canada*. Ottawa, Ontario, Canada: Department of Justice Canada. Retrieved June 22, 2014, from http://www.justice.gc.ca/eng/rp-pr/cj-jp/victim/rr06_vic3/rr06_vic3.pdf

Roberts, J. V., & Manikis, M. (2011). *Victim personal statements at sentencing: A review of the empirical research*. London, UK: Office of the Commissioner for Victims and Witnesses of England and Wales. Retrieved June 22, 2014, from http://www.justice.gov.uk/downloads/news/press-releases/victims-com/vps-research.pdf

Sherman, L. W., & Berk, R. A. (1984). The specific deterrent effects of arrest for domestic assault. *American Sociological Review, 49*, 261–272.

Sims, B., Yost, B., & Abbott, C. (2005). Use and nonuse of victim services programs: Implications from a statewide survey of crime victims. *Criminology and Public Policy, 4*, 361–384.

Wasserman, E., & Ellis, C. A. (2007). *Impact of crime on victims*. Retrieved March 7, 2015, from http://www.ccvs.state.vt.us/sites/default/files/resources/VVAA%20Ch%206%20Impact%20of%20Crime.pdf

Zweig, J., & Yahner, J. (2014). Providing services to victims of crime. In R. C. Davis, A. J. Lurigio, & S. Herman (Eds.), *Victims of crime* (4th ed., pp.325–348). Thousand Oaks, CA: Sage.

CHAPTER 13

Fear of Criminal Victimization

CHAPTER OUTLINE

LEARNING OBJECTIVES

- Describe the concepts of fear and perceived risk of victimization, and how they are related but separate concepts.
- Explain how fear of victimization has been measured and how the measures used affect estimates of fear.
- Identify patterns associated with fear of victimization.
- Discuss major theoretical explanations of fear of victimization.
- Explain the concept of "fear spots" and describe important environmental cues that generate these places.
- Identify the major consequences of fear of victimization for crime victims and nonvictims.

Fear of crime affects far more people in the United States than crime itself, and there are sound reasons for treating crime and fear of crime as distinct social problems.

Warr, 2000, p. 451

Introduction

It was not until the 1960s that criminologists first identified fear of criminal victimization as a serious social problem and the subject of legitimate study. As a result of the turbulence of this period in history, it is not surprising that the public identified crime as the most serious social problem in the United States. Despite being a local phenomenon, crime even featured prominently in the 1964 presidential election between Lyndon Johnson and Barry Goldwater. After his election, President Johnson created the President's Commission on Law Enforcement and the Administration of Justice (see Chapter 1) with the purpose of studying and recommending policies for addressing crime. In its 1967 report, the Commission remarked that "The most damaging of the effects of violent crime is fear, and that fear must not be belittled" (President's Commission on Law Enforcement and the Administration of Justice, 1967, p. 3). They further noted that fear of being attacked by a stranger was *the* primary concern related to crime for a significant portion of Americans, and that one third of Americans surveyed felt unsafe walking alone in their own neighborhoods at night (President's Commission on Law Enforcement and the Administration of Justice, 1967).

Following the Commission's report, researchers began acknowledging the importance of investigating fear of victimization as an academic field. Over the past 50 years, many criminologists and victimologists alike have focused on measuring and explaining the patterns, predictors, and consequences of fear of victimization. In part, their sustained interest has been fueled by an interesting paradox: In general, while the number of people who actually become crime victims is relatively small, the number of people who are afraid of becoming crime victims is much larger.

In other words, while people fear becoming a victim, their actual chance of becoming a victim is relatively small. Elected officials also have seized upon citizens' fear of victimization to rally support for "law and order" policies. Even today, addressing the public's fear of becoming crime victims is at the forefront of government officials' initiatives to ensure the public's level of fear does not reach the problematic levels it did during the 1960s. Despite continued efforts on multiple fronts to reduce fear of victimization, many Americans today continue to live in fear of becoming a victim.

This chapter focuses on fear of criminal victimization as a social problem—both related to and distinct from crime and victimization. In describing the current state of knowledge on fear of victimization, this chapter reviews the extent, measurement, and factors identified as influencing fear of victimization, theoretical perspectives developed to explain fear, and the policy implications of research that has been conducted on fear of criminal victimization. We use the terms *fear of crime* and *fear of criminal victimization* interchangeably throughout the chapter.

Fear of Criminal Victimization

Fear is a primal emotion characterized by a feeling of dread and an anticipation of danger in the immediate environment. Fear is not only a feeling; it results in physiological changes in the body, such as sweating, muscle contraction, increased respiration, and elevated heart rate. Fear of victimization certainly existed long before the President's Commission recognized it as a serious social problem in the United States, but research examining fear of criminal victimization did not. In the years since the Commission's report, social scientists studying fear have realized that fear of victimization is not solely a reaction to having *been* victimized, as was once assumed. While fear is among the common responses to being criminally victimized, even those who have not been victimized are frightened by the possibility. This suggests that fear of victimization is a complex and multidimensional concept, characterized by a strong emotional response but driven by related cognitive elements as well.

Defining Fear and Perceived Risk of Victimization

There is no universal definition of fear of crime, but Randy LaGrange and Kenneth Ferraro, leading fear-of-crime researchers, provided a widely used definition that illustrates its emotional aspects. They defined ***fear of crime*** as "a negative emotional reaction to crime or symbols associated with crime" (LaGrange & Ferraro, 1987, p. 72). One of the key elements of this definition is that it highlights the fear felt by crime victims. As discussed in Chapter 11, the emotional toll suffered by victims of crime is substantial, including fearing another victimization. LaGrange and Ferraro's definition also suggests that individuals can be fearful of crime through exposure to crime-related symbols and crime-conducive situations. Put differently, causes of fear of crime can be both direct and indirect. *Direct* causes include experiencing a victimization and fearing another will happen in the future. *Indirect* causes, such as exposure to crime through secondary victimization, stories in the media, or symbols in one's surroundings such as graffiti, can increase one's estimation of one's own likelihood of experiencing a victimization, or what criminologists call one's perceived risk of victimization.

This ***perceived risk of victimization*** is not fear of becoming a victim, but it has been identified as a counterpart to fear of crime. That is, compared to others, individuals who perceive themselves to be likely victims are typically more fearful of crime. For example, walking alone at night and suddenly hearing footsteps from behind can induce fear because of the perception that the person behind you is following you for no good reason other than to perhaps attack. While the sound of footsteps, by itself, is not frightening, the perceived risk of victimization associated with being followed typically provokes fear.

A related issue to perceived risk of victimization is actual victimization risk. One's ***actual victimization risk*** represents one's objective likelihood of becoming a crime victim. To illustrate these two concepts, consider an example from a recent National Crime Victimization Survey (NCVS) report related to identity theft victimization. According to results from the 2010 NCVS, 7% of households in the United States were affected by identity theft, with one or more household members over the age of 12 experiencing at least one type of identity theft (Langton, 2011). Victimization risk also varied by household characteristics. For instance, residents living in urban and suburban locations had higher rates of victimization (6%) than did residents living in rural settings (4%). In distinguishing between perceived and actual victimization risk, then, it would be accurate to say that urban and suburban residents have higher actual victimization risks than do those living in rural areas. Upon reading these statistics, if you have convinced yourself that you are likely to be a victim of identity theft, then you have just estimated your perceived risk of victimization to be high.

The distinction between these concepts is important because the conceptual and empirical distinctions were absent in early fear-of-crime research, resulting in conflicting results about the extent and nature of fear of crime. A criticism of early studies is that many researchers were effectively studying perceived risk but using the fear-of-crime label (Lane, Rader, Henson, Fisher, & May, 2014). Indeed, much of the initial research into fear of crime did not distinguish or even recognize a difference between fear and perceived risk of crime. As the next section explains, how concepts are defined influences how they are measured, and measurement directly affects research findings. Today, it is well accepted among scholars that fear and perceived risk of crime are related but conceptually distinct phenomena. Perceived and actual risk also exert powerful influences on one's overall level of fear of crime.

Measuring Fear of Criminal Victimization

As Chapter 4 explained, how researchers measure concepts such as crime and victimization directly affects their studies' results. Research on fear of victimization is no different. Therefore, before discussing the prevalence and levels of fear of crime in society and how fear is distributed across demographic groups, we need to first consider how researchers have measured fear of victimization.

Early research into fear of crime relied on questions asked of respondents participating in the National Crime Survey (NCS) and the General Social Survey (GSS). Both surveys were first used in the early 1970s, although each was not solely designed to study fear of crime. The NCS was intended to complement the UCR by collecting data on victimization in the United States, and the GSS was designed

Box 13-1: NCS and GSS Fear Questions

National Crime Survey:
"How safe do you feel or would you feel being out alone in your neighborhood at night?"

General Social Survey:
"Is there any place right around here—that is, within a mile—where you would be afraid to walk alone at night?"

primarily to collect information on public opinion and social change in American society. Both surveys used similar questions to measure fear of crime, which are provided in Box 13-1. While each of these questions captures the emotional state of *fear,* neither specifically mentions *crime,* leading many to doubt whether the survey items accurately measure the concept. Despite the rather obvious shortcomings, these measures of fear have been and currently are routinely adopted by fear-of-crime researchers (see Lane et al., 2014).

Contemporary fear-of-crime research has worked to overcome the problems inherent in the NCS and GSS measures by specifically including the word *crime* in survey questions. For example, in a study exploring the frequency of fear of crime, Stephen Farrall and David Gadd (2004, p. 128) asked study participants: "In the past year, have you ever felt fearful about the possibility of becoming a victim of crime?" This measure and others like it are an improvement over the NCS and GSS questions but may still be flawed in ways that influence respondents' interpretations of the question. As a thought exercise, consider Farrall and Gadd's question and answer based on your own circumstances. Regardless of whether your answer was *yes* or *no,* think about how you arrived at your answer. In thinking about fear of crime, which crime(s) did you consider? Murder, rape, burglary, arson, identity theft, cyberstalking? Each person who responds to this question is left to determine for himself or herself what "crime" means and thus may be thinking about much different offenses than others responding to the same question. Measures such as these are referred to as ***formless measures*** of fear of crime because they reflect only a general fear of victimization and do not specify a particular type of crime (Farrall, Bannister, Ditton, & Gilchrist, 1997). For this reason, researchers now typically investigate crime-specific fears, such as how fearful one is of being murdered or robbed.

Researchers who devise measures based on the assumption that feelings of fear of crime depend on the type of crime under study are using ***concrete measures*** (Farrall et al., 1997). For example, Bonnie Fisher and John Sloan (2003) asked college students to rate their fear of five types of victimization: larceny/theft, robbery, simple assault, aggravated assault, and rape. Their results supported the idea that fear of crime differs, in some instances dramatically, depending on the *type of crime* about which one is being asked, and that different factors influence one's feelings of fear of different types of crime. In another fear-of-victimization study, Ashley Marie Nellis (2009) examined fear of terrorism among adults living in the New York City and Washington, DC, metropolitan statistical areas in 2006. Nellis (2009, p. 327) measured fear of terrorism through a telephone survey, asking respondents how worried they were of becoming a victim of a terrorist attack on a 10-point scale (1 = no fear to 10 = great fear). The average score among the 527 participants was 3.82, indicating a moderate level of fear of terrorism.

Other important measurement issues surrounding fear-of-crime research include measuring its frequency, its intensity, and the context in which it occurs. For instance, in their study of fear of in-school victimization, Kristin Swartz and colleagues (2011) asked middle- and high-school students: "In the current school year, how often are you afraid that you will be ______?" Students then rated their fear from *never* to *always* for the offenses of physical assault, robbery, theft, being threatened with a gun, and being threatened with another weapon such as a knife. This fear measure reflects fear of the ***frequency*** of crime, or how regularly it occurs. Similarly, contemporary fear-of-crime researchers will also measure the ***intensity*** of fear of victimization, revealing *how afraid* individuals are of criminal victimization compared to some standard. For example, in the previously described study by Fisher and Sloan (2003), students rated their fear of victimization for the five different types of crime on a scale from one (low fear) to ten (high fear). Other researchers have used scales ranging from *very unafraid* to *very afraid*, which also assesses the intensity of fear (Farrall & Gadd, 2004; Fox, Nobles, & Piquero, 2009; Wilcox, Jordan, & Pritchard, 2007). Fisher and Sloan's study also highlights the significance of the temporal element of fear—that is, when the crime might take place. In their study, participants rated their fear of each crime both during the day and at night; students expressed higher levels of fear of crime at night than during the day.

Measurement issues are important to keep in mind throughout the remainder of the chapter as research findings related to fear of crime are discussed. Whether fear of crime is gauged by researchers using a formless or concrete measure or whether the measure includes frequency, intensity, or context, or some combination of these considerations, how fear of victimization is measured determines how study results can be interpreted. In sum, the conclusions researchers reach about the extent and nature of fear of crime will be significantly influenced by the wording and responses to their survey items. Put simply, measurement matters!

Extent of Fear of Criminal Victimization

With the salience of measurement issues in mind, available data suggest that a significant percentage of individuals in the United States live in fear of criminal victimization. Earliest estimates of the extent of fear of crime were provided by the President's Commission on Law Enforcement and the Administration of Justice. The survey sponsored by the Commission reported that one in three Americans felt unsafe about walking alone in their neighborhoods at night (President's Commission on Law Enforcement and the Administration of Justice, 1967). This survey also revealed that:

- 43% avoided the streets at night due to fear of crime.
- 35% did not speak to strangers anymore because of fear of crime.
- 21% used cars and cabs at night as a result of fear of crime.
- 20% said they would like to move to another neighborhood because of fear of crime.

Research undertaken in the years since the Commission's report generally supports the conclusion that fear of crime is pervasive in the United States. For example, Hindelang, Gottfredson, and Garofalo's (1978) research on lifestyle-exposure theory, reviewed in Chapter 2, also estimated the extent of fear of crime among respondents. In their analysis of an eight-city survey that was administered as a precursor to the NCVS, Hindelang and colleagues reported that a large majority of U.S. residents, approximately 90%, felt comfortable being alone in their neighborhoods *during the day*. However, this was not the case when they were asked about being alone at night: Only 55% of respondents answered this question in the affirmative. In other words, about 45% did *not* feel safe being alone in their neighborhoods at night.

When it comes to estimating how prevalent fear of crime is today, available data suggest little has changed. To paraphrase Warr's (2000) quote that opened this chapter, fear of crime affects more people in the United States than crime itself. As Chapter 4 explained, even though victimization rates in the United States have mostly declined since the 1990s, fear of crime has not. Public opinion surveys suggest that the prevalence of fear has fluctuated some but essentially remains at comparable levels to estimates reported from studies conducted in the 1960s and 1970s. The GSS, for instance, reports that fear of crime among residents of the United States has remained steady at about 41% for nearly 40 years from 1972 to 2010 (National Opinion Research Center, 2013). As previously discussed, GSS estimates of fear of crime are based on whether respondents reported that they would be afraid to walk alone at night "within a mile of [their residence]." Another long-running public opinion survey, conducted by the Gallup Organization, uses the same question language as the GSS in its measure of fear and has reported comparable results. According to Gallup, on average, nearly four in ten Americans are fearful of walking alone at night, with 37% of respondents completing the survey in 2010 indicating that they would be afraid to walk in nearby areas alone at night. Figure 13-1 illustrates a 45-year trend in how this question has been answered in Gallup's surveys.

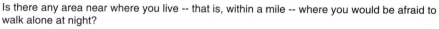

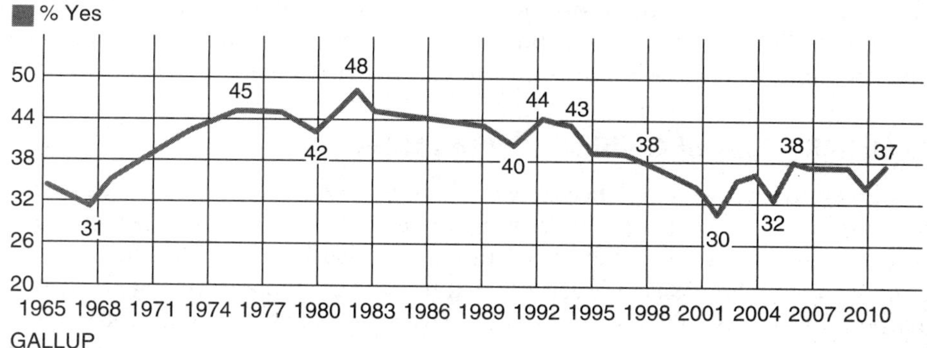

Figure 13-1 Fear of Crime in the United States, 1965–2010
Source: Gallup (2010).

Wesley Skogan (2011) used a measure of fear similar to that used by Gallup to study trends in fear of crime in Chicago from 1994 to 2003. His study estimated the prevalence of fear of crime among city residents through eight citywide telephone surveys by asking participants "How safe do you feel or would you feel being alone outside in your neighborhood at night?" (Skogan, 2011, p. 103). The results revealed several interesting findings. First, fear declined over the study period. In 1994 about 50% of females and 30% of males indicated some degree of fear in response to this survey question, whereas by 2003 female fear had declined by 20% and male fear by 10%. Second, beyond gender-based differences, fear of victimization varied with home ownership, income, age, and race. Skogan found that a larger percentage of homeowners, those making less than $40,000 a year, those over the age of 60, and minorities (Latinos and blacks) were more fearful of victimization than were their counterparts. Third, Skogan reported that although individuals' characteristics are linked to their level of fear of crime, when considering an entire city's population, these characteristics do not change fast enough to account for the declines in fear of crime in Chicago from 1994 to 2003. Instead, factors such as improved neighborhood conditions (e.g., cleaner streets, less crime) throughout the city and growing confidence in police throughout the study period were likely drivers of the changes in fear of crime.

Aside from these public opinion surveys and Skogan's study, estimates of the prevalence of fear in the United States are somewhat limited. That is, reports on levels of fear of crime are frequently limited to specific populations such as students, women, and minorities and are not necessarily representative of either the general adult or entire population of the United States. While the NCVS no longer regularly includes questions about fear of crime, other surveys administered by the Bureau of Justice Statistics (BJS) often estimate fear among specific groups in the United States. For example, BJS, in partnership with the National Center for Education Statistics, recently published a report on school crime and safety that included fear-of-crime estimates. The report revealed that 4% of students ages 12 to 18 were afraid of attack or harm while at school; 2% were afraid of attack or harm away from school (Robers, Kemp, Rathbun, Morgan, & Snyder, 2014). Further, 6% of students avoided school activities or certain places in the school (e.g., restrooms) as a consequence of fear. The report also noted that patterns in fear and avoidance behaviors varied by sex, race, and whether the school was located in an urban, suburban, or rural area. As Figure 13-2 illustrates, fear among both male and female students has declined over time, but female students are generally more fearful than male students.

Explaining Fear of Criminal Victimization

Besides studying the prevalence of fear of crime, researchers have also examined why individuals are fearful to determine influences on fear of crime. An extensive body of research indicates that like victimization, fear has distinctive patterns. For example, research consistently reports that females are more fearful of crime than males, a finding discussed in Skogan's early work (Skogan & Maxfield, 1981) and in his most recent study of fear of crime in Chicago (Skogan, 2011). Likewise, older individuals are often reported to be more fearful than younger individuals,

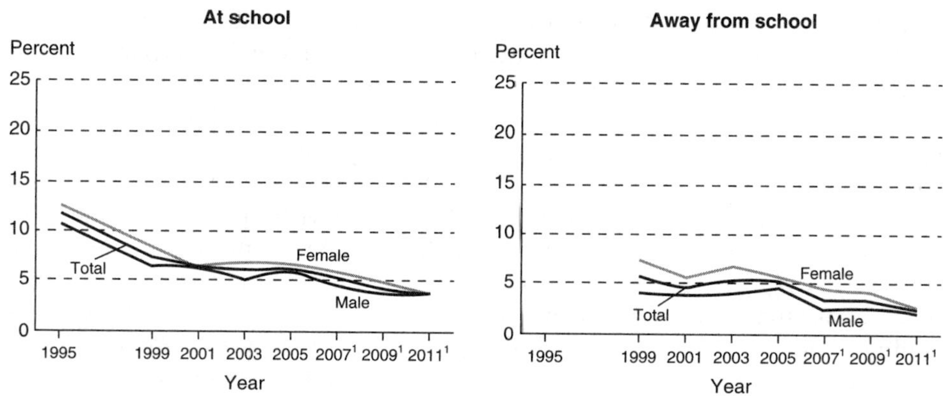

[1]In 2007, 2009, and 20011, the reference period was the school year, whereas in prior survey years the reference period was the previous 6 months. Cognitive testing showed that estimates from 2007, 2009, and 2011 are comparable to previous years.
NOTE: "At shool" includes the school buillding, on school property, on a school bus, and from 2001 onward, going to and from school. Fear of attack away from school was not collected in 1995. For more information, please see appendix A.
SOURCE: U.S. Department of justice, Bureau of justice Statistics, School Crime Supplement (SCS) to the National Crime Victimization Survey, Various years, 1995–2011.

Figure 13-2 Fear Among Students Ages 12–18 by Location and Sex, 1995–2011
Source: Robers et al. (2014).

although not all studies agree on this point. Further, theories of fear of crime have developed to explain not only what causes fear of crime, but also why it is varies with individuals' characteristics, in different populations, and across contexts. This section discusses the patterns and theories that have been advanced to explain and understand fear of crime.

Patterns of Fear of Criminal Victimization

Patterns in fear of crime have primarily been examined with respect to individuals' demographic characteristics, especially their gender and age, but also in terms of their race and income. As is the case with patterns in victimization, the task of victimologists is to try to understand why these patterns in fear exist by developing hypotheses to test their theories.

Gender

Study after study has reported that gender is one of the most consistent predictors of fear, with females always having higher fear of crime than males (Hale, 1996; Henson & Reyns, 2015; Lane et al., 2014). The relationship between gender and fear seems to persist even when other possible explanations of fear are considered. This is especially puzzling given that females, with certain exceptions discussed in Chapter 6, generally have much *lower* victimization levels than do males. This apparent disconnect between actual victimization and fear of crime has been labeled the ***paradox of fear*** and has been uncovered in a number of studies (e.g., Clemente & Kleiman, 1977; Stafford & Galle, 1984; Warr, 1984). For example, Wesley Skogan and Michael Maxfield (1981) conducted one of the earliest studies of fear of crime in the United States to examine the relationships between individuals' characteristics and their fear of crime. Based on telephone survey data obtained in 1977 from residents of Chicago, Philadelphia, and San Francisco, they reported that women were nearly 3.5 times more likely than men to feel "very unsafe" if they were to walk alone in the nearby community. In another influential early study, LaGrange and Ferraro (1989) investigated fear of crime and perceived risk among 320 residents of a metropolitan area from the southeastern United States by means of a telephone survey. They reported that women who participated in the study were significantly more fearful than men for virtually every type of crime they were asked about, including, among others, mugging, car theft, burglary, sexual assault, and murder.

More recent research also has found that females are generally more fearful of crime than males. In one such study, Joseph Schafer, Beth Huebner, and Timothy Bynum (2006) estimated the fear of victimization among men and women in a large community in the Midwest. They reported that women had a higher general fear of victimization than did men. When study participants were asked about personal and property victimization specifically, men and women had similar levels of fear of property victimization, but women expressed greater fear of personal victimization. A study by David May, Nicole Rader, and Sarah Goodrum (2010) focused on fear among residents of Kentucky and also reported significantly higher fear of crime and perceived risk of victimization among females in their sample.

The question that emerges from this body of research is this: *Why are females on average more fearful than males?* Mark Warr (1984), a leading fear-of-crime scholar, has suggested that for females fear of crime is synonymous with fear of rape. In other words, rape is a *master offense* that overshadows considerations of all other types of fear of crime. This would explain why females consistently have higher fear of crime than males, an idea that has since been developed into what Ferraro (1996) labeled "the shadow of sexual assault hypothesis."

The ***shadow of sexual assault hypothesis*** explains that fear of crime in females is driven by fear of sexual victimization for two reasons. First, any face-to-face form of criminal victimization can potentially escalate into other types of victimization. For example, a robbery can turn into a sexual assault, as could a burglary if the female resident walks in on the burglary. Therefore, the shadow of sexual assault hypothesis contends that the possibility of face-to-face crimes (e.g., a robbery, a burglary while the victim is home) escalating into sexual assault or rape *overshadows* all other considerations of fear of crime more generally. Second, sexual victimizations overwhelmingly affect females. According to the shadow hypothesis, since females are far more frequent targets of sexual victimization than are males, and since many personal crimes can take a turn for the worse and result in a sexual victimization, females usually express greater overall levels of fear of crime than do males. Or, as Warr (1984, p. 700) put it in describing fear of crime among females, "fear of crime *is* fear of rape."

The shadow of sexual assault hypothesis has been supported in many studies. For example, in his test of the shadow hypothesis, Ferraro (1996) reported that females were more fearful than men when queried about 10 different offenses (e.g., car theft, vandalism, panhandling). Further, not only were females nearly four

Table 13-1: Fear of Crime at Night

Type of Crime	Level of Fear	
	Women	Men
Larceny/theft	2.71	2.39
Robbery	3.08	2.02
Simple assault	3.08	1.94
Aggravated assault	3.01	1.92
Rape	3.54	1.26

Note: Scale is from "1" ("not afraid at all") to "10" ("very afraid").
Source: Fisher and Sloan (2003).

times more afraid of sexual assault than males, but they were also more fearful of being sexually assaulted than they were of being murdered. Finally, in support of the shadow hypothesis, Ferraro reported that fear of rape was a significant predictor of fear of murder, robbery, assault, and burglary. Many studies have since investigated the shadow thesis and generally confirm that much of the gender gap in fear can be explained as a function of female fear of rape or sexual victimization (e.g., Fisher & Sloan, 2003; Hilinski, 2009; Wilcox, Jordan, & Pritchard, 2006). Table 13-1 provides fear-of-victimization estimates for the five types of victimization included in Fisher and Sloan's (2003) study. In rating their fear of victimization at night for these five types of crime on a 10-point scale, female students consistently reported higher fear for every type of crime, particularly fear of rape.

Age

As was the case when examining gender, a pattern has been repeatedly observed for the relationship between fear of crime and age (Hale, 1996; Henson & Reyns, 2015; Lane et al., 2014). Many studies have reported that the elderly have higher fear of crime than younger individuals (Clemente & Kleiman, 1977; Skogan & Maxfield, 1981; Warr, 1984). The finding that older individuals are more afraid of victimization is another illustration of the *paradox of fear* in that for most types of crimes the elderly have relatively low victimization risks. For example, Frank Clemente and Michael Kleiman (1977) used data from the GSS to examine relationships between fear of crime and gender, age, race, socioeconomic status, and community size. They reported that older individuals generally had greater fear, with 50% of those over 65 expressing fear of victimization. However, in explaining this fear, age was not as strong an indicator as gender. In another study to explore the issue, Skogan and Maxfield (1981) found that residents of Chicago, Philadelphia, and San Francisco over the age of 60 had the highest levels of fear of crime. That is, about 41% of those 60 years or older indicated they would feel "very unsafe" being in the community alone. The authors concluded that fear of crime generally rises with age, with some variation.

While there is near-universal agreement in the fear-of-crime research that females have greater fear of crime than males, the patterns relating to age are less clear. In the previously discussed study by LaGrange and Ferraro (1989), 41% of those who were 65 years and older said they would feel either *somewhat* or *very unsafe* walking alone on the streets at night. However, LaGrange and Ferraro pointed out that estimates of fear across age groups depend upon the measure of fear being used and argued that the relationship between age and fear was not so clear-cut. Their findings suggested that if age were considered in terms of crime-specific fears such as burglary, murder, and vandalism, not only was the relationship between age and fear fairly weak, but younger persons were actually *more* fearful of victimization than older persons. This study questions the conventional wisdom that fear of crime increases with age and indicates that it may not be age that matters so much as other correlates of crime, such as perceived risk of victimization (see also Ferraro & LaGrange, 1992; McCoy et al., 1996). Table 13-2 provides the patterns in fear of crime related to age from these three studies.

In light of LaGrange and Ferraro's (1989) findings that it is often young people who most fear victimization, many studies have specifically focused on fear among adolescents and college students. In one of these studies, Lynn Addington (2003) examined fear of crime among 12- to 18-year-old students to assess the effects the April 20, 1999, Columbine High School mass shooting had on students' fear of victimization in the United States. Based on her analysis of NCVS school crime data, Addington concluded that students' fear of victimization while at school significantly increased after Columbine. Notably, 4% more students reported fear at school after the shooting compared to students before the shooting. Other studies examining fear of crime among youth will be discussed throughout the remainder of the chapter (e.g., Rader, Cossman, & Allison, 2009; Randa & Wilcox, 2010; Swartz et al., 2011; Tillyer, Fisher, & Wilcox, 2011).

Table 13-2: The Relationship Between Fear of Crime and Age

Clemente and Kleiman (1977)		Skogan and Maxfield (1981)		LaGrange and Ferraro (1989)	
Age	% Afraid	Age	% Afraid	Age	% Afraid
18–34	41	18–20	7.1	18–29	20
35–49	40	21–26	6.3	30–45	15
50–64	43	27–32	6.3	46–64	22
65 and older	50	33–39	9.3	65 and older	41
		40–49	10.6		
		50–59	22.2		
		60 and older	40.7		

Sources: Clemente and Kleiman (1977); Skogan and Maxfield (1981); LaGrange and Ferraro (1989).

Race

Race has not been examined in reference to fear of crime to the extent that gender and age have. Nevertheless, the studies that have been undertaken suggest that under some circumstances fear of crime does vary with race (Baumer, 1979; Hale, 1996). For instance, in the study by Clemente and Kleiman (1977) that was previously discussed, the authors also estimated the extent of fear among whites and African Americans. Their findings indicated that African Americans had a higher relative fear of crime, with 57% of this group experiencing fear of crime compared to 40% of whites. Likewise, in his examination of the NCS, James Garofalo (1979) reported that 41% of whites were fearful compared to 54% of African Americans. These patterns also were observed by Skogan (2011) in his study of Chicago and Skogan and Maxfield (1981) in their study of residents of Chicago, Philadelphia, and San Francisco.

Not all studies agree that minority citizens are the most fearful. For instance, research by Suzanne Ortega and Jessie Myles (1987) found that whites were actually more fearful than African Americans. Yet, when these researchers estimated fear of crime based on multiple individual characteristics (e.g., white females, African American males), they reported that the most fearful group was African American females. Further, among both African American females and males, fear increased with age, whereas among white females and males, fear generally decreased with age. Similar findings were reported by Mark Stafford and Omer Galle (1984) in their study of Chicago residents using the NCS. They reported that with few exceptions fear increased with age among all four of these groups, but that African American females experienced the most fear, followed by white females, African American males, and white males. Overall, then, while patterns in fear have been observed across race groups, the research is not in agreement about which race groups are the most fearful or why. It is possible that race is not a determinant of fear but rather is related to other characteristics that better explain fear of victimization.

Income

Research suggests that fear of victimization also is influenced by an individual's income (Baumer, 1979). Although recent research has not explored the relationship between income and fear of crime in much depth, early research on the issue revealed an inverse relationship between income and fear. Put differently, as one's income increases, fear of victimization generally decreases. This finding has been reported in several studies (e.g., Clemente & Kleiman, 1977; Garofalo, 1979). The potential reason that is often proposed is that those with higher incomes can afford to protect themselves and their property, which affords them peace of mind and less worry about victimization. For this reason, more contemporary research has concentrated on other possible influences on fear such as the wider social context (e.g., neighborhood conditions, school conditions) and previous victimization experiences rather than income per se (Brunton-Smith & Sturgis, 2011; Ferraro, 1995; McGarrell, Giacomazzi, & Thurman, 1997). These other potential correlates of fear are discussed along with the leading theoretical perspectives to explain why individuals are fearful of crime.

Theories of Fear of Criminal Victimization

Theories of fear of victimization are divided into three distinct perspectives that attempt to explain why individuals are fearful and why the previously reviewed patterns in fear exist. These perspectives are the vulnerability perspective, which is based on individuals' perceptions of their susceptibility to victimization; the environmental perspective, which is grounded in the contexts that generate feelings of fear; and an integrated multilevel perspective, which combines the two perspectives, suggesting that generators of fear exist at multiple levels (i.e., individual and contextual).

The Vulnerability Perspective

The vulnerability perspective is used for explaining fear of crime at the individual or micro-level. According to the ***vulnerability perspective***, fear of crime is a consequence of individuals' perceived vulnerabilities to victimization stemming from their personal characteristics (e.g., gender, race), their previous experiences with criminal victimization, and even their lifestyles and daily routine activities. More simply put, individuals fear crime because they believe that they are vulnerable to experiencing it. The nature of that vulnerability has been approached by researchers in a number of ways, but for the most part vulnerability can be divided into two types: physical and social.

Physical vulnerability represents an individual's capacity or ability to prevent a personal victimization, such as a robbery or an assault, from occurring. As such, the previously discussed gender- and age-based patterns in fear of crime involving greater fear among females and the elderly can both be explained using this theoretical approach. For example, females may perceive that in an altercation with a male offender they will be unable to defend themselves or their property due to the likely size or strength difference between them and the offender. This theoretical premise also is compatible with the shadow of sexual assault hypothesis insomuch as perceived physical vulnerability only increases the threat or worry that a nonsexual victimization can escalate into one that is sexual. In reference to age, the elderly and the very young may both judge themselves to be incapable of defending or protecting themselves if confronted by a criminal, and thus may be more fearful of criminal victimization. Further, physical attacks against the elderly can have more severe or long-lasting consequences than similar attacks against younger persons, perhaps providing even greater fear or anxiety about the possibility of being victimized (Killias, 1990).

Although the ***social vulnerability*** perspective is more complex because it includes a greater range of factors as explanations of fear, the overarching premise is that fear of crime is associated with social characteristics that may actually or be perceived to be related to one's ability to respond to criminal victimization should it occur. This perspective is useful in understanding fear patterns related to race, income, and other characteristics such as education or social class. Therefore, minorities, those living in poverty, those with less education, or those with less income should have higher levels of fear of crime because members of these groups would estimate their chances of preventing or responding to criminal victimization to be diminished, given their status. However, the meaning of social vulnerability will be different depending on the social characteristic. For example, immigrants may have greater fear of crime because of ignorance of the law, distrust of law enforcement, confusion about what they should do if they witness or are victims of crime, or language barriers that make reporting the crime more difficult. In a different vein, the homeless may have greater fear of victimization because of their persistent exposure to risk and lack of both social *and* financial resources needed to respond to and recover from victimization.

Beyond individual characteristics of persons such as demographics, vulnerability also can be a function of exposure to risk, target suitability, or absent or ineffective guardianship as the lifestyle–routine activities perspective suggests. For example, certain occupations require a high degree of public exposure, such as those in the transportation field (e.g., taxi drivers, bus drivers), the criminal justice system (e.g., police officers, correctional officers), or the medical profession (e.g., emergency department doctors, nurses, and medical support staff). Increased exposure to victimization risk may increase perceived risk and fear of crime for those working in these occupations.

Target suitability also may affect fear of crime. Individuals who possess expensive goods or other valuables may be targeted by offenders because of this increased target attractiveness. In this context, target suitability may be a reflection of lifestyle, such as wearing expensive jewelry, or routine activities, such as handling cash in the course of a job (e.g., bank teller, cashier). Lack of guardianship also can be a form of vulnerability that can affect fear of victimization. Indeed, this is the underlying assumption of the original NCS and GSS measures of fear that asked individuals whether they would be afraid to walk in their communities alone at night.

Having been a crime victim is another dimension of vulnerability that may influence fear of victimization; however, the research that has sought to address this hypothesis has not arrived at a definitive conclusion (Farrall, Jackson, & Gray, 2009; Hale, 1996). Some studies report that prior victimization increases fear, others find that it has no effect, and still others indicate that whether victimization influences fear depends on other variables. For instance, in Garofalo's (1979) examination of the NCS, it was revealed that there was a significant relationship between victimization and fear of crime. However, in a study of fear of criminal victimization at school among adolescents, David May and Gregory Dunaway (2000) found that previous victimization had no effect on fear at school unless it was examined in conjunction with other social characteristics, such as gender. May and Dunaway reported that prior victimization significantly affected fear of crime among females, but not males. It is also possible that characteristics of the environment, such as the school, incite fear of crime. This idea is addressed by the environmental perspective.

The Environmental Perspective

The vulnerability perspective is complemented by the ***environmental perspective***, which explains fear of crime as the result of factors beyond the individual. According to this perspective, environmental cues signal to individuals in those settings that danger may be looming and/or that they are susceptible to criminal victimization. Much of the research that has tested the environmental perspective is grounded in criminological theories, especially "broken windows theory." ***Broken windows theory*** explains that "broken windows" left unrepaired over time signal that problems in the community (i.e., the environment) are not being addressed by the residents and/or site users (Wilson & Kelling, 1982). Imagine you are on a street where you see windows broken out of the buildings, graffiti on the walls, litter on the street, overgrown yards, and abandoned cars. Do you feel safe from victimization? The theory contends these ***physical incivilities*** alert site users that the environment may not be safe because criminal behavior, like the signs of physical disorder, will go ignored by those who live or work there. ***Social incivilities*** are another aspect of the environment that can increase individuals' feelings of fear of crime. As is the case with physical incivilities, an environment containing social incivilities such as loiterers, panhandlers, drunks, high levels of noise, or the presence of prostitutes suggests such behaviors are tolerated by the community. Environments in which physical and social disorder are tolerated alert both potential criminals and victims that these are places where criminal opportunities flourish, resulting in elevated levels of fear of crime among would-be victims.

Another aspect of the environment that can influence fear of crime is referred to as social integration. Although it is more difficult to actually "see" than physical or social incivilities, the ***social integration hypothesis*** states that communities (environments) that are socially cohesive or closely knit will be characterized as having much less fear of victimization among residents because they have a sense of personal and collective security. Unlike communities or places suffering from incivilities described by broken windows theory, residents of these communities know that such problems will not be tolerated and will be promptly addressed. In socially cohesive neighborhoods, for example, residents are willing to intervene to tell youths breaking curfew to go home, or call police when they see a suspicious person or activity. At its core, the social integration perspective argues that fear will be lower in these environments because residents are willing to work together, trust each other, and serve their mutual interests in keeping themselves, their neighbors, and their community safe from crime.

The theoretical propositions related to the effects of physical incivilities, social incivilities, and social integration on fear of victimization have been examined across a wide range of environmental contexts, such as neighborhoods, secondary schools, and college campuses. For example, LaGrange, Ferraro, and Supancic (1992) estimated the effects of neighborhood perceptions of physical and social incivilities on perceived risk and fear of crime among residents from throughout the United States. They found that both physical incivilities (e.g., trash and litter, vacant houses) and social incivilities (e.g., unsupervised youth, too much noise) were statistically significant predictors of perceived risk of personal and property crime, but fear of crime itself was not. However, perceived risk exhibited powerful positive effects on fear of victimization, suggesting that the effects of incivilities may be indirect. In a study of fear among youth ages 10 to 16 from throughout the United States, Chris Melde and Finn-Aage Esbensen (2009) examined how perceived school disorder and perceived risk of school victimization affected fear of school-based victimization. They found that if students believed their school to be disorderly, they generally also had increased chances of victimization, perceived risk of victimization, and fear of in-school victimization.

Many other studies have been undertaken to better understand how incivilities and social integration affect fear of crime. Yet, a primary focus of contemporary fear of crime research has been to integrate or combine the vulnerability perspective with the environmental perspective to attain a more complete picture of factors that give rise to fear of victimization.

The Multilevel Perspective

The ***multilevel perspective*** presumes that a complete understanding of fear of crime requires a consideration of both *individual-level* vulnerability and *macro-level* disorder and social integration. Ferraro (1995) brought together these two explanations of fear with his model of fear of crime based on what he called risk interpretation. ***Risk interpretation*** refers to the process by which individuals ascertain whether they are at risk of being victimized. Ferraro explained that structural conditions that are present at the macro-level such as neighborhood incivilities or crime rates are interpreted by individuals in light of their individual situations (e.g., their age, gender, income). As attitudes about their safety or danger in the community take shape, individuals consider ways to prevent victimization by adapting their behavior. Behavioral adaptations to fear of crime are discussed further toward the conclusion of the chapter. Ferraro's model is provided in Figure 13-3.

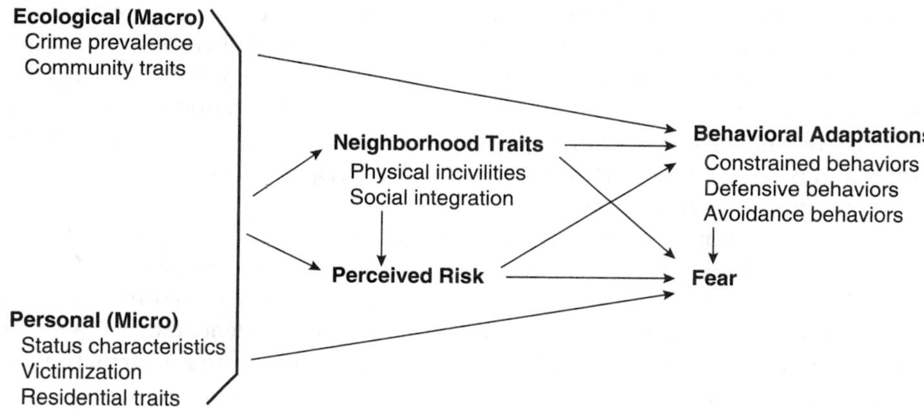

Figure 13-3 Ferraro's Model of Fear of Crime
Source: Ferraro (1995).

Much research has built on Ferraro's conceptualization of fear of crime and investigated the simultaneous effects of the macro- and micro-level predictors of fear. A few examples of these studies and their findings follow. For instance, one of these studies was conducted by Travis Franklin, Cortney Franklin, and Noelle Fearn (2008) among residents from 21 cities across Washington State. Their results suggested that while vulnerability and social cohesion were important influences on both perceived risk and fear of victimization, perceptions of neighborhood disorder exhibited the strongest effects. In other words, neighborhood factors such as noise, traffic, and youth gangs were more important predictors of perceived risk and fear than demographic characteristics or neighborhood social ties. In another study of the effects of neighborhood conditions on fear of crime, Ian Brunton-Smith and Patrick Sturgis (2011) used data from the British Crime Survey (BCS) and arrived at similar conclusions about the importance of the environment in affecting fear among residents. Their analysis found that indicators of vulnerability, including gender, race, age, education, and previous victimization, affected feelings of fear, but so did neighborhood characteristics such as the local crime rate and residents' perceptions of neighborhood disorder.

Researchers also have expanded the scope of these theoretical ideas beyond neighborhoods and studied fear of criminal victimization in other social settings, such as schools. The concepts of disorder, incivilities, social cohesion, and vulnerability can be applied to school settings, but in some cases they require reconceptualization. For instance, abandoned cars are a sign of disorder in neighborhoods, but not within school buildings, where litter, graffiti, metal detectors, or school security may be more important indicators of disorder. Considering these types of issues, researchers have applied the core concepts of the vulnerability and environmental perspectives to school fear but adapted them to school settings. For example, Swartz and colleagues (2011) addressed how student vulnerability and school disorder and social cohesion shaped feelings of fear among seventh- to 10th-grade students in Kentucky. They further divided their sample of students into males and females to explore possible gendered effects on fear. Their results indicated that previous victimization and perceptions of risk were related to fear of school crime among both males and females. Not only were there no differences between males and females with respect to the effects of school disorder or social cohesion on fear, but these variables were not statically significant predictors of fear. Overall, then, the study by Swartz and colleagues supported the vulnerability perspective but not the environmental perspective.

Marie Tillyer, Bonnie Fisher, and Pamela Wilcox (2011) also examined multilevel correlates of fear in schools but included an additional focus on school crime prevention measures. Recall that perceptions of risk are closely tied to fear, so if prevention measures such as metal detectors are in place, students may feel safer at school. They reported that vulnerability in the form of gender and prior victimization were both related to perceived risk and fear of victimization, but school cohesion was not. Although the strongest predictor of fear was perceived risk of victimization, the presence of metal detectors in the school also was found to be an important factor in understanding students' fear of crime. Metal detectors were associated with decreased fear of victimization among students, while other crime prevention efforts (e.g., locker checks, banning backpacks and book bags) proved ineffective at reducing students' fears. The finding that metal detectors reduce fear is particularly interesting considering that the authors reported that metal detectors did not reduce actual school crime.

The vulnerability, environmental, and multilevel perspectives are useful frameworks for understanding fear of crime in society and fear of crime in specific contexts, such as neighborhoods and schools. Contemporary research also has begun to investigate the extent and nature of fear of victimization online. Full-fledged tests of these perspectives have not yet been undertaken, but as Box 13-2 illustrates, cyberspace is another context that may generate unique explanations of fear of online victimization.

The environmental perspective, the findings related to contextual fear, and the discussion in Box 13-2 about online fear all indicate that settings are an important component in explaining fear of crime. Most of the research that has been undertaken has focused on the macro-environment and its characteristics, such as neighborhood disorder or a school's social cohesion. A final framework that is useful for understanding fear of crime also emphasizes the importance of the environment or setting, but does so by considering places where fear concentrates.

Box 13-2: Fear of Crime Online

Few studies have explored the extent or nature of fear of online crimes. It is not currently known whether online experiences, such as being threatened, have the same fear-inducing effects on people that face-to-face or offline experiences generate. It is possible that online behaviors are less likely to produce fear because of the physical space separating the offender and the potential victim. However, it is also possible that such encounters make individuals as afraid or even more so because of the anonymous nature of the online environment. Very few studies have been undertaken to study fear of crime online, but those that have been published suggest it is not that different from fear of offline crimes.

Research by Billy Henson, Bradford Reyns, and Bonnie Fisher (2013) asked college students how afraid they were of online interpersonal victimization by (1) intimate partners, (2) friends/acquaintances, and (3) strangers. They found that fear of online victimization was relatively low but that students were most afraid of being targeted online by strangers, then intimate partners, and the least afraid of being victimized by friends and acquaintances. Henson and his colleagues also reported that perceived risk of victimization was a strong predictor of fear of online victimization, regardless of who the offender was.

Using survey responses from the Australian Survey of Social Attitudes, Lynne Roberts, David Indermaur, and Caroline Spiranovic (2013) examined fear of a different type of online victimization: online identity theft. They concluded that routine Internet use, including how often individuals used the Internet, where they used it, age, and fear of offline crime were significant predictors of whether residents of Australia feared online identity theft victimization. In this same survey, over 50% of participants rated themselves as either "fairly" or "very" worried about having their credit cards misused on the Internet. Further, 57% of participants in the 2005/2006 British Crime Survey indicated they were either "fairly" or "very" worried about credit fraud victimization. These figures suggest that fear of online victimization may be even greater than fear of most forms of offline victimization.

As more features of daily life require routine Internet use, opportunities for cybercrimes will likewise increase. It will be up to victimologists to research how afraid individuals are of online victimization, what causes that fear, and what the consequences of online fear might be.

Hot Spots of Fear

Recall that hot spots of crime are places where crimes concentrate. For example, a suburban community can be a hot spot for burglaries because some houses do not have alarms on doors and windows and no one is home to guard the property. Specific places such as a local bar may have a high concentration of drug dealers and prostitutes as well as many suitably intoxicated or drug-influenced patrons that invite both vice and more crime.

In a like manner, ***hot spots of fear***, or fear spots, are places where fear of crime concentrates. Although fear spots could theoretically be generated in very large places, such as countries, or at more targeted locations, such as cities, they have thus far only been studied at the micro-level. ***Micro environments*** are the immediate sites that individuals occupy, such as recreation areas, shopping centers, or parking lots. These places possess various features, such as blind alleys, tall walls, or dead ends, and these types of site features have been linked to the formation of hot spots of fear. Three specific categories of site features give rise to fear spots: prospect, refuge, and escape (Fisher & Nasar, 1995).

First, ***prospect*** refers to a sense of openness about one's surroundings, as would be the case in a wide-open field or park. Theoretically, sites that have prospect should allow individuals to feel safe in their surroundings because they can see any potential threats or dangers as they approach. It follows, then, that sites with low prospect are more likely to produce fear in individuals because they cannot see or anticipate potential dangers.

The second important type of site feature to create fear spots is refuge. Areas with ***refuge*** offer places to hide—as in areas for potential criminals to hide before striking. Therefore, sites with high walls, blind alleys, or tall shrubs will have many places of refuge for would-be offenders and bring about feelings of fear among those who occupy or use the space. On the other hand, individuals should feel safe in places that do not offer refuge to would-be offenders.

The final type of site feature that generates hot spots of fear is escape. ***Escape*** refers to a way for individuals to flee if they encounter danger. Consequently, sites with avenues of escape bring about feelings of safety, while confined areas with few options for escape from threats lead to fear. The two ideal scenarios in which micro environments either make individuals feel fearful or safe based on levels of prospect, refuge, and escape are provided in Figure 13-4. Of course, there are other combinations that could lead site users to feel moderately or a little fearful as well, such as an environment with high prospect and easy escape, but also high refuge.

Level of Prospect	Level of Refuge	Level of Escape	Effect on Fear
High Prospect	Low Refuge	High Escape	Low Fear High Safety
Low Prospect	High Refuge	Low Escape	High Fear Low Safety

Figure 13-4 Effect of Site Features on Fear of Crime

The theoretical basis for sites with low prospect, high refuge, and low escape becoming hot spots of fear is Jay Appleton's (1996) prospect–refuge theory. ***Prospect–refuge theory*** contends that assessing a location in terms of its prospect and refuge is an evolutionary survival mechanism that humans still possess. Bonnie Fisher and Jack Nasar (1992) adapted this theory and used it to explain how micro environments generate or reduce fear of crime depending on the existence of prospect, refuge, and escape. In 1989, the Ohio State University constructed the Wexner Center for the Visual Arts, a building that was praised in architectural circles but not necessarily embraced by the public. Fisher and Nasar identified eight specific areas of the Wexner Center that exemplified the concepts of prospect, refuge, and escape. Using a site map, they surveyed college students who visited or passed by the Center to rate their fear of crime in those specific areas. As expected, students reported the highest fear of crime in those areas with low prospect and escape for potential crime victims and high refuge for would-be offenders. Further research has supported the initial findings of Fisher and Nasar and raised the possibility that fear spots could effectively be designed out of micro environments if an environment's design featured high prospect, low refuge, and high escape (Wang & Taylor, 2006).

The Wexner Center for the Visual Arts, The Ohio State University
Source: Panoramio (n.d.).
Photo Credit: aceshot1/Shutterstock.com

The Consequences of Fear of Crime

Fear of crime has significant consequences for individuals and for society. Among individuals, fear is a necessary emotion: It alerts danger and ensures survival. However, any fear beyond what is necessary can result in decreased quality of life, such as unnecessarily avoiding certain areas or specific locations. It also can lead to the adoption of protective behaviors, such as carrying weapons or changing daily routines or lifestyles.

Balancing Fear Against Risk

Throughout this chapter, the differences among fear of crime, perceived risk of victimization, and actual victimization risk have been highlighted. Ideally, these three elements will be in balance or harmony, with individuals accurately estimating their actual victimization risk and carrying themselves accordingly (Warr, 2000). An accurate appraisal of one's chances of becoming a victim may result in experiencing some fear of crime, but, as was discussed previously, fear is often a useful emotion.

Fear is beneficial when it signals danger and helps keep individuals out of harm's way. Therefore, one who has properly estimated one's personal victimization risk will have a "healthy" and balanced level of fear sufficient to keep safe. This possibility is illustrated in scenario 1 of Figure 13-5. Appropriate precautionary behaviors are represented by the dashed line. In scenario 1, individuals accurately estimate their likelihood of becoming victims of crime, which instills enough fear in them to ensure that they are reasonably cautious.

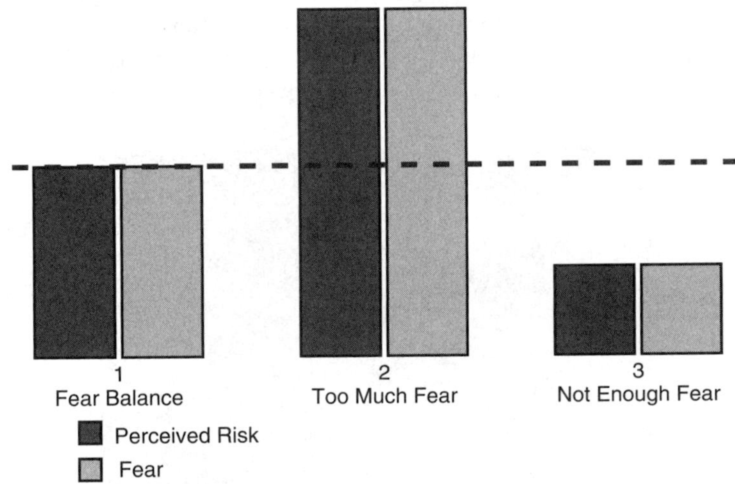

Figure 13-5 Balancing Fear and Risk

Consider the implications of having an imbalance of fear and risk. For example, scenario 2 demonstrates that those individuals who overestimate their risks for victimization will experience more fear than is needed to stay safe and avoid criminal opportunities. These individuals may take extra precautions, avoid certain places or activities, or otherwise alter their daily routines to the point that they are unnecessarily constraining their behaviors. This may even result in a lowered quality of life. Scenario 3 shows an imbalance in the other direction, that of individuals underestimating victimization risk. Here, individuals who do not acknowledge their risks for becoming victims have low levels of fear and consequently do not take enough precautions to protect themselves from victimization.

In these three scenarios, fear of crime and perceptions of victimization risk intersect to determine how individuals behave in protecting themselves and their property from criminal victimization. These precautionary behaviors, like fear and risk, have been extensively studied by criminologists and victimologists. This research suggests that fear and risk influence protective practices, but other factors, such as the type of victimization being considered and the individual's characteristics, also are important predictors. Further, the types of protective behaviors individuals adopt vary widely. Some individuals will choose to carry weapons if they are fearful, while others will stay home from school or work to avoid risky situations. The types of adaptive behaviors and influences on these precautionary actions are discussed in the next section.

Avoidance and Protective Behaviors

The President's Commission on Law Enforcement and the Administration of Justice (1967, p. 51) stated: "Perhaps the most revealing findings on the impact of fear of crime on people's lives were the changes people reported in their regular habits of life." The changes that the Commission was referring to are avoidance behaviors and protective behaviors. ***Avoidance behaviors*** are changes to one's daily routines that involve evading or avoiding certain people, places, or situations. For example, a student who is afraid of being bullied may avoid certain areas of the school or stay home from school altogether. ***Protective behaviors*** are actions designed to prevent victimizations. Carrying mace to fight off a sexual predator is an example of a self-protective behavior. Other examples of protective behaviors include purchasing security systems for a residence or vehicle, buying a watchdog, or learning self-defense techniques. These lifestyle adjustments in response to fear of crime are together referred to as ***constrained behaviors*** because of the restrictions they place on individuals' daily activities.

Researchers have hypothesized that high levels of perceived risk and fear of crime result in the adoption of avoidance or protective behaviors, or both. The expectation among individuals is that this will reduce their risk of victimization, and perhaps their fear of crime. It has also been suggested that both fear of crime and these behavioral adaptations are the result of perceived risk (Ferraro, 1995). Here, those who perceive themselves to be likely victims will be fearful, as has already been discussed, but they will also deem it necessary to take measures to protect themselves or their property. Still others suggest that the relationship is reciprocal, with fear affecting protective behaviors, and protective behaviors generating further fear (e.g., Liska, Sanchirico, & Reed, 1988). Although at this time it is not clear exactly which of these three possibilities is best supported by research, it may be the case that they are all correct, and are determined by the individual, contextual, and situational characteristics. Nicole Rader (2004) has proposed an alternative explanation about the relationship among fear of crime, perceived risk, and constrained behaviors, arguing that all of these are dimensions of the *threat of victimization*.

The ***threat of victimization***, which is depicted in Figure 13-6, is an umbrella term that Rader developed to explain the overarching construct that includes fear as its emotional dimension, perceived risk as its cognitive dimension, and constrained behaviors as its behavioral dimension. According to Rader, these three dimensions should be considered simultaneously, and focusing on only the emotional aspects of the threat of victimization (fear of crime), as most researchers have done provides an incomplete picture of how these concepts are related. Rader and her colleagues (2007)

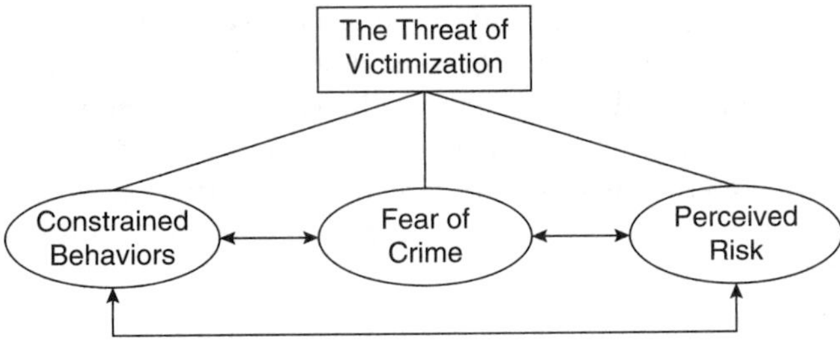

Figure 13-6 The Threat of Victimization Concept
Source: Rader (2004).

empirically examined the threat of victimization concept by using survey data from adult residents of Kentucky. Their results expressed support for the threat of victimization hypothesis, because fear of crime was related to perceived risk and constrained behaviors in reciprocal ways, meaning they simultaneously influenced each other. However, perceived risk did not affect constrained behaviors, which does not support Rader's hypothesis. Subsequent research also revealed that these three dimensions of the threat of victimization may affect each other differently depending on the individual's gender. For instance, later research by Rader and colleagues found that fear of crime influenced whether women adopted defensive precautions to protect against victimization, but this relationship did not exist for men (Rader, Cossman, & Allison, 2009).

Summary

Fear of crime is a persistent social problem that affects both victims and nonvictims, and since the 1960s criminologists and victimologists have studied its extent and nature. In doing so, researchers have consistently reported that fear of criminal victimization is more common in the United States than actual criminal victimization. This is an important contrast to make because it indicates that a substantial portion of the population suffers the consequences of fear of criminal victimization, perhaps unnecessarily. Fear-of-crime researchers also have investigated potential explanations of fear. This research has reported that certain patterns in individual characteristics identify those who are most likely to be fearful. Gender appears to play a key role, but patterns in age, race, and income also have been uncovered. Beyond patterns in individuals' characteristics, fear-of-crime scholars also have focused on developing theories to explain why and how individuals are fearful, including the vulnerability perspective, the environmental perspective, and the multilevel perspective. Fear also can be explained as a function of the micro environment, with specific site features (i.e., prospect, refuge, and escape) provoking fear, thereby causing hot spots of fear to develop. "Spotlight on Policy: Reducing Fear of Crime at a Railway Station" box provides an example of how theory and research can culminate to suggest policy solutions for reducing fear of crime on public transportation.

Spotlight on Policy: Reducing Fear of Crime at a Railway Station

Much of the research and theory reviewed throughout this chapter has identified characteristics of persons or places that explain fear of crime. A study by Paul Cozens, Richard Neale, and David Hillier (2004) assessed how strategies based on crime prevention through environmental design (CPTED) (see also Chapters 3 and 14) might reduce fear of crime for passengers waiting at Britain's railway stations. Briefly, CPTED strategies include manipulating the environment in ways that reduce opportunities for crime and fear of crime. Some of these include

- Assisting natural surveillance—improving visibility of one's surroundings
- Fostering territorial reinforcement—using site features that communicate ownership of places and encourage their maintenance
- Providing access control—using signs, exits, fences, landscaping, and lighting to guide people entering and existing the environment
- Improving image and space management—promotes a positive image of the environment or place and reinforces its purpose

The research team used an innovative technology called Quick Time Virtual Reality (QTVR) to simulate for study participants the conditions found at certain railway stations. After their virtual panoramic walkthrough of six selected stations and their access routes using QTVR, 47 respondents were interviewed about their perceptions of the environment and their consequent fear of crime. Six site improvements were identified by study participants as ways of reducing fear of crime by changing characteristics of the built environment: (1) improved lighting, (2) closed-circuit television (CCTV), (3) more staff, (4) transparent shelters, (5) cleaner stations, and (6) cutting back vegetation.

With these data in hand, improvements, such as transparent shelters for those waiting for their train, were implemented at several stations. A customer satisfaction survey later indicated that 93% of respondents noticed the new shelters, and 71% of these individuals said they reduced their fear of crime because of the improved visibility they provided.

In terms of consequences of fear of crime, it is important that individuals keep their fear in balance to ensure that they take proper precautions to protect themselves without unnecessarily constraining their behavior. Such precautionary measures may include avoiding certain places where crime may be more likely, such as streets at night, or adopting other protective measures, such as taking self-defense lessons. Yet another way to conceptualize each of these important issues in understanding fear of crime is to view fear, perceived risk, and constrained behaviors as part of an overarching concept called threat of victimization. According to the threat of victimization hypothesis, these concepts are interrelated and must be studied simultaneously to truly understand their nature.

KEYWORDS

Fear	Fear of crime	Perceived risk of victimization
Actual victimization risk	Formless measures	Concrete measures
Frequency	Intensity	Paradox of fear
Shadow of sexual assault hypothesis	Vulnerability perspective	Physical vulnerability
Social vulnerability	Environmental perspective	Broken windows theory
Physical incivilities	Social incivilities	Social integration hypothesis
Multilevel perspective	Risk interpretation	Hot spots of fear
Micro environments	Prospect	Refuge
Escape	Prospect–refuge theory	Avoidance behaviors
Protective behaviors	Constrained behaviors	Threat of victimization

DISCUSSION QUESTIONS

1. Describe the difference between fear of crime and perceived risk of victimization. How might perceived risk influence fear of criminal victimization? Provide a scenario you have experienced as an example.
2. Do the NCS and GSS survey questions about "fear" actually measure fear of crime or something else? What other types of survey questions might better measure fear of crime? Explain your answer and provide examples.
3. Why is fear of crime considered to be a persistent social problem?
4. Why does it appear that more people fear criminal victimization than are actually crime victims? Does this paradox exist for all types of personal and property crime? Argue why or why not.
5. Explain the paradox of fear. Why do those with lower victimization risks often have greater fear of victimization?
6. Besides gender and age, what other physical characteristics would the vulnerability perspective predict influence fear of victimization?
7. How can lifestyle–routine activities theory, a theory of criminal victimization, be used to understand fear of victimization?
8. Tillyer, Fisher, and Wilcox found that having metal detectors in schools reduced students' fear of crime. What else could school administrators do to make students (and teachers) feel safe at school?
9. Think about the site features on your college campus. Are there any locations that you would expect to be hot spots of fear? Find examples of features related to prospect, refuge, and escape and describe how each characteristic might influence students' fear of crime.

REFERENCES

Addington, L. (2003). Students' fear after Columbine: Findings from a randomized experiment. *Journal of Quantitative Criminology, 19*, 367–387.

Appleton, J. (1996). *The experience of landscape* (Revised Edition). West Sussex: John Wiley & Sons.

Baumer, T. L. (1979). Research on fear of crime in the United States. *Victimology, 3*, 254–264.

Brunton-Smith, I., & Sturgis, P. (2011). Do neighborhoods generate fear of crime? An empirical test using the British Crime Survey. *Criminology, 49*, 331–369.

Clemente, F., & Kleiman, M. B. (1977). Fear of crime in the United States: A multivariate analysis. *Social Forces, 56*, 519–531.

Cozens, P., Neale, R., & Hillier, D. (2004). Tackling crime and fear of crime while waiting at Britain's railway stations. *Journal of Public Transportation, 7*, 23–41.

Farrall, S., Bannister, J., Ditton, J., & Gilchrist, E. (1997). Questioning the measurement of the 'fear of crime': Findings from a major methodological study. *British Journal of Criminology, 37*, 658–679.

Farrall, S., & Gadd, D. (2004). The frequency of fear of crime. *British Journal of Criminology, 44*, 127–132.

Farrall, S., Jackson, J., & Gray, E. (2009). *Social order and the fear of crime in contemporary times.* New York: Oxford University Press.

Ferraro, K. F. (1995). *Fear of crime: Interpreting victimization risk.* Albany: State University of New York Press.

Ferraro, K. F. (1996). Women's fear of victimization: Shadow of sexual assault? *Social Forces, 75*, 667–690.

Ferraro, K. F., & LaGrange, R. L. (1992). Are older people most afraid of crime? Reconsidering age differences in fear of victimization. *Journal of Gerontology, 47*, S233–S244.

Fisher, B. S., & Nasar, J. L. (1992). Fear of crime in relation to three exterior site features: Prospect, refuge, and escape. *Environment and Behavior, 24*, 35–65.

Fisher, B. S., & Nasar, J. L. (1995). Fear spots in relation to microlevel physical cues: Exploring the overlooked. *Journal of Research in Crime and Delinquency, 32*, 214–239.

Fisher, B. S., & Sloan, J. J. (2003). Unraveling the fear of victimization among college women: Is the "shadow of sexual assault hypothesis" supported? *Justice Quarterly, 20*, 633–659.

Fox, K. A., Nobles, M. R., & Piquero, A. R. (2009). Gender, crime victimization and fear of crime. *Security Journal, 22*, 24–39.

Franklin, T. W., Franklin, C. A., & Fearn, N. E. (2008). A multilevel analysis of the vulnerability, disorder, and social integration models of fear of crime. *Social Justice Research, 21*, 204–227.

Gallup. (2010). Nearly 4 in 10 Americans still fear walking alone at night. Retrieved February 10, 2013, from http://www.gallup.com/poll/144272/Nearly-Americans-Fear-Walking-Alone-Night.aspx

Garofalo, J. (1979). Victimization and fear of crime. *Journal of Research in Crime and Delinquency, 16*, 80–97.

Hale, C. (1996). Fear of crime: A review of the literature. *International Review of Victimology, 4*, 79–150.

Henson, B., & Reyns, B. W. (2015). The only thing we have to fear is fear itself . . . and crime: The current state of the fear of crime literature and where it should go next. *Sociology Compass, 9*, 91–103.

Henson, B., Reyns, B. W., & Fisher, B. S. (2013). Fear of crime online? Examining the effect of risk, previous victimization, and exposure on fear of online interpersonal victimization. *Journal of Contemporary Criminal Justice, 29*, 475–497.

Hilinski, C. M. (2009). Fear of crime among college students: A test of the shadow of sexual assault hypothesis. *American Journal of Criminal Justice, 34*, 84–102.

Hindelang, M. J., Gottfredson, M. R., & Garofalo, J. (1978). *Victims of personal crime: An empirical foundation for a theory of personal victimization*. Cambridge, MA: Ballinger Publishing Company.

Killias, M. (1990). Vulnerability: Towards a better understanding of a key variable in the genesis of fear of crime. *Violence and Victims, 5*, 97–108.

LaGrange, R. L., & Ferraro, K. F. (1987). The elderly's fear of crime: A critical examination of the research. *Research on Aging, 9*, 372–391.

LaGrange, R. L., & Ferraro, K. F. (1989). Assessing age and gender differences in perceived risk and fear of crime. *Criminology, 27*, 697–719.

LaGrange, R. L., Ferraro, K. F., & Supancic, M. (1992). Perceived risk and fear of crime: Role of social and physical incivilities. *Journal of Research in Crime and Delinquency, 29*, 311–334.

Lane, J., Rader, N., Henson, B., Fisher, B., & May, D., (2014). *Fear of crime in the United States: Causes, consequences, and contradictions*. Durham, North Carolina: Carolina Academic Press.

Langton, L. (2011). *Identity theft reported by households, 2005–2010*. Washington, DC: Bureau of Justice Statistics.

Liska, A. E., Sanchirico, A., & Reed, M. D. (1988). Fear of crime and constrained behavior: Specifying and estimating a reciprocal effects model. *Social Forces, 66*, 827–937.

May, D. C., & Dunaway, R. G. (2000). Predictors of fear of criminal victimization at school among adolescents. *Sociological Spectrum, 20*, 149–168.

May, D. C., Rader, N. E., & Goodrum, S. (2010). A gendered assessment of the "threat of victimization": Examining gender differences in fear of crime, perceived risk, avoidance, and defensive behaviors. *Criminal Justice Review, 35*, 159–182.

McCoy, H. V., Wooldredge, J. D., Cullen, F. T., Dubeck, P. J., & Browning, S. L. (1996). Lifestyles of the old and not so fearful: Life situation and older persons' fear of crime. *Journal of Criminal Justice, 24*, 191–205.

McGarrell, E. F., Giacomazzi, A. L., & Thurman, Q. C. (1997). Neighborhood disorder, integration, and fear of crime. *Justice Quarterly, 14*, 479–500.

Melde, C., & Esbensen, F. A. (2009). The victim-offender overlap and fear of in-school victimization: A longitudinal examination of risk assessment models. *Crime and Delinquency, 55*, 499–525.

National Opinion Research Center. (2013). General Social Survey. Retrieved February 10, 2013, from http://www.norc.org/Research/Projects/Pages/general-social-survey.aspx

Nellis, A. M. (2009). Gender differences in fear of terrorism. *Journal of Contemporary Criminal Justice, 25*, 322–340.

Ortega, S. T., & Myles, J. L. (1987). Race and gender effects on fear of crime: An interactive model with age. *Criminology, 25*, 133–152.

Panoramio (n.d.). *Robert Maihofer II – Ohio State University Wexner Center for the Arts, GLCT*. Retrieved February 10, 2013, from: http://www.panoramio.com/photo_explorer # view=photo&position=5190&with_photo_id=47757181&order=date_desc&user=5023543

President's Commission on Law Enforcement and Administration of Justice. (1967). *The challenge of crime in a free society*. Washington, DC: U.S. Government Printing Office.

Rader, N. E. (2004). The threat of victimization: A theoretical reconceptualization of fear of crime. *Sociological Spectrum, 24*, 689–704.

Rader, N. E., Cossman, J. S., & Allison, M. (2009). Considering the gendered nature of constrained behavior practices among male and female college students. *Journal of Contemporary Criminal Justice, 25*, 282–299.

Rader, N. E., May, D. C., & Goodrum, S. (2007). An empirical assessment of the "threat of victimization:" Considering fear of crime, perceived risk, avoidance, and defensive behaviors. *Sociological Spectrum, 27*, 475–505.

Randa, R., & Wilcox, P. (2010). School disorder, victimization, and general v. place-specific avoidance. *Journal of Criminal Justice, 38*, 854–861.

Robers, S., Kemp, J., Rathbun, A., Morgan, R. E., & Snyder, T. D. (2014). *Indicators of school crime and safety: 2013*. Washington, DC: National Center for Education Statistics, U.S. Department of Education, and Bureau of Justice Statistics, Office of Justice Programs, U.S. Department of Justice.

Roberts, L. D., Indermaur, D., & Spiranovic, C. (2013). Fear of cyber-identity theft and related fraudulent activity. *Psychiatry, Psychology and Law, 20*, 315–328.

Schafer, J. A., Huebner, B. M., & Bynum, T. S. (2006). Fear of crime and criminal victimization: Gender-based contrasts. *Journal of Criminal Justice, 34*, 285–301.

Skogan, W. G. (2011). Trends in crime and fear: Lessons from Chicago, 1994–2003. In S. Karstedt, I. Loader, & H. Strang (Eds.), *Emotions, crime and justice* (pp. 101–122). Oxford: Hart Publishing.

Skogan, W. G., & Maxfield, M. (1981). *Coping with crime: Individual and neighborhood reactions*. Beverly Hills, CA: Sage Publications, Inc.

Stafford, M. C., & Galle, O. R. (1984). Victimization rates, exposure to risk, and fear of crime. *Criminology, 22*, 173–185.

Swartz, K., Reyns, B. W., Henson, B., & Wilcox, P. (2011). Fear of in-school victimization: Contextual, gendered, and developmental considerations. *Youth Violence and Juvenile Justice, 9*, 59–78.

Tillyer, M. S., Fisher, B. S., & Wilcox, P. (2011). The effects of school crime prevention on students' violent victimization, risk perception, and fear of crime: A multilevel opportunity perspective. *Justice Quarterly, 28*, 249–277.

Wang, K., & Taylor, R. B. (2006). Simulated walks through dangerous alleys: Impacts of features and progress on fear. *Journal of Environmental Psychology, 26*, 269–283.

Warr, M. (1984). Fear of victimization: Why are women and the elderly more afraid? *Social Science Quarterly, 65*, 681–702.

Warr, M. (2000). Fear of crime in the United States: Avenues for research and policy. In D. Duffee (Ed.), *Measurement and analysis of crime and justice* (Vol. 4, pp. 452–489). Washington, DC: National Institute of Justice.

Wilcox, P., Jordan, C. E., & Pritchard, A. J. (2006). Fear of acquaintance versus stranger rape as a "master status": Towards refinement of the "shadow of sexual assault." *Violence and Victims, 21*, 357–373.

Wilcox, P., Jordan, C. E., & Pritchard, A. J. (2007). A multidimensional examination of campus safety: Victimization, perceptions of danger, worry about crime, and precautionary behavior among college women in the post-*Clery* era. *Crime and Delinquency, 53*, 219–254.

Wilson, J. Q., & Kelling, G. (1982) The police and neighborhood safety: Broken windows. *Atlantic Monthly, 127*, 29–38.

PART IV

The Prevention of Victimization in the 21st Century

Part IV of this textbook contains one chapter, Chapter 14, which reviews victimization prevention from both theoretical and applied viewpoints within the framework of environmental criminology. Environmental criminology is a perspective that developed separately but alongside victimology, and offers many insights into ways in which criminal victimization might be prevented or its negative impacts minimized. After all, one of the primary purposes of victimology is to recognize and remedy the plight of crime victims. Learning more about victimization experiences and the consequences associated with victimization is, therefore, a critical step toward that well-meaning goal.

We also recognize that including such a chapter in a victimology textbook may be considered somewhat novel. No other victimology textbook on the market includes an entire chapter devoted to prevention, but we believe that the earlier chapters of this textbook have prepared readers to take the next logical step aimed at critically examining prevention efforts. We also hope that Part IV in future editions of this textbook will include other chapters that describe cutting-edge prevention strategies and present findings about their effectiveness to reduce, and minimize the effects of, criminal victimization.

Before these chapters can be written, the next generation of victimologists will have to apply what is known about the correlates and predictors of different types of criminal victimization toward the development of prevention strategies. Rigorous evaluations of these strategies, measuring a range of outcomes from fear of crime, to victimization, to the emotional, psychological, and physical effects of victimization, will bear out their effectiveness.

CASE STUDY #4

Crime Prevention in the 21st Century: Project Green Dot

> Too often official responses to crime . . . have been reactive, instituting tougher criminal justice responses and harsher penalties, razing poor housing areas, or destroying areas of informal street trading and dispersing the informal traders. Such approaches are often reinforced by public demand, or inscribed in urban planning principles which aim to modernize or sanitize urban spaces. *While such responses may bring short-term relief, they do not provide long-term, sustainable solutions to [preventing victimization]*. . . (emphasis added; Shaw & Carli, 2011, p. 11)

Part IV examines different theoretically informed approaches to *preventing* criminal victimization. As described in Chapter 14, there is strong theoretical and empirical evidence that criminal victimizations *can be prevented* through various measures. In some instances prevention occurs because the *routine activities* of victims are changed; this disrupts the coming together in time and space of suitable targets, lack of guardians, and motivated offenders (Cohen & Felson, 1979). There are also prevention strategies targeting the built environment, known as *crime prevention through environmental design* (CPTED) (Jeffrey, 1977), which prevent victimization by changing sightlines, through lighting enhancements, by reducing hiding places, and so forth. In short, a variety of empirically verified activities can prevent criminal victimization across people, places, and time.

Preventing Violence on College Campuses: Bystander Intervention and Project Green Dot

Increasingly, victimologists and criminologists alike are demanding that programs or policies aimed at reducing criminal victimization be evaluated using the strongest possible design (e.g., experiments or quasi-experiments), which can rule out rival hypotheses as explanations for the results. Because of this shift, both groups are unlikely to recommend a particular program or policy simply because "it *seems* to work" based on anecdotal evidence compiled by proponents. Rather, recommendations for specific programs or policies most likely arise when strong designs, combined with results of sophisticated statistical modeling, indicate a particular policy or program works to prevent or reduce victimization. Crime prevention in the 21st century has thus become more theoretically and empirically driven than at any other point in its history.

One recent illustration of a theoretically informed and empirically driven evaluation involves *Project Green Dot*, a *bystander intervention program* designed to reduce sexual assault and rape on college campuses. According to Coker and colleagues (2014, pp. 2–3), "bystander strategies engage others in prevention through increasing awareness of the nature and frequency of violence and behaviors to safely and effectively intervene to reduce the risk of violence." Victimologists know, for example, that disrupting the coming together in time and space of attractive targets, motivated offenders, and lack of guardians helps reduce the chances for crime to occur (Cohen & Felson, 1979). In Green Dot, efforts are directed to enhance *guardianship*, the presence of people, which makes a target less attractive to offenders and thus reduces the chance for a victimization to occur. The "guardians" then engage in various tactics to address the victimization.

Coker and colleagues describe bystander intervention as involving *directing, distracting, delegating,* and *delaying*—the "four Ds." *Directed intervention* involves a bystander becoming explicitly involved in a situation to stop violence from occurring. For example, the manager at a restaurant observes escalating conflict occurring between a couple seated in one of the restaurant's booths. In response, the restaurant manager inserts himself between the two parties and suggests the aggressor quiet down, and he calls a cab for the other party. Other direct tactics include objecting to sexist remarks or to boasting about sexual or physical aggression. *Distracting tactics* divert the attention of the aggressor and remove the potential victim from harm. Returning to the restaurant example, the manager might mention to a colleague within earshot of the couple, "Gee, Tony, I wonder why Officer Smith is late today? He's usually here about this time to have lunch," or "Hey, Megan, whose car is that parked in front that's being ticketed by the meter maid?" *Delegation tactics* occur when people work as a team and follow a plan to disrupt the situation. For example, again using the restaurant scenario, the manager after observing the conflict between the patrons calls aside the server waiting on the couple and plans with him or her to address the aggressor while the server speaks with the prospective victim. *Delaying tactics* are implemented *after* the violence has occurred and are reactive in nature. Here, providing emotional support to the victim and/or finding the victim resources would be examples. According to Coker and colleagues (2014), bystander intervention training is intended to engage all who may observe potential or actual violence, with the goal being to diffuse the situation and prevent the violence or, if the violence has already occurred, respond to the victim in a way that helps reduce the impact of the violence.

Coker and colleagues (2014) evaluated Project Green Dot by comparing rates of violent victimization among undergraduate students attending a college with Green Dot in place with rates of violence among undergraduate students at two comparison campuses that did not implement Green Dot. The researchers found that rates of unwanted sex, sexual harassment and stalking, and psychological dating violence were lower among students at the campus with Green Dot compared to rates at the two comparison campuses. Their results suggest that bystander intervention programs can reduce violence among college students.

Efforts to prevent victimization though bystander intervention projects like Green Dot, and empirical results showing such efforts can prove effective, signal that successes are possible and that victimization, whether involving offenses against the person or against property, can be prevented.

References

Cohen, L., & Felson, M. (1979). Social change and crime rate trends: A routine activities approach. *American Sociological Review, 44*, 588–608.

Coker, A., Fisher, B., Bush, H., Swan, S., Williams, C., Clear, E., & DeGue, S. (2014). Evaluation of the Green Dot bystander intervention to reduce interpersonal violence among college students across three campuses. *Violence Against Women*, in press. http://vaw.sagepub.com/content/early/2014/08/13/1077801214545284

Jeffrey, C. R. (1977). *Crime prevention through environmental design*. Thousand Oaks, CA: SAGE Publications.

Shaw, M., & Carli, V. (Eds.) (2011). *Practical approaches to urban crime prevention*. Montreal: United Nations Office on Drugs and Crime.

CHAPTER 14

Preventing Victimization with Environmental Criminology

CHAPTER OUTLINE

Introduction

Victimization Prevention Theories

- Foundations of Environmental Criminology
- Defensible Space
- Crime Prevention Through Environmental Design
- Situational Crime Prevention

Applied Victimization Prevention

- Defensible Space
- Crime Prevention Through Environmental Design
  - Natural Surveillance
  - Territorial Reinforcement
  - Access Control
  - Target Hardening
  - Activity Support
  - Image and Space Management
  - Summary
- Situational Crime Prevention
  - Increase the Effort
  - Increase the Risks
  - Reduce the Rewards
  - Reduce Provocations
  - Remove Excuses
  - Summary
- Displacement, Diffusion of Benefits, and Anticipatory Benefits

LEARNING OBJECTIVES

- Identify and describe the theoretical foundations of environmental criminology.
- Describe defensible space, crime prevention through environmental design (CPTED), and situational crime prevention.
- Explain how defensible space, CPTED, and situational crime prevention can be used to prevent criminal victimization.
- Based on evaluations discussed in the chapter, assess the effectiveness of defensible space, CPTED, and situational crime prevention as victimization prevention strategies.
- Define displacement, diffusion of benefits, and anticipatory benefits.

If it could be determined with sufficient specificity that people or businesses with certain characteristics are more likely than others to be crime victims, and that crime is more likely to occur in some places than in others, efforts to control and prevent crime would be more productive.

President's Commission on Law Enforcement and Administration of Justice, 1967, p. 38

Introduction

As a field of study, victimology has experienced rapid growth and significant changes in a short period. In the field's early years, victimologists primarily focused on describing the victim's role in the criminal event, which often resulted in typologies of victims and studies that explained the degree to which victims were responsible for criminal events (see Chapter 1). This approach has been criticized as "victim blaming" and transferring accountability from offenders to victims (Johnson, Mullick, & Mulford, 2002). Thus, a paradigm shift has occurred in the field, and as previous chapters demonstrate, many victimologists now work toward identifying risk factors for victimization and developing theories that explain how and why targets are selected for victimization. This valuable knowledge has direct implications for preventing initial and subsequent victimizations, which early victimologists did not address.

This chapter is divided into two sections. First, it reviews the theoretical foundations underlying the prevention of victimization. Recall that the opportunity perspective has been repeatedly presented in previous chapters (see Chapters 2 and 3) as a leading theoretical explanation for victimization; this perspective is also the keystone of most theory relating to preventing crime and victimization. Thus, the implication of identifying risk factors for victimization is that if circumstances can be altered or avoided, opportunities for victimization can be reduced, and victimization may be prevented. Several theories from environmental criminology, notably defensible space, crime prevention through environmental design (CPTED), and situational crime prevention theory, provide the rationale for why this is the case, as well as identifying the mechanisms that can be manipulated to prevent victimization in a variety of settings.

The second section of the chapter concentrates on application of these theories as part of efforts to prevent victimization in the community. Researchers and practitioners alike have tested the effectiveness of theoretically informed victimization prevention strategies that focus on reducing opportunities for crime. Evaluations of strategies based on defensible space, CPTED, and situational crime prevention are discussed. The chapter concludes with an overview of what are known as the ***collateral consequences*** of preventing victimization; they occur in the form of crime displacement, diffusion of benefits, and anticipatory benefits.

Victimization Prevention Theories

Readers have been introduced to theories from environmental criminology in previous chapters (see Chapters 2 and 3) in terms of their usefulness for understanding where victimization occurs and how and why targets are victimized. The perspective is also useful for developing crime prevention strategies based on identified patterns. ***Crime patterns*** are concentrations of crime or victimization within certain areas, places, individuals, products, or other targets. Understanding how crime and victimization are patterned requires unpacking the circumstances under which crimes occur, especially the places, times, and targets involved. By identifying these key features, ***environmental criminology*** suggests that victimization can be prevented by manipulating or changing factors that are associated with criminal events.

Environmental criminology is theoretically informed by several perspectives, including (1) rational choice theory, (2) crime pattern theory, and (3) routine activity theory. These theories provide underlying principles used by researchers to recognize the environmental factors affecting criminal circumstances. Below, these frameworks are reviewed as they apply to strategies for preventing crime and victimization. Environmental criminology also includes three important stand-alone applied theoretical perspectives: (1) defensible space, (2) CPTED, and (3) situational crime prevention. The following sections describe these three perspectives from both theoretical and applied standpoints.

Foundations of Environmental Criminology

As Chapter 3 noted, ***rational choice theory*** is primarily concerned with offender decision making. From a victimization prevention perspective, understanding how offenders make their decisions to select targets to victimize suggests methods for discouraging criminals from acting and, therefore, preventing victimizations. Viewed in this light, the theory makes three primary assertions that have implications for crime prevention. First, offenders have goals in mind when they commit crimes and they take into account the potential risks ("costs") and rewards ("benefits") associated with their behavior. Risks may include considerations such as the target's level of resistance, the target's level of protection, or the possible punishments if the offender is caught. The reward, of course, is succeeding in the criminal act and accomplishing the associated goals. Second, the theory presumes these risks and rewards vary across different types of crime, and that to understand how decisions are made requires thinking about specific offenses. For example, the costs and benefits associated with perpetrating a bank robbery differ from those involved in either a convenience store robbery or robbing an individual on the street. Thus, for rational choice theory to suggest practical strategies for prevention, the strategy must be offense-specific. Third, as part of the offender's decision-making process, he or she considers the setting in which the crime would occur. As an example, a residential burglar searching for a suitable target at night may look for a house with no lights on. This suggests that no one is home, which to a would-be offender implies that perpetrating the crime involves a low risk of being caught. Environmental criminology adopts these three assertions from rational choice theory to inform crime prevention efforts. However, before discussing prevention strategies we must review how crime pattern and routine activity theories contribute to crime prevention theory.

Crime pattern theory was introduced in Chapter 3 as an explanation for how victimization is patterned and, like rational choice theory, is used in the development of crime prevention techniques. According to crime pattern theory, crime is not random but rather is patterned across several dimensions (e.g., victim, place). Victimizations result from daily patterns of activity—or how people and things involved in crime move around and interact with each other. These activity patterns are primarily explained through the concepts of nodes, paths, and edges. As Chapter 3 discussed, nodes are places of primary activities; paths connect nodes; and edges are the boundaries of nodes. Potential offenders, just like other people, become familiar with areas by going about their everyday routines. To the extent that the nodes, paths, and edges visited by motivated offenders present criminal opportunities, the theory suggests these are the areas in which crime will concentrate—where it will occur most often. Although certain activity nodes, like one's residence, will be unique to the individual, other nodes, paths, and edges will be shared. For instance, at the city level, places like shopping malls, grocery stores, gas stations, and even schools become nodes because they attract large numbers of individuals. In terms of crime prevention, busy places (e.g., shopping centers) that are likely to be nodes shared by many individuals can be designed in ways that reduce the likelihood of crime occurring at those locations. A related concept that is useful in understanding crime patterns is known as the ***journey to crime***, which hypothesizes that offenders choose targets in areas with which they are most familiar, especially those close to their residence or other locations of their primary activities. Since the journey to crime hypothesizes that offenders are unlikely to focus their criminal intentions on unfamiliar places, preventing crimes at nodes is likely to have a lasting impact on reducing opportunities for victimization.

Routine activity theory has been discussed extensively throughout the text because of its usefulness in identifying opportunity-based risk factors for victimization. In short, the theory suggests that when (1) a motivated offender and (2) a suitable target converge in (3) an environment lacking guardianship, (4) an opportunity for victimization is created. An extensive body of research has tested the theory and identified risk factors for victimization that represent these core elements of the theory. For this reason, routine activity theory also is used to devise crime prevention strategies that are based on reducing opportunities for victimization by eliminating or minimizing these elements. If any of the three essential elements of victimization opportunities can be manipulated and opportunities reduced, then victimizations should be preventable. Perhaps the clearest way of reducing opportunities for victimization based on this theory is by increasing guardianship. Since absent or ineffective guardianship facilitates criminal opportunities, enhanced guardianship should disrupt criminal opportunities and reduce victimization. It is possible that the second element of the theory, target suitability, also can be altered to discourage crime. In particular, if targets can be made less attractive or suitable to offenders, the opportunity perspective suggests that they are less likely to be victimized. Further, the theory hypothesizes that exposure and proximity to motivated offenders increase victimization risk. Therefore, limiting one's exposure and/or proximity to likely offenders will correspondingly reduce victimization risk.

These three theoretical perspectives from environmental criminology share several features that make them both compatible with and useful from a victimization prevention perspective. First, all three theories emphasize the importance of criminal opportunities in explaining victimization. Therefore, reducing opportunities correspondingly decreases victimization risks. Second, each assumes that criminals make rational decisions. Even though offenders do not always make the *best* decisions, supporters of these theories argue they still consider costs and benefits based on available information. For example, a well-protected target is less likely to be victimized because a rational offender will decide that it is too risky or requires too much effort to act. As a result, crime prevention strategies can be developed to convince would-be offenders that criminal behavior is either too risky or not rewarding enough. Third, identifying and understanding crime patterns suggests where, when, and how crime prevention efforts should best be directed. The theories propose that crime patterns exist because opportunities concentrate in specific areas, facilities, or targets. Eliminating opportunities can therefore have a significant preventive impact. Overall, the underlying principle of environmental criminology is that by recognizing these theoretical premises, the environment or setting in which crime occurs can be changed such that criminal behaviors at those locations are reduced. The remainder of the chapter focuses primarily on three crime prevention perspectives from environmental criminology: (1) defensible space, (2) CPTED, and (3) situational crime prevention.

Defensible Space

Defensible space links criminal opportunities to the characteristics of the built environment, or the human-made surroundings that allow individual activity to occur. Oscar Newman (1972, p. 3), credited with developing the notion of "defensible space," described it as "a model for residential environments which inhibits crime by creating the physical expression of a social fabric that defends itself." In other words, crime prevention can be accomplished by *designing environments that strengthen places where individuals work and live*. Newman believed that design alone does not produce maximum preventive benefits; rather, the key to addressing crime was in using design to *create social action*—where people are invested in and encouraged to take responsibility for an area. The theory behind defensible space, therefore, advocates a three-pronged strategy for preventing crimes based on the principles of (1) territoriality, (2) natural surveillance, and (3) image and milieu. These defensible space concepts are discussed below in light of their theoretical basis for crime and victimization prevention, and later in the chapter with regard to their effectiveness at accomplishing these goals.

The first dimension of defensible space, ***territoriality***, refers to the use of architectural design to create territorial feelings, or a *drive to protect one's space*. In turn, territorial feelings are hypothesized to translate into "concern for the maintenance of the law and a belief in the possibility of its enforcement" (Newman, 1972, p. 51). In short, territoriality suggests that individuals will defend their space if they feel it is theirs to defend—that is, they have ownership of the space. According to the theory, establishing territoriality and getting individuals to "take ownership" of space can be accomplished using architectural design. For this reason, territoriality can be seen as the lynchpin of defensible space theory. Territoriality can be encouraged with physical designs that clearly demarcate or divide spaces into those that are private (e.g., one's residence), semiprivate (e.g., a landing shared by two families on the same floor in an apartment building), or public (e.g., a park). These physical designs include environmental features that establish real/physical boundaries or perceived/symbolic boundaries. Physical boundaries are created through the use of fences, gates, and walls. Symbolic boundaries are conveyed by features such as signs, property markers, flower beds, pathways, or other types of landscaping.

Surveillance generally refers to monitoring behavior occurring in a particular space, such as a city park. ***Natural surveillance*** represents the ability of individuals to observe or carry out this monitoring without the use of devices such as closed-circuit television (CCTV). Building on this idea, defensible space suggests that crime can be architecturally designed out of environments if those spaces are constructed in ways that *increase* natural surveillance. For example, if apartment windows are placed to allow residents to easily and naturally observe public spaces such as a courtyard, natural surveillance will discourage offenders from using the space for criminal activities. Sketches from Newman's original work are recreated in Figure 14-1 to illustrate his vision for how high-rise housing could use this idea to discourage crime. This idea, in part, grew out of Jane Jacobs' work (1961), in which she argued that casual users of shared spaces, such as bystanders, can discourage criminal activities simply by their presence. She referred to this as having "eyes upon the street," noting that "A well-used city street is apt to be a safe street" (Jacobs, 1993, p. 44). Natural surveillance creates defensible space by increasing the chances that unwanted behaviors will be observed and reducing fear of crime. It also has the effect of encouraging territoriality by extending the radius of control over observable spaces.

Image and milieu, the final dimensions of defensible space theory, focus on the appearance of the area and its surroundings. An area's *image* denotes a certain lifestyle among its residents, while also signaling the degree of control and care they exert over the space. *Milieu* represents the placement of the space within the context

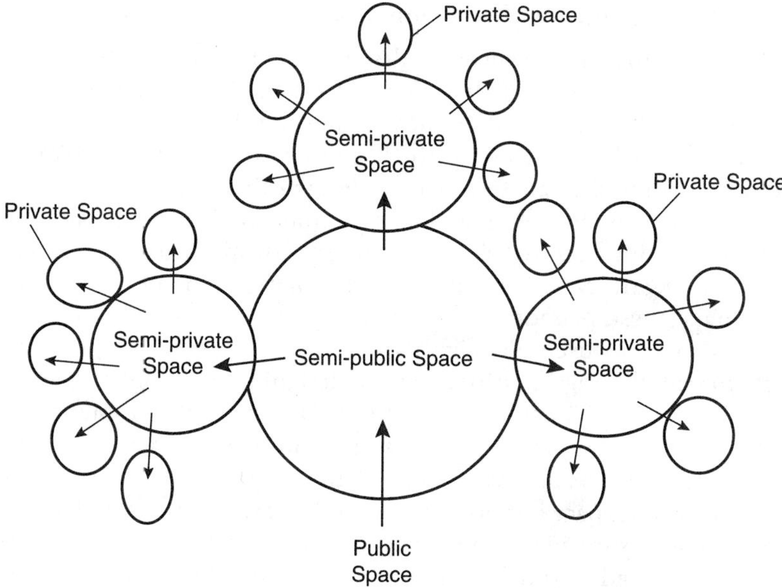

Figure 14-1 Natural Surveillance of a High-Rise
Source: Adapted from Newman (1972).

of its larger surroundings. According to defensible space theory, areas that are well maintained and have a pleasant appearance will engender territoriality, while those that are rundown and shabby (e.g., are plagued with litter, graffiti, and broken windows) stifle it. Along those lines, the placement of spaces in their larger context (i.e., milieu) can also affect opportunities for crime to occur within those spaces. For example, a building is more likely to be vandalized in a neighborhood with existing graffiti than is a building in a neighborhood that has no graffiti. In both cases, the principle is the same: Spaces and areas that are regularly maintained will be "defended" by residents and other users, and those that are allowed to deteriorate or do not promote territorial feelings are more likely to be targeted by offenders. Undefended spaces signal to offenders that no one is going to intervene to prevent crimes from occurring therein.

Newman's theory was initially met with heavy criticism. Among them was that he had not fully explained how architectural design was supposed to translate into crime prevention. Further, Rob Mawby (1977) argued that the components of the theory were contradictory, as some defensible space features could effectively cancel out each other. For example, Mawby argued that building walls that enhanced territoriality could hinder surveillance. In addition, Pat Mayhew (1979) pointed out that defensible space architecture may not influence all site users in the same way, and the defensible space strategy may be ineffective against area "insiders" as compared to "outsiders." Despite these critiques, defensible space has not only survived but flourished. Its three primary components became integral to the perspective crime prevention through environmental design.

Crime Prevention Through Environmental Design

Crime prevention through environmental design (CPTED) is a place-based crime prevention strategy developed by C. Ray Jeffery (1971) and grounded in environmental criminology. CPTED is premised on ideas from cognitive and behavioral psychology that criminal behavior, victimization, and fear of victimization are partially influenced by the physical environment, including the built environment. Jeffery argued that humans interact with and adapt to their environments, and that some environments provide cues that signal offenders to the presence of criminal opportunities. This being the case, the built environment can theoretically be designed or altered to make these phenomena less likely to occur by modifying these cues. CPTED is primarily focused on neighborhoods, streets, and other properties (e.g., parks, apartment buildings) as candidates for designing crime out of spaces.

In many ways, CPTED developed alongside Newman's defensible space theory, with both placing a heavy emphasis on manipulating environmental design in ways that increase surveillance, protect victims or other targets, and control spaces. However, while defensible space is more architecturally based and oriented toward using territoriality, natural surveillance, and image and milieu, CPTED takes a more holistic approach to crime and victimization prevention. Across built environments, there are essentially six main elements that make up the CPTED philosophy to prevention: (1) natural surveillance, (2) territorial reinforcement, (3) access control, (4) target hardening, (5) activity support, and (6) image and space management (see Moffat, 1983). These six elements, which are sometimes referred to as first-generation CPTED, are depicted in Figure 14-2 and are defined and discussed below.

The natural surveillance component of CPTED is equivalent to Newman's (1972) defensible space concept of natural surveillance and involves *enhancing the visibility of places and spaces* so that behaviors therein can be monitored. Greater visibility increases the likelihood that criminal behavior will be observed by legitimate users of the space, thereby discouraging the offender's behavior. In the language of routine activity theory, natural surveillance increases the level of guardianship of potential targets. Environmental design can facilitate natural surveillance and enhance guardianship by orienting windows and doors toward public areas, or using landscaping to ensure that sight lines are clear and unobstructed. Importantly, natural surveillance is not the only available method for increasing the monitoring of spaces. CPTED also may include formal/organized surveillance such as that provided by security guards, or mechanical surveillance such as that produced through enhanced lighting and CCTV (Cozens, Saville, & Hillier, 2005). In all, surveillance should theoretically reduce opportunities for crime and hence victimization.

Territorial reinforcement, the second element of CPTED, is analogous to Newman's concept of territoriality. Here, the prevention strategy involves *nurturing a sense of ownership of spaces* by inhabitants or legitimate users. To accomplish this, CPTED suggests that there should be a clear division of public and private spaces using both physical and symbolic barriers. ***Physical barriers*** include fences, walls, gates, or other physical design elements that can divide up spaces. ***Symbolic barriers*** may be less effective as obstacles but may foster the same feeling of territoriality among users; they include signs or landscaping that visibly separate public from

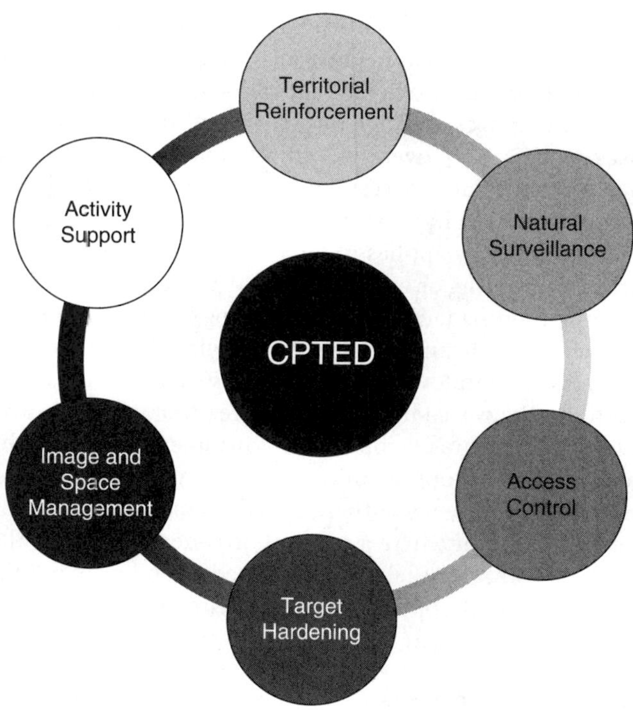

Figure 14-2 Elements of CPTED
Source: Adapted from Moffat (1983).

private property. According to both CPTED and defensible space, simply marking property as public versus private will not have crime prevention effects unless doing so results in the previously mentioned sense of ownership or territoriality. "Owned" spaces are theoretically more likely to be maintained and cared for, which promotes legitimate use of the space, enhances surveillance, and disrupts criminal opportunities. Similar to the concept of territorial reinforcement is the CPTED element of access control.

Access control is a popular crime prevention strategy that involves *restricting access to areas* to only those who have a legitimate reason for being there. CPTED suggests that by controlling access to an area, criminal opportunities are reduced, which theoretically should reduce criminal victimization. Like surveillance and territorial reinforcement strategies, access control can be natural/informal (e.g., limited access), organized/formal (e.g., security personnel), or mechanical, using physical (e.g., fences) or symbolic barriers (e.g., shrubs) (Cozens et al, 2005). Natural or informal access control involves limiting the number of entrances and/or exits to the targeted area, be it a street, building, neighborhood, or other location. For example, the Five Oaks Project, which is discussed later in the chapter, included municipal efforts to control access to the neighborhood by closing streets and alleys. This effectively made the neighborhood more difficult for outsiders to enter, exit, and navigate (Newman, 1996). Access control also can be accomplished through the use of physical or symbolic barriers such as those discussed as examples of territorial reinforcement, or through mechanical means, such as lockable gates or keycard access. This is also a case in point of the overlap that exists between CPTED concepts. Overall, access control discourages criminal behaviors within targeted environments because it increases guardianship over the location, making offending more difficult.

Target hardening is similar to access control and entails *making crime targets more difficult to victimize*. It is used in several crime and victimization prevention strategies, but for CPTED it mostly applies to targets on more of a micro-level, such as a particular apartment building or other individual property targets (e.g., homes on a city block). Target hardening tactics include placing locks on doors or windows, or enhancing existing locks; placing metal bars ("burglary bars") on windows; installing unbreakable glass in windows; putting security alarms on residences and businesses; or any other strategy that may make it more difficult for a motivated offender to victimize a target. These are examples of environmental features that can be manipulated to reduce criminal opportunities. According to the principles of environmental criminology, the presence of these measures increases the effort involved in criminal activity to the point where a rational offender will decide the effort is not worth the reward. Of course, sufficiently motivated offenders may still find a way to avail themselves of criminal opportunities by circumventing these efforts at target hardening. Target hardening also is discussed below as a tactic used in situational crime prevention.

Activity support is a CPTED strategy geared toward *encouraging particular uses for spaces*. Specifically, activity support focuses on public places, such as parks, sports fields, playgrounds, or other common areas, and uses signs and other physical design elements to promote limited use for specific purposes. Although any of these public places could potentially be locations for criminal activities (e.g., drug deals), encouraging legitimate users to make use of the space can signal to potential offenders that the location is not a welcoming or facilitating environment for crime. Apart from this, community ties and cohesion are strengthened when spaces such as these are used by the public for legitimate activities, and this discourages criminal activities and prevents crime hot spots from forming.

The final element of CPTED is image and space management. ***Image and space management*** is equivalent to the defensible space concept of image and milieu, which stress that *the physical appearance of spaces is important in preventing crime*. The overlap between defensible space concepts—including image and space management—and those of CPTED is highlighted in Table 14-1. Image and space management involves regular upkeep and maintenance of areas so they do not deteriorate and become areas of criminal activity. This idea is not unique to CPTED or defensible space; readers will perhaps recognize that a similar argument is made in broken windows theory, which suggests that physical disorder ultimately leads to a spiral of decline that encourages crime (Wilson & Kelling, 1982). When spaces are properly maintained, these signs of disorder are not allowed to take root, which signals to motivated offenders that the location is risky with respect to being caught and therefore not suitable for criminal purposes.

Collectively, these six dimensions of CPTED provide strategies for designing crime out of built environments. Each prevention strategy is oriented toward

Table 14-1: Overlap Between Defensible Space and CPTED Concepts

Concept	Defensible Space	CPTED
Territoriality	✓	✓ (Territorial reinforcement)
Natural Surveillance	✓	✓
Image and Milieu	✓	✓ (Image & space management)
Access Control		✓
Target Hardening		✓
Activity Support		✓

discouraging the rational offender from acting criminally by reducing opportunities, and making criminal behaviors riskier or more difficult to carry through. However, CPTED is not without its critics. First, as Paul Ekblom (1997) has pointed out, savvy criminals can adapt to CPTED techniques, which nullifies their preventive benefits. This is analogous to an arms race in which one side develops a successful strategy that the other side then counters. For example, CCTV may initially discourage offenders from using the monitored spaces, but as offenders identify "blind spots" into which cameras cannot see, they are no longer deterred. Thus, CPTED needs to be flexible to thwart adaptable criminals. Second, some of the CPTED strategies may conflict with each other, which limits their respective utility in preventing crimes (Reynald, 2011b). For example, access control, which often uses barriers such as gates and fences, may restrict visibility, thereby limiting natural surveillance. This line of thinking suggests that the strategies be integrated rather than implemented piecemeal. Finally, Reynald (2011b) has argued that the durability of CPTED may be limited by researchers' inadequate understanding of the specific elements that discourage crime. Since CPTED interventions are broad, with wide-reaching effects, it is difficult to pinpoint the *particular* design element or combination of elements that are most effective in preventing opportunities for victimization. However, very specific approaches to crime and victimization prevention are the focus of situational crime prevention.

Situational Crime Prevention

Ronald Clarke (1980), who applied rational choice theory to offender decision making, also developed situational crime prevention as a practical means of reducing victimization. ***Situational crime prevention*** (SCP) is a scientifically-based offense- and situation-specific approach to crime prevention based on reducing criminal opportunities in the immediate settings in which they occur. It adheres to the principles of rational choice theory by assuming that would-be offenders rationally think about the risks and rewards of their behavior before acting. Together, these two theoretical perspectives suggest techniques aimed at reducing opportunities through altering aspects of the situation and setting in ways that will discourage potential offenders (Clarke, 1980).

Originally, SCP was premised on the idea that a rational offender could be discouraged from taking advantage of opportunities in three general ways, with each method of crime prevention consisting of four specific techniques (Clarke, 1995). First, Clarke explained that opportunities could be reduced by increasing the perceived effort involved in committing the crime. SCP encourages the use of target hardening, access control, deflecting offenders, and controlling facilitators as techniques for increasing the actual or perceived effort involved in committing given crimes. Target hardening and access control have been previously discussed, but the concepts of *deflecting offenders* and *controlling facilitators* require some elaboration. To deflect offenders, SCP suggests that offenders be diverted or kept away from crime targets. For example, European soccer (*futbol*) fans of rival teams are often segregated in the stadium to reduce fighting. In short, they are kept away from each other, making it more difficult for them to brawl. Facilitators make it easier for offenders to commit crimes. So, if facilitators such as tools are controlled, it naturally increases the effort involved in the criminal behaviors. For instance, prior to the widespread use of cellphones, drug dealers would use public payphones to contact their customers and suppliers. Knowing this, cities across the United States experimented with strategies to control these payphones as facilitators of crime, such as permitting only operator-assisted or emergency calls during night hours (Clarke & Eck, 2005).

Second, SCP hypothesizes that opportunities for crime can be reduced by increasing the perceived risks associated with criminal activities. Recall that rational offenders will make decisions that minimize risks while maximizing rewards. Therefore, increasing the perceived risks of crime should theoretically convince offenders not to act in criminal ways. There are several techniques for increasing the perceived risks of crime. Those in the original iteration of SCP included entry/exit screening, formal surveillance, surveillance by employees, and natural surveillance. Those techniques using surveillance suggest that enhancing surveillance of an area (e.g., by employees, through formal means) should increase the risks of offenders being detected. In this way, SCP is comparable to CPTED and defensible space theory, which both advocate increasing surveillance and/or visibility as a means of reducing opportunities for crime. Similarly, formal methods of surveillance, such as alarm systems and security guards, make criminal behavior riskier for motivated offenders. As an example of entry/exit screening, airports screen passengers and their baggage for dangerous materials and weapons prior to boarding the aircraft. This makes carrying such materials riskier and therefore less appealing to the potential offender. Like techniques that increase the effort involved in criminal activities, these situational strategies have since undergone expansion.

Third, by reducing the anticipated rewards of crime, would-be offenders will decide that taking advantage of criminal opportunities is not worth the cost. Many historical and contemporary crime prevention practices have the effect of reducing expected criminal rewards, and the original version of SCP divided these into four broad categories: target removal, identifying property, reducing temptation, and denying benefits. A few examples will illuminate these situational strategies. For example,

Table 14-2: Evolution of Situational Crime Prevention

Increasing the Effort	Increasing the Risks	Reducing the Rewards	Inducing Guilt or Shame
1. Target Hardening 2. Access Control 3. Deflecting Offenders 4. Controlling Facilitators	5. Entry/Exit Screening 6. Formal Surveillance 7. Surveillance by Employees 8. Natural Surveillance	9. Target Removal 10. Identifying Property 11. Reducing Temptation 12. Denying Benefits	13. Rule Setting* 14. Strengthening Moral Condemnation 15. Controlling Disinhibitors 16. Facilitating Compliance
	12 Techniques 1980–1997		16 Techniques 1997–2003

*Note: "Rule setting" was initially one of the 12 techniques of SCP, housed under the category "Reducing the Rewards," but was moved to the new category "Inducing Guilt or Shame" when SCP was revised in 1997.
Source: Adapted from Clarke (1995); Clarke and Homel (1997).

the purpose of cattle branding (i.e., identifying property) is to designate livestock as property belonging to a particular owner. Cattle rustlers, then, are denied the benefit of being able to legitimately sell the stolen cattle. In the same way, certain expensive consumer products (e.g., videogame consoles) are stamped with serial numbers. Together, the original three methods of SCP based on altering perceptions of effort, risks, and rewards, consisted of 12 specific techniques, which are provided in Table 14-2.

SCP was expanded from 12 to 16 techniques in 1997 to include a category focused on inducing "guilt" or "shame" for criminal behavior (Clarke & Homel, 1997). This expansion of the theory left Clarke's original 12 techniques mostly intact but also represented a changed approach to how rational offenders might be dissuaded from committing crimes. The initial group of three strategies focused on the objective effort, risks, and rewards involved in criminal behaviors, whereas the revised version of SCP included a category reflecting how offenders might assess their circumstances. In other words, this new category of prevention techniques is aimed at convincing offenders that their prospective behaviors are wrong by altering internal behavioral controls, such as their consciences, rather than making it practically more difficult for the crime to be committed. For example, a slogan such as "real men never hit women" is designed to discourage intimate partner violence by morally condemning it. Similar tactics such as posting "shoplifting is stealing" signs serve the same function: They remind the would-be offender to think twice before acting. All told, the new techniques for inducing guilt or shame included rule setting, strengthening moral condemnation, controlling disinhibitors, and facilitating compliance. SCP consisted of the 16 preventive techniques listed in Table 14-2 until 2003, when the theory was once again expanded.

Table 14-3: Wortley's Precipitation-Control Strategies

Controlling Prompts	Controlling Pressures	Reducing Permissibility	Reducing Provocations
• Controlling Triggers • Providing Reminders • Reducing Inappropriate Imitation • Setting Positive Expectations	• Reducing Inappropriate Conformity • Reducing Inappropriate Obedience • Encouraging Compliance • Reducing Anonymity	• Rule Setting • Clarifying Responsibility • Clarifying Consequences • Personalizing Victims	• Reducing Frustration • Reducing Crowding • Respecting Territory • Controlling Environmental Irritants

Source: Adapted from Wortley (2001).

The most recent version of SCP was developed in 2003 by Derek Cornish and Ronald Clarke. Their revision of the theory followed a critique by Richard Wortley (2001) who pointed out that while situational forces affect perceived costs and benefits of crime, which are the focus of SCP, there are also situational factors that might induce or encourage individuals to offend. Wortley (2001, p. 63) persuasively argued that SCP was not addressing this underlying situational "cause" of crime and provided his own classification of techniques for controlling what he referred to as "situational precipitators." Wortley's classification of precipitation control strategies is presented in Table 14-3.

Wortley's classification included four categories: (1) controlling prompts (e.g., controlling triggers, providing reminders), (2) controlling pressures (e.g., encouraging compliance, reducing anonymity), (3) reducing permissibility (e.g., personalizing victims, clarifying consequences), and (4) reducing provocations (e.g., reducing frustration, controlling environmental irritants). Cornish and Clarke (2003) acknowledged that SCP could be adapted to address these situational precipitators and increased the number of preventive techniques to 25. The 25 techniques of SCP, along with examples, are included in Table 14-4. Readers are encouraged to visit the Center for Problem-Oriented Policing (Popcenter) website (http://www.popcenter.org/25techniques/) for an interactive version of the SCP grid.

Cornish and Clarke's (2003) 25 techniques retain the early focus on increasing the effort, increasing the risks, and reducing the rewards, while also adding two new categories: reduce provocations and remove excuses. In addition, the techniques intended to induce guilt or shame were integrated into these new categories and the existing strategies were expanded to include new techniques. In all, these 25 techniques provide strategies that can be used by law enforcement professionals and others to deter crimes by adhering to the principles of environmental criminology—namely, that criminal opportunities are largely a function of the immediate environment, and as such can be altered.

To fully understand the theoretical premises behind SCP, it is necessary to briefly discuss each preventive strategy or column in Table 14-4 along with selected examples. First, strategies that *increase the effort* for offenders can involve five distinct techniques: (1) target hardening, (2) controlling access to facilities, (3) screening exits, (4) deflecting offenders, and (5) controlling tools/weapons. For example, as the fifth cell in the table indicates, a strategy for combatting vandalism could involve restricting the sale of spray paint to juveniles. Without these tools, "tagging" becomes harder, possibly resulting in preventing the crime altogether. Second, efforts to *increase the risks* of criminal behavior also include five techniques: (1) extending guardianship, (2) assisting natural surveillance, (3) reducing anonymity, (4) using place managers, and (5) strengthening formal surveillance. Consider cell 8 of the table as an example. By reducing anonymity in certain situations, rational offenders can be deterred because the possibility of being identified makes committing crimes much more risky. Tactics such as "how's my driving?" stickers posted on the rear bumper of commercial vehicles and requiring cab drivers to post their picture identification on the dashboard of their cab also serve this purpose.

Third, methods to *reduce the rewards* perceived by potential offenders include five techniques: (1) concealing targets, (2) removing targets, (3) identifying property, (4) disrupting markets, and (5) denying benefits. Denying offenders the benefits of their criminal behaviors by definition reduces the rewards of the crime. For example, as cell 15 of Table 14-4 notes, if the previously discussed juvenile graffiti artists do acquire spray paint and tag a neighborhood building, quickly painting over it denies them the benefit of others seeing their work.

Fourth, *reducing provocations* involves five techniques that are designed to reduce the likelihood individuals are provoked into offending by something in their environment. These techniques are (1) reducing frustrations and stress, (2) avoiding disputes, (3) reducing emotional arousal, (4) neutralizing peer pressure, and (5) discouraging imitation. To illustrate, cell 17 suggests that reducing crowding in bars or pubs makes it less likely that individuals will be agitated by the uncomfortably crowded environment, thereby preventing bar fights.

The fifth and final strategy for SCP, *remove excuses*, also includes five specific techniques that can be implemented for preventive effects: (1) setting rules, (2) posting instructions, (3) alerting conscience, (4) assisting compliance, and (5) controlling drugs and alcohol. For instance, by posting instructions as cell 22 suggests, would-be offenders cannot claim their violation of the law, such as parking in a "no parking zone," was the result of ignorance.

Recently, some criminologists have suggested a sixth column called "Provide Opportunities" be added to the SCP scheme. Joshua Freilich and Graeme Newman (2014), for example, have argued that Cornish and Clarke's (2003) revisions to SCP deviated too far from its "hard" opportunity-reducing roots, instead delving into "soft" strategies that address criminal motivations. They suggested that the number of techniques should be increased from 25 to 30 situational techniques to include methods that facilitate compliance with the law, forgive past criminal offenses, offer alternatives (e.g., less harmful alternatives), subsidize alternatives to crime, and legalize (i.e., decriminalize) certain behaviors. Time will tell whether these suggestions will become part of SCP theory and practice. Regardless, a large number of crime prevention initiatives have been based on SCP. Their effectiveness

Table 14-4: The 25 Techniques of Situational Crime Prevention

Increase the Effort	Increase the Risks	Reduce the Rewards	Reduce Provocations	Remove Excuses
1. Target harden • Steering column locks and immobilizers • Anti-robbery screens • Tamperproof packaging	6. Extend guardianship • Take routine precautions: go out in a group at night, leave signs of occupancy, carry phone • "Cocoon" neighborhood watch	11. Conceal targets • Off-street parking • Gender-neutral phone directories • Unmarked bullion trucks	16. Reduce frustrations and stress • Efficient queues and polite service • Expanded seating • Soothing music/muted lights	21. Set rules • Rental agreements • Harassment codes • Hotel registration
2. Control access to facilities • Entry phones • Electronic card access • Baggage screening	7. Assist natural surveillance • Improved street lighting • Defensible space design • Support whistleblowers	12. Remove targets • Removable car radio • Women's refuges • Prepaid cards for pay phones	17. Avoid disputes • Separate enclosures for rival soccer fans • Reduce crowding in pubs • Fixed cab fares	22. Post instructions • "No parking" • "Private property" • "Extinguish campfires"
3. Screen exits • Ticket needed for exit • Export documents • Electronic merchandise tags	8. Reduce anonymity • Taxi driver IDs • "How's my driving?" decals • School uniforms	13. Identify property • Property marking • Vehicle licensing and parts marking • Cattle branding	18. Reduce emotional arousal • Controls on violent pornography • Enforce good behavior on soccer field • Prohibit racial slurs	23. Alert conscience • Roadside speed display boards • Signatures for customs declarations • "Shoplifting is stealing"

Increase the Effort	Increase the Risks	Reduce the Rewards	Reduce Provocations	Remove Excuses
4. Deflect offenders • Street closures • Separate bathrooms for women • Disperse pubs	9. Use place managers • CCTV for double-decker buses • Two clerks for convenience stores • Reward vigilance	14. Disrupt markets • Monitor pawnshops • Controls on classified ads • License street vendors	19. Neutralize peer pressure • "Idiots drink and drive" • "It's OK to Say No" • Disperse troublemakers at school	24. Assist compliance • Easy library checkout • Public lavatories • Litter bins
5. Control tools/ weapons • "Smart" guns • Disabling stolen cellphones • Restrict spray paint sales to juveniles	10. Strengthen formal surveillance • Red light cameras • Burglar alarms • Security guards	15. Deny benefits • Ink merchandise tags • Graffiti cleaning • Speed humps	20. Discourage imitation • Rapid repair of vandalism • V-chips in TVs • Censor details of modus operandi	25. Control drugs and alcohol • Breathalyzers in pubs • Server intervention • Alcohol-free events

Source: Popcenter (2014).

Table 14-5: Clarke's Rebuttals to Seven Criticisms of SCP

Criticism	Rebuttal
1. SCP is atheoretical and simplistic.	It is not atheoretical as it draws on three opportunity theories and social psychology.
2. SCP displaces crime and has not been shown to work.	Dozens of studies show that it can reduce crime, and that displacement is not guaranteed.
3. SCP does not address the root causes of crime.	It achieves immediate reductions in crime.
4. SCP is too conservative and managerial when it comes to addressing crime.	SCP solutions are economic and socially acceptable.
5. SCP is unethical because it is not available to the poor.	It protects poor and rich alike.
6. SCP restricts personal freedoms.	Small inconveniences are a worthwhile trade for crime reductions and safety.
7. SCP blames victims.	It provides victims with the means to avoid victimization risks.

Source: Adapted from Clarke (2005).

at preventing crime and victimization is discussed next, along with the effectiveness of other victimization prevention tactics, which occurs in the latter half of the chapter.

Like defensible space and CPTED, SCP has been the subject of some criticism. Clarke (2005) identified and responded to the seven most common criticisms he has encountered, or what he referred to as "misconceptions," about SCP. His primary response to these criticisms as a whole is that they come from a lack of understanding and, as a result, are either overstated or misguided. Nevertheless, they are provided along with Clarke's response in Table 14-5 to provide a balanced view of the perspective. Ultimately, each of the crime prevention theories included in this chapter should be judged on its effectiveness for preventing victimization. Therefore, applied victimization prevention is covered in the remainder of the chapter. Special emphasis is placed upon defensible space, CPTED, and SCP as prevention strategies.

Applied Victimization Prevention

With the theoretical underpinnings of victimization prevention in place, the necessary next step is to evaluate defensible space, CPTED, and SCP for their efficacy at reducing criminal victimization. We will evaluate these theoretical concepts one by one for their effectiveness. However, there is also obvious overlap between these prevention strategies, especially defensible space and CPTED. Therefore, defensible space will be discussed as a comprehensive prevention strategy first, and its shared components with CPTED will be reviewed individually as part of the evaluation of CPTED. At the same time, not all of the crime prevention activities discussed (e.g., increased street lighting) are exclusive to only one theoretical perspective. They can, therefore, be judged on their own merits. We conclude the chapter with a brief overview of three final and important concepts of (1) displacement, (2) diffusion of benefits, and (3) anticipatory benefits as they relate to crime prevention.

Defensible Space

Defensible space has been the subject of a great deal of research, which has largely found that architectural design *can* generate crime prevention benefits. Some of the most significant evaluations of defensible space were provided by Newman himself (1972, 1996). His interest in this area began with his work as an architect on large-scale public housing projects. He noticed that at two different New York City housing projects—Van Dyke and Brownsville—the resident populations were similar but the elements of physical design were quite disparate, as were the levels of crime, in the two locations. Brownsville, quite by accident as Newman pointed out, contained some elements of what he termed *defensible space*, while Van Dyke was totally devoid of them. Not coincidentally, he concluded that at least in part these defensible space characteristics of Brownsville explained why there was not only substantially less crime there, but also less turnover among residents. Box 14-1 includes two quotes from Newman's book (1972) that illustrate this disparity in design between the two projects.

Newman (1996) extended his ideas about defensible space beyond the housing level to the neighborhood level when he participated in the Five Oaks Neighborhood project in Dayton, Ohio. Based on his earlier defensible space ideas and other research at the time (e.g., White, 1990), Newman's objective was to help the residents of Five Oaks implement a number of defensible space and CPTED strategies to

Box 14-1: Newman's Defensible Space Quotes on Van Dyke and Brownsville

Van Dyke	Brownsville
"The buildings were intentionally designed tall so as to free the grounds for recreation, but the grounds go unused because they are anonymous and too distant to allow supervision from a typical apartment." "Entrance to the fourteen-story buildings is dissociated from the street, making casual surveillance by autos, pedestrians, and police impossible. Lobby areas are considered dangerous by residents, especially at night" (Newman, 1972, p. 41).	"The building's dispositions at Brownsville create triangular buffer areas which are used for play, sitting, and parking. These areas are easily observed from the street and from apartment windows. Entry to buildings is typically from the street through these buffer zones. Residents regard these areas as an extension of their own buildings and maintain active surveillance over them" (Newman, 1972, p. 45).

turn back the tide of crime that was taking over the neighborhood. Five Oaks was divided into ten mini-neighborhoods, each with its own unique name with which residents could identify. In addition, the city implemented a traffic control scheme to cut down on through traffic and also make the neighborhoods more difficult for potential outside offenders to navigate. Community watch groups ("neighborhood watch") and other neighborhood organizations, as well as added police attention, resulted in substantial reductions in crime, residents' perceptions of crime, and through traffic. In a follow-up with Five Oaks residents, Donnelly and Kimble (1997) concluded that the crime prevention measures implemented by Newman and the neighborhood residents had mostly remained stable. While crime did fluctuate with changes in the city's overall crime rate, the measures undertaken had largely taken hold and remained in place years later. Box "Spotlight on Theory: Defensible Space and CPTED in Action: The Five Oaks Project" provides more information on this project.

Spotlight on Theory: Defensible Space and CPTED in Action: The Five Oaks Project

In the late 1980s and 1990s, the Five Oaks neighborhood of Dayton, Ohio, experienced rapid increases in its crime rates. During that time, the 10-square-block neighborhood also underwent significant changes to its population, with more residents living in poverty, fewer residents owning their homes, and a greater racial diversity developing among residents. Drug crimes, gunfire, prostitution, and speeding cars were becoming major problems in the 5,000-person community, and something needed to be done (Donnelly & Kimble, 1997).

In response, a crime prevention initiative 12 months in the making and based on many ideas from environmental criminology, especially the work of Oscar Newman (1972), was designed and implemented in Five Oaks. In studying the nature of the neighborhood's problems, organizers decided that easy traffic access was a major force behind the criminal presence invading Five Oaks. The neighborhood's positioning between major commuting arteries, its proximity to highway on/off ramps, its proximity to downtown, and its grid-like layout made the neighborhood "permeable" to outsiders (Donnelly & Kimble, 1997).

According to police, Five Oaks' permeability made it an especially attractive place for drug buyers and "johns" seeking prostitutes to complete their transactions and quickly leave the scene. At the same time, the penetrable nature of the neighborhood also made it a good location to set up drug houses, and for prostitutes to advertise their services. In sum, the location and physical design of the neighborhood needed to be altered—no easy task. While the Five Oaks stabilization plan included a number of elements, including programs directed at increasing home ownership and community policing, it is perhaps best known for its street closure plan.

Five Oaks' street closure plan involved closing 35 streets and 26 alleys, including closing 11 streets leading into the neighborhood. Streets were blocked off with brick columns and metal gates and engraved with the *Five Oaks* name and logo. In effect, the street

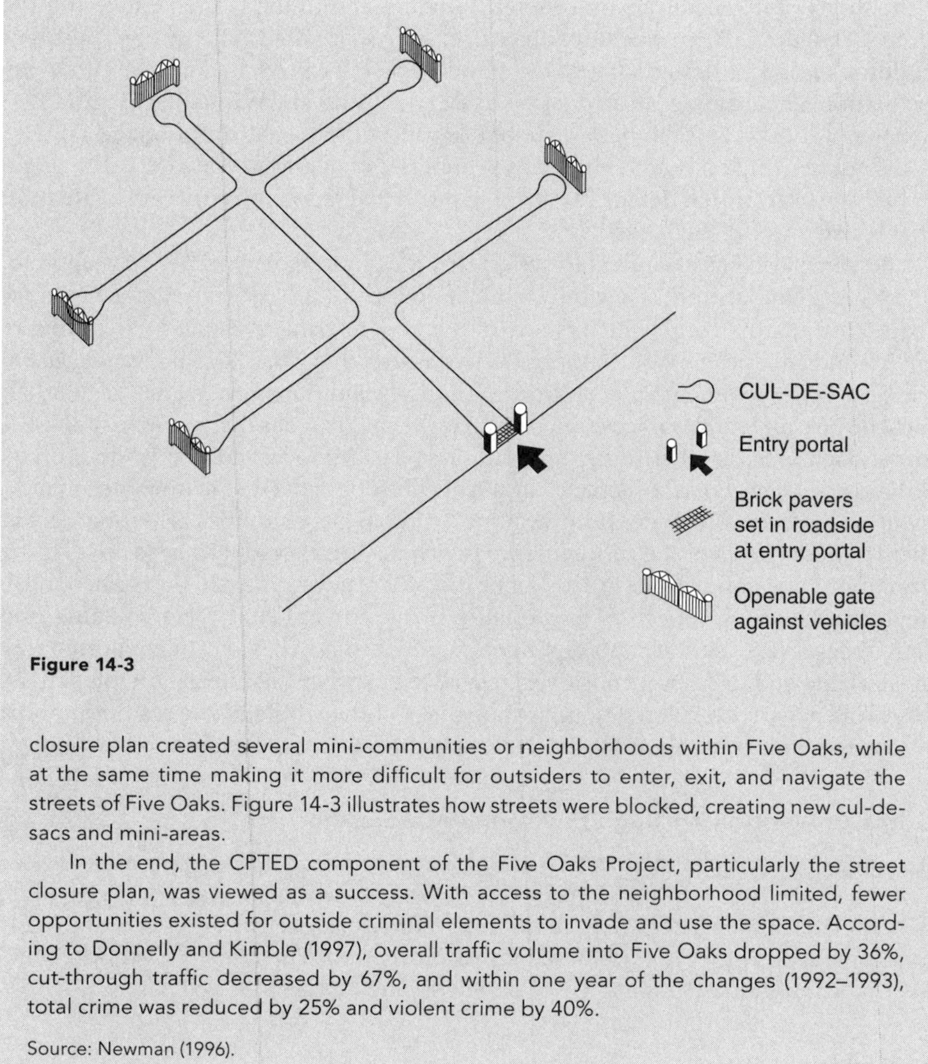

Figure 14-3

closure plan created several mini-communities or neighborhoods within Five Oaks, while at the same time making it more difficult for outsiders to enter, exit, and navigate the streets of Five Oaks. Figure 14-3 illustrates how streets were blocked, creating new cul-de-sacs and mini-areas.

In the end, the CPTED component of the Five Oaks Project, particularly the street closure plan, was viewed as a success. With access to the neighborhood limited, fewer opportunities existed for outside criminal elements to invade and use the space. According to Donnelly and Kimble (1997), overall traffic volume into Five Oaks dropped by 36%, cut-through traffic decreased by 67%, and within one year of the changes (1992–1993), total crime was reduced by 25% and violent crime by 40%.

Source: Newman (1996).

Besides Newman's own work, research validates the benefits of defensible space designs (see Jeffery & Zahm, 1993). For example, a study by Ralph Taylor, Stephen Gottfredson, and Sidney Brower (1984) investigated crime and fear of crime across Baltimore neighborhoods using defensible space, local social ties, and territoriality as potential explanations. Their analyses suggested that defensible space designs strengthened aspects of territorial functioning and directly and negatively affected crime. In other words, this study found what the theory would predict—defensible space design features encourage territoriality, which discourages crime. More recently, Brandon Welsh, Mark Mudge, and David Farrington (2010) reviewed five evaluations of defensible space programs undertaken in the United States and the United Kingdom. They concluded that defensible space reduced crime as a result of building design or design changes to public housing estates in some way in every evaluation. For example, an evaluation by Randall Atlas and William LeBlanc (1994) in Miami Shores, Florida, demonstrated significant decreases in burglary, larceny, and theft of vehicles, but no changes in robberies or aggravated assaults. The larger point, however, is that defensible space led to crime reductions in every evaluation that Welsh and colleagues assessed.

Research also has examined the effect that the physical environment has upon individuals' guardianship behaviors. Danielle Reynald (2011a) devised a scheme for measuring guardianship, which is one of the keys to crime prevention according to environmental criminology. This perspective asserts that what Reynald termed *guardianship in action* requires three conditions. The first condition is occupancy. A guardian must be present to discourage crime; however, Reynald argues that occupancy alone is not enough to stifle all criminal opportunities. The second condition is monitoring. Building on the need for occupancy, residents must be actively watching the environment to dissuade offenders from availing criminal opportunities. The final factor, then, is intervention or the willingness to intervene directly should a need arise. Using data from 21 neighborhoods in The Hague (the seat of government in the Netherlands), Reynald assessed the effects of territoriality, image and milieu, target hardening, and activity level (e.g., pedestrian flow) upon guardianship behaviors. She reported that territoriality and image were positively related to guardianship intensity, while activity level was negatively related to guardianship. On the whole, these results support Newman's arguments about the links between the environment and social action.

Crime Prevention Through Environmental Design

Research has confirmed that CPTED is a useful crime prevention strategy (see Cozens et al., 2005). Evaluations of CPTED showcase the effects of the individual components of the strategy (e.g., natural surveillance) as well as the effects of CPTED as a general strategy for place-based crime prevention. The crime prevention benefits of the individual "fragments" of the theory are briefly reviewed below.

Natural Surveillance

Physical environments that provide opportunities for natural surveillance are generally regarded as being less suitable as crime locations. For example, Sally Merry (1981) studied the effects of defensible space at a 500-apartment inner-city housing development on the East Coast, which she nicknamed "Dover Square." She conducted participant observation on site for 18 months and came to know both the complex and the residents well. Importantly, she was able to obtain valuable insights from criminals who both lived in the complex and committed robberies on its grounds. In support of the effects of natural surveillance, she explained that

> These robbers are very conscious of architectural features which constitute defensible space. They try to commit crimes where they

> will not be observed. Favorite places are the narrow and enclosed pathways where visibility is poor and witnesses nonexistent (Merry, 1981, p. 416).

A related study, although not explicitly examining the effects of CPTED, was conducted by Timothy Coupe and Laurence Blake (2006) who assessed the targeting strategies of burglars in the United Kingdom. They found that rates of night burglaries were twice those of daylight burglaries, and that daytime burglars preferred houses with dense vegetation cover in the front. Both of these findings suggest that burglars were discouraged by the threat of being seen breaking into their targets. Overall, opportunities for natural surveillance seem to signal to rational offenders that certain environments are not good places to commit crimes because of the threat of being watched. Another study of the effects of vegetation cover on crime estimated the relationship between trees (their presence and size) and crime rates in Portland, Oregon. This study found that smaller trees that obstructed natural surveillance were associated with more crime, and taller trees with reduced crime. The presence or absence of trees may also signal to offenders whether a house is cared for (i.e., territorial reinforcement) (Donovan & Prestemon, 2012).

Territorial Reinforcement

Greater territorial reinforcement, or territoriality, is associated with reductions in both crime and fear of criminal victimization (Cozens et al., 2005). Research also has reported relationships between physical site features and the behavior of users of those sites, such as increased neighborliness (e.g., Wilkerson, Carlson, Yen, & Michael, 2012). In one study, Barbara Brown and Irwin Altman (1983) examined the relationships between territoriality and residential burglary, reporting that houses that were burglarized differed from those that were not. Notably, non-burglarized houses tended to have qualities that communicated territoriality, such as identity markers; they also had greater visual contact with neighboring houses. In contrast, burglarized homes had features signaling a lack of territoriality, such as an unoccupied appearance. In a more recent example, Richard Wortley and Matthew McFarlane (2011) devised a natural experiment at Griffith University's library to determine whether territorial cues affected theft of photocopy cards (which could be redeemed for their cash value). There were two ways in which territoriality was examined: by having a signature on the back of the card (implying ownership) and by placing the cards next to two library books (implying that the owner would be back soon to use the card). The results suggested that both types of territorial reinforcement had a deterrent effect on the theft of the photocopy cards. Cards that were not signed or were not placed strategically to suggest guardianship were more likely to be stolen. Taken in the context of CPTED, this study suggests that territorial reinforcement can yield crime prevention benefits.

Access Control

Research has found that restricting or controlling access to potential crime targets or locations for crime can significantly reduce victimization risks. For example, a study by Garland White (1990) investigated the effects of neighborhood permeability, or how easily accessible the neighborhood is, on neighborhood-level burglary rates in Norfolk, Virginia. White (1990, p. 65) found that more permeable neighborhoods had higher rates of burglary victimization, explaining that more accessible neighborhoods "create the appearance of openness and vulnerability, which makes them more attractive to potential burglars." On the other hand, Barry Poyner and Barry Webb (1992) evaluated the effects of a crime prevention strategy in the United Kingdom to address theft at two large open-air retail markets. In part, the intervention involved expanding the space between vendors, giving shoppers more aisle space, and giving offenders less opportunity to use crowded conditions to access their targets (e.g., the victim's shopping bag). By controlling access in this way, theft at the markets declined precipitously. These two examples illustrate a point made by John Eck and David Weisburd (1995) that the value of access control depends on the crime. In the first case, offenders were apparently seeking permeable locations, whereas in the second case, they were avoiding them and looking for the crowded places to commit their crimes. In both cases, access control can be effective, but it should be adapted to the type of crime and the situation.

Target Hardening

Target hardening is a common method for preventing victimization that is often associated with reduced victimization risks. For example, a study by Pamela Wilcox, Tamara Madensen, and Marie Tillyer (2007) considered the effects of target hardening, place management, informal social control, and natural surveillance on burglary victimization risk in Seattle, Washington. Target hardening was measured as an index including several physical guardianship routines, such as locking doors, using burglar alarms, and having a dog in the home, among others. Wilcox and colleagues reported that target hardening efforts significantly reduced the likelihood that a residence would be burglarized. In addition, this likelihood further declined when other nearby residences took similar precautions—as expected by multilevel opportunity theory (see Chapter 3). Similar negative effects of target hardening also were reported by Terance Miethe and David McDowall (1993) in their study of Seattle neighborhoods. In a final example to make the point, David Forrester, Mike Chatterton, and Ken Pease (1988) evaluated the effects of the Kirkholt Burglary Prevention Project on residential burglary victimization, reporting that the program, which included upgrading household security along with other prevention strategies, dramatically reduced burglary generally. Chapter 9 includes a detailed description of the Kirkholt project as it relates to preventing repeat burglaries.

Activity Support

Activity support involves turning places susceptible to crime into safe havens by encouraging legitimate use of the space. For this reason, there is clear overlap here between other elements of CPTED and defensible space. However, this component of the theory has only narrowly been investigated by researchers by considering how mixed land use affects area crime. According to this line of thinking, schools, businesses, parks, or other facilities that encourage legitimate use of the space should have a dampening effect on crime—an "eyes on the street" argument. Research has not entirely supported this position, however. For example, Pamela Wilcox, Neil Quisenberry, Debra Cabrera, and Shayne Jones (2004) estimated the criminological effects of businesses, schools, and playgrounds on violence and burglary in Seattle, Washington. The results of their study indicated that neighborhoods with businesses and schools were more likely to experience violence, and neighborhoods with businesses and playgrounds had an increased likelihood of burglary victimization. Similarly, Dennis Roncek and Antoinette Lobosco (1983) reported that neighborhoods with public high schools were more likely to have burglaries and auto thefts, but not neighborhoods with private high schools. Roncek and Maier (1991) likewise reported that the presence of bars and taverns also was associated with neighborhood crime. The results of all of these studies are contrary to theoretical expectations but consistent with opportunity arguments that these amenities bring motivated offenders into proximity with potential targets. Thus, victimologists need to develop other methods for assessing the role of activity support in crime prevention.

Image and Space Management

The message that is conveyed through an environment's image and the context in which it is situated are important considerations in explaining crime and victimization. Generally, environments that promote a positive image convey a message of involvement by site users and possible intervention in problems that may arise, such as crime. Those sites with a negative image also send signals—that problems go unaddressed—and therefore suggest the location is suitable for criminal activities. One of the primary ways in which this negative image has been conceptualized is as *physical disorder*. Disorderly areas are littered, rundown, unkempt, and usually linked with a whole host of negative consequences, such as fear of crime, neighborhood dissatisfaction, high levels of residential turnover, lower housing prices, reduced trust in neighbors and in neighborliness, and increased crime and victimization (Skogan, 2012). In one study, Ralph Taylor, Sally Ann Shumaker, and Stephen Gottfredson (1985) studied how physical decay (disorder) affected neighborhood confidence across Baltimore City, Maryland, neighborhoods. They concluded that decay was important but that the effects were conditional based on the neighborhood context, especially the neighborhood's social class. Specifically, physical decay (disorder) exhibited the strongest effects in middle-income neighborhoods.

Robert Sampson and Stephen Raudenbush (1999) conducted a study of the sources and consequences of disorder in Chicago. They videotaped 23,000 street segments across 196 neighborhoods and rated them for physical and social disorder, in addition to surveying residents about neighborhood conditions and social relationships. The results suggested, among other things, that disorder was often found in areas with mixed land use, highlighting the importance of the context or space in which areas are situated. They also found that a neighborhood's level of disorder was positively associated with robbery victimization, and that collective efficacy—Sampson's term for cohesion and control over an area's shared

Table 14-6: CPTED Effectiveness

CPTED Strategy	Study Effects		
	☺	😐	☹
Lighting	10	1	0
Fencing	5	2	0
Improved surveillance by staff	5	0	0
Neighborhood cleanup	3	0	2
Physical improvement to housing	2	2	0
Landscaping	2	2	0
Security screens for staff	2	0	0
Road closure or street changes	2	0	0
Improved visibility of store interiors	2	0	0

Source: Adapted from: Poyner (1993).

spaces—was a strong deterrent against several criminal outcomes, such as violent crime. In short, this study supports the CPTED argument that image and space management can exert strong influences over opportunities for victimization within an environment.

Summary

The preceding discussion suggests that CPTED is a useful place-based method for preventing crime and victimization. A variety of techniques are available that involve manipulating environmental features to discourage criminal behaviors and therefore victimization. Several of these techniques are highlighted in Table 14-6, which summarizes an evaluation by Barry Poyner (1993) into "what works" in crime prevention. The number of studies in his evaluation supporting the use of the technique is rated as successful (☺), having no effect (😐), or actually increasing crime (☹). For example, 10 studies in Poyner's evaluation found that lighting produced crime prevention benefits. Subsequent evaluations of "what works" also speak to the effectiveness of CPTED strategies, such as lighting (Pease, 1999) and CCTV (Phillips, 1999), in preventing crime. Some of these techniques also have been implemented as part of SCP programs, to which our attention now turns.

Situational Crime Prevention

For the most part, comprehensive evaluations of SCP are hard to come by in peer-reviewed scholarly journals, but there is no shortage of research to confirm the usefulness of the strategies underlying the theory. Put differently, research is supportive of the SCP philosophy that reducing criminal opportunities prevents crime and victimization. This section reviews examples of crime prevention interventions based on SCP that have been successful. However, there are hundreds of situational crime prevention evaluations, so only select evaluations are highlighted to demonstrate the effectiveness of SCP techniques. Further, none of the evaluations contains a complete assessment of all 25 techniques. Since opportunities are situational, specific problems call for specific solutions. Readers are encouraged to review the collection of over 240 evaluations available at the Center for Problem-Oriented Policing website to read more evaluations of SCP.

Increase the Effort

Methods of increasing the effort involved in criminal behaviors have been found to significantly reduce crime and, therefore, victimization. Recall that this situational strategy includes five techniques (see Table 14-4): target harden, control access to facilities, screen exits, deflect offenders, and control tools and weapons. Two case studies, addressing violent crimes and suicide, respectively, are used as examples of crime prevention initiatives that have reduced victimization by increasing the effort.

First, *Operation Cul de Sac* (OCDS) targeted a 10-block area of Los Angeles that had been experiencing drive-by shootings, gang homicides, and street assaults. OCDS was based on the SCP theory that these violent crimes could be reduced by increasing the effort by offenders and, therefore, reducing crime opportunities. By placing traffic barriers to block motor vehicle access to the roadways where these crimes had gotten out of control, OCDS was effective at deflecting these offenders (see cell 4 of Table 14-4) and "designing crime" out of the area for two years. An evaluation of the initiative found that the number of homicides and street assaults decreased significantly during OCDS and increased again after the program ended. It also was hypothesized that the barriers increased residents' control of the area by creating defensible spaces and increasing the risks involved in trying to perpetrate drive-by shootings (Lasley, 1998).

In another classic example, Clarke and Mayhew (1988) discuss how removing carbon monoxide from the public gas supply between 1963 and 1975 in England and Wales led to a substantial decline in suicides. Prior to this period of detoxification, the presence of poisonous chemicals in the gas supply permitted those inclined toward suicide to use readily available appliances such as gas fireplaces and ovens as tools to facilitate suicide. Interestingly, the progressive removal of CO from the gas supply did not result in alternative methods of suicide, and the number of suicides declined by 35%. In short, removing the opportunity by increasing the effort involved in committing suicide practically eliminated suicide by gas poisoning in England and Wales.

Increase the Risks

Tactics that increase the risks of crime include: extend guardianship, assist natural surveillance, reduce anonymity, use place managers, and strengthen formal surveillance (see Table 14-4). In general, crime prevention research that has investigated these tactics has found that increasing the risks correspondingly reduces crime. Again, two examples demonstrate this point. First, Anthony Braga and colleagues (1999) assessed the effects of a police crime prevention intervention undertaken in Jersey City, New Jersey. The intervention targeted places that had become hot spots of violent crime (e.g., robbery, assault) with a number of prevention strategies, including situational crime prevention techniques (i.e., strengthen formal surveillance, disrupt markets, assist natural surveillance, use place managers). Examples of the tactics used included cleaning vacant lots, enforcing parking regulations, improving building security, hanging signs explaining the rules, and dozens of others. The results suggested that the number of crimes and calls for service were significantly reduced at the targeted places, and physical and social disorder both declined by 91%.

The second validation of risk-increasing prevention strategies was provided by Ronald Hunter and C. Ray Jeffery (1992). They summarized findings from several studies of crime prevention at convenience stores, which are presented in Table 14-7. According to the authors, at least 10 published evaluations have found, for example, that having two or more clerks on duty discourages convenience store robbery. Having more than one clerk on duty extends guardianship of the store in addition to increasing surveillance. On a related note, training employees to prevent crime was reportedly effective in four evaluations. Employee training is one method for using place managers. In other words, employees are encouraged to control the store and take an active role in crime prevention. Many of the crime prevention measures in the table have been identified as effective methods of preventing convenience store robbery by increasing the risks.

Reduce the Rewards

Crime prevention research suggests that reducing the rewards of crime by concealing targets, removing targets, identifying property, disrupting markets, or denying benefits also diminishes criminal opportunities and prevents victimization. Several research studies have reported these effects, but two interesting case studies carried out in New York City illustrate these SCP techniques in practice. First, Maryalice Sloan-Howitt and George Kelling (1990) described how the pervasive problem of graffiti on New York City's subway was eradicated using prevention strategies that reduced the rewards for graffiti artists by denying benefits. They explained that by 1984, graffiti covered every train in the subway system, at which time the New York City Transit Authority created the Clean Car Program. Among other things, the program implemented policies to gradually clean every train; if a new or renovated train was tagged, the program stipulated that the train be cleaned within two hours or removed from service. By immediately cleaning the graffiti, the artists were denied the fruits of their labor, and by 1989, the New York subway system was completely free of graffiti.

In the second example, Marcus Felson and colleagues (1996) discussed how New York City's Port Authority Bus Terminal was redesigned to prevent disorder, crime, and victimization. In the early 1990s, the bus terminal was one of the busiest in the world, with about 1 million passenger trips per week. It also was plagued with

Table 14-7: Preventing Convenience Store Robbery

Crime Prevention Measure	Number of Supporting Studies
Two or more clerks on duty	10
Good cash handling	8
No concealed entrances	6
Nearby other stores	5
Clear view of store front	5
Security devices in use	5
Store closed between 10 p.m. and 6 a.m.	5
Cashier in secure booth	4
Employees trained in prevention	4
Clear view of inside of store	3
Store in residential or commercial area	3
Gas pumps located at front of store	3
Cashier located in center of store	3
Store on busy street	2
Security guard present	2

Source: Hunter and Jeffery (1992).

all manner of criminal behaviors (e.g., luggage theft, pickpocketing, assault) and disorder (e.g., litter, graffiti). A prevention plan was devised to turn things around using many strategies, just a few of which involved improving crowd flow; removing niches, corners, and dark areas; and improving the restrooms. The improvements to the restrooms in particular warrant additional discussion as they show how reducing rewards can help solve problems. Felson and his coauthors (1996, pp. 26–27) described the restrooms in the terminal as follows:

> Restrooms in the Port Authority Bus Terminal had largely been taken over by illegal and disorderly activities. Transients slept on floors and in ceilings above them, dripping body fluids throughout. Drug abuse and homosexual activities made use of the toilet stalls. Fountain-shaped sinks were used as bathtubs. Drug paraphernalia littered floors or stopped up plumbing. Toilets overflowed. Travelers were afraid to enter; or when they did, would rather leave sinks running or toilets unflushed than touch grimy handles. Travelers also complained about robberies and assaults.

Improvements to the restrooms were made that used many SCP techniques, especially denying benefits and concealing targets (cells 12 and 15 in Table 14-4). For example, large six-user sinks were replaced with single-user sinks, thereby making it impossible for them to be used as bathtubs. Formerly removable ceiling panels were replaced with secure panels, eliminating the ceiling as a hiding place. Similar improvements were made throughout the terminal. For instance, benches, which were taken over for hours by transients, were replaced with individual flip seats on the walls, making them useful as seating for short periods. These examples represent only a small number of the changes made at the terminal (there were over 60) but demonstrate the utility in reducing rewards. The overall plan at the Port Authority led to many positive changes, foremost among them declines in predatory crime, fewer complaints from patrons, reduced numbers of homeless in the station, and increased sales at the terminal's retail outlets (e.g., food counters).

Reduce Provocations

Situational provocations are those environmental factors that might incite individuals into criminal behaviors who otherwise would not commit crimes. SCP strategies designed to reduce these provocations include reducing frustration and stress, avoiding disputes, reducing arousal and temptation, neutralizing peer pressure, and discouraging imitation. Although situational provocations have received less research attention than the previously reviewed SCP strategies, two case studies of crime prevention in entertainment venues have used this strategy with success. In the first study, Stuart Macintyre and Ross Homel (1997) explored how physical design features in six Australian nightclubs affected violence at those locations. They found that pedestrian flow patterns, which were a product of floor plans, often led to crowding. Crowding, in turn, was associated with aggressive incidents regardless of other potential explanations, such as staff behavior and drinking practices. In short, patrons were being agitated to the point of aggressive action when the clubs became crowded. The prevention implication is clear: Reduce crowding through architectural design and violence also will decline.

In the second case study, Arthur and Elizabeth Veno (1993) discussed the effects of a crime prevention initiative at the Australian Motorcycle Grand Prix that incorporated measures to reduce provocations. In response to significant problems with violence at the events, including clashes with police officers, Veno and Veno developed a situational crime prevention strategy in partnership with the Victoria Police. Overall, the plan aimed to prevent violence while also managing the large crowds that would attend the events. Situational techniques involving setting rules, reducing frustrations and stress, avoiding disputes, and extending guardianship were implemented. One of the tactics used was to redefine the event to include families and non-bikers. By ensuring more diverse or demographically mixed crowds, the likelihood of disputes erupting was alleviated (i.e., cell 17 of Table 14-4). Overall, the results of the evaluation indicated a significant reduction in violence at the events and higher favorability of police by spectators than in previous years.

Remove Excuses

Removing excuses for crime can be accomplished by setting rules, posting instructions, alerting conscience, assisting compliance, and controlling drugs and alcohol. Examples of techniques for carrying out these strategies are provided in Table 14-4. Two case studies, one aimed at reducing ATM robberies and the other at refund fraud at retail stores, used this SCP strategy for crime prevention gains. First, Rob Guerette and Ronald Clarke (2003) studied ATM robberies in Los Angeles and New York City. In both cities, security measures (e.g., posting safety reminders to users, increasing lighting) were mandated by recent legislation, providing a natural experiment in which to consider the effects of SCP techniques on ATM robbery. Although it was not possible to determine exactly which prevention measures were or were not effective, the collective security provisions led to substantial decreases in robberies. For example, in New York City, ATM robberies declined by 78% between 1991 and 1999. Los Angeles experienced similar declines in ATM robberies.

Second, Dennis Challinger (1996) discussed how a major Australian retailer combated refund fraud in its stores through rule setting (i.e., cell 21 of Table 14-4). Prior to changing the refund policy, fraudsters were taking advantage of opportunities provided by the existing policy to victimize stores. For example, in some cases thieves would steal easily accessible items, return them for refunds, and use the store credit to purchase items that were too difficult to steal in the first place. The retail chain made two changes to the refund policy that effectively set rules governing store refunds. First, customers were informed through store signage that receipts were required for refunds. Second, when requesting a refund without a proof of purchase, the customer would have to provide proof of identity and a signed statement; the refund also could not exceed a set amount of money. After introducing these rules, which made it difficult for opportunistic thieves to rationalize their behavior by claiming ignorance of the refund policy, fraudulent refunds decreased in both number and in dollar value.

Summary

The preceding review of several case studies highlights the effectiveness of SCP techniques at preventing crime and victimization. Yet, these case studies represent only a small portion of applied crime prevention efforts based on SCP. Police officers, security professionals, and others interested in crime prevention have used SCP in countries all over the world, especially in Europe, the United States, Canada, and Australia. In addition, although it is buttressed by environmental criminology, it also has been suggested as a means of preventing crimes in virtual environments.

Displacement, Diffusion of Benefits, and Anticipatory Benefits

One of the criticisms of crime prevention projects is that crime is merely displaced or moved to another target that is not receiving crime prevention attention. For instance, say your city implements a crime prevention program to reduce vandalism in a downtown area. The program appears to be working because the target area has seen a dramatic decrease in vandalism. However, a nearby area that was previously free of such problems starts experiencing a marked spike in graffiti and other acts of vandalism. The logical conclusion would be that graffiti and vandalism were simply shifted to another area. The arguments behind ***displacement*** assume that offenders will remain motivated to commit crimes when their initial efforts are thwarted by crime prevention measures. As a result, offenders can displace crime in five ways (Clarke & Eck, 2005):

1. *Geographical*: Offenders move to another place to offend.
2. *Temporal*: Offenders commit crimes at a different time.
3. *Target*: Offenders choose a new target.
4. *Tactical*: Offenders choose a new method for committing the same crime.
5. *Crime type*: Offenders decide to commit a different crime.

Research studies investigating whether displacement is a danger to crime prevention efforts suggest that displacement does indeed occur, but it is *not* inevitable, and when it does occur it is usually in a reduced form. Further, rational choice theory, which was discussed earlier in this chapter, suggests that the rational offender does not necessarily find a new target to victimize. For example, some offenders only act when an easy opportunity presents itself. For those who are *more* motivated to offend, crime prevention efforts may discourage them from seeking other less-protected targets, convincing them that it would be too risky, difficult, or not worth the effort (Cornish & Clarke, 1987). Rational choice theory also suggests that many offenders will be tempted to reoffend against their previous targets. From this perspective, it would be to the benefit of law enforcement and first-time victims to continue to devise prevention efforts that specifically target recurring victimization.

It is also possible that the benefits of crime prevention programs will have effects beyond their initial targets. This process, called ***diffusion of benefits***, was defined by Ronald Clarke and David Weisburd (1994, p. 169) as "the spread of the beneficial influence of an intervention" beyond the target of the intervention. For example, reconsider the situation previously described in which your city implemented a program to reduce vandalism in a downtown area. In instances of diffusion of benefits, not only would the targeted area see reductions in vandalism, but hypothetically, nearby areas that were not specifically targeted by the program would *also* see declines in problems with vandalism. Theoretically, diffusion of benefits might occur because offenders in the other locations believed they were at heightened risk of being apprehended (even though they were not) since the offenders did not know the boundaries of the intervention. In short, they were deterred from criminal behavior.

Although diffusion of benefits has been reported in crime prevention program evaluations, researchers' understanding of the phenomenon has been limited by difficulties in measuring it. To uncover diffusion of benefits, an evaluator would have to measure crime not only in the target area, for example, but also in other nearby areas that might enjoy the benefits. This is precisely what David Weisburd and his colleagues (2006) did in their evaluation of police crackdowns in Jersey City, New Jersey. For this study, two sites were targeted to reduce drug dealing and prostitution, and neighboring sites that did not receive any extra police services were monitored for displacement and/or diffusion of benefits. The results indicated that drug dealing and prostitution were not geographically displaced to the nearby areas; in fact, crime in these areas actually declined.

Overall, then, diffusion of benefits occur when crime prevention programs have effects beyond their targeted sites. A related outcome of crime prevention efforts is a prevention benefit that occurs before the program is even implemented. This possibility is known as ***anticipatory benefits***. To extend the running example, your city's crime prevention program is being discussed around town by policymakers and law enforcement and also is highlighted on the news prior to its execution. This publicity is believed to be a leading impetus for anticipatory benefits and highlights not only the role of the media and publicity in preventing crime, but also the fact that not all crime prevention is necessarily based on environmental criminology. In this case, since offenders may not know the start date of the prevention efforts, they alter their behaviors before the programs are up and running. Shane Johnson and Kate Bowers (2003) assessed the effects of publicity campaigns for 21 burglary reduction programs and concluded that publicity campaigns significantly enhanced the effectiveness of crime prevention programs, and that promoting the programs prior to their implementation actually produced anticipatory benefits.

Summary

This chapter reviewed several strategies for using environmental criminology to prevent crime and victimization. Informed by rational choice theory, crime pattern theory, and routine activity theory, environmental criminology assists in crime prevention by suggesting techniques in which opportunities for crime can be reduced by changing the immediate environment in which crimes occur. Three crime prevention frameworks from environmental criminology—defensible space, crime prevention through environmental design, and situational crime prevention—were reviewed from theoretical and applied perspectives as they relate to preventing crime and victimization. These methods of crime prevention are important additions to the field of victimology because they provide a practical means of addressing some of the known risk factors for victimization that have been identified and discussed throughout this textbook.

KEYWORDS

Collateral consequences	Journey to crime	Natural surveillance
Crime patterns	Routine activity theory	Image and milieu
Environmental criminology	Defensible space	Crime prevention through environmental design
Rational choice theory	Territoriality	Territorial reinforcement
Crime pattern theory	Surveillance	Physical barriers

Symbolic barriers	Activity support	Displacement
Access control	Image and space management	Diffusion of benefits
Target hardening	Situational crime prevention	Anticipatory benefits

DISCUSSION QUESTIONS

1. Are criminal offenders rational decision makers? Explain your answer and provide examples.
2. Apply crime pattern theory to your college or university campus. What are the nodes, paths, and edges on campus? Might crime occurring on your campus be generated by the movement and activities of individuals in these spaces? Explain why or why not and provide examples.
3. Can all types of victimization be prevented through environmental design and defensible space architecture? In other words, is one of these two theories better at explaining the prevention of some types of victimization than others? Be sure to explain what "better" means as you assess the explanatory ability of these theories.
4. Apply situational crime prevention to a specific crime and situation discussed earlier in the text. Provide examples of prevention strategies based on increasing the effort, increasing the risk, reducing the rewards, reducing provocations, and removing excuses.
5. Walk around your campus and take pictures illustrating the concepts of environmental design reviewed in this chapter. Discuss whether you think they prevent crime and explain why or why not.
6. Describe how the theories of environmental design complement or contradict each other. Provide relevant examples to support your points.
7. Apply the crime prevention theories outlined in this chapter to the neighborhood you grew up in or the one you live in now, including on campus.
8. In general, what determines whether a crime prevention program results in displacement, diffusion of benefits, or anticipatory benefits?

REFERENCES

Atlas, R., & LeBlanc, W. G. (1994). The impact on crime of street closures and barricades: A Florida case study. *Security Journal, 5*, 140–145.

Braga, A. A., Weisburd, D. L., Waring, E. J., Mazerolle, L. G., Spelman, W., & Gajewski, F. (1999). Problem-oriented policing in violent crime places: A randomized controlled experiment. *Criminology, 37*, 541–580.

Brown, B. B., & Altman, I. (1983). Territoriality, defensible space and residential burglary: An environmental analysis. *Journal of Environmental Psychology, 3*, 203–220.

Challinger, D. (1996). Refund fraud in retail stores. *Security Journal, 7*, 27–35.

Clarke, R. V. G. (1980). Situational crime prevention: Theory and practice. *British Journal of Criminology, 20*, 136–147.

Clarke, R. V. (1995). Situational crime prevention. In M. Tonry & D. P. Farrington (Eds.), *Building a safer society: Strategic approaches to crime revention, crime and justice* (Vol. 19, pp. 91–150). Chicago: University of Chicago Press.

Clarke, R. V. (2005). Seven misconceptions of situational crime prevention. In N. Tilley (Ed.), *Handbook of crime prevention and community safety* (pp. 39–70). Portland, OR: Willan Publishing.

Clarke, R. V., & Eck, J. E. (2005). *Crime analysis for problem solvers in 60 small steps.* Washington, DC: Office of Community Oriented Policing Services.

Clarke, R. V., & Homel, R. (1997). A revised classification of situational crime prevention techniques. In S. P. Lab (Ed.), *Crime prevention at a Crossroads* (pp. 17–27). Cincinnati, OH: Anderson Publishing Co.

Clarke, R. V., & Mayhew, P. (1988). The British gas suicide story and its criminological implications. *Crime and Justice, 10*, 79–116.

Clarke, R. V., & Weisburd, D. (1994). Diffusion of crime control benefits: Observations on the reverse of displacement. In R. V. Clarke (Ed.), *Crime prevention studies* (Vol. 2, pp. 165–183). Monsey, NY: Criminal Justice Press.

Cornish, D. B., & Clarke, R. V. (1987). Understanding crime displacement: An application of rational choice theory. *Criminology, 25*, 933–947.

Cornish, D. B., & Clarke, R. V. (2003). Opportunities, precipitators and criminal decisions: A reply to Wortley's critique of situational crime prevention. In M. J. Smith & D. B. Cornish (Eds.), *Crime prevention studies* (Vol. 16, pp. 41–96). Monsey, NY: Criminal Justice Press.

Coupe, T., & Blake, L. (2006). Daylight and darkness targeting strategies and the risks of being seen at residential burglaries. *Criminology, 44*, 431–464.

Cozens, P. M., Saville, G., & Hillier, D. (2005). Crime prevention through environmental design (CPTED): A review and modern bibliography. *Property Management, 23*, 328–356.

Donnelly, P. G., & Kimble, C. E. (1997). Community organizing, environmental change, and neighborhood crime. *Crime & Delinquency, 43*, 493–511.

Donovan, G. H., & Prestemon, J. P. (2012). The effect of trees on crime in Portland, Oregon, *Environment and Behavior, 44*, 3–30.

Eck, J. E., & Weisburd, D. (1995). Crime places in crime theory. In J. E. Eck & D. Weisburd (Eds.), *Crime Prevention Studies* (Vol. 4, pp. 1–34). Monsey, NY: Criminal Justice Press.

Ekblom, P. (1997). Gearing up against crime: A dynamic framework to help designers keep up with the active criminal in a changing world. *International Journal of Risk, Security and Crime Prevention, 2,* 249–265.

Felson, M., Belanger, M. E., Bichler, G. M., Bruzinski, C. D., Campbell, G. S., Fried, C. L., Grofik, K. C., Mazur, I. S., O'Regan, A. B., Sweeney, P. J., Ullman, A. L., & Williams, L. M. (1996). Redesigning Hell: Preventing crime and disorder at the Port Authority Bus Terminal. In R. V. Clarke (Ed.), *Crime prevention studies* (vol. 6, pp. 5–92). Monsey, NY: Criminal Justice Press.

Forrester, D., Chatterton, M., & Pease, K. (1988). *The Kirkholt burglary prevention project, Rochdale.* London: Home Office.

Freilich, J. D., & Newman, G. R. (2014). Providing opportunities: A sixth column for the techniques of situational crime prevention. In S. Caneppele & F. Calderoni (Eds.), *Organized crime, corruption and crime prevention* (pp. 33–42). Switzerland: Springer International Publishing.

Guerette, R. T., & Clarke, R. V. (2003). Product life cycles and crime: Automated teller machines and robbery. *Security Journal, 16,* 7–18.

Hunter, R. D., & Jeffery, C. R. (1992). Preventing convenience store robbery through environmental design. In R. V. Clarke (Ed.), *Situational crime prevention: Successful case studies* (pp. 194–204). Albany, NY: Harrow and Heston Publishers.

Jacobs, J. (1961). *The death and life of great American cities.* New York: Random House, Inc.

Jacobs, J. (1993). *The death and life of great American cities.* New York: The Modern Library.

Jeffery, C. R. (1971). *Crime prevention through environmental design.* Beverly Hills, CA: Sage.

Jeffery, C. R., & Zahm, D. L. (1993). Crime prevention through environmental design, opportunity theory, and rational choice models. In R. V. Clarke & M. Felson (Eds.), *Routine activity and rational choice* (pp. 323–350). New Brunswick, NJ: Transaction Publishers.

Johnson, L., Mullick, R., & Mulford, C. (2002). General versus specific victim blaming. *Journal of Social Psychology, 142,* 249–263.

Johnson, S. D., & Bowers, K. (2003). Opportunity is in the eye of the beholder: The role of publicity in crime prevention. *Criminology & Public Policy, 2,* 497–524.

Lasley, J. (1998). *"Designing out" gang homicides and street assaults* Washington, DC: National Institute of Justice.

Macintyre, S., & Homel, R. (1997). Danger on the dance floor: A study of interior design, crowding and aggression in nightclubs. In R. Homel (Ed.), *Crime prevention studies* (Vol. 7, pp. 91–113). Monsey, NY: Criminal Justice Press.

Mawby, R. I. (1977). Defensible space: A theoretical and empirical appraisal. *Urban Studies, 14,* 169–179.

Mayhew, P. (1979). Defensible space: The current status of a crime prevention theory. *Howard Journal of Criminal Justice, 18,* 150–159.

Merry, S. E. (1981). Defensible space undefended: Social factors in crime control through environmental design. *Urban Affairs Quarterly, 16,* 397–422.

Miethe, T. D., & McDowall, D. (1993). Contextual effects in models of criminal victimization. *Social Forces, 71,* 741–759.

Moffat, R. (1983). Crime prevention through environmental design: A management perspective. *Canadian Journal of Criminology, 25,* 19–31.

Newman, O. (1972). *Defensible space: Crime prevention through urban design.* New York: Macmillan.

Newman, O. (1996). *Creating defensible space.* Washington, DC: U.S. Department of Housing and Urban Development.

Pease, K. (1999). A review of street lighting evaluations: Crime reduction effects. In K. Painter & N. Tilley (Eds.), *Crime prevention studies* (Vol. 10, pp. 47–76). Monsey, NY: Criminal Justice Press.

Phillips, C. (1999). A review of CCTV evaluations: Crime reduction effects and attitudes towards its use. In K. Painter & N. Tilley (Eds.), *Crime prevention studies* (Vol. 10, pp. 123–155). Monsey, NY: Criminal Justice Press.

Poyner, B. (1993). What works in crime prevention: An overview of evaluations. In R. V. Clarke (Ed.), *Crime prevention studies* (Vol. 1, pp. 7–34). Monsey, NY: Criminal Justice Press.

Ponyer, B., & Webb, B. (1992). Reducing theft from shopping bags in city center markets. In R. V. Clarke (Ed.), *Situational crime prevention: Successful case studies* (pp. 99–107). Albany, NY: Harrow and Heston Publishers.

Popcenter. (2014). *Twenty-five techniques of situational crime prevention*. Retrieved February 26, 2014, from http://www.popcenter.org/25techniques/

President's Commission on Law Enforcement and Administration of Justice. (1967). *The challenge of crime in a free society.* Washington, DC: U.S. Government Printing Office.

Reynald, D. M. (2011a). Factors associated with the guardianship of places: Assessing the relative importance of the spatio-physical and sociodemographic contexts in generating opportunities for capable guardianship. *Journal of Research in Crime and Delinquency, 48*, 110–142.

Reynald, D. M. (2011b). *Guarding against crime: Measuring guardianship within routine activity theory.* Burlington, VT: Ashgate Publishing Company.

Roncek, D. W., & Lobosco, A. (1983). The effect of high schools on crime in their neighborhoods. *Social Science Quarterly, 64*, 598–613.

Roncek, D. W., & Maier, P. A. (1991). Bars, blocks, and crime revisited: Linking the theory or routine activities to the empiricism of "hot spots." *Criminology, 29*, 725–753.

Sampson, R. J., & Raudenbush, S. W. (1999). Systematic social observation of public spaces: A new look at disorder in urban neighborhoods. *American Journal of Sociology, 105*, 603–651.

Skogan, W. G. (2012). Disorder and crime. In B. C. Welsh & D. P. Farrington (Eds.), *The Oxford handbook of crime prevention* (pp. 173–188). New York: Oxford University Press.

Sloan-Howitt, M., & Kelling, G. L. (1990). Subway graffiti in New York City: "Getting up" vs. "Meanin it and cleanin it." *Security Journal, 1*, 131–136.

Taylor, R. B., Gottfredson, S. D., & Brower, S. (1984). Block crime and fear: Defensible space, local social ties, and territorial functioning. *Journal of Research in Crime and Delinquency, 21*, 303–331.

Taylor, R. B., Shumaker, S. A., & Gottfredson, S. D. (1985). Neighborhood-level links between physical features and local sentiments: Deterioration, fear of crime, and confidence. *Journal of Architectural and Planning Research, 2*, 261–275.

Veno, A., & Veno, E. (1993). Situational prevention of public disorder at the Australian Motorcycle Grand Prix. In R. V. Clarke (Ed.), *Crime prevention studies* (Vol. 1, pp. 157–175). Monsey, NY: Criminal Justice Press.

Weisburd, D., Wyckoff, L. A., Ready, J., Eck, J. E., Hinkle, J. C., & Gajewski, F. (2006). Does crime just move around the corner? A controlled study of spatial displacement and diffusion of crime control benefits. *Criminology, 44*, 549–592.

Welsh, B. C., Mudge, M. E., & Farrington, D. P. (2010). Reconceptualizing public area surveillance and crime prevention: Security guards, place managers and defensible space. *Security Journal, 23*, 299–319.

White, G. F. (1990). Neighborhood permeability and burglary rates. *Justice Quarterly, 7*, 57–67.

Wilcox, P., Madensen, T. D., & Tillyer, M. S. (2007). Guardianship in context: Implications for burglary victimization risk and prevention. *Criminology, 45*, 401–433.

Wilcox, P., Quisenberry, N., Cabrera, D. T., & Jones, S. (2004). Busy places and broken windows? Toward defining the role of physical structure and process in community crime models. *Sociological Quarterly, 45,* 185–207.

Wilkerson, A., Carlson, N. E., Yen, I. H., & Michael, Y. L. (2012). Neighborhood physical features and relationships with neighbors: Does positive physical environment increase neighborliness? *Environment and Behavior, 44,* 595–615.

Wilson, J. Q., & Kelling, G. (1982) The police and neighborhood safety: Broken windows. *Atlantic Monthly, 127,* 29–38.

Wortley, R. (2001). A classification of techniques for controlling situational precipitators of crime. *Security Journal, 14,* 63–82.

Wortley, R., & McFarlane, M. (2011). The role of territoriality in crime prevention: A field experiment. *Security Journal, 24,* 149–156.

INDEX